Interpersonal Communication
Relating to Others

Third Canadian Edition

- **Steven A. Beebe**
  Southwest Texas State University

- **Susan J. Beebe**
  Southwest Texas State University

- **Mark V. Redmond**
  Iowa State University

- **Terri M. Geerinck**
  Sir Sandford Fleming College

PEARSON
AB and
Toronto

Dedicated to our families

Mark and Matthew Beebe
Peggy, Nicholas, and Eric Redmond, and Beth Maroney
Skyler, Adelaide, and Rod Manley

National Library of Canada Cataloguing in Publication

   Interpersonal communication: relating to others / Steven A. Beebe . . . [et al.]. —3rd Canadian ed.

Includes index.
ISBN 0-205-36074-2

1. Interpersonal communication. 2. Interpersonal relations. I. Beebe, Steven A., 1950–

BF637.C45I68 2003   153.6   C2002-905962-3

Copyright © 2004, 2000, 1997 Pearson Education Canada Inc., Toronto, Ontario

Original U.S. edition published by Allyn & Bacon, Inc., a division of Pearson Education, Boston, MA 02116. Copyright © 2002. This edition is authorized for sale in Canada only.

All Rights Reserved. This publication is protected by copyright, and permission should be obtained from the publisher prior to any prohibited reproduction, storage in a retrieval system, or transmission in any form or by any means, electronic, mechanical, photocopying, recording, or likewise. For information regarding permission, write to the Permissions Department.

ISBN 0-205-36074-2

Vice President, Editorial Director: Michael J. Young
Acquisitions Editor: Marianne Minaker
Senior Developmental Editor: Lise Dupont
Marketing Manager: Christine Cozens
Production Editor: Cheryl Jackson
Copy Editor: Ann McInnis
Proofreader: Wayne Jones
Senior Production Coordinator: Peggy Brown
Formatter: Christine Velakis
Art Director: Julia Hall
Cover and Interior Design: Gillian Tsintziras
Cover Image: Illustration by Joe Fleming

2 3 4 5 08 07 06 05 04

Printed and bound in United States

Brief Contents

List of Features   ix
Preface   xi

Part I   Foundations of Interpersonal Communication   3

Chaper 1
Introduction to Interpersonal Communication   4

Chapter 2
Interpersonal Communication and Self   36

Chapter 3
Interpersonal Communication and Perception   66

Part II   Interpersonal Communication Skills   97

Chapter 4
Listening and Responding   98

Chapter 5
Emotions and Interpersonal Communication   132

Chapter 6
Communicating Verball   160

Chapter 7
Communicating Non-Verbally   192

Chapter 8
Conflict Management Skills   224

Part III   Interpersonal Communication Relationships   263

Chapter 9
Interpersonal Communication and Cultural Diversity: Adapting to Others   264

Chapter 10
Understanding Interpersonal Relationships   300

Chapter 11
Developing and Maintaining Interpersonal Relationships   332

Notes   383
Index   395

Contents

List of Features   ix
Preface   xi

Part I   Foundations of Interpersonal Communication   3

Chapter 1

Introduction to Interpersonal Communication   4

What Is Interpersonal Communication?   6

Interpersonal Communication Is a Distinctive Form of Communication   6
- Interpersonal Communication Involves Mutual Influence between Individuals   7
- Interpersonal Communication Is the Fundamental Means We Use to Manage Our Relationships   8

The Importance of Interpersonal Communication to Our Lives   9
- Improve Relationships with Family   9
- Improve Relationships with Friends and Lovers   10
- Improve Relationships with Colleagues   10
- Improve Your Physical and Emotional Health   11

An Evolving Model for Human and Interpersonal Communication   12
- Human Communication as Action: Message Transfer   12
- Human Communication as Interaction: Message Exchange   13
- Human Communication as Transaction: Message Creation   14

Mediated Interpersonal Communication: A New Frontier   16

Principles of Interpersonal Communication   21
- Interpersonal Communication Connects Us to Others   21
- Interpersonal Communication Is Irreversible   22
- Interpersonal Communication Is Complicated   23
- Interpersonal Communication Is Governed by Rules   23
- Interpersonal Communication Involves Both Content and Relationship Dimensions   25

Interpersonal Communication Myths   25
- Myth: "More Words Will Make the Meaning Clearer"   25
- Myth: "Meanings Are in Words"   26
- Myth: "Information Equals Communication"   26
- Myth: "Interpersonal Relationship Problems Are Always Communication Problems"   26

How to Improve Your Own Interpersonal Communication Effectiveness   27
- Become Knowledgeable   28
- Become Skilled   28
- Become Motivated   28
- Become Flexible   28
- Become Ethical   29
- Become Other-Oriented   29

Summary   32
For Discussion and Review   32
For Your Journal   33
Learning with Others   34
Weblinks   34
Suggested Readings   35

Chapter 2

Interpersonal Communication and Self   36

Self-Concept: Who Are You?   38
- One or Many Selves?   40
- How Your Self-Concept Develops   42

Self-Esteem: Your Self-Worth   49

Improving Your Self-Esteem   51
- Self-Talk   51
- Visualization   51
- Avoiding Comparisons   52
- Reframing   52
- Developing Honest Relationships   53
- Letting Go of the Past   53
- Seeking Support   53

How Self-Concept and Self-Esteem Affect Interpersonal Communication and Relationships   54
- Self and Others   54
- Self-Fulfilling Prophecy   55
- Self and Interpretation of Messages   58
- Self and Interpersonal Needs   59
- Self and Communication Style   60

Summary   62
For Discussion and Review   63
For Your Journal   64
Learning with Others   64
Weblinks   65
Suggested Readings   65

Contents v

Chapter 3

Interpersonal Communication and Perception 66

Understanding the Interpersonal Perception Process 68
- *Stage One: Selecting* 69
- *Stage Two: Organizing* 71
- *Stage Three: Interpreting* 73

Perception and Interpersonal Communication 75

Perceiving Others 76
- *How We Form Impressions of Others* 77
- *How We Describe Others* 79
- *How We Interpret the Behaviour of Others* 81

Identifying Barriers to Accurate Perceptions 83
- *Ignoring Information* 84
- *Overgeneralizing* 84
- *Holding on to Preconceptions* 84
- *Imposing Consistency* 84
- *Oversimplifying* 85
- *Stereotyping* 85
- *Ignoring Circumstances* 86
- *Focusing on the Negative* 86

Improving Your Perceptual Skills 87
- *Link Details with the Big Picture* 88
- *Become Aware of Others' Perceptions of You* 88
- *Increase Your Awareness* 88
- *Recognize the Elements to Which You Attribute Meaning* 88
- *Become Other-Oriented* 89
- *Use Perception Checking* 90
- *Be Sensitive to Cultural Differences* 91

Summary 92
For Discussion and Review 92
For Your Journal 93
Learning with Others 93
Weblinks 94
Suggested Readings 94

Part Two   Interpersonal Communication Skills 97

Chapter 4

Listening and Responding 98

Listening Defined 100
- *Selecting* 100
- *Attending* 101
- *Understanding* 101
- *Remembering* 102
- *Responding* 103

Listening Styles 103
- *People-Oriented Listeners* 103
- *Action-Oriented Listeners* 104
- *Content-Oriented Listeners* 104
- *Time-Oriented Listeners* 104

Listening Barriers 105
- *Being Self-Absorbed* 107
- *Emotional Noise* 108
- *Criticizing the Speaker* 109
- *Speech Rate vs. Thought Rate* 110
- *Information Overload* 110
- *External Noise* 110

Improving Your Listening Skills 112
- *Stop* 112
- *Look* 113
- *Listen* 113
- *Ask Questions* 114
- *Reflect Content by Paraphrasing* 115

Improving Empathic Listening and Responding Skills 116
- *Understand Your Partner's Feelings: Imagine How You Would Feel* 118
- *Paraphrase Emotions* 119

Improving Critical Listening and Responding Skills 122
- *Look for Faulty Logic: Wrong Reasoning* 123
- *Avoid Jumping to Conclusions: Fact–Inference Confusion* 125

Improving Your Responding Skills 126
- *Provide Well-Timed Responses* 126
- *Provide Useable Information* 126
- *Avoid Unnecessary Details* 127
- *Be Descriptive Rather Than Evaluative* 127

Summary 127
For Discussion and Review 128
For Your Journal 129
Learning with Others 129
Weblinks 130
Suggested Readings 131

Chapter 5

Emotions and Interpersonal Communication 132

Characteristics of Emotions 134
- *Physiological Effects of Emotions* 134
- *Cognitive Effects of Emotion* 135
- *Behavioural Effects and Emotions* 136

The Depth and Breadth of Emotions   138
   How Many Emotions?   138
   Intensity of Emotions   139

Factors That Influence Emotional Expression   139
   Culture   139
   Gender   140
   Etiquette   142
   Roles   142

Skills for Recognizing and Sharing Emotions   143
   Skills for Dealing with Others' Emotions   143
   Suggestions for Expressing and Managing Your Own Emotions   144
   Dealing with Some Difficult Emotional States   147

Managing Difficult Emotions When You Experience Them   153
   Be Aware That You Are Becoming Angry and Emotionally Volatile   153
   Seek to Understand Why You Are Angry and Emotional   154
   Breathe   154
   Restructure Your Thoughts and Feelings   154
   Use Positive Self-Talk   155
   Get Help   155

Summary   156
For Discussion and Review   157
For Your Journal   157
Learning with Others   158
Weblinks   159
Suggested Readings   159

Chapter 6

Communicating Verbally   160

Words and Meaning   161
   Words Are Symbols   162
   Words Are Arbitrary   162
   Words Are Context Bound   162
   Words Are Culturally Bound   163
   Words Have Denotative and Connotative Meaning   165
   Words Communicate Concrete or Abstract Meaning   166

Recognizing the Power of Words   167
   Words Have Power to Create   167
   Words Have Power to Affect Thoughts and Actions   168
   Words Have Power to Affect and Reflect Culture   169

Avoiding Word Barriers   170
   Bypassing: One Word, Two Thoughts   170
   Bafflegab: High-Falutin' Use of Words   172
   Lack of Precision: Uncertain Meaning   172
   Allness: The Language of Generalization   174
   Static Evaluation: The Language of Rigidity   175
   Polarization: The Language of Extremes   176
   Biased Language: Insensitivity Toward Others   176

Using Words to Establish Supportive Relationships   177
   Avoid Sexist Language   179
   Avoid Ethnic or Racially Biased Language   180
   Avoid Language That Demeans One's Age, Ability, or Social Class   181
   Describe Your Own Feelings Rather Than Evaluate the Behaviour of Others   181
   Solve Problems Rather Than Control Others   182
   Be Genuine Rather Than Manipulative   182
   Empathize Rather Than Remain Detached from Others   183
   Be Flexible Rather Than Rigid Toward Others   183
   Present Yourself as Equal Rather Than Superior   183

Using Words to Value Others   184
   Confirming Responses   184
   Disconfirming Responses   186

Summary   188
For Discussion and Review   189
For Your Journal   190
Learning with Others   190
Weblinks   191
Suggested Readings   191

Chapter 7

Communicating Non-Verbally   192

Why Learn about Non-Verbal Communication?   193
   Non-Verbal Messages Communicate Our Feelings and Attitudes   194
   Non-Verbal Messages Are More Believable   194
   Non-Verbal Communication Plays a Major Role in Interpersonal Relationships   195

The Challenge of Interpreting Non-Verbal Messages   197
   Non-Verbal Messages Are Often Ambiguous   197
   Non-Verbal Messages Are Continuous   198
   Non-Verbal Cues Are Multi-Channelled   198
   Non-Verbal Interpretation Is Culture Based   198

Non-Verbal Communication Codes   200
   Body Movement, Posture, and Gestures   200
   Eye Contact   204
   Facial Expressions   206
   Vocal Cues   207
   Personal Space   208
   Territory   210
   Touch   211

Contents

Appearance 211

Interpreting Non-Verbal Communication 212
Immediacy 213
Arousal 213
Dominance 214

Improving Your Ability to Interpret Non-Verbal Messages 216
Consider Non-Verbal Cues in Context 216
Look for Clusters of Non-Verbal Cues 216
Consider Past Experiences When Interpreting Non-Verbal Cues 217
Check Your Perceptions with Others 218

Summary 220
For Discussion and Review 221
For Your Journal 221
Learning with Others 222
Weblinks 223
Suggested Readings 223

Chapter 8

Conflict Management Skills 224

What Is Conflict? 226
Goals and Conflict 226
Experiences and Conflict 227

Types of Conflict 227
Pseudo Conflict 229
Simple Conflict: Different Stands on the Issues 230
Ego Conflict: Conflict Gets Personal 231

Myths about Conflict 232
Myth 1: Conflict Should Always Be Avoided 233
Myth 2: Conflict Always Occurs Because of Misunderstandings 233
Myth 3: Conflict Is Always a Sign of a Poor Interpersonal Relationship 233
Myth 4: Conflict Can Always Be Resolved 233
Myth 5: Conflict Is Always Bad 234

Conflict as a Process 234
Source: Prior Conditions 234
Beginning: Frustration Awareness 235
Middle: Active Conflict 235
End: Resolution 236
Aftermath: Follow-Up 236

Conflict Management Styles 237
Non-Confrontational Style 238
Confrontational Style 239
Cooperative Style 241

Conflict Management Skills 242
Manage Your Emotions 242

Manage Information 245
Manage Goals 247
Manage the Problem 249

When Others Aren't Other-Oriented: How to Be Assertive 253
Assertiveness Defined 253
Five Steps in Assertive Behaviour 254

Summary 258
For Discussion and Review 258
For Your Journal 259
Learning with Others 259
Weblinks 261
Suggested Readings 261

Part Three Interpersonal Communication Relationships 263

Chapter 9

Interpersonal Communication and Cultural Diversity: Adapting to Others 264

The Nature of Culture 267
Cultural Elements 267
Cultural Values 270
Cultural Contexts 274

Barriers to Effective Intercultural Communication 275
Ethnocentrism 276
Different Communication Codes 278
Stereotyping and Prejudice 278
Assuming Similarity 280

Improving Intercultural Competence 280
Developing Knowledge: Strategies to Understand Others Who Are Different from Us 280
Developing Motivation: Strategies to Accept Others Who Are Different from Us 284
Developing Skills: Strategies to Adapt to Others Who Are Different from Us 286

Summary 294
For Discussion and Review 295
For Your Journal 296
Learning with Others 297
Weblinks 298
Suggested Readings 298

Chapter 10

Understanding Interpersonal Relationships 300

An Interpersonal Relationship as a System and a Process 302

Relationships of Circumstance and Relationships of Choice 303

Trust, Intimacy, and Power in Relationships 304
- Trust 304
- Intimacy 305
- Power 306

Attraction in Relationships 309
- Short-Term Initial Attraction and Long-Term Maintenance Attraction 310
- Elements of Interpersonal Attraction 310

Self-Disclosure: A Foundation for Relational Escalation 314

Two Models for Self-Disclosure 317
- Understanding the Depth and Breadth of Self-Disclosure: The Social Penetration Model of Self-Disclosure 318
- Understanding How We Learn about Ourselves: The Johari Window Model of Self-Disclosure 319

Characteristics of Appropriate Self-Disclosure 321
- Self-Disclosure Usually Moves in Small Increments 321
- Self-Disclosure Moves from Less Personal to More Personal Information 322
- Self-Disclosure Is Reciprocal 322
- Self-Disclosure Involves Risk 323
- Self-Disclosure Involves Trust 323

Interpersonal Relationship Development Theories 324
- Social Exchange Theory 324
- Dialectical Theory 326

Summary 328
For Discussion and Review 328
For Your Journal 329
Learning with Others 329
Weblinks 330
Suggested Readings 331

Chapter 11

Developing and Maintaining Interpersonal Relationships 332

Stages of Interpersonal Relationships 334
- Relational Escalation 335
- Relational De-Escalation 337

Skills for Starting Relationships 338
- Gather Information to Reduce Uncertainty 339
- Adopt an Other-Oriented Perspective 340
- Observe and Act upon Approachability Cues 340
- Identify and Use Conversation Starters 340
- Follow Initiation Norms 341
- Provide Information about Yourself 341
- Present Yourself in a Positive Way 342
- Ask Questions 343
- Don't Expect Too Much from the Initial Interaction 343

Interpersonal Communication Skills for Escalating and Maintaining Relationships 344
- Communicate Attraction 344
- Monitor Your Perceptions, Listen Actively, and Respond Confirmingly 346
- Be Open and Self-Disclose Appropriately 347
- Express Emotions 347
- Engage in Relationship Talk 348
- Socially Decentre and Adapt 348
- Be Tolerant and Show Restraint 349
- Manage Conflict Cooperatively 350

De-Escalating and Ending Relationships 351
- Responses to Relational Problems 352
- The Decision to End a Relationship 353
- How Relationships End 354
- Causes of De-Escalating and Ending Relationships with Friends and Lovers 354
- Strategies for Ending Relationships 356

Interpersonal Relationships on the Internet 358
- Types of Computer-Mediated Communication (CMC) 359
- Comparing Face-To-Face (Ftf) Communication to CMC 361
- Using CMC to Initiate New Relationships 364
- Using CMC to Maintain Existing Relationships 366

Interpersonal Relationships at Work 369
- Upward Communication: Talking with Your Boss 371
- Downward Communication: Talking with Your Subordinates 372
- Horizontal Communication: Talking with Your Colleagues 373
- Outward Communication: Talking with Your Customers 373
- Sexual Harassment 374
- Enhancing Leadership Skills 376
- Enhancing Followership Skill 377

Summary 378
For Discussion and Review 379
For Your Journal 380
Learning with Others 381
Weblinks 381
Suggested Readings 382

Notes 383

Index 395

List of Features

Recap

Comparing Key Definitions   7
Components of the Human Communication Process   16
An Evolving Model for Interpersonal Communication   16
How Can You Improve Your Communication Effectiveness?   32
Who You Are Is Reflected in Your Attitudes, Beliefs, and Values   39
William James's Dimensions of Self   42
Strategies for Improving Your Self-Esteem   54
How Self-Concept and Self-Esteem Affect Interpersonal Communication and Relationships   62
The Interpersonal Perception Process   75
How We Organize and Interpret Interpersonal Perceptions to Perceive Others   83
Barriers to Accurate Perceptions   87
What Is Listening?   103
Overcoming Barriers to Listening   111
How to Improve Your Listening Skills   116
How to Respond with Empathy   122
Suggestions for Improving Responding Skills   127
Effects of Emotions   138
The Depth and Breadth of Emotions   139
Factors That Influence Emotional Expression   142
Guidelines for Expressing Emotions   147
Dealing with Difficult Emotional States   153
Managing Your Own Difficult Emotions   156
Word Barriers   176
Using Words to Establish Supportive Relationships   184
Using Words to Value Others   186
Reasons to Study Non-Verbal Communication   197
Categories of Movement and Gestures   204
Functions of Eye Contact   206
Edward T. Hall's Classification of Spatial Zones   209
Codes of Non-verbal Communication   212
Dimensions for Interpreting Non-Verbal Behaviour   215
How to Check Your Perceptions of Others' Non-Verbal Cues   219
Types of Conflict   232
Conflict Myths   234
Understanding Conflict as a Process   236
Conflict Management Styles   242
Assertiveness versus Aggressiveness   253
How to Assert Yourself   257
Dimensions of Cultural Values   274
The Nature of Culture   275
Develop Knowledge to Enhance Understanding   284
Develop Motivation to Accept Others   286
Develop Skill to Adapt to Others   294
Types of Power   309
Elements of Interpersonal Attraction   314
Characteristics of Appropriate Self-Disclosure   323
Skills for Starting Relationships   343
Interpersonal Skills for Escalating and Maintaining Relationships   351
Strategies for De-Escalating and Ending Relationships   358
Comparing FtF Communication to CMC   364
Using CMC to Initiate and Maintain Relationships   368

Canadian Issues

What Skills Will I Need for Employment?   11
Campus Drinking: An Attempt to Improve Low Self-Esteem?   50
Perceiving Our Neighbours to the South: How Similar or Different Are We?   70
Buzz Hargrove: What's Your Impression?   78
Listening to Francophones and Allophones   118
Dealing with Your Emotions in the Wake of a Traumatic Event   148
Labels Are Words That Affect Our Evaluation of Others   168
Rules for Non-Verbal Communication in Canada   199
Managing a Monumental Goal: Communities and Families Working to Prevent Youth Crime   247
Aboriginal Wages: An Indication of Discrimination?   279
Who Chooses Common-law as a First Conjugal Relationship?   350
Workplace Skills in a Global Economy   369

e-connections

Impersonal America   17
An Electronic Relationship   18
Emoticons   19
What's Your Personality Type?   49
The Accuracy of Our Electronic Perceptions of Others   80
What's Your EQ?   118
Japanese Turn E-mail "Smiley Faces" Right Side Up   141
Netiquette: Network Etiquette   146
What's Your Style of Arguing with Others?   150
Cyber Shorthand   164
Avoiding Bafflegab   172
Avoiding Sexist Language   180
Interpreting Non-Verbal Messages   213
A World of Differences in Your Own Backyard   275
Breaking Up   352
Cyberspace and Relationships   359

Building Your Skills

Role Play: Other-Oriented or Self-Focused   30
Who Are You?   38
Dimensions of Your Self   40
Assessing Your Willingness to Communicate   48
Perceptual Differences   68

Perceptual Interpretations   75
Preconceived Explanations   86
Identifying Your Biases   89
Using Perception Checking   91
Assessing Your Listening Skills   105
Identifying Emotional "Hot Buttons"   109
Sympathy versus Empathy   120
Listening and Paraphrasing Content and Emotion   121
The Emotions Alphabet   138
How Comfortable Are You Expressing Your Emotions to Others?   140
Describing Feelings Using "I Messages"   145
Dealing with Your Anger   150
Assessing Your Verbal Aggressiveness   151
Denotative versus Connotative Definitions   166
Practise Using "I" Language   182
Supportive-Defensive Communication Charades   187
Communicating Interest   202
Facial Expression Quiz   207
Non-Verbal Skill Assessment   217
Checking Perceptions   219
Identifying Your Conflict Management Style   239
Practising Conflict Management Skills   252
How to Assert Yourself   256
Intercultural Encounters   266
Assessing Your Communication with Strangers   268
Assessing Your Ethnocentricism   277
Can You Tolerate Ambiguity?   284
Measuring Mindfulness   285
Predicting How Others Feel   287
Whom Do You Trust?   305
Power in Your Relationships   308
Are Your Needs Complementary?   313

Self-Disclosure Patterns   317
Graphing Your Relationship Changes   336
Anxiety Level and Familiarity   339
Affinity Seeking Observation   346
How Your Relationships Have Ended   358
What Is Sexual Harassment?   375

Understanding Diversity
Cultural Differences Can Lead to Misinterpretation   31
Being Other-Oriented in Other Cultures   44
Who Listens Better: Men or Women?   107
He Said, She Said: Gender Styles Differ at Work   164
Cultural Differences in Interpreting Non-Verbal Messages   199
Gender Differences and Non-Verbal Communication   215
Gender and Conflict   228
Diversity Almanac   266
Our Range of Differences   268
Dating Customs Around the World   271
Ethnocentric Thinking   281
Interracial Relationships: Hollywood Style   290
Mind Your Manners–and Theirs   293
Gender and Ending Relationships   352
Empathy and Sexual Orientation   354

Considering Others
Three Letters from Teddy   56
Test Your Empathy Ability   117
How Can You Tell When Someone Is Lying?   137
The Talkaholic Scale   171
Communicating Ethics in the Workplace   178
Essential Guidelines   188
Empathy Can Span the Abyss   243

Preface

If we could distill the central focus of this book into a bumper sticker, it would be this: "Become other-oriented." We believe that the most important principle in understanding and enhancing interpersonal communication is to focus on others, rather than only on yourself. By being other-oriented, we don't mean that you are not self-reflexively aware of who you are or that you abandon any sensitivity to your own thoughts and behaviour. We do suggest, however, that being other-oriented involves the mindful process of considering the thoughts, needs, and values of others, rather than an egocentric focus on self. We didn't invent this principle of being other-oriented; it is the foundation of every major faith movement, religion, and human value system in the world. It was also the foundation of the first two Canadian editions of *Interpersonal Communication: Relating to Others*, and it continues as the central theme of the third Canadian edition.

This book was written to be the primary text for courses in interpersonal communication. Although there are many different approaches to teaching this subject, we have endeavoured to include the essential principles and skills that will help students learn to understand and improve their relationships with others. This approach is designed to help students enhance their own repertoires of communication skills, as well as give them insights into the hows and whys of human relationships. We continue to emphasize the importance of relationship development and present skills to help maintain quality interpersonal relationships.

Our Approach to Interpersonal Communication

An Emphasis on Others

Although becoming other-oriented is challenging, we believe it is worth the effort; mastering this ability will result in life-long relationship rewards. Considering the thoughts and feelings of others is a prerequisite for understanding and improving interpersonal communication. Our other-oriented approach gently but consistently reminds students about the importance of seeing the world as others see it. At the heart of understanding and developing relationships with others is the process of considering how others are affected by our communication.

Becoming other-oriented is not a single skill, but rather a composite of principles and skills. Foremost among them are self-awareness and self-knowledge; we suggest that true empathy and sensitivity are possible only when we feel secure about our own identity. In addition, becoming other-oriented includes all of the classic skills and principles typically taught in interpersonal communication courses, such as listening, giving feedback, conflict management skills, and verbal and non-verbal skills, and places additional emphasis on the importance of the perceptions, thoughts, attitudes, beliefs, values, and emotions of others. To emphasize the importance of our other-oriented approach, each chapter includes a feature called "Considering Others," which provides observations and research conclusions designed to help students connect to others. The other-oriented symbol used in the margins throughout the text will help you spot and develop this skill.

An Emphasis on Diversity

Embedded in our other-oriented approach is the theme that other people are different than we are. To help students understand and sensitively consider those differences when interpersonally communicating with others, we place considerable emphasis on presenting principles and research conclusions about communication diversity. In recent years, the body of research on gender- and culture-based differences in communication behaviour has grown significantly. We do more, however, than just point out that we are different from one another. Using a competency-based approach, we present practical, research-based strategies for increasing communication competence when interacting with people who are different from ourselves. Using research observations about both culture and gender, we stress that the competent interpersonal communicator is knowledgeable, motivated, and skilled in communicating with people from diverse backgrounds. Our

"Understanding Diversity" boxes highlight both interpersonal principles and skills that help students relate to people who are different from themselves.

An Emphasis on Relationships

We discuss how relationships work and how to improve them. Students are consistently curious about how to improve their relationships with others. We link communication skills with principles that help explain and predict how relationships begin, develop, and sometimes decline. As suggested by our subtitle, *Relating to Others*, we highlight the importance of cultivating relationships by developing an increased awareness of and sensitivity to others. Our emphasis on relationships is reflected in the broad range of relationship types we consider in our discussions, including relationships with friends, lovers, family, and co-workers, and even relationships formed and developed over the Internet. Communication researchers have contributed significant insights to relationship development and maintenance. We rely on the latest communication research to give students the benefit of state-of-the-art thinking about how relationships can be improved.

An Emphasis on How Technology Influences Interpersonal Relationships

The advent of the Internet and other technological tools has affected how we relate to others, not just online but off-line as well. We build upon our previous discussion of the role of technology by including new "E-Connections" boxes in every chapter that will help students see how relational cues are both similar to and different from their live-and-in-person connections to others. A new feature to this edition is the inclusion of several websites that can extend students' knowledge of interpersonal relationships. In addition, an expanded discussion in Chapter 1 and a new section in Chapter 11 review contemporary research conclusions about how relationships can develop, be maintained, and be terminated when people are connected by the Internet. Although our primary emphasis remains on face-to-face interactions, we can't ignore the significant role technology plays in affecting our relationships with others.

Throughout the book we emphasize that there are no sure-fire prescriptions for achieving satisfying relationships or peak communication experiences. But we do believe that, armed with a solid grasp of principles, students can adapt research-based strategies to their own purposes and become more skilled at initiating and managing interactions with others.

Features of the Third Canadian Edition

The features that made our first two editions successful have been retained in the third Canadian edition. Our other-oriented approach, emphasis on diversity, focus on relationships, and expanded coverage of technology, combined with our balanced discussion of principles and skills, are the key reasons both students and instructors praise the book.

Interpersonal Communication continues to supply Canadian contexts to provide "at home" relevance to all the topics covered in the book and to facilitate personal identification with these lessons by Canadian students. These objectives are achieved through the following features:

- special "Canadian Issues" boxes
- excerpts from reports of noted Canadian research institutions
- presentation of relevant Canadian statistics
- quotations and anecdotes from prominent Canadians
- photographic images that are identifiably Canadian (e.g., Canadian personalities, sports teams, locations, etc.)
- links to related Canadian websites

With respect to structure, the third Canadian edition continues to feature three parts containing 11 chapters, although we have included a new chapter dealing with emotions and their effects on interpersonal communication. In order to make room for the new emotions chapter (Chapter 5), we organized Chapters 9, 10, and 11 from the previous (second) Canadian edition into two final chapters without losing required content in the areas of interpersonal attraction and relational development. The result is a better-structured text with the addition of new and relevant material.

Part I: Foundations of Interpersonal Communication focuses upon the prerequisites of interpersonal communication. Chapter 1 traces the evolution of interpersonal communication theory, defines key concepts, and begins exploring the link between interpersonal communication and relationships. Chapter 2 encourages students to examine their own self-concept and self-esteem as they study theoretical frameworks and constructs. Chapter 3 examines the perception process, emphasizing tendencies that interfere with relational development and suggesting ways to combat them.

Part II: Interpersonal Skills focuses on the basic skills and competencies required for effective interpersonal relationships. Chapter 4 focuses on listening and responding with accuracy and empathy. Chapter 5, the new chapter on emotions, examines how feelings affect interpersonal communication and offers strategies to help students better understand their emotions, as well as the emotions of others. Understanding the power of language and verbal messages (Chapter 6), and perceiving and interpreting non-verbal cues (Chapter 7) continue to develop students' understanding of interpersonal skills. Chapter 8 examines conflict and suggests ways to manage conflict and solve problems as essential interpersonal skills.

Part III: Interpersonal Communication Relationships, significantly revised, examines more deeply the nature of relationships that we experience in life. "Interpersonal Communication and Cultural Diversity: Adapting to Others" (Chapter 9) gives students an opportunity to understand relationships in a diverse population and leads to a better understanding of the impact of cultural differences on communication and how to achieve positive interactions within this diverse milieu. "Understanding Interpersonal Relationships" (Chapter 10) presents the way relationships develop and unfold, and discusses how trust, intimacy, and power affect relationship development. Finally, "Developing and Maintaining Interpersonal Relationships" (Chapter 11) explores how relationships escalate and end, and offers strategies for developing and maintaining relationships. We also examine relationships in the workplace and have added exciting new research observations about how interpersonal communication research applies to online connections.

Here's a summary of some of the key revisions we've made to the third Canadian edition:

- a new chapter on emotions and how they affect interpersonal relations and communication
- updated research conclusions about interpersonal communication in every chapter, with continuing emphasis on research observation from communications scholars
- a further expanded discussion of the role of the Internet in the process of building and maintaining interpersonal relationships with others, including a new section in Chapter 11 called "Interpersonal Communication on the Internet"
- new, revised "E-Connections" boxes that highlight research conclusions and illustrations of how electronic communication affects our relationships
    - new URLs provide a wealth of additional information about interpersonal communication
    - these URLs can also be found at www.pearsoned.ca/beebe, our Companion Website
- new cartoons, stories, examples, and illustrations that apply the principles and skills discussed in the text
- revised discussion of self-disclosure in Chapter 10
- several new self-assessment tests
- new material in Chapter 4 to help students better adapt their behaviour when communicating with others who are different from themselves
- new section in Chapter 6 on people-oriented, action-oriented, content-oriented, and time-oriented listening styles
- new section in Chapter 6 called "Improving Critical Listening and Responding Skills"
- new material in Chapter 7 on using language to develop dialogue and supportive communication skills
- expanded discussion of ways to avoid biased, insensitive language in Chapter 7
- new material on detecting deceitful non-verbal communication in Chapter 7
- new information in Chapter 8 on how to better manage pseudo, simple, and ego conflict, and expanded coverage of conflict management skills
- reorganization of relational theory in Chapter 10, now including a discussion of relationships from the social exchange and dialectal perspectives
- new discussion in Chapter 11 of relational escalation and maintenance as it applies to diverse friendships and romantic relationships
- expanded material on relations at work, including a new section on sexual harassment in Chapter 11

- new section in Chapter 11 entitled "Interpersonal Relationships on the Internet"
- new suggested readings at the end of each chapter

Our Partnership with Instructors

Through this book we form a partnership with instructors to help students learn the principles and skills of interpersonal communication. We recognize that a textbook alone cannot do the job. Learning how to understand and improve interpersonal communication is an active process that involves comprehending, applying, experiencing, and ultimately evaluating the appropriateness of interpersonal communication principles and skills. But this book, along with our Instructor's Manual, provides guidance for every stage of the process. Our goal is to provide a wealth of teaching tools that can make the material applicable and memorable.

As part of the chapter openers, we've included learning objectives and content outlines. We've incorporated "Recap" boxes that help remind students of key content, "E-Connections" boxes that point out applications of technology to students, "Understanding Diversity" boxes that highlight applications of learning interpersonal communication in a diverse world, "Building Your Skills" boxes that help students see the connection between knowing and doing, "Canadian Issues" boxes that highlight Canadian material and issues, and "Considering Others" boxes that remind students about our central other-oriented theme. We conclude each chapter with a cogent summary of the key ideas, as well as discussion questions that focus on comprehension, critical thinking, and ethical issues. In addition, each chapter ends with suggestions for students who are writing an interpersonal journal, activities and exercises for collaborative learning, and a brief list of annotated suggested readings. Numerous self-assessment instruments are sprinkled liberally throughout the text.

Instructor Supplements

- *Instructor's Manual* (ISBN 0-205-36077-7) includes teaching suggestions, suggested course syllabi, guidelines for using the complete teaching-learning package, and a set of transparency masters.
- *Test Item File* in hard copy (ISBN 0-205-36075-0) or computerized format (0-205-36078-5) in TestGen 3.0 for Windows® and Macintosh®.
- *PowerPoint® Slides* (ISBN 0-205-36076-9) can be used to enhance lectures and tutorial instruction. These slides are also posted on the Companion Website (www.pearsoned.ca/beebe).

Student Supplements

- *Study Guide* (ISBN 0-205-39647-X) features chapter outlines, chapter reviews, and lists of terms to learn, as well as a host of activities, exercises, and practice tests.
- *Interactive Companion Website* (www.pearsoned.ca/beebe) includes learning objectives, practice tests, interactive exercises, and additional weblinks for every chapter.

Acknowledgments

The authors are grateful to those colleagues who acted as reviewers for this Canadian edition, including Lynda Archer, Humber College; Patricia Campbell, Red Deer College; Diana Denton, University of Waterloo; Christina Gauthier, Centennial College; Louise Jarrold, Dawson College; Colleen Kamps, Centennial College; Kathy Levine, University of Manitoba; Joseph Lucas, St. Clair College; David Reagan, Camosun College; Frank Renaud, Nova Scotia Community College; Stan Ross, Mount Royal College; as well as a couple of people who wished to remain anonymous. Also, thanks to all of the people at Pearson Education Canada who managed to keep this book on track and on schedule. A very special thanks goes out to Lise Dupont for her great insight and honest communication.

Interpersonal Communication

Nadia Richie/SIS

Part One

Foundations of Interpersonal Communication

- **Chapter 1**
  Introduction to Interpersonal Communication
- **Chapter 2**
  Interpersonal Communication and Self
- **Chapter 3**
  Interpersonal Communication and Perception

The first three chapters present fundamental concepts that frame our study of interpersonal communication. In Chapter 1 you will learn answers to these questions: What is interpersonal communication? What is the connection between interpersonal communication and interpersonal relationships? Why is it important to study relationships? What can I do to improve my relationships with others? Chapter 2 offers concepts and skills to help you understand more about who you are and how your self-concept and sense of self-worth influence your relationships. In Chapter 3 you will learn that perception plays a key role in effective interpersonal communication. By recognizing the factors that influence your perceptions and by actively analyzing the meaning of perceptual information, you can become more adept at sharing your sense of the world with others.

chapter 1

Introduction to Interpersonal Communication

After you study this chapter you should be able to...

1. Compare and contrast definitions of communication, human communication, and interpersonal communication.
2. Explain why it is useful to study interpersonal communication.
3. Compare and contrast communication as action, interaction, and transaction.
4. Describe the key components of the communication process.
5. Discuss five principles of interpersonal communication.
6. Describe four interpersonal communication myths.
7. Identify strategies that can improve your communication effectiveness.

- What Is Interpersonal Communication?
- The Importance of Interpersonal Communication to Our Lives
- An Evolving Model for Human and Interpersonal Communication
- Mediated Interpersonal Communication: A New Frontier
- Principles of Interpersonal Communication
- Interpersonal Communication Myths
- How to Improve Your Own Interpersonal Communication Effectiveness

Communication is to a relationship what breathing is to maintaining life.

VIRGINIA SATIR

Interpersonal communication is like breathing; it is a requirement for life. And, like breathing, it is inescapable. Unless you live in isolation, you communicate interpersonally every day. Listening to your roommate, talking to a teacher, meeting for lunch with a friend, or talking to your parents or your spouse are all examples of interpersonal communication.

It is impossible not to communicate with others. Even before we are born, we respond to movement and sound. With our first cry we announce to others that we are here. Once we make contact with others, we communicate, and we continue to do so until our last breath. Even though many of our messages are not verbalized, we nonetheless intentionally, and sometimes unintentionally, send messages to others. Without interpersonal communication, a special form of human communication that occurs as we manage our relationships, people suffer and even die. Recluses, hermits, and people isolated in solitary confinement dream and hallucinate about talking with others face to face.

Interpersonal communication is at the core of our existence. Think of the number of times you communicated with someone today, as you worked, ate, studied, shopped, or went about your other daily activities. Most people spend between 80 and 90 percent of their waking hours engaging in some form of interpersonal communication.[1] It is through these exchanges that we develop interpersonal relationships with others.

Because these relationships are so important in our lives, later chapters will focus on the communication skills and principles that explain and predict how we develop, sustain, and sometimes end them. We'll explore such questions as: Why do we like some people and not others? How can we interpret other people's unspoken messages with greater accuracy? Why do some relationships blossom and others deteriorate? How can we better manage disagreements with others? How can we better understand our relationships with our family, friends, and co-workers?

This chapter charts the course ahead, addressing key questions about what interpersonal communication is and why it is important. We will begin by seeing how our understanding of the interpersonal communication process has evolved. And we will conclude by examining how we initiate and sustain relationships through interpersonal communication.

The relationship between a guide dog and a visually impaired person is close, and the communication between them is precise and reliable. What distinguishes this form of communication from interpersonal communication, which is the focus of this textbook? (CP Photo/Richard Lam)

communication. The process of acting upon information.

human communication. The process of making sense out of the world and attempting to share that sense with others.

interpersonal communication. Process of interacting simultaneously with another person and mutually influencing each other, usually for the purpose of managing relationships.

impersonal communication. Communication that occurs when we treat people as objects, or when we respond to their roles rather than to who they are as unique persons.

What Is Interpersonal Communication?

To understand interpersonal communication, we must begin by understanding how it relates to two broader categories: communication in general and human communication. Scholars have attempted to arrive at a general definition of communication for decades. One research team counted more than 126 published definitions,[2] and experts cannot agree upon a single one. But, in the broadest sense, **communication** is the process of acting upon information.[3] Someone does or says something, and others think or do something in response to the action or the words as they understand them.

Communication is not unique to humans. It is possible, for example, for you to act upon information from your dog. He barks; you feed him. This definition also suggests that your dog can act upon information from you. You head for the cupboard to feed him; he wags his tail and jumps up in the air anticipating his dinner. Researchers do study communication between species as well as communication systems within single animal species, but these fields of study are beyond the scope of this book. The focus of our study is upon a form of human communication: people communicating with other people.

To refine this definition, we can say that **human communication** is the process of making sense out of the world and sharing that sense with others.[4] We learn about the world by listening, observing, tasting, touching, and smelling; then we share our conclusions with others. Human communication encompasses many media: speeches, songs, radio and television broadcasts, e-mail, letters, books, articles, poems, advertisements.

Interpersonal communication is a special form of human communication that occurs when we interact simultaneously with another person and mutually influence each other, usually for the purpose of managing relationships. Three essential elements of this definition determine the unique nature of interpersonal communication apart from other forms of human communication.

Interpersonal Communication Is a Distinctive Form of Communication

For years many scholars defined interpersonal communication simply as communication that occurs when two people interact face to face. This limited definition suggests that if two people are interacting, then they are interpersonally communicating. Today, interpersonal communication is defined not just by the number of people who communicate, but also by the quality of the communication. Interpersonal communication occurs not when you simply interact with someone, but when you treat the other as a unique human being.

Think of all human communication as ranging on a continuum from impersonal to interpersonal communication. Impersonal communication occurs when you treat people as objects, or when you respond to their roles rather than to who they are as unique people. Philosopher Martin Buber influenced our thinking about human communication when he presented the concept of true dialogue as

> ### Recap
>
> **COMPARING KEY DEFINITIONS**
>
> | Term | Definition |
> | --- | --- |
> | Communication | The process of acting on information |
> | Human communication | The process of making sense out of the world and sharing that sense with others |
> | Interpersonal communication | The process of interacting with another and mutually influencing each other, usually for the purpose of managing relationships |

the essence of true, authentic communication.[5] He described communication as consisting of two different qualities of relationships. He discussed an "I–It" relationship as an impersonal one; the other person is viewed as an "It" rather than as an authentic, genuine person. When you buy a pair of socks at a clothing store, you have a two-person, face-to-face, relatively brief interaction with someone. You communicate. Yet that interchange could hardly be described as intimate or personal. When you ask a server in a restaurant for a glass of water, you are interacting with the role, not necessarily with the individual. You know nothing personal about him (or her), and he knows nothing personal about you (unless he eavesdrops by your table).

Interpersonal communication occurs when you interact with another person as a unique, authentic individual rather than as object or "It." Buber calls this kind of relationship an "I–Thou" relationship. There is true dialogue. An "I–Thou" relationship is not self-centred. The communicators have developed an attitude toward each other that is honest, open, spontaneous, non-judgmental, and based on equality rather than superiority.[6] The exchanges with the sock-seller or server have the potential to become true interpersonal communication dialogue if you begin to interact with these people as unique individuals. If, for example, during your conversation with the server, you discover you were born in the same town and develop other personal links, the impersonal, role-oriented communication becomes more personal, and the quality of the communication moves toward the intimate end of the continuum.

We're not suggesting that the goal of every communication exchange is to develop a personal, intimate dialogue. As with buying socks or asking for a glass of water at a restaurant, it may not be appropriate to develop personal relationships with others just because you are talking with them.

Although interpersonal communication is more intimate and reveals more about the people involved than does impersonal communication, not all interpersonal communication involves sharing closely guarded personal information. As we discuss later in the book, there are degrees of intimacy when interacting with others. Table 1.1 compares and contrasts interpersonal communication with impersonal communication.

Interpersonal Communication Involves Mutual Influence between Individuals

Mutual influence means that *all* partners are affected by the interactions, not just one person. Interpersonal communication may or may not involve words. The interaction may be fleeting or enduring. While you are talking and your mother is listening, you are also simultaneously observing your mother's non-verbal

Table 1.1
The Continuum between Interpersonal Communication and Impersonal Communication

Interpersonal Communication	Impersonal Communication
● People are treated as unique individuals.	● People are treated as objects.
● People communicate in an "I–Thou" relationship. You are special.	● People communicate in an "I–It" relationship. You have a role to perform.
● There is true dialogue and honest sharing of self with others.	● There is mechanical, stilted interaction; no honest sharing of feelings.
● Interpersonal communication often involves communicating with someone you care about, such as a good friend or cherished family member.	● Impersonal communication involves communicating with people such as sales clerks and waitpersons—you have no history with them and you expect no future with them.

expressions. Just because she is not speaking does not mean she is not communicating. She not only hears *what* you have to say, but also observes *how* you say it.

The degree of mutual influence varies a great deal from interaction to interaction. You probably would not be affected a great deal by a brief smile that you receive from a travelling companion on a bus, but would be greatly affected by your lover telling you he or she is leaving you. Every interpersonal communication interaction influences us. Sometimes it changes our lives dramatically, sometimes in small ways. Long-lasting interpersonal relationships are sustained not by one person giving and another taking, but by a spirit of mutual equality. Both you and your partner listen and respond with respect for each other. There is no attempt to manipulate others. True dialogue, says researcher Daniel Yankelovich, involves a collaborative climate. It's not about winning and losing an argument. It's about being understood and accepted.[7]

Buber defines the quality of being fully "present" when communicating with another person as an "I–Thou" relationship.[8] To be present is to give your full attention to the other person. The quality of interpersonal communication is enhanced when both you and your partner are simultaneously present and focused on each other.

Interpersonal Communication Is the Fundamental Means We Use to Manage Our Relationships

An interpersonal **relationship** is the ongoing connection you make with others through interpersonal communication. Relationships go through a series of developmental stages. The initial stages of relationships often involve sharing less intimate or personal information. Later stages evolve to include more intimate conversations and behaviours.

You initiate and form relationships by communicating with others whom you find attractive in some way. You seek to increase your interactions with people with whom you wish to develop relationships, and you continually interpersonally communicate to maintain the relationship. You also use interpersonal communication to end relationships that you have decided are no longer viable.

You can usually identify the stage of a relationship by simply observing the interpersonal communication. People interact differently as they move toward or away

relationship. An ongoing connection made with another person through interpersonal communication.

from intimacy. Your interactions with a new acquaintance differ from those with a close friend. When interacting with a stranger, you stand farther away, use different words, are more likely to feel awkward, and are less certain about how to interpret body language than when you interact with a good friend. We more fully describe the nature and development of interpersonal relationships with others in Chapters 10 and 11.

In this book we define interpersonal communication as a unique form of human communication. There are other forms of communication, as well. **Mass communication** occurs when someone communicates the same message to many people at once, but the creator of the message is usually not physically present, and listeners have virtually no opportunity to respond immediately to the speaker. Messages communicated via radio and TV are examples of mass communication. **Public communication** occurs when a speaker addresses a large audience in person. **Small-group communication** occurs when a group of from three to fifteen people meet to interact with a common purpose and mutually influence one another. The purpose of the gathering could be to solve a problem, make a decision, learn, or just have fun. While communicating with others in a small group, it is also possible to communicate with others interpersonally—to communicate to manage a relationship with one or more individuals in the group. Finally, **intrapersonal communication** is communication with yourself. Thinking is perhaps the best example of intrapersonal communication. In our discussion of self and communication in Chapter 2, we discuss the relationships between your thoughts and your interpersonal communication with others.

mass communication. Type of communication that occurs when one person issues the same message to many people at once; the creator of the message is usually not present and there is virtually no opportunity for listeners to respond to the speaker.

public communication. Type of communication that occurs when a speaker addresses a large audience in person.

small-group communication. Type of communication that occurs when a group of from three to fifteen people meet to interact with a common purpose and mutually influence one another.

intrapersonal communication. Communication with yourself; thinking.

The Importance of Interpersonal Communication to Our Lives

Why study interpersonal communication? Because it touches every aspect of your life. It is not only pleasant or desirable to develop quality interpersonal relationships with others, it is vital for your well-being. Learning how to understand and improve interpersonal communication can improve relationships with family, loved ones, friends, and colleagues and can enhance the quality of physical and emotional health.

Improve Relationships with Family

Relating to family members can be a challenge. The divorce statistics in Canada document the difficulties that can occur when people live in relationship with each other: About half of all marriages end in divorce. We don't claim that you will avoid all family conflicts or that your family relationships will always be harmonious if you learn principles and skills of interpersonal communication. You can, however, develop more options for how to respond when family communication challenges come your way. You will be more likely to develop creative, constructive solutions to family conflict if you understand what's happening and can promote true dialogue with your spouse, parent, brother, or sister. Furthermore, family relationships play a major role in determining how you interact with others. Family communication author Virginia Satir calls family communication "the largest single factor determining the kinds of relationships [people make] with others."[9]

Improve Relationships with Friends and Lovers

We cannot choose our biological families, but we do choose our friends. Friends are people we choose to be with because we like them and usually they like us. We expect friends to be honest, open, and affectionate; to confide in us, respect us, and constructively work through disagreements.[10] We depend on them to fill many roles. According to one researcher, friends provide useful information (about job vacancies, where to shop, the best places to eat, etc.); needed services (help us when we need it); companionship; emotional support; and even financial assistance.[11] We also develop unique meanings, private jokes, and other coded messages that only our friends can understand.[12] Why do we choose some people as friends and develop a reciprocal mistrust of others? The quality of our relationships with others hinges on the quality of our communication. Therefore, learning communication patterns, principles, and prescriptions can help answer this question and improve our relationships with the friends we have.

For unmarried people, developing friendships and falling in love are the top-rated sources of satisfaction and happiness in life.[13] Conversely, losing a relationship is among life's most stressful events.[14] Most individuals between the ages of 19 and 24 report that they have had from five to six romantic relationships and have been "in love" once or twice.[15] Of course, the most intense human relationships involve both psychological and sexual intimacy, and they follow predictable patterns of courtship, escalation, and de-escalation. What we reveal about ourselves, the activities we pursue, and what we talk about in these relationships determine how successful they will be. Studying interpersonal communication may not unravel *all* of the mysteries of romantic love, but it can offer insight into our behaviours.

Effective interpersonal skills are essential for people to develop meaningful, caring relationships. (Lori Adamski Peek/Tony Stone Images)

Improve Relationships with Colleagues

In many ways, our colleagues at work are like family members. Although we choose our friends and lovers, we don't always have the same flexibility in choosing whom we work with or for. Understanding how relationships develop on the job can help us avoid conflict and stress and increase our sense of satisfaction. In addition, our success or failure in a job often hinges upon how well we get along with our supervisor and our peers. Most job performance reviews give the boss a chance to make comments about how well we work with others. Moreover, recent studies have shown that training workers to relate and communicate as a team improves quality and productivity in many occupations, so more and more workplaces are adopting teamwork as a management strategy. The Canadian Issues on the next page illustrates some of the interpersonal skills required by Canadian employers today. Chapter 11 includes a more comprehensive listing of these skills.

Canadian Issues

WHAT SKILLS WILL I NEED FOR EMPLOYMENT?

If your job search is going to be successful, not only do you need to know your own goals, you also need to know what employers are looking for when you start your job search. Courses that teach Interpersonal Communication Skills help you to improve your own skills and to become a more attractive candidate. The Conference Board of Canada has published a brochure that outlines an Employability Skills Profile based on information gathered from Canadian employers.

Many skills are required and they have been summarized under three headings: Academic Skills, Personal Management Skills, and Teamwork Skills. This brochure will assist you in developing skills in several of the main areas. Under the heading of Personal Management Skills, employers need a person who has self-esteem and confidence, who recognizes and respects people's diversity and individual differences, who has a positive attitude toward learning, growth, and personal health, and who has the ability to identify and suggest new ideas to get the job done in a creative way. Within the area of teamwork, many outcomes are discussed in this brochure, including respecting the thoughts and opinions of others in the group, using conflict management strategies to facilitate "give and take" to achieve group results, and planning and making decisions with others and supporting those outcomes.

Although many may view these as "soft skills," there is no doubt that in an economic climate where getting a job can be "hard," these skills may be the ones that may set you apart from other candidates.

Source: ED399484 95 Employability Skills Profile: What Are Employers Looking For? Author: Mary Ann McLaughlin.

Improve Your Physical and Emotional Health

Intimate interpersonal relationships are vital to your health. Research has shown that the lack or loss of a relationship can lead to ill health and even death. Physicians have long observed that patients who are widowed or divorced experience more medical problems such as heart disease, cancer, pneumonia, and diabetes than do married people.[16] Grief-stricken spouses are more likely than others to die prematurely,[17] especially around the time of the departed spouse's birthday or near their wedding anniversary.[18] Being childless also can shorten your life. One research team found that middle-aged, childless wives were almost two and one-half times more likely to die in a given year than those who had at least one child.[19] Terminally ill patients with a limited number of friends or no social support die sooner than those with stronger ties.[20] Loneliness can kill.

Research findings are similar for mental illness: widowed and divorced individuals are more likely to experience mental illness, especially depression, than those in ongoing relationships.[21] In fact, **depression** is the most commonly diagnosed mental illness. The Canadian Mental Health Association has estimated that 15 percent of the population will have a major depressive episode at some point in their lives.[22]

On the positive side, however, establishing a quality social support system can be a major factor in improving and maintaining your health. One study suggests that the more attached we are to at least one other person, the longer we live.[23]

All of these findings show that the stress of loneliness can make us sick, but if we have support from people who care about us, we can adjust to life's tumbles and

depression. A widespread emotional disorder in which the person has problems with sadness, changes in appetite, difficulty sleeping, and a decrease in activities, interests, and energy.

challenges. By learning more about effective communication, you are paving the way for closer, more satisfying relationships, and a longer life.

An Evolving Model for Human and Interpersonal Communication

Today, we know that interpersonal communication is more than simply transferring or exchanging messages with others; it is a complex process of creating meaning. To understand this process, it is useful to see how our perspective on the human communication process has evolved over the past half century. We will begin with the simplest and oldest model of the human communication process.

Human Communication as Action: Message Transfer

"Did you get my message?" This simple sentence summarizes the communication-as-action approach to human communication. Communication takes place when a message is sent and received. Period. It is a way of transferring meaning from sender to receiver. In 1942, Harold Lasswell summarized the process as follows:

Who (sender)

Says what (message)

In what channel

To whom (receiver)

With what effect.[24]

Figure 1.1 shows a basic model formulated in 1949, seven years after Lasswell's summary, that depicts communication as a linear input/output process. Today, although they view the process differently, researchers still define most of the key components in this model in basically the same way.

In face-to-face encounters, we simultaneously exchange both verbal and non-verbal messages that result in shared meanings. Through this kind of interrelation, we build relationships with others. (Robert Brenner/Photo Edit)

Figure 1.1
A Model for Communication as Action

Source: From *The Mathematical Theory of Communication* by Claude E. Shannon and Warren Weaver. Copyright 1949 by the Board of Trustees of the University of Illinois. Used by permission of the University of Illinois Press.

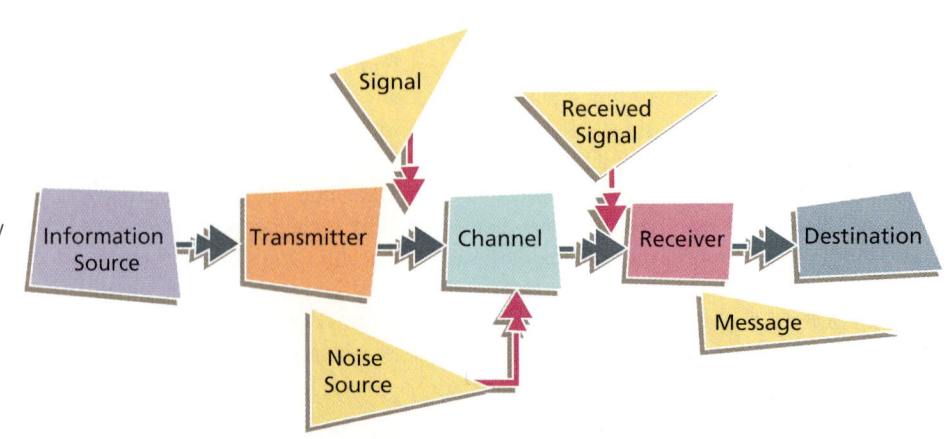

Information Source → Transmitter → Channel → Receiver → Destination

Signal, Received Signal, Noise Source, Message

Information Source and Transmitter

The **information source** for a communication can be a thought or an emotion. The transmitter (now called the **source**), the originator of that thought or emotion, puts the thought or emotion into a code that can be understood by a receiver. Translating ideas, feelings, and thoughts into a code is called **encoding**. Vocalizing a word, gesturing, or establishing eye contact are signals that we use to encode our thoughts into a message that can be **decoded** by the receiver. Decoding is the opposite of encoding. The words or unspoken signals are interpreted by the receiver.

Receiver

The **receiver** is the person who decodes and attempts to make sense out of what the source encoded. Think of a radio station with a source broadcasting to a receiver that picks up the station's signal. In human communication, however, there is something between the source and the receiver: we filter messages through past experiences, attitudes, beliefs, values, prejudices, and biases.

Signal, Received Signal, and Message

Today, all of these components are simply called the message. The **message** is the written, spoken, and unspoken elements of communication to which we assign meaning. You can send a message intentionally (talking to a professor before class) or unintentionally (falling asleep during class), verbally ("Hi. How are you?"), non-verbally (a smile and a handshake), or in written form (this book).

Channel

A message is communicated from sender to receiver via some pathway called a **channel**. Channels correspond to your senses. When you call your mother on the telephone, the channel is an auditory one. When you talk with your mother face to face, the channels are many. You see her: the visual channel. You hear her: the auditory channel. You may smell her perfume: the olfactory channel. You may hug her: the tactile channel.

Noise

Noise is interference. Without noise, all of our messages would be communicated with sublime accuracy. But noise is always present. It can be literal—the obnoxious roar of a gas-powered lawn mower—or it can be psychological. Instead of concentrating on your teacher's lecture, you may start thinking about the chores you need to finish before the end of the day. Whichever kind it is, noise gets in the way of the message and may even distort it. Communicating accurate messages involves minimizing both external and psychological noise.

Although the action approach is simple and straightforward, it has a key flaw: human communication rarely, if ever, is as simple and efficient as "what we put in is what we get out." Others cannot automatically know what you mean just because you think you know what you mean. Although by Lasswell's time, communication scholars had already begun identifying an array of key elements in the communication process, the action approach overlooked their complexity.

Human Communication as Interaction: Message Exchange

The next big leap in our understanding of human communication came in the late 1940s and early 1950s. The communication-as-interaction perspective used the

---

information source. The thought or emotion that triggers communication.

source. The originator of a thought or emotion who puts the thought or emotion into a code that can be understood by a receiver.

encode. To translate ideas, feelings, and thoughts into a code.

decode. To interpret ideas, feelings, and thoughts that have been translated into a code.

receiver. The person who decodes a message and attempts to make sense out of what the source has encoded.

message. The written, spoken, and unspoken elements of communication to which people assign meaning.

channel. The pathway by which messages are sent.

noise. Information, either literal or psychological, that interferes with the accurate reception of the communication of the message.

same elements as the action models but added two new ones: feedback and context.

Think of a table tennis game. Messages, like the ball, bounce back and forth. We talk; someone listens and responds. We respond to their response, and so forth. This perspective can be summarized using a physical principle: for every action there is a reaction.

Feedback is the response to the message. Without feedback, communication is rarely effective. When you order a black olive pizza, your server encodes the message internally and says, "That's a black olive pizza, right?" The server must provide feedback to ensure that he or she understood the message correctly.

Feedback is really a response message. Like other messages, it can be intentional (applause at the conclusion of a symphony) or unintentional (a yawn as, once again, you listen to your uncle tell his story about bears); verbal ("That's a black olive pizza, right?") or non-verbal (blushing after being asked to dance).

A second component recognized by the interaction perspective is **context**—the physical and psychological communication environment. All communication takes place in some context. As the cliché goes, "Everyone has to be somewhere." A conversation with a good friend on the beach would likely differ from one the two of you might have in a funeral home. Context encompasses not only the physical environment but also the number of people present and their relationship with the communicators, the communication goal, and the culture in which the communicators are steeped.

This approach, as shown in Figure 1.2, is more realistic, but it still has limitations if we think about interpersonal communication in specific. It still views communication as a linear, step-by-step sequence of events. Although it emphasizes feedback and context, it does not quite capture the complexity of the process if the communication takes place simultaneously. In interpersonal situations, both the source and the receiver send and receive messages at the same time.

feedback. The response to a message.

context. The physical and psychological communication environment.

Figure 1.2
A Model for Communication as Interaction
Interaction models of communication include feedback as a response to a message sent by the communication source.

Source: From *Invitation to Effective Speech* by John T. Masterson, Steven A. Beebe, and Norman H. Watson (Scott, Foresman and Company, 1989).

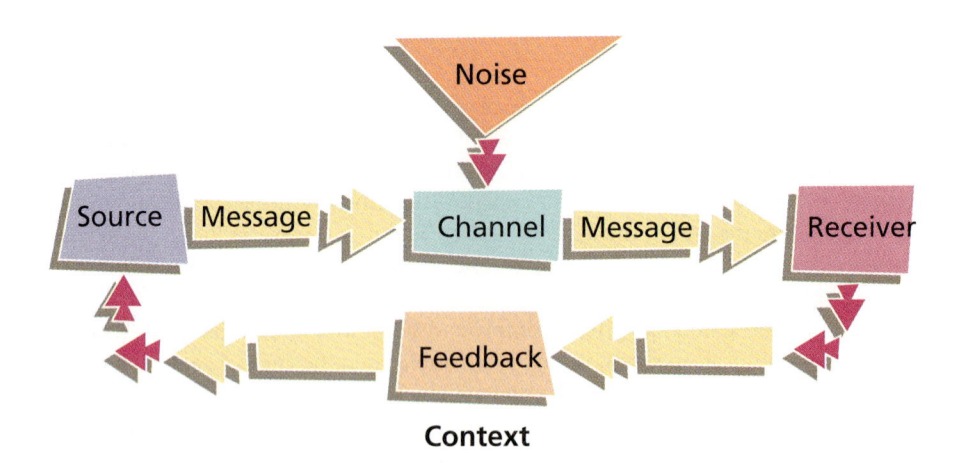

Human Communication as Transaction: Message Creation

The communication-as-transaction perspective, developed in the 1960s, acknowledges that, when we talk to each other, we are constantly reacting to what our partner is saying. The majority of scholars today view it as the most realistic model for interpersonal communication. It uses the same components to describe communication, such as action and interaction. But in this model, all of the interaction is simultaneous. As Figure 1.3 indicates, we send and receive messages concurrently. Even as we talk, we are also interpreting our partner's non-verbal and verbal responses.

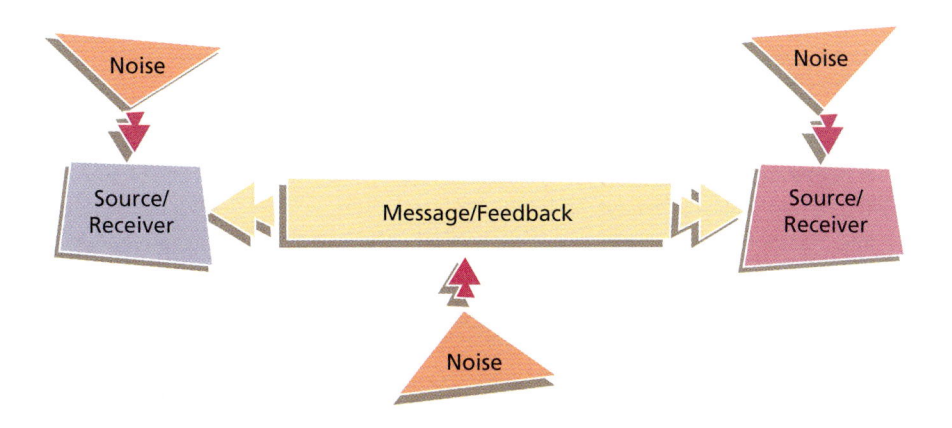

**Figure 1.3
A Model for Communication as Mutual Transaction**
The source and the receiver of a message experience communication simultaneously.

Transactional communication also occurs within a context defined more broadly than by action or interaction. Transactional communication suggests that your communication is influenced by a force that may not be immediately evident to you or your communication partner. The past experiences and culture of the people involved in the communication, the setting of the communication, and the thoughts and emotions of the communicators are all influencing how messages are being interpreted. Whereas communication as action or interaction views communication as linear—there are specific causes and effects that can explain how messages are interpreted—communication as transaction is much more complicated. An understanding of the relationships you establish changes from moment to moment as the conversation unfolds and your thoughts influence how you are responding to the message. A transactional approach to communication suggests that no single cause explains why you interpret messages the way you do. In fact, it is inappropriate to point to a single factor to explain how you are making sense of the messages of others; communication is messier than that. The meaning of messages in interpersonal relationships evolves from the past, is influenced by the present, and is affected by visions of the future.

As we communicate messages, we monitor the degree to which the other person understands each message. We mutually define the symbols we use. If one partner misunderstands a message, both can work to clarify the meaning. For example, if I ask you to hand me the book off my desk and you hand me a pad of paper, we have failed to create a shared meaning. I might then say, "No, not the pad of paper, the red book next to the phone"; you then would hand me the book. Your action would require me to explain and be more specific. We would not simply transfer or exchange meaning; we would create it during a communication transaction.

One researcher has said that interpersonal communication is "the coordinated management of meaning" through **episodes**, during which the message of one person influences the message of another.[25] Technically, only the sender and receiver of those messages can determine where one episode ends and another begins.

episode. A sequence of interaction between individuals during which the message of one person influences the message of another.

Recap

COMPONENTS OF THE HUMAN COMMUNICATION PROCESS

Term	Definition
Source	Human being who has an idea or emotion.
Receiver	Person or group toward whom the source directs messages, intentionally or unintentionally.
Message	Written, spoken, and unspoken elements of communication to which we assign meaning.
Channel	Pathway through which messages pass between source and receiver.
Noise	Anything, either literal or psychological, that interferes with the clear reception and interpretation of a message.
Encoding	Translation of ideas, feelings, and thoughts into a code.
Decoding	Interpretation of ideas, feelings, and thoughts that have been translated into a code.
Context	Physical and psychological communication environment.
Feedback	Verbal and non-verbal responses to messages.

Recap

AN EVOLVING MODEL FOR INTERPERSONAL COMMUNICATION

Human Communication as Action

Human communication is linear, as meaning is sent or transferred from source to receiver.

Human Communication as Interaction

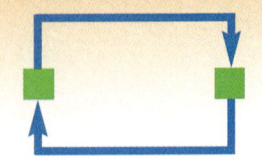

Human communication occurs as the receiver of the message responds to the source through feedback. This interactive model views communication as a linear action-reaction sequence of events.

Human Communication as Transaction

Human communication is simultaneously interactive. Meaning is created based upon a mutual, concurrent sharing of ideas and feelings. This model most accurately describes interpersonal communication.

Mediated Interpersonal Communication: A New Frontier

Today's technology allows us to expand our definition of interpersonal communication. Instead of having to rely on face-to-face contact for our interpersonal exchanges, we can now use various types of media to carry our interpersonal messages: Telephones, faxes, e-mail, and electronic chat rooms are among the sometimes bewildering assortment of devices through which we can interact, exercise mutual influence, and develop interpersonal relationships. When we use one of these media to carry the message, we are using **mediated interpersonal communication**. But as Leonard Pitts suggests in *E-Connections: Impersonal*

mediated interpersonal communication. Communication with others established or maintained by using media (such as e-mail, telephone, or a fax) rather than a face-to-face encounter.

America, mediated interpersonal communication may sometimes be less satisfying than a face-to-face encounter. Even in this electronic age, interacting with machines instead of humans may be uncomfortable for some people.

e-connections

IMPERSONAL AMERICA

A few weeks back, I bought an upgrade card for my computer. Being inexpert at such things, I soon found myself out of my depth and placed a call to the company's technical-support line. After going through the menu of options offered by the machine that answered the phone, I was connected to a recorded voice that said I would be on hold for five or ten minutes before someone could help me.

I was actually on hold for about an hour, but my ordeal finally ended.

When the machine hung up on me.

Undaunted, I called the company back—did I mention that this was long-distance?—and spent another hour listening to the same three elevator tunes repeated endlessly. Fed up, I hung up, only to repeat the sequence over the next few days without getting even a smidgen of technical support from the technical-support line.

Which brings us to the question: Where have all the human beings gone?

You know, the people who used to answer your questions, explain your options...service with a smile and all that? What happened to them?

It's not just the computer company that makes me wonder. It's the utility company, the bank, the subscription department, the telephone operator and, yes, the automated phone system at my very own office.

It wasn't always like this. Remember when you took your questions to a human who gave you a human response? Now, you listen to a menu and input information. We live in Impersonal America, an acquaintance said the other day as he swiped his money card to buy gas at the pump. Not so long ago, he mused, filling the tank meant dealing with another human being. Maybe shooting the breeze for a moment or two. Now, we just pump and run. Granted, the new way is quicker and easier.

Less painful sometimes, too. Once, years ago, I needed to get an extension on a utility bill. I'm sitting there on hold, trying to frame a hard-luck tale for the clerk, when suddenly a machine picks up the phone. It instructs me to key in some information and quickly approves my request. Never even asks for my tale of woe. It seemed a good deal to me at the time. Only

Continued

now do I find myself questioning whether the trade-off was worth it. Only now that humanity has been exchanged for cost-effectiveness and service swapped for speed.

And that's a term which seems especially apropos because I don't think this happened just because we were looking for greater efficiency. No, I think we also wanted greater uniformity. We wanted—and have made—our encounters sterile and personality-free. Know how bad it is? A cashier, an older woman who works in a cafeteria in Washington, got in hot water a while back for her habit of calling customers "honey" and "sweetie."

We wanted it to be like that. Wanted correctness over personality. Wanted one-size-fits-all customer service free from the messiness—bad moods, biases, idiosyncrasies, small talk—that characterizes human interaction. But I find that I miss the mess. Indeed, when I went through back channels and finally got a live human to answer my computer question, I was more pumped than an OPEC oil well. The guy even got snippy with me, and it was like hearing a favorite song for the first time in years.

It made me wonder: Are we really better off now than we were when human beings—snippy and otherwise—answered the phones and provided the service? OK, so maybe real live people aren't cost-effective. But I can tell you this: I wound up taking that upgrade card back to the store. Asked the clerk to recommend one from a company that could actually put a living breathing human being on the line in a reasonable amount of time. The card he showed me costs about $100 more. And you know something? It's worth it.

Source: Leonard Pitts, *Miami Herald.* Distributed by Knight-Ridder/Tribune Information Services.

At present, the most effective interpersonal communication still occurs when there are no media filters to interfere with the clarity of the message or to delay feedback from the receiver of the message. For this reason, our key focus in this book will be upon unmediated interaction between people.

But we will also begin to explore the new frontier in interpersonal communication. Can you communicate interpersonally with someone on the Internet? Can relationships be developed with another without meeting face to face? There is evidence that people can and do develop meaningful relationships with others without meeting them in person. If you are attending a college or university away from family, friends, or loved ones, you may have found that sending e-mail messages can help keep you in touch with others who are important to you. College freshmen and their parents report that e-mail connections reduce homesickness and the sadness parents often feel as their son or daughter leaves home. The past few years have seen an increase in the number of people who meet in a chat room on the Internet and eventually develop a real-time relationship. In special E-Connections features throughout this book, we will highlight the ways that today's technology is affecting our relationships. As *E-Connections:* An *Electronic Relationship* illustrates, e-mail allows intimate relationships to develop between people who are separated by thousands of miles.

e-connections

AN ELECTRONIC RELATIONSHIP

Today's technology makes it possible for people to develop relationships with others without meeting face to face. Glen is an elementary school teacher in the coastal fishing village of Port Simpson, in northern British Columbia. His wife Cathy is a full-time homemaker and mother to their five young children. They were drawn to this remote community from Vancouver eight years ago "to get away from it all." For Cathy,

> however, their alternative lifestyle quickly became one of isolation and loneliness. Three years ago, Cathy's sister visited with gifts of a computer, a modem, and a lesson on the Internet. Since that visit, Cathy has been able to "converse" daily with family and friends throughout the country. She has also made connections and formed close bonds with new acquaintances as far away as Norway. "Since I've been 'online,'" explains Cathy, "life in Port Simpson has gone from boring and lonely to worldly." For people like Cathy, e-mail provides a form of correspondence that is comparable to, yet also worlds apart from, old-fashioned letter writing. The difference, of course, is that partners can measure the intervals between these "letters" in nanoseconds instead of days or weeks. Although such exchanges are not simultaneous, they certainly can have the kind of spontaneity that we usually associate with interpersonal communication.

People have even developed new ways to communicate the feelings, emotions, and other responses that make it possible to communicate non-verbally. You are probably familiar with emoticons, keyboard symbols typed sideways, like :-O. (Note several other emoticons identified in the following E-Connections box.) You can also communicate emotions via e-mail by "screaming." In still other situations, you might respond to someone by verbally describing non-verbal behaviours: "I am frowning right now as I read what you are sending me."

e-connections

EMOTICONS

A kiss is just a : *, a sigh is just a : - (.

Electronic-mail writers have adopted a lighthearted system of shorthand known as "emoticons." These clever combinations of keyboard characters punctuate a message with just the right spirit. To read them, simply look at the line with your head tilted slightly to the left.

For example, in the most basic emoticon, the smiley face, a colon, hyphen, and a right parenthesis become the eye, nose, and mouth of glee :-).

Here's a sample of some frequently used emoticons that will help you get across the nuances of your message:

:-|)	smiley with a mustache
:D	big smile
;-	wink
:-@	scream
:X	keeping mouth shut
:-&	tongue-tied
:-J	tongue in cheek or joking
:p	sticking out tongue or giving a raspberry
:*	kiss
:**:	returning kiss
( )	hug
(((())))	lots of hugs
:-)8	sharply dressed person
:->	hey hey
|-)	hee hee
|-D	ho ho
:/	not funny
:-}	smirk
:-o	shocked (or singing the national anthem)
:I	bored
>:-<	angry
<:-)	dumb question or dumb person
(:-$	sick person or person is sick
:-(	sad
:-	really sad
:'(	crying
;-?	licking your lips

Source: Charles Bowen, *HomePC* (January 1995), 109.

Want to see more emoticons? Click on the following Web addresses to enrich your emoticon vocabulary:
www.chatlist.com/faces.html
www.pressanykey.com/emoticons.html
www.pars.com.cz/clients/smiles/index

Of course, just as not all face-to-face communication is interpersonal communication, not all mediated communication results in unique relationships with others. One of the key differences in these mediated communication situations is the reduced level of non-verbal cues. Even if you use emoticons, when you can't see the other person's facial expression, amount of eye contact, or whether he or she seems interested in what you are saying, accurately communicating your meaning, especially your feelings and emotions, can be challenging.

A growing body of research, however, suggests that when you interact with people using computer-mediated communication, you can compensate for the lack of non-verbal cues. If you've been interacting with someone over a period of several weeks or months, you begin to pick up cues about his or her emotions and feelings just from the words he or she uses and from what you have learned about that person and his or her behaviour.

Communication researcher Joseph Walther and his colleagues have developed a **social information-processing theory** that explains how you can develop quality relationships with others via e-mail and other electronic means.[26] According to this theory, a key difference between face-to-face and computer-mediated communication is the rate at which information reaches you. During live, in-person communication, you process a lot of information quickly; you process the words you hear as well as the myriad of non-verbal cues you see (facial expression and body posture) and hear (tone of voice and use of pauses). During e-mail interactions, there is less information to process, so it takes a bit longer for the relationship to develop—but it does develop as you learn more about your e-mail partner's likes, dislikes, and feelings. Also, if you expect to communicate with your electronic communication partner again, there is evidence that you will pay more attention to the relationship cues that develop. In one study, Joseph Walther and Judee Burgoon found that the development of relationships between people who met face to face differed little from those between people who had computer-mediated interactions.[27] In fact, they found the computer-mediated group actually developed *more* socially rich relationships than the face-to-face groups. Because of technology, some electronic interpersonal exchanges may not be simultaneous. Nonetheless, there is mutual understanding, and the communication can be truly personal rather than impersonal. We suggest that these electronic communication exchanges, even though not as rich in non-verbal and relational information, can mirror characteristics of face-to-face interpersonal communication in the sense that you are developing or maintaining a unique relationship with someone. In addition, electronically mediated relationships can involve mutual influence. And e-mailing someone that you'd like to marry—or divorce—that person, or just get together for a cup of coffee, illustrates how e-messages can alter both lives and relationships. Clearly, not all e-mail correspondence is interpersonal communication; today's technology, however, sometimes makes it possible to emulate in cyberspace the characteristics of interpersonal transactions.

One research team suggests that the richness of a communication channel can be measured by four criteria: (1) the amount of feedback that the communicators can receive; (2) the number of cues that the channel can convey and that can be interpreted by a receiver; (3) the variety of language that communicators use; and (4) the potential for expressing emotions and feelings.[28] Using these four criteria, researchers have developed a continuum (communication-rich to communication-lean) of communication channels. The model presented in Figure 1.4 illustrates this continuum.

social information-processing theory. Explains how people use information they receive from others via e-mail and other electronic ways to develop relationships with others.

Communication-Rich Channels

Face-to-face, one-on-one conversation
Face-to-face group discussions
Live video conference
Telephone
Interactive, live, synchronous e-mail
Non-interactive, non-synchronous e-mail
Fax
Personal letter
Impersonal memo
Posted flyer or announcement

Communication-Lean Channels

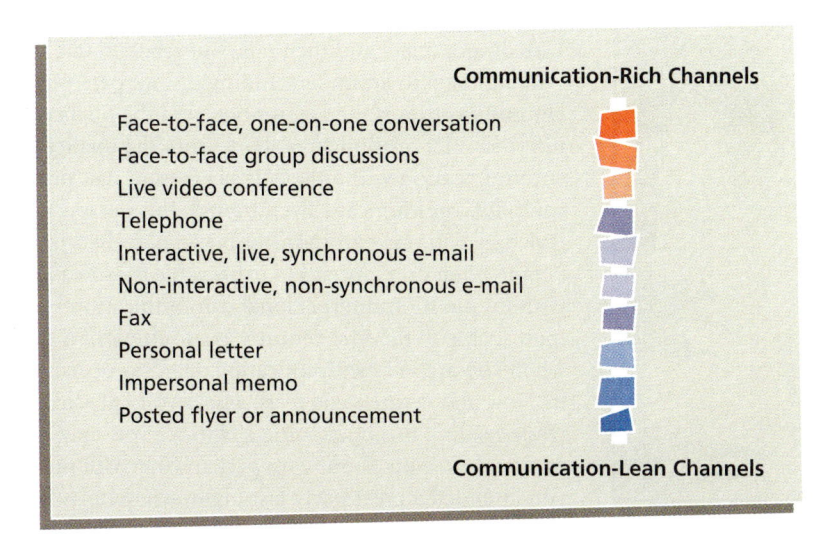

Figure 1.4
A Continuum of Communication-Rich and Communication-Lean Channels of Communication

Adapted from L. K. Trevino, R. L. Draft, and R. H. Lengel, "Understanding Managers' Media Choices: A Symbolic Interactionist Perspective." In *Organizations and Communication Technology,* edited by J. Fulk and C. Steinfield (Newbury Park, CA: Sage, 1990), 71–94.

In summary, we believe this new frontier of electronic communication makes it possible for people to develop interpersonal relationships with others who are miles away. We agree with Joseph Walther and Lisa Tidwell that

> The "Information Superhighway" is clearly not just a road for moving data from one place to another, but a roadside where people pass each other, occasionally meet, and decide to travel together. You can't see very much of other drivers at first, unless you do travel together for some time. There are highway bandits, to be sure, who are not as they appear to be—one must drive defensively—and there are conflicts and disagreements on-line as there are off-road, too.[29]

Principles of Interpersonal Communication

As we introduce the study of interpersonal communication in this chapter, it is useful to present fundamental principles that help explain the nature of interpersonal communication. Underlying our current understanding of interpersonal communication are five principles: Interpersonal communication connects us to others, is irreversible, is complicated, is governed by rules, and involves both content and relationship dimensions.

Interpersonal Communication Connects Us to Others

Unless you are a living in a cave or have become a cloistered monk, you interact with others every day. Even if you work at home in front of a glowing computer screen, you encounter other people in the course of living your life. The opportunities for interpersonal communication are ubiquitous—they are everywhere. It is through inescapable interpersonal communication with others that we affect and are affected by other human beings.

"I'm afraid you misunderstood... I said I'd like a mango."

We agree with author H. D. Duncan, who said, "We do not relate and then talk, but relate in talk." Fundamental to an understanding of interpersonal communication is the assumption that the quality of interpersonal relationships stems from the quality of communication with others. It's been said that people can't *not* communicate. Even though this perspective is debated among communication scholars because people often don't intend to express ideas or feelings, without question interpersonal communication is inescapable in the 21st century. Try to think of a time when you are *not* communicating. Hard to do, isn't it? How about when you're asleep? If you fall asleep while reading this book, others who see you may draw conclusions about you; perhaps they will think you attended a great party last night, when in reality you stayed up late studying for a biology exam. In your interpersonal conversations with others, people may similarly draw an unintended conclusion about your interest in them if you inadvertently yawn while a friend of yours is telling you about the record-size fish he caught on his recent trip to British Columbia. You didn't intend to offend him; you were just exhausted. Our point is that even when you may not be conscious of what you're doing, you are connecting to others through the ever-present process of communication.

The inescapable nature of interpersonal communication doesn't mean others will *accurately* decode your message; it does mean that others are drawing inferences about you and your behaviour—they may be right or they may be wrong. Even as you silently stand in a crowded elevator, your lack of eye contact with others communicates your unwillingness to interact with fellow passengers. Your unspoken messages, even when you are asleep, provide cues that others interpret. Remember: People often judge you by your behaviour, not your intent. Your interpersonal communication is how you develop connections to others. Even in well-established interpersonal relationships, you may be evoking an unintended response to your behaviour.

Interpersonal Communication Is Irreversible

"Disregard that last statement made by the witness," instructs the judge. Yet, the clever lawyer knows that, once her client has stated that her husband gave her a black eye during an argument, the jury cannot really "disregard" the statement. This principle applies to all forms of oral communication. We may try to modify the meaning of a spoken message by saying something like, "Oh, I really didn't mean it." But, in most cases, the damage has been done. Once created, communication has the physical property of matter; it can't be uncreated. As the

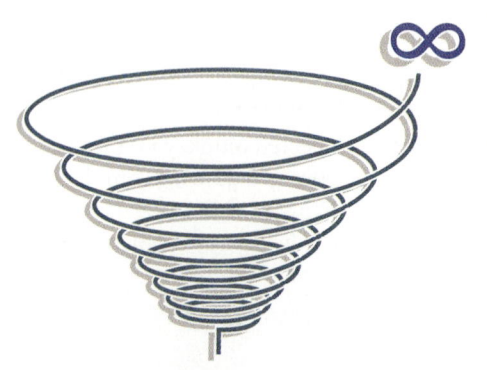

Figure 1.5 Interpersonal Communication Is Irreversible
This helical model shows that interpersonal communication never loops back on itself. It expands as the communication partners contribute their thoughts and experiences to the exchange.

Source: Copyright © F. E. X. Dance in *Human Communication Theory* (Holt, Rinehart and Winston, 1967), 294. Reprinted with permission.

helical model in Figure 1.5 suggests, once interpersonal communication begins, it never loops back on itself. Instead, it continues to be shaped by the events, experiences, and thoughts of the communication partners. A Russian proverb nicely summarizes the point: "Once a word goes out of your mouth, you can never swallow it again."

Interpersonal Communication Is Complicated

No form of communication is simple. If any were, we would know how to reduce the number of misunderstandings and conflicts in our world. Because of the number of variables involved in interpersonal exchanges, even simple requests are extremely complex. Communication theorists have noted that whenever you communicate with another person, there are really at least six "people" involved: (1) who you think you are; (2) who you think the other person is; (3) who you think the other person thinks you are; (4) who the other person thinks he or she is; (5) who the other person thinks you are; and (6) who the other person thinks you think he or she is.[30] Whew! And when you add more people to the interaction, it becomes even more involved.

Moreover, when humans communicate, they interpret information from others as symbols. A **symbol** is merely a representation of something else, and it can have various meanings and interpretations. Language is a system of symbols. In English, symbols do not resemble the words they represent. The word (symbol) for *cow* does not look at all like a cow; someone, somewhere decided that *cow* should mean a beast that chews a cud and gives milk. The reliance on symbols to communicate poses a communication challenge; you are often misinterpreted. Sometimes you don't know the code. Only if you are conversant with *Canadian* English will you know that "riding" refers to an electoral district; "allophone" refers to a Quebecker whose first language is neither French nor English; and "poutine" is french fries with cheese curds and gravy.

symbol. A representation of something else.

Messages are not always interpreted as we intend them. Osmo Wiio, a Scandinavian communication scholar, points out the messiness of communicating with others when he suggests the following maxims:

> If communication can fail, it will.
>
> If a message can be understood in different ways, it will be understood in just that way which does the most harm.
>
> There is always somebody who knows better than you what you meant by your message.
>
> The more communication there is, the more difficult it is for communication to succeed.[31]

Although we are not as pessimistic as Professor Wiio, we do suggest that the task of understanding each other is challenging.

Interpersonal Communication Is Governed by Rules

When you play Monopoly, you know that there are explicit rules about how to get out of jail, buy Boardwalk, or pass "Go" and get two hundred dollars. The rules are written down. When you play a game with others, there may even be some unwritten rules, such as when you play Monopoly with Grandpa, always let him buy Boardwalk. He gets grumpy as a bear before breakfast if he doesn't get to buy it. Similar rules govern how you communicate with others. Most of these rules are embedded in your culture or discussed verbally rather than in a written rulebook.

According to communication researcher Susan Shimanoff, a **rule** is a "followable prescription that indicates what behaviour is obligated, preferred, or prohibited in certain contexts."[32] The rules that help define appropriate and inappropriate communication in any given situation may be *explicit* or *implicit*. For your interpersonal communication class, explicit rules are probably spelled out in your syllabus. But your instructor has other rules that are more implicit. They are not written or verbalized, because you learned them long ago: Only one person speaks at a time, you raise your hand to be called, you do not pass notes.

Interpersonal communication rules are developed by the people involved in the interaction and by the culture in which the individuals are communicating. Many times we learn communication rules from experience, by observing and interacting with others.

Interpersonal relationships are also shaped by both explicit and implicit rules. You may explicitly ask your friend not to phone you after 9 P.M. But you also have implicit expectations of others. In an early stage of a relationship, for example, you do not expect to learn private family secrets. At a later stage, you might be offended if an intimate friend does not reveal such secrets. Understanding rules helps you understand what is expected in a relationship.

Rules are developed both by those involved in the interaction and by the culture in which individuals are interacting. British researcher Michael Argyle and his colleagues asked people to identify general rules for relationship development and maintenance and then rate their importance. Here are the most important rules:[33]

Partners should respect the other's privacy.

Partners should not reveal each other's secrets.

Partners should look the other person in the eye during conversation.

Partners should not criticize the other person publicly.

Although we may modify rules to achieve the goals of our relationships, these general rules remain fairly constant. In interpersonal relationships the rules of a relationship are mutually defined and agreed on. Most of us don't like to be told what to do or how to behave all the time. The expectations and rules are continually renegotiated as the relationship unfolds. Few of us learn relationship rules by copying them from a book. Most of us learn these rules from experience, through observing and interacting with family members and friends. Individuals who grow up in environments in which these rules are not observed may not know how to behave in close relationships.

rule. A followable prescription that indicates what behaviour is obligated, preferred, or prohibited in certain communication situations or contexts.

For many of us, friendships are vital to our personal well-being. By improving our interpersonal communication skills, we can learn how to improve our friendships.
(Ian Shaw/Tony Stone Images)

Interpersonal Communication Involves Both Content and Relationship Dimensions

What you say (your words) and how you say it (your tone of voice, amount of eye contact, facial expression, and posture) can reveal much about the true meaning of your message. If one of your roommates loudly and abruptly bellows, "Hey, dork! Clean this room!" and another roommate uses the same verbal message but more gently and playfully suggests, "Hey, dork. Clean this room," both are communicating a message seeking the same outcome. But the two messages have different relationship cues. The first, shouted message suggests that your roommate may be frustrated that the room still has echoes of last night's pizza party, whereas roommate number two's teasing request suggests he or she may be fondly amused by your untidiness.

The **content** of a communication message consists of the new information, ideas, or suggested actions that the speaker wishes to share. The **relationship dimension** of a communication message is usually more implied; it offers cues about the emotions, attitudes, and amount of power and control the speaker feels toward the other.[34]

Another way of distinguishing between the content and relationship dimensions of communication is to consider that the content of a message refers to *what* is said. Relationship cues refer to *how* it is communicated. This distinction explains why reading a transcript of what someone says can reveal a quite different meaning from actually hearing the person say the message.

content. New information, ideas, or suggested actions that a speaker wishes to share.

relationship dimension. The implied aspect of a communication message, which conveys information about emotions, attitudes, power, and control.

Interpersonal Communication Myths

Several common misconceptions about interpersonal communication can undermine the quality of your interpersonal relationships with others. As we embark on our study of interpersonal communication, it's just as important to unlearn some commonly held misconceptions as it is to learn research conclusions and time-tested principles of interpersonal communication. Don't believe the following myths.

Myth: "More Words Will Make the Meaning Clearer"

More is not necessarily better. Just as there is a time to talk, there is a time to be silent. Piling on more words when your interpersonal communication partner is already baffled by what you are talking about can make matters worse. If someone is confused, hurt, or angry, continuing to add verbiage may hurt, not help. Maybe you just need to stop and listen rather than talk. Or ask a question and then just silently wait for an answer. Or perhaps, rather than words, your friend needs a non-verbal message of reassurance, a hug, a smile, or a nod of your head in agreement. And just as a picture can be worth a thousand words, so demonstrating to someone what you mean can be more powerful than continuing to pile on the words. To keep going and going like the Energizer Bunny may only make matters worse. When you communicate feelings and attitudes, your non-verbal, unspoken expressions are where the action is.

Are we suggesting that more communication is always bad? No. Just don't fall into the trap of believing that more words will solve all problems, enhance the

Instead of focusing entirely on the message we want to convey, we can sometimes communicate even more effectively when we take the time to be other-oriented—to listen to what others are saying. (Masterfile/Masterfile)

quality of interpersonal relationships, and make the meaning clearer. There is a time to stop talking and listen.

Myth: "Meanings Are in Words"

In and of itself, spoken or written, a word has no meaning. It's just a sound, marks on paper, or characters on a computer screen. Meaning resides in people, not words. Others provide the meaning to connect the dots between the word you've spoken and the meaning you intend to create. But sometimes people connect the dots in a way you had not intended. Words are symbols we use to communicate with others. Because a symbol is something that represents something else, a symbol, by its very nature, can have different meanings for different people. Even the best wordsmith or professional speechwriter can use words that result in missed meaning and uncertainty. Differences in culture, background, education, and experience often explain why words create different meanings for different people. When you greet your aunt by enthusiastically demanding, "What's up?" she may find such a greeting a bit too informal and think you're being rude. But to your best buddy, offering a slurred "What's up?" is just a normal way of saying "Hello." You intended no disrespect to your aunt, but she took your colloquial welcome the wrong way. Our point: Just because you've spoken it, don't assume others will always catch what you threw to them. Meanings are in people, not in words.

Myth: "Information Equals Communication"

"How many times do I have to tell you not to use the copy machine?" "Can't you read? It's in the syllabus." "It's in the policy and procedure manual." "Are you deaf? I've told you that I love you several times." Each of these exasperated communicators seems to have thought erroneously that information is the same thing as communication. It's not. Information is not communication. This simple, yet powerful principle helps combat the myth that if you say it or write it, then communication has taken place.

Earlier in the chapter we defined communication at the most basic level as acting on information. If you say it, but no one hears it—does that mean there has been communication? Like the proverbial tree that falls silently in the forest because no one is there to hear it, the message you thought you sent is not really communication just because you've put your thoughts into a code. Encoding does not always ensure decoding. And as we already discussed, even if someone has decoded the message, it could be different from the one you intended. Information is not communication.

Myth: "Interpersonal Relationship Problems Are Always Communication Problems"

"You don't understand me!" shouts Paul to his exasperated partner Pat, "We just can't communicate anymore!" Paul seems to think the problem he and Pat are having is a communication problem. But Paul and Pat may understand each other perfectly; they may simply disagree. Although it's certainly true that conflict and discord in interpersonal relationships can occur because of misunderstandings, not *all* conflict and bumpy relationships stem from misunderstandings. There could be several explanations for why a relationship is experiencing turbulence. Perhaps the communication partners are very clear when communicating, but are so self-centred or self-absorbed that the quality of the relationship suffers. Or perhaps the communication partners just don't like each other; or, if they do like and understand each other, they just disagree. The message has been understood but rejected. Although missed meaning may be a contributing factor in interpersonal conflict, it's a myth to assume that all relational discord stems from misunderstanding.

Even though one purpose of this course is to help you enhance the quality of your relationships by becoming a better communicator, we don't claim that *all* interpersonal conflict stems from misunderstanding one another. Nor are we claiming that learning principles and skills of interpersonal communication will solve all your interpersonal relationship problems. One of this text's authors was approached by a potential client who said, "I understand you are a communication consultant. I need help with my communication skills. *Do something to me* to make me a better communicator." But communication skill development does not work like Harry Potter's magic wand; there's not something that can be "done to" someone to enhance communication ability. And even if there were a wizard's wand to make all your communication perfectly understood by others, and theirs by you, your interpersonal relationships would undoubtedly still experience stress and conflict.

How to Improve Your Own Interpersonal Communication Effectiveness

Now that we have previewed the study of interpersonal communication, you may be saying to yourself, "Well, that's all well and good, but is it possible to improve my own interpersonal communication? Aren't some people just born to have better interpersonal skills than others?" Just as some people have more musical talent or greater skill at passing a puck, evidence suggests that some people may have an inborn, biological talent for communicating with others.[35] You probably know people who have never had a course in communication, but who develop sensitive, caring interpersonal relationships with others.

A growing body of research called the **communibiological approach** to communication suggests that some people inherit certain traits or characteristics that affect the way they communicate with others. There may be a genetic basis for why people communicate as they do. For example, you or people you know may have been born to have more stage fright or anxiety when communicating with others.[36] And some people may not be as comfortable interacting in interpersonal situations as others are. Some researchers and teachers believe, however, that the communibiological approach gives too much weight to biology and not enough to how we can learn to compensate for what nature did not give us.[37]

So what are the implications of the communibiological approach to communication? Does this mean you can't improve your interpersonal communication? *Absolutely not!* The underlying premise of our study of interpersonal communication is that you can learn ways to enhance the quality of your interpersonal relationships with others. We suggest the following six-part strategy for becoming a more effective communicator.

communibiological approach. Theoretical perspective that suggests people's communication behaviour can be predicted based on personal traits and characteristics that result from their genetic or biological background.

Become Knowledgeable

By reading this chapter, you have already begun to improve your communication skills. Competent communicators are knowledgeable. They know how communication works. They understand the components, principles, and rules of the communication process. As you read on in this book, you will learn theories, principles, concepts, and rules that will permit you to explain and predict how humans communicate.

Understanding these things is a necessary prerequisite for enhancing your interpersonal effectiveness, but this kind of knowledge alone does not make you competent. You would not let someone fix your car's carburetor if he or she had only read a book on the subject. Knowledge must be coupled with skill. And we acquire skill through practice.

Become Skilled

Effective communicators know how to translate knowledge into action. You can memorize the characteristics of a good listener but still not listen well. To develop skill requires practice and helpful feedback from others who can confirm the appropriateness of your actions.

Learning a social skill is not that different from learning how to drive a car or operate a computer.[38] To learn any skill, you must break it down into subskills that you can learn and practise. "Hear it, see it, do it, correct it" is the formula that seems to work best for learning any new behaviours.[39] In this book, we will examine the elements of complex skills such as listening, offer activities that will let you practise the skill, and provide opportunities for you to receive feedback and correct your application of the skill.

Become Motivated

Practising skills requires work. You need to be motivated to use your information and skill. You must want to improve, and you must have a genuine desire to connect with others if you wish to become a competent communicator. You may know people who understand how to drive a car and have the skill to drive, yet are reluctant to get behind the wheel. Or, maybe you know someone who took a course in public speaking but is still too frightened to stand in front of a crowd. Similarly, someone may pass a test about interpersonal communication principles with flying colours, but, unless they are motivated to use their new-found skills, their interactions with others may not improve.

Become Flexible

In this book, we do not identify tidy lists of strategies that you can use to "win friends and influence people," as Dale Carnegie has. The same set of skills is not effective in every situation, so competent communicators do not assume that "one size fits all." Rather, they assess each unique situation and adapt their behaviour to achieve the desired outcome. They examine the context, the situation, and the needs, goals, and messages of others to establish and maintain relationships.

Become Ethical

Ethics are the beliefs, values, and moral principles by which we determine what is right or wrong. Ethics and ethical behaviour have long been a critical component of human behaviour. Effective interpersonal communicators are ethical. To be an ethical communicator means to be sensitive to the needs of others, to give people choices rather than forcing them to act a certain way. Unethical communicators believe that they know what other people need, even without asking them for their preferences. As we discuss in Chapter 6, being manipulative and forcing opinions on others usually results in a climate of defensiveness. Effective communicators seek to establish trust and reduce interpersonal barriers, rather than erect them. Ethical communicators keep confidences; they keep private information that others wish to be kept private. They also do not intentionally decrease others' feelings of self-worth. Another key element in being an ethical communicator is honesty. If you intentionally lie or distort the truth, then you are not communicating ethically or effectively. At the end of each chapter, we offer a section called "Focus on Ethics," in which we pose ethical questions to help you explore the ethics of interpersonal relationships.

ethics. The beliefs, values, and moral principles by which people determine what is right or wrong.

Become Other-Oriented

Most of us are egocentric—self-focused; our first inclination is to protect ourselves. Scholars of evolution might argue that it is our tendency to look out for number one that ensures the continuation of the human race. Yet, when we focus *exclusively* on ourselves, it is difficult to communicate effectively. If we fail to adapt our message to our listener, we may not be successful in achieving our intended communication goal. Adapting messages to others does not mean that we tell them only what they want to hear; that would be unethical. Nor does being considerate of others mean we abandon all concern for our own interests. Other-oriented communication suggests that we consider the needs, motives, desires, and goals of our communication partners while still maintaining our own integrity. The choices we make in forming the message and selecting the time and place to deliver it should consider the other person's thoughts and feelings.

How do you become other-oriented? Being other-oriented is really a collection of skills rather than a single skill. We devote considerable discussion throughout the book to developing this collection of essential communication skills.[40]

Focusing on others begins with an accurate understanding of your self-concept and self-esteem; we discuss these foundation principles in the next chapter. As you will learn in Chapter 3, developing an accurate perception of both yourself and others is an important element of effectively relating to others.

Being other-oriented is more than just having a set of skills or behaviours. It also includes developing positive, healthy attitudes about others. In 1951 Carl Rogers wrote a pioneering book called *Client-Centered Therapy*, which transformed the field of psychotherapy. In it Rogers explains how genuine positive regard for another person and an open and supportive communication climate lay the foundation for trusting relationships. Rogers emphasizes the importance of listening in connection to another human being, which we explore in depth in Chapter 4.

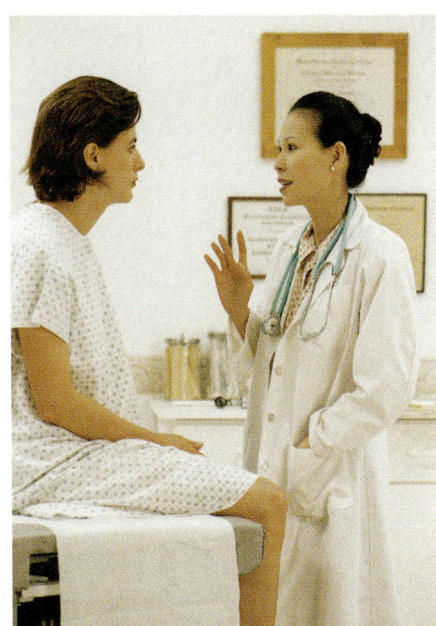

Ethical communicators are sensitive to the needs of others. (Comstock Images)

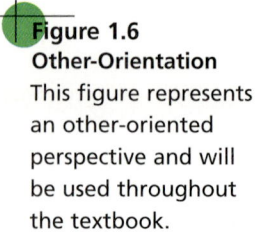

Figure 1.6
Other-Orientation
This figure represents an other-oriented perspective and will be used throughout the textbook.

Throughout the book we will emphasize the importance of developing an other-orientation in your communication activities. When we come to sections that will help you with this development, you will notice that a symbol will appear in the margin to alert you. You may already have noted a few marked passages in this chapter (see page 29). As you can see in Figure 1.6, this symbol represents the sharing of thoughts and feelings in an interpersonal exchange. We have also incorporated the special "Considering Others" feature in all of the chapters to help you understand the meaning of this important quality.

Building Your Skills

ROLE PLAY: OTHER-ORIENTED OR SELF-FOCUSED

With a communication partner, role-play the following interpersonal situations in two ways. First, role-play an interaction in which the communicators are not other-oriented; they are self-focused. Then role-play the same scene with communicators who are other-oriented; they consider the thoughts and feelings of the other person.

SUGGESTED SITUATIONS

- Try to return a broken VCR to a department store salesperson.
- Alert a grocery store cashier about an item scanned at the wrong price.
- Meet with a teacher who gave your son or daughter a failing mark.
- Ask your professor for a one-day extension on a paper that is due the next day.
- Ask someone for a donation to a worthy cause.
- Ask a professor for permission to get into a class that has reached its maximum enrolment.
- Accept an unappealing compact disc as a gift from a friend.
- Remind your son or daughter about practising the piano.

People gain insight into others' feelings by being sensitive to non-verbal messages as well as to the explicit verbal statements they make. Chapter 5, which examines emotions in detail, lays a solid ground for understanding how people feel and how we can better respond to others' feelings. We discuss verbal communication skills in Chapter 6 and non-verbal communication skills in Chapter 7. The skills and principles of managing conflict presented in Chapter 8 provide tools and ideas for understanding others when you disagree.

Becoming other-oriented also involves adapting to those who may be considerably different from you. Your communication partner may have a different cultural background, be of the opposite sex, or be older or younger than you. In Chapter 9 we explore some of these differences, especially cultural differences that can sometimes challenge effective and appropriate communication with others; we also suggest specific strategies to help you adapt to others who differ from yourself. Throughout the text, we include boxes like the one below to help you develop your sensitivity to important issues related to cultural diversity.

▲●■ Understanding Diversity

CULTURAL DIFFERENCES CAN LEAD TO MISINTERPRETATION

In a culturally diverse society, we can make mistakes without meaning to offend or confuse the other persons. Our goal is not to be insulting or misunderstood; it's just that cultures are different and sometimes those differences can lead to unintended errors.

The following true story of an international communication misunderstanding demonstrates the importance of making sure that the message being conveyed is the message intended: Not long ago a delegation of Canadian business people visited Japan to promote international trade. As a spontaneous gesture of goodwill toward their Japanese hosts, one of the Canadian delegates decided to sport a decorative shirt that bore some Japanese characters on an ornate background. Only toward the end of a dinner reception was the Canadian delegate informed by a Japanese journalist that the characters were an advertisement message equivalent to "Eat at Joe's Diner." Surely some of the Japanese business hosts must have interpreted the Canadian's "goodwill" gesture as an inappropriate form of cheap advertising.

The same kinds of misunderstandings can happen in interpersonal exchanges between people from different cultures whose mother languages can lead to misinterpretation when sharing a common language. Meanings are fragile. Consider the following exchanges between two good friends, Paula (an anglophone) and Marie-Joseph (a francophone):

Paula: It was just the way my boss *looked* at me during my presentation; he says it went well, but I'm not so sure.

Marie-Joseph: Paula, maybe you are being a bit too *sensible*.

Paula: I sure wish I could find a copy of Peter C. Newman's latest book, to buy for my father's birthday.

Marie-Joseph: Have you tried the *library* on Broadview Street?

Only if Paula knows French would she realize that *sensible* is the French word for *sensitive*, which is the message Marie-Joseph wished to convey in the first dialogue. *Librairie* is the French word for *bookstore*, which is what Marie-Joseph was actually referring to in the second dialogue. It's always wise to question your communication partners to make sure they share your understanding of a word or symbol.

Chapters 10 and 11 build on the principles of interpersonal relationships introduced in this chapter to help you understand how relationships evolve, are maintained, and sometimes end. Chapter 11 also applies our discussion of other-oriented interpersonal communication to various contexts such as families, friends, and colleagues. Our goal is to help you both to understand better how you relate to others and to develop enhanced interpersonal skill.

▶ Recap

How Can You Improve Your Communication Effectiveness?

Become Knowledgeable	Learn principles, concepts, and ideas.
Become Skilled	Translate knowledge into action.
Become Motivated	Resolve to use your knowledge and skill.
Become Flexible	Select the right behaviour; one size does not fit all.
Become Ethical	Offer choices, establish trust, and reduce barriers to interpersonal communication.
Become Other-Oriented	Focus on others rather than only on your needs.

Summary

At the most basic level, communication is the process of acting on information. Human communication is the process of making sense out of the world and sharing that sense with others. Interpersonal communication is the process of developing a unique relationship with another person by interacting and sharing mutual influence. Early models viewed human communication as a simple message-transfer process. Later models evolved to view communication as interaction and then as transaction. Contemporary approaches to interpersonal communication emphasize the simultaneous nature of influencing others. They identify seven key components in the interpersonal communication process: source, receiver, message, channel, noise, context, and feedback. Electronic media may encourage further evolution of our models for interpersonal communication.

The goal of this book is to help you improve your interpersonal skills and relationships. Interpersonal relationships range from impersonal to intimate, are complementary or symmetrical, are governed by rules, and involve both content and relationship dimensions. The most effective interpersonal communicators are not swayed by common myths about communication. Rather, they are knowledgeable, skilled, motivated, flexible, ethical, and other-oriented. Learning to connect with others is the key to establishing satisfying relationships.

For Discussion and Review

Focus on Comprehension

1. Discuss key differences among the communication as action, interaction, and transaction models.
2. Define communication, human communication, and interpersonal communication. Discuss the differences among them.
3. What are the principles of communication discussed in this chapter?

Chapter 1   Introduction to Interpersonal Communication

4. Identify the characteristics of interpersonal relationships.
5. Explain how to improve your interpersonal communication.

Focus on Critical Thinking

6. Analyze a recent interpersonal exchange with someone that did not go well. Write down some of the dialogue. Did the other person understand you? Did your communication have the intended effect? Was your message ethical?
7. Make a relationship scale on a piece of paper and label it "impersonal" at one end and "intimate" at the other. Place your family members and closest friends on the scale; then compare and discuss your entries with your classmates.
8. What rules govern your relationship with your mother? Your father? Your communication teacher? Your roommate or spouse?

Focus on Ethics

9. Think about your primary goal for this course. Is it to develop strategies to achieve your own personal goals? Is it to develop sensitivity to the needs of others? What is behind your desire to achieve your goal? Is your purpose ethical?
10. Your parents want you to visit them for the holidays. You would rather spend the time with a friend. You don't want to hurt your parents' feelings so you tell them that you have an important project that you are working on; you won't be able to come home for the holidays. Your message is understood. It achieves the intended effect; you don't go home. Explain why you think your message is ethical or unethical.

For Your Journal

1. Try to identify at least three personal goals for improving your interpersonal relationships. Write several specific objectives that you hope to accomplish by the end of this course.
2. Briefly, describe a recent communication exchange that was not effective. Perhaps you or your communication partner did not understand the message, or the message may not have achieved its intended goal, or it may have been unethical. Analyze the communication exchange, applying the components of communication discussed in this chapter. For example, what was the communication context? What were sources of internal and external noise? Did you have problems encoding and decoding? Were there problems with the communication channel?
3. Keep a one-day log of your electronically mediated interactions (e.g., phone calls, e-mail messages, fax messages). Describe each one, noting whether there was a greater emphasis on the content or emotional elements of the messages you exchanged during the interaction.

Learning with Others

1. Working with a group of your classmates, develop a five-minute lesson to teach one of the following concepts to your class:
   a. How interpersonal relationships range from impersonal to intimate
   b. Human communication as action
   c. Human communication as interaction
   d. Human communication as transaction
   e. How interpersonal relationships are governed by rules
   f. How to improve communication effectiveness

2. Working with a group of your classmates, develop your own model of interpersonal communication. Include all of the components that are necessary to describe how communication between people works. Your model could be a drawing or an actual object (like a Slinky toy) that symbolizes the communication process. Share your model with the class, describing the decisions your group made in developing it. Illustrate your model with a conversation between two people, pointing out how elements of the conversation relate to the model.

Weblinks

www.changedynamics.com/samples/commun.htm Although this is a company advertising its workshops for businesses, there are some interesting mini-lectures at this site. This one is on the elements of communication and includes charts of the communication process.

www.vlib.org/Overview.html This is a large site, called the WWW Virtual Library. This site has access to thousands of articles including sociology, psychology, and other major topics, and includes Canadian articles.

www.gov.nf.ca/nlwin/HOME/LGUIDE.HTM This is the guide topic page for Work*info*NET. Access Canadian information about jobs and job skills today.

www.icomm.ca/cmhacan/english/tentips.htm From the Canadian Mental Health Association: Ten tips for mental health.

www.depression.com This is a site devoted to depression and has a wealth of information about this common mental illness.

Suggested Readings

Argyle, M. *The Psychology of Interpersonal Behaviour.* London: Penguin, 1983.
    This is a classic book about interpersonal relationships.

Wallace, P. *The Psychology of the Internet.* Cambridge, England: Cambridge University Press, 1999.
    A text about the Internet and its effect on human relationships.

chapter 2

Interpersonal Communication and Self

After you study this chapter

you should be able to ...

1. Define, compare, and contrast the meanings of self-concept and self-esteem.

2. Identify factors that shape the development of your self-concept.

3. List and describe strategies for improving your self-esteem.

4. Describe how your self-concept affects your relationships with others.

- Self-Concept: Who Are You?

- Self-Esteem: Your Self-Worth

- Improving Your Self-Esteem

- How Self-Concept and Self-Esteem Affect Interpersonal Communication and Relationships

There's only one corner of the universe you can be certain of improving, and that's your own self.

ALDOUS HUXLEY

Philosophers suggest that there are three basic questions to which we all seek answers: (1) Who am I? (2) Why am I here? and (3) Who are all these others? In this chapter we will focus on these essential questions. We view them as progressive. Grappling with the question of who you are and seeking to define a purpose for your life are fundamental to understanding others and becoming other-oriented in your interpersonal communication and your relationships.

Fundamentally, all of your communication starts or ends with you. When you are the communicator, you intentionally or unintentionally code your thoughts and emotions to be interpreted by another. When you receive a message, you interpret the information through your own frame of reference. Your self-image and self-worth, as well as your needs, values, beliefs, and attitudes, serve as filters for your communication with others. As you develop and establish relationships, you may become more aware of these filters, and, perhaps, you will have the desire to alter them. A close relationship often provides the impetus for change.

To better understand the role that self-concept plays in interpersonal communication, we will explore the first two basic questions, "Who am I?" and "Why am I here?" by trying to discover the meaning of self. We will examine the multifaceted dimensions of our self-concept, learn how it develops, and compare self-concept to self-esteem. Then we will move to the third basic question, "Who are all these others?" We will discuss the effect of our self-concept on our communication with others, focusing on how our individual communication styles affect our interpersonal relationships.

Self-Concept: Who Are You?

You can begin your journey of self-discovery by trying the following exercise in Building Your Skills: Who Are You?

Building Your Skills

WHO ARE YOU?

Consider this question: Who are you? More specifically, ask yourself this question ten times. Write your responses in the spaces provided here or on a separate piece of paper. It may be challenging to identify ten aspects of yourself; the Spanish writer Cervantes said, "…to know thyself… is the most difficult lesson in the world." Your answers will help you begin to explore your self-concept and self-esteem in this chapter.

I am _____   I am _____

I am _____   I am _____

I am _____   I am _____

I am _____   I am _____

I am _____   I am _____

---

self. The sum total of who a person is; a person's central inner force.

self-concept. A person's subjective description of who the person thinks he or she is.

attitudes. Learned predispositions to respond to a person, object, or idea in a favourable or unfavourable way.

How did you answer the question, "Who are you?" Perhaps your self-descriptions identify activities in which you participate. Or, you may describe groups and organizations to which you belong or some of the roles you assume, such as student, child, or parent. All of these things are, indeed, a part of your **self**, the sum total of who you are. Karen Horney defines self as "that central inner force, common to all human beings and yet unique in each, which is the deep source of growth."[1]

Your answers are also part of your **self-concept**. Your self-concept is your subjective description of who you *think* you are—it is filtered through your own perceptions. For example, you may have great musical talent, but you may not believe in it enough to think of yourself as a musician. We can view self-concept as the labels we consistently use to describe ourselves to others.

Who you are is also reflected in the attitudes, beliefs, and values that you hold. These are learned constructs that shape your behaviour and self-image. An **attitude** is a learned predisposition to respond to a person, object, or idea in a favourable or unfavourable way. Attitudes reflect what you like and what you don't like. If you like school, butter pecan ice cream, and your mother, you hold positive attitudes toward these things. You were not born with a fondness for butter pecan ice cream; you learned to like it, just as some people learn to enjoy the taste of snails, raw fish, or puréed turnips.

Chapter 2 Interpersonal Communication and Self

Beliefs are the ways in which you structure your understanding of reality—what is true and what is false. Most of your beliefs are based on previous experience. You trust that the sun will rise in the morning and that you will get burned if you put your hand on a hot stove.

How are attitudes and beliefs related? They often function quite independently of one another. You may have a favourable attitude toward something and still believe negative things about it. You may believe, for example, that your college hockey team will not win the provincial championship this year, though you may be a big fan. Or you may believe that a God exists, yet not always like what that God does. Beliefs have to do with what is true or not true; attitudes reflect likes and dislikes.

Values are enduring concepts of good and bad, right and wrong. Your values are more resistant to change than either your attitudes or your beliefs. They are also more difficult for most people to identify. Values are so central to who you are that it is difficult to isolate them. For example, when you go to the supermarket, you may spend a few minutes deciding whether to buy regular or cream-style corn, but you probably do not spend much time deciding whether you will steal the corn or pay for it. Our values are instilled in us by our earliest interpersonal relationships; for almost all of us, our parents shape our values. The chart in Figure 2.1 shows that values are central to our behaviour and concept of self, and that what we believe to be true or false stems from our values. Attitudes are at the outer edge of the circle because they are the most likely to change. You may like your co-worker today but not tomorrow, even though you *believe* the person will come to work every day and you still *value* the concept of friendship.

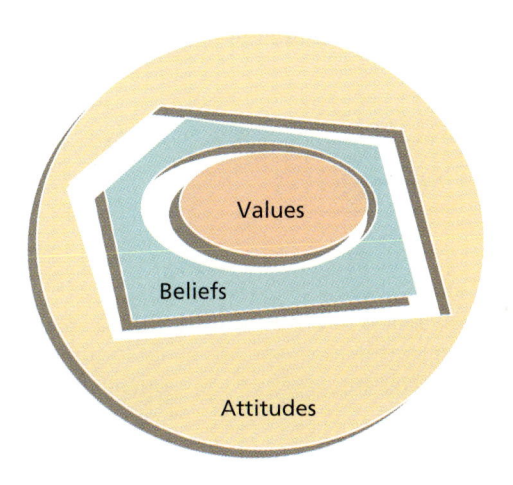

beliefs. The ways in which you structure your understanding of reality—what is true and what is false.

values. Enduring concepts of good and bad, right and wrong.

Figure 2.1
Values, Beliefs, and Attitudes in Relation to Self

▶ Recap

WHO YOU ARE IS REFLECTED IN YOUR ATTITUDES, BELIEFS, AND VALUES

	Definition	Dimensions	Example
Attitudes	Learned predispositions to respond favourably or unfavourably toward something.	Likes–Dislikes	You like ice cream, incense, and cats.
Beliefs	The way in which we structure reality.	True–False	You believe your parents love you.
Values	Enduring concepts of what is right and wrong.	Good–Bad	You value honesty and truth.

One or Many Selves?

Shakespeare's famous line, "To thine own self be true," suggests that you have a single self to which you can be true. But do you have just one self? Or is there a more "real you" buried somewhere within? "I'm just not myself this morning," sighs Sandy, as she drags herself out the front door to head for her office. If she is not herself, then *who is she*? Most scholars conclude that we have a core set of behaviours, attitudes, beliefs, and values that constitute our self—the sum total of who we are. But our *concept* of self can and does change, depending upon circumstances and influences.

In addition, our self-concepts are often different from the way others see us. We almost always behave differently in public than we do in private. Sociologist Erving Goffman suggests that, like actors and actresses, we have "on stage" behaviours when others are watching and "backstage" behaviours when they are not.

Perhaps the most enduring and widely accepted framework for describing who you are was developed by the philosopher William James. He identified three components of the self: the material self, the social self, and the spiritual self. We will continue our exploration by examining these components.

Building Your Skills

DIMENSIONS OF YOUR SELF

Take another look at your responses to the question "Who are you?" Divide your list according to James's description of self-concept as a material, social, or spiritual self. If, for example, nothing on your original list relates to your spiritual self, make an entry here so you have a response for each of the three "selves."

Material Self
References to the physical elements that reflect who you are.

Example:
I collect antiques.

Social Self
References to interactions with others that reflect who you are.

Example:
I am a member of the Chess Club.

Spiritual Self
References to your reflections about values, morals, and beliefs.

Example:
I believe the *Book of Mormon* is an inspired book.

🟠 The Material Self

Perhaps you've heard the statement, "You are what you eat." The **material self** goes a step further by suggesting, "You are what you have." The material self is a total of all of the tangible things you own: your possessions, your home, your body. As you examine your list of responses to the question, "Who are you?" note whether any of your statements refers to one of your physical attributes or something you own.

One element of the material self gets considerable attention in our culture: the body. Do you like the way you look? Most of us, if we're honest, would like to change something about our appearance. When there is a discrepancy between our desired material self and our self-concept, we may respond to eliminate the discrepancy. We may try to lose weight, change the shape of our nose, or acquire more hair. The multi-billion-dollar diet industry is just one of many that profit from our collective desire to change our appearance. We also attempt to keep up with the proverbial Joneses by wanting more expensive clothes, cars, and homes. By extension, what we own becomes who we are. The bigger, better, and more luxurious our possessions, we may subconsciously conclude, the better *we* are.

🟠 The Social Self

Look at your "Who are you?" list once more. How many of your responses relate to your **social self,** the part of you that interacts with others? William James believed that you have many social selves—that depending on the friend, family member, colleague, or acquaintance with whom you are interacting, you change the way you are. A person has, said James, as many social selves as there are people who recognize him or her.

For example, when you talk to your best friend, you are willing to "let down your hair" and reveal more thoughts and feelings than you would in a conversation with your communication professor, or even your parents. Each relationship that you have with another person is unique because you bring to it a unique social self.

🟠 The Spiritual Self

Your **spiritual self** consists of all your internal thoughts and introspections about your values and moral standards. It is not dependent upon what you own or with whom you talk; it is the essence of who you *think* you are, and of your *feelings* about yourself, apart from external evaluations. It is an amalgam of your religious beliefs and your sense of who you are in relationship to other forces in the universe. Your spiritual self is the part of you that answers the question, "Why am I here?"

---

material self. Your concept of self as reflected in a total of all the tangible things you own.

social self. Your concept of self as developed through your personal, social interactions with others.

spiritual self. Your concept of self based upon your thoughts and introspections about your values and moral standards.

Peter Blake sought to explore his self-dimensions by painting his self-portrait. What qualities does this self-portrait reveal about the artist? (Tate Gallery, London/Art Resources)

Recap

WILLIAM JAMES'S DIMENSIONS OF SELF

	Definition	Examples
Material Self	All of the physical elements that reflect who you are.	Possessions, car, home, body, clothes.
Social Self	The self as reflected through your interactions with others; actually, a variety of selves that respond to changes in situations and roles.	Your informal self interacting with your best friend; your formal self interacting with your professors.
Spiritual Self	Introspections about values, morals, and beliefs.	Religious belief or disbelief; regard for life in all its forms.

How Your Self-Concept Develops

James's three elements define the dimensions of the self, but they do not tell us where our "Who am I?" responses come from. In truth, we can only speculate about their origins. But some psychologists and sociologists have advanced theories that suggest we learn who we are through four basic means: (1) our interactions with other individuals, (2) our association with groups, (3) roles we assume, and (4) our own labels. Like James's framework, this one does not cover every base in our study of self, but its constructs can provide some clues about how our own self-concepts develop.

Interaction with Individuals

In 1902, Charles Horton Cooley first advanced the notion that we form our self-concepts by seeing ourselves in a kind of figurative **looking glass**: we learn who we are by interacting with others, much as we look into a mirror and see our reflection. This is also referred to as **reflected appraisal**. In other words, we develop self concepts that often match or correspond to the ways in which we believe others see us. Like Cooley, George Herbert Mead also believed that our behaviour and our sense of who we are, are a consequence of our relationship with others. And Harry Stack Sullivan theorized that from birth to death our self changes primarily because of how people respond to us. One sage noted, "We are not only our brother's keeper; we are our brother's maker."

The process begins at birth. Our names, one of the primary ways we identify ourselves, are given to us by someone else. During the early years of our lives, our parents are the key individuals who shape who we are. If our parents encouraged us to play the piano, we probably play now. As we become less dependent on our parents, our friends become highly influential in shaping our attitudes, beliefs, and values. And friends continue to provide feedback on how well we perform certain tasks. This, in turn, helps us shape our sense of identity as adults—we must acknowledge our talents in math, language, or art in our own minds before we can say that we are mathematicians, linguists, or artists.

Fortunately, not *every* comment affects our sense of who we think we are or our own self-worth. We are likely to incorporate the comments of others into our self-concept under three conditions:

looking-glass self. Concept that suggests you learn who you are based on your interactions with others, which are reflected back to you.

reflected appraisal. Another term for the looking-glass self. You learn who you are based on how others treat you.

- First, we are more likely to believe another's statement if he or she repeats something we have heard several times. If one person casually tells us we have a talent for singing, we are not likely to launch a search for an agent and a recording contract. But if several individuals tell us on many different occasions that we have a talent for singing, we may decide to do something about it.

- Second, we are more likely to value another's statements if he or she has already earned our confidence. If we believe the individual is competent, trustworthy, and qualified to make a judgment about us, then we are more likely to believe it. You would be more likely to think you were a talented singer if you heard it from singing star Céline Dion rather than your Aunt Sally. Again, while we are very young, our parents are the dominant voices of credibility and authority. If they tell us repeatedly that we are spoiled and sloppy, then we will probably come to view ourselves that way. If they tell us we are loving, gifted, and charming, we are likely to believe it.

- Third, we are likely to incorporate another's comments into our own concept of self if the comments are consistent with other comments and our own experience. If your boss tells you that you work too slowly, but for years people have been urging you to slow down, then your previous experience will probably encourage you to challenge your boss's evaluation.

Others also influence our beliefs about who we are through **social comparison**, assessing ourselves in relations to others' skills, abilities, traits, and behaviours. We use social comparison to further understand ourselves in relation to others. We compare ourselves against **reference groups**. Obviously, the groups that we choose and measure ourselves against have a major impact on our self-concept. For example, if you wish to find out if you are smarter than other students in a particular course, you ask others how they did on a recent test. If you scored higher than everyone else, you may label yourself "smart" and if you scored lower than everyone else, you may label yourself "dumb." This type of social comparison is around deciding whether we are *superior* or *inferior* to others. We also use social comparison to gauge how much we are like (*same as*) others or much we *differ* from others. For example, if you enjoy classical music and peers at school belittle you for this music preference, you may decide that you have strange taste in music.

Obviously, the outcome of these social comparisons depends very much upon the people or groups we use for measurement. Unfortunately, some of us compare ourselves to inappropriate reference groups. Several research studies have illustrated the power of reference groups in developing poor self-concepts and self-esteem. Recent research on body image has illustrated the "quest for thin" and how many people try vainly to reach target weights that are unrealistic or even dangerous to their health. A recent Canadian study demonstrates the power of wanting to be thin in young people: 27 percent of girls aged 12–18 years had disordered attitudes and behaviours including thinking they were fat, binge eating, self-induced vomiting, and current dieting.[2]

Association with Groups

I'm a Liberal. I'm a Girl Guide. I'm a rabbi. I'm a coach. I'm a member of the Sweet Adelines. Each of these self-descriptive statements has something in common. They answer the "Who are you?" question by providing identification with a group or organization. Reflect once more on your responses to the "Who are you?"

social comparison. A process whereby we assess our traits, skills, beliefs, and so on by comparing ourselves to selected others.

reference groups. Groups selected by an individual to compare his/her abilities, characteristics, or some other aspect of personality.

Understanding Diversity

BEING OTHER-ORIENTED IN OTHER CULTURES

How we view others is an extension of how we view ourselves. Most religions of the world emphasize a common spiritual theme known in Christianity as the Golden Rule: Do unto others what you would have others do unto you. This "rule" is the basis for most ethical codes throughout the world. This fundamental principle of other-orientation is expressed in similar ways among the world's people.

Hinduism	This is the sum of duty: Do nothing to others which would cause pain if done to you.
Buddhism	One should seek for others the happiness one desires for one's self.
Taoism	Regard your neighbour's gain as your own gain, and your neighbour's loss as your loss.
Confucianism	Is there one principle which ought to be acted upon throughout one's whole life? Surely it is the principle of loving-kindness: do not unto others what you would not have them do unto you.
Zoroastrianism	The nature alone is good which refrains from doing unto another whatsoever is not good for itself.
Judaism	What is hateful to you, do not do to others. That is the entire law: all the rest is but commentary.
Islam	No one of you is a believer until he desires for his brother that which he desires for himself.
Christianity	Do unto others what you would have others do unto you.

Adapted from Wayne Ham, *Man's Living Religions* (Independence, MO: Herald Publishing House, 1966), 39–40.

---

question. How many associate you with a group? Religious groups, political groups, ethnic groups, social groups, study groups, and occupational and professional groups play important roles in determining our self-concept. Some of these groups we are born into; others we choose on our own. Either way, these group associations are significant parts of our identities.

As we have already noted, peer pressure is a powerful force in shaping attitudes and behaviour, and adolescents are particularly susceptible to it. But adolescents are not alone in allowing the attitudes, beliefs, and values of others to shape their expectations and behaviour. Most adults, to varying degrees, ask themselves, "What will the neighbours think? What will my family think?" when they are making choices.

Roles We Assume

Look again at your answers to the "Who are you?" question. Perhaps you see words or phrases that signify a role you often assume. Father, aunt, sister, uncle, manager, salesperson, teacher, and student are labels that imply certain expectations for behaviour, and they are important in shaping self-concept. Couples who live together before they marry often report that marriage alters their relationship. Before, they may have shared domestic duties, such as doing dishes and laundry. But when they assume the labels of "husband" and "wife," they may slip into traditional roles. Husbands don't do laundry. Wives don't mow the grass. These stereotypical role expectations that they learned long ago may require extensive discussion and negotiation. Couples who report the highest satisfaction with marriage have similar role expectations for themselves and their spouses.[3]

Chapter 2 Interpersonal Communication and Self

One reason we assume traditional roles automatically is that our gender group asserts a powerful influence from birth on. As soon as parents know the sex of their child, many begin placing their children in the group by following cultural rules. They may paint the nursery pink for a girl, blue for a boy. Boys may get a catcher's mitt, a train set, or a football for their birthdays; girls may get dolls, frilly dresses, and tea sets. These cultural conventions and expectations play a major role in shaping our self-concept and our behaviour. We describe male babies as strong, solid, and independent; female babies are cute, cuddly, and sweet.[4] Recent research suggests that, until the age of three, children themselves are not acutely aware of sex roles. Between the ages of three and five, however, masculine and feminine roles begin to emerge,[5] and they are usually solidified between the ages of five and seven.

In North American culture it is often accepted, or even encouraged, for boys to exhibit rough-and-tumble, aggressive behaviour when they interact with one another. (Tony Freeman/ PhotoEdit)

Stereotypical Labels for Males and Females

Terms for Males	Terms for Females
Aggressive	Appreciative
Arrogant	Considerate
Assertive	Cooperative
Conceited	Dependent
Dominant	Feminine
Forceful	Fickle
Frank	Friendly
Handsome	Frivolous
Hard-headed	Helpful
Outspoken	Submissive
Strong	Timid

Source: From Judy C. Pearson, Lynn H. Turner, and William Todd-Mancillas, *Gender and Communication* (Dubuque, IA: William C. Brown, 1991).

Although it is changing, North American culture is still male-dominated. What we consider appropriate and inappropriate behaviour is often different for males than it is for females. In group and team meetings, for example, task-oriented, male-dominated roles are valued more than feminine, relationship-building roles.[6] We applaud fathers who work 60 hours a week as "diligent and hard working," but criticize mothers who do the same as "neglectful and selfish." Although this kind of example is becoming outdated and is slowly changing, it can still be seen found in many workplaces. The list on pages 45–46 illustrates more of these contrasts.

The groups we choose are our microenvironments, but our gender groups represent the expectations of an even larger group: the culture into which we are born. We do, however, make choices about our gender roles. One researcher developed an inventory designed to assess whether you play traditional masculine, feminine, or androgynous roles.[7] Because an **androgynous role** is both masculine and feminine, this role encompasses a greater repertoire of actions and behaviours.

Self-Labels

Although our self-concept is deeply affected by others, we are not blank slates for them to write on. The labels we use to describe our own attitudes, beliefs, values, and actions also play a role in shaping our self-concept.

Where do we acquire our labels? One way that we label ourselves is through a process of self-reflexiveness. We interpret what we experience; we are self-reflexive. **Self-reflexiveness** is the human ability to think about what we are doing while we are doing it. We talk to ourselves about ourselves. We are both participants and observers in all that we do. This dual role encourages us to use labels to describe who we are.

When you were younger, perhaps you dreamed of becoming an NHL hockey player or a movie star. Your coach or your teacher may have told you that you were a great player or a terrific actor, but, as you matured, you probably began observing yourself more critically. You scored no goals; you did not get the starring role in local theatre productions. So you self-reflexively decided that you were not, deep down, a hockey player or an actor, even though others may have labelled you as "talented." But sometimes, through this self-observation, we discover strengths that encourage us to assume new labels. A woman we know never thought of herself as "heroic" until she went through 72 hours of labour before giving birth and then nursed her baby right after delivery.

We all have the ability to view ourselves almost as if we were another person. We may be harsher on ourselves than we are on others in judging skills, talents, and virtues, or we may have an inflated self-concept. Either way, the point is that we make judgments about ourselves and simplify them into labels we use to describe ourselves to others. Labels have a powerful effect on our feelings and behaviour.

Your Personality

The concept of personality is central to **psychology**, the study of how your thinking influences how you behave. According to psychologist Lester Lefton, your **personality** consists of a set of enduring internal predispositions and behavioural characteristics that describe how you react to your environment.[8] Understanding

---

androgynous role. A gender role that includes both masculine and feminine qualities.

self-reflexiveness. The human ability to think about what we are doing while we are doing it.

psychology. Study of how thinking influences behaviour.

personality. Set of enduring internal predispositions and behavioural characteristics that describe how people react to their environment.

the forces that shape your personality is central to increasing your awareness of your self-concept and how you relate to others. Your personality influences whether you are outgoing or shy, humorous or serious, mellow or nervous, and a host of other descriptions that could be used to describe general traits or characteristics about you. There remains a considerable debate as to how much of your personality is influenced by genetics—traits you inherit from your ancestors—and how much is learned behaviour. Does nature or nurturing play the predominant role in your personality? As we noted in Chapter 1, the **communibiological approach** to communication suggests that a major factor affecting how people communicate with others is genetic makeup.[9] Others argue that although it's true that communication behaviour is influenced by genes, we should not forget that humans can learn to adjust and adapt.[10]

One personality characteristic that communication researchers have spent considerable time studying is whether you are comfortable or uncomfortable interacting with other people. Some people just don't like to talk with others.[11] In interpersonal communication situations, we may say someone is shy. **Shyness** is the behavioural tendency not to talk with others. One study found that about 40 percent of adults reported they were shy.[12] In public-speaking situations we say a person has stage fright; a better term to describe this feeling is *communication apprehension*. **Communication apprehension**, according to communication experts James McCroskey and Virginia Richmond, is "the fear or anxiety associated with either real or anticipated communication with another person or persons."[13] One study found that up to 80 percent of the population experiences some degree of nervousness or apprehension when they speak in public.[14] Another study found that about 20 percent of people are considerably anxious when they give a speech.[15] What makes some people apprehensive about communicating with others? Again, we get back to the nature–nurture issue. Heredity plays an important role in whether you are going to feel nervous or anxious when communicating with someone else. But so does whether you were reinforced for talking with others as a child, as well as other experiences that are part of your culture and learning.

Your overall **willingness to communicate** with others is a general way of summarizing the shyness or apprehension that you feel when talking with others in a variety of situations, including interpersonal conversations. If you are unwilling to communicate with others, you will be less comfortable in a career that forces you to interact with others. To assess your willingness to communicate, take the self-test developed by McCroskey and Richmond in the Building Your Skills box on page 48. The test will give you an overall score as well as a score in specific communication situations such as meetings, interpersonal conversations, communicating with strangers, and communicating with friends.

Understanding the factors that influence your self-concept—such as your interactions with individuals and groups, the roles you assume, your self-labels, and your personality, including your overall comfort level in communicating with others—can help you understand who you are and why you interact (or don't interact) with others. But it's not only who you are that influences your communication, it's your overall sense of self-esteem or self-worth that affects how you express yourself and respond to others.

communibiological approach. Perspective that suggests that genetics and biological influences play a major role in influencing communication behaviour.

shyness. Tendency not to talk or interact with other people. A discomfort or inhibition in interpersonal situations that interferes with the pursuit of goals.

communication apprehension. Fear or anxiety associated with either real or anticipated communication with other people.

willingness to communicate. General characteristic that describes an individual's tendencies to be shy or apprehensive about communicating with others.

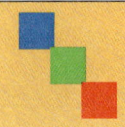

Building Your Skills

ASSESSING YOUR WILLINGNESS TO COMMUNICATE

Willingness-to-Communicate Scale

Directions: In the following 20 situations, a person might choose to communicate or not to communicate. Presume you have **completely free choice.** Determine the percentage of times you would **choose to initiate communication** in each type of situation. Indicate in the space at the left what percentage of the time you would choose to communicate. Choose any numbers between 0 and 100.

_____ 1. Talk with a service station attendant.
_____ 2. Talk with a physician.
_____ 3. Present a talk to a group of strangers.
_____ 4. Talk with an acquaintance while standing in line.
_____ 5. Talk with a salesperson in a store.
_____ 6. Talk in a large meeting of friends.
_____ 7. Talk with a police officer.
_____ 8. Talk in a small group of strangers.
_____ 9. Talk with a friend while standing in line.
_____ 10. Talk with a waiter/waitress in a restaurant.
_____ 11. Talk in a large meeting of acquaintances.
_____ 12. Talk with a stranger while standing in line.
_____ 13. Talk with a secretary.
_____ 14. Present a talk to a group of friends.
_____ 15. Talk in a small group of acquaintances.
_____ 16. Talk with a garbage collector.
_____ 17. Talk in a large meeting of strangers.
_____ 18. Talk with a spouse (or girl/boy friend).
_____ 19. Talk in a small group of friends.
_____ 20. Present a talk to a group of acquaintances.

Source: James C. McCloskey and Virginia P. Richmond, _Fundamentals of Human Communication: An Interpersonal Perspective_ (Prospect Heights, IL: Waveland Press, 1996), 53.

Computing Scores on the Willingness-to-Communicate Scale

Scoring: The WTC permits computation of one total score and seven subscores. The range for all scores is 0–100. Follow the procedures outlined below.

1. Group discussion—add scores for items 8, 15, and 19; divide sum by 3.
   Scores 89 = high WTC, scores below 57 = low WTC in this context.
2. Meetings—add scores for items 6, 11, and 17; divide sum by 3.
   Scores 80 = high WTC, scores below 39 = low WTC in this context.
3. Interpersonal—add scores for items 4, 9, and 12; divide sum by 3.
   Scores 94 = high WTC, scores below 64 = low WTC in this context.
4. Public speaking—add scores for items 3, 14, and 20; divide sum by 3.
   Scores 78 = high WTC, scores below 33 = low WTC in this context.
5. Stranger—add scores for items 3, 8, 12, and 17; divide sum by 4.
   Scores 63 = high WTC, scores below 18 = low WTC with these receivers.
6. Acquaintance—add scores for items 4, 11, 15, and 20; divide sum by 4.
   Scores 92 = high WTC, scores below 57 = low WTC with these receivers.
7. Friends—add scores for items 6, 9, 14, and 19; divide sum by 4.
   Scores 99 = high WTC, scores below 71 = low WTC with these receivers.

To compute the total score for the WTC, add the totals for stranger, friend, and acquaintance; then divide by 3. Scores above 82 = high WTC, below 52 = low WTC.

Chapter 2 Interpersonal Communication and Self

> ### e-connections
>
> #### WHAT'S YOUR PERSONALITY TYPE?
>
> Is it possible to learn what personality type you are by taking a simple test? The Myers-Briggs Personality Test is one of the most common ways to describe your personality. Based on Jung's theory of personality, the test assumes that each of us has a preference for how we like to process what we experience. According to the test, there are four dimensions to your personality. The first dimension, Extroversion–Introversion (E or I), describes whether you tend to focus your energy in the outside world or the inner world. The second dimension, Sensing–Intuition (S or N), describes whether you prefer to rely on more objective data or subjective impressions when interpreting what you experience. The third dimension is Thinking–Feeling (T or F); this dimension describes your preference for emphasizing cognitive or emotional information. The final dimension is Judging–Perceiving (J or P); this dimension describes the way you evaluate what you experience. There are 16 possible combinations of personality types. For example, an INFP is someone who is more introverted, intuitive, emotional, and perceptive. Psychologists debate, however, how accurately this test can measure your personality.[16] Although some research suggests it is a quick and valid way to identify how you interact with others, other studies suggest it may not be accurate, especially because it was designed for students in grades 4 through 12. To take a very brief inventory based on the Myers-Briggs test, go to the following website and determine for yourself whether your score accurately describes you.
>
> www.halconline.com/psych
>
> Do you want to explore other personality tests? Check out the following website, which is packed with more tests and links to other tests:
>
> www.mbtypeguide.com/Type/index.html

Self-Esteem: Your Self-Worth

Your **self-esteem** is closely related to your self-concept. Through your self-concept you *describe* who you are. Through your self-esteem, you *evaluate* who you are. The term **self-worth** is often used interchangeably with *self-esteem*. We derive our sense of self-worth from comparing ourselves to others: "I'm good at playing soccer" (because I beat others); "I can't cook" (because others cook better than I do); "I'm not good at meeting people" (most people I know seem to be more comfortable interacting with others); "I can't fix a broken toilet" (but my brothers and my mom and dad can). Each of these statements implies a judgment about how well or badly you can perform certain tasks, with implied references to how well others perform the same tasks. A belief that you cannot fix a broken toilet or cook like a chef may not in itself lower your self-esteem. But if there are *several* things you cannot do well, or *many* important tasks that you cannot seem to master, these shortcomings may begin to colour your overall sense of worth.

Psychologist Eric Berne developed the concept of a **life position** to describe our overall sense of our own worth and that of others.[17] He identified four life positions: (1) "I'm OK, you're OK," or positive regard for self and others; (2) "I'm OK, you're not OK," or positive regard for self and low regard for others; (3) "I'm not OK, you're OK," or low self-regard and positive regard for others; and (4) "I'm not OK, you're not OK," or low regard for both self and others. Your life position is

self-esteem (self-worth). Your evaluation of your worth or value as reflected in your perception of such things as your skills, abilities, talents, and appearance.

life position. Your feeling of being either "OK" or "not OK" as reflected in your sense of worth and self-esteem.

a driving force in your relationships with others. People in the "I'm OK, you're OK" position have the best chance for healthy relationships because they have discovered their own talents and also recognize that others have been given talents different from their own.

Canadian Issues

CAMPUS DRINKING: AN ATTEMPT TO IMPROVE LOW SELF-ESTEEM?

How many students start college or university unsure of themselves? Perhaps everything is new and unfamiliar—living in residence or an apartment, new city or town, no friends on the new campus. Many colleges start the new semester with orientation activities so that students can meet each other and get to know the campus. How many of these activities involve alcohol and do students have a drink or two to relax or feel better about themselves so that they can meet others more easily?

While we cannot answer all those questions, recent research points out that drinking and drug use among many students continues to be a problem. A recent ongoing study from the Centre for Addiction and Mental Health continues to monitor drinking and drug use among Canadian university students. The Canadian Campus Survey is done every two years. The latest results from the survey from the fall of 1998 and released in 2000 continues to report that heavy drinking among students is a significant cause for concern. With little change, alcohol use continues to be the highest among first-year students and those living in residence.

These most recent results indicate that over 63 percent of students reported drinking five or more drinks on a single occasion and more than 34 percent reported consuming more than eight drinks in one sitting at least once a month. When drinking to get drunk, students drank the most (8.9 drinks), which was followed by the reasons of celebrating or being at a party (5.7 drinks), to forget their worries (5.5 drinks), and to feel good (5.4 drinks). Among the alcohol-related problems reported by students were missed classes due to a hangover, missed classes due to drinking, hangovers, memory loss, and regretting their actions. The lead researcher, Louis Gliksman, stated that heavy drinking for this age group could result in a number of problems. Among the list of problems, he included broken relationships, academic difficulties, accidents, and legal and administrative problems, all of which could affect students' futures. Obviously, high alcohol consumption and alcohol abuse appear to be an ongoing "campus" problem.

For Discussion

1. What are some reasons for the heavy drinking by university students? Could attempting to improve self-esteem be one of the reasons?
2. Is it a university student problem only or is it a problem for college students as well?
3. Are drinking and partying part of a higher education culture? If so, how can this culture be changed to promote lower alcohol abuse? What is your campus doing about this problem?

Source: "First National Study of Drug Use among University Students Released by the Centre for Addiction and Mental Health Shows 'Heavy' Drinking to Be a Significant Concern," *Centre for Addiction and Mental Health, News Release,* March 29, 2000.

Read the full release at

www.camh.net/press_releases/can_campus_survey_pr29300.html

Improving Your Self-Esteem

We have already seen how low self-esteem can affect our own communication and interactions. In recent years, teachers, psychologists, ministers, rabbis, social workers, and even politicians have suggested that many of our societal problems as well stem from our collective feelings of low self-esteem. Our feelings of low self-worth may contribute to our choosing the wrong partners; to becoming dependent on drugs, alcohol, or other substances; and to experiencing problems with eating and other vital activities. So we owe it to society, as well as to ourselves, to maintain or develop a healthy sense of self-esteem.

Although no simple list of tricks can easily transform low self-esteem into feelings of being valued and appreciated, you can make improvements in the ways you think about yourself and interact with others. We'll explore seven proven techniques that have helped others.

Self-Talk

Intrapersonal communication is communication within yourself. Your level of self-esteem influences the way you talk to yourself about your abilities and skills. Perhaps you remember the children's story *The Little Engine That Could*, in which the pint-sized hero repeated, "I think I can. I think I can," to overcome a seemingly impossible challenge. Although becoming your own cheerleader may not enable you to climb your own metaphorical mountains quite so easily, there is evidence that self-talk, both positive and negative, does influence behaviour. Realistic, positive self-talk can have a reassuring effect upon your level of self-worth and, therefore, your interactions with others. Conversely, repeating negative messages about your lack of skills and abilities can keep you from trying and achieving.

For example, imagine that you have an algebra test coming up. If you are not optimistic about your performance on the test, you may be tempted to let your self-fulfilling prophecy come true by not studying. But, by reminding yourself (talking to yourself) about the importance of study and effort, you may be able to change your defeatist outlook. If you tell yourself, "I don't have to fail if I study," or "If I seek help from the teacher and spend more time on algebra, I can master these formulas," you may motivate yourself to improve your performance. Improved performance can enhance your confidence and self-worth. Of course, blind faith without hard work won't succeed. Self-talk is not a substitute for effort; it can, however, keep you on track and help you, ultimately, to achieve your goal.

Visualization

Visualization takes the notion of self-talk one step further. Besides just telling yourself that you can achieve your goal, you can actually try to "see" yourself conversing effectively with others, performing well on a project, or emphasizing some other desirable behaviour. Recent research suggests that an apprehensive public speaker can manage his or her fears not only by developing skill in public speaking but also by visualizing positive results when speaking to an audience. If you are one of the many people who fears speaking in public, try visualizing yourself walking to the lectern, taking out your well-prepared notes, and delivering an interesting,

---

intrapersonal communication. Communication within yourself that includes your self-talk.

visualization. A technique of imagining that you are performing a particular task in a certain way. Positive visualization can enhance your self-esteem.

well-received speech. This visualization of positive results enhances confidence and speaking skill. The same technique can be used to boost your sense of self-worth about other tasks or skills. Of course, your visualization should be realistic and coupled with a plan to achieve your goal. Visualizing yourself performing well can yield positive results in changing long-standing feelings of inadequacy.

Avoiding Comparisons

Even before we are born, we are compared with others. The latest medical technology lets us see sonograms of fetuses still in the womb, so parents may begin comparing children with their siblings or other babies before birth. For the rest of our lives we are compared with others, and, rather than celebrating our uniqueness, comparisons usually point up who is bigger, brighter, and more beautiful. Most of us have had the experience of being chosen last to play on a sports team, passed over for promotion, or standing unasked against the wall at a dance.

In North American culture we may be tempted to judge our self-worth by our material possessions and personal appearance. If we know someone who has a newer car (or simply a car, if we rely on public transportation), a smaller waistline, or a higher grade point average, we may feel diminished. Comparisons such as "He has more money than I have," or "She looks better than I look," are likely to deflate our self-worth. One-hundred-and-one-year-old Sadie and 103-year-old Bessie Delaney, sisters who have endured racial prejudice, have inspired many by their refusal to let what they did not have deter their sense of personal accomplishment. In their best-seller, *Having Our Say*, these two family matriarchs write of the value of emphasizing what we have, rather than comparing our lack of resources with others who have more.

Rather than focusing on others who seemingly are better off, focus on the unique attributes that make you who you are. Avoid judging your own value in comparison to that of others. A healthy, positive self-concept is fuelled not by judgments of others, but by a genuine sense of worth that we recognize in ourselves.

Reframing

reframing. The process of redefining events and experiences from a different point of view.

Reframing is the process of redefining events and experiences from a different point of view. Just as reframing a work of art can give the painting a whole new look, reframing events that cause us to devalue our self-worth can change our perspective. Research suggests that in times of family stress, individuals who are able to engage in self-talk and describe the event from someone else's perspective manage stress more successfully. If, for example, you get a report from your supervisor that says you should improve one area of your performance, instead of listening to the self-talk that says you're bad at your job, reframe the event within a larger context: tell yourself that one negative comment does not mean you are hopeless as a worker.

Of course, all negative experiences should not be lightly tossed off and left unexamined, because you can learn and profit from your mistakes. But it is important to remember that our worth as human beings is not contingent on a single letter grade, a single response from a prospective employer, or a single play in a football game. Looking at the big picture—what effect this small event will have on your whole life, on society, on history—places negative experiences that we all have in a realistic context.

Developing Honest Relationships

Having at least one other person who can help you objectively and honestly reflect on your virtues and vices can be extremely beneficial in fostering a healthy, positive self-image. As we noted earlier, other people play a major role in shaping our self-concept and self-esteem. The more credible the source of information, the more likely we are to believe it. Having a trusted friend, colleague, religious leader, or counsellor who can listen without judging you and give you the straight scoop about yourself can help you avoid "pity parties." Prolonged periods of self-pity left unchecked and unconfirmed can lead to feelings of inferiority. Later in this book, we will discuss how honest relationships are developed through the process of self-disclosure.

Letting Go of the Past

Your self-concept is not a fixed construct. Nor was it implanted at birth to remain constant for the rest of your life. Things change. You change. Others change. Individuals with low self-esteem may be locking on to events and experiences that happened years ago and tenaciously refusing to let go of them. Someone wrote, "The lightning bug is brilliant, but it hasn't much of a mind; it blunders through existence with its headlight on behind." Looking back at what we can't change only reinforces a sense of helplessness. Constantly replaying negative experiences in our mental VCR only serves to make our sense of worth more difficult to change. Becoming aware of the changes that have occurred, and can occur, in your life can assist you in developing a more realistic assessment of your value. If you were overweight as a child, you may have a difficult time accepting that your worth does not hinge upon the pounds you carried years ago. Being open and receptive to change in self-worth is important to developing a healthy self-concept. Longfellow's advice to let go of the past remains wise advice today: "Look not mournfully into the past. It comes not back again. Wisely improve the Present. It is thine. Go forth to meet the shadowy future, without fear. . . ."

Seeking Support

Some of your self-image problems may be so ingrained that you need professional help. A trained counsellor, religious leader, or therapist can help you sort through them. Therapists usually take a psychoanalytic approach, inviting you to search for experiences in your past that may help you first to understand your feelings and then to change them. Other counsellors use different techniques. If you are not sure to whom to turn for a referral, you can start with your school counselling services. Or, if you are near a medical school teaching hospital, you can contact the counselling or psychotherapy office there for a referral.

Because you have spent your whole lifetime developing your self-esteem, it is not easy to make big changes. But, as we have seen, talking through our problems can make a difference. As communication researchers Frank E. Dance and Carl Larson see it, "Speech communication empowers each of us to share in the development of our own self-concept and the fulfillment of that self-concept."[18]

> ## Recap

STRATEGIES FOR IMPROVING YOUR SELF-ESTEEM

Self-Talk	If you're having a bad hair day, tell yourself that you have beautiful eyes and lots of friends who like you anyway.
Visualize	If you feel nervous before a meeting, visualize everyone in the room congratulating you on your great ideas.
Avoid Comparisons	Focus on what you can do to enhance your own talents and abilities.
Reframe	If you experience one failure, keep the larger picture in mind rather than focusing on that isolated incident.
Develop Honest Relationships	Cultivate friends in whom you can confide and who will give you honest feedback for improving your skills and abilities.
Let Go of the Past	Talk yourself out of your "old tapes"; focus on ways to enhance your abilities in the future.
Seek Support	Talk with professional counsellors who can help you identify your gifts and talents.

How Self-Concept and Self-Esteem Affect Interpersonal Communication and Relationships

Your self-concept and self-esteem act as filters in every interaction with others. They determine how you approach, respond to, and interpret messages. Specifically, your self-concept and self-esteem affect your ability to be sensitive to others, your overall expectations through self-fulfilling prophecy, your interpretation of messages, and your typical communication style.

Self and Others

We have suggested the importance of becoming other-oriented—being sensitive to the thoughts and feelings of others—as a requisite for developing quality interpersonal relationships with others. As we saw in Chapter 1, the process of becoming other-oriented begins with decentring—consciously thinking about another person's thoughts and feelings. But before you begin to decentre—to try to understand another person from another perspective—it is important for you to feel centred—to know yourself and to understand how others see you.

To become other-oriented involves recognizing that your "self" is different from others. As the Peanuts cartoon at the bottom of next page reminds us, the world does not revolve around our solitary selves. Others influence our actions and our self-image. George Herbert Mead suggests that we develop an "I," which is based upon our own perspective of ourselves, and a "Me," which is an image of ourselves based upon the collective responses we receive and interpret from others. Being aware of how your concept of self ("I") differs from the perceptions others have of you ("Me") is an important first step in developing an other-orientation.

When we begin the **decentring** process, we often interpret our assumptions about others using our own selves as a frame of reference, especially if we do not know the other person well.[19] For example, if you are nervous and frightened when you have to take a test, you might assume that your friend will react the same way. You may need to remind yourself that the other person is separate from yourself and has a different set of responses.

When you use a **specific-other perspective**, you rely on information that you have observed or that you can imagine about a particular person to predict his or her reactions. If, for example, you know firsthand that your sister hates it when someone eats off her plate during dinner, you may use that experience to conclude that she would dislike sharing a bag of popcorn at the movies.

Sometimes a **generalized-other perspective** will be more useful. When you decentre, you can apply knowledge and personal theories that you have about people in general or about specific subgroups to the person with whom you are interacting. For example, you might think that your economics professor, who holds a Ph.D., would prefer to be addressed as *Professor* rather than as *Mister* because almost all of your other professors with doctorates prefer to be called *Professor*.

Your ability to predict how others will respond to you is based upon your ability to understand how your sense of the world is similar to, and different from, their own. First you must know yourself well. Then you can know and understand others. The best way to improve your ability to decentre is to notice how others respond when you act on the predictions and assumptions you have made about them. You may discover that you have not moved out of your own frame of reference enough to make an accurate prediction about another person.

decentring. Cognitive process in which you take into account another person's thoughts, feelings, values, background, and perspective.

specific-other perspective. The process of relying upon observed or imagined information about another person that is used to predict that person's behaviour.

generalized-other perspective. The process of relying upon observed or imagined information about many people or people in general to predict a person's behaviour.

Self-Fulfilling Prophecy

While you are considering whether a person's behaviour matches the predictions that you make about him or her, it is also important to remember that people interpret messages in a way that confirms what they already think of themselves. Suppose, for example, you think of yourself as an overly controlling person. If your sister surprises you by offering to share her popcorn at the movies, you may feel guilty and wonder if she is just giving in to your bullying, instead of assuming that she is expressing affection for you. This extends into the realm of action as well. What we believe about ourselves often comes true because we expect it to come

PEANUTS

self-fulfilling prophecy.
The notion that predictions about your future actions are likely to come true because you believe that they will come true.

true. We refer to this as **self-fulfilling prophecy**. If you think you will fail the math quiz because you have labelled yourself inept at math, then you must overcome not only your math deficiency but also your low expectations of yourself. As Professor Henry Higgins argues in George Bernard Shaw's play *Pygmalion*, "If you treat a girl like a flower girl, that's all she will ever be. If you treat her like a princess she may be one." Your attitudes, beliefs, and general expectations about your performance have a powerful and profound effect upon your behaviour.

The self-fulfilling prophecy can have a powerful impact on people in both positive and negative ways. Treated like someone who can do nothing right, a person may eventually be unable to do "anything right." These expectations have a powerful impact on behaviour. Read the story of little Teddy Stallard below to more fully understand how the expectations of others can influence us in both positive and negative ways.

Considering Others

THREE LETTERS FROM TEDDY

Teddy's letter came today and now that I've read it, I will place it in my cedar chest with the other things that are important in my life.

"I wanted you to be the first to know."

I smiled as I read the words he had written and my heart swelled with pride that I had no right to feel.

I had not seen Teddy Stallard since he was a student in my fifth-grade class, fifteen years ago. It was early in my career, and I had only been teaching for two years.

From the first day he stepped into my classroom, I disliked Teddy. Teachers (although everyone knows differently) are not supposed to have favorites in a class, but most especially are they not to show dislike for a child, any child.

Nevertheless, every year there are one or two children that one cannot help but be attached to, for teachers are human, and it is human nature to like bright, pretty, intelligent people, whether they are ten years old or twenty-five. And sometimes, not too often fortunately, there will be one or two students to whom the teacher just can't seem to relate.

I had thought myself quite capable of handling my personal feelings along that line until Teddy walked into my life. There wasn't a child I particularly liked that year, but Teddy was most assuredly one I disliked.

He was dirty. Not just occasionally, but all the time. His hair hung low over his ears and he actually had to hold it out of his eyes as he wrote his papers in class. (And this was before it was fashionable to do so!) Too, he had a peculiar odor about him which I could never identify.

His physical faults were many, and his intellect left a lot to be desired, also. By the end of the first week I knew he was hopelessly behind the others. Not only was he behind; he was just plain slow! I began to withdraw from him immediately.

Any teacher will tell you that it's more of a pleasure to teach a bright child. It is definitely more rewarding for one's ego. But any teacher worth her credentials can channel work to the bright child, keeping him challenged and learning while she puts major efforts on the slower ones. Any teacher *can* do this. Most teachers *do* it, but I *didn't*. Not that year.

In fact, I concentrated on my best students and let the others follow along as best they could. Ashamed as I am to admit it, I took perverse pleasure in using my red pen; and each time I came to Teddy's papers, the cross-marks (and there were many) were always a little larger and a little redder than necessary.

"Poor work!" I would write with a flourish.

While I did not actually ridicule the boy, my attitude was obviously quite apparent to the class, for he quickly became the class "goat," the outcast— the unlovable and unloved.

He knew I didn't like him, but he didn't know why. Nor did I know— then or now—why I felt such an intense dislike for him. All I know is that he was a little boy no one cared about, and I made no effort on his behalf.

The days rolled by and we made it through the Fall Festival, the

Thanksgiving holidays, and I continued marking happily with my red pen.

As the Christmas holidays approached, I knew that Teddy would never catch up in time to be promoted to the sixth-grade level. He would be a repeater.

To justify myself, I went to his cumulative folder from time to time. He had very low grades for the first four years, but no grade failure. How he had made it, I didn't know. I closed my mind to the personal remarks:

First grade: "Teddy shows promise by work and attitude, but has poor home situation."

Second grade: "Teddy could do better. Mother terminally ill. He receives little help at home."

Third grade: "Teddy is a pleasant boy. Helpful, but too serious. Mother passed away end of the year."

Fourth grade: "Very slow, but well behaved. Father shows no interest."

Well, they passed him four times, but he will certainly repeat fifth grade! Do him good! I said to myself.

And then the last day before the holiday arrived. Our little tree on the reading table sported paper and popcorn chains. Many gifts were heaped underneath, waiting for the big moment.

Teachers always get several gifts at Christmas, but mine that year seemed bigger and more elaborate than ever. There was not a student who had not brought me one. Each unwrapping brought squeals of delight and the proud giver would receive effusive thank-yous.

His gift wasn't the last one I picked up; in fact it was in the middle of the pile. Its wrapping was a brown paper bag and he had colored Christmas trees and red bells all over it. It was stuck together with masking tape.

"For Mrs. Thompson—From Teddy" it read.

The group was completely silent and for the first time I felt conspicuous, embarrassed because they all stood watching me unwrap that gift.

As I removed the last bit of masking tape, two items fell to my desk. A gaudy rhinestone bracelet with several stones missing and a small bottle of dime-store cologne—half empty.

I could hear the snickers and whispers and I wasn't sure I could look at Teddy.

"Isn't this lovely?" I asked, placing the bracelet on my wrist. "Teddy, would you help me fasten it?"

He smiled shyly as he fixed the clasp and I held up my wrist for all of them to admire.

There were a few hesitant *ooh*'s and *ahh*'s but as I dabbed the cologne behind my ears, all the little girls lined up for a dab behind their ears.

I continued to open the gifts until I reached the bottom of the pile. We ate our refreshments and the bell rang.

The children filed out with shouts of "See you next year!" and "Merry Christmas!" but Teddy waited at his desk.

When they had all left, he walked towards me clutching his gift and books to his chest.

"You smell just like Mom," he said softly. "Her bracelet looks real pretty on you, too. I'm glad you liked it."

He left quickly and I locked the door, sat down at my desk and wept, resolving to make up to Teddy what I had deliberately deprived him of—a teacher who cared.

I stayed every afternoon with Teddy from the end of the Christmas holidays until the last day of school. Sometimes we worked together. Sometime he worked alone while I drew up lesson plans or graded papers.

Slowly but surely he caught up with the rest of the class. Gradually there was a definite upward curve in his grades.

He did not have to repeat the fifth grade. In fact his final averages were among the highest in the class, and although I knew he would be moving out of the state when school was out, I was not worried for him. Teddy had reached a level that would stand him in good stead the following year, no matter where he went. He had enjoyed a measure of success and as we were taught in our teacher training: "Success builds success."

I did not hear from Teddy until seven years later, when his first letter appeared in my mailbox.

"Dear Mrs. Thompson,

I just wanted you to be the first to know. I will be graduating second in my class next month.

Very truly yours,

Teddy Stallard"

I sent him a card of congratulations and a small package, a pen and pencil gift set. I wondered what he would do after graduation.

Four years later, Teddy's second letter came.

"Dear Mrs. Thompson,

I wanted you to be the first to know. I was just informed that I'll be graduating first in my class. The university has not been easy, but I liked it.

Very truly yours,

Teddy Stallard"

I sent him a good pair of sterling silver monogrammed cuff links and a card, so proud of him I could burst!

And now—today—Teddy's third letter.

"Dear Mrs. Thompson,

I wanted you to be the first to know. As of today I am Theodore J. Stallard, M.D. How about that!!??

I'm going to be married in July, the twenty-seventh, to be exact. I wanted to ask if you could come and sit where Mom would sit if she were here. I'll have no family as Dad died last year.

Very truly yours,

Teddy Stallard"

I'm not sure what kind of gift one sends to a doctor on completion of medical school and state boards. Maybe I'll just wait and take a wedding gift, but my note can't wait.

"Dear Ted,

Congratulations! You made it and you did it by yourself! In spite of those like me and not because of us, this day has come for you.

God bless you. I'll be at the wedding with bells on!"

—Elizabeth Silance Ballard

Questions

1. What events influenced Teddy's self-concept in his early years?
2. How did Mrs. Thompson help Teddy?
3. What important lessons did you learn from this story about how others influence our self-concept and self-esteem?

Source: "Three Letters from Teddy," from *Home Life*, March 1976. Copyright 1976, The Sunday School Board of the Southern Baptist Convention (now LifeWay Christian Resources of the Southern Baptist Convention). All rights reserved. Used by permission of the author.

The medical profession is learning the power that our attitudes and expectations have over healing. Dr. Bernard Siegel, in his book *Love, Medicine, and Miracles*,[20] provides convincing evidence that patient attitudes about the healing process have a direct effect upon becoming well. Patients who have a positive, cooperative spirit are likely to recover from illness more quickly than those who assume the worst. As the article below about positive attitudes and heart disease illustrates, your state of mind may influence your state of health.

Self and Interpretation of Messages

Do you remember Eeyore, the donkey from the stories about Winnie-the-Pooh and his friends? Eeyore lived in the gloomiest part of the Hundred Acre Wood and had a self-image to match. In one story, which used to be a favourite of one of your author's sons, all of the animals congregated on a stormy night to check on Eeyore:

> ... they all came to the part of the forest known as Eeyore's gloomy place. On this stormy night it was terribly gloomy indeed—or it would have been were it not for Christopher Robin. He was there with a big umbrella.
>
> "I've invited Eeyore to come and stay with me until the storm is over," said Christopher Robin.
>
> "If it ever is," said Eeyore, "which doesn't seem likely. Not that anybody asked me, you understand. But then, they hardly ever do."[21]

Perhaps you know, or have known, an Eeyore—someone whose low self-esteem colours how he or she interprets messages and interacts with others. According to research, such people are more likely to have the following traits:[22]

- Be more sensitive to criticism and negative feedback from others.
- Be more critical of others.
- Believe they are not popular or respected by others.

- Expect to be rejected by others.
- Dislike to be observed when performing.
- Feel threatened by people who they feel are superior.
- Expect to lose when competing with others.
- Be overly responsive to praise and compliments.
- Evaluate their overall behaviour as inferior to that of others.

The Pooh stories offer an antidote to Eeyore's gloom in the character of the optimistic Tigger, who assumes that everyone shares his exuberance for life:

> . . . when Owl reached Piglet's house, Tigger was there. He was bouncing on his tail, as Tiggers do, and shouting to Piglet. "Come on," he cried. "You can do it! It's fun!"[23]

If, like Tigger, your sense of self-worth is high, research suggests you will:

- Have higher expectations for solving problems.
- Think more highly of others.
- Be more likely to accept praise and accolades from others without feeling embarrassed.
- Be more comfortable having others observe you when you perform.
- Be more likely to admit you have both strengths and weaknesses.
- Be more comfortable when you interact with others who view themselves as highly competent.
- Expect other people to accept you for who you are.
- Be more likely to seek opportunities to improve skills that need improving.
- Evaluate your overall behaviour more positively than would people with lower self-esteem.[24]

Reflecting the assumption that our self-concept influences our behaviour is the principle of **selective exposure**, which suggests that we tend to place ourselves in situations consistent with who we think we are. Whom do you usually find at a Baptist church on Sunday morning? Baptists. Who are the attendees at a Liberal convention? Liberals. If you view yourself as a good student who wants an A in the class, where are you likely to be during class time? We behave in ways that reinforce our perception of self, both in our interpretation of messages and in our behaviour.

Self and Interpersonal Needs

According to social psychologist Will Schutz, our concept of who we are, coupled with our need to interact with others, profoundly influences how we communicate with others. Schutz identifies three primary social needs that affect the degree of communication we have with others: the need for inclusion, the need for control, and the need for affection.[25] The **need for inclusion** suggests that each of us has a need to be included in the activities of others. We all need human contact and fellowship. We need to be invited to join others, and perhaps we need to invite others to join us. Of course, the level and intensity of this need differs from person to person, but even loners desire some social contact. Our need to include others

As Professor Henry Higgins said about Eliza Doolittle, "If you treat a girl like a flower girl, that's all she will ever be. If you treat her like a princess she may be one." (Shooting Star)

selective exposure. A principle that suggests we tend to place ourselves in situations that are consistent with our self-concept and self-esteem.

need for inclusion. Interpersonal need to be included and to include others in social activities.

need for control.
Interpersonal need for some degree of domination in our relationships as well as the need to be controlled.

need for affection.
Interpersonal need to give and receive love, personal support, warmth, and intimacy.

communication style (social style). Your consistent way of relating to others based upon your personality, self-concept and self-esteem.

social learning approach. Perspective that explains your style of communicating with others is based on learning from and modelling other people.

assertiveness. Tendency to make requests, ask for information, and generally pursue your own rights and best interests.

responsiveness. Tendency to be sensitive to the needs of others, including being sympathetic to the pain of others and placing the feelings of others above your own feelings.

and be included in activities may stem, in part, from our concept of ourselves as either a "party person" or a loner.

The second need, the **need for control**, suggests that we also need some degree of influence over the relationships we establish with others. We may also have a need to be controlled because we desire some level of stability and comfort in our interactions with others. If we view ourselves as people who are comfortable being in charge, we are more likely to give orders to others rather than take orders from them.

And finally, we each have a **need for affection**. We need to give and receive love, support, warmth, and intimacy, although the amounts we need vary enormously from person to person. If we have a high need for affection, we will more likely place ourselves in situations where that need can be met. The greater our inclusion, control, and affection needs are, the more likely it is that we will actively seek others as friends and initiate communication with them.

Self and Communication Style

Our self-concept and self-esteem affect not only the way we feel about ourselves, the way we interpret messages, and our personal performance, they also influence the way we *deliver* messages and treat other people. Each of us has a **communication style** or **social style** that is identifiable by the habitual ways in which we behave toward others. The style we adopt helps others interpret our messages. As they get to know you, other people begin to expect you to behave in a certain way, based upon previous associations with you.

How do we develop our communication style? Many communication researchers, sociologists, and psychologists believe that we have certain underlying traits or personality characteristics that influence how we interact with others. Some scholars believe these traits stem from genetics—we are born with certain personality characteristics. We are who we are because that's the way we are made.[26] Others emphasize the **social learning approach**—we communicate with others as we do because of our interactions with others such as our parents and friends. The truth is that we cannot yet explain exactly how we come to communicate as we do.

Even though we don't know the precise role of nature or nurture in determining how we communicate, most inventories of personality or communication style focus on two primary dimensions that underlie how we interact with others—assertiveness and responsiveness.[27] **Assertiveness** is the tendency to make requests, ask for information, and generally pursue our own rights and best interests. An assertive style is sometimes called a "masculine" style. By masculine, we don't mean that only males can be assertive, but that in many cultures being assertive is synonymous with being "masculine." You are assertive when you seek information if you are confused, or direct others to help you get what you need.

Responsiveness is the tendency to be sensitive to the needs of others. Being other-oriented and sympathetic to the pain of others, and placing the feelings of others above your own feelings are examples of being responsive. Researchers sometimes label responsiveness a "feminine" quality. Again, this does not mean only women are or should be responsive, only that many cultures stereotype being responsive as a traditional behaviour of females.

What is your communication style? To assess your style of communication on the assertiveness and responsiveness dimensions, take the "Sociocommunicative Orientation" test by James McCroskey and Virginia Richmond below. You may discover that you test higher on one dimension than on the others. It's also possible to be high on both or low on both. Assertiveness and responsiveness are two different dimensions; you need not have just one or the other.

Sociocommunicative Orientation*

Directions: The following questionnaire lists 20 personality characteristics. Please indicate the degree to which you believe each of these characteristics applies to you, as you normally communicate with others, by marking whether you (5) strongly agree that it applies, (4) agree that it applies, (3) are undecided, (2) disagree that it applies, or (1) strongly disagree that it applies. There are no right or wrong answers. Work quickly; record your first impression.

_____ 1. helpful
_____ 2. defends own beliefs
_____ 3. independent
_____ 4. responsive to others
_____ 5. forceful
_____ 6. has strong personality
_____ 7. sympathetic
_____ 8. compassionate
_____ 9. assertive
_____ 10. sensitive to the needs of others
_____ 11. dominant
_____ 12. sincere
_____ 13. gentle
_____ 14. willing to take a stand
_____ 15. warm
_____ 16. tender
_____ 17. friendly
_____ 18. acts as a leader
_____ 19. aggressive
_____ 20. competitive

*Items 2, 3, 5, 6, 9, 11, 14, 18, 19, and 20 measure assertiveness. Add the scores on these items to get your assertiveness score. Items 1, 4, 7, 8, 10, 12, 13, 15, 16, and 17 measure responsiveness. Add the scores on these items to get your responsiveness score. Scores range from 50 to 10. The higher your score, the higher your orientation as assertive and responsive.

Source: James C. McCroskey and Virginia P. Richmond, *Fundamentals of Human Communication: An Interpersonal Perspective* (Prospect Heights, IL: Waveland Press, 1996), 91.

What many people want to know is, "What's the best communication style? Should I be assertive or responsive?" The truth is, there is no one best style for every situation. It depends. Sometimes the appropriate thing to do is to assert yourself—to ask or even demand that you receive what you need and have a right to receive. In other situations, it may be more appropriate to be less confrontational. Maintaining the quality of the relationship by simply listening and being thoughtfully responsive to others may be best. The appropriateness of your communication style involves issues we will discuss in future chapters, such as how you adapt to culture and gender differences, your needs, the needs and rights of others, and the goal of your communication.

> ### Recap
>
> #### HOW SELF-CONCEPT AND SELF-ESTEEM AFFECT INTERPERSONAL COMMUNICATION AND RELATIONSHIPS
>
> | | Definition | Examples |
> |---|---|---|
> | **Message Interpretation and Interaction** | Feelings of high or low self-esteem affect how you understand and react to messages. | If you have high self-esteem, you are more likely to accept praise without embarrassment. |
> | **Self-Fulfilling Prophecy** | What you believe about yourself will come true because you expect it to come true. | You expect to have a rotten time at a party and you behave in such a way that you don't enjoy the party. |
> | **Communication Style** | Your self-concept and self-esteem contribute to habitual ways of responding to others. | Your image of yourself influences your expressive or assertive behaviour toward others. |

Summary

We all seek answers to three questions: Who am I? Why am I here? Who are all these others? William James answered the first question by dividing th self into three parts. The material self includes our bodies and those tangible possessions we own that give us identity. The social self is the part that engages in interaction with others. The spiritual self consists of thoughts and assumptions about values, moral standards, and beliefs about forces that influence our lives. Other theorists conclude that our self-concept develops through interaction with other people. The groups we belong to also give us identity. Our roles as sister, brother, student, and parent are important in how we view who we are; the roles we assume provide labels for who we are. We also self-reflexively make our own observations about ourselves apart from others, and about groups or roles we assume. Our gender plays a key part in affecting our view of who we are in relationship to others.

Your self-concept and self-esteem affect how you interact with others. Self-concept is who you think you are; self-esteem is your evaluation of your self-worth. It is difficult to alter your self-esteem, but seven techniques have been helpful to others: positive self-talk, visualizing success, avoiding comparisons with others, reframing events and relationships from a different perspective, developing honest relationships with others, letting go of the past, and seeking professional help.

Your self-concept and self-esteem affect your relationships with others. We use specific-other perspectives and generalized-other perspectives to predict others' behaviours. The self-fulfilling prophecy refers to predictions about your future actions that are likely to come true because you believe they will come true. We also communicate with others based on our sense of self-worth and the needs that we are attempting to fulfill. We also develop a communication style that includes how assertively we communicate to meet our own needs and how sensitive we are to others' needs.

For Discussion and Review

Focus on Comprehension

1. List and describe the three selves identified by William James.
2. Define, compare, and contrast the terms *self-concept* and *self-esteem*.
3. Identify and describe four factors that explain how our self-concept develops.

Focus on Critical Thinking

4. Joel, who is 30 years old, married, and has two children, suffers from feelings of low self-esteem. Although he has many friends and a wife who loves him, he feels that others perform much better than he does at work. What strategies would help Joel enhance his self-esteem?
5. Make a list of all of the groups, clubs, and organizations to which you belong. Rank them from most important to least important. What does your ranking of them tell you about these groups in reference to your self-concept?
6. Provide an original example of how visualization might help you enhance your self-esteem. Describe the positive scene.

Focus on Ethics

7. Discuss the ethical implications of using untrue flattery to enhance a friend's self-esteem.
8. There are many self-help books on the market that claim to enrich your social life by providing surefire techniques for enhancing self-esteem. Do you think these claims are ethical? Why or why not?
9. Aelish has long planned to attend a top-notch graduate program in psychology. Her grades, however, are only in the C and B range. Her SAT scores are average. Should she try to reframe this factual information or deal with her problem in another way?

For Your Journal

1. Record goals for your self-talk and note your self-talk messages day by day. You might want to organize your journal around specific topics such as academic achievement, personal appearance, shyness, or social skills. Under academic achievement you could write: "I will monitor my self-talk messages to keep myself on track while I study for two hours each day." Your personal appearance self-talk goal may be to tell yourself something positive about your appearance instead of thinking about only what you don't like.

2. Write in your journal the 10 responses you wrote for the Building Your Skills: Who Are You? questionnaire on page 38. At the end of the course, again write 10 responses to the "Who are you?" question without looking at your earlier responses. What are the differences in your responses? How do you explain them?

3. If someone were to walk into one of your favourite rooms in your home, residence room, or apartment, what conclusions might he or she draw about your social style? Are you neat and well organized? Or does your room have the characteristics of an expressive personality? Write a brief description of who you are from a social style perspective based upon the clues in your room.

Learning with Others

1. Place the following list of values in order from 1 to 14. In a group with other students, compare your answers. Discuss how your personal ranking of these values influences your interaction with others.

    _____ Honesty   _____ Justice

    _____ Salvation   _____ Wealth

    _____ A comfortable life _____ Beauty

    _____ Good health   _____ Equality

    _____ Human rights   _____ Freedom

    _____ Peace   _____ Personal happiness

    _____ Fulfilling work   _____ A personal code of ethics

2. You are going to make a shield of your life (like a coat of arms). Draw a large outline of a shield that fills an entire sheet of paper. Divide your shield into four equal sections. In the upper right-hand section of your shield, draw or

symbolize something at which you have skill or talent. In the upper left-hand section draw or symbolize something you are trying to improve or a new skill you are learning. In the lower right-hand section draw or symbolize your most prized material possession. Finally, in the lower left-hand section, write three words that you hope someone would use to describe you.

Share your shield with other students. Tell your classmates why you drew what you did. Discuss how your shield reflects your attitudes, beliefs, and values.

3. Go through your personal music library of tapes or CDs and identify a selection that best symbolizes you. Your selection may be based upon either the lyrics or the music. Bring your selection to class and play it for your classmates. (Your instructor will bring a tape or CD player.) Tell why this music symbolizes you. Discuss with classmates how today's music provides a glimpse of our culture and a vehicle for self-expression.

Weblinks

www.social-anxiety.com   This is an excellent site by the Berent Associates. It contains a great deal of information about shyness and social phobias and includes case studies.

www.shyness.com   This site, from The Encyclopedia of Mental Health, defines shyness, and discusses symptoms, causes, consequences, and treatment.

www.mindbodysoul.com   This is a fascinating site. You can get entrance to many services for free simply by registering. This site has everything from astrology (which you pay for) to food recipes (free) and exercise tips (free).

www.queendom.com   This site is devoted to tests including personality tests. Some of the tests are for fun while others have good reliability and validity.

Suggested Readings

Kiener, Robert. "Just a Prairie Girl." *Reader's Digest,* 159(956), (December 2001): 66–72. Montreal, PQ: Reader's Digest Magazines Canada.

Read the full interview with Pamela Wallin about her 20-year career in radio, print, and television. Ms. Wallin is an example of a woman who believes in herself and in what she can do.

Jones, J. J., S. Bennett, M. P. Olmsted, M. L. Lawson, and G. Rodin. "Disordered Eating Attitudes and Behaviours in Teenaged Girls: A School-Based Study." *Canadian Medical Association Journal,* 165(5), (2001): 547–553.

A disturbing study about the quest for thinness by young women in Canadian society.

chapter 3

Interpersonal Communication and Perception

After you study this chapter

you should be able to ...

1. Define perception and interpersonal perception.
2. Identify and explain the three stages of interpersonal perception.
3. Describe the relationship between interpersonal communication and interpersonal perception.
4. Explain how we form impressions of others, describe others, and interpret others' behaviour.
5. Identify the eight factors that distort the accuracy of our interpersonal perceptions.
6. Identify six suggestions for improving your interpersonal perceptions.

- Understanding the Interpersonal Perception Process
- Perception and Interpersonal Communication
- Perceiving Others
- Identifying Barriers to Accurate Perceptions
- Improving Your Perceptual Skills

People only see what they are prepared to see.

RALPH WALDO EMERSON

Look at the painting in Figure 3.1. What is happening and what has happened? What is the relationship among the individuals in the painting? You probably have deduced that the boy was running away from home, the police officer found him, and then took the boy into the local coffee shop for ice cream or some other treat. Perhaps you think that the server is wistfully recalling his own days of running away as a child. What are your feelings about the police officer? Do you see him as a friendly and caring person who has a good understanding of kids?

As human beings we interpret and attribute meaning to what we observe or experience, particularly if what we are observing is other people. We tend to make inferences about their motives, personalities, and other traits based on their physical qualities and behaviours. The types of conclusions you draw from observing the painting shown in Figure 3.1 exemplify the process we call *interpersonal perception*. Through interpersonal perception we piece together various bits of information about other people and draw conclusions that may or may not be accurate. Because our feelings and responses to other people are based on our perceptions, those who are skilled at making observations and interpretations have a head start in developing effective interpersonal relationships.

Most of the time, we are unaware of our own perception process. For example, you may not have realized that you were drawing conclusions about the painting until you read the questions above. But we may become aware of the process when differences in perception cause a conflict or disagreement. In truth, no two individuals ever perceive the same thing in exactly the same way. Fortunately, communication tools, such as conversation, allow us to create shared meanings despite the differences in our perceptions.

Our perceptions are influenced by who we are, including the accumulation of our experiences. If you have had several bad experiences with the police, for example, you may not view the police officer in the painting in Figure 3.1 as a friendly person. Or if you know something about the life and work of Norman Rockwell, the illustrator who painted the picture, you may view all his works as representations of an idyllic North American culture and society that existed only in his mind. As we saw in Chapter 2, everything we perceive is filtered through our self-concept.[1] It is important to recognize and examine factors that might distort the

Figure 3.1

The Runaway. Original oil painting for a *Saturday Evening Post* cover, September 20, 1958. Old Corner House Collection, Stockbridge, Massachusetts.

Source: Printed by permission of the Rockwell Family Trust. Copyright © The Runaway, the Norman Rockwell Family Trust.

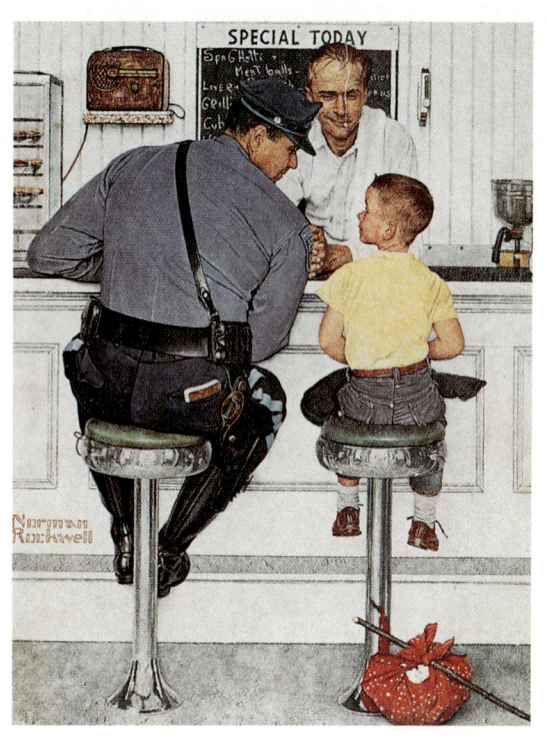

accuracy of our interpretations. We can also reduce inaccuracies by applying an other-oriented approach as we interact with people. By focusing on how others perceive the world, we can reduce the amount of distortion that our own self-concepts impose on our perceptions.

Before we turn to the role that perception plays in interpersonal communication, let's first take a closer look at the interpersonal perception process itself.

Building Your Skills

PERCEPTUAL DIFFERENCES

Think of two instances in which you and a friend had a very similar perception of something—perhaps the food in a restaurant, a scene in a movie, or some behaviour you observed in some other person. How did you know that you and your friend had similar perceptions? What factors in your backgrounds influenced the way you each perceived the experience?

Now think of two instances in which you and a friend had different perceptions of the same thing. How did you discover that you and your friend had different perceptions? To what factors in each of your backgrounds do you attribute these different perceptions? What effects did the differences in perception have upon your interactions?

Understanding the Interpersonal Perception Process

What is perception? We collect information about our world through our five senses. We make sense of the world through perception. **Perception** is the process of understanding or making sense of your experiences. For example, a sound travels through the air, vibrates on your eardrum, activates the nerves, and sends a signal to the brain. Perception allows you to define what that sound means. A

perception. Experiencing your world and making sense out of what you experience.

similar sequence of events takes place when you see, smell, feel, or taste something. The process of perception also includes organizing and interpreting information provided by the senses. You come out of a building and see wet pavement and puddles of water, hear thunder, smell a distinct odour caused by ions, and observe drops of falling water. You integrate all those bits of information and conclude that it is raining, and has been for a while.

Our perceptions of people, however, include analysis and interpretation that go beyond simple interpretation of sensory information. **Interpersonal perception** is the process by which we decide what people are like and give meaning to their actions. It includes making judgments about personality and drawing inferences from what we observed.[2] When you meet someone new, you *select* certain information to attend to (you note whether the person is male or female, has an accent, smiles, uses a friendly tone of voice), as well as particular personal information (the person is from Lunenburg, Nova Scotia). You then *organize* the information under some category that is recognizable to you, such as "a friendly Maritimer." Then you *interpret* the organized perceptions: this person is trustworthy, honest, hardworking, and likeable.

In our discussion, we will focus on this kind of interpersonal perception, which relates to understanding our observations of other people. We will begin by examining the three stages of the interpersonal perception process that we described above: selecting, organizing, and interpreting what we observe.

interpersonal perception. The process of selecting, organizing, and interpreting our observations of other people.

selective perception. Directing our attention to specific stimuli and consequently ignoring other stimuli.

Stage One: Selecting

Sit for a minute after you read this passage and try to tune in all the sensory input you are receiving: consider the feel of your socks against your feet, the pressure of the floor on your heels, the pressure of the piece of furniture against your body as you sit, the buzzing sounds from various sources around you—this "white noise" might come from a refrigerator, personal computer, fluorescent lights, water in pipes, voices, passing traffic, or your own heartbeat or churning stomach. What do you smell? What do you see? Without moving your eyes, turn your awareness to the images you see in the corner of your vision. What colours do you see? What shapes? What taste is in your mouth? How do the pages of this book feel against your fingertips? Now stop reading and consider all these sensations. Try to focus on all of them at the same time. You can't. You have to select what you are going to pay attention to. Without this ability to select, life would be chaos.

The number of sensations we can attend to at any given time is limited. We are, therefore, selective about which sensations make it through to the level of awareness. Perhaps you close your eyes or sit in the dark as you listen to music. This allows you to select more auditory sensations because you are eliminating visual ones. This selectivity can also cause us to fail to perceive information that is important. Imagine that you are standing with your back to an open hallway door talking to a friend and complaining about your roommate or spouse just as that roommate or spouse walks in the door. Your friend hand-signals that the other person has just entered, but you miss this cue and go on to say things that you later wish your roommate or spouse had not heard. You missed the signal because you failed to perceive the gesture. Because you were simplifying the stimuli to which you attended, you did not process the hand gesture.

Directing our attention to specific stimuli and consequently ignoring others is called **selective perception**. In our interactions with others we may choose to focus on specific cues such as gestures or foot movement. What specific qualities or features do you tend to focus on when you first meet others? Do you pay particular attention to handshakes, smiles, eye contact, body posture, gestures, or tone of voice? Sometimes we exercise selective perception when we are listening for a specific piece of information. As in the example of missing your friend's hand signal, our selective focus might prevent us from perceiving other important cues.

During this selection stage, we also attempt to simplify the stimuli that flood in through our senses by using various techniques. We use perceptual filters to screen out constant sensations that we have learned are unimportant, such as the sensations of our clothes against our skin and the surrounding white noise and smells. We do, however, attend to the sensation of the elastic bands of our underclothes if they pull too tight, because a threshold of arousal is crossed, forcing the brain to attend to that stimulus. Each of our senses has such a threshold. As long as sensations stay below this threshold, we can then attend to the stimuli that we have actively selected and pay attention to these stimuli only.

We also select stimuli by categorizing. In many ways this is also used for organizing and interpreting stimuli. For example, I notice in a supermarket that there is a vegetation that I have never seen before. It is beside the apples. Based on this I tell myself it must be a fruit (simplification) and is probably a type of apple or apple-like (categorization). I would also interpret that it is edible. Don't let this confuse you. Categorizing is an important part of the entire perception process so we will revisit it in several different ways! We create categories to reduce or simplify the amount of information to which we have to attend or remember. We also use categories to organize information.

We also categorize using current labels such as nationality. The Canadian Issues box below examines the perceived differences between two nationalities: Canadians and Americans.

Canadian Issues

PERCEIVING OUR NEIGHBOURS TO THE SOUTH: HOW SIMILAR OR DIFFERENT ARE WE?

Often we hear the line that Canadians are the same as Americans. After all, we watch many of the same TV shows, listen to the same music, dress similarly, watch American sports, eat "American" food, and on the list goes. After the terrorist attacks of September 11, 2001, our empathy for our American neighbours was high, as hundreds of thousands of Canadians donated money, and thousands offered help. Many Canadians actively participated in the long and arduous clean up effort. We wept for our neighbours as well as for the many Canadians that were touched with this tragedy in personal ways. The Canadian government was one of the first to offer help. The latest year-end poll offers some surprising results.

While we perceive ourselves as being very similar to our neighbours, surveys point out that there are several subtle and real differences and that the perception of similarity is not quite accurate in all respects. The latest annual *Maclean's* year-end poll undertaken with CBC TV's *The Magazine*, conducted in November of 2001, indicates that we vary from our American neighbours in some significant ways. For instance, Canadians feel that the war on terrorism will last longer that two or three years (70 percent) while 40 percent feel it will last longer than the Second World War. On the other hand, the American majority believes that it will last only months, a year at the most. (1) A real difference with this poll from other years is that Canadians are now prepared to give more money to the military. (2) In the 1999 poll Americans were more concerned with world issues, war, and peace than were Canadians. In fact, this problem did not appear in the top seven for Canadians, but was number four for the Americans. (3)

In the most recent poll, 47 percent of Canadians described our relations with the United States as "friends, but not especially close." Canadians were almost evenly divided in the belief that the September 11th attacks were aimed at the U.S. only (49%) or Western democratic societies including Canada (48%).

For Canadians, the two most important national issues were health/education and unemployment/economy. Over 60 percent believed that if Canada went into a recession the terrorist attacks and aftermath were to blame. (4) Canadians also responded that they felt closer to the Americans following September 11, the top three reasons being "We share a common set of values and beliefs," "We are facing a common threat," and "We are tied together economically."

Past polls, such as the 1999 *Maclean's* poll, were more focused on our differences rather than our similarities. In 1999, the most important issue for Canadians was social services, especially health and education (then also ranked as number one); for Americans, it was social and moral issues. Canadians ranked unemployment and the economy as number two while the Americans gave crime and violence the number two spot. Crime and violence were ranked sixth out of the top eight problems by Canadians. The economy was ranked third by our neighbours. Another major difference appears to centre on religion and religious beliefs. Americans go to church more often. Also, more Americans believe that there is a hell (73 percent agreed) than do Canadians (49 percent). (5)

While these past polls indicate differences, we are also similar to our neighbours in a number of ways. September 11th has shown that we have a great deal of empathy toward our neighbours, while still wanting to preserve our distinctiveness. It will be interesting to read next year's polls, and polls to come, to see the impact of the terrorist attacks on future years. Will these attacks bring the two nations together and encourage further similarities or will Canadians (and Americans) still pride themselves on their differences? Maybe number one on both lists will be safety for all.

For Discussion

1. Why do you think we perceive ourselves as being similar to our neighbours when in actuality there are several important differences?
2. Do you think there are other major differences between Canadians and Americans?
3. In what ways do you think we are very similar to Americans?
4. How do you think the disaster of September 11, 2001, will change our views of Americans and of the world?

Sources

1., 2. Robert Sheppard, "Keeping Our Distance," *Maclean's*, December 31, 2001, 26–28.
3. Chris Wood, "The Vanishing Border," *Maclean's*, December 20, 1999, 20–23.
4. *Maclean's*/CBC Poll, "Since Sept. 11," *Maclean's*, December 31, 2001, 38–40.
5. *Maclean's*/CBC Poll, "Peering Inward and Outward," *Maclean's*, December 20, 1999, 48–49.

Stage Two: Organizing

Look at the four items in Figure 3.2. What does each of them mean to you? If you are like most people, you will perceive item A as the word *interpersonal*, item B as a circle, C as a rabbit, and D as a telephone number. Strictly speaking, none of those perceptions is correct. We'll discuss why after we explore this second stage of perception: organization.

Patterning

After we select what stimuli we are going to attend to and process, we start to organize them into convenient, understandable, and efficient patterns that allow us

Figure 3.2
What Do You See?

A. NTRPRSNL

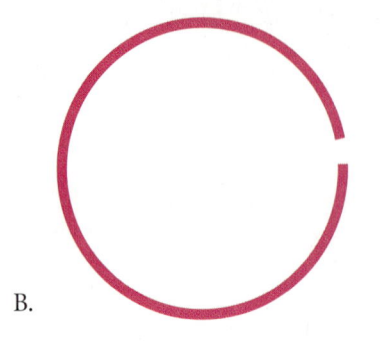

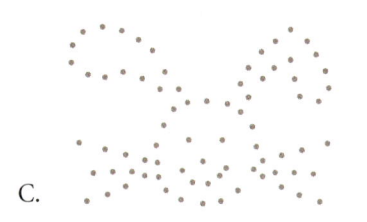

B. ◯

C. ⁖⁘⁙ (rabbit pattern of dots)

D. 555 4433

to make sense of what we have observed. Organizing makes it easier for us to process complex information, because it allows us to impose the familiar onto the unfamiliar, and because we can easily store and recall simple patterns. For example, when you looked at item C in Figure 3.2, you see the pattern of dots that you label a rabbit because *rabbit* is a concept you know and to which you attach various meanings. The set of dots would not have meaning for you in and of themselves, nor would it be meaningful for you to attend to each particular dot or to the dots' relationship to one another. It would be possible to create a mathematical model of the dots indicating their placement on an X–Y grid, but such a model would be extremely complex and difficult to observe and remember. It's much easier to organize the dots in a way that refers to something stored in your memory: a rabbit. For similar reasons, we organize patterns of stars in the sky into various animals and familiar shapes like the bear, the crab, and the Big and Little Dippers. As we do for the pattern of dots making up the rabbit, we search for and apply patterns to our perceptions of people.

Punctuating

The way we organize information depends partly upon the way we punctuate it. Item D in Figure 3.2 looks like a telephone number because it has three numbers followed by four numbers. You might also remember that 555 is the prefix you use for calling long-distance information. However, the digits could just as easily represent two totally independent numbers: 555 followed by the number 4433. How we interpret the numbers depends upon how we punctuate[3] or separate them. When we record information, we use commas, periods, dashes, and colons to signal meanings and interpretations. In our minds, sometimes we impose punctuation marks where we believe they should be. We may, for example, have put a hyphen between 555 and 4433 even though no hyphen appeared there.

When it comes to punctuating relational events and behaviours, we each develop our own separate set of standards. You will sometimes experience difficulties and disagreements because of differences in how you and your partner choose to punctuate a conversational exchange or shared sequence of events.[4] Suppose you and a friend have been talking about her recent school problems. After a few moments of silence, you assume that your conversation on that topic has ended, so you start talking about your recent job interview. Later on, you find out that you offended your friend because she had not punctuated the conversation the same way. She believed that her problems should still have been the focus of the conversation.

Superimposing

Looking again at Figure 3.2, you can see that our inclination to **superimpose**, or place a familiar structure on information we select, also leads us to create a

superimpose. To place a familiar structure on information you select.

familiar word from the meaningless assemblage of letters in item A, and to label the figure in item B a circle, even though circles are continuous lines without gaps on the right side. We apply the same principles and search for and apply patterns in our perception of people. When we have an incomplete picture of another human being, we impose a pattern or structure, classify the person on the basis of the information we do have, and fill in the gaps. Filling in these gaps is known as **closure**. We apply these principles to our interaction with other people. We fill in "gaps" based on how people dress, how they speak, the manner in which they speak, and other bits and pieces of incomplete information.

Categorizing

Two important ways that we categorize stimuli in our interactions—prototypes and stereotypes—help us to organize large amounts of stimuli and to understand our experiences by placing them in contexts that we can more easily manage.

Prototypes are knowledge structures that represent the best or most clear example of some category. For example, the word "grandmother" may represent to you an older woman with grey hair, who wears sensible shoes, has wrinkles in her skin, and bakes wonderful pies. To you this portrait is the ideal of "grandmother" and, as such, is labelled as a prototype. You have many prototypes for a wide variety of categories, such as best teacher, true friend, car salesperson, and great doctor. Once you have placed an individual into a prototype, you may automatically attribute qualities to this person. You learn, for instance, that the person sitting beside you is a parent. You then automatically assume characteristics that you associate with parenthood: being loving, committed, responsible, and tired.

Despite its efficiency, however, this simplification process can create significant problems. One of these potential problems is stereotypes. Stereotypes are different than prototypes and are based on overgeneralizing characteristics to predict the behaviour of the person in a specific category. **Stereotypes** are cognitive simplifications that allow us to predict the behaviour of an individual we have placed in that category. If, for instance, you find out that someone is conservative, you may stereotype that person as being anti-welfare, against gun control legislation, and supportive of new cuts in social program spending. Note that you have made these predictions without having any real interaction with the person. Stereotypes are based on our perceptions of similarities of people who belong to a specific group, not on actual interaction with people from these groups. Stereotypes lead to labelling of others based on the category in which we perceive those people to belong.

closure. The process of filling in missing information.

prototypes. Cognitive structures that represent the best or clearest example of a category.

stereotypes. Predictive generalizations about people or situations based on the category in which they have been placed.

Stage Three: Interpreting

Once we have selected and organized stimuli into familiar patterns, we are ready to interpret what they mean. We attach meaning to all that we observe. It is not enough to simply select and organize material, we have to make sense of it. We learn through socialization and our own recurring experiences to attribute particular meaning to particular stimuli. In some cases the meanings are fairly standardized, as they are for language, for example. But others are much more personalized. As the excerpt from "The Greek Interpreter" shows, the fictional detective Sherlock Holmes was noted for his ability to apply exacting interpretations to what he observed. In general, the heroes in mysteries usually excel in their ability to observe, organize, and interpret the stimuli around them. Sherlock and Mycroft Holmes possess an ability to attend to specific cues that you and I may miss. They also are able to organize the cues to create a unique meaning and interpretation. Seeing that the man in dark mourning clothes is carrying a baby's toy and a picture book takes on special meaning when the various cues are combined.

Sherlock Holmes and His Brother Mycroft Make Some Observations

In this excerpt, Sherlock Holmes is visiting his brother Mycroft. Both are looking out a window when Mycroft asks Sherlock what he makes of a very small, dark fellow with his hat pushed back and several packages under his arm standing on the street corner. Dr. Watson records their conversation:

"An old soldier, I perceive," said Sherlock.
"And very recently discharged," remarked his brother.
"Served in India, I see."
"And a non-commissioned officer."
"Royal Artillery, I fancy," said Sherlock.
"And a widower."
"But with a child."
"Children, my dear boy, children."
"Come," said I, laughing, "this is a little too much."

"Surely," answered Holmes, "it is not hard to say that a man with that bearing, expression of authority, and sun-baked skin, is a soldier, is more than a private, and is not long from India."

"That he has not left the service long is shown by his still wearing his ammunition boots, as they are called," observed Mycroft.

"He had not the cavalry stride, yet he wore his hat on one side, as is shown by the lighter skin on that side of his brow. His weight is against his being a sapper [army engineer]. He is in the artillery."

"Then, of course, his complete mourning shows that he has lost someone very dear. The fact that he is doing his own shopping looks as though it were his wife. He has been buying things for children, you perceive. There is a rattle, which shows that one of them is very young. The wife probably died in childbed. The fact that he has a picture book under his arm shows that there is another child to be thought of."

Source: From Sir Arthur Conan Doyle, "The Greek Interpreter."

Although all of us may not possess Sherlock Holmes's perceptual talents, we do all attribute meaning to what we observe. If you shake someone's hand and it feels like a wet, dead fish, what is your reaction and interpretation? If you notice someone you don't know winking at you from across a room, what do you think? If a toddler is crying in a room full of people and a woman comes over and picks the child up, what do you assume about the woman? If you see a student glance over at another student's exam paper and then record an answer, what do you think the student has done? All of these are examples that show we impose meaning on what we observe to complete the perceptual process.

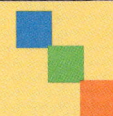

Building Your Skills

PERCEPTUAL INTERPRETATIONS

Find a place where you can sit and watch people for a while. Write down as many points as you can that you are able to observe about the people that pass by or that are seated nearby. Try to make some interpretations based upon your observations, just as Sherlock Holmes might have. What do you notice about their clothing, their shoes, the manner in which they walk? What are they carrying with them? Do they seem to be in a hurry? Can you tell which are students, teachers, or members of other professions? If you are watching other students, can you tell what their majors are?

If you get the chance, you might approach some of these people and see how accurate your observations are. People are generally open to hearing positive perceptions about themselves. You may want to hold back on sharing negative perceptions.

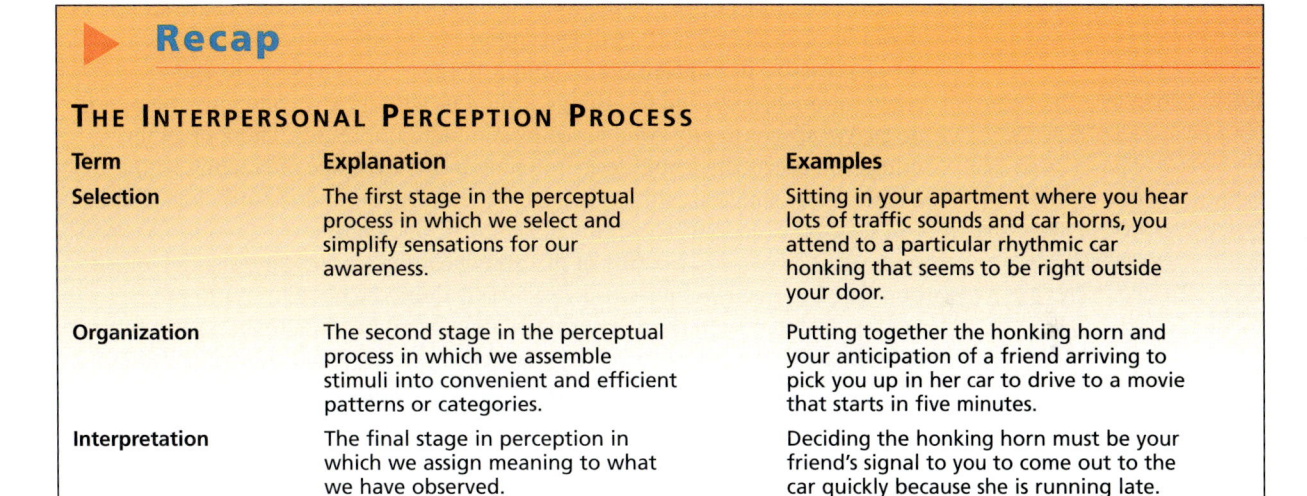

▶ Recap

THE INTERPERSONAL PERCEPTION PROCESS

Term	Explanation	Examples
Selection	The first stage in the perceptual process in which we select and simplify sensations for our awareness.	Sitting in your apartment where you hear lots of traffic sounds and car horns, you attend to a particular rhythmic car honking that seems to be right outside your door.
Organization	The second stage in the perceptual process in which we assemble stimuli into convenient and efficient patterns or categories.	Putting together the honking horn and your anticipation of a friend arriving to pick you up in her car to drive to a movie that starts in five minutes.
Interpretation	The final stage in perception in which we assign meaning to what we have observed.	Deciding the honking horn must be your friend's signal to you to come out to the car quickly because she is running late.

Perception and Interpersonal Communication

Interpersonal perception is a two-way street when it comes to interpersonal communication. Our perceptions of others affect the ways in which we communicate with them, and their perceptions of us affect the way they communicate with us.

We continually modify the topics, the language, and the manner in which we communicate according to the perceptions we have of others. For example, if you observe a woman dressed in a tracksuit running in a park, you may conclude that she is a physical fitness fanatic. Then, if you strike up a conversation with her, you may bring up topics such as physical fitness, sports, and diet. But if she informs you that she knows nothing about those things and has just started jogging to offset the time she spends watching videos and eating potato chips, then you would probably shift your focus according to a revised perception. You might start talking about movies and the relative merits of rippled versus plain potato chips. Similarly, if you were talking to a child, you would probably use simple language rather than complex technical terminology. If you were talking to a person who is hearing impaired, you might slow down your speech and raise your speaking volume. The way that others talk and behave also tells us a great deal about how they perceive us. Maybe you can remember the first time someone younger than you called you Mister, Ms., Mrs., or Miss (if it hasn't happened yet, it will). It probably surprised you to realize that someone perceived you as "old," or as someone with authority. We also analyze others' reactions to us for clues about their conception of who we are. As an example, suppose your new college friends go out to play basketball, your favourite sport, but do not invite you. When you later ask them why, they say they always thought of you as the unathletic, studious type. Sometimes others' perceptions of us are surprising. If we never ask, we may never discover that they are inaccurate. The degree to which others have a conception of us that is different from our own is often a measure of the quality of the relationship. The stronger the interpersonal relationship, the closer our self-perceptions are to the perceptions others have of us.[5]

How much we notice about another person's communication behaviour relates to our level of interest and need. Perception can be either a passive or an active process. **Passive perception** occurs simply because our senses are in operation. We see, hear, smell, taste, and feel things around us without any conscious attempt to do so. We are constantly bombarded by stimuli to our senses. Think of all the things you potentially could select for your awareness while interacting with a friend: words you hear with variations in the tone, rate, and so forth; behaviours you see with variations in eye contact, gestures, body movement, and facial expressions. As we have seen, because of the overwhelming amount of potential information that is available to our senses, we usually don't catch it all.

If we feel uncertain about a given situation or interaction, we become motivated to select particular information through active perception. **Active perception** is the process of seeking out specific information by intentionally observing and questioning; we make a conscious effort to figure out what we are experiencing. We've all heard noises that startle us and make us wonder, "What was that?" We then try to recall the sound and identify it, or we might investigate—seek out additional information.

If you can gain information and reduce your uncertainty about others, then you can predict their reactions and behaviours, adapt your behaviours and strategies, and therefore maximize the likelihood of fulfilling your social needs.[6] Although this might sound calculating, it really isn't. If you enjoy outdoor activities, such as camping and hiking, one of your goals in establishing social relationships is probably to find others who share your interest. So observing, questioning, and processing information to determine a potential friend's interests can help you assess whether the relationship will meet your goals. In Chapter 4 we discuss ways to improve your ability to gain information through more effective listening.

passive perception. Perception that occurs because your senses are in operation.

active perception. Perception that occurs because you seek out specific information through intentional observation and questioning.

Perceiving Others

As we collect information about others, we organize and interpret that information in various ways. Interpersonal perception involves three processes: forming impressions of others; applying implicit personality theories and the use of mental constructs, which we use to organize information about people; and finally, developing attribution theories, which help us explain why people behave the way they do.

How We Form Impressions of Others

Impressions are collections of perceptions about others that we maintain and use to interpret their behaviours. Impressions tend to be very general: "She seemed nice," "He was very friendly," or "What a nerd!" According to **impression formation theory**, we form these impressions through perceptions of physical qualities and behaviour, information people disclose about themselves, and information that third parties tell us. We select, organize, and interpret all of these perceptions to create a general impression. In the Canadian Issues box on pages 78–79, there is a brief history and some facts about Buzz Hargrove. What is your current impression of this CAW leader? After you read the feature, did your impressions change at all? We tend to form these impressions readily and part with them reluctantly. When we first meet someone we form a **first impression** without having much information, and we often hold on to this impression throughout the relationship.

In one study conducted by Solomon Asch, individuals were asked to provide an evaluation of two people based on two lists of adjectives.[7] The list for the first person had the following adjectives: *intelligent, industrious, impulsive, critical, stubborn,* and *envious*. The list for the other person had the same adjectives, but in reverse order. Although the content was identical, respondents gave the first person a more positive evaluation than the second. One explanation for this is that the first words in each list created a first impression that respondents used to interpret the remaining adjectives. In a similar manner, the first impressions we form about someone often affect our interpretation of subsequent perceptions of them.

This effect of attending to the first pieces of information that we observe is called the **primacy effect**. We also tend to put a lot of stock in the last thing we observed, which is called the **recency effect**.[8] For example, if you think for years that your friend is honest, but today you discover that she lied to you about something important, that lie will have a greater impact on your impression of her than the honest behaviour she has displayed for years. The primacy and recency effects explain why you are more likely to remember information at the beginning or end of a paragraph than you are to remember information in the middle.

We also attempt to manage the impressions others form of us. We make guesses about how other people will interpret our own physical displays and behaviours; as a result, we attempt to manipulate those displays and behaviours to our advantage. Think about the first day of classes this semester. Did you think about what clothes you were going to wear to classes? Did you worry about how your hair looked, or your breath smelled? Most of us choose clothes that we think will create a positive statement and reflect who we are. In this way we attempt to manage the impressions others form of us. Our ability to manage such impressions effectively depends on our ability to socially decentre (as discussed in the next chapter) by looking at ourselves from other people's perspectives. The more accurate you are at determining how others will react to

impression. A collection of perceptions about others that you maintain and use to interpret their behaviours.

impression formation theory. Theory that explains how you develop perceptions about people and how you maintain and use those perceptions to interpret their behaviours.

first impression. The product of a set of perceptions we gather upon meeting another person.

primacy effect. Placing heavy emphasis upon the first pieces of information that we observe about another to form an impression.

recency effect. Placing heavy emphasis on the most recent information we have observed about another to form or modify our impression.

When we're not sure about the meaning intended by another's message, it is wise to actively check out the meaning by asking what he or she meant by the words. (Bob Daemmrich/Stock Boston)

Canadian Issues

BUZZ HARGROVE: WHAT'S YOUR IMPRESSION?

What is your impression of Buzz Hargrove, leader of the Canadian Auto Workers Union? (CP Photo/Frank Gunn)

According to one source, you either love him or hate him. Or maybe some people just love to hate him. He has been called a lot of things from showman to bully to bluffer. Whatever your perceptions are of Buzz Hargrove, he is one of the most influential and powerful public figures in Canada today. As the leader of the Canadian Auto Workers (CAW), he has fought many battles during his leadership that began in 1992 and has been re-elected for several three-year terms.

He was born Basil Eldon Hargrove in 1944 in Bath, New Brunswick, and was the sixth of 10 children. His father, Percy, was a carpenter who worked at logging camps during the winter. The family was poor and his mother, Eileen, grew potatoes to pay for the children's clothes. His mother left the family by 1958, leaving him and his siblings with their difficult father. At 16, Buzz dropped out of school after finishing Grade 10 and drifted from job to job. Finally, in 1964, he landed in the Windsor Chrysler plant in Ontario while visiting his older brother. Ken Gerrard, the plant chairman for the union local, helped him to get a job on the line making seat cushions. In 1965, he won in an election to become shop steward, the same year the Canada–U.S. Auto Pact was rectified. Here he met Bob White. Buzz was at White's side during the rebellion against their American UAW leaders, eventually breaking away to create the new union, the CAW. Until White left the CAW for the presidency of the Canadian Labour Congress, the two worked closely together with Buzz as White's special assistant. Since 1992, Buzz has taken over the helm of the CAW. Since his takeover, he has made friends and enemies in management and union alike. (1) Also, it should be noted that he is a member of the NDP and is quite vocal in his views on what he thinks the party should or should not do. Here are just a few of the events in the history of Buzz Hargrove's leadership of the CAW. Consult your local newspaper's business section and you will continue to find Buzz in the news.

- In 1995, according to one source, the NDP convinced themselves that it was Buzz and the public-sector unions that were responsible for the NDP vote declining from 39 percent to 21 percent. By 1999, the vote collapsed to 12 percent. Blame it on Buzz? (2)

- In 1996, after finishing the last round of negotiations with the "Big Three" car companies (Chrysler, General Motors, and Ford), he announced the final deal with Ford complete with a box of Pablum and a baby spoon. He was quoted as saying that the company would take to his demands "like babies to their first solid foods: they spit it out at first but learn to like it." (3)

- Shortly after signing a new collective agreement in October of 1998, the Canadian National Railway Co. announced that it was eliminating 3000 jobs from its current payroll of 6000 employees. Labour leaders, including Buzz Hargrove, expressed their outrage. Buzz in particular was vocal as investors rewarded the company by driving up its share price in the face of such "fiscal responsibility." This was not the first time that company shares have appreciated in the wake of major layoffs or plant closures. According to Hargrove the corporations and the government are to blame: "What corporations have achieved is nothing less than the systematic dismantling of the socio-economic system that Canadians have built over the last four decades." (4)

- In December of 2000, Buzz and Ken Georgetti were feuding over shop-floor raiding. Georgetti is the chief of the Canadian Labour Congress (CLC), an umbrella

> organization to which the CAW belongs. The CLC was not pleased with how the CAW "robbed" the memberships of two other unions (the Service Employees International Union and the Public Service Alliance of Canada). Such "poaching" is prohibited by the CLC constitution. Hargrove's position is that all working people should have a say as to what union they belong to. According to this article, Hargrove is right, as unions provide a service for which customers pay (union dues). (5)
>
> **Sources**
>
> 1. Deirdre McMurdy and Luke Fisher, "Big Bad Buzz," *Maclean's*, December 16, 1996, 22–24; CBC TV's *Life and Times* biographies, "Buzz Hargrove: Labour of Love," www.tv.cbc.ca/lifeandtimes/bio2000/hargrove.htm
> 2. Geoff Bickerton, "Buzz, Battles and Bombs," *Canadian Dimension*, Fall 1999, Vol. 33 (4/5), 16.
> 3. Canadian Press, "Big Three Talks End with Ford Deal," *Canadian News Digest*, Wednesday, November 6, 1996, www.canoe.ca/NewsArchiveNov96/candigest_nov6.html
> 4. Deirdre McMurdy, "Passionate, but Wrong," *Maclean's*, November 30, 1998, 64.
> 5. Derek DeCloet, "Brother Against Brother," *Canadian Business*, June 12, 2000, 103.

people's looks and behaviours, the more potential you have for adapting your own looks and behaviours.

How We Describe Others

Do you like to "people watch"? If you have some time on your hands while waiting for a friend, you may just start looking at people and make guesses about what these strangers may do for a living, or whether they are friendly or grumpy, peaceful or petulant, kind or mean. We make assumptions about their personality. Even with people we know well, we don't know everything about them. When attempting to understand others, we rely on these guesses or assumptions to describe their characteristics and personalities.

These hunches help us to develop an **implicit personality theory**, a pattern of associated qualities that we attribute to people, which allows us to understand them—whether we met them 10 minutes ago or 10 years ago. We make guesses about who they are, based on what information we already have about them. Implicit personality theory provides a way of organizing the vast array of information we have about people's personalities.[9] Implicit personality theories are essentially stereotypes that we apply to people in general. We accomplish perceptual closure through the use of implicit personality theory; that is, we are able to fill in the blanks about a person's personality without actually having to observe additional qualities. Once you have determined that someone is a "warm" person, you automatically associate other related terms. Your implicit personality theory may be similar to that held by others in your culture, but each person forms his or her own individual theory. There is more consistency between the personality frameworks you would use to judge two strangers than there is between the personality framework you use and the one another person uses to describe the same stranger.

Implicit personality theories allow us to manage a lot of information effectively, but they also can lead us to incorrect conclusions about other people. How accurately does "happy" actually describe a "warm" person? There are probably

implicit personality theory. Our own set of beliefs and hypotheses about what people are like.

unhappy warm people. In assuming a connection between these two concepts, you might have reached an erroneous conclusion about the other person. When you assume the warm person is happy, you might not perceive the person's need for support and nurturing. As a result, your responses will be inappropriate and lead to ineffective interpersonal communication. Therefore, while implicit personality theories may fill some of the blanks in about a person, the danger is that we operate under the theory and do not attempt to gather more information or check out what may be incorrect perceptions.

---

e-connections

THE ACCURACY OF OUR ELECTRONIC PERCEPTIONS OF OTHERS

More and more people first "meet" in cyberspace before interacting face to face. Precisely how does communicating with someone via e-mail affect how accurately we make impressions of their personality or predict how our electronic partner feels about other issues? Researcher Rodney Fuller asked people to identify a person they hadn't met in person but with whom they had an e-mail exchange. He then asked them several questions to assess how sensitive they were to their Internet partner's feelings about several issues; the subjects answered the same questions about themselves. He also asked people to complete the same questions about people they had met live and in person. The results: People who interacted with others face to face were more likely to accurately assess how their colleagues would answer the questions. The e-mail-only group, in general, perceived their electronic partners to be more logical and analytical than they actually were. Patricia Walker, in her excellent book *The Psychology of the Internet*, concludes that we relate to others in type differently from the way we do in person. "Online," concludes Walker, "we appear to be less inclined to perform those little civilities common to social interactions. Predictably, people react to our cooler, more task-oriented impression and respond in kind." Our perception of others is based on the information we discern from our interactions with them. When communicating by e-mail, we have a more limited array of information to share. Electronic perceptions of others may be more "cool" than when meeting others face to face.

Source: Rodney Fuller, "Human-Computer-Human Interaction: How Computers Affect Interpersonal Communication," in D. L. Day, and D. K. Kovacs (Eds.), *Computers, Communication and Mental Models* (London: Taylor & Francis, 1996); and Patricia Walker, *The Psychology of the Internet* (Cambridge, England: Cambridge University Press, 1999), 17.

---

halo effect. Attributing a variety of positive qualities to those we like.

horn effect. Attributing a variety of negative qualities to those we dislike.

personal constructs. Specific qualities or attributes we associate with each person we know.

One feature common to most of our implicit personality theories is the tendency to put people into two categories: those we like and those we don't like. When we observe people we like, there is often a **halo effect**; we attribute a variety of positive qualities to them because we like them. If you like me, then you will assume I have nothing except angelic qualities: I am nice to other people, warm and caring, fun to be with, and have a great sense of humour. On the other hand, if you don't like me, you may think of me as the Devil, attributing to me a variety of negative qualities. This is called the **horn effect**.

Although implicit personality theory describes how we organize and interpret our perceptions of people's personalities in general, we develop categories for people called *constructs*, which help us explain our perceptions of a specific person. When constructs are used to categorize people, they are referred to as personal constructs. Constructs are bipolar in their dimensions. **Personal constructs** represent qualities that allow us to categorize people into one of two groups of polar opposites: friendly or unfriendly, intelligent or unintelligent, graceful or clumsy, extrovert or introvert, funny or serious, conservative or liberal, overachiever or underachiever, playful or studious. These personal constructs help us to make more detailed assessments of particular qualities, rather than the more broad categories of prototypes.

Think about a close friend of yours. What qualities or constructs would you use to describe this person? What qualities differentiate this person from others? People differ in their ability to describe others. In other words, people differ in their **cognitive complexity**, the ability to develop a long list of personal constructs to describe people. Cognitive complexity varies in terms of differentiation, elaboration, and integration. Because we differ in cognitive complexity, these differences affect the accuracy of our perceptions. A person with a highly developed set of constructs is aware of the motives and causes of people's actions and is able to pick up on their emotional states. People with lower cognitive complexity have difficulty understanding information that does not fit into a previous construct and they see the world in simpler terms. Most importantly, a highly developed construct system enables us to take on another person's perspective, to empathize, and to orient toward the other person.

To help us understand the people we know, we develop a set of personal constructs for each person. A highly perceptive person may see a whole array of constructs for this woman: whimsical, warm, dependable, friendly, generous, and kind. A person with a less developed set of constructs may see only the whimsical side of her. (Brigid Allig/Tony Stone Images)

How We Interpret the Behaviour of Others

"I know why Alice didn't come to our meeting. She just doesn't like me," says Cathy. "She also just wants people to think she's too busy to be bothered with our little group." Cathy seems not only to have made a negative impression of Alice, but Cathy also seems to harbour a hunch as to why Alice didn't come to the meeting. Cathy is attributing meaning to Alice's behaviour. Even though Alice could have just forgotten about the meeting, Cathy thinks Alice's absence is caused by feelings of superiority and contempt. Cathy's assumptions about Alice can be explained by attribution theory.

Attribution theory explains how we ascribe specific motives and causes to the behaviours of others. It helps us interpret what people do and why they are doing it. Suppose a student sitting next to you in class gets up in the middle of the lecture and walks out. Why did the student leave? Did the student become angry at something the instructor said? No, the lecturer was simply describing types of cloud formations. Was the student sick? You remember noticing that the student looked a little flushed and occasionally winced. Maybe the student had an upset stomach. Or maybe the student is a bit of a rebel, and often does things like leaving in the middle of a class.

Fritz Heider said that we are "naive psychologists,"[10] because we all seek to explain the motives people have for their actions. We are naive because we do not create these explanations in a systematic or scientific manner, but rather by applying common sense to our observations. Developing the most credible explanation for the behaviour of others is the goal of the **attribution** process. According to one attribution theory, **correspondent inference theory**, we try to determine the intentionality of the person in causing the effect.[11] In determining how intentional

cognitive complexity. The level of ability to develop a sophisticated set of personal constructs.

attribution theory. Theory that explains how you generate explanations for people's behaviours.

attributions. The reasons we develop to explain the behaviours of others.

correspondent inference theory. One theory of attribution that is based on determining how intentional a person's actions are.

causal attribution theory. One theory of attribution that is based upon determining whether a person's actions are caused by circumstance, a stimulus, or the person.

self-serving bias. Attributing our successes to internal dispositions and attributing our failures to external circumstances beyond our control.

self-handicapping strategy. Preparing for possible failure in the future by setting up an external reason for such failure.

the act was, we may take into account what other choices the person had available to him or her, how desirable the action was, and whether we believe the person changed his or her behaviour in an attempt to impress us. What did the student intend to accomplish in leaving the class?

Causal attribution theory identifies three potential causes for any person's action: circumstance, a stimulus, or the person her- or himself.[12] Attributing to *circumstance* means that you believe a person acts in a certain way because the situation leaves no choice. This way of thinking places responsibility for the action outside the person. You would be attributing to circumstance if you believed the student quickly left the classroom because of an upset stomach. Concluding that the student left because the instructor said something inappropriate would be attributing the student's action to the *stimulus* (the instructor). But if you knew the instructor hadn't said anything out of line, and that the student was perfectly healthy, you would place the responsibility for the action on the student. Attributing to the *person* means that you believe there is some quality about the person that caused the observed behaviour. Attributions to the person are the ones we are most concerned with in this text because they are factors in our impressions of others.

We also use attributional processes to interpret our own behaviours, often in selfish ways. The **self-serving bias** and **self-handicapping strategy** are two related attributional biases that allow individuals to construct attributions for self-interest (or self-preservation) purposes.[13] The self-serving bias attributes success to internal dispositions, such as intelligence, wit, and personality, and attributes failure to external circumstances beyond personal control, such as various factors about the event. These external factors may be weather, time, being disliked by the other party involved, and other personal traits of the other party. It may be easier to say a professor does not like you and that's why you failed a test, rather than to blame the failure on your lack of preparation. The self-serving bias may help protect and maintain a positive self-esteem because it allows us to take credit for our successes and to blame external reasons for our failures.

The self-serving bias usually occurs after we have done something. The self-handicapping strategy occurs prior to the event or situation. When people engage in self-handicapping, they set up an external cause for possible failure in the near future. It may be easier to announce to your friends that you will probably fail a test because the professor does not like you. By using self-handicapping, an external reason for the possible failure has been set up and may even contribute to the eventual outcome. Now if you do not study, you have already established a reason for the failure.

Both biases assist individuals in attributing external causes to behaviour, particularly behaviour with negative outcomes. As just stated earlier, we are most interested in how we attribute causes to others as it helps form our impressions of others. If individuals can blame others for their own failure or suspected future problems, it has major impact on how these individuals are perceived and treated. If you blame a travel agent for a poor holiday, are you likely to use this travel agent again? A number of other factors affect the accuracy of our attributions: our ability to make effective and complete observations; the degree to which we are able to directly observe the cause and the effect; the completeness of our information; our level of self-interest; and our ability to rule out other causes. It is also helpful to know how unique the person's response is to the particular stimulus, to compare the person's response to how other people typically respond, and to know whether the person usually responds each time in the same way to the stimulus. Even with the most complete information, however, we can never completely understand another person's action because we cannot become the other person. Fortunately, we can improve our level of understanding by developing our other-orientation and by becoming more sensitive to the assumptions or theories we use to make attributions.

▶ Recap

HOW WE ORGANIZE AND INTERPRET INTERPERSONAL PERCEPTIONS TO PERCEIVE OTHERS

Term	Definition	Examples
Impression Formation	We form global perspectives we have of others based upon general physical qualities, behaviours, and disclosed information.	Categorizing people as nice, friendly, shy, or handsome.
Implicit Personality	We form our own personal general theory about the way people think and behave.	"I've never met a person I didn't like."
Attribution Theory	We develop reasons to explain the behaviours of others. We attribute others' actions to the circumstance, a stimulus, or to the person.	"I guess she didn't return my call because she doesn't like me." "He's just letting off steam because he had a bad week of exams."

Identifying Barriers to Accurate Perceptions

Think about the most recent interaction you have had with a stranger. Do you remember the person's age, sex, race, or body size? Did the person have any distinguishing features such as a beard, wild clothing, or a loud voice? The qualities you recall will most likely serve as the basis for attributions you make about that person's behaviour. But these attributions, based upon your first impressions, might be highly inaccurate. We each see the world from our own unique perspective. That perspective is clouded by a number of distortions and barriers that contribute to inaccurate interpersonal perception. We'll examine these barriers next.

Ignoring Information

People sometimes don't focus on important information, because we give too much weight to information that is obvious and superficial.[14] Why do we ignore important information that may be staring us in the face? It's because of what we learned about attribution theory. We tend to explain the motives for a person's actions on the basis of the most obvious information rather than on in-depth information we might have. When meeting someone new, we perceive his or her physical qualities first: colour of skin, body size and shape, age, sex, and other obvious physical characteristics. We overattribute to these qualities because they are so vivid and available. We have all been victims of these kinds of attributions, some of us more than others. Often, we are unaware that others are making biased attributions because they do not express them openly. But sometimes we can tell by the way others react to us and treat us.

One female student described a job interview in which the male interviewer talked at her for 15 minutes and then abruptly dismissed her without asking a single question. A male friend of hers with less distinguished academic qualifications and work experience spent 40 minutes fielding questions from this same interviewer. Did the interviewer have a sex bias? Probably. Looking only at the female student's gender, he attributed qualities to her that he decided would make her unsuitable for the job. Instead of looking at the more specific information her résumé provided, he simply disregarded it. As discussed earlier, this tendency reflects our desire to simplify stimuli, but it can be dangerous and unfair.

Overgeneralizing

We treat small amounts of information as if they were highly representative.[15] This tendency also leads us to draw inaccurate, prejudicial conclusions. Your authors, for example, may talk to two students from your school, and then generalize the impression we have of those two students to the entire student population. In a similar way, we tend to assume that the small sampling we have of another person's behaviour is a valid representation of who that person is. As we saw in Figure 3.2, we create a rabbit even when we have only a few dots on which to base our perception.

Holding on to Preconceptions

We distort or ignore information that violates our expectations or preconceptions.[16] We see what we want to see, hear what we want to hear. Earlier in this chapter we talked about how we develop impressions and constructs. Once we develop them, we have preconceptions about what we expect from another person. These preconceptions can be so strong that we will distort the way we process our perceptions so that we can remain constant to them. The halo and horn effects discussed earlier are reflections of this tendency.

Imposing Consistency

We overestimate the consistency and constancy of others' behaviours. When we organize our perceptions, we also tend to ignore fluctuation in people's behaviours, and see them as consistent. We believe that if someone acted a certain way one day, he or she will continue to act that way in the future. In fact, everyone's behaviour varies from day to day. Some days we are in a bad mood, and our behaviour on those days does not represent what we are generally like. As intimacy develops in relationships, we interact with our partners in a variety of activities that provide a more complete picture of our true nature.

Oversimplifying

We prefer simple explanations to complex ones. When Terry picks you up late to go to a movie, she says, "Sorry, I lost track of the time." The next day, Christine also picks you up late to go to a movie. She says, "Sorry. You wouldn't believe how busy I've been. I ran out of hot water when I was showering and my hair dryer must be busted. It kept shutting off. Then I stopped to get something to eat and it took forever to get my order. And then it turned out they had it all messed up and had to redo it." Whose explanation can you accept more easily—Terry's or Christine's?

Usually, we prefer simple explanations; they tend to be more believable and easier to use in making sense of another's actions. But, in reality, our behaviours are affected by a multitude of factors, as Christine's explanation indicates. Unfortunately, it takes a lot of effort to understand what makes another person do what he or she does—more effort than we are typically willing to give.

stereotype. Set of qualities that you attribute to a person because of the person's membership in some category.

Stereotyping

Preconceived notions about what they expect to find may keep people from seeing what's before their eyes and ears. We see what we want to see, hear what we want to hear. We stereotype others. To **stereotype** someone is to place someone in a rigid category and then interpret all the person's behaviour from the framework of that category. The word *stereotype* was originally a printing term, referring to a metal plate that was cast from type set by a printer. The plate would print the same page of type over and over again. When we stereotype people, we place them into inflexible, all-compassing categories. We "print" the same judgments on anyone placed into a given category. We may even choose to ignore contradictory information that we receive directly from the other person. Instead of adjusting our conception of that person, we adjust our perception. The halo and horn effects discussed earlier are reflections of this tendency. For example, if an instructor gets an excellent paper from a student who she has concluded is not particularly bright or motivated, she may tend to find errors and shortcomings that are not really there, or she may even accuse the student of plagiarism.

Categorizing individuals is not an inherently bad thing to do, but it is harmful to hang on to an inflexible image of another person in the face of contradictory information. For example, not all mothers are responsible or loving. But because

Stereotypes can help us make sense out of the wide range of stimuli we encounter every day. But we also need to be sure that we don't overuse stereotypes and fail to see people as individuals. (Bill Bachmann/The Image Works)

North American culture reveres motherhood, we may not easily process our perceptions of a mother who is abusive or negligent.

Ignoring Circumstances

We diminish the effect of external circumstances on another's behaviour.[17] Although we tend to explain our own negative actions in terms of circumstances, we tend to attribute others' actions to their personality. If we are late for an appointment, it is because of traffic or the need to wrap up a project, and so on. But if others are late, it is because they are not punctual and have intentionally chosen to treat us rudely. Again, this tendency represents our desire for simplification. We are often unaware of the circumstances that affect others, and we do not want to take the trouble to investigate them.

We also fail to compare one person's behaviour with that of others under the same circumstances. Suppose you have a close friend who has flunked out of school because of personal problems, financial difficulties, and insufficient college preparation. You gain many insights into his motives and emotions as you spend time providing support. However, if you meet someone else who flunked out of school, you may not compare this other person's situation with your friend's. Usually, we come to appreciate the effect of circumstances on the behaviours of those we know intimately, but we discard that knowledge when we encounter it in someone else, preferring to attribute the behaviour to the person.

Focusing on the Negative

We give more weight to negative information than to positive information.[18] Job interviewers often ask interviewees to describe their strengths and weaknesses. If you describe five great strengths and one weakness, it is likely that the interviewer will attend more to the one weakness you mention than to the strengths. We seem to recognize this bias and compensate for it when we first meet someone by sharing only positive information about ourselves.

Building Your Skills

PRECONCEIVED EXPLANATIONS

Think about your own preconceptions about cause-effect relationships. For each of the following, think about what your first explanation of the cause would be:

- A person not calling back after a first date.
- A server giving you lousy service.
- Your car not being repaired after you have paid a high service fee.
- A teacher being late for class.
- A child who beats up other kids.
- A student who copies test answers from the student next to him.
- A mother who refuses to let her teenage son drive the car on Friday nights.

Now go back and generate as many alternative explanations for each behaviour as you can. How can you be sure which explanation is correct?

In another of the Solomon Asch experiments on impression formation, participants heard one of the following two lists of terms describing a person: (1) intelligent, skillful, industrious, warm, determined, practical, cautious; or (2) intelligent, skillful, industrious, cold, determined, practical, cautious.[19] The only difference in these two lists is the use of "warm" in the first list, and "cold" in the second. Despite the presence of six other terms, those with the "cold" list had a much more negative impression of the person than those with the "warm" list. One piece of negative information can have a disproportionate effect on our impressions and negate the effect of several positive pieces of information.

> ### Recap
>
> **BARRIERS TO ACCURATE PERCEPTIONS**
>
> | | |
> |---|---|
> | **Ignoring Information** | We give too much weight to information that is obvious and superficial. |
> | **Overgeneralizing** | We treat small amounts of information as if they were highly representative. |
> | **Holding on to Preconceptions** | We distort or ignore information that violates our expectations or preconceptions. |
> | **Imposing Consistency** | We overestimate the consistency and constancy of others' behaviours. |
> | **Oversimplifying** | We prefer simple explanations to complex ones. |
> | **Stereotyping** | We rely on our pre-existing rigid expectations about others to influence our perceptions. |
> | **Ignoring Circumstances** | We diminish the effect of external circumstances on another's behaviour. We fail to compare one person's behaviour to that of others under the same circumstances. |
> | **Focusing on the Negative** | We give more weight to negative information than to positive information. |

Improving Your Perceptual Skills

With so many barriers to perceiving and interpreting other people's behaviour accurately, what can you do to improve your perceptual skills? Increasing your awareness of the factors that lead to inaccuracy will help initially, and you will find further suggestions in this section. Ultimately, your improvement will depend upon your willingness to do three things: (1) to grow as you expand your experiences, (2) to communicate about your perceptions with others, and (3) to seek out and consider others' perceptions of you. And just by reading this chapter you've gained greater understanding of how the perception process affects your relationship with others. Emulate Sherlock Holmes: Use your knowledge of the perceptual process to sharpen your own perceptions and conclusions. Here are additional strategies to help you become a more accurate perceiver.

Link Details with the Big Picture

Any skilled detective knows how to take a small piece of information or evidence and use it to reach a broader conclusion. Skilled perceivers keep the big picture in mind as they look for clues about a person. In this chapter we have encouraged you to become more sensitive to details when observing others. But be cautious of taking one scrap of evidence and spinning out inaccurate conclusions about a person. Just because someone may dress differently from you, or have a pronounced accent, don't rush to judgment about the person's competence based on such few snatches of information. Look and listen for other cues about your new acquaintance that can help you develop a more accurate understanding of who that person is. As we noted in this chapter, what we see first (primacy) or last (recency) may have the most powerful effect on our overall conclusion. Try not to use the early information to cast a quick or rigid judgment that may be inaccurate. Look at all the details you've gathered.

Become Aware of Others' Perceptions of You

The best athletes don't avoid hearing criticisms and observations from their coaches. Instead, they seek out as much feedback as they can about what they are doing right and wrong. Olympic training often involves the use of videotaped replays and computer analysis so athletes can see themselves as others see them and use that perspective to improve their performance. It is difficult to be objective about our own behaviour, so feedback from others can help us with our self-perceptions. The strongest relationships are those in which the partners are both willing to share and be receptive to the perceptions of the other.

Increase Your Awareness

Your senses are constantly bombarding you with information, much of which you ignore. You can increase the amount of information that you process from your senses by consciously attending to the input. When you interact with others, try to identify one new thing to focus on and observe each time. Watch their gestures, their eyes, the wrinkles around their eyes, their foot movements; listen to their tone of voice. Each observation will provide information that potentially can improve the quality of your interactions. You may create additional problems, however, if you focus so narrowly on one element that you miss others or overestimate the meaning of irrelevant information. Try to notice as much detail as possible, but keep the entire picture in view.

Recognize the Elements to Which You Attribute Meaning

As we have seen, the third stage in the perception process involves attributing meaning to what we perceive. We do this so automatically that we often fail to realize that we have attributed meaning to something. Therefore, we also fail to recognize the effect it might have on what we do and say. Try to become aware of the stimuli to which you attribute meaning. If, for instance, you shake a person's hand that is weak and clammy, you might quickly withdraw your hand and form an impression of the person as wimpy and aloof without realizing that you have attributed meaning to the handshake. Take an inventory of your own perceptual tendencies. Do you pay particular attention to eye contact, gestures, facial expressions, clothing, accents, or vocal intonations? When you become more aware of what you attend to and when you are attributing meaning, you can then decide whether you are giving proper weight to the elements you are perceiving.

Building Your Skills

IDENTIFYING YOUR BIASES

Write down a list of some recent interpretations you've made about others' behaviours. Identify the specific behaviour or quality that you have observed and the resulting interpretation. For example, Joe is a really big man (quality), therefore he must be a football player (interpretation).

Identify which interpretations might have been affected by any of the biases we've talked about (e.g., giving weight to information that is obvious and superficial).

See if you can confirm the validity of those interpretations by collecting additional information. Ask Joe if he plays football or look on the football roster for his name.

Become Other-Oriented

Effective interpersonal perception depends on the ability to understand where others are coming from, to get inside their heads, to see things from their perspectives.

Becoming other-oriented involves a two-step process: social decentring (consciously *thinking* about another's thoughts and feelings) and empathizing (*responding emotionally* to another's feelings).[20] What does your boss think and feel when you arrive late for work? What would your spouse think and feel if you brought a dog home as a surprise gift? Throughout this book we offer suggestions for becoming other-oriented, for reminding yourself that the world does not revolve around you. Being other-oriented enables you to increase your understanding of others and improve your ability to predict and adapt to what others do and say.

To improve your ability to socially decentre, and to empathize, strive for two key goals: (1) Gather as much information as possible about the circumstances that are affecting the other person; and (2) gather as much information as possible about the other person. In the next chapter we expand on these ideas as we discuss in more detail how to adapt to others by decentring and empathizing. As we've emphasized before, being other-oriented is not a single skill, but a family of related communication skills (such as socially decentring, empathizing, listening, responding, interpreting verbal and non-verbal messages, appropriately adapting to others, and managing conflict).

Ten Questions That Can Help You Become Other-Oriented

How to Take the Perspective of Another Person

1. What factors or circumstances are affecting the person?
2. How can I determine whether there are factors I don't know about or don't fully understand?
3. What do I know about this person that explains his or her behaviour and feelings?
4. What is going through the other person's mind at this time?
5. What are the other person's feelings at this time?
6. What other explanations could there be for the person's actions?
7. What would I think if I were in the same situation?
8. How would I feel if I were in the same situation?
9. What would other people think if they were in that situation?
10. What would other people feel if they were in that situation?

Use Perception Checking

indirect perception checking. Seeking additional information to confirm or refute interpretations you are making through passive perception.

direct perception checking. Asking for confirmation or refutation from the observed person of an interpretation of a perception about him or her.

When we observe others' behaviour and make attributions about why they are doing what they are doing, we can be inaccurate and make mistakes. These mistakes can affect your relationships with others and lead to serious miscommunication. You can check out the accuracy of your perceptions and attributions indirectly and directly. Checking out your perceptions also displays your other-orientation and allows you to more fully understand the motives and causes of others' behaviours. By checking your perceptions you reduce uncertainty and clarify that your perceptions are accurate. **Indirect perception checking** involves seeking additional information through passive perception to either confirm or refute your interpretations. If you suspect someone is angry with you but is not admitting it, for example, you could look for more cues in his or her tone of voice, eye contact, and body movements to find more cues to confirm your suspicion. You could also ask questions or listen more intently to the person's words and language.

Direct perception checking involves asking straight out if your interpretations of a perception are correct. This often is not easy to do for several reasons: We don't like to admit uncertainty or suspicions to others; we might not trust that they will respond honestly; if our interpretations are wrong, we might suffer embarrassment or anger. But asking someone to confirm a perception shows that you are committed to understanding his or her behaviour. If your friend's voice sounds weary and her posture is sagging, you may assume that she is depressed or upset. If you ask, "I get the feeling from your tone of voice and the way you're acting that you are kind of down and depressed; what's wrong?" your friend can then either provide another interpretation: "I'm just tired; I had a busy week," or expand on your interpretation: "Yeah, things haven't been going very well . . ." Your observation might also be a revelation: "Really? I didn't realize I was acting that way. I guess I am a little down." The Building Your Skills box on page 91 outlines a straightforward method of perception checking. The real key is to be honest and direct with the other person while using tact, diplomacy, and empathy.

Chapter 3   Interpersonal Communication and Perception

Building Your Skills

USING PERCEPTION CHECKING

Perception checking is a method to assist you in making more accurate interpretations of others' behaviours. It is based on describing the behaviour you have noticed or that is troubling you, interpreting that behaviour tentatively including more than one interpretation, and asking for some clarification about the interpretation and some sort of closure about the issue. For example, you stop to chat with a friend in the hall at school but she cuts you off and rushes away. You are left feeling hurt and want to find out why she did not stop to talk. When you see her later in the day in the cafeteria, you decide to ask about the behaviour. Using perception checking, here is the way the conversation might go.

"Hi, there. Do you have a minute to talk?" (Your friend responds positively, so you continue.)

"When I saw you earlier today, I was trying to talk to you and you dashed off. I figured that maybe you had other things on your mind or maybe something was upsetting you. Can you tell me if you are OK?"

Your friend responds that she forgot her purse in the last class and was really upset that it may have been stolen. Luckily, the teacher had retrieved it for her. You then respond supportively stating, "Whew, I knew that you must be upset at something. I'm glad that you were not upset with me and that you retrieved that purse!"

So let's review the four steps. However, keep in mind that this is just one method of perception checking using these four elements. There are other techniques and considerations that also work (such as Adler et al., 2001).[21]

1. Describe the behaviour that is of concern or puzzling to you. Remember that it is the behaviour that you are describing and not the person. For example, you do not want to say, "When you were rude to me," as this is not the behaviour but your interpretation of the behaviour. Instead say, "When you did not answer me" or "When you rushed away." These latter statements describe the actual behaviour. Be as clear as possible when describing the behaviour.

2. Offer two possible interpretations of the behaviour that you have described. Make sure to voice these interpretations as tentative. See above: "I figured that maybe you had other things on your mind, or that something was upsetting you."

3. Ask for clarification. Often at this step, you can also voice concern about the person or the behaviour. Clarification can be requested in a number of different ways such as, "Could you clear this up for me? I want us to continue to be good friends."

4. After the behaviour has been clarified and you have the correct interpretation, use some sort of closure. See above: "I knew that you must be upset at something. I'm glad that you were not upset with me and that you retrieved that purse!"

Try to use some of these steps the next time you need to examine your perceptions about someone else's behaviour.

Be Sensitive to Cultural Differences

Although Chapter 9 deals with diversity and cultural differences in greater detail, it is worthwhile to increase some understanding of culture and perceptual differences as a method of improving the accuracy of your perception. Cultures can influence perception in many ways. For example, in some Asian cultures eye contact is seen as disrespectful especially to those in authority. Yet, in North America, if no eye contact is given, many people may feel the person is lying or hiding something. By simply realizing that cultures differ in what is acceptable or unacceptable behaviours, you will be less likely to make perceptual errors. The potential for interpersonal communication problems will diminish if you keep these simple ideas with you when interpreting a person's behaviour if he or she is from a culture different from your own.

Summary

Interpersonal perception is a fundamental element of interpersonal communication. Our communication and interpersonal relationships are affected by the way we perceive those with whom we interact. Interpersonal perception is more than just the arousal of the senses; it also involves selecting, organizing, and interpreting what we observe to decide what people are like and to give meaning to their actions.

Our perceptions of others affect how we communicate, and how others perceive us affects how they communicate with us. Interpersonal perception can be a passive or active process. It is passive when only our senses are in operation; it is active when we feel a need for information and intentionally seek it. We are motivated to seek information in situations that have high amounts of uncertainty. Perception of information helps reduce uncertainty and provides us with more control of the situation.

Interpersonal perception affects and is affected by the development of impressions, our own implicit personality theories, constructs, and attributions. Our general impressions of individuals are often affected by primacy and recency effects; we pay particular attention to the first things we notice and the most recent things we notice about others. In our interactions with others we all seem to operate as "naive psychologists," developing and applying our own implicit personality theories. These implicit personality theories represent the general way we believe people behave. We develop specific personal constructs that represent the qualities we associate with specific people we know. Finally, we try to explain the actions and behaviours of others through the process of attribution. According to attribution theorists, we seek to find out the intent and cause of a person's action; we see a person's action as a response to a given circumstance, a particular stimulus, or the person's own personality. To make rational and accurate attributions, we must overcome perceptual barriers. We can identify nine specific tendencies that distort the accuracy of our attributions, such as ignoring information or overgeneralizing.

The following suggestions will help you to improve your interpersonal perception: (1) link details with the big picture; (2) become aware of others' perceptions of you; (3) increase your awareness; (4) recognize the elements to which you are attributing meaning; (5) become other-oriented; (6) use perception checking; and (7) be sensitive to cultural differences.

For Discussion and Review

Focus on Comprehension

1. In what ways does interpersonal perception affect our interpersonal communication and relationships?
2. Identify and describe the three stages of the interpersonal perception process.
3. Explain the relationships among impressions, implicit personality theory, constructs, and attributions.

Chapter 3 Interpersonal Communication and Perception   93

4. Identify and explain eight barriers to accurate perception.
5. How can you improve your perceptual skills?

Focus on Critical Thinking

6. Think about some of your recent interpersonal conflicts. How would you describe your perception of the problem? How do you think the others would describe their perceptions of it? What role did perception play in contributing to or resolving the conflict?
7. What do you think contributes to the development of the tendencies that cause us to perceive people inaccurately? How might the effects of those factors be minimized or eliminated?

Focus on Ethics

8. Do you have a right in an intimate relationship to expect your partner to share his or her perceptions of you, whether those perceptions are positive or negative? Explain your reasoning.
9. If you are aware of how you are distorting your own perceptions and attributions, should you try to change them? Is it a moral obligation? Explain your reasoning.

For Your Journal

1. As you interact with a friend, try to assess your awareness level of the cues that are being communicated. Ask your friend to confirm your interpretation of the cues that you have observed. How effective and accurate were you at picking up information?
2. Use the list of barriers to accurate perception to do a self-analysis. Which barriers influence your perceptions the most? What problems do those distortions create in your interactions with others?
3. Choose two of the suggestions for improving your perceptions. Develop a plan for what you will do in your next interaction to apply that suggestion. Try the suggestion; then write an evaluation of how well you applied the suggestion, how well the suggestion worked, and how you might modify your plan to apply the suggestion in the future.

Learning with Others

1. Choose an advertisement, magazine illustration, photograph, or painting that shows a group of people and bring it to class. In groups of four or five, pass around the pictures. For each picture, write down a few words to describe your perceptions about what you see in the picture. What are the people doing? What is their relationship to one another? What is each one like? How is each one feeling? Why are they doing what they are doing? After you have finished, share with one another what you wrote down. Try to determine why there were differences. What factors influenced your perceptions?

2. Pair up with someone in class whom you do not know and have not interacted with before. Without saying anything to each other, write down the words from the following list that you think apply to the other person. Now converse for five minutes. In a separate section of your paper, write down any additional words that you believe apply to the person. You can go back and put a line through any of the words in the first list that you now think are inaccurate. Share with your partner what words you put down before and during the conversation, and what words you changed. Have your partner share his or her perceptions of you. Discuss, as best you can, the reasons you chose each word.

intelligent	athletic	artistic	studious
nice	funny	conceited	friendly
introvert	extrovert	hard worker	shy
talented	popular	inquisitive	moody
emotional	happy	brave	responsible
leader	follower	uncertain	confused

Weblinks

www.server.bmod.athabascau.ca/html/aupr/psycres.htm This is Canada's Athabasca University psychology resources online.

www.canoe.ca This is a Canadian site that has up-to-the-minute news and access to many publications, including *Maclean's* magazine.

www.macleans.ca Read the most current issue of *Maclean's* or search the magazine's archives.

www.selfgrowth.com/index.html This is a site devoted to personal growth, self-improvement, and self-help. You can sign up to receive a free newsletter.

Suggested Readings

Gregg, Allan R. "Scary New World." *Maclean's,* December 31, 2001.
    Read this interesting article about the effects of terrorism on Canadians from the latest *Maclean's*/CBC year-end poll.

McMurdy, Deirdre. "Jobs You Don't Want." *Maclean's,* August 28, 2000, 27–28.
    Read about three people, including Buzz Hargrove, and why you may not want their jobs.

Hargrove, Buzz. *Labour of Love: The Fight to Create a More Humane Canada.* Stoddart Publishing Company, 1998.
    This interesting book by Hargrove details his work in the CAW and his interesting ideas and opinions about Canadian industry, politics, and unions.

Ashton Hinrichs/Super Stock

Part Two

Interpersonal Communication Skills

- **Chapter 4** Listening and Responding
- **Chapter 5** Emotions and Interpersonal Communication
- **Chapter 6** Communicating Verbally
- **Chapter 7** Communicating Non-Verbally
- **Chapter 8** Conflict Management Skills

People judge you by your behaviour, not by your intentions. The following five chapters focus on research-based communication skills that will help you monitor and shape your behaviour to improve the quality of your relationships. Chapter 4 offers tips and strategies for listening to others and confirming your understanding of what you hear. In Chapter 5, a new chapter, the focus is on your emotions: what they are, ways to more fully understand and be aware of your emotions, and strategies to help manage your emotions and the emotions of others. We communicate to others how we feel and our feelings influence interpersonal communication just as how others feel influences their communication with us. Chapter 6 explores how the words we use, and misuse, affect our relationships with others. Meanings, as we'll learn, are in people, not in words themselves. Becoming other-oriented involves both listening to the words and reading the behaviour cues of others. Chapter 7 focuses on the scope and importance of unspoken messages. We will explore the implications of the adage, "Actions speak louder than words." Chapter 8 then discusses conflict and teaches some basic strategies to manage conflict and disagreements with others.

chapter 4
Listening and Responding

After you study this chapter you should be able to...

1. Describe five elements of the listening process.
2. Identify characteristics of four listening styles.
3. Understand why we listen and list several important barriers to effective listening.
4. Identify ways to improve other-orientation and listening skills.
5. Identify responding skills and understand strategies for improving them.

- Listening Defined
- Listening Styles
- Listening Barriers
- Improving Your Listening Skills
- Improving Empathic Listening and Responding Skills
- Improving Critical Listening and Responding Skills
- Improving Your Responding Skills

The friends who listen to us are the ones we move toward, and we want to sit in their radius.

KARL MENNINGER

Conversation overheard at Jimmy's Bar and Grill last Thursday:

Carmen: So, let's get down to the details. Where are we gonna hold this party?

Bonnie: I can't think about it now, Carmen. I'm too upset over a fight I had with Alex this morning.

Carmen: Why don't you get rid of that husband, kiddo? You're always fighting. Find someone who treats ya with more respect. Now come on, just think about the best place—here at Jimmy's or over at Nathan and Yasuko's house?

Caitlyn: What did you fight about, Bonnie?

Bonnie: He wants me to quit my job—which I don't like so much anyway—and have a baby. But I'm not sure I feel ready for such a big move, although I'd love to stop working there.

Caitlyn: So you're feeling torn because you'd like to quit your job, but not to have a baby.

Bonnie: Well, I don't know. But if I did decide to have a baby, I wouldn't want to do it just to please him.

Carmen: Don't give in to him, Bonn. He'll never stop pushing you around. I think maybe Nathan and Yasuko's. They've got that big barbecue pit.

Caitlyn: Let's go over to my house where there's no jukebox and talk this over, Bonnie. It sounds like you're not really dismissing the idea, are you?

Bonnie: No. I would like to talk.

Figure 4.1
What You Do with Your Communication Time

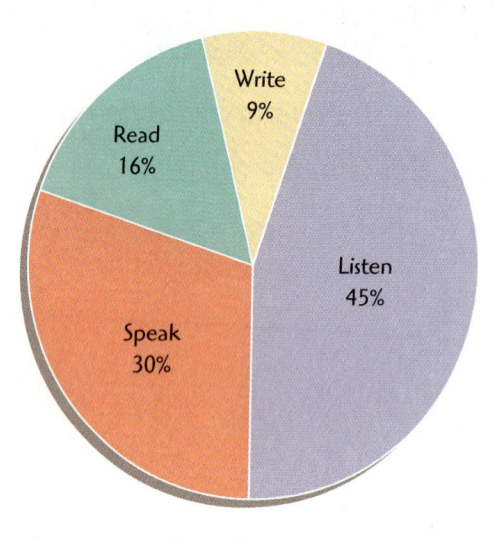

Pie chart: Listen 45%, Speak 30%, Read 16%, Write 9%

Can you identify the skilled listener in this snatch of conversation? Probably. Can you describe the skills that she is using? Probably not. But you will be able to by the time you finish this chapter.

You spend more time listening to others than almost anything else you do. As the pie chart in Figure 4.1 shows, people typically spend more than 80 percent of an average day communicating with other people, and they spend 45 percent of that communication time listening to others.[1] Ironically, most people's formal communication training focuses on writing, the activity to which we devote the least amount of communication time. Chances are that, up until now, you have had no training in listening. In this chapter, we will focus on this often neglected yet quintessential skill for developing quality interpersonal relationships. As we have seen, becoming other-oriented means learning about the needs, hopes, concerns, and joys of another to enhance the quality of your relationship. And listening is the process by which you can learn the most about another person. In addition, we will explore ways to respond to others and check your perceptions of their comments.

Listening Defined

"Did you hear what I said?" demanded a father who had been lecturing his teenage son on the importance of hanging up his clothes. In fact, the boy did *hear* him, but he may not have been *listening*. **Listening** is a complex process we use to make sense out of what we hear. **Hearing** is the physiological process of decoding sounds. You hear when the sound vibrations reach your eardrum and buzz the middle ear bones: the hammer, anvil, and stirrup. Eventually, the sound vibrations are translated into electrical impulses that reach the brain. To listen to something, you must first select that sound from competing sounds. To truly listen involves four activities—selecting, attending, understanding, and remembering. We confirm that listening occurs by responding.

listening. The process of selecting, attending, understanding, remembering, and responding to sounds and messages.

hearing. The physiological process of decoding sounds.

selecting. The process of sorting through various sounds competing for your attention.

Selecting

To **select** a sound is to focus on one sound as you sort through the various sounds competing for your attention. As you listen to another in an interpersonal context, you focus on the words and non-verbal messages of your partner. Even now, as you are reading this book, there are undoubtedly countless noises within earshot. Stop reading for a moment and sort through the various sounds around you. Do you hear music? Is there noise from outside? How about the murmur of voices, the tick of a clock, the hum of a computer, the whoosh of an air conditioner or furnace? To listen, you must select which of these sounds will receive your attention.

Attending

After selecting a sound, you then focus on it. Attention can be fleeting. You may **attend** to the sound for a moment and then move on or return to other thoughts or other sounds. Typically, you attend to those sounds and messages that meet your needs or are consistent with what you think you should be focusing on. If you are hungry, you may select and then attend to a commercial for a sizzling burger or a crispy-crust pizza. Information that is novel, humorous, intense, or that somehow relates to you, also may capture your attention. Almost 30 years later, many Canadians still recall Prime Minister Trudeau's "fuddle-duddle": The prime minister had been accused of violating parliamentary rules by mouthing a particular four-letter word, while making a matching hand gesture, in the House of Commons. Trudeau's quick response to his accusers ("I may have just mouthed 'fuddle-duddle'") became a shared joke among the Canadian media and public alike, even sparking a boom in "fuddle-duddle" T-shirts. The collective attention of the nation had been temporarily drawn away from more pressing issues of the time, which, by now, are forgotten by most.

In general, conflict, humour, new ideas, and real or concrete things command your attention more easily than abstract theories that do not relate to your interests or needs. In addition, when someone invites you to participate or respond, you listen much more attentively than you do when someone just talks at you. One of your authors recently attended a day-long series of lectures at Oxford University on life in England during the Middle Ages. As a paleoanthropologist droned on about femur measurements and Harris lines, I struggled to stay awake. But when the lecturer produced several recently unearthed skeletons and invited the audience to participate in drawing conclusions about their lives and environment, I was all ears.

Healthy family relations result when parents and children are able to develop people-oriented listening styles.
(Michael Newman/PhotoEdit)

attending. The process of focusing on a particular sound or message.

understanding. Assigning meaning to messages.

Understanding

Whereas hearing is a physiological phenomenon, **understanding** is the process of assigning meaning to the sounds you select and to which you attend. There are several theories about how you assign meaning to words you hear, but there is no universally accepted notion of how this process works. We know that people understand best if they can relate what they are hearing to something they already know. For this reason the use of analogy and comparison is effective when explaining complex material or abstract ideas.

A second basic principle about how people understand others is that the greater the similarity between individuals, the greater the likelihood for more accurate understanding. Individuals from different cultures who have substantially different religions, family lifestyles, values, and attitudes often have difficulty understanding each other, particularly in the early phases of a relationship.

You understand best that which you also experience. Perhaps you have heard the Montessori school philosophy: I hear, I forget; I see, I remember; I experience, I understand. Hearing alone does not provide us with understanding. We hear over one billion words each year, but we understand only a fraction of that number. In Chapter 3 we discussed the processes involved in perception and observed that different people can reach dramatically different conclusions about the same events and messages, based on their previous experiences. A key to establishing relationships with others is trying to understand those differences in experience to arrive at a common meaning for the messages we exchange.

remembering. Recalling information that has been communicated.

Remembering

To **remember** is to recall information. Some researchers theorize that you store every detail you have ever heard or witnessed; your mind operates like a video camera. But you cannot retrieve or remember all of the tapes. Sometimes you are present, yet you have no recollection of what occurred.

Our brains have both short-term and long-term memory storage systems. Short-term memory is where you store almost all the information you hear. You look up a phone number in the telephone book, mumble the number to yourself, then dial the number only to discover that the line is busy. Three minutes later you have to look up the number again because it did not get stored in your long-term memory. Our short-term storage area is very limited. Just as airports have only a few short-term parking spaces, but many spaces for long-term parking, our brains can accommodate only a few things of fleeting significance, but acres of important information. We forget hundreds of snips and bits of insignificant information that pass through our brains each day.

The information we store in long-term memory includes events, conversations, and other data that are significant for us. We tend to remember dramatic and vital information, as well as seemingly inconsequential details connected with such information. Many of us can recall in poignant detail how Wayne Gretzky tearfully announced his trade from the Edmonton Oilers to the Los Angeles Kings. Do you remember the day that runner Ben Johnson was detected with steroids after winning the gold medal for Canada at the 1988 Olympic Games? Donovan Bailey's world-record sprint to bring Canada an Olympic gold medal in 1996 will likely be another indelible image in the collective memory of Canadians. Information makes it to long-term memory because of its significance to us. The more recent event of the terrorist attacks of September 11, 2001, will also be well remembered by most of us. Do you remember where you were when you heard about the plane crashes?

Do you remember where you were when you heard about the plane crashes into the World Trade Center? (Reuters New Media/ Corbis/Magma)

Responding

Interpersonal communication is interactive; it involves both talking and responding. You **respond** to people to let them know you understand their messages. Responses can be non-verbal; direct eye contact and head nods let your partner know you're tuned in. Or you can respond verbally by asking questions to confirm the content of the message: "Are you saying you don't want us to spend as much time together as we once did?" or by making statements that reflect the feelings of the speaker: "So you are frustrated that you have to wait for someone to drive you where you want to go." We will discuss responding skills in more detail later in the chapter.

> ### Recap
> #### WHAT IS LISTENING?
> | | |
> |---|---|
> | Selecting | Sorting through various sounds that compete for your attention. |
> | Attending | Focusing on a particular sound or message. |
> | Understanding | Assigning meaning to messages. |
> | Remembering | Recalling information that has been communicated. |
> | Responding | Confirming your understanding of a message. |

Listening Styles

What's your listening style? Do you focus more on the content of the message than on the feelings being expressed by the speaker? Or do you prefer brief sound bites of information? Your **listening style** is your preferred way of making sense out of the spoken messages you hear. Listening researchers Kitty Watson, Larry Barker, and James Weaver found that listeners tend to fall into one of four listening styles: people-oriented, action-oriented, content-oriented, or time-oriented.[2]

People-Oriented Listeners

As you might suspect from the label, **people-oriented listeners** tend to be comfortable with and skilled at listening to people's feelings and emotions. They are likely to empathize and search for common areas of interest. People-oriented listeners embody many of the attributes of being other-oriented that we've discussed throughout the book—they seek strong interpersonal connections when listening to others. Preliminary evidence suggests that people-oriented listeners may be less apprehensive when interacting with others in small-group and interpersonal interactions.[3]

---

responding. Confirming your understanding of a message.

listening style. Preferred way of making sense out of spoken messages to which we listen.

people-oriented listener. Listener who is comfortable with and skilled at listening to people's feelings and emotions.

action-oriented listener.
Listener who prefers information that is well-organized, brief, and error free.

second-guessing.
Questioning the ideas and assumptions underlying a message; assessing whether the message is true or false.

content-oriented listener.
Listener who is more comfortable listening to complex, detailed information than are those with other listening styles.

time-oriented listener.
Listener who likes messages delivered succinctly.

Action-Oriented Listeners

An **action-oriented listener** prefers information that is well organized, brief, and error-free. An action-oriented listener doesn't like the speaker to tell lengthy stories and digress. The action-oriented listener may think, "Get to the point" or "What am I supposed to do with this information?" when hearing a message filled with too many anecdotes or rambling, disorganized bits of information. Whereas a people-oriented listener would be more likely to focus on the feelings of the person telling the story, the action-oriented listener wants to know the point or the punch line. There is new evidence to suggest that action-oriented listeners are more likely to be more skeptical when listening to information. Researchers call this skepticism **second-guessing**—questioning the ideas and assumptions underlying a message. Rather than taking the information they hear at face value, action-oriented listeners are more likely to reinterpret or evaluate the literal message to determine whether it is true or false—they make another guess (hence the term *second-guessing*) as to whether the information they are listening to is accurate.[4]

Content-Oriented Listeners

If you are a **content-oriented listener**, you are more comfortable listening to complex, detailed information than are people with other listening styles. A content-oriented listener hones in on the facts, details, and evidence in a message. In fact, if a message does not have ample supporting evidence and specific details, the content-oriented listener is more likely to reject the message. Like the action-oriented listener, content-oriented listeners are likely to make second guesses about the messages they hear. Content-oriented listeners are also less apprehensive when communicating with others in group and interpersonal situations.[5] Content-oriented listeners would make good judges or lawyers; they focus on issues and arguments and listen to see whether a conclusion that a speaker reaches is accurate or credible.

Time-Oriented Listeners

You're a **time-oriented listener** if you like your messages delivered succinctly. Time-oriented listeners are keenly aware of how much time they have to listen. Their lives are filled with many things on their "to do" list; their "in-basket" often overflows, so they want messages delivered quickly and briefly. Whereas a people-oriented listener might enjoy spending time over a cup of coffee catching up on the day's activities, a time-oriented listener is more like a drive-by listener—a time-oriented listener may think, "Give me what I need so I can keep on moving to my next task or hear my next message," "Don't ramble, don't digress, just get to the point quickly."

Knowing your listening style can help you better understand how to adapt to various listening situations. If, for example, you know that you are a time-oriented or action-oriented listener and your friend or companion is a people-oriented listener, you and your friend will need to adjust both your speaking and listening styles. When speaking to an action-oriented listener, give the listener a brief preview of what you will be talking about. You could say, "Phil, there are three things I'd like to share with you." Stick to that structure. When speaking to a people-oriented listener, realize that he or she will feel rushed or hurried if you skip information about feelings or relationships. A people-oriented listener prefers to spend more time talking about emotions than do those with other listening styles. A time-oriented listener would like information summarized like a crisply written business memo punctuated with bullets and lists of essential information.

What is the best listening style? It depends on the listening situation and the communication context and objectives. In a high-pressure, fast-paced job such as stock trading, you don't have time to listen to stories about clients' families or the latest TV show; you need information delivered quickly and efficiently. A father, listening to a daughter talk about what a rotten day at school she had, would find a people-oriented listening style the most effective way of listening to his daughter pour her heart out about life's challenges and frustrations. Being aware of your own preferred listening style and the needs of your communication partner can help you adopt a listening style that best suits the situation.

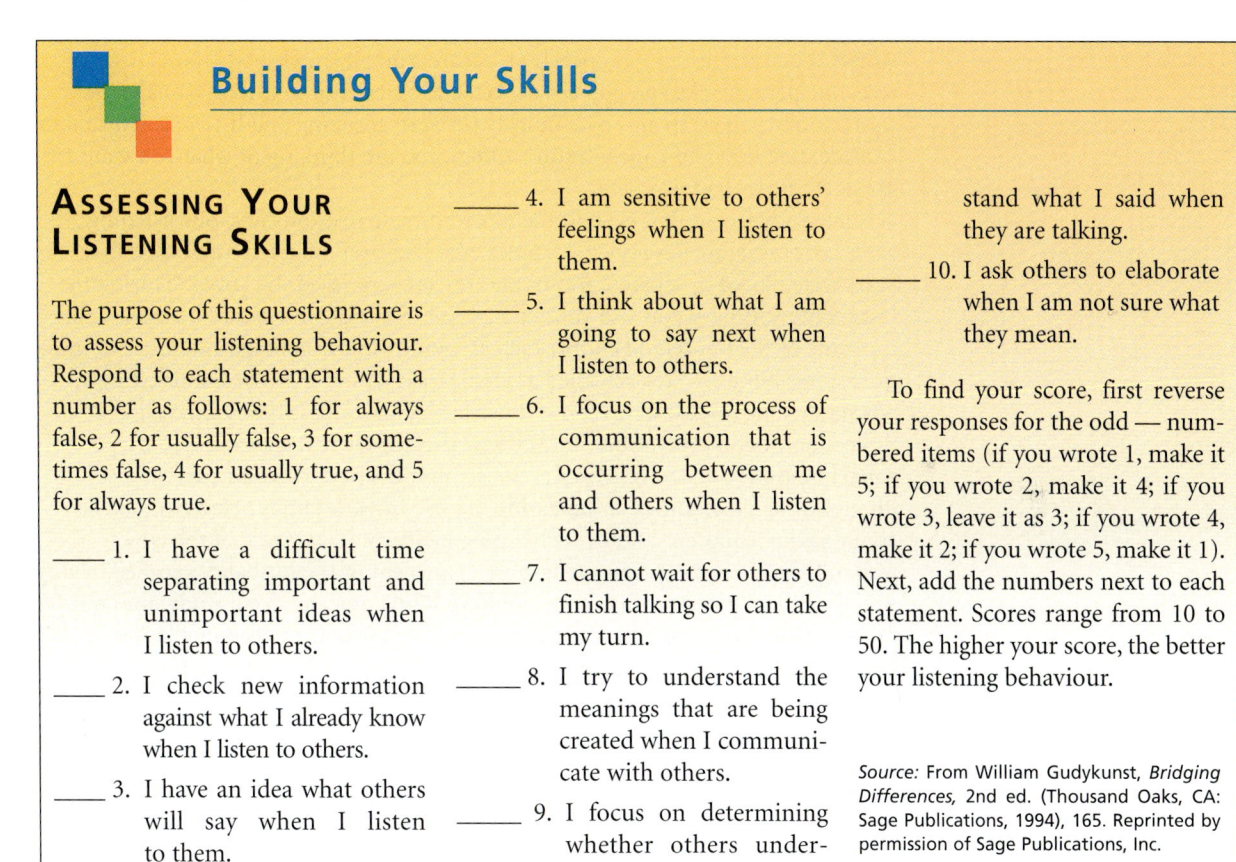

Building Your Skills

ASSESSING YOUR LISTENING SKILLS

The purpose of this questionnaire is to assess your listening behaviour. Respond to each statement with a number as follows: 1 for always false, 2 for usually false, 3 for sometimes false, 4 for usually true, and 5 for always true.

_____ 1. I have a difficult time separating important and unimportant ideas when I listen to others.

_____ 2. I check new information against what I already know when I listen to others.

_____ 3. I have an idea what others will say when I listen to them.

_____ 4. I am sensitive to others' feelings when I listen to them.

_____ 5. I think about what I am going to say next when I listen to others.

_____ 6. I focus on the process of communication that is occurring between me and others when I listen to them.

_____ 7. I cannot wait for others to finish talking so I can take my turn.

_____ 8. I try to understand the meanings that are being created when I communicate with others.

_____ 9. I focus on determining whether others understand what I said when they are talking.

_____ 10. I ask others to elaborate when I am not sure what they mean.

To find your score, first reverse your responses for the odd — numbered items (if you wrote 1, make it 5; if you wrote 2, make it 4; if you wrote 3, leave it as 3; if you wrote 4, make it 2; if you wrote 5, make it 1). Next, add the numbers next to each statement. Scores range from 10 to 50. The higher your score, the better your listening behaviour.

Source: From William Gudykunst, *Bridging Differences,* 2nd ed. (Thousand Oaks, CA: Sage Publications, 1994), 165. Reprinted by permission of Sage Publications, Inc.

Listening Barriers

Even though we spend so much of our communication time listening, most of us don't listen as well as we should. Twenty-four hours after we hear a speech, a class lecture, or a sermon, we forget more than half of what was said. And it gets worse. Within another 24 hours we forget half of what we remembered, so we really remember only a quarter of the lecture.

Our interpersonal listening skills are not much better. If anything, they may be worse. When you listen to a speech or lecture, you have a clearly defined listening role; one person talks and you are expected to listen. But in interpersonal situations, you may have to alternate quickly between speaking and listening. This takes considerable skill and concentration. Often, you are thinking of what you want to say next rather than listening.

One study found that even in the most intimate relationships, our listening skills are not highly developed. Couples who had been married for at least five years were placed in separate rooms and researchers asked the wives, "During the last six months have you and your spouse talked about who would be responsible for some of the household chores such as taking out the garbage and other domestic responsibilities?" "Yes," recalled at least 71 percent of the wives. Interestingly, when the same question was put to their husbands, only 19 percent recalled a discussion of domestic duties. Intrigued, the researchers next asked a more personal question of the wives: "In the last six months have you and your spouse discussed the possibilities of increasing the size of your family? Have you talked about having children?" An overwhelming majority, 91 percent, of the wives responded affirmatively. Curiously, only 15 percent of the husbands recalled having a conversation about having more children. While one anecdotal study does not prove conclusively that all intimate relationships suffer from listening lapses, it does illustrate the problem. And as the Understanding Diversity box on page 107 reiterates, often the problem is gender related.

Another study found that, surprisingly, we sometimes pay more attention to strangers than to intimate friends or partners.[6] Married couples in the study tended to interrupt each other more often and were generally less polite to one another than were strangers involved in a decision-making task. Apparently, we take listening shortcuts when communicating with others in close relationships.

Most interpersonal listening problems can be traced to a single source—ourselves. While listening to others, we also "talk" to ourselves. Our internal thoughts are like a play-by-play sportscast. We mentally comment on the words and sights that we select and to which we attend. If we keep those comments focused on the message, they may be useful. But we often attend to our own internal dialogues instead of to others' messages. Then our listening effectiveness plummets.

Inattentive listening is a bit like channel surfing when we watch TV—pushing the remote control button to switch from channel to channel, avoiding commercials and focusing for brief periods on attention-grabbing program "bites." When we listen to others, we may fleetingly tune in to the conversation for a moment, decide that the content is uninteresting, and then focus on a personal thought. These thoughts are barriers to communication, and they come in a variety of forms.

Understanding Diversity

WHO LISTENS BETTER: MEN OR WOMEN?

Research provides no definitive answer to this question. There is evidence that men and women listen differently and have different expectations about the role of listening and talking. Deborah Tannen suggests that one of the most common complaints wives have about their husbands is, "He doesn't listen to me anymore" along with, "He doesn't talk to me anymore." Another scholar noted that complaints about lack of communication were usually at the top of women's lists of reasons for divorce but mentioned much less often by men. Since both men and women are participating in the same conversation, why are women often more dissatisfied with the listening and talking process than men? Tannen's explanation: women expect different things from conversations than do men.

One researcher suggests that men and women may have different attention styles. When men listen, they may be looking for a new structure or organizational pattern, or to separate bits of information they hear. They continually shape, form, observe, inquire, and direct energy toward a chosen goal. Men's attention style is reported to be more emotionally controlled than women's attention style. Women are described as more subjective, empathic, and emotionally involved as they listen. They are more likely to search for relationships among parts of a pattern and to rely upon more intuitive perceptions of feelings. They are also more easily distracted by competing details. Females may hear more of the message because they reject less of it. These differences in attention styles and the way men and women process information, suggests the researcher, can potentially affect listening, even though we have no direct evidence linking attention style to listening skill.

Another researcher suggests that when men listen, they listen to solve a problem; men are more instrumental and task oriented. Women listen to seek new information to enhance understanding. There is additional evidence that men may be more goal oriented when they listen. What are the implications of these research studies? It may mean that men and women focus on different parts of messages and have different listening objectives. These differences can affect relationship development. Males may need to recognize that while they are attending to a message and looking for new structure to solve a problem or achieve a goal, they may hear less of the message and therefore listen less effectively. And even though many females may hear more of the message, they may need to make connections between the parts of the information they hear to look for major ideas, rather than just focus on the details. In any case, gender-based differences in attention style and information processing may account for some of the relational problems that husbands and wives, lovers, siblings and male-female pairs experience.[7]

Being Self-Absorbed

You're in your local grocery store during "rush hour." It appears that most of your community has also decided to forage for food at the same time. As you are trying to get in and out of the store quickly, it seems that many of the harried shoppers are oblivious to those around them. They stop in the aisle, blocking the path for others (including you). They elbow their way into crowded checkout stands. And the "express lane" that limits customers to 10 items or fewer is backed up because more than one shopper is math challenged—has difficulty counting to 10. You find yourself becoming tense—not just because you are hungry and need sustenance, but because it seems the grocery store is filled with people who are self-absorbed; they are focused on getting their needs met, but not the needs of others.

Self-absorbed listeners are focused on their needs rather than yours; the message is about *them*, not *you*. During conversations with a self-absorbed communicator, you have difficulty sustaining the conversation about anything except your self-absorbed partner's ideas, experiences, and stories. This problem is also called **conversational narcissism**. To be narcissistic is to be in love with oneself, like the mythical Greek character Narcissus, who became enamored with his reflection in a pool of water.[8]

The self-absorbed listener is actively involved in doing several things other than listening. The self-absorbed person is much more likely to interrupt others in mid-sentence. He or she is seeking ways to focus the attention on him- or herself.

The self-absorbed listener is also not focusing on his or her partner's message, but thinking about what he or she is going to say next. This focus on an internal message can keep a listener from selecting and attending to the other person's message. If you are supposed to be listening to Aunt Mae tell about her recent trip to the Elmira Fall Fair, but you are eager to hit her up for a loan, your personal agenda will serve as a barrier to your listening ability. Or you may simply decide that Aunt Mae's monologue is boring and unimportant and give yourself permission to tune out as she drones on. Like humorist James Thurber's famous daydreamer, Walter Mitty, you may eventually find yourself unable to respond cogently, lost in your own world.[9]

How do you short-circuit this listening problem? First, diagnose it. Note consciously when you find yourself drifting off, thinking about your agenda rather than concentrating on the speaker. Second, throttle up your powers of concentration when you find your internal messages are distracting you from listening well. If you notice that you are "telling" yourself that Aunt Mae's anecdote is boring, you can also mentally remind yourself to listen with greater energy and focus.

Emotional Noise

Words are powerful symbols that affect our attitudes, our behaviour, and even our blood pressure. Words arouse us emotionally. **Emotional noise** occurs when our emotional arousal interferes with communication effectiveness. If you grew up in a home in which R-rated language was never used, then four-letter words may be distracting to you. Words that insult your religious or ethnic heritage can also be fighting words. Most of us respond to certain trigger words like a bull to a waving cape; we want to charge in to correct the speaker or, perhaps, even do battle with him or her.

conversational narcissism.
Overly focusing on personal agendas and being self-absorbed rather than focusing on the needs and ideas of others.

emotional noise.
Communication interfered with by emotional arousal causes emotional noise.

Building Your Skills

IDENTIFYING EMOTIONAL "HOT BUTTONS"

Following are some listening situations and phrases that may cause you to become emotional. Check those that are "hot buttons" for you as a listener, and add others that strongly affect you, positively or negatively.

_____ "You never/always . . ."

_____ Know-it-all attitudes

_____ Individuals who smoke cigarettes or cigars while talking to you

_____ "Shut up!"

_____ Being ignored

_____ Bad grammar

_____ "You never listen."

_____ Obscene language

_____ Whining

_____ "What you should do is . . ."

_____ Being interrupted

Others:

_____

_____

_____

Knowing what your emotional hot buttons are can help prevent your overreacting when they are pushed.

Source: Adapted from Diane Bone, *The Business of Listening* (Los Altos, CA: Crisp Publications, 1995), 52.

Sometimes it is not specific words, but rather concepts or ideas that cause an emotional eruption. Some talk-radio hosts try to boost their ratings by purposely using demagogic language that elicits passionate responses. Although listening to such conflict can be interesting and entertaining, when your own emotions become aroused, you may lose your ability to converse effectively. Strong emotions can interfere with focusing on the message of another.

The emotional state of the speaker may also affect your ability to understand and evaluate what you hear. One researcher found that if you are listening to someone who is emotionally distraught, you will be more likely to focus on his or her emotions, than on the content of the message.[10] Another researcher advises that when you are communicating with someone who is emotionally excited, you should remain calm and focused, and try simply to communicate your interest in the other person.[11]

Your listening challenge is to avoid emotional sidetracks and to keep your attention focused upon the message. When your internal dialogue is kicked into high gear by objectionable words or concepts, or by an emotional speaker, make an effort to quiet it down and steer back to the subject at hand.

Criticizing the Speaker

The late Mother Teresa once said, "If you judge people, you have no time to love them." Being critical of the speaker may distract us from focusing on the message. As we learned in Chapter 3, most people are especially distracted by appearances, forming impressions of others based solely on non-verbal information. Superficial factors such as clothing, body size and shape, age, and ethnicity all affect our interpretation of a message.

It is important to monitor your internal dialogue to make sure you are focusing on the message rather than criticizing the messenger. Good listeners say to themselves,

"While it may be distracting, I am simply not going to let the appearance of this speaker keep my attention from the message."

Speech Rate vs. Thought Rate

Your ability to think faster than people speak is another listening pitfall. The average person speaks at a rate of 125 words a minute. Some folks talk a bit faster, others more slowly. You, on the other hand, have the ability to process up to 600 or 800 words a minute. The difference between your mental ability to handle words and the speed at which they arrive at your cortical centres can cause trouble, giving you time to daydream, tune the speaker in and out, and give you the illusion that you are concentrating more attentively than you actually are.[12]

You can turn your listening speed into an advantage if you use the extra time instead to summarize what a speaker is saying. By periodically sprinkling in mental summaries during a conversation, you can dramatically increase your listening ability and make the speech-rate/thought-rate difference work to your advantage.

Information Overload

We live in an information-rich age. We are all constantly bombarded with sight and sound images, and experts suggest that the volume of information competing for our attention is likely to become even greater in the future. Incoming messages and information on computers, fax machines, car phones, and other technological devices can interrupt conversations and distract us from listening to others.

Be on the alert for these information interruptions when you are talking with others. Don't assume that because you are ready to talk, the other person is ready to listen. If your message is particularly sensitive or important, you may want to ask your listening partner, "Is this a good time to talk?" Even if he or she says yes, look for eye contact and a responsive facial expression to make sure the positive response is genuine.

External Noise

As you will recall, all of the communication models we saw in Chapter 1 include the element of noise—distractions that take your focus away from the message. Many households seem to be addicted to noise. Often there is a TV on (sometimes more than one), a computer game beeping, and music emanating from another room. These, and other sounds, compete with your attention when you are listening to others.

Besides literal noise, there are other potential distractors. A headline in the evening paper about the latest details in a lurid sex scandal may "shout" for your attention, just when your son wants to talk with you about his latest science fiction story. A desire to listen to your new Nelly Furtado CD may drown out your partner's overtures to a heart-to-heart about your family's budget problems. The lure of music, TV, books, or Nintendo all can distract you from your listening task.

Distractions make it difficult to sustain attention to a message. You have a choice to make. You can attempt to listen through the labyrinth of competing distractions, or you can modify the environment to reduce them. Turning off the stereo, setting down the paper, and establishing eye contact with the speaker can help to minimize the noise barrier.

Are Cell Phones a Dangerous Listening Distraction?

Many things can distract us when we are trying to listen and respond to others. But a more recent distraction on the road is the use of cell phones. Can drivers pay attention to the road and listen and talk to others on a cell phone? As you may recall from our discussion of perception in Chapter 3, people must selectively attend to stimuli, and we cannot pay attention to all incoming sensations.

So what do you think? Can you listen and respond appropriately and drive carefully (paying close attention to other cars, staying on your side of the road, and so on)? Two researchers who surveyed people who had been in collisions have some hard data that may change your mind if you are one of those people who think that you can drive and listen and talk on a cell phone. In their research, they found that drivers were four times more likely to have a collision when using a cell phone than when not using one. Of interest, the collision statistics did not change according to the time of day (dark or light), the season, or whether the driver was making or receiving a call. Being engaged on a cell phone was much riskier than listening to the radio, talking to passengers, and other activities that commonly occur while driving.

Of interest, the study was carried out only with drivers who had experienced a collision that did not cause personal injury, so they have no data on accidents that actually caused injuries or fatalities. However, the risk of collision increased greatly at higher speeds. And the people in the study all agreed on at least one thing: They regretted the use of their cellular phones after the crash! So before making that call or receiving that call while driving, you may want to ask yourself one question: Is it worth the risk?

Source: Based on Donald A. Redelmeier and Robert J. Tibshirani, "Car Phones and Car Crashes: Some Popular Misconceptions," *Canadian Medical Association Journal*, 164 (11), (2001), 1581–1582.

▶ Recap

OVERCOMING BARRIERS TO LISTENING

Listening Barriers	To Overcome the Barrier
Being Self-Absorbed	Consciously become aware of the self-focus and shift attention.
Emotional Noise	Use self-talk to manage emotions.
Criticizing the Speaker	Focus on the message, not the messenger.
Information Rate	Use the difference between speech rate and thought rate to mentally summarize the message.
Information Overload	Realize when you or your partner is tired or distracted and not ready to listen.
External Noise	Take charge of the listening environment by eliminating the distraction.

Improving Your Listening Skills

Many of the listening problems we have identified stem from focusing on ourselves rather than on the messages of others. You can begin improving your listening skills by following three steps you probably first encountered in elementary school: (1) stop, (2) look, and (3) listen, and then (4) ask questions and (5) reflect content by **paraphrasing**. Simple as they may seem, these steps can provide the necessary structure to help you refocus your mental energies and improve your listening power. Let's consider each step separately.

paraphrasing. Checking the accuracy of your understanding by offering a verbal summary of your partner's message.

Stop

To select and attend to the messages of others, we must tap into our internal dialogue and stop our own running commentary about issues and ideas that are self-focused rather than other-focused. As we learned in Chapter 1, *decentring* is the term that describes the process of stepping away from our own concerns to think about the thoughts and feelings of our partner. If we treat decentring as a skill, we can learn to shift our internal dialogue to focus on others, although, at first, it will require conscious effort.

A model of how we learn any skill, attributed by many to Abraham Maslow, suggests that we operate at one of four skill levels:

- Unconscious incompetence
- Conscious incompetence
- Conscious competence
- Unconscious competence

The first level—*unconscious incompetence*—means we are unaware of our own incompetence. We don't know that we don't know. For example, before you read this chapter, you may simply not have been aware that you are distracted by your internal dialogue when you interact with others.

The second level is *conscious incompetence*. Here, we become aware or conscious that we are not competent; we know that we don't know. You may now be aware that you are an easily distracted listener, but you do not know how to solve the problem.

Level three is *conscious competence*; we have become aware that we know something, but it has not yet become an integrated habit. You might have to work at decentring when you first begin using it as you listen.

The final level of skill attainment is *unconscious competence*. At this level your skills have become second nature to you. After the age of six, most people who were raised in Canada are unconsciously competent at tying their shoes; it is automatic. In the same way, you may become so skilled in the decentring process that you do it as the rule rather than as an exception. At this level, you will also probably have the capacity to empathize, or "feel," with others as you listen.

Look

Non-verbal messages are powerful. As the primary ways that we communicate feelings, emotions, and attitudes, they play a major role in the total communication process, particularly in the development of relationships. Facial expressions and vocal cues, as well as eye contact, posture, and use of gestures and movement, can dramatically colour the meaning of a message. When the non-verbal message contradicts the verbal message, we almost always believe the non-verbal message. In listening to others, it is vital that you focus not only on the words but also on the non-verbal messages. Listen with your eyes as well as your ears.

Another reason to look at someone is to establish eye contact, which signals that you are focusing your interest and attention on him or her. If your eyes are glancing over your partner's head, looking for someone else, or if you are constantly peeking at your watch, your partner will rightfully get the message that you're not really listening. One researcher found that we telegraph our desire to change roles from listener to speaker by increasing our eye contact, using gestures such as a raised finger, and shifting our posture.[13] So it is important to maintain eye contact and monitor your partner's non-verbal signals when you are speaking as well as listening.

It is important, however, not to be distracted by non-verbal cues that may prevent us from interpreting the message correctly. A research team asked one group of college students to listen to a counsellor, and another group to both view and listen.[14] The students then rated the counsellor's effectiveness. Students who both saw and heard the counsellor perceived him as *less* effective because his distracting non-verbal behaviours affected their evaluations. We will provide more information about how to enhance your skill in interpreting the non-verbal messages of others in Chapter 7.

Listen

After making a concerted effort to stop distracting internal dialogue and to look for non-verbal cues, you will then be in a better position to understand the verbal messages of others. To listen is to do more than focus on facts; it is to search for the essence of the speaker's thoughts. We recommend the following strategies to help you improve your listening skill.

1. *Determine your listening goal.* You listen to other people for several reasons—to learn, to enjoy yourself, to evaluate, or to provide empathic support. With so many potential listening goals and options, it is useful to decide consciously what your listening objective is.

    If you are listening to someone give you directions to the city park, then your mental summaries should focus on the details of when to turn left and how many streets past the courthouse you go before you turn right. The details are crucial to achieving your objective. If, in contrast, your neighbour is telling you about her father's triple bypass operation, then your goal is to empathize. It is probably not important that you be able to recall when her father checked into the hospital or other details. Your job is to listen patiently and to provide emotional support. Clarifying your listening objective in your own mind can help you use appropriate skills to maximize your listening effectiveness.

2. *Transform listening barriers into listening goals.* If you can transform into listening goals the listening barriers you read about earlier, you will be well on your way to improving your listening skill. Make it a goal not to focus on your personal agenda. Make it a goal to use self-talk to manage emotional noise. Set a goal not to criticize the speaker. Remind yourself before each conversation to do mental summaries that capitalize on the differences between your information-processing rate and the speaker's verbal delivery rate. And make it your business to choose a communication environment that is free of distraction from other incoming information or noise.

3. *When your listening goal is to remember a message, mentally summarize the details of the message.* This suggestion may seem to contradict the suggestion to avoid focusing only on facts, but it is important to have a grasp of the details your partner provides. As we noted earlier, you can process words much more quickly than a person speaks. So, periodically, summarize the names, dates, and locations in the message. Organize the speaker's factual information into appropriate categories or try to place events in chronological order. Without a full understanding of the details, you will likely miss the speaker's major point.

4. *Mentally weave these summaries into a focused major point or series of major ideas.* Facts usually make the most sense when we can use them to help support an idea or major point. So, as you summarize, try to link the facts you have organized in your mind with key ideas and principles. Use the facts to enhance your critical thinking as you analyze, synthesize, evaluate, and finally summarize the key points or ideas your listening partner is making.[15]

5. *Practise listening to challenging material.* To improve or even maintain any skill, you need to practise it. Listening experts suggest that listening skills deteriorate if people do not practise what they know. Listening to difficult, challenging material can sharpen listening skills, so good listeners practise by listening to documentaries, debates, and other challenging material rather than mindless sitcoms and other material that entertains but does not engage them mentally.

Ask Questions

Sometimes when others share a momentous occurrence, the story may tumble out in a rambling, disorganized way. You can help sort through the story if you ask questions to identify the sequence of events. "What happened first?" and "Then what happened?" can help both you and your partner clarify what happened.

If your partner is using words or phrases that you don't understand, ask for definitions. "He's just so lackadaisical!" moans Meghan. "What do you mean by *lackadaisical*? Could you give me an example?" asks Mikhail. Sometimes asking for an example helps the speaker sort through the events as well.

Of course, if you are trying to understand another's feelings, you can ask how he or she is feeling, or how the event or situation made him or her feel. Often, however, nonverbal cues are more revealing than a verbal disclosure about feelings and emotions.

Reflect Content by Paraphrasing

After you try to imagine how you would feel under similar circumstances and to make sure you have an accurate understanding of the events that occurred, you need to check your understanding of the facts. Respond with a statement such as:

"Are you saying. . . ?"

"You seem to be describing. . ."

"So, the point you are making seems to be. . ."

"Here is what I understand you to mean. . ."

"So, here is what seemed to happen. . ."

Then, summarize the events, details, or key points you think the speaker is trying to convey. This is not a word-for-word repetition of what the speaker has said, nor do you need to summarize the content of *each* phrase or minor detail. Rather, it is a paraphrase to check the accuracy of your understanding. Here is an example:

Jamal: This week I have so much extra work to do. I'm sorry if I haven't been able to help keep this place clean. I know it's my turn to do the dishes tonight, but I have to get back to work. Could you do the dishes tonight?

Brigid: So you want me to do the dishes tonight and for the rest of the week. Right?

Jamal: Well, I'd like you to help with the dishes tonight. But I think I can handle it for the rest of the week.

Brigid: OK. So I'll do them tonight and you take over tomorrow.

Jamal: Yes.

Research conducted in clinical counselling settings found that when a listener paraphrases the content and feelings of a speaker, the speaker is more likely to trust and value the listener.[16] Remember the conversation at the beginning of this chapter? Caitlyn cultivates trust by paraphrasing, whereas Carmen focuses on her own issues and dispenses unsolicited advice. Paraphrasing to check understanding is also a vital skill to use when you are trying to reconcile a difference of opinion. Chapter 8 will show you how to use it in that context.

> **Recap**

HOW TO IMPROVE YOUR LISTENING SKILLS

Listening Skills	Definition	Action
Stop	Tune out distracting competing messages.	Become conscious of being distracted; use self-talk to remain focused.
Look	Become aware of the speaker's non-verbal cues; monitor your own non-verbal cues to communicate your interest in the speaker.	Establish eye contact; avoid fidgeting or performing other tasks when someone is speaking to you. Listen with your eyes.
Listen	Create meaning from your partner's verbal and non-verbal messages.	Mentally summarize details; link these details with main ideas.
Ask questions	Clarify words, events, and feelings by questioning the speaker.	Ask for definitions and examples; clarify sequences of events.
Reflect content by paraphrasing when appropriate	Briefly state the essence of what the speaker has said to ensure the accuracy of your understanding.	Summarize the key events, details, or points of what the speaker has said.

Improving Empathic Listening and Responding Skills

Above all, good listening is an other-oriented ability. The heart of being other-oriented is cultivating **empathy**—feeling what someone else is feeling. Empathy and the companion skill of socially decentring—the cognitive process of taking into account another person's thoughts, feelings, and background—are often primary listening goals. Sometimes the purpose of listening to a friend, relative, or colleague is not just to remember what is said, but to demonstrate that you care and are compassionate toward your partner. The Canadian Issues box on page 118 demonstrates our need to be empathic with those who speak different languages.

Good listening, especially listening to empathize with another, is active, not passive. To listen passively is to avoid displaying any behaviour that lets the speaker know we are listening.[17] Passive listeners sit with a blank stare or a frozen facial expression. Their thoughts and feelings could be anywhere, for all the speaker knows. **Active listeners**, in contrast, respond mentally, verbally, and non-verbally to a speaker's message. This serves several specific functions. First, it can be a measure of how accurately you understood the message. If you burst out laughing as your friend tells you about losing his house in a flood, he'll know you misunderstood what he was saying. Second, your responses indicate whether you agree or disagree with the comments others make. If you tell your friend that you do not approve of her comments on abortion, she'll know your position on the information she shared. Finally, your responses tell speakers how they are affecting others. Like radar that guides high-tech weapons, your feedback provides information to help others decide whether or not to correct the course of their messages.

As you can see, responding is something we do for others that holds out great benefits for us. It is the key to exchanging mutually understood, emotionally satisfying messages. Responding is especially critical if you are listening to provide support. Of course, listening to empathize is only one of the possible listening goals you may have. We are not suggesting that ferreting out someone's emotions is

empathizing. Feeling what others are feeling, rather than just acknowledging that they are feeling a certain way.

active listening. The interactive process of responding mentally, verbally, and non-verbally to a speaker's message.

Chapter 4 Listening and Responding

the goal of every listening encounter. That would be tedious for both you and your listening partners. But when you do want to listen empathically and respond, you must shift the focus to your partner and try to understand the message from his or her perspective.[18] We will discuss four strategies you can use to accomplish this.

Empathy is not a single skill but a collection of skills that help you predict how others will respond. Daniel Goleman's book *Emotional Intelligence* is an outstanding resource that discusses the role and importance of our emotions in developing empathy with others.[19] Goleman has found evidence that people who are emotionally intelligent—sensitive to others, empathic, and other-oriented—have better interpersonal relationships. Goleman summarizes the centrality of emotions in developing empathy by quoting Antoine de Saint-Exupéry: "It is with the heart that one sees rightly; what is essential is invisible to the eye."[20]

The quiz in *Considering Others: Test Your Empathy Ability* can help you determine how effectively you empathize with others. We then discuss strategies you can use to enhance your empathy skills.

Considering Others

TEST YOUR EMPATHY ABILITY

Empathy is an emotional capability that often grows out of a conscious decentering process. It is the ability to move away from yourself enough to "feel for" another person. But it does not mean abandoning your own self. On the contrary, empathic people often have a strong self-concept and high self-esteem, which enable them to be generous with others. Take this short test to assess your empathy. Respond to each statement by indicating the degree to which the statement is true regarding the way you typically communicate with others. When you think of how you communicate, is the statement always false (answer 1), usually false (answer 2), sometimes false and sometimes true (answer 3), usually true (answer 4), or always true (answer 5)?

_____ 1. I try to understand others' experiences from their perspectives.

_____ 2. I follow the Golden Rule ("Do unto others as you would have them do unto you") when communicating with others.

_____ 3. I can "tune in" to emotions others are experiencing when we communicate.

_____ 4. When trying to understand how others feel, I imagine how I would feel in their situation.

_____ 5. I am able to tell what others are feeling without being told.

_____ 6. Others experience the same feelings I do in any given situation.

_____ 7. When others are having problems, I can imagine how they feel.

_____ 8. I find it hard to understand the emotions others experience.

_____ 9. I try to see others as they want me to.

_____ 10. I never seem to know what others are thinking when we communicate.

To find your score, first reverse the responses for the even-numbered items (if you wrote 1, make it 5; if you wrote 2, make it 4; if you wrote 3, leave it as 3; if you wrote 4, make it 2; if you wrote 5, make it 1). Next, add the numbers next to each statement. Scores range from 10 to 50. The higher your score, the more you are able to empathize.

Source: William Gudykunst, *Bridging Differences*, 3rd ed. (Thousand Oaks, CA: Sage, 1998), 234.

e-connections

WHAT'S YOUR EQ?

According to best-selling author psychologist Daniel Goleman, your emotional intelligence is your ability to interact with others by listening, being empathic, and generally being sensitive to others rather than being oblivious to others or self-focused. In essence, your emotional intelligence is the extent to which you are other-oriented, the central premise of this book. What's your EQ (emotional intelligence quotient)? To take a short, ten-question test, click on the following Web address and assess your EQ:

www.utne.com/azEq.tmp1

Here's another EQ test to try:

http://homearts.com/depts/relat/olegab5.htm

When your friends have "one of those days," perhaps they seek you out to talk about it. They may not have any real problems to solve—perhaps it was just a day filled with miscommunication and squabbles with their partners or co-workers. But they want to tell you the details. Do you listen empathically, without giving advice? Often that is what your friends are seeking—a listener who focuses attention on them and understands what they are saying. People are willing to listen empathically for the same reasons they like to give friends gifts. It makes people feel good to show that they value others. Psychologist and counsellor Carl Rogers summarized the value of empathy when he said, "A high degree of empathy in a relationship is possibly the most potent factor in bringing about change and learning."

Understand Your Partner's Feelings: Imagine How You Would Feel

If your goal is to empathize or "feel" with your partner, you might begin by imagining how you would feel under the same circumstances. If your partner comes home dejected from being hassled at work, try to recall how you felt when that

Canadian Issues

LISTENING TO FRANCOPHONES AND ALLOPHONES

English and French are the two predominant mother tongues in Canada. Approximately 85 percent of the Canadian population speak one or the other.[21] Anglophones speak English as a mother tongue, Francophones speak French as a mother tongue, and Allophones speak any other language as a mother tongue. Large urban centres tend to be the most linguistically diverse as 80 percent of Allophones live in these cities.[22]

With such a diversity of languages, we need to pay special attention when listening to others who may be struggling with a new language. Listening can be a challenge when we are faced with accents, missed or misplaced words, wrong phrasing, or the silence of non-comprehension. Use the suggestions in this text to improve listening to those who are trying to speak your mother tongue.

Linguistic diversity is just one of the many challenges and strengths of a multi-cultural nation.

For Discussion

1. Take a poll to find out the various mother tongues in your class.
2. What are some specific suggestions you could give to a person who is trying to understand someone who is attempting to speak a new language?

Source: Canadian Issues: Languages in Canada, 1996, www.nais.ccm.emr.ca/schoolnet/issues/html/lang001.html

happened to you. If a friend calls to tell you his or her mother died, try to imagine how you would feel if the situation were reversed. Of course, your reaction to these events might be different from your partner's or your friend's. You may need to decentre and remember how your partner felt in other similar situations, to understand how he or she is feeling now.

Paraphrase Emotions

The bottom line in empathic responding is to make certain that you accurately understand how the other person is feeling. Again, you can paraphrase, beginning with such phrases as:

"So, you are feeling . . ."

"You must feel . . ."

"So, now you feel . . ."

"Emotionally, you must be feeling . . ."

In the following example of empathic responding, the listener asks questions, summarizes content, and summarizes feelings.

David: I think I'm in over my head. My boss gave me a job to do and I just don't know how to do it. I'm afraid I've bitten off more than I can chew.

José: (Thinks how he would feel if he were given an important task at work but did not know how to complete it, then he asks for more information.) What job did she ask you to do?

David: I'm supposed to do an inventory of all of the items in the warehouse on the VAX computer system and have it finished by the end of the week. I don't have the foggiest notion of how to start. I've never even used that system.

José: (Summarizing feelings.) So, you feel panicked because you may not have enough time to learn the system *and* do the inventory.

David: Well, I'm not only panicked, I'm afraid I may be fired.

José: (Summarizing feelings.) So, your fear that you might lose your job is getting in the way of just focusing on the task and seeing what you can get done. It's making you feel like you made a mistake in taking this job.

David: That's exactly how I feel.

Note that toward the end of the dialogue José has to make a couple of tries to summarize David's feelings accurately. Also note that José does a good job of just listening and responding without giving advice. Just by being an active listener, you can help your partner clarify a problem.

You can better understand a partner's feelings—empathize with him or her—if you listen and try to recall how you might have felt in similar situations.
(Gerard Loucel/Tony Stone Images)

Building Your Skills

SYMPATHY VERSUS EMPATHY

Most card shops have a sympathy card section. Such cards let people know you realize they are feeling bad about the death of someone close to them. To **sympathize** is to say you are sorry—that you want to offer your support and acknowledge that someone is feeling bad. Empathy goes one step further than sympathy. Empathy means that you try to perceive the world from another's perspective; you attempt to feel what someone else feels.

Respond to the sample situations below both with sympathy and with empathy.

1. A good friend of yours just phoned to tell you that her dog, a well-loved 14-year-old pet, has just died.

   Respond with sympathy:
   _____
   _____
   _____

   Respond with empathy:
   _____
   _____
   _____

2. Your older brother comes to visit you and tells you that he and his wife are getting a divorce after 20 years of marriage.

   Respond with sympathy:
   _____
   _____
   _____

   Respond with empathy:
   _____
   _____
   _____

3. A friend tells you that she just got fired from her job.

   Respond with sympathy:
   _____
   _____
   _____

   Respond with empathy:
   _____
   _____
   _____

Source: From William Gudykunst, *Bridging Differences*, 2nd ed. (Thousand Oaks, CA: Sage Publications, 1994). Reprinted by permission of Sage Publications, Inc.

---

sympathizing.
Acknowledging that someone may be feeling bad.

We have discussed responding and the active listening process from a tidy step-by-step textbook approach. In practice, you may have to back up and clarify content, ask more questions, and rethink how you would feel before you attempt to summarize how someone else feels. Conversely, you may be able to summarize feelings *without* asking questions or summarizing content if the message is clear and it relates to a situation with which you are very familiar. Overusing this skill can slow down a conversation and make the other person uncomfortable or irritated. But if you use it judiciously, paraphrasing can help both you and your partner keep focused on the issues and ideas at hand.

Reflecting content or feeling through paraphrasing can be especially useful in the following situations:

- Before you take an important action.
- Before you argue or criticize.
- When your partner has strong feelings or wants to talk over a problem.

- When your partner is speaking "in code" or using unclear abbreviations.
- When your partner wants to understand *your* feelings and thoughts.
- When you are talking to yourself.
- When you encounter new ideas.[23]

If you do decide to use reflecting skills, researchers suggest you keep the following guidelines in mind:

- Use your own words.
- Don't go beyond the information communicated by the speaker.
- Be concise.
- Be specific.
- Be accurate.

Do *not* use reflecting skills if you aren't able to be open and accepting; if you do not trust the other person to find his or her own solution; if you are using these skills as a way of hiding yourself from another; or if you feel pressured, hassled, or tired.[24] And, as we have already discussed, overuse of paraphrasing can be distracting and unnatural.

Don't be discouraged if your initial attempts to use these skills seem awkward and uncomfortable. Any new skill takes time to learn and use well. The instructions and samples you have seen here should serve as a guide, rather than as hard-and-fast prescriptions to follow during each conversation.

Building Your Skills

LISTENING AND PARAPHRASING CONTENT AND EMOTION

Working in groups of three, ask person A to briefly identify a problem or conflict that he or she is having (or has had) with another person (co-worker, supervisor, partner, or family member). Person B should use questioning, content paraphrasing, and emotion paraphrasing skills to explore the problem. Person C should observe the discussion and evaluate person B's listening and reflecting skills, using the Observer Checklist. Make a check mark next to all of the skills that person B uses effectively.

OBSERVER CHECKLIST

Non-verbal Skills

_____ Direct eye contact

_____ Open, relaxed body posture

_____ Uncrossed arms

_____ Uncrossed legs

_____ Appropriate hand gestures

_____ Reinforcing nods

_____ Responsive facial expression

_____ Appropriate tone of voice

_____ Appropriate volume

Verbal Skills

_____ Effective and appropriate questions

_____ Accurate paraphrase of content

_____ Accurate paraphrase of emotion

_____ Timely paraphrase

_____ Didn't interrupt the speaker

> **Recap**

How to Respond with Empathy

Responding with Empathy	Action
Understand Your Partner's Feelings	Ask yourself how you would feel if you had experienced a similar situation or recall how you *did* feel under similar circumstances. Or recall how your *partner* felt under similar circumstances.
Paraphrase Emotions	When appropriate, try to summarize what you think your partner may be feeling.

Improving Critical Listening and Responding Skills

After putting it off for several months, you've decided to buy a mobile phone. As you begin to talk to your friends, you're surprised to find a bewildering number of factors to consider: Do you want digital? cellular? voice mail? How many weekend minutes, evening minutes, or daily minutes of calling time do you need? You decide to head to a store to see if a salesperson can help you sort through the maze of options. The salesperson is friendly enough, but you become even more overwhelmed with the number of options, bells, and whistles to consider. As you try to make this decision, your listening goal is not to empathize with those who extol the virtues of mobile phones. Nor do you need to take a multiple-choice test over the information they share. To sort through the information, you need to listen critically.

Critical listening involves listening to evaluate the quality, appropriateness, value, or importance of the information you hear. *The goal of a critical listener is to use information to make a choice.* Whether you're selecting a new phone, deciding whom to vote for, choosing a potential date, or evaluating a new business plan, you will be faced with many opportunities to use your critical listening skills in interpersonal situations.

A critical listener is not necessarily one who offers negative comments. A critical listener seeks to identify both good information and information that is flawed or less helpful. We call this process *information triage. Triage* is a French term that usually describes the process used by emergency medical personnel to determine which of several patients is the most severely ill or injured and needs immediate medical attention. **Information triage** is a process of evaluating and sorting out issues. An effective critical listener performs information triage; he or she is able to distinguish useful and accurate information and conclusions from information that is less useful, as well as conclusions that are inaccurate or invalid.

How do you develop the skill of information triage? Initially, listening critically involves the same strategies as listening to comprehend that we discussed earlier. Before you evaluate information, it's vital that you first *understand* the information. Second, examine the logic or reasoning used in the message. And finally, be mindful of whether you are basing your evaluations on facts—something that is observed or verifiable, or inference—a conclusion based on partial information. Although courses in logic, argumentation, and public speaking often present skills to help you evaluate information, it's also important to listen critically during interpersonal conversations.

critical listening. Listening in which the goal is to evaluate and assess the quality, appropriateness, value, or importance of information.

information triage. Ability to sort good information from less useful or valid information.

Look for Faulty Logic: Wrong Reasoning

Effective critical listeners can spot whether or not a speaker is logically reaching a valid, well-supported conclusion. **Logic** is the application of appropriate evidence to reach a valid, well-reasoned conclusion. People who are thinking illogically often use reasoning fallacies to reach a flawed conclusion. The point they are making or the conclusion they are reaching does not make logical sense. A **fallacy** occurs when someone attempts to persuade without adequate evidence or uses arguments that are irrelevant, inaccurate, or inappropriate. The study of logic and reasoning is usually included in courses in debate, argumentation, persuasion, public speaking, and philosophy. But because people often listen critically in interpersonal situations, we include a brief overview of classic reasoning fallacies.[25] You can enhance both your critical listening and responding skills if you can avoid or spot the following fallacies.

Causal Fallacy

A **causal fallacy** occurs when someone makes a faulty cause-and-effect connection between two things or events. A popular children's book titled *Wilbur, the Dog Who Chased the Sun Up* is about a dog, Wilbur, who thought that his barking every morning caused the sunrise. It made sense to him: He barked; the sun came up. But simply because one thing follows another does not mean that the first event caused the second event. Be wary of someone who claims such a cause-and-effect relationship without evidence or proof. For example, the salesperson who claims, "People who buy mobile phones make more money" cannot guarantee that buying a phone will cause you to have increased income. Another logical explanation could be that mobile phone purchasers already have well-paying jobs—that's why they need a mobile phone.

Bandwagon Fallacy

Some people will try to get your vote or money by claiming that "everybody thinks this is a good idea, so you should too." Such a person is guilty of the **bandwagon fallacy**. Because someone says that "everyone" is "jumping on the bandwagon" or agrees with an idea or supports a point of view does not necessarily make it accurate or correct. Examples of bandwagon fallacies are "Everyone knows you will be more popular if you purchase a convertible" and "Everyone believes we need to increase the sales tax to support education for our children."

Either/Or Fallacy

The **either/or fallacy** practically defines itself. It occurs when someone argues that there are only two alternatives to a problem or issue. It's a fallacy because life is rarely that simple; there are virtually always more than only two options to consider. "It's either increase taxes or fire several teachers," bellows a member of the school board. Although those may be two choices, there are undoubtedly more options than just those. Be skeptical when you hear someone boil an issue down to only two options. Another example of an either/or fallacy is "Either we put trigger locks on all guns, or we limit the sale of handguns."

Hasty Generalization

A generalization is simply a conclusion someone has reached. A **hasty generalization** is a conclusion without adequate evidence to support it. For example, Ben

---

logic. Use of appropriate evidence to reach a valid, well-reasoned conclusion.

fallacy. False reasoning that occurs when someone attempts to persuade without adequate evidence or with arguments that are irrelevant or inappropriate.

causal fallacy. Making a faulty cause-and-effect connection between two things or events.

bandwagon fallacy. Reasoning that suggests that because everyone else believes something or is doing something, then it must be valid, accurate, or effective.

either/or fallacy. Oversimplifying an issue as having only one or two outcomes or choices (either this *or* that).

hasty generalization. Reaching a conclusion without adequate evidence to support the conclusion.

claimed you shouldn't eat shrimp, because his nephew ate shrimp and became ill. Ben was guilty of using a hasty generalization fallacy. One case does not prove the point. Even if two or three out of the millions of people who eat shrimp every day became ill after dining on shrimp scampi, those instances are not adequate evidence to claim that no one should enjoy a shrimp cocktail. In another instance, your co-worker tells you, "You don't need to worry about kids joining street gangs. My two sons went through high school and were never tempted to join a gang. Gangs are no real threat in our community." This, too, is an example of making a hasty generalization.

Attacking the Person

At your office holiday party you overhear someone say, "We know Karl's idea of expanding the parking garage is stupid, because Karl grew up in the country. He just isn't sophisticated." The person making this claim is guilty of a reasoning fallacy called attacking the person. **Attacking the person** occurs when you critique someone's idea because of an irrelevant personal characteristic, rather than evaluating the idea itself. "She grew up in China. She could not possibly have an insightful thing to say about the need for a new airport." This is another example of inappropriately attacking the person rather than the idea the individual is proposing. Don't dismiss what someone says only because you have been turned against the person who presented it. Focus on the merit of the message or idea rather than on the irrelevant qualifications of the messenger.

Red Herring

When someone tries to divert attention from the real issue or idea being discussed, by using irrelevant facts or information rather than directly responding to the issue at hand, the person is using the **red herring** fallacy. This fallacy gets its name from an old trick of dragging a red herring fish across a trail to divert the dogs who were sent to track someone down. When asked a difficult or potentially embarrassing question, politicians often respond with a completely different issue or irrelevant piece of information. Here's how one politician used a red herring to divert attention from something she'd rather not talk about: "So the question is, did I illegally raise campaign money? Well, the issue is really 'Did my opponent sponsor legislation to support underage drinking?' Too many teenagers are abusing alcohol, and this abuse must stop!" Did you see how the issue of teenage drinking was used to divert attention from charges of the use of illegal campaign funds? Watch out for speakers who try to divert your attention from issues they'd rather not talk about.

Non Sequitur

Non sequitur is a Latin term for "it does not follow." A **non sequitur** fallacy occurs when one idea or conclusion does not logically follow the previous idea or conclusion. Non sequitur arguments don't make sense. "We need to hire more workers because we have fluoridated water in our community." After hearing a non sequitur argument, you may scratch your head and mentally or audibly say, "Huh?" "Because we have a new campus radio station, we should pick up the trash around city hall." Or going door to door, the mayoral candidate says, "I will make a wonderful mayor because I have five children and sixteen grandchildren." These, too, are non sequitur conclusions. There is no logical connection between radio stations and picking up trash. And it's a stretch to argue that you'd make a better mayor because you have children and grandchildren.

---

attacking the person. Critiquing irrelevant personal characteristics of the person who is proposing an idea, rather than critiquing the idea itself.

red herring. Using irrelevant facts or information to distract someone from the issue that needs to be discussed.

non sequitur. Idea or conclusion that does not logically follow the previous idea or conclusion. Latin for "it does not follow."

Being able to spot the use of faulty logic is an important ability when trying to evaluate the soundness of a speaker's conclusion. Being knowledgeable about reasoning fallacies can also help you better respond to flawed arguments developed by others.

Avoid Jumping to Conclusions: Fact–Inference Confusion

Imagine this scene. You are a detective investigating a death. You are given the following information: (1) Leo and Chantal are found lying together on the floor, (2) Leo and Chantal are both dead, (3) Leo and Chantal are surrounded by water and broken glass, (4) on the sofa near Leo and Chantal, a cat is seen with its back arched, apparently ready to defend itself.

Given these sketchy details, do you, the detective assigned to the case, have any theories about the cause of Leo and Chantal's demise? Perhaps they slipped on the water, crashed into a table, broke a vase, and died (that would explain the water and broken glass). Or maybe their attacker recently left the scene, and the cat is still distressed by the commotion. Clearly, you could make several inferences (conclusions based on partial information) as to the probable cause of death. Oh yes, there is one detail we forgot to mention: Leo and Chantal are fish. Does that help?

People often spin grand explanations and hypotheses based on sketchy details. Acting on inferences, people may act as though the "facts" clearly point to a specific conclusion. Determining the difference between a fact and an inference can help you more accurately use language to reach valid conclusions about what you see and experience.

What makes a fact a fact? Most students, when asked this question, respond by saying, "A fact is something that has been proven true." If that is the case, *how* has something been proven true? In a court of law, a **fact** is something that has been observed or witnessed. Anything else is speculation or inference.

> "Did you see my client in your house, taking your jewelry?" asks the wise attorney.
>
> "No," says the plaintiff.
>
> "Then you do not know for a fact that my client is a thief."
>
> "I guess not," the plaintiff admits.

The problem occurs when we respond to something as if it were a fact (something observed), when in reality it is an **inference** (a conclusion based upon speculation):

> "It's a fact that your mother doesn't like me."
>
> "It's a fact that you will be poor all of your life."
>
> "It's a fact that you will fail this course."

Each of these statements, although it might very well be true, misuses the term *fact*. If you cannot recognize when you are making an inference instead of stating a fact, you may give your judgments more credibility than they deserve.

Being consciously competent about whether someone is reaching a conclusion based on facts or is speculating by drawing an inference can help you improve your information triage skill. An effective critical listener considers the quality of the factual evidence used to develop ideas and opinions. You can also more effectively respond and ask questions if you are aware of whether someone is drawing conclusions based on direct observation (facts) or partial information (inferences).

fact. Something that has been directly observed to be true or can be proved to be true.

inference. Conclusion based on partial or available evidence.

Although people often reach conclusions based on inferences, being sensitive to the differences between how conclusions and observations are labelled can improve both critical listening and responding skills.

Improving Your Responding Skills

We've offered several strategies for responding to others when your goal is to comprehend information, empathize with others, or evaluate messages. Regardless of your communication goal, we'll now present several additional strategies to enhance your skill in responding to others. The timing of the response, usefulness of the information, amount of detail, and descriptiveness of the response are useful strategies to consider when responding to others.

Provide Well-Timed Responses

Feedback is usually most effective when you offer it at the earliest opportunity, particularly if your objective is to teach someone a skill. For example, if you are teaching someone how to make your famous egg rolls, you provide a step-by-step commentary as you watch your pupil. If he or she makes a mistake, you don't wait until the egg rolls are finished to say that he or she left out the cabbage. Your pupil needs immediate feedback to finish the rest of the sequence successfully.

Sometimes, however, if a person is already sensitive and upset about something, delaying feedback can be wise. Use your critical thinking skills to analyze when feedback will do the most good. Rather than automatically offering immediate correction, use the just-in-time (JIT) approach, and provide feedback just before the person might make another mistake. If, for example, your daughter typically rushes through math tests and fails to check her work, remind her right before her next test to double-check her answers, not immediately after the test she just failed. To provide feedback about a relationship, select a mutually agreeable place and time when both of you are rested and relaxed; avoid hurling feedback at someone "for his or her own good" immediately after he or she offends you.

Provide Useable Information

Perhaps you've heard this advice: Never try to teach a pig to sing. It wastes your time. It doesn't sound pretty. And it annoys the pig. When you provide information to someone, be certain that it is useful and relevant. How can you make sure your partner can use the information you share? Be other-oriented; put yourself in your partner's mindset. Ask yourself, "If I were this person, how would I respond to this information? Is it information I can act on? Or is it information that may make matters worse?" Under the guise of effective feedback, we may be tempted to reveal to others our complete range of feelings and emotions. But research suggests that

When you are teaching someone a new skill, the timing of your feedback is just as important as what you say. When should this grown-up tell the child he is helping how to improve his bicycle riding?
(Marc Romanelli/The Image Bank/Getty)

selective feedback is best. In one study, married couples who practised selective self-disclosure were more satisfied than couples who told everything they knew or were feeling.[26] Immersing your partner in information that is irrelevant or that may be damaging to the relationship may be cathartic, but it may not enhance the quality of your relationship or improve understanding.

Avoid Unnecessary Details

When you are selecting meaningful information, try to cut down on the volume of information. Don't overwhelm your listener with details that obscure the key point of your feedback. Give only the high points that will benefit the listener. Be brief.

Be Descriptive Rather Than Evaluative

"You're an awful driver!" shouts Doris at her husband Frank. Although Doris may feel she has provided simple feedback to her spouse about his skills, Frank will probably not respond warmly, or even listen closely, to her feedback. If Doris tries to be more descriptive and less evaluative, then he might be inclined to listen: "Frank, you are travelling 70 km/h in a 50 km/h zone" or "Frank, I get very nervous when you zigzag so fast through the freeway traffic" are less offensive comments. They describe Frank's behaviour rather than render judgments about him that are likely to trigger a defensive, passive listening reaction.

▶ **Recap**

SUGGESTIONS FOR IMPROVING RESPONDING SKILLS

Provide Well-Timed Responses	Sometimes immediate feedback is best; at other times provide a just-in-time (JIT) response when it will do the most good.
Provide Meaningful Information	Select information that your partner can act on, rather than making vague comments or suggestions that are beyond his or her capabilities.
Avoid Unnecessary Details	Avoid information overload; don't bombard the listener with too much information; keep your comments focused on major points.
Be Descriptive	Don't evaluate your listening partner; focus on behaviour rather than personality.

Summary

Listening effectively to others is the quintessential skill required for establishing other-oriented relationships. Listening, the process of making sense out of what we hear, includes selecting, attending, understanding, remembering, and responding to others. Preferred listening styles vary, and include those who are people-oriented, action-oriented, content-oriented, and time-oriented listeners.

Most of us don't listen effectively because we are self-oriented instead of other-oriented. Barriers to effective listening include being self-focused, being distracted by emotional noise, criticizing the speaker, wasting the difference between speech and thought rates, and being distracted by information overload and external noise.

To become better listeners, we can pursue three seemingly simple steps: stop, look, and listen. To stop means to avoid tuning in to our own distracting messages and to become mindful of what others are saying. To look is to observe and interpret unspoken messages—non-verbal communication skills and principles will be discussed in greater detail in Chapter 7. After stopping and looking, we can then listen more effectively to others by focusing on details and the speaker's key ideas. Being other-oriented does not mean you should abandon your own convictions or values, but you should make a conscious effort to pay attention to the needs and concerns of others. After we complete these three steps, we should ask questions and reflect content by paraphrasing.

We can further improve our ability to listen and respond empathically by seeking to understand our partner's feelings and paraphrasing his or her emotions. We can further improve our ability to listen and respond critically by looking for faulty logic and being consciously competent at distinguishing facts from inferences. And we can improve our skills at responding, regardless of the communication objective, by providing well-timed responses; providing usable information; avoiding unnecessary details; and being descriptive rather than evaluative.

For Discussion and Review

Focus on Comprehension

1. What are some differences between hearing and listening?
2. What strategies can we follow to respond with empathy?
3. What are key listening barriers that keep people from listening well?
4. What are some suggestions for effectively paraphrasing interpersonal messages?
5. What are reasoning fallacies? Provide examples.

Focus on Critical Thinking

6. Identify two situations during the past 24 hours in which you were an effective or ineffective listener. What factors contributed to your listening skill (or lack of skill)?
7. Miranda and Salvador often disagree about who should handle some of the child-rearing tasks in their home. When they have discussions on these issues, what are some effective listening skills and strategies that they could use to make sure they understand one another?
8. Jason and Chris are roommates. They both work hard each day and come home exhausted. What suggestions would you offer to help them listen effectively even when they are tired?

Focus on Ethics

9. Is it possible for paraphrasing and active listening to become a way to manipulate others? Support your answer.
10. Your friend asks you how you like her new dress. You really feel it is a bit too revealing. But it is time for the two of you to leave for your evening activities. Should you respond honestly, even though it may mean that you and your friend will be late for important engagements?

Chapter 4   Listening and Responding

11. Your roommate wants to tell you about his day. You are tired and really don't want to hear all of the details. Should you fake attention so that you won't hurt his feelings or should you simply tell your roommate that you are tired and would rather not hear about the details right now?

For Your Journal

1. Keep this checklist (first published in the *International Listening Association Newsletter*) with you one full day to monitor your listening problems.

   A Checklist for Listeners
   Today I . . .
   Interrupted other people _____ times.
   Misunderstood other people _____ times.
   Lost track of a conversation _____ times.
   Stopped making eye contact with a speaker _____ times.
   Asked someone to repeat himself/herself _____ times.
   Let my mind wander while listening to someone _____ times.
   Changed the subject in the middle of a conversation _____ times.
   Jumped to a conclusion about what someone was going to say _____ times.
   Reacted emotionally to what someone was saying before they finished _____ times.

   After keeping track of your personal listening statistics, what changes would you like to make in your listening behaviour?

2. Monitor and then jot down notes about your own self-talk during a conversation with another person. What competing thoughts and ideas occurred to you while you were conversing with your partner? What did you do to refocus on the message?

Learning with Others

1. Place a check mark beside all of the communication barriers that affect you. Identify the action you will take to manage the barrier. Discuss your results with your classmates.

   How Will You Overcome Listening Barriers?

Barrier	Action
Being self-absorbed	_____
Emotional noise	_____

Criticizing the speaker _____

Speech rate vs. thought rate _____

Information overload _____

Outside distractions _____

2. Charting Your Listening Cycle

Are you a morning person or an evening person? Use the chart shown here to plot your listening energy cycle. Draw a line starting at 6:00 A.M. showing the highs and lows of your potential listening effectiveness. If, for example, you are usually still asleep at 6:00 A.M., your line will be at 0 and start upward when you awake. If you are a morning person, your line will peak in the morning. Or, perhaps your line will indicate that you listen best in the evening.

After you have charted your typical daily listening cycle, gather in small groups with your classmates to compare listening cycles. Identify listening strategies that can help you capitalize on your listening "up" periods. Also, based upon this chapter and your own experiences, identify ways to enhance your listening when you traditionally have low listening energy.

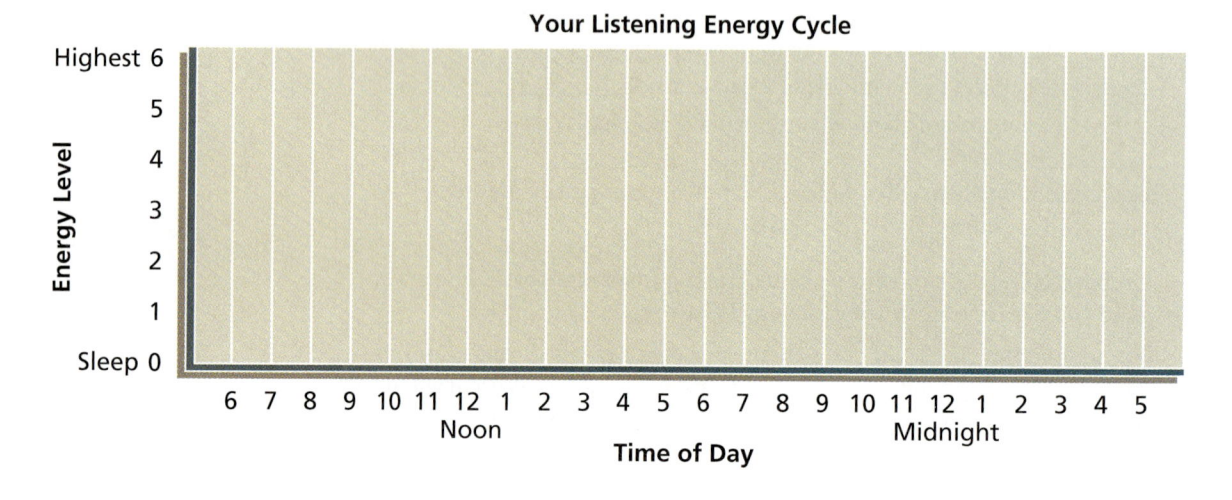

Your Listening Energy Cycle

Energy Level: Highest 6, 5, 4, 3, 2, 1, Sleep 0

Time of Day: 6 7 8 9 10 11 12 (Noon) 1 2 3 4 5 6 7 8 9 10 11 12 (Midnight) 1 2 3 4 5

Weblinks

canada.gc.ca   This is the primary Internet site for Canada with links to numerous organizations, programs, and services.

www.uiuc.edu/webclasses.html   This is the site for online classes at the University of Illinois. There are many courses listed, including some with content on Interpersonal Skills.

strategis.ic.gc.ca   Strategis is Canada's largest business site. It has extensive online resources. Find out how businesses teach communication skills, view articles on leadership, and other related articles from across Canada.

Suggested Readings

Schulz, Yogi. "Are You Really Paying Attention?" *Computing Canada,* 27(18), (2001): 23.
>This small article describes how effective listening can lead to more successful IT project completion.

Myers, Sharon. "Empathic Listening: Reports on the Experience of Being Heard." *Journal of Humanistic Psychology,* 40(2), (2000): 148–171.
>Written by a professor from the University of New Brunswick, this qualitative study explores empathic listening in a counselling environment.

Kiener, Robert. "The Nature of David Suzuki." *Reader's Digest* (February 2002): 50–57.
>An interesting interview about the life and opinions of David Suzuki including his views that the government is not listening to his (and others') warnings about environmental issues.

chapter 5

Emotions and Interpersonal Communication

After you study this chapter

you should be able to ...

1. Define emotions and explain how emotions are experienced.
2. Discuss how emotions influence cognitions.
3. Explain the factors that influence the expression of emotions.
4. Help others express their feelings.
5. Recognize and share your feelings with others.
6. Manage difficult emotions.

- Characteristics of Emotions
- The Depth and Breadth of Emotions
- Factors That Influence Emotional Expression
- Skills for Recognizing and Sharing Emotions
- Managing Difficult Emotions When You Experience Them

In wakefulness we react to events with emotions; in dreams we react to emotions with events.

ROBERT ZEND

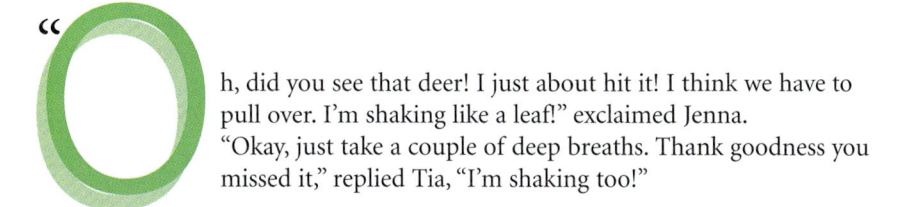

"Oh, did you see that deer! I just about hit it! I think we have to pull over. I'm shaking like a leaf!" exclaimed Jenna.
"Okay, just take a couple of deep breaths. Thank goodness you missed it," replied Tia, "I'm shaking too!"

Interpersonal communication cannot be properly discussed without including the topic of emotions. Emotions are an integral part of communication. As the above scene depicts, the two women while communicating verbally are also communicating and experiencing emotions through non-verbal channels. During communication with others, we feel and react to the messages that we receive. Often we are surprised by others' reactions to what we say—what we intended and what was received are not always the same message. Or we may communicate in order to get a specific emotional reaction such as telling a joke to make another person laugh. Emotions are displayed non-verbally as we will discuss in much more detail in Chapter 7. In this chapter, we will examine emotions. Although we cannot ignore the non-verbal components of emotion, most of our discussion of non-verbal behaviour will occur in the next chapter. We begin by defining emotions and the physiological make-up and effects of emotion. Then we will turn our attention to examining the impact of emotions on interpersonal communication and the factors that influence our emotional expression. Third, skills in two areas: skills for recognizing and dealing with the emotions of others and skills for managing your own emotions will be explored including the managing of some difficult emotions.

Characteristics of Emotions

There are several theories of emotions ranging from the earlier explanations of Canon and Bard and James and Lange to the newer theories of Singer and Schacter and Opponent-Process Theory. Here we will not examine these theories but rather examine what all of these theories have in common. These theories all conclude that emotions are triggered by environmental stimuli and that we react to these stimuli both physically and cognitively. For example, Jenna and Tia almost hit a deer and, realizing how close they were to having an accident, experience both the fear of almost hitting something and the relief of not hitting something. Physically both women are shaking, and Jenna needs to pull over to regain her composure. **Emotions**, then, are reactions to the environment and consist of physiological reactions, subjective cognitive states, and behavioural reactions. Scientists generally agree on these three characteristics of emotions.[1] Let's examine each of these three characteristics more closely.

Emotions are reactions to the environment and consist of physiological reactions, subjective cognitive states, and behavioural reactions.
(Brown W. Cannon III/Stone/Getty)

Physiological Effects of Emotions

When we encounter a situation, our bodies respond physiologically. For example, you are walking home late at night and hear a noise behind you that sounds like footsteps. Your heart rate increases, the hair on the back of your neck stands up, and your mouth suddenly goes dry. These reactions are prompted by your **autonomic nervous system**—the part of your nervous system that connects internal organs, glands, and involuntary muscles to the central nervous system. Two parts of the autonomic nervous system are active in regulating the physiological reactions that accompany emotion.[2] The activation of the *sympathetic nervous system* readies the body for vigorous action by performing such functions as increasing the heart rate, blood pressure, and respiration. The *parasympathetic nervous system* helps restore the body's resources through such actions as diverting blood from large muscles to the digestive organs for digestion. For the most part, you do not actively control these aspects of your nervous system, which include such activities as maintaining your heart rate, breathing, swallowing, digestion, and other more "automatic" physiological functioning. Part of these automatic reactions to a stimulus activated by the sympathetic nervous system is the **fight or flight response**, which prepares you for action in such situations as the example of being followed late at night or preparing the body for impact in a near car accident. While a rather simplistic explanation of the complex bodily reactions that occur during an event, it serves to illustrate the nature of emotions as having physical impact in the body that can range from extremes such as created by fear to other emotions such as happiness or sadness. For milder emotions, we may not feel that we are experiencing any physiological changes at all.

Heightened Arousal

When we are angry, frustrated, or upset, we experience physiological arousal. Recent research has examined more closely the relationship of heightened physiological arousal and emotions. In many situations the body prepares itself for "fight

emotions. Responses to events that include psychological, subjective, behavioural, and physiological components.

autonomic nervous system. The part of the nervous system that connects internal organs, glands, and involuntary muscles to the central nervous system.

fight or flight response. An emotional and physiological state of readiness that prepares an organism to fight a stressor or flee the stressor.

or flight," even though neither behaviour may be required. For example, you are rushing in your car to meet your sister at a restaurant. On the way, you are narrowly missed by a driver who swerves into your lane and barely misses you. Your heart pounds, your mouth goes dry, and your hands clench the steering wheel. If you are like many of us, you may also utter a few choice words! As you continue to drive, you feel less stressed. When you get to the restaurant 10 minutes late, your sister is not there. You wait another 10 minutes. You finally order a coffee and are still waiting. As your sister approaches, you say angrily, "It's about time you got here! What took you so long?"

A growing body of research indicates that such emotional arousal lasts long after an incident and is very slow to dissipate.[3] It also appears that under some conditions, heightened arousal can enhance aggressive responses, regardless of the source of the arousal. According to **excitation transfer theory**, because physiological arousal takes time to dissipate, this arousal can be transferred to other situations. Instead of becoming merely annoyed (a small increase in arousal) at a further small incident (your sister being late), you become enraged.[4] You are unaware of the *residual arousal* from the car experience and therefore attribute the arousal to your sister's lateness: even when you are aware of this arousal, you attribute it to the current situation. In other words, past emotionally arousing events continue to affect you long after the event is over.

This has many implications for communication. If we are not aware of this residual arousal, we may not understand why we are feeling the way we are later when we overreact to the next event. Have you ever been surprised at someone who you feel has overreacted to an event? One answer for such overreaction is the presence of this residual arousal.

> **excitation transfer theory.** Theory that explains that residual emotional arousal takes time to dissipate and thus this arousal can be transferred to other situations.

Cognitive Effects of Emotion

The second characteristic is the subjective experience of emotions based on the personality and characteristics of the person. Who you are affects your experience and interpretation of an event. In other words, your cognitions or thoughts about an event affect how you feel. If you are over 180 cm tall and weigh over 90 kg, you do not even notice the sound of the footsteps, or if you do, you may think to yourself, "Hope this person does not want any trouble, because he is going to be messing with the wrong person." But if you are just over 150 cm tall, weigh 45 kg, and are terrified of being mugged, you may well perceive this as a threatening situation and experience fear. In the first example, the increased heartbeat of the person is the thrill of a possible fight, whereas in the second example, the increased heartbeat is the fear of possibly being hurt. In both cases, the physiological symptoms are the same, but the interpretations are different. Missing the deer was a great relief for both women in our opening example. Since their sympathetic nervous systems were activated so quickly, the shaking occurs after the event as their parasympathetic nervous systems attempt to calm them down again.

While there is often a direct connection between the body and emotions, the mind and our thoughts play an important role in determining our feelings in any situation. The body reacts similarly to both fearful and joyful situations. It is up to us to determine what the physiological changes mean, which is a large component of theories of emotion proposed by various researchers.[5] Such theories concentrate on the role of cognition and use *cognitive labels* to describe what we are feeling as a result of our interpretation of the situation. When we are not sure how we are feeling, we look outward for clues to assist us in identifying our emotions. In other words, when we experience some sort of physiological arousal, we think about what

schemas. Mental representations of events, roles, or persons.

we are feeling and then add the label. For example, if you win a large sum of money, you label the physiological effects as joy! External events and cues assist us in labelling how we are feeling.

Cognition also influences emotions through the activation of *schemas.* **Schemas** are organized mental representations or a system of cognitions about something such as an event, a role, a type of person, and so on. For example, you have schemas about weddings and the characteristics of a good teacher. These schemas are organized in our minds and help us to define and understand events. Emotions are also part of schemas. At a wedding you expect people to be happy; you expect yourself to be happy for the couple. But how would you react if everyone looked sad or if the bride and groom started fighting? Chances are you would try to figure out what is going on by looking at others around you and trying to determine how they are feeling about this turn of events.

Behavioural Effects and Emotions

In many cases, we end up guessing how a person feels by watching his or her behaviour. Most of this behaviour is non-verbal and we make assumptions about how someone is feeling based on non-verbal clues which we will discuss in much greater detail in Chapter 7. This is the third component of emotions: the behavioural expression of the internal feeling or state. If someone starts shouting at you, waves his or her arms, and stomps his or her feet, you would hazard the guess that the person is angry or very upset about something. We continually assess situations based upon the behaviour of the people involved—not an easy task, especially in situations that are ambiguous or that we have little information about. For example, your roommate is angry with you but you have no idea what she could be angry about. You know she is angry because she looks angry—a red face, tight lips, and refusing to speak to you.

How do you know if someone is about to lose control? How do you know if your message is being well received or even understood? Paying close attention to non-verbal behaviour and to other uncontrolled actions will become an important skill for you to learn. Emotions are communicated non-verbally as we shall see in Chapter 7.

It is often easy to interpret strong emotions as the internal physiological changes are also manifested outwardly. For example, if someone is angry his or her blood pressure increases, which may result in "going red in the face," an easily observable behaviour. Under the influence of strong emotions, people turn red in the face (blush), perspire, grit their teeth, clench fists, pout, cry, slump in posture, and engage in other readily observable behavioural manifestations of the emotion.

But what about emotions that are not strong, or two or more emotions that can be illustrated by the same behaviours? Is the person who is red in the face angry, embarrassed, or experiencing high blood pressure? Is the person who is perspiring nervous or excited? People can also mask their emotions to some degree. We can smile even when we do not feel like it and pretend not to be angry when we are seething under the surface. In many public situations, we cannot demonstrate how we feel as social etiquette may dictate how we are to respond. Few of us yell at our bosses during a meeting. It goes against social norms and chances are it will also damage our career path. As we will see in Chapter 7, non-verbal behaviour can also be ambiguous and difficult

This person is angry, and his/her feelings are clearly observable. But mixed emotions are far more difficult to interpret. (Thomas Hoeffgen/Stone/Getty)

to read. However, one area of display of emotion has been extensively researched, including cross-cultural study, and that is the face.

The Universality of Emotional Expression

Research indicates that the expression of some emotions is universal, particularly facial expressions. Six different basic emotions are clearly expressed in the face: anger, happiness, sadness, disgust, fear, and surprise.[6] Two other emotions have recently been researched that also may be fundamental: contempt[7] and the expression of pain.[8]

Many emotional states may be more difficult to identify. Is the other person angry or bored? How can you tell if someone is lying? The Considering Others box below sheds a bit of light on the indicators of lying.

Considering Others

HOW CAN YOU TELL WHEN SOMEONE IS LYING?

How can you tell if someone is lying to you? Can you tell when someone is consciously deceiving you? Is it easier to identify lying when the person you are speaking to is someone you know, or if the liar is a stranger? People will lie to a parent or a counsellor to avoid trouble, to avoid turning in a friend, or to get someone else into trouble rather than themselves. Are lie detectors a valid means of determining whether someone is lying? Much research has been devoted to identifying deliberate deception and the accuracy of lie detector tests. It has also revealed several *external* cues that may indicate lying:

- Basic discrepancies between non-verbal channels. For example, a liar may manage to control facial expressions, but body language may betray nervousness or tell a different story.[9]
- Variations in paralanguage, such as a rise in voice pitch, or lack of verbal fluency.[10]
- More sentence repairs.[11] A liar may start a sentence, interrupt it, and then start all over again.
- An unusually low or high level of eye contact.[12]
- Averting of eyes before answering a question. This is often interpreted as an effort to hide something.[13]
- Exaggerated facial expressions.[14]
- Nervous mannerisms such as excessive self-touching and fidgeting. Touching, scratching, and rubbing suggest emotional arousal, which may be caused by lying to the other person.
- Short and recurrent pauses may signal that the liar has to be continually thinking about what he or she needs to say next.[15]

Internal responses from the autonomic nervous system that indicate deception are measured with polygraphs or lie detectors. Polygraphs record physiological reactions that occur during questioning. Results of research into the accuracy of polygraphs are mixed. While many professionals believe that polygraphs are accurate, some research has indicated otherwise.[16] Under questioning, nervousness or embarrassment may also cause arousal similar to the arousal when lying. Also, people can intentionally change their level of physiological arousal.[17] Accomplished con artists and other criminals may also be able to control their physiological responses in the same way as the subjects in research. However, polygraph testing can be one tool to detect lying and should not be ruled out as a method in crime investigation. In fact, one research report has pointed out that reviews of the reliability of polygraphs in *Introductory Psychology* may be negatively biased.[18] Because of this question of reliability, the results of polygraphs have not been admissible in Canadian courts since a Supreme Court ruling in 1987.

So how can you tell when someone is lying? As we've emphasized several times, because of the transactional nature of interpersonal communication, meaning is created as people communicate with others; behaviours do not have a fixed interpretation. Also, remember not to place too much emphasis on a single cue. As we've just noted, look for clusters of cues rather than pointing your finger when someone has less eye contact and saying, "Aha! Now I know you're a liar!"

> **Recap**

EFFECTS OF EMOTIONS

Physiological Effects	Emotions are accompanied by physical changes such as heart rate increase.
Cognitive Effects	Emotions are influenced by our thoughts such as labelling something as fear-provoking or exciting.
Behavioural Effects	Emotions may prompt behavioural responses such as smiling or crying.

The Depth and Breadth of Emotions

Before looking at the factors that influence emotional expression, we need to more closely look two other characteristics of emotion: depth and breadth. We experience emotions on many different levels. You can be overjoyed or mildly amused. How does it feel when you are apprehensive, yet happy? Just how many emotions are there, and do they differ in intensity?

How Many Emotions?

We can feel many, many emotions and even feel different emotions at the same time. Earlier we stated that there appear to be six universal emotions including happiness (joy), anger, sadness, surprise, fear, and disgust. One researcher has labelled these as **primary emotions** and adds to these two other emotions: acceptance and anticipation.[19] Plutchik defines these primary emotions as being simple or made up of just one feeling. Other emotions are more complex and are labelled as **mixed emotions** because they are blends of the primary emotions. For example, according to Plutchik, the emotion of love consists of joy and acceptance and the emotion of contempt is a combination of anger and disgust. These mixed emotions are more difficult to read accurately. The real key here is that there are a great number of emotions and emotional states that we experience and some are more complex than others. To illustrate the wide number of emotions that we experience, try the Building Your Skills exercise below.

primary emotions. The six pure emotions as represented on Plutchik's Emotion Wheel.

mixed emotions. On Plutchik's Emotion Wheel, these emotions are blends of the primary emotions.

Building Your Skills

THE EMOTIONS ALPHABET

To illustrate the number and complexity of emotions that we experience, try this activity. It is a great classroom exercise for sharing, as students will not all have the same answers. This simple exercise demonstrates the great number and blends of emotions that we all experience. It works well as a round robin. Each student is given one letter of the alphabet and tries to identify an emotion that starts with that letter. If a student can't fill one in, then the next student tries and so on. One author uses this as an introduction to emotions, and students cannot believe the number of emotions there are!

Instructions: On a blank piece of paper, write the letters of the alphabet from A to Z. For each letter of the alphabet, identify an emotion that starts with that letter. See if you can identify more than one emotion for some of them. For example, for the letter A you may choose anxious or anticipation.

Intensity of Emotions

Emotions also vary in intensity. Think of the difference between mild annoyance and rage. Mildly annoyed, you may tell a person what you think in a calm and cool manner; but, if in a rage, you may scream at the person. The more intense the emotions, the more likely you will feel the physiological effects of experiencing the emotion, and the chances are higher that others will recognize how you feel. It should be noted that people vary in how well they communicate or feel emotions. For some people, everything that happens leads to intense feelings. To them, everything is "absolutely wonderful" or, at the other extreme, everything is an "absolute disaster." Some people are very clear when they experience strong emotions, but may not be clear about how they feel when experiencing less intense emotions (hence the need to examine the situation to assist in identifying emotion).

> ### Recap
>
> #### THE DEPTH AND BREADTH OF EMOTIONS
>
> | Term | Definition |
> | --- | --- |
> | Primary emotions | The six pure emotions, according to Plutchik |
> | Mixed emotions | Emotions that are blends of primary emotions |
> | Intensity | Emotions vary in strength |

Factors That Influence Emotional Expression

We all feel emotions, so why don't we just express them? Why is that many of us readily give opinions, state facts and figures, but become tongue-tied and uncomfortable when asked to express how we feel? Obviously, people differ in this comfort level with some people telling you exactly how they feel (to the point where you want to leave the room) while others stay tight-lipped and rarely, if ever, express how they feel. There are many factors that influence how and when we express our emotions. Here we will briefly outline a few, including culture, gender, etiquette, and roles.

Culture

In Chapter 9, we will examine culture and diversity in great detail, but because of the influence of **culture** on the expression of emotion it deserves some mention here. Your culture is your learned and shared system of knowledge, beliefs, values, and norms. Earlier, you learned that some emotions are universally experienced and expressed across all cultures and are easy to identify, whereas blends of emotions are more difficult for people to identify. The culture you were born into has had profound influence upon you in many ways; one of those ways is the rules or norms of acceptable emotional expression. Cultures vary in many ways, including expressiveness of emotions, non-verbal communication of emotions, and differences in what is emotionally pleasing or displeasing.

culture. A learned system of knowledge, behaviour, attittudes, beliefs, values, and norms that is shared by a group of people.

Building Your Skills

HOW COMFORTABLE ARE YOU EXPRESSING YOUR EMOTIONS TO OTHERS?

Think of specific people for each of the following categories: an acquaintance of the same sex, an acquaintance of the opposite sex, a friend of the same sex, a friend of the opposite sex, a close friend of the same sex, a close friend of the opposite sex, a parent or relative of the same sex, and a parent or relative of the opposite sex.

Using a scale from 1 (most comfortable) to 10 (least comfortable), for each person, indicate how comfortable you would be about sharing the following feelings:

_____ liking for the other person
_____ love for the other person
_____ anger with the other person
_____ disappointment with the other person
_____ liking for a third person
_____ love for a third person
_____ anger toward a third person
_____ disappointment with a third person
_____ anger toward yourself
_____ disappointment in yourself
_____ embarrassment
_____ your fears
_____ happiness
_____ enthusiasm
_____ pride
_____ uncertainty

Compare your scores for each person. With whom are you most comfortable sharing your emotions? Compare the emotions you are most open about with the emotions you are most closed about. What makes you uncomfortable about sharing certain emotions?

---

individualistic culture.
A set of norms, values, and beliefs that emphasize the individual rather than the group.

collectivistic culture.
A set of norms, values, and beliefs that emphasize group or community rather than the individual.

high-context cultures.
Cultures that rely heavily on situational and non-verbal cues for communication of feelings.

low-context cultures.
Cultures that rely more heavily on verbal cues rather than non-verbal cues for communication of feelings.

Some cultures are more emotionally expressive than others and display their emotions more openly than other cultures. For example, one study found evidence that people from warmer climates are more emotionally expressive than those who live in cooler places.[20] **Individualistic cultures** (like Canada and the United States), which are more oriented toward the "self" rather than harmony, allow individuals to express their emotions more openly. More **collectivistic cultures** (such as Japan and China) with their emphasis on harmony, discourage members from overt displays, particularly of negative emotions such as anger or dislike.[21]

Another cultural dimension to take into consideration is the difference between **high-context** and **low-context cultures**. High-context cultures rely heavily on non-verbal cues for communication, whereas cultures classified as low-context rely more on verbal cues to communicate messages. People raised in low-context cultures may not be as adept at reading non-verbal behaviour as are individuals from high-context cultures.[22] Since many non-verbal behaviours indicate emotions, members from these cultures may fail to recognize some emotions. People from high-context cultures tend to spend less time speaking and use fewer words. High-context cultures include Japan, Greece, and Arab nations. Low-context cultures include the United States, Germany, and German-Swiss cultures.[23]

Gender

Men and women are different in how they express emotions, at least in some major areas, according to research.[24] Research continues to lend some credence to

e-connections

JAPANESE TURN E-MAIL "SMILEY FACES" RIGHT SIDE UP

TOKYO—When Yukihiro Furuse first began prowling international computer networks in the mid-1980s, he was perplexed to encounter emoticons, the strange combinations of punctuation and accent marks and letters that Westerners used in electronic mail to indicate happiness, sadness and other emotions.

But when Furuse and other network pioneers tried to incorporate symbols such as :-) into their domestic e-mail, their Japanese correspondents found the Western smiley—dare we say it—inscrutable.

"We had to write many times, 'If you tilt your head, you will see the face,'" said Furuse, who is director of the publications department at the Center for Global Communications, a research institute affiliated with International University of Japan.

So in the latest example of Japan seizing upon a Western idea, adapting it to their culture and improving upon it, Japanese computer users have evolved a unique set of emoticons. The Japanese smileys are intricate in their design, somewhat ambiguous in their expression and, in what many here would argue is a big advance, are right side up instead of sideways.

The basic smiley in Japan, (^_^), is much easier to recognize as a face than the Western version, but since the mouth doesn't curl upward (no character on the keyboard can do that), the Japanese smiley is somewhat harder to understand without knowing the context.

Source: **Andrew Pollack**, *The New York Times.*

Japanese Emoticons

Regular smile:	(^_^) (caret underscore caret)
Girl's smile:	(^.^) (caret . caret)
Banzai smiley:	\(^_^)/ backslash (caret underscore caret) /
Cold sweat:	(^^;) (caret caret ;)
Excuse me:	(^o^;>) (caret o caret; greater than symbol)
Double-byte smiley:	(^__^) (caret long underscore caret)
Exciting:	(*^o^*) (asterisk caret o caret asterisk)

---

the stereotype of the male who displays few emotions and the more emotionally expressive female. Women tend to express how they feel, whereas men are less likely to do so. Women use more emotionally expressive words than men and are quicker to express how they feel.[25] Women also tend to "show" how they feel more than men. For example, one research study found that women displayed more facial expression and had stronger physiological reactions to emotion-provoking films.[26] Also, males who scored high in masculinity on a questionnaire to assess gender identity had much less facial expressiveness than males whose results were less masculine or androgynous. Regardless of sex, people who were classified as androgynous experienced the highest levels of arousal and displayed more emotion. Interestingly, more females were androgynous than males.

Of course, these are research results; not all males lack expressiveness and not all females are expressive. Other factors must also be taken into consideration such as socialization. For instance, both men and women raised in emotionally expressive families feel stronger emotions even if only the women display the emotions.[27] Also, women and men are socialized into different gender communication cultures.[28] Games that girls favour when they are young include playing house and school, and games which include sensitivity and cooperation between players. Boys'

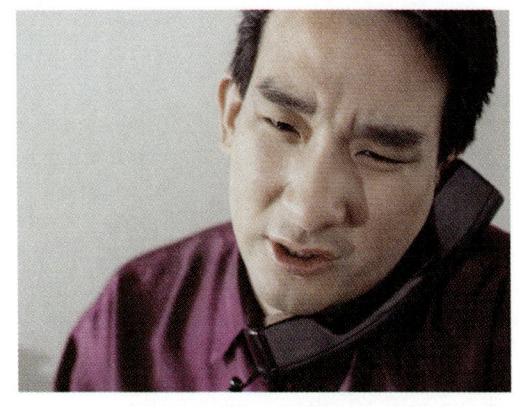

Cultures vary in many ways including expressiveness of emotions and non-verbal communication of emotions. In Japan/China individuals are discouraged from overt displays of particularly negative emotions such as anger or dislike.
(Wonderfile/Masterfile)

games, such as baseball, soccer, and war, have more clear-cut rules and rely less on talk and cooperation. Girls are taught to use talk expressively to deal with feelings, personal ideas, and problems and to build relationships. On the other hand, boys tend to use talk instrumentally to solve problems, take stands on issues, and give advice.

Etiquette

Etiquette, or the rules around what is socially appropriate or inappropriate, affects emotional expression. Many social situations have rules or norms that serve as guides to behaviour. Several of these norms also influence what constitutes appropriate emotional expression. First, many formal or public settings have social rules for emotional expression. While it may be appropriate to loudly laugh and scream in your dorm room, at a sporting event, or at a bar, few people would do the same in a funeral home or church (or other places of worship where this behaviour is frowned upon). Many workplaces also have rules that frown upon employees who are loud and boisterous when serious work is supposed to be taking place. Second, the social situation itself may dictate the type of emotional expression. People talking quietly about a recent disaster or sharing sad news would not be impressed by your latest imitation of the prime minister. This type of joking behaviour goes against the solemnity of the current topic. On the flip side, if everyone is laughing and joking, you will be seen as "bringing everyone down" if you appear glum or moody. Finally, etiquette may govern the intensity of emotional expression. When given a substantial raise by your boss, you are likely not going to literally jump up and down with joy in front of her. You will probably graciously thank your boss (then run into the washroom to jump up and down!).

Roles

The roles that people have in society also influence emotional expression. In many roles, you have to control your emotional expression. Teachers and many other professionals are expected to maintain rational behaviour and to control their emotions, particularly negative ones like anger. In other roles, such as salespeople, receptionists, and dentists, we wear a mask of pleasantry, even joviality. In other words, the roles we undertake dictate, to some extent, how much emotion we express and even what emotions we can express.

▶ Recap

FACTORS THAT INFLUENCE EMOTIONAL EXPRESSION

Factor	Definition	Example
Culture	Shared system of knowledge, beliefs, values and norms	Japan—less expressive
Gender	Masculine or feminine	Females more verbally expressive
Etiquette	Manners around how emotions should be expressed	Do not laugh at funerals
Roles	Position in society	Teacher cannot express extreme anger

Skills for Recognizing and Sharing Emotions

Since emotions range in how easily we can recognize them, we need to learn some skills to better understand the emotions of others. A second set of skills that we need to learn is to better understand our own emotions and to learn effective ways to share how we feel with others. This final and critical section will cover both areas including a special section on recognizing and dealing with difficult emotions.

Skills for Dealing with Others' Emotions

Have you ever had the experience where you completely misunderstood another person and what he or she was trying to tell you? Instead of building communication bridges, you widen the gap of misunderstanding. Here we offer some tips to help you become more skilled in understanding how others feel and how you can more appropriately respond to their emotional states. Part of being an other-oriented communicator is to try to understand and respond to how others are feeling.

Recognize Individual Differences in How Emotions Are Experienced

It can be difficult to understand another person's feelings, because the same event may have made you feel differently. This is of paramount importance for you to realize; we all respond differently even to the same event including catastrophes, losses, and even the death of loved ones. Often we make an assumption that because we are sad or happy about an event, others will also feel similarly. While one person may be sad at the loss of a parent, another person can be relieved at the death of a parent. While the event is the same, the circumstances may be very different. Some events may evoke the same emotional response, such as a beautiful ballet or a nostalgic movie, but do not assume that others will react as you do.

Be Aware That Non-verbal Expression of Emotion Is Contagious

Have you ever noticed that when you watch a funny movie, you are more likely to laugh out loud if other people around you are laughing? That when you are around people who are sad or remorseful, you are more likely to feel and express sadness? There's a reason this happens. Non-verbal emotional expressions are contagious. People often display the same emotions that a communication partner is displaying. **Emotional contagion theory** suggests that people tend to "catch" the emotions of others.[29] Interpersonal interactions with others can affect your non-verbal expression of emotions. The ancient Roman orator Cicero knew this when he gave advice to public speakers. He said, if you want your audience to experience joy, you must be a joyful speaker. Or, if you want to communicate fear, then you should express fear when you speak. Knowing that you tend to catch or imitate the emotions of others can help you interpret your own non-verbal messages and those of others; you may be imitating the emotional expression of others around you.

emotional contagion theory. Theory that emotional expression is contagious; people can "catch" emotions just by observing each other's emotional expressions.

Use Perception Checking

We have covered perception checking in Chapter 3 and will revisit it in the next chapter. Here we will illustrate its use in checking the emotions of another person. When you are unclear how another person is feeling, you can ask the person or tentatively interpret the other person's emotions. For example, if you arrive home from classes and see that your partner is "looking angry," you can check this out in a very non-threatening way by saying something like, "You look like you have had a rough day and something is troubling you. Want to talk about it?" Notice that this statement allows the other person to report back specifically how he or she is feeling without you "putting words into his or her mouth." Another way is to state what you think the person is feeling, but do so in a way that allows the other person to correct you. For example, using the above situation, you could say, "You look like you're having a bad day and something may have made you angry." By using the word *may*, the statement and hence your interpretation are not carved in stone. Perception checking opens the door for communication while minimizing the chances of the other person becoming defensive.

Use Humour

When others are feeling sadness, anger, frustration, fatigue, and other negative emotions, your use of humour can brighten a dismal day and encourage sharing. For example, a statement such as "Who let the bear in and where did my friend go?" might lighten your friend's mood and encourage talk. However, do not trivialize how another person feels with such comments or make fun of someone who is feeling low. Humour is best used when you know a person well.

Suggestions for Expressing and Managing Your Own Emotions

At home and work, we experience a broad range of feelings. Part of being an effective interpersonal communicator is to manage and communicate how you feel appropriately. Have you ever lost your temper and regretted your words later? Or did you not tell someone how you really felt only to lose the friendship or damage the relationship? If you have said yes to these questions, then you are already on your way to becoming a better "emotions manager." You have recognized that self-expression is not always an easy task, especially when you are feeling strong emotions. The following suggestions will assist you to become an even better "emotions manager" by providing you with some guidelines for expression.

Recognize Your Feelings

Sometimes, our lives get so busy and things get so hectic that we do not stop long enough to ask ourselves, "How do I feel?" When you do not take the time to gauge your emotions, they can take you by surprise. You can monitor your feelings by paying attention to the physiological signs that we discussed earlier. Your physiological state can be a clear indicator of how you are feeling. For example, your professor has requested a meeting with you after class in her office. If your hands are sweaty, your heart is beating wildly, and your mouth is dry prior to talking to your professor you may discover that you are nervous. Also, you can use your non-verbal language as a gauge of how you are feeling and how intense the emotion you are experiencing is. Before talking to your professor, are you pacing the hallway, clenching and unclenching your fists? Also, pay attention to what you are thinking. What are the thoughts that are causing this nervousness? For example, do you think you failed the last test or are in some other trouble? Maybe she wishes to speak to you about a possible summer job.

Chapter 5   Emotions and Interpersonal Communication   145

🟠 Take Ownership for Your Feelings

Often, we blame others for how we feel as if they were personally responsible for our emotional state. Have you ever said things like, "You make me so mad/happy/frustrated"? (Or fill in whatever feeling you like.) In reality, you make yourself feel the way you do; it is your perception and cognitions that often lead to your emotional state. A good example is "road rage," a term coined to refer to incidents where a driver (or drivers) engages in behaviour dangerous to others. We have all read about incidents where one driver has even stopped the other and hurt or killed the other person! In many "road rage" incidents, the victim may be unaware of his or her transgression. In other words, the driver made himself or herself angry and, as a result, behaved in dangerous, rude, or even illegal ways. We own our feelings and need to express them in that way. Instead of saying "You make me so mad," change this to "I feel mad when . . ." These "I messages" clearly state who owns the feelings: you. If you own the feelings, then you can change them by re-examining the precipitating factors or event. The Building Your Skills exercise below will assist you with a review of active listening by using "I messages." If you recall, in Chapter 2 we examined perception checking and in Chapter 6 we will look more closely at active listening which includes a component of using "I messages."

By changing your perception of an event, you can also modify your feelings. If you remember that not all drivers are out to get you, then you will likely not feel angry when someone cuts you off or turns into your path. If a co-worker continually requests help, change your perception of frustration to one a little more soothing. This co-worker requests your help because you are good at what you do and admires your skill. Later in this chapter, we will go into this strategy in more depth under Cognitive Restructuring, which is also a valuable conflict management tool. If you own your emotions, then you can change them.

Building Your Skills

DESCRIBING FEELINGS USING "I MESSAGES"

Below are statements that need rewording into "I messages." Work alone or in small groups and come up with a sentence or two that uses "I language" to describe the feeling and place ownership where it belongs. You can also try to reword the phrase to take the "sting" out so that a conflict may not occur. Remember that you are not trying to fix the problem here; you are simply going to change each statement with one that reflects correct ownership.

1. You statement: "You make me so mad when you come in so late!"

   I statement: _____

   _____

2. You statement: "There you go again! You never ask my opinion. You are so exasperating!"

   I statement: _____

   _____

3. You statement: "You continually upset me when you ask for work to be done with such short notice."

   I statement: _____

   _____

4. You statement: "You're disappointing me. You promised to have your share of the project done by today."

   I statement: _____

   _____

Think, Before You Speak

While this tip seems obvious, this suggestion is not always followed, especially when we are under the influence of powerful emotions such as anger, frustration, or sadness. We launch out with a tirade about how we feel without really thinking about our feelings or even labelling them correctly. In the earlier exercise, you had to think about feelings according to the alphabet. Instead of using simple terms like *mad, happy, great,* and *terrible,* expand your thoughts and describe your feelings in more detail. You can even use descriptions about how your body feels, such as "I'm shaking like a leaf," or "I feel all tied up in knots." These statements are more accurate and do not leave the person you are speaking to wondering what you really are feeling in a situation.

Also, use phrases so that you describe how you are feeling in more detail. Feelings do not only happen one at a time. You can be feeling many emotions simultaneously. You may not just be mad at your partner. You may also be disappointed or embarrassed. If your roommate gets drunk at a party and shares a confidence loudly to everyone, you may feel angry and disappointed at the betrayal. You might also feel embarrassed to watch a friend act so foolishly. These are the feelings that you want to describe, not just the anger.

---

e-connections

NETIQUETTE: NETWORK ETIQUETTE

While we may want to think before we speak, we may also want to think before we "write." The Internet offers us many chances to express ourselves to others in an environment that is very different from face-to-face communication (see Chapter 11 for much more information on the use of the Internet for interpersonal communication and relationship development). While it may be easier for some people to "let loose" while communicating with others in cyberspace, we still have to remember that it is a person on the other end. It may be wise to think about what you are saying before you hit the "send" button.

There are various prescriptive lists describing how to behave appropriately on the Internet. The following is one such list that provides 10 rules of "Netiquette":

Rule 1. Remember the human.
Rule 2. Adhere to the same standards of behavior online that you follow in real life.
Rule 3. Know where you are in cyberspace.
Rule 4. Respect other people's time and bandwidth.
Rule 5. Make yourself look good online.
Rule 6. Share expert knowledge.
Rule 7. Help keep flame wars under control.
Rule 8. Respect other people's privacy.
Rule 9. Don't abuse your power.
Rule 10. Be forgiving of other people's mistakes.

Source: The above core rules of Netiquette by Virginia Shea appear courtesy of the author and Albion.com. For a further discussion and explanation of these and other rules for behaviour on the Internet, you can find Netiquette at the following website: www.albion.com/netiquette/book/index.html

---

Know When to Feel, Talk, or Act

Sometimes we need to get in touch with how we feel before expressing ourselves or acting on those feelings. When something happens to you, you may have many feelings that you need to sort out. For example, if your girlfriend breaks up with you, you can experience a lot of feelings—anger, sadness, confusion, disbelief—and you need time to sort these feelings out. Talking about your feelings can help you understand them and it may be appropriate to confide in a friend or family member to help you sort through your feelings. If you are experiencing a trauma or cannot understand your feelings, professional counselling can be a valuable way to talk about your experiences.

Often, people act too quickly, even rashly, without thinking about their feelings or even talking about them with another. People who rebound into other relationships, for example, have not worked through their feelings and are often headed toward further relationship disaster.

▶ Recap

GUIDELINES FOR EXPRESSING EMOTIONS

Suggestion	Examples
Recognize Your Feelings	"My hands are sweaty. I think I'm nervous."
Own Your Feelings	"I'm the one who is getting angry."
Think, Before You Speak	"I'm not really mad; I'm more frustrated."
Know When to Feel, Talk, or Act	"I'm going to count to 10, before I say anything."

Dealing with Some Difficult Emotional States

During many situations in our lives, we may experience a wide range of emotions, including frustration, sadness, hopelessness, surprise, and anger. These emotions are classified as difficult because we do not (usually) enjoy experiencing them and may have problems managing them. We also do not enjoy dealing with people who are very angry, frustrated, or sad. Here we will examine three of the more common difficult emotional states that you may experience personally or encounter when working or assisting others: frustration, anger, and sadness. As well, we will briefly look at aggression within the topic of anger, because extreme anger or rage can easily result in aggression. Clients or others that you work with or have contact with may behave aggressively.

Frustration

Frustration occurs when an individual is blocked from doing something he or she wants to do; behaviour toward a goal is thwarted. For example, if you are headed for an important appointment and have to drive behind a very slow driver, you may experience frustration, thinking you may be late. The experience of frustration may be the antecedent to conflict. For example, people who feel frustrated when driving may act out their frustration by tailgating or honking their horn, which may create conflict with the other driver.

According to some research, frustration can lead to anger and subsequent aggression. The original **frustration-aggression hypothesis**[30] proposed that frustration led to a tendency toward aggression. In other words, aggression was preceded by frustration. Later theories[31] have included the cognitive component of appraisal. People think about the event and, based on their appraisal of it, decide whether or not the event is frustrating. If they appraise it as extremely frustrating, they may become angry and aggressive. In other words, how you perceive the event and the extent to which it arouses negative feelings influence how much aggression

frustration. The feeling that occurs when an individual is blocked from achieving a goal.

frustration-aggression hypothesis. The hypothesis that aggression occurs as a result of frustration.

you will display, if any. For example, if the appointment is not that important to you or is perhaps distasteful (such as having a root canal), you may experience less frustration.

Canadian Issues

DEALING WITH YOUR EMOTIONS IN THE WAKE OF A TRAUMATIC EVENT

What would it be like to have something so horrible happen to you that you could not even imagine the consequences? How would you feel? Ian Stewart knows all too well the feelings that ran through his mind in the weeks and months after his terrible ordeal. These are a few excerpts from the story of Ian Stewart, a Canadian journalist, who was shot on January 9, 1999, while covering a civil war in Africa. His award-winning story from November 24, 1999, is his account of what he has gone through and what he is going through as he courageously struggles back towards health after being shot in the head:

I floated in a grey fog illuminated by the flickering of fluorescent lights. Someone was calling my name over and over, but the voice sounded far away. Blurry faces hovered over me. Shadows, then gone . . .

Wavering on that boundary between sleep and awareness, I couldn't lift my head from the pillow. . . . Something was awfully wrong. Why couldn't I feel my leg?

Weeks drifted by. The mist that had enshrouded my brain began to lift. Destruction and death haunted my hospital dreams. Silhouettes of palm trees swayed against a cobalt sky streaked red and yellow by tracer bullets. Waking hours were no better. Lying on rubber sheets, I struggled to stop the walls as they spun by.

Adding to the torment, I have never been able to remember what happened when we were shot. With no recollection of the most cataclysmic moment of my life, each day is a battle against the incomprehensible.

Of course, I have been told how it happened. Our station wagon turned a corner and came upon five armed men in American-style jeans and flip-flops. Oddly, one was wearing a bowler hat. He raised his automatic rifle and fired a burst. Our escort returned fire, killing the shooter and another rebel. It was over in seconds. David had been cut by flying glass. I had been shot in the head. Myles had been killed instantly, the 24th AP journalist to die in the line of duty in the organization's 151 years. . . .

Over the next several hours, David and AP Abidjan correspondent Tim Sullivan (now bureau chief) saved my life, pleading and cajoling my way onto a succession of airplanes that would hop across Africa and on to England and modern medical care. It was late Monday night by the time I was carried into London's Hospital for Neurology and Neurosurgery. With the dirty field dressing still around my head, I was wheeled past a shocked couple who had just rushed from Toronto. . . .

I can't say when I began to realize the gravity of my wound. Because of the very nature of a brain injury, patients often find it hard to understand and almost impossible to accept. The consequences of my injury were almost entirely physical. My left arm and hand were paralysed, my left leg impaired. . . .

But there were other complications. For days, I struggled just to understand where I was. . . . My brain was a crystal goblet shattered into a million slivers of fading dreams and dashed hopes. I have been piecing it back together, one sliver at a time. . . . Ten weeks after the shooting, I returned to my parents' home on Toronto's Lake Ontario waterfront.

For months I have struggled to adjust to life with a disability. I don't ever want to forget even the smallest detail of this experience. Two months after returning to Toronto, I have improved enough to walk with a cane. On June 3, a Thursday, I walk into a medical supply centre to return my wheelchair.

Once I was an athlete, a football player. Now I shuffle a few yards, stop to catch my breath, sit for a spell. As a wire service reporter, I used to whip out several stories a day. Now I spend months on this one, pecking at the keys with my one good hand. My therapist says that in time, my left arm will regain some function. How much is impossible to say. . . .

Myles, David and I were naive to hope our reporting could make people care about a little war in Africa. In fact, Freetown might never have made your daily newspaper had it not been for the death of one western journalist and wounding of another.

Will I continue to work as a journalist when I am well enough to work? Yes, and most likely I'll go back overseas.

Will I risk my life for a story again? No. Not even if the world cares next time.

Source: Ian Stewart, "A Long Journey Home." Associated Press, November 24, 1999, www.apme.com/writing_awards/stewart_story.html. Used with permission of the Associated Press.

🔶 Anger

Anger is a common experience during a conflict. We all know that feeling—anger. It can build slowly or suddenly ignite, and it can make it hard to maintain control of oneself. **Anger** is a feeling of extreme hostility, indignation, or exasperation. Anger is stimulated when appraisal indicates that others are responsible for the achievement of an individual's goal. If you feel that someone is getting in the way of achieving something, you may become angry. Anger creates stress and brings about a number of physiological changes that were discussed earlier. Internally, the heart rate increases, blood pressure increases, galvanic skin responses change, and breathing becomes shallower and quicker. But we cannot see these changes and need the help of other indicators that we can see when standing at a distance.

Recent research has shed some light on two types of maladaptive anger, termed anger-in and anger-out.[32] According to Martin and Wan, people prone to anger-in responses suffer frequent, ruminative angry feelings. These feelings do not go away and colour future judgments and appraisals. Those who experience anger-out lash out at others, doing such things as slamming doors, striking out at others, and being verbally abusive and threatening. Both types of anger contribute to the development of cardiovascular disease.

Non-verbal Signals of Anger Outwardly, there may be several physical non-verbal indicators of anger that you can see if you are close enough. If the person is breathing more rapidly, you may notice it if the individual is wearing tighter-fitting clothing around the chest. While most people do not lose control when they are angry, it is good to know levels of anger and when to identify clues that someone's angry behaviour is escalating. One noticeable indicator of anger is enlargement of the pupils, which creates the look known as "wide-eyed with rage."[33]

According to Ouellette,[34] a trainer in managing aggressive behaviour, there are three areas of non-verbal behaviour that can reveal anger. Gestures, including facial colour, can give many clues about anger. A person's face may redden if the person is light-skinned. However, when a person becomes extremely angry (rage), the face may drain of all colour—a sign of possible physical attack. Opening and closing fists and baring teeth are two other important gestures to examine.

Second, he recommends that the person's eyes be closely monitored. Eyes that dart from side to side or up and down may indicate that the person feels trapped. "Target glances" occur when a person looks at a target person before attack. For example, the person may look at your chin before trying to hit it. If the person is going to attempt to flee, he or she may glance at possible exits.[35]

The third area that can reveal anger is the use of space. A person may try to close the distance when angry. People who are more aggressive try to intimidate by controlling personal space such as moving closer to the individual they are trying to control or manipulate. Have you ever had the experience with someone who is angry when they move closer to you and jab you in the shoulder with a finger? How do you feel? Do you feel angry yourself? Do you feel defensive?

It is also important that we learn to recognize the signs of our own anger. By recognizing when we are becoming angry, we can work on controlling our anger so that we don't do something that we may regret later. Being in control of such strong emotions will decrease the chances of doing or saying something that may have personal and/or professional repercussions. The Building Your Skills activity on page 150 discusses some techniques to help manage anger.

---

anger. A feeling of hostility, indignation, or exasperation.

Building Your Skills

DEALING WITH YOUR ANGER

There is no doubt about it: we all get angry both on and off the job. Your ability to manage your anger is crucial for a successful career in any number of fields. There will be plenty of opportunities for you to feel angry: the uncooperative client, the store clerk who calls you names, the person who wants to take you on physically after jumping out of her car. And these are just a few examples! So what can you do about all of this anger? Here are a few tips to manage it:

1. **Channel your anger.** Anger can be an energizing force and this force can be used in positive ways. If you are still angry after an encounter with a hostile customer or client, use the energy to finish paperwork.
2. **Make a conscious decision about whether to express your anger.** Rather than just letting anger and frustration build and erupt out of control, make a conscious choice about whether you should express your frustration and irritation. We're not denying that there are valid reasons for you to express anger and frustration or suggesting that you should not express your feelings. Sometimes there is no way to let someone know how important an issue is to you other than by forcefully expressing your irritation or anger. If you do decide to express your anger, don't lose control. Be direct and descriptive. The guidelines for listening and responding that we provided in Chapter 4 can serve you well. Keep your anger focused on issues rather than personalities.
3. **Express your anger before it reaches a peak.** Sometimes people are unaware that you are angry. If you decide to express your anger, discuss it right away rather than letting it simmer. If it simmers too long, it can boil over. If your partner insults someone you like, let him or her know right away about your feelings.
4. **Think before you act.** The old standard of "counting to 10" may not be a bad idea. Remember that all actions and words have consequences. You can lose your job or your credibility by acting rashly.
5. **Recognize when you are angry.** This may sound simple to do, but some people are not aware that they are angry. By being sensitive to your own physiological signs, you can learn to recognize anger long before it overwhelms you.
6. **Realize that you are responsible for how you feel.** While such a suggestion can be difficult to believe, you do make yourself angry. By changing your perception, you can change the feeling. By owning your feelings, you can change them.

---

e-connections

WHAT'S YOUR STYLE OF ARGUING WITH OTHERS?

When we are angry we often argue with others, even letting the argument get out of hand. How do you argue with others? Do you tenaciously keep arguing even at the expense of someone's feelings or do you back down if you sense you're crossing the line of fair fighting or arguing with others? To assess your arguing style, click on the following Web address:

www.psychtests.com/arguingstyle.html

---

verbal aggressiveness.
Using words in a way that causes pain and attacks another person's self-concept.

Verbal Aggression When some people are very angry, they may also become verbally aggressive. Why are some people verbally aggressive? There may be any of several reasons.[36] As noted in Chapters 1 and 2, recent research emphasizing what is called the "communibiological approach to communication" suggests that we are each born with certain traits or characteristics.[37] It's just the nature of some people to be verbally aggressive. Being verbally aggressive is also closely linked to the concept of seeking power in a relationship.[38] Verbally aggressive people often use hurtful language as a way of gaining or maintaining power over others. They may learn that they can get what they want by bullying others. As long as they continue to get what they want and are reinforced for their heavy-handed verbal aggressiveness, they will continue to do it. Still other people are verbally aggressive as a way of expressing bottled-up emotions and frustrations. And finally, verbal aggressiveness is contagious. When one person is verbally aggressive, the other person is likely to reciprocate.[39]

What should you do if you are a victim of verbal aggressiveness? The simple and obvious answer is to avoid relationships with people who are verbally aggressive. The verbally aggressive person may need more power and confirmation of his or her own worth; trying to find constructive strategies to let the aggressor know he or she is valued may help. But if long-held patterns of being verbally aggressive are present, don't expect quick or dramatic changes in the aggressive person by just offering him or her compliments. Verbally aggressive comments by others are often triggered by anger just as the non-verbal elements are triggered. The Building Your Skills activity below will help you to assess your own verbal aggressiveness.

Verbally aggressive people often use hurtful language as a way of gaining or maintaining power over others. (PhotoDisc)

Building Your Skills

ASSESSING YOUR VERBAL AGGRESSIVENESS

The following scale is designed to assess your verbal aggressiveness. Use the following scale:

1 = Almost never true
2 = Rarely true
3 = Occasionally true
4 = Often true
5 = Almost always true

HOW VERBALLY AGGRESSIVE ARE YOU?

_____ 1. I am extremely careful to avoid attacking individuals' intelligence when I attack their ideas.

_____ 2. When individuals are very stubborn, I use insults to soften the stubbornness.

_____ 3. I try very hard to avoid having other people feel bad about themselves when I try to influence them.

_____ 4. When people refuse without good reason to do a task I know is important, I tell them they are unreasonable.

_____ 5. When others do things I regard as stupid, I try to be extremely gentle with them.

_____ 6. If individuals I am trying to influence really deserve it, I attack their character.

_____ 7. When people behave in ways that are in very poor taste, I insult them in order to shock them into proper behavior.

_____ 8. I try to make people feel good about themselves even when their ideas are stupid.

_____ 9. When people simply will not budge on a matter of importance, I lose my temper and say rather strong things to them.

_____ 10. When people criticize my shortcomings, I take it in good humor and do not try to get back at them.

_____ 11. When individuals insult me, I get a lot of pleasure out of really telling them off.

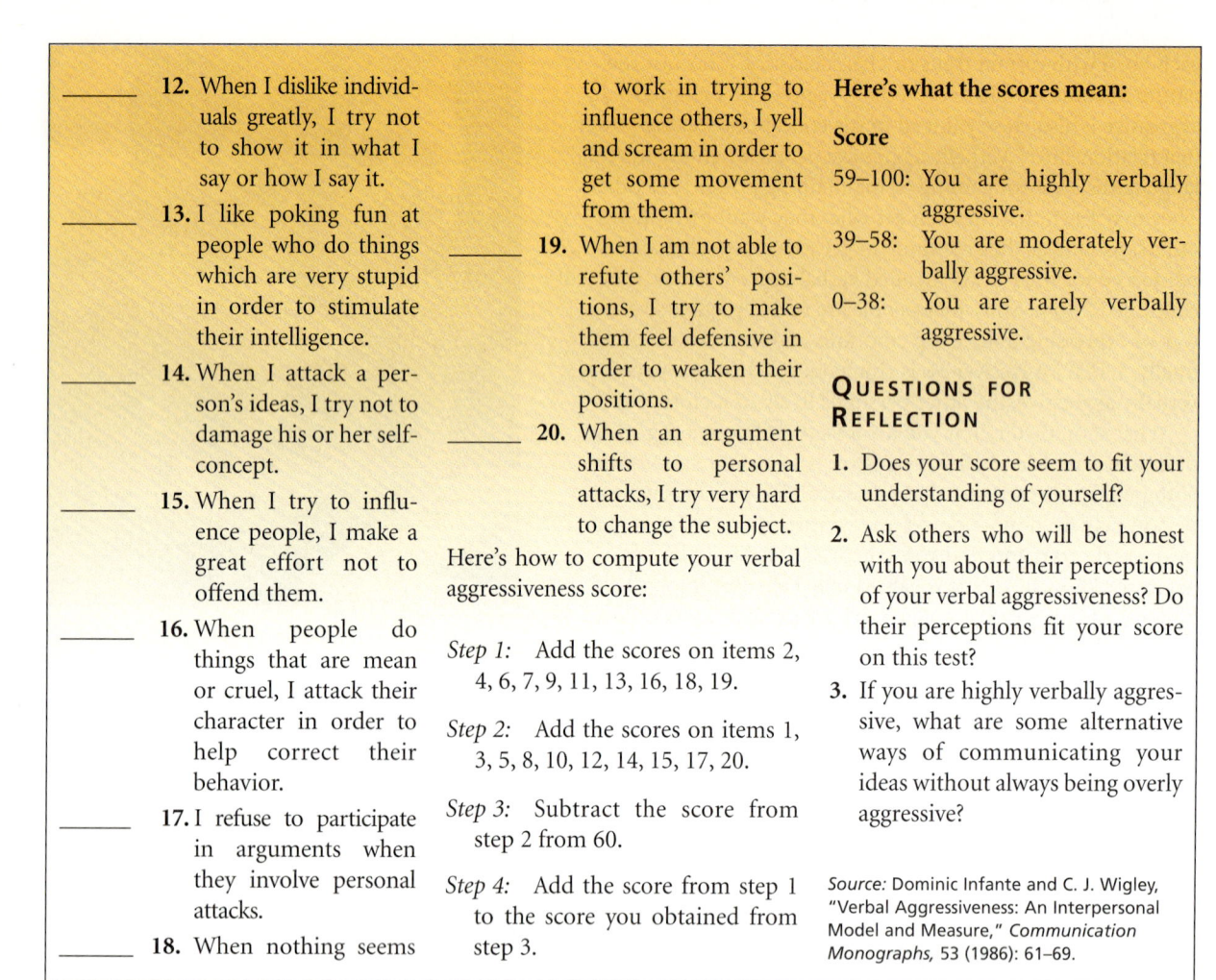

_____ 12. When I dislike individuals greatly, I try not to show it in what I say or how I say it.

_____ 13. I like poking fun at people who do things which are very stupid in order to stimulate their intelligence.

_____ 14. When I attack a person's ideas, I try not to damage his or her self-concept.

_____ 15. When I try to influence people, I make a great effort not to offend them.

_____ 16. When people do things that are mean or cruel, I attack their character in order to help correct their behavior.

_____ 17. I refuse to participate in arguments when they involve personal attacks.

_____ 18. When nothing seems to work in trying to influence others, I yell and scream in order to get some movement from them.

_____ 19. When I am not able to refute others' positions, I try to make them feel defensive in order to weaken their positions.

_____ 20. When an argument shifts to personal attacks, I try very hard to change the subject.

Here's how to compute your verbal aggressiveness score:

Step 1: Add the scores on items 2, 4, 6, 7, 9, 11, 13, 16, 18, 19.

Step 2: Add the scores on items 1, 3, 5, 8, 10, 12, 14, 15, 17, 20.

Step 3: Subtract the score from step 2 from 60.

Step 4: Add the score from step 1 to the score you obtained from step 3.

Here's what the scores mean:

Score

59–100: You are highly verbally aggressive.

39–58: You are moderately verbally aggressive.

0–38: You are rarely verbally aggressive.

QUESTIONS FOR REFLECTION

1. Does your score seem to fit your understanding of yourself?

2. Ask others who will be honest with you about their perceptions of your verbal aggressiveness? Do their perceptions fit your score on this test?

3. If you are highly verbally aggressive, what are some alternative ways of communicating your ideas without always being overly aggressive?

Source: Dominic Infante and C. J. Wigley, "Verbal Aggressiveness: An Interpersonal Model and Measure," *Communication Monographs,* 53 (1986): 61–69.

Sadness

While sadness may not be the first emotion that crosses your mind as being a part of conflict, during or after a heated argument many people display sadness. **Sadness** covers a range of feelings from slight gloominess to overwhelming grief.

All of us experience sadness and it can be a difficult emotion to manage. Sadness is a normal emotion and does not mean that something is wrong with us. Events that provoke sadness are often ones where we experience a loss: a friend, a romantic partner, a cherished possession, death of someone close to us. We can even become sad when we think about how things should have been or how things used to be. And how many of us have a "good" cry during a movie? Do not confuse normal sadness with **depression**. Depression is characterized by overwhelming feelings of gloom, despondency, and dejection. While you may feel depressed, only if there are several other long-term symptoms, such as diminished interest in everyday activities and pleasures, significant weight gain or loss, profound changes in sleeping habits (sleeping too much or insomnia), or loss of energy, would you be classified as experiencing depression. If these feelings and symptoms become extreme, you should get help immediately. If you notice these symptoms in someone you know well, you may want to encourage this person to also gain assistance.[40]

sadness. A range of emotions that include feelings of gloominess and grief.

depression. Refers to a sad and despairing mood or a clinical disorder characterized by feelings of sadness, loss of energy, fatigue, and appetite and sleeping changes.

Chapter 5 Emotions and Interpersonal Communication   153

Other than these obvious signs, what are the non-verbal indicators of sadness? A person who is sad may "droop" with sloping shoulders and appear to be "hunched into himself or herself." The mouth is downturned, and the chin may wobble as if the person were about to cry. A sad person may have difficulty with eye contact, and any talk about the problem may evoke an outpour of crying. The person may breathe irregularly as he or she tries to maintain control and keep emotions in check.

One research study that focused on women found that sadness was an indicator in depression and was the dominant mood and emotion of the subjects.[41] Other symptoms of depression include low mood, feelings of helplessness and hopelessness, negative attitudes about the self, and an inability to experience happiness or joy.

> ## Recap

DEALING WITH DIFFICULT EMOTIONAL STATES

Emotion	Definition	Example
Frustration	Blocked from a goal	Slow traffic when you are late for work and you tailgate the car in front of you
Anger	Feeling of extreme hostility, indignation, or exasperation	Friend is thirty minutes late for lunch date
Sadness	Feelings ranging from mild gloominess to grief	News of a friend's death causes you to feel very gloomy

Managing Difficult Emotions When You Experience Them

Many of the earlier suggestions about managing your own emotions will also assist in helping you deal with these difficult emotions. However, emotions that are experienced frequently and interfere with you functioning effectively can be extremely debilitating. **Debilitating emotions** are intense and last a long time. For example, if I am angry at a co-worker because she is always late and I have to do extra work until she comes in, I can handle that anger appropriately through confrontation. I can say, "Sheila, you are consistently late and I end up doing your work. If it happens again, I will go the boss. I will no longer pick up your slack." But what if I become enraged or let it bubble up inside me over a long period of time? This becomes a debilitating emotion. There have been many cases of such rage in the workplace leading a disgruntled worker to come back and shoot his co-workers. So how can you manage these debilitating emotions so that you do not become depressed, engraged, or so frustrated that you cannot cope? Here we offer several suggestions to assist you in managing powerful emotions such as anger.

debilitating emotions. Emotions that are very intense and long-term, and can ultimately negatively affect behaviour.

Be Aware That You Are Becoming Angry and Emotionally Volatile

One characteristic of people who "lose it" is that they let their emotions get the best of them. Before they know it, they are saying and doing things that they later regret. Unbridled and uncensored emotional outbursts rarely enhance the quality of an interpersonal relationship. An emotional purge may make you feel better, but your partner is likely to reciprocate, which will only escalate the conflict spiral.

Before that happens, become aware of what is happening to you. As we described earlier, your body will start to react to your emotions with an increased heart rate. Be mindful of such changes. Be sensitive to what is happening to you physically.

Seek to Understand Why You Are Angry and Emotional

Understanding what's behind your anger can help you manage it. Earlier we discussed that we need to recognize our emotions. The same is true for anger. Realize that it is normal and natural to be angry. It's a feeling everyone experiences. You need not feel guilty about it. Anger is often expressed as a defence when you feel violated. Two powerful anger triggers are (1) you don't think you have been treated fairly, and (2) you feel entitled to something that you are being denied. Think about the last time you became very angry. Chances are your angry outburst stemmed from a sense that you were not treated fairly or that someone denied you something you were entitled to. Often there is a sense of righteous indignation when you are angry. You are being denied something you feel you should have.

Breathe

One of the simplest yet most effective ways to avoid overheating is to breathe. As you become aware that your emotions are starting to erupt, take a slow, deep, calm, unnoticeable breath. Then breathe again. This can help calm you and manage the physiological changes that adrenaline creates. Deep breathing—the prime strategy women use to manage the pain of childbirth—can powerfully help restore calmness to your spirit. Focusing on your breathing is also one of the primary methods of meditation. We're not suggesting that you hyperventilate. But unobtrusively breathing, a deep, slow breath that doesn't just fill your upper lungs, but starts in your diaphragm—the muscles that support your lungs—is an active strategy to help you regain rational control.

Restructure Your Thoughts and Feelings

Albert Ellis, the "father" of *rational emotive therapy,* believes that the thoughts we have about ourselves influence our feelings, and ultimately our behaviour.[42] Ellis believes that we often hold on to irrational beliefs and that these beliefs can cause us many problems. Some of these beliefs include setting and worrying about impossible goals, believing that one event will affect our lives forever, believing we should be perfect, believing that everyone should like us, or believing that we can't control how we feel. If we hold these irrational beliefs long enough, we experience emotional and psychological problems (such as depression) and will start to behave in maladaptive ways. He believes that by changing irrational thoughts we can change or restructure our feelings. To change these irrational thoughts, we have to recognize these thoughts as irrational and change the thoughts to rational ones. One irrational thought is to hold onto the notion that everyone should like you. Ask yourself why this should be so. Such a thought can lead to a large amount of stress as you attempt to get others to like you. But what if you could change this thought to something like, "Not everyone has to like me. I know that I am a good person. I will meet people who are not going to like me or want to get to know me and that's okay."

Since our emotions come from within through our own "self-talking" based on irrational thoughts, changing what you tell yourself can change how you feel. For example, if someone cuts you off while you are driving, instead of thinking, "You @#$@E###" and feeling angry, try to reframe or restructure the event. You could say to yourself, "Maybe he is in a hurry because he is on his way to an emergency," or "It was not me personally he was cutting off; it was my car and he's just a lousy driver."

Use Positive Self-Talk

If we can make ourselves feel bad through negative self-talk, then positive self-talk should help us feel better. When we talk to students, we often hear the outcomes of negative self-talk. "I'll never pass the final," "I'm not smart enough for this course," or "I can't do it." Prior to telling us these things, students have been telling themselves these things. Inside, they are saying over and over, "I can't do it," "I'm not smart enough," and a host of other negative things. After a while these negative statements lead to negative beliefs, and unfortunately negative outcomes. But what if you say to yourself, "I can pass this course," "I am smart enough," and "I can do it." When you feel positive, you may be more likely to try rather than to give up and feel sad or angry. These positive beliefs that you can do something are also referred to as **self-efficacy**—an individual's belief that he or she can perform some behaviour or task successfully.[43] If you tell yourself that you can pass an exam, and study for the exam while you continue to engage in positive self-thoughts, you are more likely to pass that exam! Research on self-efficacy has been found to play a role in success on many tasks[44] and in managing stress,[45] and is linked to personal happiness and life satisfaction.[46]

self-efficacy. An individual's belief that he or she can perform some behaviour or task successfully.

Get Help

If you have been feeling frustrated, angry, or sad for a long period of time, do not hesitate to get help. Talking to others is an excellent way to more fully understand your feelings. People who have had similar experiences can help you deal with your emotions while providing a supportive environment. Just sharing your feelings often puts them into perspective and gives you ideas about how to manage the events that are triggering such feelings. For example, a student talked to one author about her problems with her roommate. The roommate never cleaned up and the apartment was a mess. She was angry and frustrated. After talking about the problem, she felt calmer and a couple of strategies were developed to assist in coping with the "sloppy roommate."

As we stated earlier, many emotional states such as sadness may also be a symptom of more debilitating states such as depression. Debilitating emotions can be a sign that something is wrong, such as too much stress. Talk to a counsellor, your religious leader, your doctor, friends, or your family. Intense emotions experienced over a long period of time can ruin both your mental and physical health. Talk to someone who will listen and who has the knowledge and experience to help you.

Talking to others is an excellent way to more fully understand your feelings. Others who have had similar experiences can help you deal with your emotions while providing a supportive environment.
(Amy Etra/PhotoEdit)

▶ Recap

MANAGING YOUR OWN DIFFICULT EMOTIONS

Suggestion	Example
Be Aware That You Are Becoming Emotional	"I can feel the anger welling up in me."
Seek to Understand Why You Are Angry and Emotional	"I feel that I'm not being given a chance."
Breathe	"Okay, I'm going to relax my body."
Restructure Your Thoughts and Feelings	"I can look at this another way."
Use Positive Self-Talk	"I'm a good person and I can handle this crisis."
Get Help	"I'm going to talk to Mom about this one!"

Summary

In this chapter, we have examined emotions. Emotions are reactions to the environment and involve three different components. First, there are physiological effects, influenced by the autonomic nervous system creating various levels of arousal. Second, emotions are influenced by our thoughts or interpretation of the event and of the arousal. Third, emotions are displayed through behaviour, which is how we interpret the emotions of others. Some research indicates that some emotions are universal or expressed similarly across cultures. Emotions can be divided up into primary emotions and mixed or blended emotions. Mixed emotions are more difficult to interpret as they are more complex. Emotions also vary in intensity and are influenced by individual differences.

Culture, gender, and roles are factors that influence emotional expression. Your culture influences how you are to express your emotions and how intensely you are allowed in that expression. Individualistic cultures allow more emotional expression than collectivistic cultures. High-context cultures rely more heavily on non-verbal cues for message communication than do low-context cultures.

To help you recognize others' emotions, you need to learn to recognize individual differences in expression, be aware that non-verbal expression of emotions is contagious, use perception checking to ensure that you accurately understand how the other person feels, and use humour when appropriate. To manage your own emotions, you should recognize when you are experiencing an emotion, take ownership of your feelings, think before speaking, and know when to feel, talk, and act on emotions. Some emotions may be difficult to experience or manage in others. These emotions include frustration, anger and aggression, and sadness. To manage these more debilitating emotions, be aware that you are becoming angry and emotionally volatile, seek to understand why you are angry and emotional, breathe, try cognitive restructuring, and use positive self-talk. If necessary, get help to assist you in managing difficult emotions.

Chapter 5   Emotions and Interpersonal Communication

For Discussion and Review

Focus on Comprehension

1. What are emotions?
2. Identify the three components of emotions.
3. Why are some emotions so difficult to manage? Discuss two difficult emotions, citing examples from your own experiences.

Focus on Critical Thinking

4. Do you think that men are becoming more emotionally expressive over the last few years or are they still less expressive than women? Support your answer.
5. Pierre is taking a business trip to Korea. He has never been to Asia. What advice would you give Pierre so that he will fit in with the business people he will be meeting with in Korea?

Focus on Ethics

6. Is it ethical to pretend to feel emotions that you are not experiencing, such as pretending to be happy when you are not? Why or why not?
7. Twelve-year-old Nathan consistently does not get along with his other brothers and sisters. He also is not doing well in school. He appears to be angry all the time. His parents want to take him to a counsellor, but Nathan does not want to go. Should Nathan's parents insist that he attend counselling? Why or why not?

For Your Journal

1. Select two TV situation comedies or dramas that revolve around people working or living together. Observe how characters manage each other's emotions. Draw on the principles and skills presented in this chapter as you describe the techniques. You may even want to discuss which of your TV characters seem to do the most effective job of communicating with one another.
2. Describe what someone would learn about your family in regards to emotions and emotional expression if they were to view only the non-verbal elements of the way your family interacts. For example, imagine someone viewing a videotape of your family's daily activities, with the "sound turned off." Consider not only such factors as facial expression of emotion, eye contact, touch, and use of personal space, but also the way your home is arranged and the overall appearance of your family's dwelling.

Learning with Others

1. Although this is a leadership exercise and will be referred to in a later chapter, it is also a good activity to further understand emotions in a group process. Read the following case study and complete the instructions. Then compare your group's task list and communication strategies with those of other groups.

Hurricane Preparedness Case

Although you have idly watched local meteorologists track Hurricane Bruce's destructive course through the Caribbean for several days, you have not given any serious thought to the possibility that the number 3–rated storm might directly affect your coastal city. However, at about 7:00 A.M. today, the storm suddenly veered northward, putting it on course for a direct hit. Now the National Hurricane Center in Miami has posted a hurricane warning for your community. Forecasters are predicting landfall in approximately 9 to 12 hours. Having taken no advance precautions, you are stunned by the amount of work you now must do to secure your three-bedroom suburban home, which is about a kilometre from the beach, and to protect your family—your spouse and two children ages 5 and 12.

You have enough food in the house for two days. You also have one candle and a transistor radio with one weak battery. You have no other hurricane supplies, nor have you taken any hurricane precautions. Your group's task is to identify specific strategies for (1) ensuring the survival and safety of your family and property, (2) assigning appropriate tasks to family members to carry out these strategies, and (3) identifying your feelings as if you were really experiencing such a natural disaster. First, brainstorm a list or sequence of events or lists of tasks that you need to accomplish. Then arrange them in priority order. Finally, decide the best way to assign and explain these tasks to various family members. Make notes about your decisions. As you go through this experience, have one person record all of the emotions you might be feeling if this was really happening.

Weblinks

www.canoe.ca/CNEWSFeatures9911/34-long.html Read the entire story by Ian Stewart of his long road to recovery from being shot in Africa.

www.seorf.ohiou.edu/~af313/Brain/EmotionalQ/eq.htm Find out about your emotional IQ!

http://fccjvm.fcci.cc.us/~jwisner/face.htm This website is about facial feedback and experiencing emotions.

Suggested Readings

Goldshmidt, Orly Tugeman. "'Talking Emotions': Gender Differences in a Variety of Conversational Contexts." *Symbolic Interaction,* 23(2), (2000): 117–135.
   This article discusses a study about gender differences in language and emotions.

Kring, Ann M., and Albert H. Gordon. "Sex Differences in Emotional Expression." *Harvard Mental Health Letter,* 16(3), (1999): 6–8.
   This is a short overview of an experiment examining the differences of males and females in experiencing and expressing emotions.

chapter 6

Communicating Verbally

After you study this chapter

you should be able to...

1. Describe the relationship between words and meaning.
2. Understand how words influence us and our culture.
3. Identify word barriers and know how to manage them.
4. Discuss how the words we use affect our relationships with others.
5. Understand supportive approaches to relating to others.
6. Understand how to confirm other people's sense of themselves.

- Words and Meaning
- Recognizing the Power of Words
- Avoiding Word Barriers
- Using Words to Establish Supportive Relationships
- Using Words to Value Others

Words can destroy. What we call each other ultimately becomes what we think of each other, and it matters.

JEANNE J. KIRKPATRICK

Words are powerful. Those who use them skillfully can exert great influence with just a few of them. Consider these notable achievements:

Shakespeare expressed the quintessence of the human condition in Hamlet's famous "To be or not to be" soliloquy—363 words long.

Several of our great religions adhere to a comprehensive moral code expressed in a mere 297 words: the Ten Commandments.

Words have great power in our private lives as well. We have seen that emotions can also be powerful. We express those emotions verbally with words and non-verbally with actions. In this chapter we will examine ways to use words more effectively in interpersonal relationships. We'll investigate how to harness the power that words have to affect your feelings, thoughts, and actions, and we'll describe links between language and culture. We will also identify communication barriers that may keep you from using words effectively and note strategies and skills for managing those barriers. Finally, we will examine the role of speech in establishing supportive relationships with others. In one of his pessimistic moments, the poet Robert Frost said, "Half the world is composed of people who have something to say and can't, and the other half who have nothing to say and keep on saying it." This chapter is designed to help you become that person who has something to say and can say it well.

Words and Meaning

As you read the printed words on this page, how are you able to make sense out of these black marks? When you hear words spoken by others, how are you able to interpret those sounds? Although there are several theories that attempt to explain how we learn language and ascribe meaning to both printed and uttered words, there is no single universally held view that neatly clarifies the mystery. We can, however, better understand the nature of words by taking a closer look at what words are and how they function.

Words Are Symbols

symbol. A word, sound, or visual device that represents a thought, concept, or object.

referent. The thing that a symbol represents.

thought. The mental process of creating a category, idea, or image triggered by a referent or symbol.

As we noted in Chapter 1, words are **symbols** that represent something else. A printed word triggers an image, sound, concept, or experience. Take the word *cat*, for instance. The word may conjure up in your mind's eye a hissing creature with bared claws and fangs. Or, perhaps you envision a cherished pet curled up by a fireplace.

The classic model in Figure 6.1 was developed by one pair of researchers to explain how we use words as symbols, noting relationships between *symbols* (words), *referents*, and *thoughts*.[1] **Referents** are the things the symbols (words) represent. **Thought** is the mental process of creating a category, idea, or image triggered by the referent or the symbol. So, these three elements, words, referents, and thoughts, become inextricably linked. Although some scholars find this model too simplistic to explain how we link all words to a meaning, it does illustrate the process for most concepts, people, and tangible things.

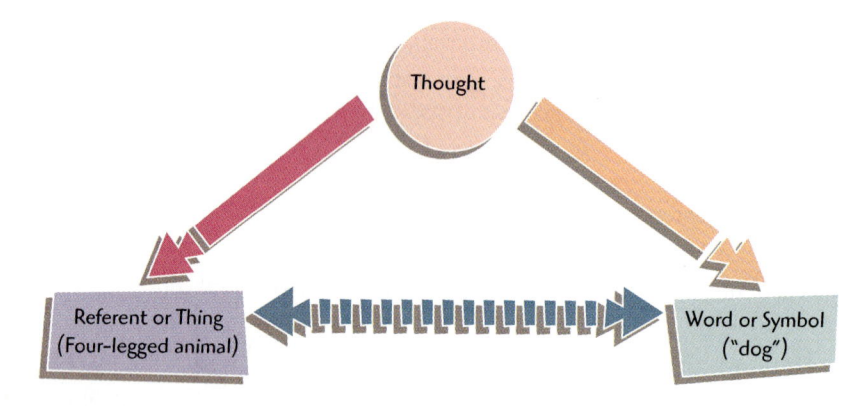

Figure 6.1 Triangle of Meaning

Thought

Referent or Thing (Four-legged animal) ↔ Word or Symbol ("dog")

Words Are Arbitrary

In English, as in all languages, words arbitrarily represent something else. The word *dog*, for example, does not *sound* like a dog or *look* at all like a dog. There is no longer a logical connection between the beast and the symbol. Figure 6.2 shows the language tree that charts the evolution of, and links among, one group of human languages. As you can see, the English language evolved from a mixture of Indo-European tongues. It will continue to evolve as we develop the need to name and describe new phenomena. *E-Connections: Cyber Shorthand* on page 164 illustrates how the use of "words" continues to evolve.

Words Are Context Bound

Your English or speech communication teacher has, undoubtedly, cautioned you that taking something out of context changes its meaning. Symbols derive their meaning from the situation in which they are used. The words *old man* could refer to a male over the age of 70, your father, your teacher, your principal, or your boss. We would need to know the context of the two symbols *old* and *man* to decipher their specific meaning. The transactional nature of communication emphasizes how meaning is created through discussion.

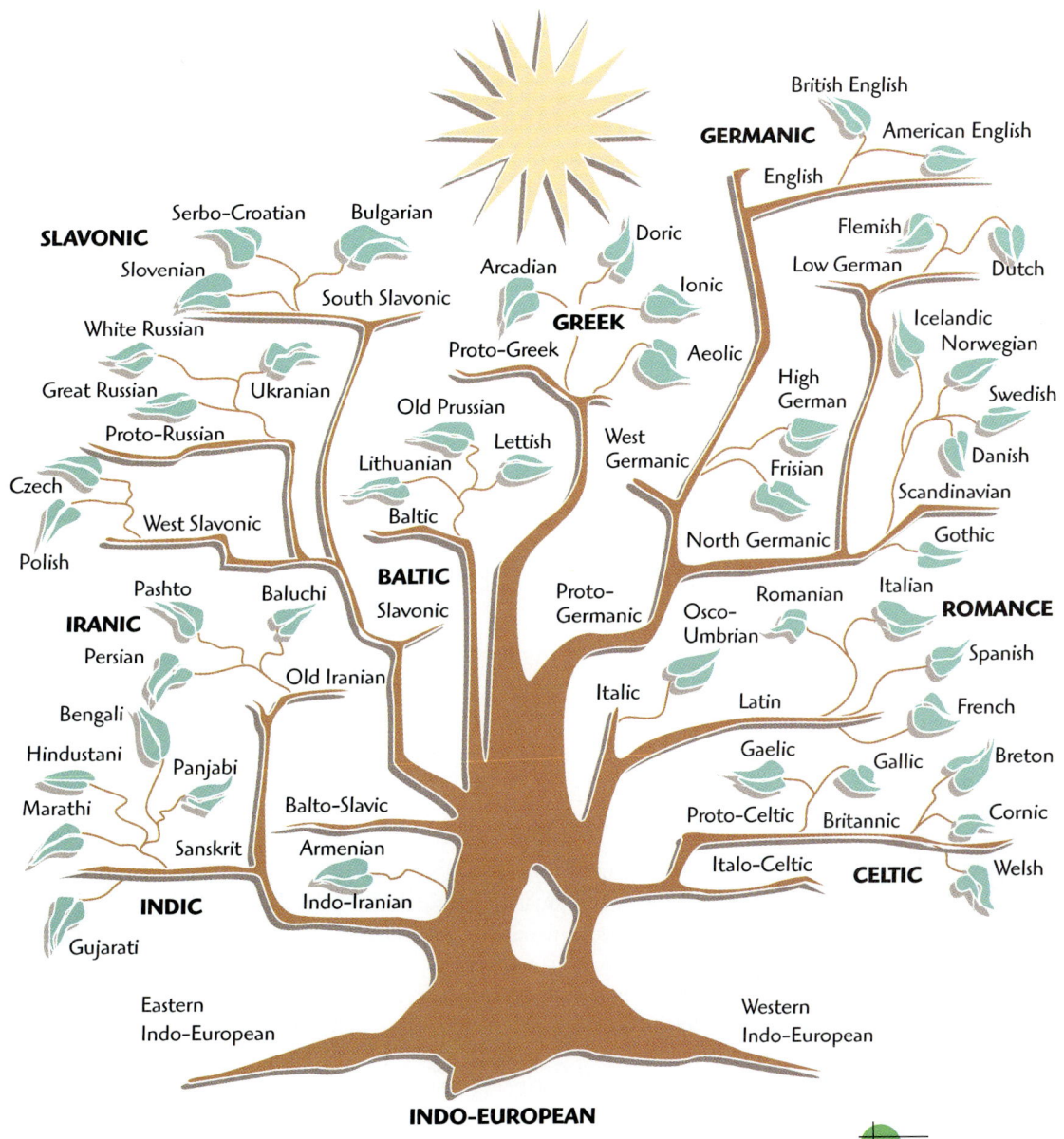

Chapter 6 Communicating Verbally

**Figure 6.2
The Language Tree**

The "Language Tree," Caputo, et al., *Interpersonal Communication*, Kendall-Hunt, 1997.

Words Are Culturally Bound

Culture consists of the rules, norms, values, and mores of a group of people, which have been learned and shaped from one generation to the next. The meaning of a symbol such as a word can change from culture to culture. Some years ago General Motors sold a car called a Nova. In English, *nova* means bright star—an appropriate name for a car. In Spanish, however, the spoken word *nova* sounds like the words "no va," which translates, "It does not go." As you can imagine, this name was not a great sales tool for the Spanish-speaking market. Men and women have also been grouped into different cultures and have different styles in conversation. The Understanding Diversity box on the next page further explains these differences.

e-connections

CYBER SHORTHAND

People who connect online have developed a host of verbal shortcuts to save time and keystrokes when communicating with others. Here's a list of some popular cyber shorthand that reflects the evolving use of language.

PPL	=	people	BTW	=	by the way
LOL	=	laughing out loud	J/K	=	just kidding
ROLF	=	rolling on the floor laughing	S2S	=	skin to skin
AFK	=	away from the keyboard	IMHO	=	in my humble opinion
BAK	=	back at the keyboard	OIC	=	oh, I see
BRB	=	be right back	TTYL	=	talk to you later
BBL	=	be back later (logging off)	GMTA	=	great minds think alike
			TTFN	=	ta ta for now
			ISO	=	in search of

▲●■ Understanding Diversity

HE SAID, SHE SAID: GENDER STYLES DIFFER AT WORK

So you think you're bilingual, do you? You say you speak English and French—or Spanish, or German.

Impressive, but not good enough—not in today's workplace anyway. To be truly successful in the '90s, you also must be fluent in Femalespeak and Malespeak.

Conversation is rife with ritual, according to Deborah Tannen, author of *You Just Don't Understand* and *Talking from 9 to 5*. And men and women's conversational rituals often clash, leading to misinterpretation and, in the worst cases, hindering women's progress up the male-dominated corporate ladder.

On page after page in her latest tome, Tannen reiterates her theme: Both conversational styles—men tend to be direct, blunt; women indirect and vague—are valid. Either style can work well with others who share that style. But neither works well in every situation.

Tannen repeatedly pleads for both sexes to understand each other's style and to develop flexibility within those styles.

Men and women have very definite expectations of how members of their own sex should behave, Tannen writes.

Studies show that "individuals of both sexes who departed from the norms for their own sex were viewed negatively by subordinates of the same sex," she says.

In one study, "a male manager whose style approximated those of the women was seen as 'fairly meek' and 'weak' by men who worked for him, though he was highly praised by women subordinates," Tannen writes.

Conversely, or perversely, women managers whose style was more like those of the men in that study were criticized by female subordinates who saw them as cold and haughty.

What's a person to do?

Adapt to your audience, Tannen and others say.

For Moira Jamieson, an Orlando business consultant, the adapting has taken the form of becoming more comfy with Femalespeak, since Malespeak is her natural style.

"One of the comments I've received throughout my life is that I'm blunt, I'm direct, I'm domineering like a man," says Jamieson, 39. "For this reason, I've had great relationships with men."

But not so great with women.

"Most women find me too pushy, assertive, forceful," she says. "On several occasions, I've been called a bitch for just being blunt."

So Jamieson is modifying her style.

"It takes a great deal of conscious effort," she says. "I think about things for a couple days before I know I'll have to say them."

'TIL SPEECH DO WE PART

According to Deborah Tannen, these are the conversational rituals of women and men:*

WOMEN

- Speaking indirectly, couching criticism and commands in praise or vagueness to avoid causing offence or hurt feelings.

- Maintaining an appearance of equality.
- Playing down their authority to avoid appearing egotistical or "bossy."
- Saying "I'm sorry" not as an apology but as a way of restoring balance to a conversation.
- Feeling discomfort with boasting; downplaying their accomplishments.
- Asking questions to elicit more information.

MEN

- Speaking directly, whether giving criticism or orders.
- Using banter, teasing, and playful put-downs.
- Striving to maintain a one-up position in any interaction.
- Perceiving "I'm sorry" as putting oneself down or accepting blame.
- Boasting or "blowing their own horn" to highlight their accomplishments.
- Seeking information elsewhere rather than asking questions, for fear of appearing to lack knowledge.

According to Tannen and other researchers, here are some ways to bridge the gap between these different rituals:

TIPS FOR WOMEN

- Be cautious in offering unsolicited advice. Often, when men are given advice, they take it as criticism.
- Don't soften your opinions with qualifiers such as "I think" or "Maybe we should" or "Wouldn't it be a good idea if." Using such qualifiers weakens your message.
- Be wary of going into long explanations. Get to the point quickly—if more explanation is needed, provide it.

TIPS FOR MEN

- Don't minimize the importance of women's feelings with statements such as, "Why are you so upset about that?" Women express their feelings more quickly and easily and need to have those feelings taken seriously.
- Don't remain silent and assume a woman will know you're absorbing what she's saying. Ask questions to show that you're interested and listening.

* Note: Remember that these generalizations do not represent all men or all women.

Source: Excerpted and adapted from: Loraine O'Connell, *Austin American-Statesman* (January 24, 1995).

The study of words and meaning is called semantics. One important body of semantic theory, known as **symbolic interaction**, suggests that as a society we are bound together because of our common use of symbols. Originally developed by sociologists as a way of making sense out of how societies and groups are linked together,[2] the theory of symbolic interaction also illuminates how we use our common understanding of symbols to form interpersonal relationships. Common symbols foster links in understanding and, therefore, lead to satisfying relationships. Of course, even within a given culture we misunderstand each other's messages. But the more similar the cultures of the communication partners, the greater the chance for a meeting of meanings.

symbolic interaction. A theory that suggests societies are bound together through common use of symbols.

Words Have Denotative and Connotative Meaning

Language is the vehicle through which we share our sense of the world with others. Through language we transfer our experience into symbols and then use the symbols to share our experience. But, as we learned in Chapter 1, the process of symbol sharing through language is not just a simple process of uttering a word and having its meaning clearly understood by another. Messages convey both

Most of us can agree on the denotative meaning for the word *school*. But the connotative meaning will be different for everybody. (Ellen Senisi/The Image Works)

content and feelings. So, our language conveys meaning on two levels: the denotative and the connotative.

The **denotative** level conveys content. The denotation of a word is its restrictive or literal meaning. For example, here is one dictionary definition for the word *school*:

An institution for the instruction of children; an institution for instruction in a skill or business; a college or a university.[3]

This definition is the literal or denotative definition of the word *school*; it describes what the word means in North American culture.

The **connotative** level of language conveys feelings. Words also have personal and subjective meanings for us. The word *school* to you might mean a wonderful, exciting place where you meet your friends, have a good time, and occasionally take tests and perform other tasks that keep you from enjoying fellowship with your chums. To others, *school* could be a restrictive, burdensome obligation that stands in the way of making money and getting on with life. The connotative meaning of a word is more specialized. The denotative or objective meaning of the word *school* can be found in your *Oxford*, *Gage*, or *Webster's* dictionary; your connotative subjective response to the word is probably not contained there.

Words Communicate Concrete or Abstract Meaning

Words can be placed along a continuum from abstract to concrete. We call a word concrete if we can experience its referent with one of our senses; if we can see it, touch it, smell it, taste it, or hear it, then it's concrete. If we cannot do these things

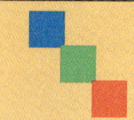

denotative meaning. The restrictive or literal meaning of a word.

connotative meaning. The personal and subjective meaning of a word.

Building Your Skills

DENOTATIVE VERSUS CONNOTATIVE DEFINITIONS

1. Provide both denotative (literal) and connotative (personal) definitions for the following terms. Compare your answers with those of your classmates.

	DENOTATIVE DEFINITION	CONNOTATIVE DEFINITION
Winter	_____	_____
Prom	_____	_____
Piano	_____	_____
Car	_____	_____
Spring Break	_____	_____

2. Practise describing something, starting with an abstract description, and then becoming more concrete. Make this a game you play with one or more of your classmates. Think of something concrete, such as the name of your communication teacher or your provincial premier. Make your first clue an abstract hint such as "person" or "human," and then provide increasingly more concrete clues.

with the referent, then the word is abstract. We can visualize the progression from abstract to concrete as a ladder:

Abstract	Shelter	Something that protects you from the elements.
	Building	A structure designed to protect you from the elements.
	House	A structure that serves as a primary residence.
	Your home	The specific place in which you live.
Concrete	Lumber, nails, and bricks	The building material used to construct your home.

In general, the more concrete the language, the easier it is for others to understand.

Recognizing the Power of Words

Sticks and stones may break my bones,
But words can never hurt me.

This old schoolyard chant may provide a ready retort for the desperate victim of name-calling, but it is hardly convincing. With more insight, the poet Robert Browning wrote, "Words break no bones; hearts though sometimes." And in his book *Science and Sanity*, mathematician and engineer Alfred Korzybski argued that the words we use (and misuse) have tremendous effects upon our thoughts and actions.[4] Browning and Korzybski were right. As we said at the beginning of this chapter, words have power.

Words Have Power to Create

"To name is to call into existence—to call out of nothingness,"[5] wrote French philosopher Georges Gusdorff. Words give us a tool to create our world by naming and labelling what we experience. You, undoubtedly, learned in your elementary science class that Sir Isaac Newton discovered gravity. Perhaps it would be more accurate to say that he labelled rather than discovered it. His use of the word *gravity* gave us a cognitive category; we now converse about the pull of the earth's forces that keeps us from flying into space. Words give us the symbolic vehicles to communicate our creations and discoveries to others.

When you label something as "good" or "bad," you are using language to create your own vision of how you experience the world. If you tell a friend that the movie you saw last night was vulgar and obscene, you are not only providing your friend with a critique of the movie, you are also communicating your sense of what is appropriate and inappropriate.

As we noted in Chapter 2, you create your self-worth largely with self-talk and with the labels you apply to yourself. One theorist believes that you also create your moods and emotional state with the words you use to label your feelings.[6] If you get fired from a job, you might say that you feel angry and helpless, or you might declare that you feel liberated and excited. The first response might lead to depression, and the second to happiness. One fascinating study conducted over a 35-year period found that people who described the world in pessimistic terms when they were younger were in poorer health during middle age than those who had been optimistic.[7] Your words and corresponding outlook have the power to affect your health.

Words Have Power to Affect Thoughts and Actions

How about some horse meat for supper tonight? Most of us find such a question disgusting. Why? Horse meat is not something we typically eat. One theorist argues that horse meat is not a featured delicacy at the local supermarket simply because we have no other word for it. Your butcher does not advertise pig meat or cow meat; labelling the meat as pork chops, ham, and sausage, or as steak and ribs, makes it sound more appetizing. Advertisers have long known that the way a product is labelled affects our propensity to purchase it.

Words can distort how we view and evaluate others. When we label someone as good, bad, chic, or in any other way, it distorts our perception of the other person. Read the Canadian Issues box for research findings on the use of labels to signify a cultural group and how these labels may affect our perceptions of a group.

Canadian Issues

LABELS ARE WORDS THAT AFFECT OUR EVALUATION OF OTHERS

The words that we use to label other people and cultures affect how we evaluate a group. A recent study examined labels and the effects that these labels had on people's attitudes toward Canada's native peoples. The labels of Aboriginal Peoples, Native Peoples, Native Indians, First Nations People, and Native Canadians were used in the study to assess attitudes, stereotypes, and emotions towards several target groups including Native Canadians. The results indicate that how groups are labelled affects our perceptions in both positive and negative ways.[8] These labels affect whether or not a group or a person with a particular label will be evaluated more positively or negatively. Once we have evaluated another group, our behaviour may be based on that label and evaluation. Of interest, the labels Native Canadians and First Nations People elicited the least favourable evaluations compared to the other three labels in this study.[9] Although attitudes cannot always predict behaviour, there is little doubt that attitudes often do influence behaviour in positive and negative ways.[10] To learn more about the attitude-behaviour relationship, you may want to examine some texts in social psychology, such as the one listed here.

Sources: Darrell W. Donakowski and Victoria M. Esses, "Native Canadians, First Nations, or Aboriginals: The Effect of Labels on Attitudes Toward Native Peoples." *Canadian Journal of Behavioural Science*, 28(2), (1996): 86–91. Copyright 1996 Canadian Psychological Association. Reprinted with permission. Also J. E. Alcock, D. W. Carment, and S. W. Sadava, *A Textbook of Social Psychology* (Scarborough, ON: Prentice-Hall Canada, 1998).

Words also have the power to affect policies and procedures. Consider the words of Supreme Court of Canada judge Claire L'Heureux-Dubé, who participated in a human rights conference on the topic of government budget cuts. How are Justice L'Heureux-Dubé's personal values about human rights reflected in the words of her speech? What power do these words have in shaping Canadian policy on human rights protection? What is the ultimate power of a judge's words or court rulings on the making and interpretation of laws in Canada?

Human Rights Outweigh Debt Cutting, Top Judge Says

VICTORIA—A Supreme Court of Canada judge says the push to cut government debt and deficits is one of the greatest threats to human rights in Canada.

In an interview Tuesday, Justice Claire L'Heureux-Dubé said the protection of equality should supersede short-term economic considerations.

"In the short term you may think that you are saving money, but in the long term the damage that it does to society without human rights creates more problems and it costs more.

"You have no justification to ask the cost of justice when you haven't figured out the cost of injustice.

"When you don't see the results [of human rights commissions] immediately . . . then there's a great temptation to cut resources. Justice should be at the forefront of politicians' agendas. . . .

"In an era of diminishing public resources and increasing global competition, the real question is not whether we can afford to eliminate discrimination but whether we can afford not to. . . . [T]he equal dignity of every member of the community is a value of the highest order, and I would hope that money is not a measure of that dignity."

Source: From an article by Jim Beatty, Southam Newspapers *(The Vancouver Sun),* as it appeared in *The Ottawa Citizen,* June 5, 1996, A1.

In the late 1960s, a California sociology professor conducted an experiment to demonstrate that words have power to affect behaviour.[11] He divided his class into two groups. To one group he distributed a bumper sticker that boldly displayed the words, "I support the Black Panthers." At that time, many members of the students' local community thought the Panthers were using unnecessary force to promote their agenda. Students in this first group had to drive around for a week with the stickers on their cars. The other group drove around as usual, without stickers.

It took only a few hours to prove the professor's point: words do affect attitudes and behaviour. Students who had the stickers were harassed by other motorists and issued traffic tickets at an alarming rate. The other group had no increase in hassles. By the end of the study, 17 days later, the "Panther" group had received 33 traffic citations.

Words Have Power to Affect and Reflect Culture

About a decade before the sociology professor's bumper sticker experiment, two anthropologists simultaneously began to refine a theory called **linguistic determinism**, which had originated in the 19th century.[12] Their version is based on a hypothesis of reciprocity: language shapes your culture and culture shapes your language. To understand your culture, theorize these anthropologists, you should study the words you use. If an impartial investigator from another culture were to study a transcript of all of your spoken utterances last week, what would he or she learn about you and the culture in which you live? If you frequently used

linguistic determinism.
A theory that describes how use of language determines or influences thoughts and perceptions.

words like *CD* and *download*, the investigator would know that these things are important to you. But he or she might not know what they mean if they are not also part of his or her culture.

Words not only reflect your culture; there is evidence that they mould it. When Wendell Johnson, a speech therapist, noticed that very few Indians in a certain tribe stuttered, he also found that their language had no word for stuttering.[13] He concluded that few people had this affliction because it never entered their minds as a possibility. Perhaps you've heard that the Inuit have 23 different words for snow. Even though they really don't have quite that many, there is evidence that they have more words for snow than someone native to Miami, Florida.[14]

These examples also show that the words we use and listen to affect our **world view**—how we interpret what we experience. If you were to don someone else's prescription glasses, the world would literally look different to you, and the glasses would either enhance or inhibit your ability to see the world around you. In a sense, your world view is your own set of prescription glasses, which you formulate over time, based upon your experiences, attitudes, beliefs, values, and needs. The words you use to describe your view of the world reflect and further shape your perspective. And you, in turn, help to shape your culture's collective world view through your use of language.

The "tech-speak" spoken here may help to create the special culture these individuals share.
(Mark Richards/PhotoEdit)

Avoiding Word Barriers

According to theologian and educator Ruel Howe, a communication barrier is "something that keeps meaning from meeting."[15] Words have the power to create monumental misunderstandings as well as deep connections. Although it is true that meanings are in people, not in words, sometimes assumptions or inaccurate use of words hinders understanding. Let's identify some of the specific barriers to understanding that we can create through language.

Bypassing: One Word, Two Thoughts

A student pilot was on his first solo flight. When he called the tower for flight instructions, the control tower said, "Would you please give us your altitude and position?"

The pilot said: "I'm 180 cm tall, and I'm sitting up front."

Bypassing occurs when the same words mean different things to different people. Meaning is fragile. And the English language is imprecise in many areas. One researcher estimated that the 500 words we use most often in our daily conversations with others have over 14 000 different dictionary definitions. And this number does not take into account personal connotations. So, it is no wonder that bypassing is a common communication problem.

world view. A culturally acquired perspective for interpreting experiences.

bypassing. The same words mean different things to different people.

Chapter 6 Communicating Verbally

We all know that Pavlov's dog salivated when he heard the bell that he had learned to associate with food. Sometimes we respond to symbols the way Pavlov's dog did to the bell, forgetting that symbols (words) can have more than one meaning.

Considering Others

THE TALKAHOLIC SCALE

Are you a "talkaholic," or do you know someone who is? The simple description of a "talkaholic" is someone who talks more than most people. Being other-oriented means not only being a good listener, as we discussed in Chapter 5, but it means being sensitive to how much you talk. "Talkaholics" often ververbalize. They are sometimes insensitive to others' need for information. No, we're not suggesting that you should not contribute to the conversation, and at times it is appropriate and expected that you'll talk and others listen, but consider whether you may be a conversation dominator. Take the following test developed by communication researchers James McCroskey and Virginia Richmond to determine your "talkaholic" quotient. The higher your score, the higher your tendency to be a "talkaholic" when relating to others.

The Talkaholic Scale

Directions: The questionnaire below includes sixteen statements about talking behavior. Please indicate the degree to which you believe each of these characteristics applies to you by marking, on the line before each item, whether you (5) strongly agree that it applies, (4) agree that it applies, (3) are undecided, (2) disagree that it applies, or (1) strongly disagree that it applies. There are no right or wrong answers. Work quickly; record your first impression.

_____ 1. Often I keep quiet when I know I should talk.
_____ 2. I talk more than I should sometimes.
_____ 3. Often I talk when I know I should keep quiet.
_____ 4. Sometimes I keep quiet when I know it would be to my advantage to talk.
_____ 5. I am a "talkaholic."
_____ 6. Sometimes I feel compelled to keep quiet.
_____ 7. In general, I talk more than I should.
_____ 8. I am a compulsive talker.
_____ 9. I am not a talker; rarely do I talk in communication situations.
_____ 10. Quite a few people have said I talk too much.
_____ 11. I just can't stop talking too much.
_____ 12. In general, I talk less than I should.
_____ 13. I am **not** a "talkaholic."
_____ 14. Sometimes I talk when I know it would be to my advantage to keep quiet.
_____ 15. I talk less than I should sometimes.
_____ 16. I am **not** a compulsive talker.

Scoring: To determine your score on this scale, complete the following steps:

Step 1. Add the scores for items 2, 3, 5, 7, 8, 10, 11, and 14.
Step 2. Add the scores for items 13 and 16.
Step 3. Complete the following formula: Talkaholic score = 12 + total from step 1 − total from step 2.

A score of 40 or above suggests that you are a talkaholic.

Source: James C. McCroskey and Virginia P. Richmond, *Fundamentals of Human Communication: An Interpersonal Perspective* (Prospect Heights, IL: Waveland Press, 1996), 66.

Bafflegab: High-Falutin' Use of Words

Do you suffer from bafflegab? Here is an example of it: Bafflegab is multiloquence characterized by consummate interfusion of circumlocution or periphrasis, inscrutability, incognizability, and other familiar manifestations of abstruse expatiation commonly used for promulations implementing procrustean determinations by governmental bodies. Whew! What a mouthful. Why do some people use such highly abstract language? Perhaps they are just trying to dazzle their listener with evidence of their education, or they may simply not be other-oriented. Bafflegabbers may be focused on impressing the receiver rather than on conveying meaning. Other-oriented speakers use clear words that the listener can understand. Another reason people use big words, overly formal language, or evasive phrases is to hide their ignorance.

---

e-connections

AVOIDING BAFFLEGAB

Uncertain of the meaning of a word that you find on the Internet? Look it up on the "Webopaedia." The following website will help you interpret words you don't understand:

www.pcwebopaedia.com

Here's another site that can help you avoid bafflegab. Here you'll find a comprehensive dictionary of technical jargon, especially computer jargon, that appears on the Web:

www.netmeg.net/jargon

Lack of Precision: Uncertain Meaning

Alice Roosevelt Longworth writes about the investigation of a merchant sailor. "Do you," asked the interrogator, "have any pornographic literature?"

"Pornographic literature!" the sailor burst out indignantly. "I don't even have a pornograph!"

At a ceremony in a university chapel, an old lady buttonholed an usher and commanded, "Be sure you get me a seat up front, young man. I understand they've always had trouble with the agnostics in the chapel!"

Each of these examples, along with the Far Side cartoon to the right, illustrates a **malapropism**—a confusion of one word or phrase for another that sounds similar to it. You have probably heard people confuse such word pairs as *construction* and *instruction*, and *subscription* and *prescription*. Although this confusion may at times be humorous, it may also result in failure to communicate clearly. So, too, can using words out of context, using inappropriate grammar, or putting words in the wrong order. Confusion is the inevitable result, as these sentences taken from a letter to a welfare department illustrate:

> I want my money as quickly as I can get it. I've been in bed with the doctor for two weeks, and it didn't do me any good. If things don't improve, I will have to send for another doctor.

And the following statements appeared in church bulletins:

> The eighth-graders will be presenting Shakespeare's *Hamlet* in the church basement on Friday at 7:00 P.M. The congregation is invited to attend this tragedy.

> This afternoon there will be meetings in the North and South ends of the church—children will be baptized on both ends.

Ha ha ha, Biff. Guess what? After we go to the drugstore and the post office, I'm going to the vet's to get tutored.

These are funny examples, but, in fact, unclear language can launch a war or sink a ship. It is vital to remember that *meanings are in people, not in words*. We give symbols meaning; we do not receive inherent meaning *from* symbols. If you are other-oriented, you will assess how someone else will respond to your message and you will try to select those symbols that he or she is most likely to interpret as you intend.

For most communication, the object is to be as specific and concrete as possible. Vague language creates confusion and frustration. Consider this example:

Sasha: Where's the aluminum foil?

Pam: In the drawer.

Sasha: What drawer?

Pam: In the kitchen.

Sasha: But where in the kitchen?

Pam: By the fridge.

Sasha: But which one? There are five drawers.

Pam: Oh, the second one from the top.

Sasha: Why didn't you say so in the first place?

Is it possible to be too precise? It is if you use a restricted code that has a meaning your listener does not know. A **restricted code** involves the use of words that have a particular meaning to a subgroup or culture. For example, most children

malapropism. The confusion of one word or phrase for another that sounds similar to it.

restricted code. Using words that have a particular meaning to a person, group, or culture.

jargon. Another name for restricted code; specialized terms or abbreviations whose meaning is known only to members of a specific group.

allness. The tendency to use language to make unqualified, often untrue generalizations.

grow up learning their own family's secret words. Sometimes, we develop abbreviations or specialized terms that make sense and save time when we speak to others in our group. Musicians, for example, use special terms that relate to reading and performing music. Most computer hackers know that a "screamer" is someone whose messages in cyberspace are all in CAPITAL LETTERS. Ham radio operators use codes to communicate over the airwaves. Yet, in each instance, this shorthand language would make little sense to an outsider. In fact, groups that rely upon restricted codes may have greater cohesiveness because of this shared "secret" language or **jargon**. Whatever your line of work, guard against lapsing into phrases that can be interpreted only by a few.

When people have known one another for a long time, they also may use restricted codes for their exchanges. The Blondie cartoon below is an example of how married couples can communicate using a code that no outsider could ever interpret.

Allness: The Language of Generalization

The tendency to use language to make unqualified, often untrue generalizations is called **allness**. Allness statements deny individual differences or variations. Statements such as "All women are poor drivers" and "People from the South love iced tea" are generalizations that imply that the person making the pronouncement has examined all the information and has reached a definitive conclusion. Although our world would be much simpler if we *could* make such statements, reality rarely, if ever, provides evidence to support sweeping generalizations. For example, although research conclusions document differences between the way men and women communicate, it is inaccurate to say that all women are more emotional and that all men are task oriented. Empathic, other-oriented speakers avoid making judgments of others based only upon conventional wisdom or traditionally held attitudes and beliefs. If you respond to others (of a different gender, sexual orientation, or ethnicity) based on stereotypical concepts, you will diminish your understanding and the quality of the relationship.

One way to avoid untrue generalizations is to remind yourself that your use and interpretation of a word is unique. Saying the words "to me" either to yourself or out loud before you offer an opinion or make a pronouncement can help communicate to others (and remind yourself) that your view is uniquely yours. Rather than announcing, "Curfews for teenagers are ridiculous," you could say, "To me, curfews for teenagers are ridiculous."

Indexing your comments and remarks is another way to help you avoid generalizing. To index is to acknowledge that each individual is unique. Rather than announcing that all doctors are abrupt, you could say, "My child's pediatrician spends a lot of time with me, but my internist never answers my questions." This helps you remember that doctor number one is not the same as doctor number two.

Static Evaluation: The Language of Rigidity

You change. Your world changes. An ancient Greek philosopher said it best: "You can never step in the same river twice." A **static evaluation** is a statement that fails to recognize change; labels, in particular, have a tendency to freeze-frame our awareness. Ruth, known as the class nerd in high school, is today a successful and polished businessperson; the old label does not fit.

In addition, some of us suffer from hardening of the categories. Our world view is so rigid that we can never change or expand our perspective. But the world is a technicolour moving target. Just about the time we think we have things neatly figured out and categorized, something moves. Our labels may not reflect the buzzing, booming, zipping process of change. It is important to acknowledge that perception is a process and to avoid trying to nail things down permanently into all-inclusive categories.

General semanticists use the metaphorical expression "the map is not the territory" to illustrate the concept of static evaluation. Like a word, a map symbolizes or represents reality. Yet, our road system is constantly changing. New roads are built, old ones are closed. If you were to use a 1949 map to guide you from St. Andrews, New Brunswick, to Winnipeg, Manitoba, the current highway system would not even be on it, and you would probably lose your way. Similarly, if we use old labels and do not adjust our thinking to accommodate change, we will be semantically lost.

Perhaps you have a parent who still uses "old maps." When you come home to visit, your parent expects that you will be there for dinner each night and will still eat four helpings at every meal. Your parent may not understand that you have changed, and his or her old map does not function well in your new territory. You may have to help construct a new one.

To avoid static evaluation yourself, try dating your observations and indicate to others the time period from which you are drawing your conclusion. If your second cousin comes to town for a visit, say, "When I last saw you, you loved to listen to Céline Dion." This allows for the possibility that your cousin's tastes may have changed since you saw her last. But most importantly, try to observe and acknowledge changes in others. If you are practising what you know about becoming other-oriented, you are unlikely to erect this barrier.

indexing. A way of avoiding allness statements by separating one situation, person, or example from another.

static evaluation. Pronouncing judgment on something without taking changes into consideration.

Polarization: The Language of Extremes

Describing and evaluating what we observe in terms of extremes, such as good or bad, old or new, beautiful or ugly, brilliant or stupid, is known as **polarization**. General semanticists remind us that the world in which we live comes not in black and white but in a variety of colours, hues, and shades. If you describe things in extremes, leaving out the middle ground, then your language does not accurately reflect reality. And because of the power of words to create, you may believe your own pronouncements.

polarization. Describing and evaluating what we observe in extremes, such as good or bad, old or new, beautiful or ugly.

"You either love me or you don't love me," says Kamal.

"You're *always* trying to control me," replies Lise.

Both people are overstating the case, using language to polarize their perceptions of the experience.

Family counsellors who listen to family feuds find that the tendency to see things from an either-or point of view is a classic symptom of a troubled relationship. Placing the entire blame on your partner for a problem in your relationship is an example of polarizing. Few relational difficulties are exclusively one-sided.

Biased Language: Insensitivity Toward Others

Using words that reflect your biases toward other cultures, ethnic groups, gender, sexual orientation, or people who are simply different from you can create a word barrier for your listeners. Because words, including the words used to describe people, have power to create and affect thoughts and behaviour, they can affect the quality of relationships with others. Although TV, radio, and magazine articles may debate the merits of political correctness, it is clear that sexist or racially stereotypical language can offend others. Three issues in language use can reflect poorly on the speakers and impact interpersonal relationships with others: sexist language, ethnic or racially biased language, and elitist language—language that assumes superiority.

▶ Recap

WORD BARRIERS

Barrier	Definition	Examples
Bypassing	Misinterpreting a word that evokes different meanings for different people.	*W.C.* might mean wayside chapel to a person who is Swiss and water closet to someone who is English.
Bafflegab	Unnecessary use of many abstract words	"Please extinguish all smoking materials" instead of "No Smoking."
Lack of Clarity	Words used inappropriately or in imprecise ways.	Sign in Acapulco hotel: The manager has personally passed all the water served here.
Allness	Lumping things or people into all-encompassing categories.	All Maritimers rely on the sea for their livelihood.
Static Evaluation	Labelling people, objects, and events without considering change.	You call your 28-year-old nephew a "juvenile delinquent" because he spray-painted your fence when he was 11.
Polarization	Description in either-or terms—good or bad, right or wrong.	You're either for me or against me.
Biased Language	Language that reflects gender, racial, or ethnic biases.	My mom is a mailman.

Using Words to Establish Supportive Relationships

"I'm going to win this argument."

"You're wrong and I'm right. It's as simple as that."

"You're going to do it my way or else!"

"Listen, you're a woman, so how would you know?"

None of these statements is likely to result in a positive communication climate. All four are likely to result in debate rather than true dialogue. The words you hear and use are central to your establishing a quality or positive relationship with others. Author and researcher Daniel Yankelovich suggests that the goal of conversations with others should be to establish a genuine dialogue rather than to verbally arm-wrestle a partner in order to win the argument.[16] A true dialogue involves establishing a climate of equality, listening with empathy, and trying to bring assumptions into the open. Expressing equality, empathy, openness and avoiding biases are more likely to occur if you approach conversations as dialogue rather than debate. As shown in Table 6.1, in true dialogue people look for common ground rather than using a war of words to defend a position.

For more than three decades Jack Gibb's observational research has been used as a framework for both describing and prescribing verbal behaviours that contribute to feelings of either supportiveness or defensiveness.[17] Gibb spent several years listening to and observing groups of individuals in meetings and conversations, noting that some exchanges seemed to create a supportive climate, whereas others created a defensive one. Words and actions, he concluded, are tools we use to let someone know whether we support them or not.

In Chapter 7, we will see how non-verbal cues can affect the quality of relationships. But now, let us consider how you can use words to create a supportive climate rather than an antagonistic one.

Table 6.1
Debate and Dialogue Compared

Debate	Dialogue
There is one right answer, and you have it.	Many people have pieces of the answer; together you can find the best solution.
The goal is to win.	The goal is to seek common ground and agreement.
The focus is on combat; prove that you are right and the other person is wrong.	The focus is on collaboration; seek common understanding.
Search for weakness and errors in others' positions.	Search for strengths and value the truth in what others say.
Defend your views.	Use the contributions of others to improve your thinking.

Source: Adapted from Daniel Yankelovich, *The Magic of Dialogue: Transforming Conflict into Cooperation* (New York: Simon & Schuster, 1999), 39–40.

Considering Others

COMMUNICATING ETHICS IN THE WORKPLACE

This chapter has been about verbal communication. Each chapter includes a section that focuses on ethics—personal ethics. But what about business ethics? How do companies communicate to potential customers, clients, and other companies that they are ethical in their business practices? There are many examples of ethical companies in Canada—companies that treat employees fairly, treat customers with dignity and respect, and offer products that are safe, reliable, fairly priced, and do what they are supposed to do. How do you identify an "ethical company"? Perhaps one way to identify an ethical company is to find out whether or not the company practises ethical behaviour within the company.

A November 1996 survey by KPMG of Canada (KPMG LLP is the Canadian member firm of KPMG International, a global network of professional service firms), surveyed 1000 Canadian public and private companies to get an up-to-date picture of current ethics-related practices and issues in Canada. Companies included health care, hospitality and tourism, financial institutions, retail and wholesale, and insurance, to name a few. Of the 251 responses, the results showed some interesting trends:

- Several areas were identified from academic research and respondents were asked to indicate the level of its importance as a source of ethical "risk." These areas included conflict of interest, external relationships, handling company assets, customer relations, relations with suppliers, relations with competitors, and employee and workplace issues.
- The most important sources of risk were identified as Employee and Workplace Issues and Company Assets.
- "Integrity of Books" ranked as the top individual issue, with 71% of respondents rating this issue as "Very Important."
- 83% of the companies have a published mission statement.
- 66% of the companies have a published code of ethics, practice, or conduct; however, only 21% claimed any kind of training in connection in connection with their code.
- Of companies with over $1 billion in revenues, 90% reported a published code of ethics.
- Just over 40% of respondents indicated that they had someone who was "in charge" or responsible for their ethics program and most were referred to as a "Human Resources Manager."

Of interest, according to this survey 78% of respondents stated that their companies had no formal policy to protect employees who report ethical violations. Those that did have a policy used confidential hotlines (such as Sears) or the like. It appears that many companies desire to have ethical employees but have no real means for violations to be reported—an interesting finding.

These are only some of the results from this survey. When being interviewed by prospective employers, you may want to ask if there is a published code of ethics, who oversees the implementation of the code, what happens to employees who violate the code, how violations are reported, and whether the code extends to ensuring that you will receive fair treatment as an employee.

Another way to find "ethical companies" is to do a Web search. Many companies such as Compaq Canada and QLT Inc. have extensive websites with mission statements and other policies posted for the public. These mission statements often include statements about how the company conducts its business and its treatment of both customers and employees. As a customer, check into mission statements and ask about customer relations. Ask questions regarding customer satisfaction and make sure that the mission statement and policies are not just "words."

Questions

1. What areas of ethical conduct are particularly important to you when you are considering making a major purchase such as a computer or automobile? Why?
2. While many companies have ethics policies, very few have procedures for reporting violations. Why do you think this happens? How should violations be reported?
3. Design a sample ethics policy for a fictitious company.
4. Other than through mission statements, how can ethical companies communicate their ethical behaviour to the general public?

Sources: KPMG, 1997 KPMG fsiness Ethics Survey Report. www.itcilo.it/english/actrav/telearn/global/ilo/code/1997kpmg.html, and QLT Inc. www.qlt.inc.com, and Compaq Canada www.compaq.ca

Avoid Sexist Language

Sexist language is the use of words that reflect stereotypical attitudes or that describe roles in exclusively male or female terms.

Words such as congress*man*, alder*man*, and *man*kind ignore the fact that women are part of the workforce and the human race. Contrast these with *city councillor, letter carrier,* and *humankind,* which are gender neutral and allow for the inclusion of both men and women. Or, rather than eliminating the word *man* from your vocabulary, try to use appropriate labels when you know the gender of the subject. A male police officer is a policeman; a female police officer is a policewoman. Rather than salesperson, you could say salesman or saleswoman, depending on the gender of the seller.

O'Donnell found that even dictionaries fall into patterns of describing men and women with discriminatory language.[18] Included in the *Oxford English Dictionary* definition for *woman* are (1) an adult female being, (2) a female servant, (3) a ladylove or mistress, and (4) a wife. Men are described in more positive and distinguished terms: (1) a human being, (2) the human creation regarded abstractly, (3) an adult male endowed with many qualities, and (4) a person of importance of position.

Many of our social conventions also diminish or ignore the importance of women:

Sexist	Unbiased
I'd like you to meet Dr. and Mrs. John Chao.	I'd like you to meet Dr. Susan Ho and Dr. John Chao. They are husband and wife.
	or
	I'd like you to meet John Chao and Susan Ho. They're both doctors at Hôtel Dieu Hospital.
Let me introduce Mr. Tom Bertolone and his wife Beverly.	Let me introduce Beverly and Tom Bertolone.

We have, however, made more substantial progress in reflecting changes and changed attitudes toward women in the professional arena. Compare the terms we now use to describe workers with those used in the 1950s:

Terms Used Today	Terms Used in 1950s
Flight attendant	Stewardess
Firefighter	Fireman
Police officer	Policeman
Physician	Female doctor
Office workers	Girls at work
Ms.	Miss/Mrs.
People/humans/humankind	Mankind

Consciously remembering to use non-sexist language will result in several benefits.[19] First, non-sexist language reflects non-sexist attitudes. Your attitudes are reflected in your speech and your speech affects your attitudes. Monitoring your speech for sexist remarks can help you monitor your attitudes about sexist assumptions. Second, using non-sexist language will help you become more other-oriented. Monitoring your language for sexist remarks will reflect your sensitivity to others. Third, non-sexist language will make your speech more contemporary and unambiguous. By substituting the word *humankind* for *mankind*, for example, you can communicate that you are including all people, not just men, in your observation or statement. And, finally, your non-sexist language will empower others. By eliminating sexist bias from your speech, you will help confirm the value of all the individuals with whom you interact.

e-connections

AVOIDING SEXIST LANGUAGE

Although we've identified a rationale for avoiding biased language and offered several tips for using non-sexist language, you still may want additional strategies to help you using words that won't offend others. The following websites offer links to several sites that offer a wealth of strategies and suggestions for avoiding sexist language:

www.researchpaper.com/writing center/26.html

www.utexas.edu/student/lsc/handouts/1284.html

In addition to the debate over language that reflects on one's gender, there is considerable and controversial discussion about the way in which people talk about someone's sexual orientation. Regardless of your personal view about sexual orientation, the principle of being other-oriented suggests that you can be sensitive to the way you speak of it. Your approval or disapproval of someone's sexual preferences should not undermine your goal of being an effective communicator. Labelling someone a *fag, queer,* or *dyke* may not only be offensive and hurtful to the person being labelled but may also reflect on the sensitivity of the person doing the labelling. In most circles, the preferred terms for someone who is homosexual are *gay* for men and *lesbian* for women. We're not suggesting that certain words be expunged from dictionaries or never be uttered; we are suggesting that when describing others, people should be sensitive to how they wish to be addressed and discussed.

Avoid Ethnic or Racially Biased Language

In addition to monitoring your language for sexual stereotypes, avoid racial and ethnic stereotypes. Monitor your speech so you are not, even unconsciously, using phrases that depict a racial group or ethnic group in a negative, stereotypical fashion. How do you feel about being called a Canuck? A student writer of an American University paper who used the term "Canuck" to refer to the large number of Canadians moving into the entertainment field in the United States was fired for using the term. He was later rehired after a large number of Canadians expressed that they did not find the term offensive.[20] Phrases such as "There are too many Indians and not enough chiefs," or "I jewed him down" (to negotiate a good price), demonstrate an insensitivity to members of other cultural groups. The underlying principle in avoiding biased language is to be other-oriented and to imagine how the listener might react to your words. As in the Canadian Issues box on page 168 demonstrates, how we label others can affect our perceptions. A sensitive other-oriented communicator keeps abreast of changes in preferred labels and adopts the designations currently preferred by members of the ethnic groups themselves.

Avoid Language That Demeans One's Age, Ability, or Social Class

Language barriers are created not only when someone uses sexist or racially biased language, but also when someone disparages a person's age, mental or physical ability, or social standing. Calling someone a "geezer," "retard," or "trailer trash" may seem to some harmless or humorous, but may be perceived by others as disparaging.[21]

Discriminating against someone because of age is a growing problem in the workplace. In some occupations, as a worker moves into his or her 50s, it may be difficult to change jobs or find work. Despite laws designed to guard against age discrimination, such discrimination clearly exists. As we have noted, the language that people use has power to affect attitudes and behaviour. That's why using negative terms to describe the elderly can be a subtle—or sometimes not-so-subtle—way of expressing disrespect toward the older generation.

Similarly, the way someone describes people with disabilities can negatively impact how they may be perceived. A study by researcher John Seiter and his colleagues found that when people with a disability were called demeaning or disparaging names, they were perceived as less trustworthy, competent, persuasive, and sociable than when the same people were described in more positive or heroic terms.[22] At the end of their study, the authors note, "communicators who want to be effective should avoid using derogatory language." Guard against calling attention to someone as a "cripple," "retarded," "dim-witted," or "mental"; these terms are offensive. As one common expression puts it: Much truth's spoken when you're just jokin'. Even though it may seem innocent to use such words to label others, it can alter your perceptions of others, as well as reflect poorly on you. Although there clearly are differences in ability among people, because of a variety of factors, be sensitive to your use of language. As suggested by communication researcher Dawn Braithwaite, the preferred terms are "disabled people" or "people with disabilities."[23]

Also monitor the way you talk about someone's social class. Although some societies and cultures make considerable distinctions among classes, it is nonetheless offensive today to use words that are intended to demean someone's social class. Terms such as "welfare recipients," "manual labourers," and "blue-collar workers" are often used derogatorily. Avoid labelling someone in such a way that shows disrespect toward the person's social standing, education, or socioeconomic status.

Describe Your Own Feelings Rather Than Evaluate the Behaviour of Others

Most of us don't like to be judged or evaluated. Criticizing and name-calling, obviously, can create relational problems, but so can our attempts to diagnose others' problems or win their affection with insincere praise. In fact, any form of evaluation creates a climate of defensiveness. As Winston Churchill declared, "I am always ready to learn, although I do not always like being taught." Correcting others, even when we are doing it "for their own good," can raise their hackles.

One way to avoid evaluating others is to eliminate the accusatory *you* from your language. Statements such as, "You always come in late for supper," or "You need to pick up the dirty clothes in your room," attack a person's sense of self-worth and usually result in a defensive reaction.

Instead, use the word *I* to describe your own feelings and thoughts about a situation or event: "I find it hard to keep your supper warm when you're late," or "I don't enjoy the extra work of picking up your dirty clothes." When you describe your own feelings instead of berating the receiver of the message, you are in essence taking ownership of the problem. This approach leads to greater openness and trust because your listener does not feel rejected or that you are trying to control him or her.

> ## Building Your Skills
>
> ### Practise Using "I" Language
>
> An essential skill in being supportive rather than defensive is describing what you want with "I" language rather than "you" language. Rephrase the following "you" statements into "I" statements.
>
> | "You" Language | "I" Language |
> |---|---|
> | 1. You are messy when you cook. | _____ |
> | 2. Your driving is terrible. | _____ |
> | 3. You never listen to me. | _____ |
> | 4. You just lie on the couch and never offer to help me. | _____ |
> | 5. You always decide what movie we see. | _____ |

Solve Problems Rather Than Control Others

When you were younger, your parents gave you rules to keep you safe. Even though you may have resented their control, you needed to know what was hot, when not to cross the street, and not to stick your finger in a light socket. Now that you are an adult, when people treat you like a child, it often means they are trying to control your behaviour, to take away your options. In truth, we have little or no control over someone else's behaviour.

Most of us don't like to be controlled. Someone who presumes to tell us what's good for us, instead of helping us puzzle through issues and problems, is likely to engender defensiveness. Open-ended questions such as, "What seems to be the problem?" or "How can we deal with the issue?" create a more supportive climate than critical comments such as, "Here's where you are wrong" or commands such as, "Don't do that!"

Be Genuine Rather Than Manipulative

To be genuine means that you honestly seek to be yourself rather than someone you are not. It also means taking an honest interest in others and considering the uniqueness of each individual and situation, avoiding generalizations or strategies that focus only on your own needs and desires. A manipulative person has hidden agendas; a genuine person uses words to discuss issues and problems openly and honestly.

Carl Rogers, the founder of person-centred counselling, suggests that true understanding and dialogue occur when people adopt a genuine or honest positive regard for others.[24] If your goal is to look out only for your own interests, your language will reflect your self-focus. At the heart of being genuine is being other-oriented—being sincerely interested in those with whom you communicate. Although it's unrealistic to assume you will become best friends with everyone you meet, you can, suggests Rogers, work to develop an unselfish interest, or what he called an unconditional positive regard for others. That's hard to do. But the effort will be rewarded with a more positive communication climate.

An essential skill in being supportive rather than defensive is describing what you want with "I" language rather than "you" language. Could the use of "I" language help this couple? (Chip Henderson/Tony Stone Images)

Empathize Rather Than Remain Detached from Others

Empathy is one of the hallmarks of supportive relationships. As we learned earlier, empathy is the ability to understand the feelings of others and to predict the emotional responses they will have to different situations. The opposite of empathy is neutrality. To be neutral is to be indifferent or apathetic toward another. Even when you express anger or irritation toward another, you are investing some energy in the relationship.

After an unsuccessful attempt to persuade his family to take a trip to Banff National Park, Preston declared, "I don't care what you think, that's where we're going." His proclamation reflects a disregard for the feelings of others in his family. This insensitivity is self-defeating. The defensive climate Preston creates with his words will probably prevent the whole family from enjoying the vacation.

Be Flexible Rather Than Rigid Toward Others

Most people don't like someone who always seems certain that he or she is right. A "you're wrong, I'm right" attitude creates a defensive climate. This does not mean that you should have no opinions and go through life blithely agreeing to everything. And it doesn't mean that there is *never* one answer that is right and others that are wrong. But instead of making rigid pronouncements, you can use phrases such as, "I may be wrong, but it seems to me . . . " or "Here's one way to look at this problem." This manner of speaking gives your opinions a softer edge that allows room for others to express a point of view.

Present Yourself as Equal Rather Than Superior

You can antagonize others by letting them know that you view yourself as better or brighter than they are. You may be gifted and intelligent, but it's not necessary to announce it. And although some people have the responsibility and authority to manage others, "pulling rank" does not usually produce a cooperative climate. With phrases such as, "Let's work on this together," or "We each have a valid perspective," you can avoid erecting walls of resentment and suspicion.

Also, avoid using bafflegab to impress others. Keep your messages short and clear, and use informal language. When you communicate with someone from another culture, you may need to use an **elaborated code** to get your message across. This means that your messages will have to be more explicit, but they should not be condescending. Two of your authors remember vividly trying to explain to a French exchange student what a fire ant is. First, we had to translate *ant* into French, and then we had to provide scientific, descriptive, and narrative evidence to help the student understand how these tiny, biting insects terrorize people in the southern part of the United States.

elaborated code. Using many words and various ways of describing an idea or concept to communicate its meaning.

▶ Recap

USING WORDS TO ESTABLISH SUPPORTIVE RELATIONSHIPS

- Avoid language that is sexist, ethnic or racially biased, or demeaning of another's age, ability, or social class.
- Describe your feelings instead of evaluating the behaviour of others.
- Keep the focus on problem solving, not control.
- Be genuine rather than manipulative in your approach.
- Show that you understand another person's point of view.
- Make it clear that you do not have all the answers.
- Present yourself as equal rather than as superior.

Using Words to Value Others

"I just don't feel appreciated any more," confides Gillian during her counselling session. "My husband Ryan doesn't let me know he cares for me." One of the key skills in maintaining a long-term relationship is to know how to demonstrate that you value the other person. It's not just *nice* to know that someone cares about us; it is vital that we know others have genuine feelings of concern for us. In addition to acts of kindness, it is our words that let others know we appreciate them.

Researchers have identified ways we use language to confirm or disconfirm others.[25] A **confirming response** is a statement that causes others to value themselves more. Conversely, a **disconfirming response** is one that causes others to value themselves less.

confirming response. A statement that causes another person to value himself or herself more.

disconfirming response. A statement that causes another person to value himself or herself less.

Confirming Responses

The adage, "People judge us by our words and behaviour rather than by our intent," summarizes the underlying principle of confirming responses. Those who receive your messages determine whether they have the effect you intended. Formulating confirming responses requires careful listening and attention to the other person. We will describe several kinds of confirming responses here:

🟠 Direct Acknowledgment

When you respond directly to something another person says to you, you are acknowledging not only the statement, but also that the person is important.

Jen: It certainly is a nice day for a canoe trip.

Midori: Yes, Jen, it's a great day to be outside.

🟠 Agreement about Judgments

When you confirm someone's evaluation of something, you are also affirming that person's sense of taste and judgment.

Nancy: I think the steel guitar player's riff was fantastic.

Denis: Yes, I thought it was the best part of the performance.

🟠 Supportive Response

When you express reassurance and understanding, you are confirming a person's right to his or her feelings.

Joel: I'm disappointed that I scored only a 60 on my interpersonal communication test.

Greta: I'm sorry to see you so sad, Joel. I know that test was important to you.

🟠 Clarifying Response

When you seek greater understanding of another person's message, you are confirming that he or she is worth your time and trouble. Clarifying responses also encourage the other person to talk in order to explore his or her feelings.

Dilip: I'm not feeling very good about my family situation these days.

Tyrone: Is it tough with you and Ann working different shifts?

🟠 Expression of Positive Feeling

We feel confirmed or valued when someone else agrees with our expression of joy or excitement.

Lorraine: I'm so excited! I was just promoted to associate professor.

Dorette: Congratulations! I'm so proud of you! Heaven knows you deserve it.

🟠 Compliment

When you tell people you like what they have done or said, what they are wearing, or how they look, you are confirming their sense of worth.

Jean-Christophe: Did you get the invitation to my party?

Huong: Yes! It looked so professional. I didn't know you could do calligraphy. You're a talented guy.

In each of these examples, note how the responder provides comments that confirm the worth or value of the other person. But we want to caution that confirming responses should be sincere. Offering false praise is manipulative, and your communication partner will probably sniff out your phoniness.

> ### Recap
>
> #### USING WORDS TO VALUE OTHERS
> - Directly acknowledge something someone has said.
> - Agree with the person's judgments.
> - Be supportive; let the other person know you are trying to understand how he or she feels.
> - Ask questions to help clarify another person's statements if you are not sure you understand.
> - Express positive feelings to echo those of the other person.
> - Compliment the person if you can be sincere.

Disconfirming Responses

Some statements and responses can undermine another person's self-worth. Note the following so that you can avoid using them and can also recognize when someone using them is trying to chip away at your self-image and self-esteem.

Impervious Response

When a person fails to acknowledge your statement or attempt to communicate, even though you know he or she heard you, you may feel a sense of awkwardness or embarrassment.

Rosa: I loved your speech, Harvey.

Harvey: (No response, verbal or non-verbal.)

Interrupting Response

When people interrupt you, they may be implying that what they have to say is more important than what you have to say. In effect, they could also be implying that they are more important than you are.

Anna: I just heard on the financial news that . . .

Sharon: Oh yes. The stock market just went down 100 points.

Irrelevant Response

An irrelevant response is one that has nothing at all to do with what you were saying. Chances are your partner is not listening to you at all.

Arnold: First we're flying down to Rio, and then to Quito. I can hardly wait to . . .

Chin-Lee: They're predicting a hard freeze tonight.

The real message Chin-Lee is sending is, "I have more important things on my mind."

Tangential Response

A tangential response acknowledges you but is only minimally related to what you are talking about. Again, it indicates that the other person isn't really attending to your message.

Kurt: This new program will help us stay within our budget.

Samantha: Yeah. I think I'll save some bucks and send this letter by regular mail.

Impersonal Response

A response that intellectualizes and uses the third person distances the other person from you and has the effect of trivializing what you say.

Diana: Hey, Bill. I'd like to talk with you for a minute about getting your permission to take my vacation in July.

Bill: One tends to become interested in recreational pursuits about this time of year, doesn't one?

Incoherent Response

When a speaker mumbles, rambles, or makes some unintelligible effort to respond, it may leave you wondering if what you said was of any value or use to the listener.

Paolo: George, here's my suggestion for the merger deal with Canatech. Let's make them an offer of $48 a share and see how they respond.

George: Huh? Well... So... Well... hmmm... I'm not sure.

Incongruous Response

When a verbal message is inconsistent with non-verbal behaviour, we usually believe the non-verbal message, but we usually feel confused as well. An incongruous response is like a malfunctioning traffic light with flashing red and green lights—you're just not sure whether the speaker wants you to go or stay.

Sue: Honey, do you want me to go grocery shopping with you?

Steve: (Shouting) OF COURSE I DO! WHY ARE YOU ASKING?

Although it may be impossible to eliminate all disconfirming responses from your repertoire, becoming aware of the power of your words and monitoring your conversation for offensive phrases may help you avoid unexpected and, perhaps, devastating consequences.

Building Your Skills

SUPPORTIVE-DEFENSIVE COMMUNICATION CHARADES

Divide into groups of two to four people. Each team or group should prepare a short play depicting one of the supportive or defensive communication responses described in this chapter. Perform your play for the class or another team to see if they can identify the type of supportive or defensive communication behaviour your team is portraying. Consider one of the following situations or develop one of your own:

- Speaking with a professor about a grade.
- Returning a broken item to a store.
- Talking with your child about his or her marks.
- Responding to a telemarketing salesperson who calls you during dinner.
- Talking with one of your employees who made a work-related mistake.
- Rebooking a flight because your flight was cancelled by the airline.
- Taking an order from a customer at a fast-food restaurant.
- Receiving a complaint from a customer about poor service.
- Talking with someone who has knocked on your door inviting you to his or her church.
- Asking someone to turn down the stereo or TV while you are trying to study.

Variation: Instead of illustrating supportive and defensive communication, roleplay an example of one of the confirming or disconfirming communication behaviours discussed in this chapter.

Considering Others

ESSENTIAL GUIDELINES

The key to shared understanding is to focus on the needs, goals, and mindset of your communication partner. Throughout this chapter we have emphasized how to develop an other-oriented approach to communicating verbally. You can use a few slogans to remind yourself of what you have read:

Slogan # 1: *Meanings are in people not in words.*

Words are arbitrary, contextually and culturally bound symbols that can have denotative and connotative, concrete or abstract meaning. Focus on what the words may mean to your partner.

Slogan # 2: *Think before you speak.*

Words have power to create and affect feelings and actions, as well as to affect and reflect culture. Before you speak, consider the impact your words will have on others. Remember that words can hurt—and once spoken, words cannot be taken back.

Slogan # 3: *Say what you mean and mean what you say.*

Given the complexity of the meaning creation process, it is a wonder that we communicate as accurately as we do. When speaking with others, be mindful of the potential for miscommunication and misunderstanding. Use precise language and be accurate in conveying your true feelings. Remember that you are responsible for what you communicate. The spoken word belongs half to the person who speaks and half to the person who understands.

Slogan # 4: *Speak to others as you wish to be spoken to.*

Our words can engender a supportive communication climate or create defensiveness, which can lead to misunderstanding. Always try to put yourself in your partner's place.

Summary

The words we use have great power to affect our self-image and to influence the relationships we establish with others. English words are symbols that refer to objects, events, people, and ideas. They are arbitrary. We interpret their meaning through the context and culture to which they belong. Communication is complex because most words have both denotative (literal) meanings and connotative (subjective) meanings, and because words range from concrete to abstract.

The power of words stems from their ability to create images and to influence our thoughts, feelings, and actions. There is also an important link between the words we use and our culture. Language shapes culture and culture shapes language. Our view of the world is influenced by our vocabulary and the categories we have created with words.

Several word barriers can contribute to misunderstanding in interpersonal communications. Bypassing occurs when a word means one thing to one person and another thing to someone else. Our verbal expressions may lack clarity, either because we make language errors or because the meaning we want to convey is not clear to us. Allness statements can mislead and alienate listeners because the speaker falsely implies that he or she knows all there is to know about something. Another barrier, static evaluation, fails to take changes into account and uses outdated labels and categories. Polarization is the language of extremes; when someone thinks in black and white, many shades of meaning disappear. Finally, biased language that is insensitive to others creates noise that interferes with the meaning of a message.

The words you use can enhance or detract from the quality of relationships you establish with others. People who use supportive communication avoid using language that in any way labels or demeans others. Supportive communication is descriptive rather than evaluative, problem oriented rather than control oriented, genuine rather than contrived or manipulative, empathic rather than neutral, flexible rather than rigid, and equal rather than superior. The words we use can either confirm or undermine another's sense of self-worth. If you directly acknowledge people, agree with their judgments, voice support when they feel bad, ask them to clarify their messages, affirm their positive feelings, and compliment them sincerely, then you may help them boost their self-image. Conversely, our responses can be disconfirming if we are impervious, interrupt someone, or use irrelevant, tangential, impersonal, incoherent, or incongruous messages.

For Discussion and Review

Focus on Comprehension

1. How do words create meaning for others?
2. What power do words have in our relationships with others?
3. What are some barriers to effective understanding, and what are some strategies for overcoming these barriers?
4. What are the characteristics of a supportive communicator?
5. What are confirming communication responses? Describe a few.
6. What are disconfirming communication responses? Describe a few.

Focus on Critical Thinking

7. Yasmina and Paul are having an argument. Paul shouts, "You're constantly criticizing me! You don't let me make any important decisions!" How could Paul communicate how he feels in a more supportive way?
8. Allan asked Jessie to pick him up after work at the circle drive at 5:30 P.M. Jessie waited patiently at the circle drive on the other side of campus and finally went home at 6:30 P.M., having seen no sign of Allan. Allan was waiting at the circle drive behind his office rather than at the one on the other side of the campus. What word barriers do you think led to this misunderstanding?
9. Rephrase the following statements to use less biased language:
    a. I'd like to introduce Mr. Russell Goldberg and his wife Muriel.
    b. In an office memo: "Several gals have been leaving their purses at their desks."
10. Rephrase the following statements, using the skill of indexing.
    a. All politicians want power and control over others.
    b. All teachers are underpaid.
    c. All Vancouverites like to brag about how great their city is.

Focus on Ethics

11. If you really don't want to listen to your co-worker go into details about her latest vacation trip or the recent escapades of her children or grandchildren, is it appropriate to tell her that you'd rather not hear her "news"? Support your response.
12. Is it ethical to correct someone when he or she uses sexist language or makes a stereotypical remark about someone's race, gender, or sexual orientation? What if that person is your boss or your teacher? Explain your answer.
13. Is it ethical to mask your true feelings of anger and irritation with someone by using supportive statements or confirming statements, when what you really want to do is tell him or her "the truth" in no uncertain terms?

For Your Journal

1. Keep a log of examples of word barriers you experience or encounter. Note examples of bypassing, lack of precision in language, bafflegab, and other uses of words that inhibit communication. The examples could come from your own verbal exchanges or those that you observe in the conversations of others.
2. Make a list of words that are in your vocabulary today but were not in your vocabulary five years ago. Include new words that you may have learned in school as well as words that were not generally used or that have been coined in the last half-decade (e.g., *CD-ROM*, *ebay*).
3. Record a sample dialogue between you and a good friend that illustrates some of the confirming responses described on page 185.

Learning with Others

1. Think of a bypass miscommunication that you've experienced. Share your recollection with a small group and compare your feelings and responses with those of others.
2. In your group, think of biased language that is still being currently used. For each term, discuss why this term may be offensive and offer alternate terms or phrases.
3. In your group, choose one person to play a recently divorced person whose ex-spouse is not abiding by a child custody agreement and insists on seeing the children at odd hours. Another person should play the role of a trusted friend who only listens and responds. Ask the trusted friend to use the skills he or she learned in this chapter along with the effective listening skills presented in Chapter 4. Then, do a group evaluation of his or her response.

Weblinks

strategis.ic.gc/sc_mangb/abc/engdoc/homepage.html   This is the home page for Aboriginal Business Canada.

www.psych.hanover.edu/Krantz/journal.html   A site dedicated to electronic journals and periodicals in psychology and related fields. A great site for research.

www.statcan.ca   This is the site for Statistics Canada. There are statistics on everything the Canadian government collects, such as demographics, exercise frequency, family size, and so on. Also, there is access from this site to a number of other links including research and other Canadian sites.

www.vandruff.com/art_converse.html   Conversational Terrorism: How NOT to Talk: This site offers several types and examples of "conversational cheapshots" that are both informative and humorous.

www.ethic.ubc.ca/resources   This is a site from the University of British Columbia about ethics and has several links to other such sites.

www.cbsr.bc.ca   This is the site for Canadian Business for Social Responsibility. Businesses join this group and promote the ethical conducting of business. Among current members are Alcan and Bell Canada.

www.mgmt.utoronto/CCBE   This is the website of Clarkson Centre for Business Ethics.

www.itcilo.it/english/actrav/telearn/global/ilo/code/1997kpmg.htm   From KPMG, read the results of a *1997 Business Ethics Survey*.

Suggested Readings

Mowat, Jeff. "Making Connections." *Canadian Manager*, 25(3), (2000): 26–28.
   This short article presents several suggestions on how to create rapport with another person in less than 30 seconds. Well worth 30 seconds of your time.

Polanyi, Margaret. "Atwood on Atwood." *Reader's Digest* (April 2002): 58–67.
   An interview with Margaret Atwood about her upbringing and her writing career. Ms. Atwood has some interesting thoughts about the writing process.

(no author recorded). "Meeting the PEOPLE Challenge." *Canadian Manager*, 24(2), (1999): 20–25.
   Discusses the challenges that will face the workplace by 2005 and how employees can be prepared. Includes an interesting self-assessment including communication and problem-solving abilities.

chapter 7

Communicating Non-Verbally

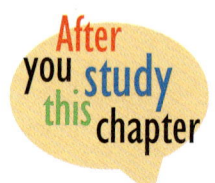

After you study this chapter you should be able to ...

1. Explain why non-verbal communication is an important and challenging area of study.
2. Describe the functions of non-verbal communication in interpersonal relationships.
3. Summarize research findings that describe codes of non-verbal communication behaviour.
4. Describe three dimensions for interpreting non-verbal behaviour.
5. Formulate a strategy for improving your ability to interpret non-verbal messages accurately.

- Why Learn about Non-Verbal Communication?
- The Challenge of Interpreting Non-Verbal Communication
- Non-Verbal Communication Codes
- Interpreting Non-Verbal Communication
- Improving Your Ability to Interpret Non-Verbal Messages

*What you are speaks so loudly that
I cannot hear what you say.*

RALPH WALDO EMERSON

Pierre: Lisa, will you get the telephone?

Lisa: Get it yourself!

Pierre: Hey! Why so testy? All I asked you to do was answer the phone!

If we could view a videotape of Pierre and Lisa's interaction, we could more clearly see the source of the conflict. Pierre's tone of voice and his scowling facial expression made his simple request seem more like an order.

As we noted in Chapter 1, communication has both content and emotional dimensions. Our tone of voice, eye contact, facial expressions, posture, movement, vocal cues, appearance, use of personal space, manipulation of the communication environment, and other non-verbal clues reveal how we feel toward others. We can define **non-verbal communication** as behaviour other than written or spoken language that creates meaning for someone. In this chapter we will focus on how non-verbal communication affects the quality of our interpersonal relationships. As we identify the functions and codes of non-verbal cues, we will also explore ways to improve our skill in interpreting the non-verbal messages of others.

non-verbal communication. Behaviour other than written or spoken language that creates meaning for someone.

Why Learn about Non-Verbal Communication?

When you are sitting in a public place, such as a shopping mall, airport, or bus stop, do you make assumptions about what other people might be like as you observe their non-verbal behaviour? Most of us are people watchers, and we rely on non-verbal communication clues to predict how others may feel about and react to us. Non-verbal communication plays a major role in relationship development because it is also the main channel we use to communicate our feelings and attitudes toward others. But, because much of our non-verbal communication behaviour is unconscious, most of us have limited awareness or understanding of it. We begin examining non-verbal communication by looking at the ways we use it.

Non-Verbal Messages Communicate Our Feelings and Attitudes

Constantine knew that he was in trouble the moment he walked into the room. His wife Sandra gave him a steely stare. Her brow was furrowed and her arms were crossed. On the table was a dish of cold lobster Newburg, candles burnt to nubs, and dirty dishes at all but one place setting: his. Constantine was in the doghouse for forgetting the dinner party his wife had planned, and he needed no words from her to sense the depth of her displeasure.

Albert Mehrabian concluded that as little as 7 percent of the emotional meaning of a message is communicated through explicit verbal channels.[1] The most significant source of emotional communication is our face—according to Mehrabian's study, it channels as much as 55 percent of our meaning. Vocal cues such as volume, pitch, and intensity, communicate another 38 percent of our emotional meaning. In all, we communicate approximately 93 percent of the emotional meaning of our messages non-verbally. Although these percentages do not apply to every communication situation, the results of Mehrabian's investigation do illustrate the potential power of non-verbal cues in communicating emotion.[2]

When we interact with others, we base our feelings and emotional responses not upon what our partner says, but, rather, upon what he or she does. We also alter our non-verbal communication to suit different relationships. With good friends you let down your guard; you may slouch, scratch, and take off your shoes to show you trust them. But if you were interviewing for a job or meeting your future in-laws for the first time, your posture would probably be stiffer and your smiles more carefully controlled as you try to convey the impression that you are mature, competent, and respectable.

Non-Verbal Messages Are More Believable

"Honey, do you love me?" asks Brenda.

"OF COURSE I LOVE YOU! HAVEN'T I ALWAYS TOLD YOU THAT I LOVE YOU? I LOVE YOU!" shouts Jim, keeping his eyes glued to his morning newspaper.

Brenda will probably feel less than reassured by Jim's pledge of affection. The contradiction between his spoken message of love and his non-verbal message of irritation and lack of interest will leave her wondering about his true feelings.

Actions speak louder than words. This cliché became a cliché because non-verbal communication is more believable than verbal communication. Non-verbal messages are more difficult to fake. One research team concluded that we use the following cues, listed in order of most to least important, to help us discern when a person is lying:[3]

- Greater time lag in response to a question
- Reduced eye contact
- Increased shifts in posture
- Unfilled pauses
- Less smiling
- Slower speech
- Higher pitch in voice
- More deliberate pronunciation and articulation of words

It is difficult to manipulate an array of non-verbal cues, so a skilled other-oriented observer can see when our true feelings leak out. One research team has identified the face, hands, and feet as key sources of non-verbal leakage cues.[4] Are you aware of what your fingers and toes are doing as you are reading this book? Even if we become experts at masking and manipulating our faces, we may first signal lack of interest or boredom with another person by finger wiggling or toe wagging. Or, we may twiddle a pen or pencil. When we become emotionally aroused, the pupils of our eyes dilate, and we may blush, sweat, or change our breathing patterns.[5] Lie detectors rely on these unconscious cues. A polygraph measures a person's heart and breathing rate, as well as the electrical resistance of the skin (called galvanic skin response), to determine whether he or she is giving truthful verbal responses.

Non-Verbal Communication Plays a Major Role in Interpersonal Relationships

As we learned in Chapter 1, communication is inescapable; one researcher suggests that as much as 65 percent of the social meaning in our messages is based upon non-verbal communication.[6] Of course, the meaning that others interpret from your behaviour may not be the one you intended, and the inferences they draw based upon non-verbal information may be right or wrong.

We learned in Chapter 3 that we begin making judgments about strangers just a fraction of a second after meeting them, based upon non-verbal information. Within the first four minutes of interaction we scope the other out and draw conclusions about him or her.[7] Another research team found that you may decide whether a date is going to be pleasant or dull during the first 30 seconds of meeting your partner, before your partner has had time to utter more than "Hello."[8] Non-verbal cues are the ones that form first impressions, accurate or not.

Non-verbal cues are important not only when we initiate relationships but also as we maintain and develop mature relationships with others. In fact, the more intimate the relationship, the more we use and understand the non-verbal cues of our partners. Couples that have been together for years spend less time verbalizing their feelings and emotions to each other than they did when they first met; each learns how to interpret the other's subtle non-verbal cues. If your partner is silent during dinner, you may know that the day was a tough one, and you should give her or him a wide berth. If, when a woman puts on new bright green pants, the man grimaces and asks, "New pants?" she may understand that he does not like them. In fact, all of us are more likely to use non-verbal cues to convey negative messages than to explicitly announce our dislike of something or someone. We also use non-verbal cues to signal changes in the level of satisfaction with a relationship. When we want to cool things off, we may start using a less vibrant tone of voice and cut back on eye contact and physical contact with our partner.

Even though we've discussed verbal messages and non-verbal messages in separate chapters in this book, verbal and non-verbal cues often work together to create meaning. Also keep in mind that interpersonal communication, especially the expression of non-verbal messages, is a transactional process. Meaning is created simultaneously between those communicating. **Interaction adaptation theory** describes the transactive process of how people adapt to the communication behaviour of others.

Portrait artists pay close attention to non-verbal cues such as posture, facial expression, and gesture to capture their subjects' personalities. What do the non-verbal cues reveal about this Spanish dancer?
(John Singer Sargeant, *Belle Epoque*. Erich Lessing/Art Resource)

interaction adaptation theory. Theory suggesting that a predictor of how you interact with others is your tendency to adapt to what others are doing.

Based on interaction adaptation theory, Judee Burgoon and her colleagues have concluded that non-verbal cues play a key role in how people adapt to others.[9] If, for example, your friend leans forward to tell a story, you may reciprocally lean forward to listen. Or if during a meeting you sit with folded arms, unconvinced of what you are hearing, you may look around the conference table and find others with similarly folded arms. Like an intricate dance, when we communicate, we relate to others by responding to movement, eye contact, gestures, and other non-verbal cues. Sometimes we relate by mirroring the posture or behaviour of others. Or we may find ourselves gesturing in sync with someone's vocal pattern. The rhythm of life is often conveyed as we respond and adapt to others through our non-verbal behaviour.

Although we do rely heavily on non-verbal messages, they do not operate independently of spoken messages in our relationships. Instead, verbal and non-verbal cues work together in two primary ways to help us make sense of others' messages.

First, non-verbal cues substitute for, repeat, contradict, or regulate verbal messages. An extended thumb signals that a hitchhiker would like a ride. A circle formed by the thumb and index finger can either signal that everything is A-OK or convey an obscene message. When someone asks, "Which way did he go?" we can silently point to the back door. In these instances, we are substituting non-verbal cues for a verbal message.

We can also use non-verbal cues to repeat or reinforce our words. "Where is the personnel department?" asks a job applicant. "Three flights up. Take the elevator," says the security guard, pointing to the elevator. The guard's pointing gesture repeats the verbal instruction and clarifies the message.

"Sure, this is a good time to talk about the Henrikson merger," says the business executive, nervously looking at her watch, stuffing papers into her attaché case, and avoiding eye contact with her co-worker. In this instance, the non-verbal cues contradict the verbal ones. And, as we learned earlier, the non-verbal message is almost always the one we believe.

We also use non-verbal cues to regulate our participation in verbal exchanges. In most informal meetings it is not appropriate or necessary to signal your desire to speak by raising your hand. Yet, somehow you are able to signal to others when you'd like to speak and when you'd rather not talk. How does this happen? You use eye contact, raised eyebrows, an open mouth, or, perhaps, a single raised index finger to signal that you would like to make a point. If your colleagues do not see these signals, especially the eye contact, they know you are not interested in talking.[10]

The second way in which non-verbal cues work together with verbal ones is in accenting and complementing emotional messages. "Unless we vote to increase our tax base," bellows Mr. Coddlington, "we will not have enough classroom space to educate our children." While delivering his impassioned plea to the school board, Mr. Coddlington also loudly slaps the lectern to accent his message and reinforce its intensity. A scolding mother's wagging finger and an angry supervisor's frown are other non-verbal cues that accent verbal messages.

Complementary non-verbal messages that we deliver simultaneously with a verbal message can also help to colour the emotion we are expressing or the attitude we are conveying. The length of a hug while you tell your son you are proud of him provides complementary information about the intensity of your pride. The firmness of your handshake when you greet a job interviewer can complement your verbal claim that you are eager for employment.

> ## Recap
>
> ### REASONS TO STUDY NON-VERBAL COMMUNICATION
>
> - Non-verbal communication is the primary way in which we communicate feelings and attitudes toward others.
> - Non-verbal messages are usually more believable than verbal messages.
> - Non-verbal communication plays a major role in relationship development.
> - Non-verbal cues substitute for, repeat, contradict, or regulate verbal messages.
> - Non-verbal cues accent and complement emotional messages.

The Challenge of Interpreting Non-Verbal Messages

Even though we have made great claims for the value of studying non-verbal behaviours, it is not always easy to decipher unspoken messages. We have dictionaries to help us interpret words, but we have no handy reference book to help us decode non-verbal cues. To help you with the decoding process, we are going to classify some common types of non-verbal behaviours. But first, you should be aware of some of the difficulties inherent in attempting a classification.

Non-Verbal Messages Are Often Ambiguous

Most words carry a meaning that everyone who speaks the same language can recognize. But the meaning of non-verbal messages may be known only to the person displaying them. Perhaps even more importantly, that person may not intend for the behaviour to have any meaning at all. And some people have difficulty expressing their emotions non-verbally. They may have a frozen facial expression or a monotone voice. Or they may be teasing you, but their deadpan expressions lead you to believe that their negative comments are heartfelt. Often, it is tough to draw meaningful conclusions about another person's behaviour, even if we know him or her quite well.

Non-Verbal Messages Are Continuous

Words are discrete entities; they have a beginning and an end. You can point to the first word in this sentence and underline the last one. Our non-verbal behaviours are not as easily dissected. Like the sweep of a second hand on a watch, non-verbal behaviours are continuous. Some, such as a slap or a hand clap, have definite beginnings and endings. But more often than not, your non-verbal behaviour unfolds without clearly defined starting and stopping points. Gestures, facial expressions, and even eye contact can flow from one situation to the next with seamless ease. Researchers have difficulty studying non-verbal cues because of this continuous stream, so trying to categorize and interpret them will be challenging for us as well.

Non-Verbal Cues Are Multi-Channelled

Have you ever tried to watch two or more TV programs at once? Some televisions let you see as many as eight programs simultaneously so that you can keep up with three ball games and two soap operas and view commercials on the three other channels. Like the multi-channel TV, non-verbal cues come simultaneously to our perception centre from a variety of sources. And just as you can really watch only one channel at a time on your multi-channel television—although you can move among them very rapidly—so, too, can you actually attend to only one non-verbal cue at a time. One researcher suspects that negative non-verbal messages (frowns, grimaces, lack of eye contact) command attention before positive messages when the two compete.[11] Moreover, if the non-verbal message contradicts the verbal message, then we may have trouble interpreting either one correctly.[12]

Non-Verbal Interpretation Is Culture Based

As you read in the last chapter, some emotions and their non-verbal expressions are universal. For example, humans from every culture smile when they are happy and frown when they are unhappy.[13] We also all raise or flash our eyebrows when meeting or greeting others, and young children in many cultures wave to signal they want their mothers, raise their arms to be picked up, and suck their thumbs for comfort.[14] All this suggests that there is some underlying basis for expressing emotion and that there are some universal non-verbal emotional expressions. Yet, each culture also develops unique rules for displaying and interpreting these gestures and expressions.

Understanding Diversity

CULTURAL DIFFERENCES IN INTERPRETING NON-VERBAL MESSAGES

Research investigating non-verbal communication in a variety of cultures confirms that individuals interpret non-verbal messages from their unique cultural perspective. Note the following conclusions:[15]

FACIAL EXPRESSIONS One research team found that facial expressions conveying happiness, sadness, anger, disgust, and surprise were the same in 68 to 92 percent of the cultures examined. All humans probably share the same neurophysiological basis for expressing emotions, but we learn different rules for sending and interpreting the expressions. For example, the Japanese culture does not reinforce the show of negative emotions; it is important for Japanese to "save face" and to help others save face as well.

EYE CONTACT There seems to be more eye contact in interpersonal interactions between Arabs, South Americans, and Greeks than between people from other cultures. There is evidence that some African-Americans look at others less often than do whites when sending and receiving messages. One of the most universal expressions among cultures appears to be the eyebrow flash (the sudden raising of the eyebrows when meeting someone or interacting with others).

GESTURES Hand and body gestures with the most shared meaning among Africans, North Americans, and South Americans include pointing, shrugging, head nodding, clapping, thumbs down, waving hello, and beckoning. There are, however, regional variations within cultures; it is not wise to assume that all people in a given culture share the same meaning for certain gestures. The OK gesture made by forming a circle with the thumb and finger has sexual connotations for some South American and Caribbean countries. In France, the OK sign means worthless.

SPACE Arabs, Latin Americans, and Southern Europeans seem to stand closer to others than people from Asia, India, Pakistan, and Northern Europe. If you have been to Britain you know that people queue or wait for buses in orderly straight lines. In France, however, queuing is less orderly and individuals are more likely to push forward to be the next customer or get the next seat on the bus. As with gestures, however, there are regional variations in spatial preferences.

There is no common cross-cultural dictionary of non-verbal meaning. There are well-established norms for non-verbal behaviour for each culture, however, and conscientious travellers will make an effort to learn these norms for the culture they are visiting. How accurate is the advice given in the Canadian Issues box on pages 199 and 200 for visitors to Canada? Given Canada's rapidly changing immigrant population (discussed in Chapter 9), how long can these norms be expected to remain valid?

Canadian Issues

RULES FOR NON-VERBAL COMMUNICATION IN CANADA

What are the rules for non-verbal communication in Canada? In a "bible" of protocol for doing business in 60 different countries, readers are provided the following advice on non-verbal rules of behaviour with Canadians (note that this is not the complete list). This book was written in 1994. Do you see any changes in these rules or are they still the same now? Do you think the divisions between French Canadians and British Canadians is a fair one given the country's diversity today?

- In Canada, the standard greeting is a smile, often accompanied by a nod, wave, and/or verbal greeting.

- In business situations, a handshake is used upon greetings or introductions.
- Canadian businesspeople expect a firm handshake (web-to-web contact), direct eye contact, and an open, friendly manner. A weak handshake may be taken as a sign of weakness.
- Older men usually wait for women to offer their hand before shaking.
- French Canadians also have a fairly firm handshake. And they shake hands more often: upon greetings, introductions, and departures, even if the person has been greeted earlier that day.
- Good friends and family members sometimes embrace, especially among the French. A kissing of both cheeks may also occur, especially among the French.
- The standard distance between you and your conversation partner should be 60 cm. British Canadians are uncomfortable standing any closer to another person. French Canadians may stand slightly closer.
- Canadians, especially those of British descent, do not tend toward frequent or expansive gesturing.
- The backslap is a sign of close friendship among British Canadians. It is rarely used among the French.
- Direct eye contact shows that you are sincere, although it should not be too intense. Some minorities look away to show respect.
- When sitting, Canadians often look very relaxed. Men may sit with the ankle of one leg on the knee of the other or prop their feet up on chairs or desks.
- In business situations, maintain good posture and a less casual pose.
- In most of Canada, to call the waiter or waitress over, briefly wave to get his or her attention. To call for the cheque, make a writing gesture. In Quebec, it is only necessary to nod the head backwards or to make a discreet wave of the hand.

Source: From T. Morrison, W. A. Conaway, and G. A. Borden, *Kiss, Bow, or Shake Hands: How to Do Business in Sixty Different Countries* (Holbrook, Mass.: Bob Adams, Inc., 1994).

Non-Verbal Communication Codes

Keeping all of these challenges to our understanding in mind, we can begin looking at the categories of non-verbal information that researchers have studied: movement and gestures, eye contact, facial expressions, use of space and territory, touch, and personal appearance. Although we will concentrate on the codes that fall within these categories in mainstream Western culture, we will also try to look at codes for other cultures and subcultures.

Body Movement, Posture, and Gestures

In 1771, when English explorer Captain Cook arrived in the New Hebrides, he didn't speak the language of the natives. His only way of communicating was sign language. Through gestures, pointing, and hand waving, he established contact with the natives. There is evidence that people have used gestures to communicate since ancient times—especially to bridge cultural and language differences. The first record of using sign language to communicate is found in Xenophon's *The March Up Country*, in which unspoken gestures were used to help the Greeks cross Asia Minor in about 400 B.C. Even when we do speak the same language as others, we use gestures to help us make our point.[16]

Kinesics is the study of human movement and gestures. It was Francis Bacon who noted, "As the tongue speaketh to the ear, so the hand speaketh to the eye." We have long recognized that the movement and gestures we exhibit provide valuable

kinesics. The study of human movement and gestures.

information to others. Various scholars and researchers have proposed paradigms for analyzing and coding these movements and gestures, just as we do for spoken or written language.[17]

One paradigm identifies four stages of "quasi-courtship behaviour."[18] The first stage is *courtship readiness*. When we are attracted to someone, we may suck in our stomach, tense our muscles, and stand up straight. The second stage includes *preening behaviours*: we manipulate our appearance by combing our hair, applying makeup, straightening our tie, pulling up our socks, and double-checking our appearance in the mirror. In the third stage we demonstrate *positional cues*, using our posture and body orientation to be seen and noticed by others. Here, the classic Norman Rockwell painting shows teenagers illustrating typical preening and positional cues.

One researcher recently found 52 gestures and non-verbal behaviours that women use to signal an interest in men. Among the most common unspoken flirting cues were: smiling and surveying a crowded room with the eyes, and moving closer to the object of affection.[19] These cues intensify in the fourth stage, *appeals to invitation*, using close proximity, exposed skin, open body positions, and eye contact to signal availability and interest. Subjects in one study reported that they were aware of using all these techniques to promote an intimate relationship. In fact, we use these quasi-courtship behaviours to some extent in almost any situation in which we are trying to gain favourable attention from another.

Another team of researchers focused on non-verbal behaviours that make us label a person warm and friendly or cold and distant.[20] They found that "warm" people face their communication partners directly, smile more, make more direct eye contact, fidget less, and generally make fewer unnecessary hand movements. "Cold" people make less eye contact, smile less, fidget more, and turn away from their partners.

Posture and body orientation reveal important information. Open body posture (uncrossed arms and legs) communicates that we are receptive and responsive listeners. When we are trying to decrease our contact with someone, say at a party or family gathering, we are likely to turn away from the individual we want to avoid. As you will find when you participate in the following *Building Your Skills: Communicating Interest*, your body orientation and posture provide important cues to your interest and willingness to continue or end communication with someone.

Albert Mehrabian has identified the non-verbal cues that contribute to perceptions of liking.[21] He found that an open body and arm position, a forward lean, and a more relaxed posture communicate liking. When we are attempting to persuade someone, we typically have more eye contact and a more direct body orientation; we are more likely to lean forward and closer to others.

Another team of researchers tried to classify movement and gestures according to their function. They identified five categories: emblems, illustrators, affect displays, regulators, and adaptors.[22]

Can you identify the quasi-courtship behaviour in this painting? (Printed by permission of the Norman Rockwell Family Trust. Copyright © *Soda Jerk,* The Norman Rockwell Family Trust)

Building Your Skills

COMMUNICATING INTEREST

Non-verbally play the roles of both a good listener and a poor listener. First, imagine that you are listening to someone talk. As a good listener, how would you communicate your interest in what the person is saying without uttering a word? Note your posture, eye contact, presence or lack of hand movement. Are your arms and legs crossed?

Now role-play a poor listener—someone who appears to be bored or even irritated by what a speaker is saying. What are the differences in the cues you use? Use the space here or write your responses on a sheet of paper to describe the differences.

Nonverbal Behaviours of a Good Listener

Posture: _____
_____
_____

Body orientation: _____
_____
_____

Eye contact: _____
_____
_____

Gestures: _____
_____
_____

Movement: _____
_____
_____

Nonverbal Behaviours of a Poor Listener

Posture: _____
_____
_____

Body orientation: _____
_____
_____

Eye contact: _____
_____
_____

Gestures: _____
_____
_____

Movement: _____
_____
_____

---

emblems. Non-verbal cues that have specific, generally understood meanings in a given culture and that may substitute for a word or phrase.

illustrators. Non-verbal behaviour that accompanies a verbal message and either contradicts, accents, or complements it.

🟠 Emblems

Non-verbal cues that have specific, generally understood meanings in a given culture and may actually substitute for a word or phrase are called **emblems**. When you are busy typing a report that is due the next day and your young son rushes in to ask for permission to buy a new computer game, you turn from your computer and hold up an open palm to indicate your desire for uninterrupted quiet. To communicate your enthusiastic enjoyment of a violin soloist at a concert, you applaud wildly. You want your children to stop talking in the library, so you put an index finger up to your pursed lips.

🟠 Illustrators

We frequently accompany a verbal message with **illustrators** that either contradict, accent, or complement the message. Slamming a book closed while announcing, "I don't want to read this anymore" or pounding a lectern while proclaiming, "This point is important!" are two examples of non-verbal behaviours that accent the verbal message. Typically, we use non-verbal illustrators at the beginning of clauses or phrases.[23] TV newscasters, for example, turn a page to signal that they are moving to a new story or topic. Most of us use illustrators to help us communicate information about the size, shape, and spatial relationships of objects. You probably even use them when you talk on the phone, though probably not as many as you use in face-to-face conversation.[24]

🟠 Affect Displays

Non-verbal movements and postures used to communicate emotion are called **affect displays**, which as we saw in the last chapter are used to display how we feel. Our facial expressions, vocal cues, posture, and gestures convey the intensity of our emotions.[25] If you are happy, for example, your face will telegraph your joy to others. But the movement of your hands, the openness of your posture, and the speed with which you move will tell others *how* happy you are. Similarly, if you are feeling depressed, your face will probably reveal your sadness or dejection, while your slumped shoulders and lowered head will indicate the intensity of your despair. When we are feeling friendly, we use a soft tone of voice, an open smile, and a relaxed posture.[26] When we feel neutral about an issue, we signal that feeling by putting little expression on our face or in our voice. When we feel hostile, we use a harsh voice, frown with our teeth showing, and keep our posture tense and rigid.

🟠 Regulators

We use **regulators** to control the interaction or flow of communication between ourselves and another person. When we are eager to respond to a message, we make eye contact, raise our eyebrows, open our mouth, raise an index finger, and lean forward slightly. When we do not want to be part of the conversation, we do the opposite: we avert our eyes, close our mouth, cross our arms, and lean back in our seats or away from the verbal action.

🟠 Adaptors

When we are cold, we reach for a sweater or wrap our arms around our chests to keep warm. When the temperature is 36 degrees Celsius in the shade and there is no breeze, we reach for a fan to make our own breeze. These behaviours are examples of **adaptors**—non-verbal behaviours that help us to satisfy a personal need and adapt to the immediate situation. When you adjust your glasses, scratch a mosquito bite, or comb your hair, you are using movement to help you manage your personal needs.

🟠 The Five Categories and Interpersonal Communication

How will understanding these five categories of non-verbal behaviour help you understand others and your own interpersonal communication? They give you a new and more precise way to think about your own behaviour. By noting how often you use emblems instead of words to communicate a message, you can recognize how important emblems are in your relationships with others. The more you rely upon emblems that have unique meanings for you and your partner, the more intimate the interpersonal relationship. Also, start to notice whether your non-verbal behaviour contradicts what you say. Monitoring your use of illustrators can help you determine whether you are sending mixed signals to others. Be aware of how you display affect. Knowing that your face and voice communicate emotion, and that posture and gesture indicate the intensity of your feelings, can help you understand how others make inferences about your feelings and attitudes. If other people have difficulty interpreting your emotional state, you may not be projecting your feelings non-verbally. And finally, notice how you use adaptors. Individuals who do not learn the cultural norms of displaying adaptors can have a difficult time socially. For example, if you were never taught not to comb your hair or belch at the table, you may find you receive few dinner invitations.

---

affect display. Non-verbal behaviour that communicates emotions.

regulators. Non-verbal messages that help to control the interaction or level of communication among people.

adaptors. Non-verbal behaviours that help satisfy a personal need and help a person adapt or respond to the immediate situation.

Since non-verbal cues are ambiguous, it's not a good idea to use them to achieve a specific objective. But, as you have seen, people are more likely to respond in predictable ways if you use behaviours they can recognize and interpret easily.

▶ Recap

CATEGORIES OF MOVEMENT AND GESTURES

Category	Definition	Examples
Emblems	Behaviours that have specific, generally understood meaning.	Raising a thumb to hitchhike a ride.
Illustrators	Cues that accompany verbal messages and provide meaning for the message.	Pounding the podium to emphasize a point.
Affect Displays	Expressions of emotion.	Hugging someone to express love.
Regulators	Cues that control and manage the flow of communication between others.	Looking at someone when you wish to speak.
Adaptors	Behaviours that help you adapt to your environment.	Scratching, combing your hair.

Eye Contact

Subtle power. Whether you choose to look at someone or avert your gaze has an enormous impact on your relationship with that person. Researchers have identified four functions for eye contact in interpersonal interactions.[27]

First, it serves a *cognitive* function because it gives you information about another person's thought processes. For example, if your partner breaks eye contact after you ask him or her a question, you will know that he or she is probably thinking of something to say.

Second, we use eye contact to *monitor* the behaviour of others. We receive a major portion of the information we obtain through our eyes. We look at others to determine whether they are receptive to our messages. In fact, this search for feedback is implicit in the word for the centre part of the eye, *pupil*, which comes from the Latin word *pupilla* or "little doll." When you look into someone's eyes, you can see a miniature reflection of yourself.[28]

Third, eye contact is one of the most powerful *regulatory* cues we use to signal when we want to talk and when we don't want to communicate. Your authors have noticed that when they ask questions such as, "Who can tell me the four functions of eye contact?" students quickly, yet unobtrusively, avert their eyes to signal, "Don't call on me." When we do want to communicate with others, say when we're standing in line at the bakery, we fix our eyes on the clerk to signal, "My turn next. Please wait on me."

Finally, the area around our eyes serves an *expressive* function. The eyes have been called the "mirror of the soul" because they reveal our emotions to others. We may cry, blink, and widen or narrow our gaze to express our feelings.

Researchers Mark Knapp and Judith Hall have summarized conclusions on non-verbal communication that predict when you are most and least likely to have eye contact with someone, as shown in Table 7.1.[29]

Table 7.1

When Are You Most and Least Likely to Have Eye Contact with Someone?

You Are More Likely to Have Eye Contact When You	You Are Less Likely to Have Eye Contact When You
• Like or love your partner	• Do not like your partner
• Are physically distant from him or her	• Are physically close to your partner
• Are discussing easy, impersonal topics	• Are discussing difficult, intimate topics
• Have nothing else to look at	• Have other things to look at
• Are interested in your partner's reactions	• Are not interested in your partner's reactions
• Are trying to dominate or persuade your partner	• Are not trying to dominate or persuade your partner
• Are from a culture that emphasizes eye contact	• Are from a culture that de-emphasizes eye contact
• Are an extrovert	• Are an introvert
• Have a high need to affiliate or to be included	• Have a low need to affiliate or do not need to be included
• Are dependent on your partner (and your partner is not responsive)	• Are more independent of your partner (and your partner is responsive to you)
• Are listening rather than talking	• Are talking rather than listening
• Are female	• Are male

Source: Adapted from Mark L. Knapp and Judith A. Hall, *Nonverbal Communication in Human Interaction* (Fort Worth, Texas: Harcourt Brace, 1997), 390–391.

When we do establish eye contact with others, it may seem that our gaze is constant. Yet, research suggests that we actually spend the majority of our time looking at something other than the person's eyes. One research team found that we focus on something else, including our partner's mouth, 57 percent of the time.[30] Not surprisingly then, facial expressions are another rich source of information in our communication with others.

> **Recap**
>
> **FUNCTIONS OF EYE CONTACT**
>
> | | |
> |---|---|
> | Cognitive | Provides cues about our thinking and thought processes. |
> | Monitoring | Provides information about how others are responding to us; we monitor to seek feedback. |
> | Regulatory | Manages the flow of communication; we use eye contact to signal when we do and do not want to interact with another person. |
> | Expressive | Provides information about feelings, emotions, and attitudes. |

Facial Expressions

You tell your parents that you will not be able to spend the holidays with them because you have decided to take your children skiing. You present your partner with a new abstract art painting that you would like to hang in your bedroom. As the personnel director reviews your résumé, you sit in silence across the desk from her or him. In each of these situations you would be eagerly awaiting some reaction from the other person. And what you would be scanning is his or her face. The face is the exhibit gallery for our emotional displays. And although we often try to manipulate our facial cues to project a premeditated feeling, our faces may still betray our true emotions to others.[31]

To interpret our partner's facial expressions accurately, we need to put our other-orientation skills to work, focusing on what the other person may be thinking or feeling. It helps if we know the person well, can see his or her whole face, have plenty of time to watch it, and understand the situation that prompted the emotion.[32] But, it is also helpful to know the cues for "reading" facial expressions.

Your face is versatile. According to one research team, it is capable of producing over 250 000 different expressions.[33] Research suggests that women have greater variety in their emotional expressions and spend more time smiling than men.[34] But all of our expressions can be grouped under six primary emotional categories; the following list describes the changes that occur on our faces for each one.[35]

Surprise:	Wide-open eyes; raised and wrinkled brow; open mouth.
Fear:	Open mouth; tense skin under the eyes; wrinkles in the centre of the forehead.
Disgust:	Raised or curled upper lip; wrinkled nose; raised cheeks; lowered brow; lowered upper eyelid.
Anger:	Tensed lower eyelid; either pursed lips or open mouth; lowered and wrinkled brow; staring eyes.
Happiness:	Smiling; mouth may be open or closed; raised cheeks; wrinkles around lower eyelids.
Sadness:	Lip may tremble; corners of the lips turn downward; corners of the upper eyelid may be raised.

The face is an exhibit gallery for our emotions. The messages we convey through thousands of different expressions are usually more powerful and direct than verbal ones.
(Bob Daemmrich/Stock Boston)

How accurately do we interpret emotions expressed on the face? Several studies have attempted to measure subjects' skill in identifying emotional expressions of others. They have found that reading facial expression is a tricky business. According to one research team, even though our faces provide a great deal of information about emotions, we have learned how to control our facial expressions.[36]

Building Your Skills

FACIAL EXPRESSION QUIZ

Divide into teams of two people. Person A should select one of the six primary emotions communicated by the face and attempt to display the emotion to person B by using the phrase, "May I help you?" The six primary emotions are happiness, sadness, surprise, disgust, anger, and fear. Communicate all six emotions in random order while verbalizing this phrase. Some will be easier to identify and do than others!

Person B should attempt to identify the emotions expressed by person A and list them in order.

When person A has communicated all six emotions, he or she can reverse roles with person B.

1. _____
2. _____
3. _____
4. _____
5. _____
6. _____

Vocal Cues

Try this. Say "John" to communicate the following emotions: anger, sadness, disgust, happiness, fear, surprise. If you are reading this in a public place, stop reading for a moment and give it a try, even if you have to whisper. What happened to your voice? Like your face, your voice is a major vehicle for communicating your emotions. The pitch, rate, and volume at which we speak, and our use of silence, all provide important clues to our feelings.

Your voice is a primary tool for communicating information about the nature of relationships between you and others.[37] We use our voices to present one message on the surface (with words) and usually a more accurate expression of our feelings with our vocal quality. Say the following sentence out loud: "This looks great." Now say it sarcastically; you really don't think it looks great: "This looks great." Clearly, your vocal cues provide the real meaning.

Some vocal expressions of emotion are easier to identify than others. Expressions of joy and anger are obvious ones, whereas shame and love are the most difficult emotions to identify based on vocal cues alone.[38] We are also likely to confuse fear with nervousness, love with sadness, and pride with satisfaction.

Our voices also provide information about our self-confidence and our knowledge of the subject matter in our messages. Most of us would conclude that a speaker who mumbles, speaks slowly, consistently mispronounces words, and uses "uhs" and "ums" is less credible and persuasive than one who speaks clearly, rapidly, and fluently.[39] Even though mispronunciations and vocalized pauses ("ums" and "ahs") seem to have a negative effect on credibility, they do not seem to be a major impediment to attitude change. People may, for example, think that you are less knowledgeable if you stammer, but you may still be able to get your persuasive message across.

In addition to providing information about emotions, self-confidence, and knowledge, vocal cues also serve a regulatory function in interpersonal situations, signalling when we want to talk and when we don't. When we are finished talking, we may lower the pitch of our final word. When we want to talk, we may start by interjecting sounds such as "I . . . I . . . I . . ." or "Ah . . . Ah . . . Ah . . ." to interrupt the speaker and grab the verbal ball. We also may use more cues such as, "Sure," "I understand," "Uh-huh," or "OK" to signal that we understand the message of the other person and now we want to talk or end the conversation. These *back channel* cues are particularly useful in telephone conversations when we have no other non-verbal cues to help us signal that we would like to get off the phone.

Sometimes it is not what we say, or even how we say it, that communicates our feelings. Being silent may communicate volumes. One researcher, in commenting about the importance of silence in speech, said: "Silence is to speech as white paper is to this print. . . . The entire system of spoken language would fail without [people's] ability to both tolerate and create sign sequences of silence-sound-silence units."[40]

Why are we sometimes at a loss for words? There are many possible reasons. We may simply not know what to say. Or, there is evidence that when someone tells a lie, he or she may need a few moments to think of a credible ruse. We may be silent because we want to distance ourselves from those who are around us; we want to communicate that we really don't want to be involved in the conversation. Or, perhaps, we just need some time to think about what we want to contribute to the conversation. Silence, too, may be a sign of respect. Some children were raised with the message, "Be seen and not heard." They were taught that those in authority should maintain control of the talking process. At other times you are silent with someone because words would diminish the experience you are sharing. Walking hand in hand on the beach, watching the sun set, or sitting on a balcony overlooking a spectacular mountain vista may call for silence; trying to translate the experience into words would diminish it.

Would you be comfortable just sitting silently with a good friend? Sidney Baker's theory of silence suggests that the more at ease we are when we share a silence with a close friend, the more comfortable we are with just being together and enjoying each other's companionship. People need to talk until there is nothing left to say; the uncertainty has been managed. In most long-term relationships, partners may not feel a need to fill the air with sound. Just being together to enjoy each other's company may be most fulfilling. Baker calls such moments "positive silence."[41]

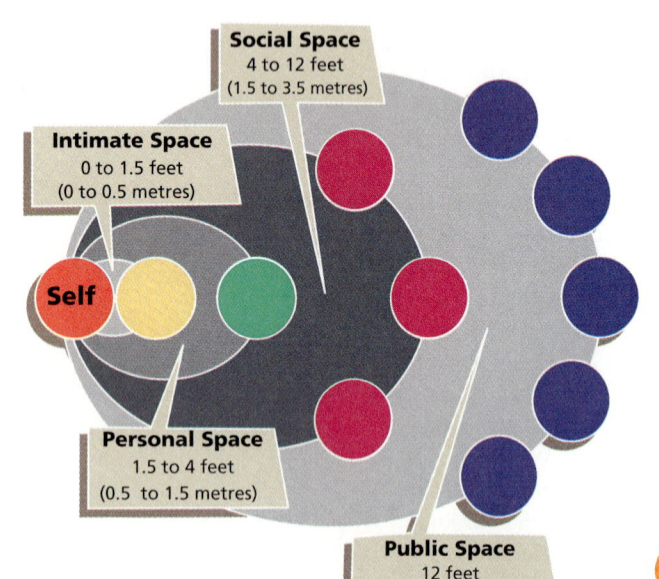

Personal Space

Imagine that you are sitting alone in a booth at your local pizza parlour. As you sit munching your thin-and-crispy pepperoni pizza, you are startled when a complete stranger sits down in your booth directly across from you. With several empty tables and booths in the restaurant, you feel very uncomfortable that this unknown individual has invaded "your" area.

Figure 7.1
Edwin T. Hall's Four Zones of Space

- Intimate Space: 0 to 1.5 feet (0 to 0.5 metres)
- Personal Space: 1.5 to 4 feet (0.5 to 1.5 metres)
- Social Space: 4 to 12 feet (1.5 to 3.5 metres)
- Public Space: 12 feet (3.5 metres and beyond)

Chapter 7 Communicating Non-Verbally

Normally, we do not think much about the rules we observe regarding personal space, but in fact every culture has fairly rigid ways of regulating space in social interactions. Violations of these rules can be alarming and, as in the preceding scenario, even threatening. How close we are willing to get to others relates to how well we know them and to considerations of power and status.

One of the pioneers in helping us understand the silent language of personal space was Edward T. Hall. His study of **proxemics** investigated how close or how far away we arrange ourselves around people and things.[42] Hall identified four spatial zones that we unconsciously define for ourselves, as shown in Figure 7.1. When we are between zero and one and one half feet (0–0.5 m) from someone, we are occupying **intimate space**. This is the zone in which the most intimate interpersonal communication occurs. It is open only to those with whom we are well acquainted, unless we are forced to stand in an elevator, a fast-food line, or some other crowded space.

The second zone, which ranges from one and one half to four feet (0.5–1.5 m), is called **personal space**. Most of our conversations with family and friends occur in this zone. If someone we don't know well invades this space on purpose, we may feel uncomfortable.

Zone Three, called **social space**, ranges from four to twelve feet (1.5–3.5 m). Most group interaction, as well as many of our professional relationships, take place in this zone. The interaction tends to be more formal than that in the first two zones.

Public space, the fourth zone, begins at twelve feet (3.5 m). Interpersonal communication does not usually occur in this zone, and many public speakers and teachers position themselves even farther from their audience.

The specific space that you and others choose depends upon several variables.[43] The more you like someone, the closer to them you will stand. We allow individuals with high status to surround themselves with more space than we allow for people with lower status. Large people also usually have more space around them than smaller people, and women stand closer to others than do men.[44] All of us tend to stand closer to others in a large room than we do in a small room.

In a group, who's in charge, who's important, and who talks to whom are reflected by the spatial arrangement we self-select. The more dominant group members tend to select seats at the head of a table, while the shyer individuals often select a corner seat at a rectangular table.[45]

---

proxemics. The study of how close to or far away from people and objects we position ourselves.

intimate space. Zone One—space most often used for very personal or intimate communication, ranging from zero to one and one half feet (0–0.5 m).

personal space. Zone Two—space most often used for conversation with family and friends, ranging from one and one half to four feet (0.5–1.5 m).

social space. Zone Three—space most often used for group discussion, ranging from four to twelve feet (1.5–3.5 m).

public space. Zone Four—space most often used by public speakers or one speaking to many people, ranging from twelve feet (3.5 m) and beyond.

▶ Recap

EDWARD T. HALL'S CLASSIFICATION OF SPATIAL ZONES

	Definition	Examples
Zone One	Intimate space	Zero to one and one half feet (0–0.5 m)
Zone Two	Personal space	One and one half to four feet (0.5–1.5 m)
Zone Three	Social space	Four to twelve feet (1.5–3.5 m)
Zone Four	Public space	Twelve feet (3.5 m) and beyond

Territory

territoriality. The study of how animals and humans use space and objects to communicate occupancy or ownership of space.

Territoriality is the study of how humans and animals use space and objects to communicate occupancy or ownership of space. You assumed "ownership" of the booth in the pizza parlour and the accompanying "right" to determine who sat with you because you and your pizza were occupying the booth. In addition to invading your personal space, the intrusive stranger broke the rules that govern territoriality.

We announce our ownership of space with territorial markers—things that signify that the area has been claimed—much as explorers once planted a flag claiming uncharted land for their king. When you are studying at the library, for example, and need to get up and check a reference at the computerized card catalogue, you might leave behind a notebook or a pencil. In rural areas, landowners post signs at the borders of their property to keep hunters off their territory. Signs, locks, electronic security systems, and other devices secure our home and office territories.

We also use markers to indicate where our space stops and someone else's starts. "Good fences make good neighbours," wrote the poet Robert Frost. When someone

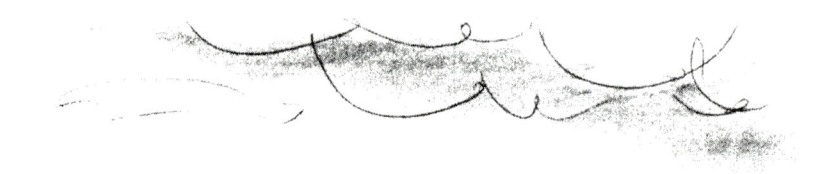

"Excuse me, sir. I am prepared to make you a rather attractive offer for your square."

sits too close, we may try to erect a physical barrier, such as a stack of books or a napkin holder, or we might use our body as a shield by turning away. If the intruder does not get the hint that "this land is our land," we ultimately resort to words to announce that the space is occupied.

Touch

Standing elbow to elbow in a crowded elevator, you may find yourself in physical contact with total strangers. As you stiffen your body and avert your eyes, a baffling sense of shame floods over you. If you are sitting at a conference table and you accidentally brush the toe of your shoe against your colleague's ankle, you may jerk away and may even blush or apologize. Why do we react this way to unpremeditated touching? Normally, we touch to express intimacy. When intimacy is not our intended message, we instinctively react to modify the impression.

Countless studies have shown that intimate touching is vital to our personal development and well-being.[46] Infants and children need it to confirm that they are valued and loved. Many hospitals invite volunteers in to hold and rock newborns whose mothers cannot do it themselves. Advocates of breastfeeding argue that the intimate touching it entails strengthens the bond between mother and child.[47]

The amount of touch we need, tolerate, receive, and initiate depends upon many factors. The amount and kind of touching you receive in your family is one big influence. If your mother or father greets you with hugs, caresses, and kisses, then you probably do this to others. If your family is less demonstrative, you may be restrained yourself. Studies show that most of us are more likely to touch people when we are feeling friendly, happy, or under other specific circumstances:[48]

- when we ask someone to do something for us
- when we share rather than ask for information
- when we try to persuade someone to do something
- when we are talking about intimate topics
- when we are in social settings that we choose rather than in professional settings that are part of our job
- when we are thrilled and excited to share good news
- when we listen to a troubled or worried friend

Appearance

In all of our interactions with others, appearance counts. Our culture places a high value upon our weight, our hairstyle, and our clothes; these things are particularly important in the early stages of relationship development. Attractive females have an easier time persuading others than do those who are perceived as less attractive. In general, we think attractive people are more credible, happier, more popular, more sociable, and even more prosperous than less attractive people.[49]

Appearance Counts. What role do you think appearance plays in the selection of television hosts? **(CBC)**

Clothes Affect Perceptions. How is the superior status of senior-ranking R.C.M.P. officers conveyed through their orders of full dress? (© RCMP/1995-041 (G))

It was in Chapter 2 that we discussed the link between our self-concept and personal appearance. The shape and size of your body also affects how others perceive you. Heavier and rounder individuals are often perceived to be older, more old-fashioned, less good-looking, more talkative, and more good-natured than thin people, who are perceived to be more ambitious, more suspicious of others, more uptight and tense, more negative, and less talkative. Muscular and athletically fit individuals are seen as better looking, taller, and more adventurous. These perceptions are, in fact, so common that they have become easily recognizable stereotypes, on which casting directors for movies, TV shows, and plays rely when selecting actors.

Aside from keeping us warm and within the legal bounds of decency, our clothes also affect how others perceive us. In institutional settings, an individual's rank is typically denoted by his or her uniform, as with the orders of dress for the Royal Canadian Mounted Police. On a less formal level, "social" rank is also inferred by the clothes we wear. For example, one study found that a man who jaywalked while dressed in nice clothes attracted more fellow violators than he did when he was shabbily attired.[50] Studies have attempted to identify a "power" look and magazines are constantly giving us prescriptions for ways to be attractive and stylish; however, outside of uniformed institutions, there really is no formula for dressing for success. Styles and expectations about appearances change. We have only to look at the clothing norms of the 1950s, 1960s, or 1970s to note how they are different from those of today.

▶ Recap

CODES OF NON-VERBAL COMMUNICATION

Movements and Gestures	Communicate information, status, warmth, credibility, interest in others, attitudes, liking.
Eye Contact	Serves cognitive, monitoring, regulatory, and expressive functions.
Facial Expressions	Express emotions.
Vocal Cues	Communicate emotion through pitch, rate, volume, and quality, and modify the meaning of messages.
Personal Space	Provides information about status, power, and intimacy.
Territory	Provides cues to use, ownership, or occupancy of space.
Touch	Communicates intimacy, affection, or rejection.
Appearance	Influences perceptions of credibility and attraction.

Interpreting Non-Verbal Communication

So what does it all mean? How do we make sense out of the postures, movements, gestures, eye contact, facial expressions, uses of space and territory, touch, and appearance of others? Albert Mehrabian has found that we synthesize and interpret non-verbal cues along three primary dimensions: *immediacy, arousal,* and *dominance*.[51]

Immediacy

Sometimes, we are not able to put our finger on the precise reason we find a person likeable or unlikeable. Mehrabian believes that immediacy cues are a likely explanation. **Immediacy** cues are behaviours that communicate liking and engender feelings of pleasure. The principle underlying immediacy is simple: we move toward persons and things we like and avoid or move away from those we dislike. Immediacy cues physically increase our sensory awareness of others.

Our use of space and territory is not the only cue that contributes to positive or negative feelings. Mehrabian has noted several other non-verbal cues that increase immediacy. One of the most powerful is touch; others include a forward lean, increased eye contact, and an open body orientation. The meaning of these behaviours is usually implied rather than explicitly spelled out in words.

In brief, to communicate that we like someone, we use these cues:[52]

Proximity:	Close, forward lean
Body Orientation:	Direct, but could be side by side
Eye Contact:	Eye contact and mutual eye contact
Facial Expression:	Smiling
Gestures:	Head nods, movement
Posture:	Open, arms oriented toward others
Touch:	Cultural- and context-appropriate touch
Voice:	Higher pitch, upward pitch

immediacy. The feelings of liking, pleasure, and closeness communicated by such non-verbal cues as eye contact, forward lean, touch, and open body orientation.

arousal. The feelings of interest and excitement communicated by such non-verbal cues as vocal expression, facial expressions, and gestures.

---

e-connections

INTERPRETING NON-VERBAL MESSAGES

Is there a dictionary of non-verbal cues? Although there are no agreed-on standard meanings for gestures, there are some widely held interpretations of selected gestures. Click on the following website:

http://members.aol.com/nonverbal12/diction.htm

Here you'll find a summary of several gestures with some common interpretations. After looking at gestures and their interpretations in the website, check the accuracy of this "dictionary" by seeing whether you and your friends or classmates agree with the interpretation presented.

Arousal

The face, voice, and movement are primary indicators of **arousal**. If we see arousal cues, we conclude that another person is responsive to and interested in us. If the person acts passive or dull, we conclude that he or she is uninterested.

When you approach someone and ask whether he or she has a minute or two to talk, that person may signal interest with a change in facial expression and more animated vocal cues. People who are aroused and interested in you show animation in their face, voice, and gestures. A forward lean, a flash of the eyebrows, and a nod of the head are other cues that implicitly communicate arousal. Someone who says, "Sure, I have time to talk with you," in a monotone and with a flat, expressionless face is communicating the opposite. Think of arousal as an on/off switch. Sleeping is the ultimate switched-off state.

Dominance

The third dimension of Mehrabian's framework for implicit cues communicates the balance of power in a relationship. **Dominance** cues communicate status, position, and importance. A person of high status tends to have a relaxed body posture when interacting with a person of lower status.[53] When you talk to a professor, he may lean back in his chair, put his feet on the desk, and fold his hands behind his head during the conversation. But unless your professor is a colleague or a friend, you will maintain a relatively formal posture during your interaction in his office.

Another dominance cue is the use of space. High-status individuals usually have more space around them; they have bigger offices and more "barriers" protecting them. A receptionist in an office is usually easily accessible, but to reach the president of the company you may have to navigate through several corridors, and past several administrative assistants and an executive assistant who are "guarding" the door.

Other power cues that communicate feelings of dominance include the use of furniture, clothing, and locations. You study at a table in the library; the college president has a large private desk. You may wear jeans and a T-shirt to class; the head of the university wears a business suit. Your dorm may be surrounded by other dorms; the president's residence may be a large house surrounded by a lush, landscaped garden in a prestigious neighbourhood. We use space, territory, posture, and artifacts such as clothing and furniture to signal feelings of dominance or submissiveness in the presence of others.

Michael Argyle summarizes the non-verbal cues that communicate dominance:[54]

Use of Space:	Height (on a platform or standing) Facing a group More space
Eye Contact:	Less with lower status More when talking More when initially establishing dominance More when staring to establish power
Face:	No smile, frown, mature adult features
Touch:	Initiating touch
Voice:	Loud, low pitch, greater pitch range Slow, more interruptions, more talk Slight hesitation before speaking
Gesture:	Pointing at the other or at his or her property
Posture:	Standing, hands on hips, expanded chest, more relaxed

dominance. The feelings of power, status, and control communicated by such non-verbal cues as a relaxed posture, greater personal space, and protected personal space.

Understanding Diversity

Gender Differences and Non-Verbal Communication

There is evidence that men and women display and interpret non-verbal cues differently.[55]

Eye Contact

Women usually have a more prolonged gaze with others than do men. Women, however, are less likely to just stare at someone; they break eye contact more frequently than men. In general, women receive more eye contact from others than do men.

Space

Men tend to have more space around them than do women. Women both approach and are approached more closely than men. And when conversing with others, women seem to prefer side-by-side interactions.

Facial Expression

Research suggests that women smile more than men. It is also reported that women tend to be more emotionally expressive with their faces than men; this is, perhaps, related to the conclusion that women are more skilled at both sending and interpreting facial expressions.

Gesture and Posture

Overall, women appear to use fewer and less expansive gestures than men. Women are more likely, for example, to rest their hands on the arms of a chair while seated; men are more likely to use gestures. Men and women position their legs differently: women cross their legs at the knees or ankles while men are more likely to sit with the ankle of one leg on the knee of the other or with their legs apart.

Touch

Men are more likely to initiate touch with others than are women. Women are touched more than men. Men and women also attribute different meaning to touch; women are more likely to associate touch with warmth and expressiveness than are men. (We should add a note of caution here. It is wise to take care about whom and when we touch. Touch can easily be misinterpreted as harassment and may be seen as unwelcome. It may be appropriate to hug a friend who has just received a promotion but it may not be appropriate to hug a co-worker who conveys similar news.)

Vocal Cues

Vocal patterns may be more related to biological differences in the vocal register than other non-verbal behaviours. Women speak in both higher and softer tones than do men. Women also use their voice to communicate a greater range of emotions than do men. Women are also more likely to raise their pitch when making statements; some people interpret the rising pattern (as in asking a question) as an indication of greater uncertainty.

▶ Recap

Dimensions for Interpreting Non-Verbal Behaviour

Dimension	Definition	Non-Verbal Cues
Immediacy	Cues that communicate liking and pleasure.	Eye contact, touch, forward lean, close distances.
Arousal	Cues that communicate active interest and emotional involvement.	Eye contact, varied vocal cues, animated facial expressions, forward lean, movement.
Dominance	Cues that communicate status and power.	Protected space, relaxed posture, status symbols.

Improving Your Ability to Interpret Non-Verbal Messages

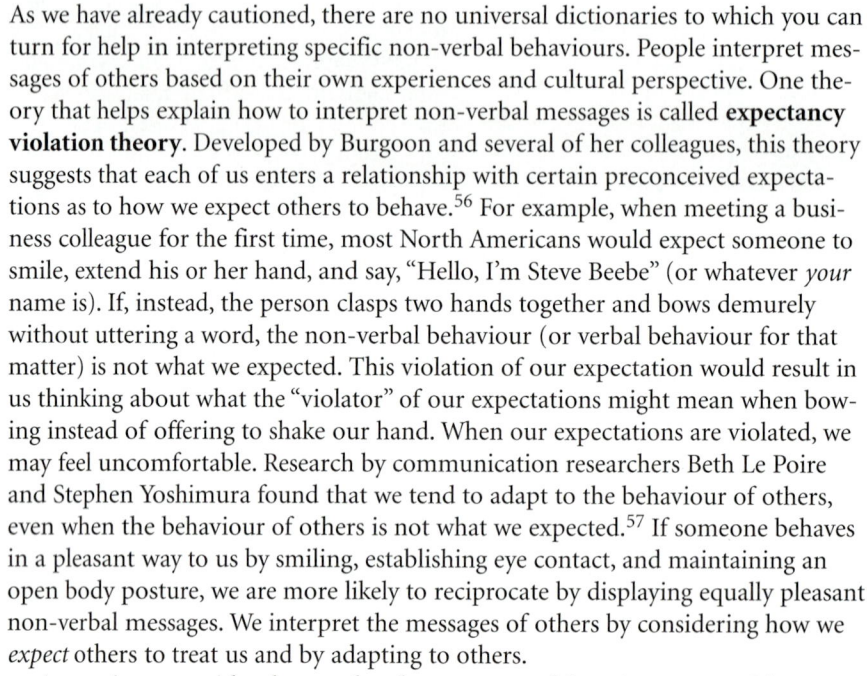

As we have already cautioned, there are no universal dictionaries to which you can turn for help in interpreting specific non-verbal behaviours. People interpret messages of others based on their own experiences and cultural perspective. One theory that helps explain how to interpret non-verbal messages is called **expectancy violation theory**. Developed by Burgoon and several of her colleagues, this theory suggests that each of us enters a relationship with certain preconceived expectations as to how we expect others to behave.[56] For example, when meeting a business colleague for the first time, most North Americans would expect someone to smile, extend his or her hand, and say, "Hello, I'm Steve Beebe" (or whatever *your* name is). If, instead, the person clasps two hands together and bows demurely without uttering a word, the non-verbal behaviour (or verbal behaviour for that matter) is not what we expected. This violation of our expectation would result in us thinking about what the "violator" of our expectations might mean when bowing instead of offering to shake our hand. When our expectations are violated, we may feel uncomfortable. Research by communication researchers Beth Le Poire and Stephen Yoshimura found that we tend to adapt to the behaviour of others, even when the behaviour of others is not what we expected.[57] If someone behaves in a pleasant way to us by smiling, establishing eye contact, and maintaining an open body posture, we are more likely to reciprocate by displaying equally pleasant non-verbal messages. We interpret the messages of others by considering how we *expect* others to treat us and by adapting to others.

As you interact with others and make sense out of these interpersonal interactions, several principles and key skills can help you to interpret others' non-verbal messages more accurately. Before reading these skills, try the non-verbal skills assessment in the Building Your Skills box on page 217.

expectancy violation theory. Theory that you interpret the messages of others based on how you expect others to behave.

Consider Non-Verbal Cues in Context

Just as quoting an expert out of context can change the meaning of a statement, trying to draw conclusions from an isolated snatch of behaviour or a single cue can lead to misinterpretations. Beware of looking at someone's folded arms and concluding that he or she does not like you or is not interested in what you are saying. It could be that the air conditioner is set too low and the person is just trying to keep warm.

Look for Clusters of Non-Verbal Cues

Instead of focusing on a specific cue, look for corroborating cues that can lead to a more accurate conclusion about the meaning of a behaviour. Is the person making eye contact? Is he or she facing you? How far away is he or she standing from you?

Always consider non-verbal behaviours in conjunction with other non-verbal cues, the environment, and the person's verbal message.

Building Your Skills

Non-Verbal Skill Assessment

Rate your current level of skill attainment (10 = High; 1 = Low) on the following factors:

	Rating Today	Desired Rating
1. I know the functions of non-verbal messages when I communicate with others.	_____	_____
2. I know how to interpret other people's postures and movements to determine whether people like me or feel more powerful than I am.	_____	_____
3. I know how to interpret the use of space around me and others to assess whether people like me or feel more powerful than I am.	_____	_____
4. I know the role voice plays in communicating my emotions and others' emotions.	_____	_____
5. I know the role facial expressions play in communicating and interpreting emotions.	_____	_____
6. I know how to interpret the eye contact of other people to assess dynamics of power, control, leadership, and credibility.	_____	_____
7. I know the non-verbal cues that communicate that people like me and that I like them.	_____	_____
8. I know the non-verbal cues that communicate power and status relationships.	_____	_____
9. I know the non-verbal cues that communicate that people are interested and responsive to me and my message.	_____	_____

Overall Non-Verbal Assessment

| 10. I do an excellent job of interpreting non-verbal messages. | _____ | _____ |

Consider Past Experiences When Interpreting Non-Verbal Cues

Familiarity may breed contempt, but it also increases our ability to interpret another's non-verbal behaviour. You may have learned, for example, that when your mother started crying when you played the piano, it meant she was proud of you, not melancholy. Family members can probably interpret one another's non-verbal cues more accurately than can those from outside the family. But after knowing someone over a period of time, you begin to increase your sensitivity to certain glances, silences, movements, and vocal cues that might be overlooked or misunderstood by others.

Check Your Perceptions with Others

You judge others by their behaviour, not by their intent. The only way to know what people intend is to ask them whether you have interpreted their behaviour correctly. But before you blurt out a hunch, first consider the context and confirming cues; think about this person's previous behaviour. Then, if you are still confused or uncertain about the meaning of a behaviour, ask for clarification. For example, if you receive a tremendous job offer that requires you to move to a new province, and your partner greets your enthusiastic announcement with silence, you could ask, "Does your silence mean that you're opposed to the move, or are you speechless with excitement?" Then wait for a response.

Or suppose you work in the kitchen all day to make a turkey dinner for your friend from Japan. After her first bite you see her eyes open wide and her lips purse up. So you ask, "Does that mean you don't like it, or did you taste something new and different?"

This key skill is called **perception checking**. As we saw in Chapter 3, you can follow four steps to check someone's perception. First, observe and describe the non-verbal cues, making a point to note such variables as amount of eye contact, posture, use of gestures, facial expression, and tone of voice. Second, try to interpret what the individual is expressing through his or her non-verbal behaviour. Next, check your perception by asking him or her if it is accurate by asking for clarification. End by using some sort of closure that indicates you understand the behaviour as in the example below. Of course, we are not suggesting that you need to go through life constantly checking everyone's non-verbal cues. Overusing this skill would be irritating to most people. We are suggesting, however, that when you are uncertain of how someone feels, and it is important to know, a perception check may be in order. Consider this example:

perception check. The skill of asking someone whether your interpretation of his or her non-verbal behaviour is accurate.

Dana: Hi, Mum. I'm sorry Erik and I missed the family reunion last week. It's been a hectic week. The kids had something goin' on every night and we just needed to rest.

Muriel: (Frowns, has little eye contact, folds her arms, and uses a flat voice.) Oh, don't worry about it.

Dana: I know you said don't worry about it, Mum, but it looks like you are still upset. I know that look of yours. I also hear in your voice that you are not really pleased. Is it really OK, or are you still a little miffed?

Muriel: Well, yes, to be honest, Dad and I were really looking forward to getting all of the kids together.

Dana: I'm sorry, Mum. We will make an effort to be at the next one. Thanks for sharing with me how you really felt.

Addressing your question to a specific non-verbal cue will help you interpret your partner's behaviour in future interactions as well. As we noted earlier, evidence suggests that the longer couples are together, the more they rely upon non-verbal behaviour to communicate. One study claims that most couples spend less than 11 minutes a week in sustained conversation.[58] Even after 50 years, however, conversation is still required occasionally to clarify non-verbal responses.

Chapter 7   Communicating Non-Verbally   219

> ▶ **Recap**
>
> ## How to Check Your Perceptions of Others' Non-Verbal Cues
>
> | Steps | Consider |
> |---|---|
> | 1. Observe their non-verbal behaviour. | Are they frowning? |
> | | Do they have eye contact? |
> | | Are their arms crossed? |
> | | What is their tone of voice? |
> | | What is their posture? |
> | 2. Form a mental impression of what you think they mean. | Are they happy, sad, angry? |
> | | Is the non-verbal message contradicting the verbal message? |
> | 3. Ask to check whether your perception is accurate. | "Are you upset? You look angry." |
> | | "Your expression and your voice suggest you don't believe me. Do you think I'm lying?" |
> | | "The look on your face tells me you really like it. Do you?" |
> | 4. Closure | "Thanks for letting me know how you really feel about this." |

Building Your Skills

Checking Perceptions

Practise checking your perceptions of non-verbal information by asking questions. Look at the photographs below. Then formulate the perception-checking question requested next to each photograph.

Photo One
Perception-checking question the teacher could ask her student:

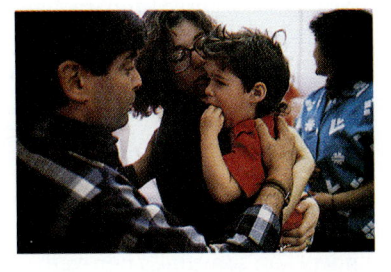

_____
_____
_____
_____
_____

Photo Two
Perception-checking question the father could ask his son:

_____
_____
_____
_____
_____

PHOTO THREE
Perception-checking question the salesperson could ask his customer:

_____
_____
_____
_____
_____
_____

Summary

Unspoken messages have a major effect upon interpersonal relationships. The primary way in which you communicate feelings, emotions, and attitudes is through non-verbal cues. When there is a contradiction between your verbal and non-verbal messages, others almost always believe the non-verbal one. But non-verbal messages are usually more ambiguous than verbal messages. Although some non-verbal messages have a definite beginning and ending, most are part of a seamless flow of movement, gestures, glances, and inflections. Also, there are culture-based differences in the way we learn and interpret unspoken messages.

Non-verbal cues can be categorized and studied to reveal the codes to our unspoken communication. Movement, posture, and gestures communicate both content and expressive information when we use them as emblems, illustrators, affect displays, regulators, and adaptors. Eye contact is an important code for regulating interaction in interpersonal exchanges. Facial expressions and vocal cues provide a wealth of information about our emotions. Our use of personal space and territory communicates a variety of messages relating to power, status, and other relational concerns. Touch is one of the most powerful cues to communicate liking; and our appearance telegraphs to others how we wish to be treated and how we perceive our role in relation to them.

One of the prime fascinations with non-verbal messages is the potential to understand hidden meaning communicated through unspoken codes. It is more difficult to read non-verbal cues than the words on this page, but there is a general framework that can help you assess the non-verbal messages of others, as well as your own non-verbal expressions. Researchers have identified three primary dimensions for interpreting non-verbal messages: immediacy cues provide information about liking and disliking; arousal cues alert others to our interest and level of engagement with them; and position, power, and status are communicated through dominance cues.

To enhance your skill in interpreting non-verbal messages, always consider the context in which you observed the cues and look for clusters of non-verbal behaviours. The longer you have known someone, the easier it is to interpret his or her unspoken messages. But, to verify whether you understand someone's non-verbal behaviour, you should ask whether your interpretation is accurate.

For Discussion and Review

Focus on Comprehension

1. What is non-verbal communication?
2. Why is it important to study non-verbal communication?
3. Describe non-verbal emblems, illustrators, affect displays, regulators, and adaptors.
4. What are the non-verbal communication codes presented in this chapter?
5. What are the non-verbal cues that communicate immediacy, arousal, and power?

Focus on Critical Thinking

6. Gabriella has had difficulty getting hired as a manager. One of her best friends suggested that she pay more attention to her non-verbal behaviour when she is interviewed for a job. What advice would you give Gabriella to ensure that she monitors her non-verbal interview behaviour?
7. Greg has been told that he sometimes comes across as cold, aloof, and standoffish. What could Greg do to communicate his sincere desire to be interpersonally warm and approachable?

Focus on Ethics

8. Antonio really wants to be hired as a salesperson. He hires a fashion consultant to recommend what he should wear and determine how he should look when he interviews for a job. In general, is it ethical to manipulate your appearance to impress others?
9. Is it appropriate to draw definitive conclusions about another's personality and attitudes based only upon a "reading" of his or her other non-verbal cues? Support your answer.
10. Is it ethical for salespersons, politicians, and others who wish to make favourable impressions to alter their non-verbal messages to get you to like them, vote for them, or buy their products? Explain your answer.

For Your Journal

1. Videotape 15 minutes of a TV drama or situation comedy. View the program with the sound turned off. Using the four principles of interpreting non-verbal messages, describe the meaning of the non-verbal messages you watch. After you have made written observations in your journal, view the program with full sound and determine how accurate your interpretations were.
2. Mehrabian has suggested that we convey 55 percent of our emotional meaning through facial expressions, 38 percent through vocal cues, and only 7 percent through verbal statements. Spend 30 minutes observing four or five people in a

public place, such as a mall, airport, or student centre, and attempt to prove or disprove Mehrabian's conclusions. Before you begin your people watching, design a method for recording your observations in your journal.

Learning with Others

1. Go on a non-verbal communication scavenger hunt. Your instructor will ask you to observe your family members and friends to find one or more of the following sets of non-verbal communicators:
   a. Examples of emblems, illustrators, affect displays, regulators, and adaptors.
   b. Examples of how people use the four zones of personal space.
   c. Examples of immediacy, arousal, and dominance.
   d. Examples of the cognitive, monitoring, regulatory, and expressive functions of eye contact.
   e. Examples of clothing that reveals intentions or personality traits.

2. Spend some time observing people in a public place, such as a restaurant, airport terminal, student centre, or bar, and write examples of quasi-courtship behaviour as discussed in this chapter on page 201. List the four phases we described (courtship readiness, preening, positional cues, appeals to invitation) on a sheet of paper, and describe several examples to illustrate each of these phases.

3. Divide into groups of three or four people. Use the following evaluation form to evaluate a room or public space. Each person in your group should evaluate the same room. It could be your own room, a cafeteria, classroom, fast-food restaurant, or even a hotel lobby. Compare your answers with other group members. You could also give a report to the class on your results.

Environment Analysis

A. Briefly describe the environment you analyzed:
   a. How big is the space?
   b. Describe the moveable objects. (A brief diagram may clarify your description.)
   c. Describe the predominant colours.
   d. Describe the sounds in the environment; what did you hear?
   e. Describe the lighting.
   f. Make a note of any unique structural or aesthetic design features (artwork, plants, windows, etc.).

B. Rate the room using the following scales:

formal	___	___	___	___	___	___	informal
warm	___	___	___	___	___	___	cold
pleasant	___	___	___	___	___	___	unpleasant
useful	___	___	___	___	___	___	not useful
beautiful	___	___	___	___	___	___	ugly

C. Describe the probable effects the room design has upon communication interaction patterns (e.g., does it encourage or discourage communication?).

D. Based upon your observations, is the room appropriately designed for its intended use? Explain.

Weblinks

www.coe.uh.edu/~shortam/lesson8.html This is an online lesson on non-verbal communication which is very well done. It has extra material and other links to related topics.

www.ablecom.net/users/kaaj/psych/home.html This is the home page for Dr. Albert Mehrabian's work. There are outlines for several of his books and other research.

www.collegejournalprofiles/countryprofiles/canada.html Read this article to learn how Canadians are perceived and the etiquette that should be practised when meeting and greeting a Canadian.

www.hcc.hawaii.edu/intranet/committees/FacDevCom/guidebk/teachtip/commun-1.htm This is a lesson on non-verbal communication designed for faculty. It is informative and adds to the text material.

www.deafcan.org/communication.html This is an interesting online article from the Deaf Advocacy Network about American Sign Language (ASL), Pidgin Signed English (PSE), and how to get a deaf person's attention for communication.

Suggested Readings

Axtell, Roger E. *The Do's and Taboos of Hosting International Visitors.* New York: John Wiley and Sons, 1989.
   This classic describes how different cultures vary in their body language and interpretation of it.

Mehrabian, A. *Nonverbal Communication.* Chicago: Aldine Atherton, 1972.
   Another classic, well worth the read!

chapter 8

Conflict Management Skills

After you study this chapter you should be able to...

1. Define conflict.
2. Compare and contrast three types of interpersonal conflict.
3. Identify commonly held myths about interpersonal conflict.
4. Describe differences between destructive and constructive approaches to managing conflict.
5. List and describe five stages of conflict.
6. Describe three types of conflict management styles.
7. Identify and use conflict management skills to help manage emotions, information, goals, and problems when attempting to resolve interpersonal differences.

- What Is Conflict?
- Types of Conflict
- Myths about Conflict
- Conflict as a Process
- Conflict Management Styles
- Conflict Management Skills
- When Others Aren't Other-Oriented: How to Be Assertive

Outside noisy, inside empty.

CHINESE PROVERB

"This house stinks," said Paul, wrinkling up his nose. "It smells like day-old garbage."

"Take it out yourself. It's your job," said Simone, turning her back on him to scrub furiously at an imaginary morsel of food on a frying pan that was already polished clean.

"Hey, hey," said Paul, holding up both hands in front of him, "I wasn't accusing you. I just said it smelled bad in here. Don't be so touchy."

"Oh, no? Well, you're always criticizing me. You think just because you have a big important job that you can come in here and say anything you like. And I come home from work feeling tired, too, you know, but you don't do anything to help, not even the things you agree to!" shouted Simone, turning around to confront him with her soapy hands on her hips.

"Well, you're always knocking me for no reason. I'm not putting up with this bad treatment from you anymore," snarled Paul. As he turned on his heel to stalk out of the kitchen, Simone burst into tears.

Does this conflict have a ring of familiarity? Do you know why Paul and Simone reached an impasse in their attempt to communicate? Eventually all relationships experience conflict. Paul and Simone's exchange is complicated, seething with conflicting goals and underlying resentments. How do we avoid the same kind of outcome in our own complicated exchanges?

Conflict management is not a single skill but a set of skills. But to manage conflict effectively involves more than learning simple techniques.

The best route to success in resolving conflict effectively is to acquire knowledge about what conflict is, what makes it happen, and what we can do about it. We begin by defining conflict, examining some of the myths about it, and focusing on some of its constructive functions. We also discuss the relationship among conflict, power, and conflict management styles.

In addition, we will discuss how learning about your typical style of managing conflict can give you insight into managing interpersonal differences. And finally, we will present conflict management skills that draw upon listening, emotions, and verbal and non-verbal communication that we discussed in the previous chapters, to help manage the inevitable interpersonal conflicts that arise in the best of relationships.

What Is Conflict?

Simply stated, **interpersonal conflict** is a struggle that occurs when two people cannot agree upon a way to meet their needs. When the needs are incompatible, if there are too few resources to satisfy them, or if the individuals opt to compete rather than to cooperate to achieve them, then conflict occurs. The intensity level of a conflict usually relates to the intensity of the unmet needs. One researcher developed the "struggle spectrum," shown in Figure 8.1, to describe conflicts ranging from mild differences to fights.[1] But the bedrock of all conflicts is differences—different goals, experiences, genders, cultures, and other factors.

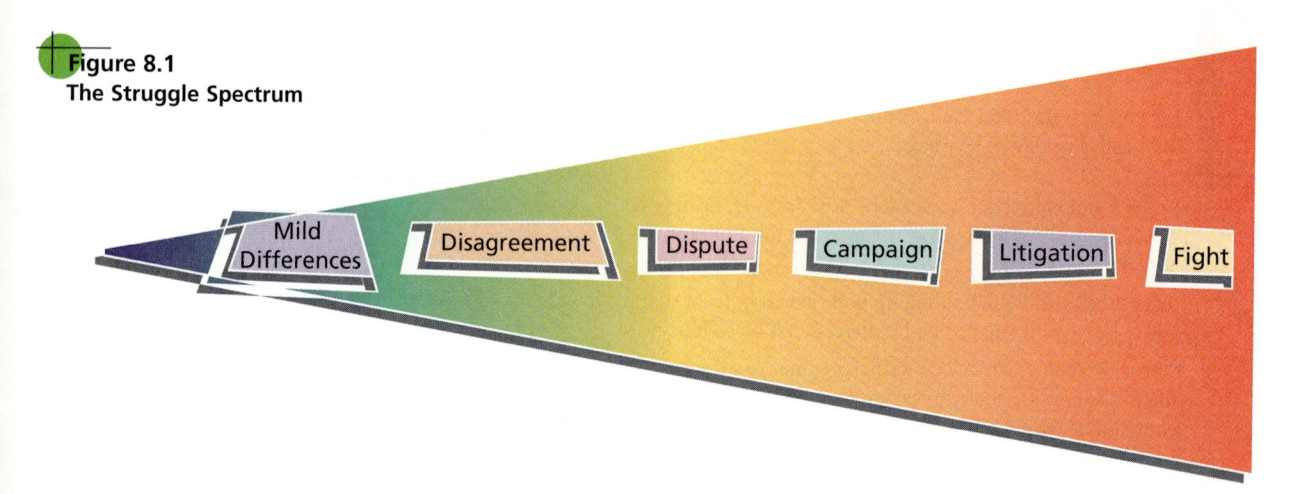

interpersonal conflict.
A struggle that occurs when two people cannot agree upon a way to meet their needs or goals.

**Figure 8.1
The Struggle Spectrum**

Mild Differences — Disagreement — Dispute — Campaign — Litigation — Fight

Assertively expressing honest ideas may mean that a person feels safe and comfortable enough with his or her partner to disagree. As we will discuss later, conflict in interpersonal relationships can play a constructive role in focusing on issues that may need attention. The ebb and flow of interpersonal psychological intimacy and separation inevitably leads to some degree of conflict in any relationship. When conflict happens in your relationships, don't immediately assume that the relationship is doomed.

Goals and Conflict

Psychologists agree that we are need-driven, goal-oriented individuals. Because most of what we do is based upon achieving a desirable goal, it is not surprising that most conflict is goal driven. You want something; your partner wants something else. If your partner interferes with your achievement of your goal, there may be a fight.

Suppose you are trying to find a parking spot in a busy shopping centre. Just as you find one, another shopper zips into "your" space. Your blood boils, and you get out of your car fighting mad. Or, suppose you have had a difficult day at work. All you want to do is hunker down with a bowl of popcorn and watch MTV. But your partner announces that a friend and his six-year-old son are coming over for dinner. "That's not what *I* feel like doing tonight. Why didn't you ask *me* before you invited them?" you shout. In both instances, your goals are colliding head on with those of someone else, and you feel as if you have lost control of the situation.

Of course, if Wile E. Coyote and Roadrunner ever found a way to resolve their conflicts, we'd stop watching their cartoons. But humans might prefer to find ways to resolve their conflicts. (Shooting Star ©All rights reserved.)

Experiences and Conflict

Our inherent differences, coupled with our experiences, provide fuel for conflict. Consider the conflict that newlyweds Christy and Matt are having about how to celebrate the upcoming winter holidays. They have only two days to spend in their parents' town before returning to their new home in another city. Christy's family always exchanges presents and has a huge gathering on Christmas Eve and a family dinner on Christmas Day. Matt's family is Jewish. They celebrate Hanukkah quietly and do not feel comfortable either exchanging gifts for Christmas or trying to fit in at someone else's traditional celebration. Matt would like to celebrate Hanukkah on either Christmas Eve or Christmas Day at his parents' house, but Christy cannot understand why his family does not want to join her family's festivities. The conflict between Christy and Matt is not based upon different goals: they both want to see each set of parents and both want to celebrate the holidays. The conflict stems from their different backgrounds and experiences.

Types of Conflict

At some time or another, many close relationships go through a conflict phase. "We're always fighting," complains a newlywed. But if she were to analyze these fights, she would discover important differences among them. One research duo found that most conflicts fit into three different categories: (1) **pseudo conflict**—triggered by a lack of understanding; (2) **simple conflict**—stemming from different ideas, definitions, perceptions, or goals; and (3) **ego conflict**—based upon personal differences.[2]

Understanding Diversity

GENDER AND CONFLICT

Throughout our discussion of interpersonal relationships we have noted that men and women learn different ways of relating to others. Research suggests that women are more likely to focus on relationship issues, whereas men typically focus on tasks.[3] Women often interact with others to achieve intimacy and closeness, but men interact to get something done or to accomplish something apart from the relationship. Men are often more aggressive and assertive than women when pursuing a goal or conquest.[4] The following list summarizes key differences that researchers have observed between some men's and women's responses to conflict.

PERCEIVED GENDER DIFFERENCES IN RESPONDING TO CONFLICT[5]

Females	Males
Concerned with equity and caring; connect with and feel responsible to others.	Concerned with equality of rights and fairness; adhere to abstract principles, rules.
Interact to achieve closeness and interdependence.	Interact for instrumental purposes; seek autonomy and distance.
Attend to interpersonal dynamics to assess relationship's health.	Are less aware of interpersonal dynamics.
Encourage mutual involvement.	Protect self-interest.
Attribute crises to problems in the relationship.	Attribute crises to problems external to the relationship.
Concerned with the impact of the relationship on personal identity.	Neither self- nor relationship-centred.
Respond to conflict by often focusing mainly on the relationship.	Respond to conflict by often focusing on rules and being evasive until a unilateral decision is reached.

Although these findings provide a starting point for analyzing our conflicts with members of the opposite sex, we caution you against lapsing into "allness" statements such as, "Oh, you're just like all women. That's why you disagree with me." Or, "You're just like all men. You never want to focus on how I feel." Even thinking in these ways can prevent you from listening to what your partner is saying.

The most recent perspective on analyzing gender differences is called the *partnership perspective*. Rather than viewing gender differences as a gulf to be bridged, this perspective suggests that men and women are not locked into particular styles or approaches.[6] The partnership approach emphasizes the importance of keeping channels open and avoiding the tendency to stereotype communication styles by gender.

CULTURE AND CONFLICT

An individual's culturally learned assumptions influence his or her conflict behaviour. In some cultures, most of the conflict is **expressive;** it focuses on the quality of relationships, and on managing interpersonal tension and hostility. In other cultures, conflict is more instrumental. It centres less on relationships and more on achieving a specific goal or objective.[7] One

> researcher noted that for people from low-context cultures (those who derive more meaning from words than from the surrounding context), conflicts are most often instrumental. Most North Americans come from low-context cultures. Many Asian cultures, on the other hand, are high-context cultures. They are also collectivist: they value group effort over individual achievement.[8] For people from these cultures, conflicts often centre on expressive, relational concerns. Keeping peace in the group or saving face is often a higher priority than achieving a goal.
>
> Managing culture-based conflict requires a strong other-orientation. One research team suggests that North Americans of European descent receive little training in how to develop solutions to problems that are acceptable to an entire group.[9] They are often socialized to stick up for their own rights at any cost, and they approach conflict as a win-lose situation. In contrast, people from collectivist cultures approach conflict management situations from a win-win perspective; it is important that both sides save face and avoid ridicule. Such differences in approaches provide a double challenge. In addition to disagreeing over the issue at hand, people from different cultures may also have different strategies for reaching agreement.

Pseudo Conflict

Will: Meet me at the fountain.

Sean: No, that's too far. Meet me by the administration building.

Will: The fountain is closer and more convenient.

Sean: No, it's not.

Will: Yes, it is. It's just off Market Street.

Sean: Oh, you mean the fountain by the administration building.

Will: Sure, that's exactly what I mean.

Sean: Oh, no problem. That's the place I had in mind.

Pseudo means false or fake. Pseudo conflict occurs when we simply miss the meaning in a message. But unless we clear up the misunderstanding by asking for more information, a real conflict might ensue. Note that in this example, Will offers helpful information ("It's just off Market Street") and Sean checks it with feedback ("Oh, you mean the fountain by the administration building").

How can you avoid pseudo conflict? A key strategy is to clarify the meaning of words and expressions that you don't understand. Keep the following strategies in mind to minimize misunderstandings before they occur:

- *Check your perceptions:* Ask to clarify what you don't understand; seek to determine whether your interpretation is the same as your partner's.
- *Listen between the lines:* Look for puzzled or quizzical facial expressions of your partner. People may not voice their misunderstanding, but may express their uncertainty non-verbally.
- *Establish a supportive rather than a defensive climate for conversation:* Avoid evaluating, controlling, using manipulative strategies, being aloof, acting superior, or rigidly asserting that you're always right. These classic behaviours are like pushing the button to increased defensiveness and misunderstanding.

---

pseudo conflict. Conflict triggered by a lack of understanding and miscommunication.

simple conflict. Conflict that stems from different ideas, definitions, perceptions, or goals.

ego conflict. Conflict that is based upon personal issues; conflicting partners attack one another's self-esteem.

expressive conflict. Conflict that focuses on issues about the quality of the relationship and managing interpersonal tension and hostility.

instrumental conflict. Conflict that centres on achieving a particular goal or task and less on relational issues.

Simple Conflict: Different Stands on the Issues

Simple conflict stems from differences in ideas, definitions, perceptions, or goals. You want to go to Lake Louise for your vacation; your partner wants to go to Quebec City. Your partner wants to fly; you would rather take the train. You understand each other, but you disagree.

A key to unravelling a simple conflict is to keep the conversation focused on the issues at hand so that the expression of differences does not deteriorate into a battle focusing on personalities.

The following exchange between Marc and Nick illustrates a conflict over a simple difference of opinion; notice how both partners stick to the issues and figure out a way to resolve their differences.

Marc: I want to watch *The Simpsons* tonight. It's their Christmas show.

Nick: No way, man. I have to watch a documentary about textiles for my history class. It's an assignment.

Marc: But I've worked all weekend. I'm beat. The last thing I want to watch is some stuffy old documentary on the history of weaving.

Nick: Tell you what. Go ahead and watch *The Simpsons*. I'll videotape the documentary and watch it later. Deal?

Marc: Okay. Thanks. And I'll go grill some burgers so we can have supper together first.

This next exchange between Sue and Nadia is a bumpier one. What starts as a simple conflict deteriorates into a series of personal attacks.

Nadia: Sue, can I borrow your black skirt? I have a date tonight. It would look great with my new jacket.

Sue: Sorry, Nadia. I'm going to wear it tonight. I've got to give a presentation to the school board about our new volunteer program.

Nadia: In case you don't remember, when you brought it home you said I could borrow it anytime. Besides, you haven't paid back the $20 I loaned you to buy it.

Sue: Yes, but I bought the skirt especially for this occasion.

Nadia: Well, don't ask to borrow anything from me ever again. You're just plain selfish.

Sue: Oh, yeah? Well *you're* the one who hogs all the space in the refrigerator. Talk about someone who's selfish. If that's not the pot calling the kettle black!

Nadia: All right, now that we're being honest about who hogs what, *you're* the one who monopolizes the bathroom in the morning.

And so it escalates. The original disagreement about the skirt is forgotten and egos become attacked and bruised.

You can avoid pseudo or false conflict if you ask for clarification, listen between the lines, and work to establish a supportive climate. (B. Daemmrich/The Image Works)

Chapter 8 Conflict Management Skills

To keep simple conflict from escalating into personal vendettas, consider the following strategies:

- *Clarify your and your partner's understanding of the issues and your partner's understanding of the source of the disagreement.*
- *Keep the discussion focused on facts and on the issue at hand, rather than drifting back to past battles and unrelated personal grievances.*
- *Look for more than just the initial solutions that you and your partner bring to the discussion; generate many options.*
- *Don't try to tackle too many issues at once.* Perform "issue triage"—identify the important issues and work on those.
- *Find the kernel of truth in what your partner may be saying.* Find agreement where you can.
- *If tempers begin to flare and conflict is spiralling upward, cool off.* Come back to the discussion when you and your partner are fresh.

Ego Conflict: Conflict Gets Personal

As you can see from the preceding example, a personal attack puts your partner on the defensive, and many people behave according to the adage, "The best defence is a good offence." When you launch a personal attack, you are "picking a fight." And as Sue and Nadia's exchange illustrates, fights that begin as pseudo or simple conflicts can easily lapse into more vicious ego conflicts. Here's another example:

Michael: I don't think you should allow students to wear Halloween costumes to school. What can I do with a bunch of monsters and witches in gym class?

Katrina: Well, all the parents are calling me up about it, and the kids are excited.

Michael: Is that how you make decisions? By responding to pressure from parents and kids?

Katrina: You're just disagreeing with me because you wanted to be chair of this committee.

Michael: Not true! I just don't think *you* have the ability to chair it!

Note that as each person in the conflict becomes more defensive about his or her position, the issues become more tangled.

Remember Paul and Simone's argument at the beginning of this chapter? It started with what was probably an offhand remark and escalated into a major argument because both participants began attacking each other and bringing up other sensitive issues instead of focusing on the original comment.

If you find yourself involved in ego conflict, try to refrain from hurling personal attacks and emotional epithets back and forth. Instead, take turns expressing your feelings without interrupting each other, then take time to cool off. It is difficult to use effective listening skills when your emotions are at a high pitch.

Here are additional strategies to consider when conflict becomes personal:

- *Try to steer the ego conflict back to simple conflict.* Stay focused on issues rather than personalities.
- *Make the issue a problem to be solved rather than a battle to be won.*
- *Write down what you want to say.* It may help you clarify your point, and you and your partner can develop your ideas without interruption. A note of caution: Don't put angry personal attacks in writing. Make your written summary rational, logical, and brief rather than emotion-laden.
- *When things get personal, make a vow not to reciprocate.* Use "I" messages that we talked about in Chapter 4 ("I feel uncomfortable and threatened when we yell at each other.") rather than "you" messages ("You're such a creep. You never listen.") to express how you are feeling.

▶ Recap

TYPES OF CONFLICT

	Pseudo Conflict	**Simple Conflict**	**Ego Conflict**
What It Is	Individuals misunderstand each other.	Individuals disagree over which action to pursue to achieve their goals.	Individuals feel personally attacked.
What to Do	Check your perceptions.	Clarify understanding.	Return to issues rather than personal attacks.
	Listen between the lines; look for non-verbal expressions of puzzlement.	Stay focused on facts and issues.	Talk about a problem to be solved rather than a fight to be won.
	Be supportive rather than defensive.	Generate many options rather than arguing over one or two options.	Write down rational arguments to support your position.
	Listen actively.	Find the kernel of truth in what your partner is saying; emphasize where you agree.	Use "I" messages rather than "you" messages.

Myths about Conflict

conflict myths.
Inappropriate assumptions about the nature of interpersonal conflict.

Although not all conflict is destructive to our relationships, many cultures have taboos against displaying it in public. According to one researcher, many of us were raised with five **conflict myths** that contribute to our negative feelings about conflict.[10] As you read the following sections, you may shake your head and say, "That's not where I came from." In some families, conflict is expressed openly and often. But even if your experience has been different, reading about these prevailing myths may help you understand your emotional responses to conflict or your partner's response when conflict occurs.

Myth 1: Conflict Should Always Be Avoided

"If you can't say anything nice, don't say anything at all." Many of us learned early in our lives that conflict is unnatural and that we should eliminate it from our conversations and relationships. Yet, evidence suggests that conflict arises in virtually every relationship. Because each of us has a unique perspective on our world, it would be extraordinary for us *always* to see eye to eye with another person. One researcher found that contentment in marriage relates not to the amount of conflict, but to the way in which partners manage it.[11] Conflict is also a normal and productive part of interaction in group deliberations.[12] It is a myth that we should view conflict as inherently unproductive and something to be avoided. It happens, even in the best of relationships.

Myth 2: Conflict Always Occurs Because of Misunderstandings

"You just don't understand what my days are like. I need to go to sleep!" shouts Janice as she scoops up a pillow and blanket and stalks off to the living room. "Oh yeah? Well, you don't understand what will happen if I don't get this budget in!" responds Ron, who is hunched over the desk in their bedroom. It is clear that Ron and Janice are having a conflict. They have identified the cause of their problem as a lack of understanding between them, but in reality they *do* understand each other. Ron knows that Janice wants to sleep; Janice knows he wants to stay up and work. Their problem is that they disagree about whose goal is most important. This disagreement, not lack of understanding, is the source of the conflict.

Myth 3: Conflict Is Always a Sign of a Poor Interpersonal Relationship

It is an oversimplification to assume that all conflict is rooted in underlying relational problems. Conflict is a normal part of any interpersonal relationship. Although it is true that constant bickering and sniping can be symptomatic of deeper problems, disagreements do not necessarily signal that the relationship is on the rocks. In fact, overly polite, stilted conversation is more likely to signal a problem than are periodic disagreements. The free expression of honest disagreement is a hallmark of a healthy relationship. Assertively expressing honest ideas may mean that a person feels safe and comfortable enough with his or her partner to disagree. As we will discuss later, conflict in interpersonal relationships can play a constructive role in focusing on issues that may need attention. The ebb and flow of interpersonal psychological intimacy and separation inevitably leads to some degree of conflict in any relationship. When conflict happens in your relationships, don't immediately assume that the relationship is doomed.

Myth 4: Conflict Can Always Be Resolved

Consultants and corporate training experts, and self-help book authors often offer advice about how to eliminate conflict so that all will be well and harmony will prevail. Some people claim that with the application of a few skills and how-to techniques, conflicts can disappear, much like a stain from a shirt laundered with the right kind of detergent. This is simply not true. Not all differences can be resolved by listening harder or paraphrasing your partner's message. Some disagreements are so intense and the perceptions so fixed that individuals may have to agree to disagree and live with it.

Myth 5: Conflict Is Always Bad

It's a common fantasy to dream of eliminating all interpersonal conflict from our relationships. It would be bliss, we think, if we could live without disagreement, hassle, haggling, and tension. But conflict is a healthy component of our relationships. In fact, if a relationship is conflict-free, the individuals are probably not being honest with each other. Although it can be destructive, conflict can also help us identify issues that need further discussion and can lead to negotiations that give us fresh insights into the relationship.

> ### Recap
>
> #### CONFLICT MYTHS
>
> **Myth 1:** Conflict should always be avoided.
> **Myth 2:** Conflict always occurs because of misunderstandings.
> **Myth 3:** Conflict is always a sign of a poor interpersonal relationship.
> **Myth 4:** Conflict can always be resolved.
> **Myth 5:** Conflict is always bad.

Conflict as a Process

Cathy was reading the Sunday paper, enjoying a second cup of coffee, and listening to her favourite classical music station. All seemed well. Suddenly, for no apparent reason, her roommate Kai brusquely stormed into the room and shouted, "I can't stand it anymore! We have to talk about who does what around here." Cathy was taken completely off guard. She had no idea her roommate was upset about the division of household chores. To her, this outburst seemed to come out of the blue; in reality, however, several events led up to it.

Most relational disagreements have a source, a beginning, a middle, an end, and an aftermath.[13] Just as in the Beetle Bailey comic on page 235, conflicts have a process or series of stages. Let's find out how they function.

Source: Prior Conditions

The first phase in the conflict process is the one that sets the stage for disagreement; it begins when you become aware that there are differences between you and another person. The differences may stem from role expectations, perceptions, goals, or resources. In the previous example, Kai perceived that she and Cathy played different roles in caring for the household.

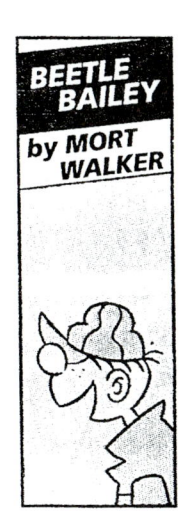

In interpersonal relationships, *many* potential sources of conflict may be smouldering below the surface. It may take some time before they flare up into overt conflict. Moreover, they may be compounded with other concerns, making them difficult to sort out.

Beginning: Frustration Awareness

At this stage, at least one of you becomes aware that the differences in the relationship are increasingly problematic. You may begin to engage in self-talk, noting that something is wrong and creating frustration. Perhaps you realize that you won't be able to achieve an important goal or that someone else has resources you need to achieve it. Or you may become aware of differences in perceptions. Kai knew that Cathy's family always used weekends for relaxation. In Kai's family, on the other hand, everyone pitched in on weekends to get household chores done for the week. She may have recognized that difference, even as her frustration level rose.

Becoming aware of differences in perception does not always lead to increased frustration. But when the differences interfere with something you want to accomplish, then your frustration level rises. In Kai's case, she wanted to get the house clean so she could turn her attention to studying for a test she had the next day. Cathy's apparent indifference to helping Kai achieve that goal was a conflict trigger.

Middle: Active Conflict

When you bring your frustration to the attention of others, a conflict becomes an active, *expressed struggle*.[14] If frustrations remain only as thoughts, the conflict is passive, not active. Active conflict does not necessarily mean that the differences are expressed with shouting or emotional intensity. An expression of disagreement may be either verbal or non-verbal. Calmly asking someone to change an attitude or behaviour to help you achieve your goal is a form of active conflict; so is kicking your brother under the table when he starts to reveal your secret to the rest of the family.

Cathy was not aware of the division of labour problem until Kai stormed into the room demanding a renegotiation of roles. Kai had been aware of her frustration for some time, yet had not acted on it. Many experts advocate that you do not wait until your frustration level escalates to peak intensity before you approach someone with your conflict. Bottled-up frustration tends to erupt like pop in a bottle that has just been shaken. Intense emotions can add to the difficulty of managing a conflict.

End: Resolution

When you begin to try managing the conflict, it has progressed to the resolution stage. Of course, not all conflicts can be neatly resolved. Couples who divorce, business partners who dissolve their corporation, or roommates who go their separate ways have all found solutions, even though they may not be amicable.

After Kai's outburst, she and Cathy were able to reach a workable compromise about the division of their household labour. Cathy agreed to clean the house every other week; Kai promised not to expect her to do it on weekends.

Aftermath: Follow-Up

As Yogi Berra once said, "It ain't over 'til it's over." After a conflict has been resolved, the follow-up stage involves dealing with hurt feelings or managing simmering grudges, and checking with the other person to confirm that the conflict has not retreated into the frustration awareness stage. As we noted in Chapter 1, interpersonal relationships operate as transactive processes rather than as linear, step-by-step functions. Conflict does progress in stages, but your resolutions can backslide unless you confirm your understanding of the issues with your partner.

The Friday after their discussion, Cathy proudly showed off a spotless apartment to Kai when she came home from class. Kai responded with a grin and a quick hug and privately resolved to get up early on Sunday morning so that she could go out to get Cathy some pastries and the newspaper before she awoke. This kind of mutual thoughtfulness exemplifies a successful follow-up in a conflict.

▶ Recap

UNDERSTANDING CONFLICT AS A PROCESS

Prior Conditions Stage	The stage is set for conflict because of differences in the individuals' actions or attitudes.
Frustration Awareness Stage	One individual becomes aware that the differences are problematic and becomes frustrated and angry.
Active Conflict Stage	The individuals communicate with each other about the differences; the conflict becomes an expressed struggle.
Resolution Stage	The individuals begin seeking ways to manage the conflict.
Follow-Up Stage	The individuals check with themselves and each other to monitor whether both are satisfied with the resolution.

Understanding the stages of conflict can help you better manage the process. You'll also be in a better position to make the conflict a constructive rather than a destructive experience. Conflict is **constructive** if it helps build new insights and establishes new patterns in a relationship. Airing differences can lead to a more satisfying relationship in the long run. David W. Johnson lists the following as benefits of conflict in interpersonal relationships. Interpersonal conflict

- Focuses attention on problems that may have to be solved
- Clarifies what may need to be changed
- Focuses attention on what is important to you and your partner
- Clarifies who you are and what your values are
- Helps you learn more about your partner
- Keeps relationships interesting
- Strengthens relationships by increasing your confidence that you can manage disagreements[15]

constructive conflict. Conflict that helps build new insights and establishes new patterns in a relationship.

destructive conflict. Conflict that dismantles relationships without restoring them.

Although conflict can be constructive, we don't want to oversell the value or function of conflict in relationships with others. Conflict can also be **destructive**. The hallmark of destructive conflict is a lack of flexibility in responding to others.[16] Conflict can become destructive when people view their differences from a win-lose perspective, rather than looking for solutions that allow both individuals to gain. If the combatants assume that one person will lose, the resulting competitive climate precludes cooperation and flexibility.

One way to minimize destructive conflict cycles is to understand the sequence of conflict-triggering causes so that you can address them at an early stage. It's important to perceive interpersonal conflict not just as something you react to once an issue has surfaced; becoming aware of underlying frustrations before they blossom into active expressions of conflict can help maintain both honesty and trust in a relationship. Also, diagnosing whether the conflict is a misunderstanding, a simple disagreement, or a personal vendetta can give you insight into managing disagreements before they move closer to a fight on the struggle spectrum.

By focusing on the problem at hand rather than assuming a defensive attitude, this machinist and foreman may reach a constructive solution to their conflict. (Richard Pasley/Stock Boston)

Conflict Management Styles

What's your approach to managing interpersonal conflict: fight or flight? Do you tackle conflict head-on or seek ways to remove yourself from it? Most of us do not have a single way of dealing with differences, but we do have a tendency to manage conflict by following patterns that we have used before. The pattern we choose depends on several factors: our personality, the individuals with whom we are in conflict, the time and place of the confrontation, and other situational factors. For example, if your boss gives you an order, you respond differently than if your partner gives you an order.

Several researchers have attempted to identify the patterns or styles of conflict. One model distinguishes only two dimensions: (1) how concerned you are for others and (2) how concerned you are for yourself.[17] Another more widely accepted approach organizes conflict styles into three types: (1) non-confrontational (avoiding, withdrawing, being indirect); (2) confrontational (attempting to use controlling strategies to influence or manipulate outcomes); and (3) cooperative (seeking a solution that both individuals will find acceptable).[18]

Non-Confrontational Style

One approach to handling conflict is to back off, either by avoiding the conflict or by giving in to the other person. Virginia Satir, author of *Peoplemaking*, a popular book about family communication, suggests that we learn conflict response patterns early in life.[19] Placating, distracting, computing, withdrawing, and giving in are responses that typify a **non-confrontational style.**

A *placating* response is an attempt to please; generally, placaters are uncomfortable with negative emotions and may adopt this approach because they fear rejection if they rock the boat. Typically, they seek approval and try to avoid threats to their self-worth. Placaters never seem to get angry, are so controlled that they seem unresponsive to the intensity of the situation, quickly agree with others to avoid conflict, and try to avoid confrontation at all costs. They appear to be other-oriented, but, in fact, they are simply seeking self-protection. Satir describes them as "syrupy, martyrish, and bootlicking." In the following exchange, note Hilary's placating response to Lesley's complaint:

Lesley: Hilary, I'm not in agreement with you on the QCN merger. I think the merger should be called off.

Hilary: OK. Whatever you think is best. I just want you to feel good about your decision.

Another non-confrontational style that Satir identifies is *distracting*. Distracters attempt to change the subject and avoid conflict or stress, rather than face issues directly. They hope that eventually the problem will just go away if it can be put off long enough.

A third non-confrontational style is called *computing*; computers remove themselves from conflict by remaining aloof and cool. They avoid emotional involvement and refuse to be provoked or ruffled, even under intense pressure. This detachment allows them to avoid expressing genuine feelings about issues and ideas. Instead, they respond to emotional issues with impersonal words and phrases, such as "One would tend to become angry when one's car is dented, wouldn't one?" The computing style is characterized by low empathy and minimal involvement with the issues at hand.

Withdrawing from conflict, either physically or psychologically, is another non-confrontational approach. "I don't want to talk about it," "It's not my problem," "Don't bother me with that now," or "I'm not interested in that" are typical responses from someone who uses this style.

---

non-confrontational style.
A style of managing conflict that includes placating, distracting, computing, withdrawing, and giving in.

Finally, some people consistently *give in* when faced with conflict. They are so uncomfortable that they surrender before the conflict escalates. Evan hates western movies. Yet, when Pam wants to rent *How the West Was Won*, Evan says, "OK, fine," just to avoid a confrontation.

Confrontational Style

"You're wrong!" shouts Ed. "Here's how to get our project in on time. We can't waste time in the library. We just have to write up what we have."

"But Ed," suggests Derek, "the assignment calls for us to have three library sources."

"No. We don't have time. Just do it," argues Ed.

Ed wants to *control*, not *collaborate*.

You will learn in Chapter 10 that each of us has some need to control and be controlled by others. But some people almost always want to dominate and make sure that their objectives are achieved. In managing conflict, **confrontational** people have a win-lose philosophy. They want to win at the expense of the other person, to claim victory over their opponents. They are focused on themselves and

confrontational style. A style of managing conflict motivated by a desire to dominate. Behaviours include blaming, threatening, warning, and other forms of verbal abuse.

Building Your Skills

IDENTIFYING YOUR CONFLICT MANAGEMENT STYLE

We each learn to manage conflict in different ways. This exercise helps you increase your awareness of your conflict management style.

1. Complete the following questionnaire, "What Would I Do in a Conflict?"
2. After you've completed and scored the questionnaire, rank-order the five conflict strategies from the one you use most, to the one you use least.
3. Your instructor may ask you to discuss your results with another person or with a group of your classmates. Think of examples that illustrate each of the conflict styles.

WHAT WOULD I DO IN A CONFLICT?

1. You and a classmate both want to use the computer at the same time.
   a. I would give up wanting it and give up on the classmate as a friend.
   b. I would try to force the classmate to let me use the computer first.
2. You and a classmate both want the same library book at the same time.
   a. I would give up on wanting it and give up on the classmate as a friend.
   b. I would listen carefully to why my classmate needed the book, and if his reasons were more important than mine, I would let him have it, because a good friend is important.
3. You and a classmate both want to sharpen your pencil at the same time.
   a. I would let the classmate go first and give up on her as a friend.
   b. I would ask for us to solve the problem by one person sharpening both pencils so both of us have to wait an equal amount of time.
4. You and a classmate both want to be first in the lunch line.
   a. I would let the classmate go first and give up on him as a friend.
   b. I would compromise by agreeing to alternate who goes first for an equal number of days.
5. You and a classmate both want the same chair at your favourite table in the library.
   a. I would try to force the classmate to let me have the

chair, not caring if she was angry or upset with me.
   b. I would listen carefully to why my classmate wanted the chair, and if her reasons were more important than mine, I would let her have it, because a good friend is important.
6. You and a classmate are working on a group project. Both of you want to draw the illustrations, and neither wants to write the report.
   a. I would try to force the classmate to let me draw the illustrations, not caring if he was angry or upset with me.
   b. I would compromise by agreeing for each of us to draw half of the illustrations and write half of the report.
7. You and a classmate have been playing ball. Neither of you wants to put the equipment away.
   a. I would try to force the classmate to do it, not caring if she was angry or upset with me.
   b. I would ask for us to solve the problem by putting the equipment away together.
8. You and a classmate are making a video. Both of you want to run the camera, and neither wants to narrate.
   a. I would listen carefully to why my classmate wanted to do the filming, and if his reasons were more important than mine, I would let him do it, because a good friend is important.
   b. I would ask the classmate to compromise so that each of us filmed half of the time and each narrated half of the time.
9. You told a classmate a secret, and she told it to several other people.
   a. I would listen carefully to why my classmate told my secret, and if her reasons were more important than mine, I would forgive her, because a good friend is important.
   b. I would try to solve the problem by asking my classmate what happened and by working out an agreement about keeping secrets in the future.
10. You and a classmate both believe you did most of the work on a joint report.
   a. I would compromise by agreeing that we both did half.
   b. I would try to solve the problem by reviewing each aspect of the paper and decide who did how much on that aspect.

SCORING PROCEDURE

Circle the letters below that you circled on each question. Then total the number of letters circled in each column.

Question	Withdrawing	Forcing	Smoothing	Compromising	Negotiating
1.	a	b			
2.	a		b		
3.	a			b	
4.	a				b
5.		a	b		
6.		a		b	
7.		a			b
8.			a	b	
9.			a		b
10.				a	b
Total	____	____	____	____	____

Your score for withdrawing reflects your *non-confrontational* approach to conflict. If you scored high on forcing, you may tend to have a more *confrontational* style. If you scored high on smoothing, compromising, and negotiating, you are more likely to seek *cooperative* ways of managing conflict. *Remember:* There is no one best style to use all of the time. Although the cooperative approach is more likely to result in dialogue, there are times when it is best to be non-confrontational. And in some situations it may be appropriate and ethical to confront the issues. Throttling up your listening skills is important when forcing or confronting issues.

Source: David W. Johnson, *Reaching Out: Interpersonal Effectiveness and Self-Actualization* (Allyn & Bacon, 2000), 253–255.

usually ignore the needs of others. Confronters often resort to blaming, or seeking a scapegoat, rather than assuming responsibility for a conflict. "I didn't do it," "Don't look at me," and "It's not my fault" are typical statements.

If this strategy does not work, confronters may try hostile name-calling, personal attacks, or threats and warnings. Threats refer to actions they can actually carry out.[20] Warnings are negative prophecies they cannot actually control. The boyfriend who says, "If you don't stop calling me names, I'm going to leave you," has issued a threat; he has the power to leave. If he were to say, "Don't call your parents names or they'll write you out of their will," that would be a warning. In reality, he has no control over his girlfriend's parents.

Obviously, threats are more powerful than warnings in changing behaviour, and then only if the other person would genuinely find the threatened actions punishing or disruptive. If a parent threatens a spanking, a child will take the threat seriously only if he or she knows the parent will carry it out. If, in the past, the parent has administered only light raps on the wrist, the child will probably not pay much attention to the threat.

Cooperative Style

Those who take a **cooperative** approach to conflict management view conflicts as a set of problems to be solved, rather than as games in which one person wins and another loses. They use other-oriented strategies and foster a win-win climate by using the following techniques:[21]

- *Separate the people from the problem.* They leave personal grievances out of the discussion, describing problems without making judgmental or evaluative statements about personalities.

- *Focus on shared interests.* They ask questions such as "What do we both want?" "What do we both value?" "Where are we already agreeing?" to emphasize common interests, values, and goals.

- *Generate many options to solve the problem.* They use brainstorming and other techniques to generate alternative solutions. (You will learn more about problem-solving techniques later in this chapter).

- *Base decisions on objective criteria.* They establish standards for an acceptable solution to a problem—these standards may involve cost, timing, and other factors. Suppose, for example, that you and your neighbour are discussing possible ways to stop another neighbour's dog from barking all night. You decide upon these criteria: the solution must not harm the dog; it must be easy for the owner to implement; the owner must agree to it; it should not cost more than $50; and it must keep the dog from disturbing the sleep of others. Your neighbour suggests, "Maybe the dog can sleep in the owner's garage at night." This solution meets all but one of your criteria, so you call the owner, who agrees to put the dog in the garage by 10:00 P.M. Now everyone wins because the solution meets a sound, well-considered set of objective criteria.

cooperative style. A style of managing conflict that seeks win-win solutions to problems. Cooperative people separate the people from the problem, focus on shared interests, generate multiple solutions, and base decisions on objective criteria.

> **Recap**

CONFLICT MANAGEMENT STYLES

Non-Confrontational Style Avoids conflict by placating (agreeing), distracting, computing (becoming emotionally detached), or withdrawing from the conflict.

Confrontational Style Wants to manipulate others by blaming and making threats; sets up a win-lose framework.

Cooperative Style Seeks mutually agreeable resolutions to manage differences.

Works within an other-oriented, win-win framework:
- Separates people from the problem.
- Focuses on shared interests.
- Generates many options to solve problems.
- Bases decisions upon objective criteria.

Conflict Management Skills

As we saw in the previous section, the non-confrontational and confrontational styles of conflict management do not solve problems effectively, nor do they foster healthy long-term relationships. The skills we will review here are those we touched upon in our discussion of the cooperative style.[22]

Managing conflict, especially emotion-charged ego conflict, is not easy. Even with a fully developed set of skills, you should not expect to melt tensions and resolve disagreements instantaneously. The following skills can, however, help you generate options that promote understanding and provide a framework for cooperation.

Manage Your Emotions

For weeks you have been working on a brochure with a tight deadline. You turned it over to the production department with instructions two weeks ago. Today, you call to check on its progress, and you discover that it is still sitting on the production coordinator's desk. You feel angry and frustrated. How should you respond? You may be tempted to march into her office and scream at her, or to shout at her supervisor.

Try to avoid taking action when you are in such a state. You may regret what you say, and you will probably escalate the conflict.

Often, the first sign that we are in a conflict situation is a feeling of anger, frustration, fear, or even sadness (as we explained in Chapter 5), which sweeps over us like an ocean wave. If we feel powerless to control our own fate, then we will have difficulty taking a logical or rational approach to managing the conflict. Expressing our feelings in an emotional outburst may make us feel better for the moment, but it may close the door to logical, rational negotiation.

As we also saw in Chapter 5, when we are emotionally charged, we experience physical changes as well. These changes also trigger the fight-or-flight response. If we choose to stay, verbal or physical violence may erupt; if we flee from the

Considering Others

EMPATHY CAN SPAN THE ABYSS

Intergenerational conflicts and misunderstandings can cause pain and emotional bruises. Instead of finding nurturing and love within the family circle, some people encounter exactly the opposite.

For example, one elderly reader writes: "I don't look forward to family gatherings because I come back with my self-esteem reduced to zero and feeling like a stereotypical old geezer. I'm rebuffed by my own children, giggled at, and made to feel my thoughts aren't important."

Another elderly reader describes in detail a truly unhappy situation. "I gave my money to my children, trusting them to take care of my needs when I grew older. But now that I have no money left, they have discarded me. How stupid I was not to take care of my security! I'm alone now, really alone, I need to understand what I did wrong. I guess I gave too much, cared too much."

Many letters from elderly people tell similar stories. I also hear from their sons and daughters, members of the so-called sandwich generation, whose reports have a different focus. A 54-year-old woman writes about the "hard burden" she bears in caring for her 88-year-old mother: "I'm angry that I am increasingly having to be a parent to someone whose self-centredness and narcissism made her unable to be a mother to me. The simple, awful fact is that I respect my mother and love her as my flesh and blood, but I don't like her and I wish she weren't in my life. My fear is that she's going to live on and on, growing more and more needful of my 'parenting,' and that I won't be free of her presence until I'm approaching 70 myself."

Another letter from a member of the sandwich generation reads: "My challenge involves my relationship with my mother-in-law of 29 years. She's 89. She has lost all semblance of a positive outlook. She speaks only of her aches and pains and the bleakness of her life. I cannot deal with this negative approach to living. Whatever I try to do for her, nothing is ever right."

Reflecting on these letters, I find the key word for what *both* sides need is empathy—which the dictionary defines as identification with and understanding of the situation, feelings, and motives of another person. Without this empathy, a great abyss can exist where there should be communication. Can we overemphasize that there's no substitute for honest communication between people? *Tell* others what you feel! Try to explain *why* you feel as you do. This can lead to real understanding.

One woman offers a promising, creative role model for others: "Sometimes I'm not delighted to hear what my mother needs and wants because it impinges on my time and energy. However, I prefer to know what she's thinking and feeling, even if it results in conflict. The resolution of such conflicts has strengthened our friendship and the community that is our family. Love, I believe, is being open and seeking a resolution that may require mutual sacrifice."

An extremely helpful, sound definition. Speaking of love, one reader writes: "Many years ago my mother gave me a book that set my life on a self-respecting, self-valuing course. It says it's quite okay to love yourself. If you don't, how can anyone else love you? If you think you're not worth loving, then, by cracky, you're not. If you think you're not worth much, you will always be a problem—if not a pain—to be around. Is that what you want for yourself? Not I."

A final intergenerational note from a grandmother: "My life was lonely after I lost my husband. I volunteered at the hospital, bowled twice a week, was active at my church and kept my home. But there was still a terrible void in my life. Then my 23-year-old granddaughter told me to keep Wednesday evenings open for her. We take turns cooking, or sometimes we go out. You have no idea what this has done for me. We share a meal, talk, and just enjoy our friendship. Our talk may be about her work or what I've done the past week—just nice conversation. We sometimes cry together. But we laugh together as well."

This grandmother and granddaughter have found a happy way to bridge the generation gap. Others could profit from their example.

Source: From Malcolm Boyd, *Modern Maturity.* Reprinted with permission from *Modern Maturity.* Copyright © 1992, American Association of Retired Persons.

conflict, we cannot resolve it. Until we can tone down (not eliminate) our emotions, using some of the suggestions from Chapter 5, we will find it difficult to apply other skills. Let's look at some additional specific strategies that you can draw upon when an intense emotional response to conflict clouds your judgment and hampers your decision-making skills.[23]

Select a Mutually Acceptable Time and Place to Discuss a Conflict

If you are upset, or even tired, you are at risk for an emotion-charged shouting match. If you ambush someone with an angry attack, don't expect him or her to be in a productive frame of mind. Instead, give yourself time to cool off before you try to resolve a conflict. In the case of the lapsed deadline, for example, you could call both the production coordinator and her boss and schedule an appointment to meet with them later in the day. By that time you could gain control of your feelings and also think the issue through. Of course, sometimes issues need to be discussed on the spot; you may not have the luxury to wait. But whenever it is practical, make sure the other person is ready to receive you and your message.

Plan Your Message

If you are approaching someone to discuss a disagreement, take care to organize your message. Identify your goal and determine what outcome you would like; do not barge in and pour out your emotions.

You might also consider talking with a trusted friend or colleague first. A good friend with empathic listening skills can help you clarify the issues in the conflict. If you don't talk with a friend, consider writing down the key ideas you want to express to help you prepare for your face-to-face discussion. The purpose of the notes is not to deliver a speech when you meet your conflict partner. But taking time to plan your message by talking with a friend or by writing it down can help you frame the issues of the disagreement.

Monitor Non-Verbal Messages

As you learned in Chapter 7, your actions play a key role in establishing the emotional climate in any relationship. Monitoring your non-verbal messages can help to de-escalate an emotion-charged situation. Speaking calmly, using direct eye contact, and maintaining a natural facial expression will signal that you wish to collaborate rather than control. Your non-verbal message should also support your verbal response. If you say you are listening to someone, but you continue to read the paper or work on a report, you are communicating a lack of interest in the speaker and the message.

Avoid Personal Attacks, Name-Calling, and Emotional Overstatement

Using threats and derogatory names can turn a simple conflict into an ego conflict. When people feel attacked, they will respond by protecting themselves. As we in saw in Chapter 5, verbal aggression does not solve problems or conflict and may escalate the situation. Also, try to avoid exaggerating your emotions. If you say you are irritated or annoyed rather than furious, you can still communicate your feelings, but you will take the sting out of your description.

Use Self-Talk

When Tom was chairing the committee meeting, Monique accused him of falsifying the attendance numbers at the last fine arts festival. Instead of lashing back at Monique, he paused, took a slow, deep, yet unnoticed breath, and thought, "I'm tired. If I snarl back, all we will do is escalate this issue out of proportion. I'll talk with Monique later after we have both cooled down." Perhaps you think that talking to yourself is an eccentricity. Nothing could be further from the truth. As you saw in Chapters 2 and 5, thoughts are directly linked to feelings,[24] and the messages we tell ourselves play a major role in how we feel and respond to others. Ask yourself whether an emotional tirade and an escalating conflict will produce the results you want. When Eleanor Roosevelt noted that "No one can make you feel inferior without your consent," she was acknowledging the power of self-talk in affecting our emotional response to what others say and do. Also, as we noted in Chapter 5, positive self-talk will help you in coping with a wide variety of emotions.

What strategies do this mother and daughter seem to have drawn on to manage their conflicts? (Rhonda Sidney/PhotoEdit)

Manage Information

Because uncertainty, misinformation, and misunderstanding are often by-products of conflict and disagreement, skills that promote mutual understanding are an important component of cooperative conflict management. Based on the describing, listening, and responding skills discussed in Chapter 4, the following specific suggestions can help you reduce uncertainty and enhance the quality of communication during conflict.

Clearly Describe the Conflict-Producing Events

Instead of just blurting out your complaints in random order, think of delivering a brief, well-organized mini-speech. When Lise almost had a car accident, she came home and told her husband, "Last week you said you would get the brakes fixed on the car. On Monday, when you still hadn't taken the car in, you said you would do it on Wednesday. Now it's Friday and the brakes are in even worse shape. I had a close call this afternoon when the car almost wouldn't stop. We've got to get those brakes fixed before anyone drives that car again."

"Own" Your Statements by Using Descriptive "I" Language

"I feel upset when you post the week's volunteer schedule without first consulting with me," reveals Natasha. Her statement describes her feelings as her own. If she had said, "You always prepare a schedule without telling anyone first. All of us who volunteer are mad about that," her statement would have had an accusatory sting. Beginning the statement with "you" sets the listener up for a defensive response. Also, notice that in the second statement, the speaker does not take responsibility for the anger; she suggests that it belongs to other unidentified people as well. If you narrow the issue down to a conflict between you and the other person, you put the conflict into a more manageable framework.

Use Effective Listening Skills

Managing information is a two-way process. Whether you are describing a conflict situation to someone, or that individual is bringing a conflict to your attention, good listening skills will be invaluable.

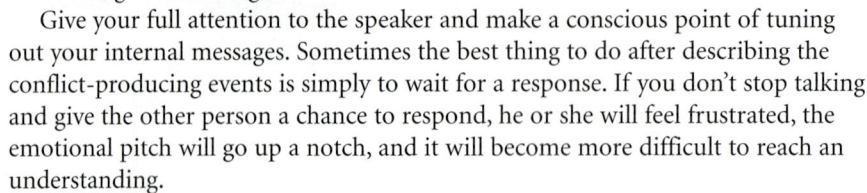

Give your full attention to the speaker and make a conscious point of tuning out your internal messages. Sometimes the best thing to do after describing the conflict-producing events is simply to wait for a response. If you don't stop talking and give the other person a chance to respond, he or she will feel frustrated, the emotional pitch will go up a notch, and it will become more difficult to reach an understanding.

Finally, do not just focus on the facts or details, but analyze them so you can understand the major point the speaker is making. Use your understanding of the details to interpret the speaker's major ideas. Remember to stay other-oriented and "seek to understand rather than to be understood."[25]

Check Your Understanding of What Others Say and Do

Respond clearly and appropriately. Your response and that of your conflict partner will confirm that you have understood each other. Checking perceptions is vital when emotions run high.

If you are genuinely unsure about facts, issues, or major ideas addressed during a conflict, ask questions to help you sort through them instead of barging ahead with solutions. Then, summarize your understanding of the information; do not parrot the speaker's words or paraphrase every statement, but check key points to ensure that you have understood the message. Note how Kamal adeptly paraphrases to check his understanding:

Maggie: I don't like the conclusion you've written to the conference report. It doesn't mention anything about the ideas suggested at the symposium. I think you have also misinterpreted the CEO's key message.

Kamal: So, if I understand you, Maggie, you're saying the report missed some key information and may also include an inaccurate summary of the CEO's speech.

Maggie: Yes, Kamal. Those are the concerns I have.

Manage Goals

As we have seen, conflict is goal-driven. Both individuals involved in an interpersonal conflict want something. And for some reason, be it competition, scarce resources, or lack of understanding, the goals appear to be in conflict. To manage conflict, it is important to seek an accurate understanding of these goals and to identify where they overlap.

Identify Your Goal and Your Partner's Goal

After you describe, listen, and respond, your next task should be to identify what you would like to have happen. What is your goal? Most goal statements can be phrased in terms of wants or desires. Consider the following examples:

Problem	Goal
Your boss approaches you and wants you to work overtime; you need to pick up your son from day care.	You want to leave work on time; your boss wants the work completed ASAP.
Your partner wants to sleep with the window open; you like a warm room and sleep better with the window closed.	You want a good night's rest; your partner wants a good night's rest.
Your six-year-old son wants to go to a swim party where there are no lifeguards.	You want your son to be safe; your son wants to have a good time.

Canadian Issues

MANAGING A MONUMENTAL GOAL: COMMUNITIES AND FAMILIES WORKING TO PREVENT YOUTH CRIME[26]

When it comes to trying to achieve goals; many Canadian communities are working on achieving a large one: preventing youth crime. While communities share the same goal, different strategies are being used to prevent youth crime. These small but articulate movements are starting to snowball in communities across Canada. The issue is public concern over youth crime. You don't need a pollster to know that one of the "hot buttons" for widespread public insecurity is youth crime. Public panic grows as headlines report sensational crimes.

Despite the harsh climate, there is growing support for youth crime remedies that focus not on punishment and reprisal but on the root causes of crime.

Many believe we need to "get tough with young people," says Memorial University of Newfoundland professor Joan Pennel, a member of Canada's National Crime Prevention Council. "'Getting tough' means locking young people up, and when you lock them up, you disrupt their position in the community. This approach hasn't decreased criminal activity."

Another simple answer that some have seized on is to send offending youth to strict, military-style "boot camps." "[But] the research finds that it really doesn't reduce re-offending, or reduce the prison population," according to Barb Hill of the John Howard Society in Kingston, Ontario.

What are the most appropriate ways to address youth crime? Anne Sherman, also of the National Crime Prevention Council, believes that justice system reform begins with community involvement. She also believes that "a restorative justice system is more appropriate than a punitive justice system, something that combines community involvement, victim involvement and restoration to the victim." Sherman believes that alternatives to court trials and incarceration must provide offending youth with meaningful ways to take responsibility and to make amends.

For example, the Ambassador Program in downtown Toronto has been described as a "retrieval program" for street youth who have dropped out of school and lived through drug abuse. Youth in the program spend their mornings in class working toward high school credits. Additional credits are earned in the afternoons by doing work placements in various job settings. In the "Speak Out" component of the program, the youth are trained to visit senior elementary schools in high-risk neighbourhoods and talk about life on the street and on drugs, based on their own experiences.

The Bent Arrow Traditional Healing Society's program for Aboriginal youth in Edmonton is aimed at urban youth who have had some involvement with the criminal justice system. The program draws heavily upon traditional Aboriginal culture and spirituality, while the students also do a five-week placement with employers who agree to hire them if they meet the requirements of the workplace. At the heart of the project, however, are the personal relationships with the students. "This place is more like an extended family," says Executive Director Shauna Seneca, "and that's by design. These kids need people in their lives who will care for them, come hell or high water. Many have never known that before."

In Prince Edward Island, "CRIME BEAT" was initiated to show youth that the rest of the community recognizes the good they are doing. "A lot of youth think the rest of the world is down on them," says coordinator Diane Barnes. One group of program youth produced a musical play about the impact of drunk driving among youth. Another group organized a successful "taxi-token" campaign during the Christmas season: tokens worth $5 (enough to get anyone in Charlottetown a ride home) were sold throughout the community for use as gifts.

Another "restorative" community solution to youth crime across Canada includes "family conferences," which are based on Aboriginal traditions. In a family conference, a young offender meets with a group of family and community members to discuss his or her offence, its impact on victims, and means to make amends.

Barb Hill, of the John Howard Society, sees hope that local crime prevention councils are springing up across Canada. "People are starting to say 'we want to do something different here.' . . . [They] want to talk about what their community can do instead of sending their youth away."

For Discussion

1. What do you feel are the main causes of youth crime today?
2. What are other goals that communities should develop to assist in the development of youth?

Source: Excerpts from *Transition*, Vanier Institute of the Family, Ottawa (March 1996), 4–10. The website for the Vanier Institute of the Family is www.cf-efc.ca

---

Often in conflicts you will be faced with balancing the achievement of your goal against the goal of maintaining the relationship that you have with your partner. Eventually, you may decide that the latter goal is more important than the substantive conflict issue.

Next, it is useful to identify your partner's goal. In each of the problems on page 247 you would need to know what the other person wants so that you can manage the conflict. Use effective describing, listening, and responding skills to determine what each of you wants and to verbalize your goals. Obviously, if you both keep your goals hidden, it will be difficult to manage the conflict.

Identify Where Your Goal and Your Partner's Goal Overlap

Roger Fisher and William Ury stress the importance of focusing on shared interests when seeking to manage differences.[27] Armed with an understanding of what you want and what your partner wants, you can then determine whether the goals overlap. In the conflict over whether the window should be open or closed, the goal of both parties is the same: each wants a good night's sleep. Framing the problem as "how can we achieve our mutual goal," rather than arguing over whether the window should be open or closed, moves the discussion to a more productive level.

If you focus on shared interests (common goals) and develop objective, rather than subjective, criteria for the solution, there is hope for finding a resolution that will satisfy both parties.

Manage the Problem

If you can structure conflicts as problems to be solved (see Table 8.1 below) rather than battles to be won or lost, you are well on your way to seeking strategies to manage the issues that confront you and the other person involved in the conflict. There are many models of problem solving that can be used to arrive at a solution that everyone can live with in all kinds of conflicts. Most models rely on a set of defined steps that help clarify the problem, analyze the problem, generate and evaluate possible solutions, implement the chosen solution, and then evaluate the solution at a given date. These models can be found in business texts and counselling texts, and are actively used by many organizations such as the Ontario Provincial Police and many corporations such as IBM Canada. Here, we will focus on a very straightforward model: Define the problem, analyse the problem's causes and effects, generate many possible solutions, select a solution that best achieves the goals of the conflicting parties, and then evaluate the solution at a mutually agreed upon date.

Table 8.1
Solving Problems: One Method of Organizing Problem-Solving Discussions

1.	Define the Problem	What is the issue?
2.	Analyze the Problem	What are the causes, symptoms, effects, and obstacles?
3.	Determine the Goals	What do you want? What does your partner want? How do the goals overlap?
4.	Generate Multiple Solutions	List many options rather than debating one or two strategies for achieving the goal.
5.	Select the Best Solution and Try It	Eliminate options that are not mutually agreeable. If possible, take the best ideas from several generated to reach an amicable resolution.
6.	Set a Time to Evaluate the Chosen Solution	Periodically, revisit your solution to see if it is appropriate to your current situation.

Define the Problem

Most problems boil down to something you want more of or less of. You can think of a problem as a "deviation" from where you would like to be or what you want regarding a specific issue. If you feel you are putting in too many hours at the office, the deviation is the difference between the number of hours you feel you should be working and the number of hours you are actually working.

Make sure that you *define the "real" problem* and not just the symptoms. Cara and Ian have been living together for over a year. Lately, they have been fighting over small issues. They decide to spend some time talking about what is wrong and trying to understand each other. Rather than just dealing with symptoms (Cara complains that Ian snores at night), they keep talking until they get at the "real" or root problem. Cara wants to get married to Ian now. Ian wants to stay with Cara, but he wants to wait until he feels ready for marriage. He also wants to feel financially secure before he marries.

🔸 Analyze the Problem

Next, *analyze the problem*. To analyze is to break something down into its components. With the other party, begin by describing the conflict-producing events in chronological order (see page 245). Then, decide what type of conflict it is. If your analysis reveals it as a pseudo conflict, keep on with the analysis process. Attempt to ferret out the rest of the symptoms, effects, and obstacles; decide whether the conflict stems from several subproblems or from one major issue. As you proceed, you and the other party may decide that you need more information to help clarify the issues.

After some discussion, Cara and Ian analyze their problem. They realize they come from different family backgrounds and have different expectations about marriage. Cara's parents were high school sweethearts, were married when both were 18, and are still happily married after almost 25 years together. Ian's parents are older; they met after each of them had been divorced, and they married after a long, slow-paced relationship. Cara's and Ian's different frames of reference help explain their feelings about the timing of marriage. Often, it is these different frames of reference, or perceptions of how events should be timed or completed, that can be at the root of interpersonal conflict.

🔸 Determine the Goals

The next step in managing the problem is to *determine the goals of you and your partner* by following the previous information on managing goals. Generate objective criteria for a solution using the previous guidelines about identifying goals of you and your partner. The more measurable, verifiable, and objective the criteria, the greater the likelihood that both parties will agree when the criteria have been met. Cara and Ian decide that, ultimately, they have the same goal—to get married. The issue boils down to timing. They decide to seek a course of action that will make them both feel secure.

🔸 Generate Multiple Solutions

Their next step is to *generate multiple solutions*. Simply understanding the issues and the causes, effects, symptoms, and history of a problem will not enable you to manage a conflict. It takes time and creativity to find mutually satisfactory solutions to most problems. It stands to reason that the more solutions you generate, the greater the probability that you can manage the conflict constructively. One way to generate options is through brainstorming. To use brainstorming, try the following suggestions:

1. Make sure the problem and the goals are clear to both of you.
2. Try to temporarily suspend judgment and evaluation; do not censor your thoughts.
3. Specify a certain time period for brainstorming.
4. Consider having each partner brainstorm ideas separately before a meeting, or write ideas down before verbalizing solutions.
5. Try to develop at least one unique or far-out idea. You can always tame wild ideas later.

6. Piggyback off the ideas of your partner. Encourage your partner to use or modify your ideas.
7. Write down all of the ideas suggested.
8. Review each idea, noting ways to combine, eliminate, or extend them.

If the goal is to find the best way to manage the difficulty, it may take only one good idea to help move the conflict forward to a constructive resolution.

When they brainstorm, Cara and Ian generate the following options: save money for a year and then get married; take turns going to college; take turns working to support the family while the other gets a degree; get married now, get jobs and postpone college; get married now and take out student loans.

Select the Best Solution and Try It

Cara and Ian decide to *select the best solution.* Sometimes, it may take several attempts at defining, analyzing, goal-setting, and generating multiple ideas before a mutually agreeable solution emerges. It is always appropriate to recheck your understanding of the issues and goals. Cara and Ian decide to combine the best of several ideas. They agree to get engaged, but not to set a date. Instead, they set a financial goal of $5000 in savings. When they reach that goal, they will set a wedding date. If they are both attending college, they will get part-time jobs so that they have income, and they will also apply for student loans.

If, after repeated attempts, you cannot arrive at a mutually acceptable solution, you may decide to keep trying. Or you may agree to take the issue to an impartial person who can help you identify conflict management strategies and solutions. At work, your immediate superior may be called in to help settle the matter. Or, occasionally, you may agree to disagree and drop it.

Set a Time to Evaluate the Chosen Solution

To agree to a solution is not enough. Each of the parties must live up to his or her end of the agreement. What if, after a year, Cara and Ian have not saved any money? What might happen if they have to attend different colleges? Once a solution has been agreed upon and implemented, many variables can get in the way of the intended goals. Periodic checking, particularly with long-term solutions, is necessary to keep the parties focused and to examine if other problems are creeping into the solution. Cara and Ian may have to go back to any of the previous steps and work through more problems and differences.

Even though we have presented these conflict management steps as prescriptive suggestions, it is important to remember that *conflict rarely follows a linear, step-by-step sequence of events.* These skills are designed to serve as a general framework for collaboratively managing differences. But if your partner does not want to collaborate, your job will be more challenging.

In reality, you don't simply manage your emotions and then move neatly on to developing greater understanding with another person. Sorting out your goals and your partner's goals is not something that you do once and then put behind you. It will take time and patience to balance your goal of maintaining a relationship with your immediate achievement goals. In fact, as you try to manage a conflict, you will more than likely bounce forward and backward from one step to another. This framework gives you an overarching perspective for understanding and actively managing disagreements, but the nature of interpersonal relationships means that you and your partner will respond—sometimes in unpredictable ways—to a

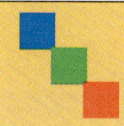

Building Your Skills

PRACTISING CONFLICT MANAGEMENT SKILLS

In this activity you will be paired with another person and invited to role-play a conflict that you have had with another person. A third person will observe and provide feedback about the communication skills you use to manage the conflict.

Person A
Think about a recent incident in which someone offended you. Make a few notes about the conflict. Then approach person B, who will play the person who has offended you. Describe the conflict, remembering to manage your emotions.

Person B
You have offended person A. Your job is to listen, reflect, and help to manage the conflict. Start a dialogue to identify each other's goals and see how they overlap; then try to generate strategies to achieve the goals.

Person C
Your job is to observe the role play. Use the following checklist to help you evaluate the participants. When the role play is over, tell the participants what they did well. Ask them how they could improve, and offer suggestions as well.

If time permits, switch roles and conduct another role play.

CONFLICT MANAGEMENT ROLE PLAY CHECKLIST

Managing Emotions	Person A	Person B
Makes direct eye contact.	_____	_____
Maintains open body posture.	_____	_____
Uncrosses arms and legs.	_____	_____
Leans forward slightly.	_____	_____
Uses a calm voice.	_____	_____
Uses reinforcing head nods.	_____	_____
Has appropriate facial expressions.	_____	_____

Managing Information		
Paraphrases content accurately.	_____	_____
Paraphrases feelings accurately.	_____	_____
Clearly describes the problem.	_____	_____
Uses appropriate lead-in ("So," or "You seem to be saying").	_____	_____

Managing Goals		
States the goals clearly.	_____	_____
Identifies how goals overlap.	_____	_____

Managing the Problem		
Use the six steps of problem solving.	_____	_____

variety of cues (psychological, sociological, physical) when communicating. Think of the skills you have learned as options to consider rather than as hard-and-fast rules to follow in every situation.

When Others Aren't Other-Oriented: How to Be Assertive

Even if you master collaborative conflict management skills, others may make irrational, inappropriate demands that create conflict and tension. In these instances, you will need to assert yourself, especially if someone has aggressively violated your rights.

Assertiveness Defined

Assertiveness was defined in Chapter 2 as the tendency to make requests, ask for information, and generally pursue one's own rights and best interests. Assertive people let their communication partners know when a behaviour or message is infringing on their rights. Each individual has rights. In interpersonal communication, you have the right to refuse a request someone makes of you, the right to express your feelings as long as you don't trample on the feelings of others, and the right to have your personal needs met if they don't infringe on the rights of others.

Some people confuse the terms *assertiveness* and *aggressiveness*. **Aggressiveness** means pursuing your interests by denying the rights of others. Assertiveness is other-oriented; aggressiveness is exclusively self-oriented. Aggressive people are coercive. They blame, judge, and evaluate to get what they want. They use intimidating non-verbal cues such as steely stares, a bombastic voice, and flailing gestures. Assertive people can ask for what they want without judging or evaluating their partner.

In Chapter 6 we talked about using "I" messages to express your thoughts and feelings rather than "you" messages. "I" messages describe what you want by expressing your feelings and goals. "You" messages lead with an attack on the other person. "You creep! You ate the last breakfast taco" is an aggressive "you" statement. "I asked you to save one taco for me; now I won't have anything to eat for breakfast" is an assertive statement that states your rights and describes the consequences of violating them.

assertiveness. Pursuing your best interests without denying your partner's rights.

aggressiveness. Pursuing your interests while denying the rights of others by blaming, judging, and evaluating the other person.

▶ Recap

ASSERTIVENESS VERSUS AGGRESSIVENESS

Assertiveness	Aggressiveness
Expresses your interests without denying the rights of others.	Expresses your interests and denies the rights of others.
Is other-oriented.	Is self-oriented.
Describes what you want.	Evaluates the other person.
Discloses your needs, using "I" messages.	Discloses your needs, using "you" messages.

How to Assert Yourself If You Are Harassed

What Is Harrassment?

In Canada, the *Canada Labour Code*, the *Human Rights Act*, and provincial and territorial human rights codes are intended to protect individuals from harassment and to guarantee equal treatment. The *Human Rights Act* asserts that all employees in the workplace have a right to be free from harassment of any kind on the grounds of sex, race, ancestry, creed, handicap, age, family status, marital status, the receipt of public assistance, and record of offences. A pamphlet prepared by the Canadian Human Rights Commission in 1992 states: "The provisions of the Code apply to trade unions and self-governing professions as well as employers."[28]

The *Human Rights Act* (now R.S.C. 1985, c. H-6) became law in March, 1978. As a result of this act, the provinces implemented their own codes and legislation and set up commissions to handle complaints. In Ontario, for example, a complaint may be filed by contacting the nearest office of the Ontario Human Rights Commission.

Often, such drastic measures may not need to be taken. Large companies and organizations usually have their own policies and procedures to assist individuals who feel they are being harassed on the job. A good example of such a policy can be found at many universities and colleges.

What to Do If You Are Being Harrassed

What should you do if you are being harassed at work or school? First, you should use the five steps in assertive behaviour which are discussed next. Be firm and repeat yourself, if necessary. If the person persists with the harassment, go to your supervisor, department head, or coordinator. If this person is the harasser, report the harassment to his or her supervisor. Make sure that you keep a thorough written record of all incidents. A harassment advisor, a school counsellor, or a member of the Human Resources Department will help you formulate a strategy to deal with the harasser. Often, a meeting with the supervisor and a firm stand using the organizational policy will succeed in stopping the harassment. If these strategies do not work, a formal investigation will be initiated and investigated by a team. This team will make recommendations about any further action, if necessary, to resolve the dispute.

Five Steps in Assertive Behaviour

Many people have a tendency to withdraw in the face of controversy, even when their rights are being violated or denied. But you can develop skill in asserting yourself by practising five key suggestions.[29]

Describe

Describe how you view the situation. To assert your position, you first need to describe how you view the situation. You need to be assertive because the other person has not been other-oriented. For example, Doug was growing increasingly frustrated with Laurie's tardiness at the weekly staff meeting. He first approached Laurie by describing his observation: "I have noticed that you are usually 15 minutes

Chapter 8 Conflict Management Skills   255

late to our weekly staff meetings." A key to communicating your assertive message is to monitor your non-verbal message, especially your voice. Avoid sarcasm or excessive vocal intensity. Calmly, yet confidently, describe the problem.

🔸 Disclose

Disclose your feelings. After describing the situation from your perspective, let the other person know how you feel.[30] Disclosing your feelings will help to build empathy and avoid lengthy harangues about the other person's unjust treatment. "I feel as if you don't take our weekly meetings seriously," continues Doug as he asserts his desire for Laurie to be on time to the meeting. Note that Doug does not talk about how others are feeling ("Every member of our group is tired of you coming in late"); he describes how *he* feels.

🔸 Identify Effects

Identify effects. Next, you can identify the effects of the other person's behaviour upon you or others. "When you are late it disrupts our meeting," says Doug.

🔸 Be Silent

Wait. Then you can simply wait for a response. Non-assertive people find this step hard. Again, be sure to monitor your non-verbal cues. Make sure your facial expression does not contradict your verbal message. Delivering an assertive message with a broad grin might create a double bind for your listener, who may not be sure what the primary message is—the verbal one or the non-verbal one.

🔸 Paraphrase

Paraphrase content and feelings. After the other person responds appropriately, reflect your understanding of both the content and feelings of the message. Laurie may respond: "Oh, I'm sorry. I didn't realize I was creating a problem. I have another meeting that usually goes overtime. It's difficult for me to arrive at the start of our meeting on time." Doug could then reply, "So, the key problem is a time conflict with another meeting. That must make you feel frustrated to try to do two things at once."

If the other person is evasive, unresponsive, or aggressive, you'll need to go through the steps again: clearly describe what the other person is doing that is not acceptable; disclose how you feel; identify the effects; wait; then reflect and clarify as needed. A key goal of an assertive response is to seek an empathic connection between you and your partner. Paraphrasing feelings is a way of ensuring that both parties are connecting.

If you tend to withdraw from conflict, how do you become assertive? Visualizing can help. Think of a past situation in which you wished you had been more assertive and then mentally replay the situation, imagining what you might have said. Also practise verbalizing assertive statements. When you are appropriately assertive, consciously congratulate yourself for sticking up for your rights. To sharpen your assertiveness skills, try *Building Your Skills: How to Assert Yourself*.

Building Your Skills

HOW TO ASSERT YOURSELF

Working with a partner, describe a situation in which you could have been more assertive. Ask your partner to assume the role of the person toward whom you should have been more assertive. Now replay the situation, using the following skills:

1. *Describe:* Tell the other person that what he or she is doing bothers you. Describe rather than evaluate.

2. *Disclose:* Tell the other person how you feel. For example, "I feel X, when you do Y...."

3. *Identify Effects:* Tell the other person the effects of his or her behaviour upon you or your group. Be as clear and descriptive as you can.

4. *Wait:* After you have described, disclosed, and identified the effects, wait for a response.

5. *Paraphrase:* Use reflective listening skills: question, paraphrase content, paraphrase feelings.

OBSERVATION OF ASSERTIVENESS SKILLS

Ask your classmates to observe your role play and provide feedback, using the following checklist. When you have finished asserting your point of view, reverse roles.

_____ Clearly describes what the problem was.

_____ Effectively discloses how he or she felt.

_____ Clearly describes the effects of the behaviour.

_____ Pauses or waits after describing the effects.

_____ Uses effective questions to promote understanding.

_____ Accurately paraphrases content.

_____ Accurately paraphrases feelings.

_____ Has good eye contact.

_____ Leans forward while speaking.

_____ Has an open body posture.

_____ Has appropriate voice tone and quality.

Fighting Fairly

Consider the following suggestions to keep you focused on issues rather than on personalities when you experience interpersonal conflict:

1. Be specific when you introduce a complaint.
2. Don't just complain; ask for a reasonable change that will make the situation better.
3. Give and receive feedback about the major points of disagreement to make sure you are understood by your partner.
4. Try tolerance. Be open to your own feelings, and equally open to your partner's feelings. Openness means that you accept change and can verbalize that attitude to your partner.
5. Consider compromise if appropriate. Many conflicts involve issues that are neither right nor wrong. Your partner may even have some good ideas.
6. Deal with one issue at a time.
7. Don't "mind rape." Don't assume to tell your partner what he or she knows or feels. Never assume you know what your partner thinks. Ask.
8. Attack the issue, not each other.
9. Don't call each other names or use sarcasm.
10. Don't "**gunny sack**." Just as farmers use a gunny sack to carry feed, many people carry past hurts into the conflict and then unleash them from the gunny sack. Forget the past and stay with the issue at hand.
11. Don't burden your partner with too many issues.
12. Think about your thoughts and feelings before speaking.

Source: Adapted from George R. Bach and Ronald M. Deutsch, *Pairing* (New York: Peter Wyden, 1970).

gunny sacking. Dredging up old problems and issues from the past, like pulling them out of an old bag or gunny sack, to use against your partner.

Recap

HOW TO ASSERT YOURSELF

Step	Example
1. Describe	"I see that you haven't completed the report yet."
2. Disclose	"I feel that the work I ask you to do is not a priority with you."
3. Identify Effects	"Without that report, our team will not achieve our goal."
4. Be Silent	Wait for a response.
5. Paraphrase	Paraphrase content: "So, you were not aware that the report was late."
	Paraphrase feelings: "Perhaps you feel embarrassed."

Summary

Interpersonal conflict is an expressed struggle that occurs when two people cannot agree upon a way to meet their needs or goals. At the root of all conflicts are our individual perspectives, needs, and experiences.

Conflict can result from misunderstanding someone (pseudo conflict), or it can stem from a simple difference of opinion or viewpoint (simple conflict). Ego conflict occurs when personalities clash; the conflict becomes personal and you may feel a need to defend your self-image.

Myths about the conflict management process tell us that conflict should always be avoided; that conflict always occurs because of misunderstandings; that conflict always occurs because of a poor interpersonal relationship; and that conflict can always be resolved. But conflict in interpersonal relationships is not always destructive. It can actually play a constructive role by identifying areas that need attention and transformation.

Although conflict seems to erupt suddenly, it often originates in events that occur long before the conflict manifests itself. It evolves from these prior conditions into frustration awareness, active conflict, resolution, and follow-up stages. Understanding conflict as a process also involves recognizing how people seek and are given control over others.

Non-confrontational approaches to conflict include placating, distracting, computing, and withdrawing. Confrontational approaches employ blaming, controlling, threats, and warnings. Cooperative approaches involve separating the person from the problem, focusing on shared interests, generating many options to seek a solution, and basing the decision on objective rather than subjective criteria. Skills for managing conflict focus on managing emotions, information, goals, and, ultimately, on managing the problem. Even if you master collaborative conflict management skills, in some instances you may need to assert yourself firmly.

The goal of this chapter is not to eliminate conflict from your interpersonal relationships; that would be unrealistic and even undesirable. But knowing principles and skills for bridging differences can give you greater flexibility in maintaining satisfying relationships with others.

For Discussion and Review

Focus on Comprehension

1. What are pseudo, simple, and ego conflict?
2. What are five myths about conflict?
3. What are the five stages of the conflict management process?
4. What are the four essential skills of managing conflict?

Focus on Critical Thinking

5. Richard has an explosive temper. He consistently receives poor performance evaluations at work because he lashes out at those who disagree with him. What strategies might help him manage his emotional outbursts?

Chapter 8 Conflict Management Skills

6. Melissa and Antonio always seem to end up making personal attacks and calling each other names when they get into a disagreement. What type of conflict are they experiencing when they do this, and how can they avoid it?
7. Analyze the opening dialogue in this chapter. What are Simone and Paul doing wrong in managing their differences? Are they doing anything right?

Focus on Ethics

8. Is it ethical to mask your true emotions in order to get along with others? Is honesty in a relationship always the best policy? Explain your response.
9. Are there situations when you should *not* assert your point of view? Provide an example to support your answer.
10. Are there situations in which you should *not* assert your point of view? Provide an example to support your answer.

For Your Journal

1. Consider a recent conflict you have had with someone. Determine whether it was a pseudo, simple, or ego conflict. Describe the strategies you used to manage the conflict. Now that you have read this chapter, discuss the other strategies you could have used to help manage the disagreement.
2. Identify a current or recent conflict you are having or have had with a friend or acquaintance. Use the problem-solving steps presented in this chapter to seek a solution to the problem that is creating the conflict. Define the problem: Identify the issues. Analyze the problem: What are the causes, symptoms, effects, and obstacles that keep you from achieving your goal? Determine your goal: What do you want? What does your partner want? Generate many possible solutions that would solve the problem. Select the solution(s) that would permit each person to achieve his or her goal. Finally, select a time that you can review the solution(s) and make any necessary changes.
3. Briefly, describe a conflict during which you did *not* do a good job of managing your emotions, that is, one in which you became angry and upset and lost your cool. Respond to the following questions: Why did you lose control of your emotions? If you could go back in time, what would you do differently to better manage your emotions before and during the conflict? Consider incorporating some of the suggestions discussed in this chapter.

Learning with Others

1. **Win As Much As You Can**[31]

This activity is designed to explore the effects of trust and conflict on communication. You will be paired with a partner. There will be four partner teams working in a cluster.

4 Xs: Lose $1 each
3 Xs: Win $1 each 1 Y: Lose $3
2 Xs: Win $2 each 2 Ys: Lose $2 each
1 X: Win $3 3 Ys: Lose $1 each
4 Ys: Win $1

Directions: Your instructor will provide detailed instructions for playing this game. For ten successive rounds you and your partner will choose either an X or a Y. Your instructor will tell all partner teams to reveal their choices at the same time. Each round's payoff will depend on the decision made by others in your cluster. For example, according to the scoring chart shown above, if all four partner teams mark X for round one of this game, each partner team loses $1. You are to confer with your partner on each round to make a joint decision. Before rounds 5, 8, and 10, your instructor will permit you to confer with the other pairs in your cluster. Keep track of your choices and winnings on the score sheet below. When you finish the game, compare your cluster's results with those of others. Discuss the factors that affected your balances. There are three key rules:

1. Do not confer with the other members of your cluster unless you are given specific permission to do so. This applies to non-verbal and verbal communication.
2. Each pair must agree on a single choice for each round.
3. Make sure that the other members of your cluster do not know your pair's choice until you are instructed to reveal it.

Round	Time Allowed	Confer with	Choice	$ Won	$ Lost	$ Balance	
1	2 min.	partner	_____	_____	_____	_____	
2	1 min.	partner	_____	_____	_____	_____	
3	1 min.	partner	_____	_____	_____	_____	
4	1 min.	partner	_____	_____	_____	_____	
5	3 min.	cluster					Bonus Round:
	1 min.	partner	_____	_____	_____	_____	Pay x 3
6	1 min.	partner	_____	_____	_____	_____	
7	1 min.	partner	_____	_____	_____	_____	
8	3 min.	cluster					
	1 min.	partner	_____	_____	_____	_____	Pay x 5
9	1 min.	partner	_____	_____	_____	_____	
10	3 min.	cluster					
	1 min.	partner	_____	_____	_____	_____	Pay x 10

2. Agree/Disagree Statements about Conflict

Read each statement once and mark whether you agree (A) or disagree (D) with it. Take five or six minutes to do this.

_____ 1. Most people find an argument interesting and exciting.

_____ 2. In most conflicts someone must win and someone must lose. That's the way conflict is.

Chapter 8 Conflict Management Skills

_____ 3. The best way to handle a conflict is simply to let everyone cool off.

_____ 4. Most people get upset at a person who disagrees with them.

_____ 5. If people spend enough time together, they will find something to disagree about and will eventually become upset with one another.

_____ 6. Conflicts can be solved if people just take the time to listen to one another.

_____ 7. If you disagree with someone, it is usually better to keep quiet than to express your personal difference of opinion.

_____ 8. To compromise is to take the easy way out of conflict.

_____ 9. Some people produce more conflict and tension than others. These people should be restricted from working with others.

After you have marked the above statements, break up into small groups and try to agree or disagree unanimously with each statement. Especially try to find reasons for differences of opinion. If your group cannot reach agreement or disagreement, you may change the wording in any statement to promote consensus. Assign one group member to observe your group interactions. After your group has attempted to reach consensus, the observer should report how effectively the group used the guidelines suggested in this chapter.

Weblinks

www.chrc.ca   This is the site for the Canadian Human Rights Commission. It includes the Canadian Human Rights Act, a reference library, recent news releases, and other sources of human rights information.

www.arista.nisa.com/fairjustice   This is the site for the British Columbia–based Fair Justice Society. This society provides a number of services to victims and families and has offices spanning the country from British Columbia to Ontario. A good source of information on violence and other conflict situations.

www.flemingc.on.ca/hod/POLPROC/3-311.htm   This is the site for the Prevention of Harassment Policy for Sir Sandford Fleming College in Peterborough, Ontario.

Suggested Readings

Fisher, R. and W. Ury. *Getting to Yes: Negotiating Agreement Without Giving In.* Boston: Houghton Mifflin, 1988.
   This is a must-read for any person who wishes to learn more about the negotiation process.

Stevenson, Kathryn, Jennifer Tufts, Dianne Hendrick and Melanie Kowalski. Youth and Crime, *Canadian Social Trends.* Catalogue No. 11-008 (1999): 17–21.
   Read more about youth crime in Canada.

Kong, Rebecca. Criminal Harassment in Canada, Canadian Social Trends. Catalogue No. 11-008-XPE (1997): 29–33.
   Read about criminal harassment in Canada and who gets harassed by whom.

Hyacinth Manning/SuperStock

Part Three

Interpersonal Communication Relationships

■ **Chapter 9**
Interpersonal Communication and Cultural Diversity: Adapting to Others

■ **Chapter 10**
Understanding Interpersonal Relationships

■ **Chapter 11**
Developing and Maintaining Interpersonal Relationships

Why are we attracted to some people and not to others? Do cultural differences have an impact on our understanding of our relationships with others? How do we begin relationships, and what are the best strategies for keeping them alive? What makes some relationships last for years and others fall apart? These are just some of the questions we will explore in Part III as we build upon our understanding of interpersonal communication skills and principles. Chapter 9 explores the impact that diversity has on communication in relationships. Chapter 10 discusses how we initiate and nurture relationships. Chapter 11 explains the sometimes mysterious process of how relationships mature and die, and discusses the application of relationship principles and skills in interactions with others including computer-mediated communication. Relationships at work are also explored in this final chapter.

chapter 9

Interpersonal Communication and Cultural Diversity: Adapting to Others

After you study this chapter

you should be able to ...

1. Define culture.
2. Identify four components of culture.
3. Discuss differences and similarities in verbal and non-verbal communication in different cultures.
4. Discuss barriers that inhibit effective intercultural communication.
5. Identify strategies to improve intercultural competence.

- The Nature of Culture
- Barriers to Effective Intercultural Communication
- Improving Intercultural Competence

Culture is communication, and communication is culture.

EDWARD T. HALL

Overheard before class begins: "I've had it with all this cultural diversity stuff. It seems like every textbook in every class is obsessed with it.

My history textbook talks about all these obscure people I've never heard of before. In English lit all we're reading is stuff by people from different cultures. I'm tired of all this politically correct nonsense. I mean, we're all Canadians. Why don't they just teach us what we need to know and cut all this diversity garbage?"

Perhaps you've encountered this kind of "diversity backlash" among some of your classmates, or, perhaps, you even share this attitude yourself. It may seem unsettling that textbooks are changing, and that educators are so concerned with cultural diversity. But these changes are not motivated by an irrational desire to be politically correct. They are taking place because Canada is changing. As the statistics in the Diversity Almanac on page 266 suggest, it is becoming an increasingly culturally diverse country. And with this growing diversity, there is also a growing awareness that learning about cultural differences can affect every aspect of our lives in positive ways. You may not plan on travelling the world, but the world is travelling to you. Your boss, teacher, religious leader, best friend, or partner may have grown up with different cultural traditions than your own. Textbooks and courses are reflecting the change, not initiating it. Try the Building Your Skills exercise on page 266. You may be surprised by the number of intercultural elements you have experienced in just a single week!

A goal in our study of interpersonal communication is to learn how we can put aside differences in age, gender, race, or ability that might cause a barrier to effective communication. (Esbin-Anderson/The Image Works)

Building Your Skills

INTERCULTURAL ENCOUNTERS

Identify the intercultural encounters you have had during the past week. Use the space below to organize your experiences.

Friends or family members who are from a culture other than my own:

_____

_____

_____

People I have met from a culture other than my own:

_____

_____

_____

Ethnic foods I have eaten (not counting pizza):

_____

_____

_____

Situations in which I have heard someone speaking a language other than my own:

1. _____

2. _____

3. _____

4. _____

Understanding Diversity

DIVERSITY ALMANAC

If the trends that were established in 1996 continue, Canada will continue to grow in both ethnic and racial diversity. (Unfortunately, at the time of writing the new census data were unavailable). Of interest, one release from the census reports that the large cities are experiencing the most rapid growth in ethnic and racial diversity, with Montreal, Toronto, and Vancouver leading the growth patterns.

- While Canada holds a widespread public perception of soaring immigration over the past years, there has actually been little deviation from Canada's 1994 rate of accepting 5.9 new immigrants per 1000 people. In fact, this rate is lower than Canada's historical "peaks," including 1957 (16 per 1000), 1966 (11 per 1000), and 1974 (8 per 1000).

- In 1996, 95 percent of Canada's total population were Canadian citizens. The majority obtained their citizenship by birth, while 13 percent were naturalized citizens.

- Canada's current rate of immigration is nonetheless still higher than in the other two leading immigration destinations, the United States (2.8 per 1000) and Australia (3.5 per 1000), and of the same order of magnitude as New Zealand (6.2 per 1000).

- In 1996, Europeans made up the largest share of all immigrants living in Canada, accounting for 47 percent of all immigrants.

  ... But the picture is changing.

- The proportion of new immigrants to Canada who are European-born has declined steadily since 1961. Before 1961, 91 percent of new immigrants to Canada were born in Europe. This proportion fell dramatically to 20 percent for those new immigrants who arrived between 1991 and 1996.

  Where are the recent immigrants to Canada coming from?

- Between 1991 and 1996, Asian-born persons, most from Hong Kong, China, the Philippines, and India, represented 57 percent of Canada's new immigrants.

  Where are Canada's recent immigrants planning to settle?

- In 1996, 42 percent of Canada's new immigrants settled in Toronto, while 18 percent settled in Vancouver, and 13 percent settled in Montreal.

Source: From *Report on the Demographic Situation in Canada 1995: Current Demographic Analysis,* 91–209; *Annual Demographic Statistics,* Cat. No. 91–213 and *The Daily,* November 4, 1997, Statistics Canada, Cat. No. 11-001.

Chapter 9   Interpersonal Communication and Cultural Diversity 267

Throughout this book we present examples and research conclusions that emphasize how cultural differences affect our interpersonal relationships. In this chapter we examine in more detail the impact culture has upon our lives and suggest some skills for bridging cultural differences in your interpersonal communications and relationships. With these skills, you will be equipped to understand and value the diversity inherent in our population. To live comfortably in the 21st century, we can learn ways to accommodate and understand cultural differences instead of ignoring them, suffering because of them, or wishing that they would disappear.

Canada is a multicultural country.
(Kerr/*Toronto Sun*)

The Nature of Culture

Exactly what is culture? **Culture** is a learned system of knowledge, behaviour, attitudes, beliefs, values, and norms that is shared by a group of people.[1] According to noted anthropologist Edward T. Hall, communication and culture are inseparable. How you interact with others is inextricably linked to how you learned to be a member of your group. Basically, we derive our cultural identity from three factors: elements, values, and contexts.

Sometimes when we speak of culture, we may be referring to a co-culture. A **co-culture** is a distinct cultural group within a larger culture. Some co-cultures in Canada would include members of minority groups such as Black Canadians and Asians. In a large city such as Toronto, many co-cultures live and/or work in a specific area, adding a distinct ethnic flavour to the city. Many communication researchers consider gender one of the most important co-cultures that significantly affects our communication with others. Gays and lesbians constitute another important co-culture in our society. The Amish, Islamic, and Jewish religious groups are examples of important religious co-cultures.

culture. A learned system of knowledge, behaviour, attitudes, beliefs, values, and norms that is shared by a group of people.

co-culture. A culture that exists within a larger cultural context (e.g., the gay and lesbian culture).

cultural elements. Categories of things and ideas that identify the most profound aspects of cultural influence (e.g., schools, governments, music, theatre, language).

enculturation. The process of communicating a group's culture from generation to generation.

Cultural Elements

Categories of things and ideas that identify the most profound aspects of cultural influence are known as **cultural elements**. According to one research team, cultural elements include the following:

- *Material culture:* things and ideas
- *Social institutions:* schools, governments, religious organizations
- *Individuals and the universe:* system of beliefs
- *Aesthetics:* music, theatre, art, dance
- *Language:* verbal and non-verbal communication systems[2]

As we grow, we learn to value these cultural elements. You were not born with a certain taste in music, clothes, and automobiles. Through **enculturation**, the process of communicating a group's culture from generation to generation, you learned what you liked by choosing from among the elements that were available within your culture. Your friends, colleagues, the media, and most importantly, your family, communicate information about these elements and advocate choices for you to make.

Pomp and Circumstance. Which elements of culture are conveyed through Canada's changing of the guard ceremony on Parliament Hill? How do these cultural elements combine to shape the identity of Canadians? (Ottawa Citizen/Chris Mikula)

Building Your Skills

ASSESSING YOUR COMMUNICATION WITH STRANGERS

Your comfort level in communicating with strangers is related to your ability to communicate with people from other cultures. Respond to each statement by indicating the degree to which it is true of your communication with strangers: Always False (answer 1), Usually False (answer 2), Sometimes True and Sometimes False (answer 3), Usually True (answer 4), or Always True (answer 5).

_____ 1. I accept strangers as they are.

_____ 2. I express my feelings when I communicate with strangers.

_____ 3. I avoid negative stereotyping when I communicate with strangers.

_____ 4. I find similarities between myself and strangers when we communicate.

_____ 5. I accommodate my behaviour to strangers when we communicate.

To find your score, add the numbers you wrote next to each statement. Scores range from 5 to 25. The higher your score, the greater your potential for developing a strong relationship with someone from a different background.

Source: From William B. Gudykunst, *Bridging Differences: Effective Intergroup Communication* (Newbury Park: Sage, 1991), 143.

Understanding Diversity

OUR RANGE OF DIFFERENCES

Cultural diversity includes more than differences in ethnic background or gender. To become other-oriented is to consider a range of differences that affect how we communicate and respond to others. Note the following differences that affect our interactions with others.

AGE Different generations, because they share different cultural and historical events, often view life differently. If your grandparents experienced the Great Depression of the 1930s, they may have different attitudes about savings accounts than you or even your parents. Today's explicit song lyrics may shock older North Americans who grew up with such racy lyrics as "makin' whoopee." The generation gap is real.

LANGUAGE By far the majority of Canadians outside of Quebec claim English as their "native tongue," and most Quebeckers claim French as their native tongue. However, a sizeable minority of Canadians report a wide range of other languages as their native tongue, and this range reflects the diversity of cultures that are integrally formed by their language. The following is a breakdown of the 20 most popularly reported minority languages spoken in Canada.

TOP 20 HOME LANGUAGES, CANADA, 1991, EXCLUDING ENGLISH AND FRENCH

1. Chinese
2. Italian
3. Punjabi

4. Spanish
5. Portuguese
6. Polish
7. German
8. Vietnamese
9. Arabic
10. Tagalog
11. Greek
12. Tamil
13. Cree
14. Persian
15. Korean
16. Ukrainian
17. Urdu
18. Gujarati
19. Hungarian
20. Hindi

Source: Adapted from *The Daily*, December 2, 1997, Statistics Canada, Cat. No. 11-001.

RELIGION Ways and times of prayer, observed holidays, and attitudes around appropriate attire are just a few of the factors in a person's religious beliefs and traditions that can affect relationships.

Here is a breakdown of the top denominations by percent of total population:

Roman Catholic	45.2%
Protestant	36.2%
United Church	11.5%
Anglican	8.1%
Presbyterian	2.4%
Lutheran	2.4%
Baptist	2.5%
Pentecostal	1.6%
Eastern Orthodox	1.4%
Jewish	1.2%
Islamic	.9%
Hindu	.6%
Buddhist	.6%
Sikh	.5%

Source: From *The Daily*, June 1, 1993, Statistics Canada, Cat. No. 96-304E.

DISABILITY Although you may not think of the disabled as part of the cultural diversity equation, there is evidence that we unconsciously alter our communication style when we converse with people with disabilities. For example, we make less eye contact with people who are in wheelchairs; we also afford them more personal space when conversing. We often speak more loudly and more slowly to those who are blind. Many people with disabilities find these behaviours insulting.

SOCIAL CLASS As the Canadian Charter of Rights and Freedoms says, "every individual is equal," but there is dramatic evidence that class differences do exist and affect communication patterns. Social psychologist Michael Argyle reports that the cues we use to make class distinctions are: (1) way of life, (2) family, (3) job, (4) money, and (5) education. Class differences influence whom we talk with, whether we are likely to invite our neighbours over for coffee, and whom we choose as our friends and lovers. Most of us must make a conscious effort if we want to expand beyond our class boundaries.

GENDER In this book we emphasize how gender affects the way we listen, use words, and send and interpret non-verbal messages. Sex differences are biological differences between males and females: only men can impregnate, only women can menstruate, gestate, and lactate. But gender differences focus on learned behaviour that is culturally associated with being a man or a woman. Gender role definitions are flexible: a man can adopt behaviour that is associated with a female role definition in a given culture and vice versa.

SEXUAL PREFERENCE During the past decade gays and lesbians have become more assertive in expressing their rights within society. Issues such as whether gays belong in the military, in the clergy, and in the teaching professions have stirred the passions of many. Being gay has become a source of pride for some, but it is still a social stigma for others. The incidence of suicide among gay teenagers is significantly higher than among non-gay teens. Although gays and lesbians are gaining legal rights and protections, they are still subject to discriminatory laws and social intolerance. The gay and lesbian community functions as a co-culture or a culture within the larger culture.

RACE According to the dictionary, race is based upon the genetically transmitted physical characteristics of a group of people classified together on the basis of a common history, nationality, or geographical location. Skin colour and other physical characteristics affect our responses and influence the way people of different races interact. Racial prejudice still has a devastating effect upon interpersonal communication patterns and relationships.

ETHNICITY Ethnicity refers to a social classification based upon a variety of factors such as nationality, religion, language, or ancestral heritage. Nationality and geographical location are especially important in defining an ethnic group. Those of Irish ancestry are usually referred to as an ethnic group rather than as a race. The same could be said of Britons, Norwegians, and Spaniards. Ethnicity, like race, fosters common bonds that affect communication patterns. On the positive side, ethnic groups bring vitality and variety to our society. On the negative side, members of these groups may experience persecution or rejection from members of other groups in our society.

This girl's clothing and pets reflect the esthetics and lifestyle of her Inuit culture.
(Mike Beedell)

Cultures are not static; they change as new information and new influences penetrate their stores of knowledge. We no longer believe that bathing is unhealthy, or that we can safely use makeup made with lead. These changes resulted from scientific discoveries. But other changes take place through acculturation; we acquire other approaches, beliefs, and values by coming into contact with other cultures. Today, acupuncture, yoga, tai chi, and karate studios are commonplace in most cities across Canada. Taco shells are available in every supermarket and restaurants offer a variety of fare from Mexican to Italian to Thai. In less obvious ways, "new" perspectives from other cultures have also influenced our thoughts, actions, and relationships. In the Understanding Diversity box on page 271, read about cultural differences in dating customs.

Cultural Values

Identifying what a given group of people values or appreciates can provide insight into the behaviour of an individual raised within that group. Although there are great differences among the world's **cultural values**, one researcher identified four variables for measuring values that are significant in almost every culture.[3] According to Geert Hofstede, each culture places varying degrees of value upon masculine and feminine perspectives, avoidance of uncertainty, distribution of power, and individualism (see Table 9.1). Hofstede's research conclusions have been widely summarized to describe differences among these four key cultural values. Although his research has been criticized as being dated (his information is now more than 30 years old) and based primarily on males who worked at IBM (the main source for much of his information), his research remains one of the most comprehensive, data-based studies of understanding cultural values.[4] He surveyed more than 100 000 employees in more than 50 countries; his research effort has yet to be duplicated or surpassed.

Masculine versus Feminine Perspectives

Some cultures emphasize traditional male values, whereas others place greater value on female perspectives. These values are not really about biological sex differences but overarching approaches to interacting with others. People from **masculine cultures** tend to value more traditional roles for both men and women. Masculine cultures also value achievement, assertiveness, heroism, and material wealth. Research reveals that men tend to approach communication from a content orientation, meaning that they view communication as functioning primarily for information exchange. Men talk when they have something to say. This is also consistent with the tendency for men to base their relationships, especially their male friendships, on sharing activities rather than talking.

Men and women from **feminine cultures** tend to value such things as caring for the less fortunate, being sensitive toward others, and enhancing the overall quality of life.[5] Women, as research suggests, tend to approach communication for the purpose of relating or connecting to others, of extending themselves to other people to know them and be known by them.[6] What women talk about is less important than the fact that they're talking, because talking implies relationship.

A short way of summarizing this difference: *Men often communicate to report; women often communicate to establish rapport.*[7] So the point of difference isn't in the way the sexes actually communicate, but in the motivations for or reasons they communicate. The *how* may not be that different; the *why* may be very different.[8]

cultural values. What a given group of people values or appreciates.

masculine cultural values. Achievement, assertiveness, heroism, and material wealth.

feminine cultural values. Relationships, caring for the less fortunate, and overall quality of life.

Understanding Diversity

Dating Customs Around the World

The development of relationships varies from culture to culture. The following list describes some of the dating behaviours from cultures throughout the world. How similar are these norms from the norms or ways of your social group?

These are some of the ways teens date in other countries of the world.

Afghanistan
Dating is rare because most marriages are arranged by parents, and schools are separate for boys and girls. Opportunities to meet are rare. Girls have a 7 P.M. curfew, whereas boys have an 11 P.M. curfew.

Australia
Most teens go out in large groups and don't pair off until they are 18 or 19 years old. Girls often ask boys out, and pay for the date, too. Couples often go to dinner parties, barbecues, or the beach.

Central and South America
Dating is not allowed until the age of 15. When of age, most boys and girls date in large groups, going out together to weekend dance parties. When not dancing, teens gather at local clubs to eat and talk.

Europe
Dating is usually a group event. In Finland, as many as thirty teens may attend a movie together. Slumber parties are common in Italy and Switzerland, where teens gather for parties at a home and sleep there when the party is over.

In Spain teens join a *pandilla*, a club or a group of friends with the same interests, such as cycling or hiking. Dating is done one to one, and both girls and boys ask each other out and split the cost of the evening's entertainment.

In Russia dates take place at dances or at clubs where teens eat or chat with friends. In small towns, teens meet in the streets downtown or gather around a fountain.

Iran
It is against the law to date. Teens are separated until they are of marrying age; then their families introduce them to each other and sometimes a courtship follows.

Japan and Korea
Most high school students don't date or go to parties, but spend their time studying instead. Dating begins in college, when only boys do the asking and pay for the dates.

Source: "Dating Customs Around the World." FactMonster.com. © 2000 The Learning Network Inc., **www.factmonster.com/ipka/ A0767654.html** (Sept. 26, 2000).

In Russian small towns, teens often meet in the streets downtown to socialize together. How does this compare with your experience? (Jeff Greenberg/PhotoEdit)

Of course, rarely is a culture on the extreme end of the continuum; many are somewhere in between. For centuries, most countries in Europe, Asia, and the Americas have had masculine cultures. Men and their conquests dominate history books; men have been more prominent in leadership and decision making than women. But today many of these cultures are moving slowly toward the middle—legal and social rules are encouraging more gender balance and greater equality between masculine and feminine roles.

Tolerance of Uncertainty versus Avoidance of Uncertainty

Cedric works for the phone company as a customer service representative. He grew up in Jamaica where there is sometimes a higher tolerance for bureaucratic uncertainty than there is in Canada. Jake is from Toronto; he expects (sometimes demands) that his problems be resolved quickly. Cedric's higher tolerance for uncertainty and Jake's desire for straight, prompt answers to questions created an

Table 4.1

Examples of Countries That Illustrate Four Cultural Values

Cultural Value	Examples of Countries That Scored Higher on This Cultural Value	Examples of Countries That Scored Lower on This Cultural Value
Masculinity: People from countries with higher masculinity scores prefer high achievement, men being in more assertive roles, and more clearly differentiated sex roles than people from countries with lower scores on this cultural dimension.	Japan, Australia, Venezuela, Italy, Switzerland, Mexico, Ireland, Jamaica, Great Britain	Sweden, Norway, Netherlands, Denmark, Yugoslavia, Costa Rica, Finland, Chile, Portugal, Thailand
Uncertainty Avoidance: People from countries with higher uncertainty avoidance scores generally prefer to avoid uncertainty; they like to know what will happen next. People from countries with lower scores are more comfortable with uncertainty.	Greece, Portugal, Guatemala, Uruguay, Belgium, Japan, Yugoslavia, Peru, France	Singapore, Jamaica, Denmark, Sweden, Hong Kong, Ireland, Great Britain, Malaysia, India, Philippines, United States
Power Distribution: People from countries with higher power distribution scores generally prefer greater power differences between people; they are generally more accepting of someone having authority and power than are people from countries with lower scores on this cultural dimension.	Malaysia, Guatemala, Panama, Philippines, Mexico, Venezuela, Arab countries, Ecuador, Indonesia, India	Austria, Israel, Denmark, New Zealand, Ireland, Sweden, Norway, Finland, Switzerland, Great Britain
Individualism: People from countries with higher individualism scores generally prefer individual accomplishment rather than collective or collaborative achievement.	United States, Australia, Great Britain, Canada, Netherlands, New Zealand, Italy, Belgium, Denmark, Sweden, France	Guatemala, Ecuador, Panama, Venezuela, Columbia, Indonesia, Pakistan, Costa Rica, Peru, Taiwan, South Korea

Source: Adapted from Geert Hofstede, *Cultures and Organizations: Software of the Mind* (London: McGraw-Hill, 1991).

oil-and-water confrontation. Jake phoned Cedric to complain about the slow response to his request to have a new phone line installed for his fax machine. Cedric tried to be reassuring, but Jake got the distinct impression that Cedric was not sympathetic and thought that a week's wait for a new line was perfectly reasonable. Jake expected his new line within 24 hours. Both had difficulty tuning in to the cultural difference in their expectations about how quickly a bureaucracy should respond to an individual request.

Some cultures tolerate more ambiguity and uncertainty than others. Those in which people need certainty to feel secure are more likely to have and enforce rigid rules for behaviour and to develop more elaborate codes of conduct. People from cultures with a greater tolerance for uncertainty have more relaxed, informal expectations for others. "Go with the flow" and "It will sort itself out" are phrases

Chapter 9   Interpersonal Communication and Cultural Diversity   273

that describe their attitudes. One study showed that people from Portugal, Germany, Peru, Belgium, and Japan have high certainty needs, but people from Scandinavian countries tend to tolerate uncertainty.[9]

🟠 Concentrated versus Decentralized Power

Some cultures value an equal or decentralized distribution of power, whereas others accept a concentration of hierarchical power in a centralized government and other organizations. In the latter, hierarchical bureaucracies are common, and people expect some individuals to have more power than others. Russia, France, and China are all high on the concentrated power scale. Those that often strive for greater equality and distribution of power and control include many (but not all) citizens from Australia, Denmark, New Zealand, and Israel. People from these latter countries tend to minimize differences in power between people.

🟠 Individual versus Group Achievement

Kaylie: We've got this group project to do. Let's divvy up the work and then meet back here next week to see what each of us has done.

Ayako: Wait a minute, Kaylie. It might seem to be more efficient to divide up the work into little separate pieces, but in the end we'll have a better report if we work on every section.

Kaylie: Are you kidding? We'll be here all night! Josh, you take the history of the problem. Bert, you look at problem causes and effects. Ayako, why don't you do a literature search on the CD-ROM in the library and start looking up articles.

Ayako: All right. But I still think it would be better to go to the library together. I think we'd have better luck if we worked on each aspect of the problem as a team.

Kaylie and Ayako clearly have different strategies for working together. Kaylie approaches the project from an individualistic perspective; Ayako prefers a collective or group strategy to achieve the goal. Traditionally, North Americans champion individual accomplishments and achievements. People from Asian backgrounds often value collective or group achievement more highly. One researcher summed up the North American goal system this way:

> Chief among the virtues claimed . . . is self-realization. Each person is viewed as having a unique set of talents and potentials. The translation of these potentials into actuality is concurred the highest purpose to which one can devote one's life.[10]

In a collectivistic culture, conversely, people strive to attain goals for all members of the family, group, or community. In Kenyan tribes, for example:

> . . . nobody is an isolated individual. Rather, his [or her] uniqueness is secondary fact. . . . In this new system group activities are dominant, responsibility is shared and accountability is collective. . . . Because of the emphasis on collectivity, harmony and cooperation among the group tends to be emphasized more than individual function and responsibility.[11]

Individualistic cultures tend to be more loosely knit socially; individuals feel responsible for taking care of themselves and their immediate families.[12] In collectivistic cultures, individuals expect more support from others, and more loyalty to and from the community. Because collectivistic cultures place more value on "we" than "I," teamwork approaches usually succeed better in their workplaces.

What can be inferred about the use of *cultural context* cues to enhance message and meaning in Canadian Aboriginal culture?
(Royal Canadian Mounted Police)

> **Recap**

DIMENSIONS OF CULTURAL VALUES

Masculine versus Feminine	Does the culture place the highest value on assertiveness, heroism, and wealth or on relationships, caring for others, and overall quality of life?
Tolerance of Uncertainty versus Avoidance of Uncertainty	Does the culture have a high tolerance for ambiguity and uncertainty or does it hold more rigid and explicit behavioural expectations?
Concentrated versus Decentralized Power	Does the culture tolerate or accept hierarchical power structures or does it favour a more equal distribution of power?
Individual versus Group Achievement	Does the culture value individual achievement more than collective group accomplishments or vice versa?

North American businesses, for example, have tried to adopt some of Japan's successful team strategies for achieving high productivity.

Cultural Contexts

cultural context. Information not explicitly communicated through language, such as environmental or non-verbal cues.

high-context culture. A culture that derives much information from non-verbal and environmental cues.

low-context culture. A culture that derives much information from the words of a message and less information from non-verbal and environmental cues.

As we discussed in Chapter 6, individuals from different cultures use **cultural contextual** cues in varying degrees to enhance messages and meaning. This led Edward T. Hall to categorize cultures as either high- or low-context.[13] As shown in Figure 9.1, in **high-context cultures** non-verbal cues are extremely important in interpreting messages. **Low-context cultures** rely more explicitly on language, and use fewer contextual cues to send and interpret information. Individuals from high-context cultures may perceive persons from low-context cultures as less attractive, knowledgeable, and trustworthy, because they violate unspoken rules of dress, conduct, and communication. Individuals from low-context cultures often are not skilled in interpreting unspoken, contextual messages.[14]

Figure 9.1 High/Low Contexts: Where Different Cultures Fall on the Context Scale

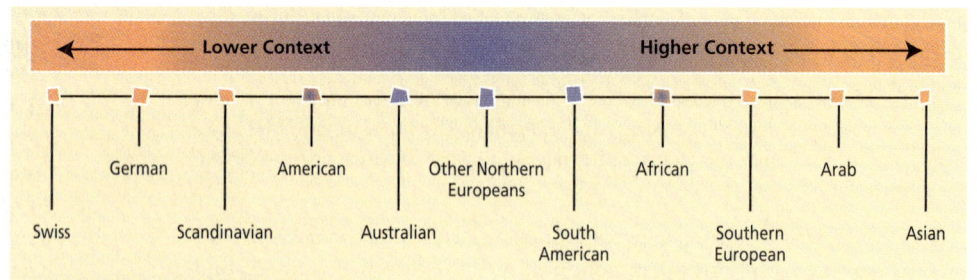

← Lower Context | Higher Context →

Swiss — German — Scandinavian — American — Australian — Other Northern Europeans — South American — African — Southern European — Arab — Asian

Low-Context Cultures
(Information must be provided explicitly, usually in words.)
- Are less aware of non-verbal cues, environment, and situation
- Lack well-developed networks
- Need detailed background information
- Tend to segment and compartmentalize information
- Control information on a "need to know" basis
- Prefer explicit and careful directions from someone who "knows"
- Consider knowledge a commodity

High-Context Cultures
(Much information drawn from surroundings. Very little must be explicitly transferred.)
- Consider non-verbal cues important
- Let information flow freely
- Rely on physical context for information
- Take environment, situation, gestures, and mood into account
- Maintain extensive information networks

Source: From Donald W. Klopf, *Intercultural Encounters: The Fundamentals of Intercultural Communication* (Englewood, CO: Morton Publishing, 1998), 33, and *Meeting News*, (June 1993).

e-connections

A WORLD OF DIFFERENCES IN YOUR OWN BACKYARD

You need not become a world traveller to observe the range of differences in ethnicity, gender, sexuality, religion, and disability. Pick a public spot on your campus or in your community. Sit there with pencil and paper for 30 minutes and make notes on the different types of people you observe. Although many of your observations will be guesses or inferences, note how many different kinds of people you can observe, based on their ethnicity, race, or culture. You may also look for cues that announce someone's religious beliefs, such as a religious symbol (perhaps a star of David or a cross) or type of clothing (perhaps a nun's habit, priest's collar, or Islamic veil).

You can also learn about the rich and varied cultural traditions of the world by exploring the resources of the Internet. For a comprehensive list of resources about human diversity, click on the following website:

http://alabanza.com/kabacoff/Inter-Links/diversity.html

Here are three additional websites that offer descriptions of cultural traditions around the world:

www.wcpworld.com:80/future/links.htm

At this site, visit the culture of any country in the world.

www.cal.org/pubs/ncrcpubs.htm

This site is used by people who teach and learn languages of other cultures.

www.execpc.com/~dboals/div-gen.html 1 #

Here you'll find links to several sites that describe cultural traditions from around the world.

▶ Recap

THE NATURE OF CULTURE

Cultural Elements	Things and ideas that represent profound aspects of cultural influence, such as art, music, schools, and belief systems.
Cultural Values	What a culture reveres and holds important.
Cultural Contexts	Information not explicitly communicated through language, such as environmental or non-verbal cues. High-context cultures (such as Japanese, Chinese, Korean) derive much information from these cues. Low-context cultures (such as North American, Western European) rely more heavily on words.

Barriers to Effective Intercultural Communication

Intercultural communication occurs when individuals or groups from different cultures communicate. The transactional process of listening and responding to people from different cultural backgrounds can be challenging. The greater the difference in culture between two people, the greater the potential for misunderstanding and mistrust.

Misunderstanding and miscommunication occur between people from different cultures because of different coding rules and cultural norms, which play a major role in shaping patterns of interaction. The greater the difference between the cultures, the more likely it is that they will use different verbal and non-verbal codes. When you encounter a culture that has little in common with your own, you may experience **culture shock**, or a sense of confusion, anxiety, stress, and loss. If you are visiting or actually living in the new culture, your uncertainty and stress may take time to subside as you learn the values and codes that characterize the culture.

intercultural communication. Communication between or among people who have different cultural traditions.

culture shock. Feeling of stress and anxiety a person experiences when encountering a culture different from his or her own.

But if you are simply trying to communicate with someone from a background very different from your own—even on your home turf—you may find the suggestions in this section helpful in closing the communication gap.[15]

The first step to bridging differences between cultures is to find out what hampers effective communication. What keeps us from connecting with people from other cultures? Sometimes it is different meanings created by different languages or by different interpretations of non-verbal messages. Sometimes it is our inability to stop focusing on ourselves and begin focusing on the other. We'll examine some of these barriers first, then discuss strategies and skills for overcoming them.

Ethnocentrism

Marilyn had always been intrigued by Russia. Her dream was to travel the country by train, spending time in small villages as well as exploring the cultural riches of Moscow, Kiev, and St. Petersburg. Her first day in Russia was a disappointment, however. When she arrived in Moscow, she joined a tour touting the cultural traditions of Russia. When the tour bus stopped at Sparrow Hills, affording them a breathtaking hilltop view of the Moscow skyline, she was perplexed and mildly shocked to see women, dressed in elegant wedding gowns, mounted on horses galloping through the parking lot. Men in suits were cheering them on as a crowd of tipsy revellers set off fireworks and danced wildly to a brass band. "What kind of people are these?" sniffed Marilyn.

"Oh," said the tour guide, "it is our custom to come here to celebrate immediately following the wedding ceremony."

"But in public with such raucousness?" queried Marilyn.

"It is our tradition," said the guide.

"What a backwards culture. They're nothing but a bunch of peasants!" pronounced Marilyn, who was used to more refined nuptial celebrations at a country club or an exclusive hotel.

For the rest of the tour Marilyn judged every Russian behaviour as inferior to those of westerners. That first experience coloured her perceptions, and her ethnocentric view served as a barrier to effective communication with the Russian people she met.

Colourful celebrations like this ritual purification ceremony in Bali can reinforce healthy ethnic pride. When this pride is taken to the extreme through ethnocentric feelings, barriers between groups may result.
(Michael Burgess/Stock Boston)

Ethnocentrism stems from a conviction that your own cultural traditions and assumptions are superior to those of others. In short, it is the opposite of an other-orientation that embraces and appreciates the elements that give another culture meaning. This kind of cultural snobbery is one of the fastest ways to create a barrier that inhibits, rather than enhances, communication.

ethnocentrism. The belief that your cultural traditions and assumptions are superior to others.

Building Your Skills

Assessing Your Ethnocentricism

The following measure of ethnocentrism was developed by communication researchers James Neuliep and James McCroskey. Answer the following questions honestly.

This instrument is composed of 24 statements concerning your feelings about your culture and other cultures. In the space provided to the left of each item indicate the degree to which the statement applies to you by marking whether you (5) strongly agree, (4) agree, (3) are neutral, (2) disagree, or (1) strongly disagree with the statement. There are no right or wrong answers. Work quickly and record your first response.

_____ 1. Most other cultures are backward compared with my culture.

_____ 2. People in other cultures have a better lifestyle than we do in my culture.

_____ 3. Most people would be happier if they didn't live like people do in my culture.

_____ 4. My culture should be the role model for other cultures.

_____ 5. Lifestyles in other cultures are just as valid as those in my culture.

_____ 6. Other cultures should try to be more like my culture.

_____ 7. I'm not interested in the values and customs of other cultures.

_____ 8. It is not wise for other cultures to look up to my culture.

_____ 9. People in my culture could learn a lot from people in other cultures.

_____ 10. Most people from other cultures just don't know what's good for them.

_____ 11. People from my culture act strange and unusual when they go into other cultures.

_____ 12. I have little respect for the values and customs of other cultures.

_____ 13. Most people would be happier if they lived like people in my culture.

_____ 14. People in my culture have just about the best lifestyles of anywhere.

_____ 15. My culture is backward compared with most other cultures.

_____ 16. My culture is a poor role model for other cultures.

_____ 17. Lifestyles in other cultures are not as valid as those in my culture.

_____ 18. My culture should try to be more like other cultures.

_____ 19. I'm very interested in the values and customs of other cultures.

_____ 20. Most people in my culture just don't know what is good for them.

_____ 21. People in other cultures could learn a lot from people in my culture.

_____ 22. Other cultures are smart to look up to my culture.

_____ 23. I respect the values and customs of other cultures.

_____ 24. People from other cultures act strange and unusual when they come into my culture.

To determine your ethnocentrism **reverse** your score for items 2, 3, 5, 8, 9, 11, 15, 16, 18, 19, 20, and 23. For these items, 5 = 1, 4 = 2, 3 = 3, 2 = 4, and 1 = 5. That is, if your original score was a 5, change it to a 1. If your original score was a 4, change it to a 2, and so forth. Once you have reversed your score for these 12 items, add up all 24 scores. This is your generalized ethnocentrism score. Scores greater than 80 indicate high ethnocentrism. Scores of 50 and below indicate low ethnocentrism.

Source: J. W. Neuliep and J. C. McCroskey, "The Development of a U.S. and Generalized Ethnocentrism Scale," _Communication Research Reports,_ 14 (1997): 393.

Different Communication Codes

You are on your first trip to Calgary. You step off the bus and look around for Stampede Park, and you realize that you have gotten off at the wrong stop. You see a corner grocery store with "Stampede Park" painted on a red sign. So you walk in and ask the man behind the counter, "How do I get to the Calgary Stampede, please?" The man smiles, shrugging his shoulders. But he points to a transit map pasted onto the wall behind the counter.

Today, even when you travel within Canada, you are likely to encounter people who do not speak your language. Obviously, this kind of intercultural difference poses a formidable communication challenge. And even when you do speak the same tongue as another, he or she may come from a place where the words and gestures have different meanings. Your ability to communicate will depend upon whether you can understand each other's verbal and non-verbal codes.

In the example above, although the man behind the counter did not understand your exact words, he noted the cut of your clothing, your backpack, and your anxiety, and he deduced that you were asking for directions. And you could understand what his gesture toward the transit map meant. Unfortunately, not every communication between the users of two different languages is this successful.

Even when language is translated, there can be missed or mangled meanings. Note the following examples of mistranslated advertisements:

- A General Motors auto ad with "Body by Fisher" became "Corpse by Fisher" in Flemish.
- A Colgate-Palmolive toothpaste named "Cue" was advertised in France before anyone realized that *Cue* also happened to be the name of a widely circulated pornographic book about oral sex.
- Pepsi-Cola's "Come Alive with Pepsi" campaign, when it was translated for the Taiwanese market, conveyed the unsettling news that, "Pepsi brings your ancestors back from the grave."
- Parker Pen could not advertise its famous "Jotter" ballpoint pen in some languages because the translation sounded like "jockstrap" pen.
- One American airline operating in Brazil advertised that it had plush "rendezvous lounges" on its jets, unaware that in Portuguese (the language of Brazil) "rendezvous" implies a special room for making love.[16]

Stereotyping and Prejudice

Europeans dress fashionably.

Asians are good at math.

Canadians are overly apologetic.

stereotype. To place a person or group of persons into an inflexible, all-encompassing category.

These statements are stereotypes. They are all inaccurate. To **stereotype** someone is to push him or her into an inflexible, all-encompassing category. In Chapter 3, we saw how our tendency to simplify sensory stimuli can lead us to adopt stereotypes as we interpret the behaviour of others. When we stereotype, we "print" the same judgment over and over again, failing to consider the uniqueness of individuals, groups, or events. This becomes a barrier to effective intercultural communication. Two anthropologists suggest that every person is, in some respects (1) like all other people, (2) like some other people, and (3) like no other people.[17] Our challenge when meeting others is to discover how they are alike and how they are unique.

Can stereotypes play a useful role in interpersonal communication? The answer is a resounding "no" if our labels are inaccurate or if they assume superiority on our part. But, sometimes, it may be appropriate to draw upon generalizations. If, for example, you are driving lost and alone in a large city at two o'clock in the morning and another car repeatedly taps your rear bumper, it would be prudent to try to drive away as quickly as possible rather than to hop out of your car to make a new acquaintance. You would be wise to prejudge that the other driver might have some malicious intent. In most situations, however, **prejudice**—prejudging someone before you know all of the facts—inhibits effective communication. If you decide that you like or dislike (usually dislike) someone simply because he or she is a member of a certain group or class of people, you will not give yourself a chance to communicate with the person in a meaningful way. Prejudice usually involves negative attitudes toward members of a specific social group or culture.

Certain prejudices are widespread. Although there are more females than males in the world, in many societies females are prejudged to be less valuable than males. One study found that even when a male and a female hold the same type of job, the male's job is considered more prestigious than the female's.[18] **Discrimination** is often a result of prejudice. When people discriminate, they treat members of groups differently from their own in negative ways. In the past, people of different gender, race, ethnicity, or sexual orientation were often victims of discrimination socially and politically. Today, gender and racial discrimination in hiring and promotion is illegal in Canada. But our social attitudes have not kept pace with the law. Stereotyping and prejudice are still formidable barriers to effective interpersonal communication. While many do not actively engage in discrimination, many people still hold negative attitudes and stereotypes of people different from themselves.

prejudice. Prejudging someone before you know all of the facts or background of that person.

discrimination. Negative behaviours directed toward members of social groups who are the object of prejudice.

Canadian Issues

ABORIGINAL WAGES: AN INDICATION OF DISCRIMINATION?

A recent study examined wage gaps between Canadian workers as a whole and four main Aboriginal groups. These Aboriginal groups were: Native peoples on reserve, Native peoples off reserve, Inuit, and Métis. The study confirmed that, on average, Aboriginal people earn less than Canadians as a whole. The most disadvantaged Aboriginal group was Native peoples living on reserves. According to this study, the wage gap between Native men living on reserves and Métis is 22 percent. Another interesting finding of this study was that there is greater disparity in the distribution of wages among Aboriginals than among Canadians as a whole. In other words, not only are Aboriginals earning less than other Canadians but they also experience more inequality in their wages. For example, the mean annual wage of a worker in the top quintile (high earning bracket) is $63 720 for Canadian workers as a whole and $48 720 for workers of Aboriginal identity. As wages increase, this gap also increases between the two groups. While we can look at mitigating factors, such as differences in educational attainment and ages of workers, this gap still remains a problem for the future of Aboriginals in Canada. More studies are needed to further examine the sources of this inequality and then steps should be taken to reduce this disparity.

For Discussion

1. List some ideas to help alleviate this disparity in wages.

2. What can the government do to increase educational and job opportunities for Aboriginals?

3. Is discrimination against Aboriginals still an issue in Canada? Do you think that this wage disparity is an example of such discrimination?

Source: Rachel Bernier, *The Dimensions of Wage Inequality among Aboriginal People.* Statistics Canada, Cat. No. 11F0019MPE 97109, December, 1997.

Assuming Similarity

Just as it is inaccurate to assume that all people who belong to another social group or class are worlds apart from you, it is usually erroneous to assume that others act and think as you do. Even if they appear to be like you, all people are not alike. While this statement is not profound, it has profound implications. We often make the mistake of assuming that others value the same things we do, maintaining a self-focused perspective instead of an other-oriented one. As you saw in Chapter 3, focusing on superficial factors, such as appearance, clothing, and even a person's occupation, can lead to false impressions. Instead, we must take the time to explore a person's background and cultural values before we can determine what we really have in common.

Improving Intercultural Competence

The remaining portion of this chapter presents three sets of strategies to help you bridge differences between yourself and people who come from a different cultural background. These three strategy sets—appropriate knowledge, motivation, and skill—are based on our understanding of how to be a competent communicator.

knowledge. One of the elements of becoming a competent communicator; information that enhances understanding of others.

Our suggestion to enhance your understanding or **knowledge** of others is based on the assumption that knowing more about others is important in quality relationships. One of the barriers to effective intercultural communication is having different communication codes. Improving your knowledge of how others communicate can reduce the impact of this barrier. We offer strategies to help you learn more about other cultures by actively pursuing information about others.

motivation. Internal state of readiness to respond to something. An element of interpersonal competence.

A second set of strategies focuses on becoming motivated to improve our intercultural communication knowledge and skills. **Motivation** is an internal state of readiness to respond to something. A competent communicator wants to learn and improve; an incompetent communicator is not motivated to develop new skills. Technically, no one can motivate you to do something; motivation comes from within. But developing strategies to appreciate others who are different from yourself may help you appreciate different cultural approaches to communication and relationships. We suggest you endeavour to be more tolerant of uncertainty and to avoid knee-jerk negative evaluations of others.

skill. Behaviour that improves the effectiveness or quality of communicating with others.

The final set of strategies—developing **skill** in adapting to others—focuses on specific behaviours that can help overcome the barriers and cultural differences we have discussed. Here, to address the barrier of ethnocentrism, we will identify the advantages of becoming a more flexible communicator. We will also describe the essential competence of becoming other-oriented—focusing on the needs, goals, and values of others instead of only on your own. As we discussed in Chapter 1, becoming other-oriented is critical to the process of relating to others.

Developing Knowledge: Strategies to Understand Others Who Are Different from Us

Knowledge is power. To increase your knowledge of others who are different from you, we suggest that you actively seek information about others, ask questions and

Understanding Diversity

ETHNOCENTRIC THINKING

All good people agree,
And all good people say,
All nice people like Us, are We,
And everyone else is They.

In a few short lines, Rudyard Kipling captured the essence of what sociologists and anthropologists call ethnocentric thinking. Members of all societies tend to believe that "All nice people like Us, are We." They find comfort in the familiar and often denigrate or distrust others. Of course, with training and experience in other climes, they may learn to transcend their provincialism, placing themselves in others' shoes. Or, as Kipling put it,

. . . if you cross over the sea,
Instead of over the way,
You may end by (think of it!)
looking on We
As only a sort of They.

In a real sense, a main lesson of the sociology of intergroup relations is to begin to "cross over the sea," to learn to understand why other people think and act as they do and to be able to empathize with their perspectives.

Source: Adapted from Faun B. Evans, Barbara Gleason, and Mark Wiley, *Cultural Tapestry: Readings for a Pluralistic Society* (HarperCollins, 1992).

---

listen to the answers, and establish common ground. Let's discuss these strategies in more detail.

Seek Information about the Culture

Prejudice stems from ignorance. Learning about another person's values, beliefs, and behaviours can help you understand his or her messages and their meaning. Every person has a **world view** based on cultural beliefs about the universe and key issues such as death, God, and the meaning of life.[19] According to Carley Dodd, "A culture's world view involves finding out how the culture perceives the role of various forces in explaining why events occur as they do in a social setting."[20] These beliefs shape our thoughts, language, and behaviour. Only through intercultural communication can we hope to understand how each individual views the world. As you speak to a person from another culture, think of yourself as a detective, watching for implied, often unspoken, messages that provide information about the values, norms, roles, and rules of that person's culture.

You can also prepare yourself by studying the culture. If you are going to another country, courses in the history, anthropology, art, or geography of that place can give you a head start on communicating with understanding. Learn not only from books, magazines, and the Internet but also from individuals whenever possible. Even in a high-context culture, no one will fault you for asking directly for help if you show a sincere desire to learn. If you are trying to communicate with someone closer to home who is from a different background, you can study magazines, music, food, and other readily available sources of information about his or her culture. Or exchange visits to one another's homes or hangouts to observe and learn more about the person.

Given the inextricable link between language and culture, the more you learn about another language, the more you will understand the traditions and customs of the culture. Politicians have long known the value of using even a few words of their constituents' language. Speaking even a few words can signify your interest in learning about the language and culture of others.

When we speak of culture we are also referring to co-cultures. As you already know, a co-culture is a cultural group within a larger culture. Learning how men

world view. Perception shared by a culture or group of people about key beliefs and issues, such as death, God, and the meaning of life, which influences interaction with others.

and women, each a separate co-culture, communicate differently can help us improve our communication with the opposite gender. Men, for example, are more likely to develop friendships through participating in common activities with other men (playing on a baseball team, working together).[21] Women are more likely to develop friendships through talking together rather than working together.

Reading books about differences between the way men and women communicate is one strategy to help both sexes improve understanding and develop insight into different approaches to communication. There are many popular books that can help create a dialogue between men and women about communication differences and, thus, promote greater knowledge about how to improve communication.

As you read about other cultures or co-cultures, it is important not to develop rigid categories or stereotypes for the way others may talk or behave. Proclaiming, "Oh, you're just saying that because you're a man" or "You women always say things like that" can increase, rather than decrease, communication barriers. Throughout this book we will discuss research-based gender differences in the way men and women communicate, in order to enhance your understanding and improve communication with members of the opposite sex. But we don't recommend that you treat men and women as completely separate species from different planets or automatically assume you will immediately misunderstand the opposite sex.

Ask Questions and Listen Effectively

When you encounter a person from another background, asking questions and then pausing to listen is a simple technique for gathering information and also for confirming the accuracy of your expectations and assumptions. Some cultures, such as the Japanese, have rigid expectations regarding gift giving. It is better to ask what these expectations are than to assume that your good old down-home manners will see you through.

When you ask questions, be prepared to share information about yourself, too. Otherwise, your partner may feel as if you are interrogating him or her as a way to gain power and dominance rather than from a sincere desire to learn about cultural rules and norms.

Communication helps to reduce the uncertainty that is present in any relationship.[22] When you meet people for the first time, you are highly uncertain about who they are and what they like and dislike. When you communicate with someone from another culture, the uncertainty level is particularly high. As you begin to interact, you exchange information that helps you develop greater understanding. If you continue to ask questions, eventually you will feel less uncertain about how the person is likely to behave.

Just asking questions and sharing information about yourself is not sufficient to bridge differences in culture and background. It is equally important to listen to what others share. In Chapter 4 we provide specific strategies for improving your listening skills.

Develop a "Third Culture"

Several researchers suggest that one of the best ways to enhance understanding when communicating with someone from a different cultural background is to develop a **third culture**. This is created when the communication partners join aspects of separate cultures to create a third, "new" culture that is more comprehensive and inclusive than either of the two separate cultures.[23] The goal of developing a third-culture mentality is to reduce our tendency to approach cultural differences as an "us" versus "them" point of view. Rather than trying to

third culture. Establishing common ground by joining separate cultures to create a third, "new," more comprehensive and inclusive culture.

Chapter 9   Interpersonal Communication and Cultural Diversity

The relationship between this Himalayan Sherpa and Western trekker can be made more comfortable for both of them if they develop a "third culture," different from both of their cultures, with its own rules and expectations.   (David Robbins/Tony Stone Images)

eliminate communication barriers stemming from two different sets of experiences, adopting a third culture framework seeks to create a new understanding of both participants for each other.[24]

Consider the example of Fiona, a businesswoman from Calgary, Alberta, and Xiaoxian, a businesswoman from Shanghai, China. In the context of their business relationship, it would be difficult for them to develop a comprehensive understanding of each other's cultural traditions. If, however, they openly acknowledged the most significant of these differences and sought to create a third culture by identifying explicit rules and norms for their interaction, they might be able to develop a more comfortable relationship with each other.

As described by Benjamin Broome, the third culture "is characterized by unique values and norms that may not have existed prior to the dyadic [two-person] relationship."[25] Broome labels the essence of this new relationship **relational empathy**, which permits varying degrees of understanding rather than requiring complete comprehension of another's culture or emotions.

One of the barriers to effective intercultural communication is having different communication codes. In seeking a third culture, you are seeking a way to develop a common code or framework to enhance understanding. Developing such a code that both individuals can understand may include each party's learning the language of the other. It can also include discussing meanings of non-verbal communication so that misunderstandings can be reduced. Further, it involves using the perception check skills we discussed in Chapter 3.

The cultural context includes all of the elements of the culture (learned behaviours and rules or "mental software") that affect the interaction. Do you come from a culture that takes a tea break each afternoon at 4:00 P.M.? Does your culture value hard work and achievement, or relaxation and enjoyment? Creating a third culture acknowledges the different cultural contexts and interactions participants have experienced and seeks to develop a new context for future interaction.

relational empathy.   The essence of the third culture, permitting varying degrees of understanding rather than complete comprehension of another's culture or emotions.

> ### Recap
>
> **DEVELOP KNOWLEDGE TO ENHANCE UNDERSTANDING**
>
> | | |
> |---|---|
> | Seek Information about the Culture | Learn about a culture's world view. |
> | Ask Questions and Listen | Reduce uncertainty by asking for clarification and listening to the answer. |
> | Develop a Third Culture | Create common ground. |

Developing Motivation: Strategies to Accept Others Who Are Different from Us

To be motivated is to want to do something. To be a competent communicator, the communicator must develop a positive mindset for enhancing his or her ability to relate to others and to also accept others as they are. A key to accepting others is to develop a positive attitude of tolerance and acceptance of those who are different from us. We suggest three strategies to help improve your acceptance and appreciation of others who are different from you: tolerate ambiguity, develop mindfulness, and avoid negative judgments about others.

Tolerate Ambiguity

Communicating with someone from another culture produces uncertainty. It may take time and several exchanges to clarify a message. Be patient and try to expand your capacity to tolerate ambiguity if you are speaking to someone with a markedly different world view.

When Ken and Rita visited Montreal, they asked their hotel concierge to direct them to a church of their faith, and they wound up at one with a predominantly Haitian congregation. They were not prepared for the exuberant chanting and verbal interchanges with the minister during the sermon. They weren't certain whether they should join in or simply sit quietly and observe. Ken whispered to Rita, "I'm

Building Your Skills

CAN YOU TOLERATE AMBIGUITY?

Respond to each statement with a number from 1 to 5: (1) Always False, (2) Usually False, (3) Sometimes False and Sometimes True, (4) Usually True, or (5) Always True.

_____ 1. I am comfortable in new situations.

_____ 2. I deal with unforeseen problems successfully.

_____ 3. I experience little discomfort in ambiguous situations.

_____ 4. I am relaxed in unfamiliar situations.

_____ 5. I am not frustrated when things do not go the way I expected.

To find your score, add the numbers you wrote next to each statement. Scores range from 5 to 25. The higher your score, the greater your tolerance for ambiguity.

Source: From William B. Gudykunst, *Bridging Differences: Effective Intergroup Communication* (Newbury Park: Sage, 1991), 121.

not sure what to do. Let's just watch and see what is expected of us." In the end, they chose to sit and clap along with the chanting rather than to become actively involved in the worship. Rita felt uncomfortable and conspicuous, though, and had to fight off the urge to bolt. But after the service, several members of the congregation came up to greet Ken and Rita, invited them to lunch, and expressed great happiness in their visit. "You know," said Rita later in the day, "I'm so grateful that we sat through our discomfort. We might never have met those terrific people. Now I understand why their worship is so noisy—they're just brimming over with joy."

Develop Mindfulness

"Our life is what our thoughts make it," said Marcus Aurelius in *Meditations*. To be **mindful** is to be consciously aware of cultural differences, to acknowledge that there is a connection between thoughts and deeds when you interact with a person from a background different from your own. William Gudykunst suggests that being mindful is one of the best ways to approach any new cultural encounter.[26] Remember that there are and will be cultural differences, and try to keep them in your consciousness. Also, try to consider the other individual's frame of reference or world view and to use his or her cultural priorities and assumptions when you are communicating.[27] Adapt your behaviour to minimize cultural noise and distortion.

You can become more mindful through self-talk, something we discussed in Chapter 2. Self-talk consists of rational messages to yourself to help you manage your emotions or discomfort with a certain situation. Imagine that you are working on a group project with several of your classmates. One classmate, Suji, was born in Iran. When interacting with you, he consistently gets about 30 cm away, whereas you are more comfortable with 90–120 cm between you. When Suji encroaches on your space, you could "be mindful" of the difference by mentally noting, "Suji sure likes to get close to people when he talks to them. This must represent a practice in his culture." This self-talk message makes you consciously aware that there may be a difference in your interaction styles. If you still feel uncomfortable, instead of blurting out, "Hey, man, why so close?" you could express your own preferences with an "I" message: "Suji, I'd prefer a bit more space between us when we talk."

mindful. To be consciously aware of cultural differences.

Building Your Skills

MEASURING MINDFULNESS

Respond to each statement with a number from 1 to 5: (1) Always False, (2) Usually False, (3) Sometimes False and Sometimes True, (4) Usually True, or (5) Always True.

_____ 1. I pay attention to the situation and context when I communicate.

_____ 2. I can describe others with whom I communicate in great detail.

_____ 3. I seek out new information about the people with whom I communicate.

_____ 4. I try to find rational reasons why others may behave in a way I perceive negatively.

_____ 5. I recognize that the person with whom I am communicating has a different point of view than I do.

To find your score, add the numbers you wrote next to each statement. Scores range from 5 to 25. The higher your score, the more mindful you are when you communicate.

Source: From William B. Gudykunst, *Bridging Differences: Effective Intergroup Communication* (Newbury Park: Sage, 1991), 120.

🟠 Avoid Negative Judgments about Another Culture

Canadian tourist on her first visit to France:	"Can you believe it. How repulsive! These people actually eat horse meat and think it's a delicacy."
Black teenager watching his white classmates dance:	"Man, they don't know anything about good music! And those dances are so dumb. I don't call this a party."
Japanese businessperson visiting Argentina:	"These people are never on time. No wonder they can never catch up to us."
German student, after watching a documentary about life in Japan:	"No wonder they work so hard. They have tiny little houses. I'd work long hours too if I had to live like that."

The kind of ethnocentrism that underlies judgments like these is a communication barrier. It is also an underlying cause of suspicion and mistrust and, in extreme cases, a spark that ignites violence. Instead of making judgments about another culture, try simply to acknowledge differences and to view them as an interesting challenge rather than as an obstacle to be eradicated.

▶ Recap

DEVELOP MOTIVATION TO ACCEPT OTHERS

Tolerate Ambiguity	Take your time and expect some uncertainty.
Develop Mindfulness	Be conscious of cultural differences rather than ignoring the differences.
Avoid Negative Judgments	Resist thinking your culture has all of the answers.

🟠 Developing Skills: Strategies to Adapt to Others Who Are Different from Us

To be skilled is to be capable of putting what you know and want to achieve into action. The underlying skill in being interculturally competent is the ability to be flexible and adapt to others.

🟠 Develop Flexibility

When you interact with someone from another background, your responding skills are crucial. You can learn only so much from books; you must be willing to learn as you communicate. Every individual is unique, so cultural generalizations that you learn from research may not always apply. It is not accurate to assume, for example, that all French people are preoccupied with food and fashion. Many members of minority groups in Canada find it draining to correct these generalizations in their encounters with others. Pay close attention to the other person's non-verbal cues when you begin conversing; then adjust your communication style and language, if necessary, to put the person at ease. Avoid asking questions or making statements based on generalizations.

Become Other-Oriented

Throughout this book we have emphasized the importance of becoming other-oriented—focusing on others rather than on yourself—as an important way to enhance your interpersonal competence. We have also discussed the problems ethnocentrism can create when you attempt to communicate with others, especially with those whose culture is different from your own. We now offer three specific ways to increase your other-orientedness: social decentring, empathy, and adaptation.

Although our focus in this discussion will be on how to increase other-orientation in intercultural interactions, the principles apply to *all* interpersonal interactions. The major difference between intercultural interactions and those that occur within your own culture is primarily the obviousness of the differences between you and the other person.

1. *Social Decentring.* **Social decentring**, the first strategy, is a *cognitive process* in which we take into account the other person's thoughts, feelings, values, background, and perspectives. This process involves viewing the world from the other person's point of view. The greater the difference between ourselves and the other person, the more difficult it is to accomplish social decentring. In doing the *Building Your Skills: Predicting How Others Feel* exercise below you may find it easier to judge your close friend than any of the other people described.

social decentring. A cognitive process in which we take into account another person's thoughts, feelings, values, background, and perspectives.

Building Your Skills

PREDICTING HOW OTHERS FEEL

Look at the descriptions and rank them from 1 (highest) to 6 (lowest) in order of how readily you could predict each person's reactions on finding out his or her mother or other close relative has just died.

_____ A. A close friend of yours of the same sex, age, race, and culture.

_____ B. A 60-year-old male Chinese farmer.

_____ C. A college student who is 20 years older than you but of the same race, sex, and culture.

_____ D. A 10-year-old B.C. girl who is the child of Asian and Hispanic parents.

_____ E. A college student of a different race than you but the same age, culture, and sex.

_____ F. A college student of the opposite sex than you but the same age, race, and culture as you.

What qualities do you feel provide you with the best information on which to base your judgments? Why? What would you need to know about each person to feel comfortable in making a prediction? How can you get that information?

The rest of your rankings depend on the various experiences you have had. Your interactions with members of the opposite sex, or with someone from another race, or of a different age are probably the next most frequent, and next highest ranked. Interactions with people from other cultures are probably the most difficult because your experiences in such interactions are often limited. It is easier to socially decentre about someone who is similar in culture and background to you.

There are three ways to socially decentre or take another's perspective: (1) develop an understanding of others, based upon how you have responded when something similar has happened to you, (2) base your understanding of others upon the knowledge you have about a specific person, or (3) make generalizations about someone, based upon your understanding of how you think most people would feel or behave.[28]

When you draw upon your direct experience, you use your past knowledge of what happened to you to help you guess how someone else may feel. To the degree that the other person is similar to you, your reactions and theirs will match. Suppose, for example, you are talking to a student who has just failed a midterm exam in an important course. You have also had this experience. Your reaction was to discount it because you had confidence you could still pull a passing grade. You might use this self-understanding to predict your classmate's reactions. To the degree that you are similar to the classmate, your prediction will be accurate. But, suppose your classmate comes from a culture with high expectations for success. Your classmate might feel upset over having dishonoured his or her family by a poor performance. In this situation, understanding your own reaction needs to be tempered by your awareness of how similar or dissimilar the other person is to you. Recognition of differences should lead you to recognize the need to socially decentre in another way.

The second way we socially decentre—or take the perspective of another—is based on specific knowledge we have of the person with whom we are interacting. Drawing on your memory of how your classmate reacted to a previous failed midterm gives you a basis to more accurately predict his or her reaction. Even if you have not observed your classmate's reaction to the same situation, you project how you think he or she would feel based on similar instances. As relationships become more intimate, we gain more information to allow us to more readily socially decentre. Our ability to accurately predict and understand our partners usually increases as relationships become more intimate. In intercultural interactions, the more opportunity you have to interact with the same person and learn more about the person and his or her culture, the more your ability to socially decentre will increase.

The third way we socially decentre is to apply our understanding of people in general, or of categories of people from whom we have gained some knowledge. Each of us develops implicit personality theories, constructs, and attributions of how people act, as discussed in Chapter 3. You might have a general theory to explain the behaviour of men and another theory for women. You might have general theories about Mexicans, Chinese, Aboriginals, Slovenians, Americans, or Black Canadians. As you meet someone who falls into one of your categories, you draw upon that conceptualization to socially decentre. The more you can learn about a given culture, the stronger your general theories can be, and the more effectively you can use this method of socially decentring. The key, however, is to avoid developing inaccurate, inflexible stereotypes of others and basing your perceptions of others only on those generalizations.

2. *Empathy.* Besides thinking about how another may feel (socially decentring), we can have an emotional reaction to what others do or tell us. We feel empathy for another. **Empathy**, a second strategy for becoming other-oriented, is an emotional reaction that is similar to the one being experienced by another person, as compared to social decentring, which is a cognitive reaction. Empathy is feeling what another person feels. Our emotional reaction can be either similar to, or different from, the emotions the other person is experiencing. You might experience mild pity for your classmate who has failed the midterm, in contrast to his or her stronger feelings of anguish and dishonour. On the other hand, you might share his or her same feelings of anguish and dishonour.

Some emotional reactions are almost universal and cut across cultural boundaries. You might experience empathy when seeing photos or videos depicting emotional scenes occurring in other countries. Seeing a mother crying while holding her sick or dying child in a refugee camp might move you to cry and feel a deep sense of sadness or loss. You empathize with the woman. You might also experience empathy for your brother, who has just received the devastating news that his best friend has been killed in an automobile accident. You grieve with him. Empathy can enhance interpersonal interactions in a number of ways: it can provide a bond between you and the other person; it is confirming; it is comforting and supportive; it can increase your understanding of others; and it can strengthen the relationship. We can empathize most easily with those who are similar to us, and in situations with which we have had a similar emotional experience.

empathy. Process of developing an emotional reaction that is similar to the reaction being experienced by another person. Feeling what another person is feeling.

Grief for the loss of a loved one is a universal emotion that cuts across all cultures. (David Barnett/Stock Boston)

Understanding Diversity

INTERRACIAL RELATIONSHIPS: HOLLYWOOD STYLE

What do Whoopi Goldberg, Woody Allen and Puff Daddy have in common? The same hairstylist or fashion designer, maybe? Not quite. But they are all currently involved in interracial relationships. Interracial couples are nothing new in Hollywood. From early pairings like Dorothy Dandridge and Jack Dennison to the abundance of interracial couples gracing today's awards shows and magazine pages, interracial couples have made their mark in tinsel town. So if real-life Hollywood couples are comfortable enough with mixed relationships, why isn't art imitating life?

Hollywood's portrayal of interracial relationships, on the big and small screens, are few and far between. And it seems when they are represented, it is too often met with controversy. Recently David E. Kelly, the creator of the hit Fox show *Ally McBeal* came under fire for what he calls his "consciously color-blind show." In the series, the lead character, played by Calista Flockhart, had an ongoing relationship with a black man. Two other main characters have had an interracial relationship, as well. Ling and Richard, characters played by Lucy Liu and Greg Germann, also have carried on a relationship throughout much of the recent seasons. The onscreen interracial relationships have since ended, but not before a flurry of criticism from those who thought Kelly's angst-less portrayals of interracial relationships resemble a fairy tale more than real life.

And speaking of fairy tales, perhaps that is one place where it is safe to cast characters in interracial relationships. In the Disney remake of Rodgers and Hammerstein's *Cinderella* starring Brandy and Whitney Houston, diversity was the theme of the day. With Whoopi Goldberg and Victor Garber pairing up as the king and queen and Brandy playing Cinderella to Paolo Montalban's prince, interracial couples abounded. This piece of work was actually praised by the critics for its multicultural cast. But then, I suppose it's easier to believe that mixed marriages can work in a world where pumpkins can turn into carriages.

Another show that has tackled the interracial relationship issue head on is ABC's *Boy Meets World*. On this show, Rider Strong and Trina McGee-Davis play a college-aged couple in an interracial relationship with all the typical pains of young love—except the racial ones. In fact, the show's executive producer, Michael Jacobs, made a point of informing the actors that the race issue would not be addressed. McGee-Davis, for one, is all for the representation of interracial couples on prime time. She even went as far as to come to David E. Kelley's defense when critics attacked *Ally McBeal*. In a letter to the *Los Angeles Times*, Ms. McGee-Davis eloquently commended Kelly's approach to the relationship on his show. She went on to refer to the uncomplicated interracial relationships on television as "search engines" and "portals" to the future.

But not all actors are so hip to the idea of interracial relationships on the tube. Eriq LaSalle of NBC's hit drama *ER* had a problem with it. LaSalle's character, Dr. Peter Benton, had an ongoing relationship with Alex Kingston's character, Dr. Elizabeth Corday, on the show. LaSalle reportedly pushed for an end to their characters' interracial relationship as it was something he was "not comfortable" with. LaSalle's character had a string of dysfunctional relationships with black women. In the interracial relationship, however, he felt his character was written to be more warm and loving than in the previous ones. He felt it was sending the wrong message to African-American viewers; that interracial relationships allowed black men to be more tender than relationships with black women. Kingston, on the other hand, felt the characters' relationship was "a wonderful thing."

As rare as interracial relationships are on primetime television, the big screen tends to have even fewer examples of interracial couples. *Guess Who's Coming to Dinner* is an obvious example of a Hollywood classic with an interracial theme, but since its 1967 release, there haven't been many to follow. Spike Lee took a stab at the issue in his *Jungle Fever,* but this film wasn't a huge box office draw. There are higher expectations for the recently released *Snow Falling on Cedars*, based on a novel by David Guterson. This film follows the forbidden relationship of a white man and a Japanese woman in the 1950s.

In an article called "Black Men Can't Kiss" E! Online addressed the issue of interracial relationships in the movies. The author, Ken Neville, raises the question of why black men and white women who are

> paired up in films like *The Pelican Brief* and *Kiss the Girls* don't develop the sexual relationships that viewers have come to expect of similar pairings of same-race couples. Neville defers to the author of a book on the subject of race in the movies who was quoted by the *New York Post* as saying, "Who is this a taboo for? Not for regular people. It's just a taboo for people in Hollywood who are shaping these images." With interracial marriages continuing to rise, perhaps it's time for Hollywood television and film producers to take their cues from society.
>
> *Source:* © 2000 by Kimberly Hohman, http://racerelations.about.com. Licensed to About, Inc. Used by permission of About, Inc. which can be found on the Web at www.About.com. All rights reserved.

Developing empathy is different than sympathizing with others. When you offer **sympathy**, you tell others that you are sorry that he or she feels what he or she is feeling. Here are examples and statements of sympathy: "I'm sorry your Uncle Joe died," or "I'm sorry to hear you failed your test." When you sympathize with others, you acknowledge their feelings. But when you empathize, you experience an emotional reaction that is similar to the other person's; you, too, feel grief or sadness. Recall the strategies for developing empathic listening skills in Chapter 4.

● Appropriately Adapt Your Communication to Others

The logical extension of being flexible and becoming other-oriented is to adapt your communication to enhance the quality and effectiveness of your interpersonal communication. To **adapt** means to adjust your behaviour to others to accommodate differences and expectations. Appropriate adaptation occurs in the context of the relationship you have with the other person and what is happening in the communication environment. Adapting to others has its roots in **communication accommodation theory**, which suggests that all people adapt their behaviour to others to some extent. Those who appropriately and sensitively adapt to others are more likely to experience more positive communication.[29] Adapting to others doesn't mean you only tell others what they want to hear and do what others want you to do. Such placating behaviour is not wise, effective, or ethical. Nor are we suggesting that you adapt your behaviour only so that you can get your way; the goal is effective communication, not manipulation. We are suggesting, however, that you be aware of what your communication partner is doing and saying, especially if there are cultural differences, so that your message is understood and you don't unwittingly offend others. Although it may seem common sense, being sensitive to others and adapting behaviours to others are not as common as you might think.

Sometimes people adapt their behaviour based on what they think someone will like. At other times they adapt their communication after realizing they have done something wrong. When you modify your behaviour in anticipation of an event, you **adapt predictively**. For example, you might decide to buy a friend flowers to soften the news about breaking a date because you know how much your friend likes flowers. When you modify your behaviour after an event, you **adapt reactively**. For example, you might buy your friend flowers to apologize for a fight.

There are a number of reasons we adapt our communication to the other person. We often adapt our messages in an attempt to make them more understandable. In talking to an individual with limited understanding of English, for instance, you would probably choose simple words and phrases (we have a tendency to make our voices louder in these situations under the false assumption that the other person isn't "hearing" what we say). We also adapt our messages to accomplish our goals more effectively. In our intercultural interactions, we frequently adapt our communication behaviour in response to the feedback or reactions we are receiving. Table 9.2 lists a variety of ways we adapt our verbal messages to others.

---

sympathy. To acknowledge that someone may be feeling bad; to be compassionate toward someone.

sympathy. To acknowledge that someone may be feeling bad; to be compassionate toward someone.

adaptation. Adjusting behaviour to accord with what someone else does. We can adapt based upon the individual, the relationship, and the situation.

communication accommodation theory. Theory that suggests that all people adapt their behaviour to others to some extent.

adapt predictively. Modifying or changing behaviour in anticipation of an event.

adapt reactively. Modifying or changing behaviour after an event.

Table 9.2
Communication Adaptation Behaviours

Type	Examples
Topical: Choosing a topic or issue to discuss because you know it will interest the other person.	Talking about a mutual friend, talking about a party you both went to, asking if he or she saw a particular play that was in town.
Explanatory/Elaboration: Providing additional information or detail because you recognize that the other person does not know it.	Explaining your mother's eating habits to a new friend, explaining to a neighbour who has squirrel problems how you keep them away from your bean plants.
Withholding Explanation or Information: Not providing explanation because your partner already knows the information; because it might hurt or anger your partner; because of fear of how the other person might misuse it; or to avoid violating a confidentiality.	Not elaborating on the parts of an auto engine when you describe a car problem because you know the listener is knowledgeable about cars; not telling a friend you saw his or her lover with another person because he or she would be hurt; not telling someone about your interest in a mutual friend because you are afraid that person would blab about it to the mutual friend.
Examples/Comparisons/Analogies: Choosing examples that you know your partner will find relevant.	Explaining roller blading by comparing it to ice skating, something your partner knows how to do.
Personal Referencing: Referring to your partner's specific attitudes, interests, personality, traits, ethnic background, etc.	"I've got something to tell you I think you'll find funny." "Could you help me balance my chequebook; you're so good at math." "That's a behaviour I'd expect from you, given the way your parents raised you."
Vernacular/Language: Choosing or avoiding certain words because of their potential effect on the receiver. Using words that have a unique meaning for you and your partner. Using words that you think are appropriate to the other person's level of understanding.	A wife asking her husband if he was catching flies during a movie, meaning he was asleep with his mouth wide open. A father telling his child that a criminal is someone who does bad things. Two computer jocks talking about "bytes," "ram," and "chips."
Disclosure: Consciously deciding to share information about yourself that the other does not know about you.	Telling your lover about your sexual fantasies. Telling your instructor about family problems.
Immediate Follow-Up Questioning: Seeking additional information from the other person about information he or she shares during the interaction.	"So, what was it like growing up in small-town Alberta?" "Tell me more about your vacation in Toronto." "Where are you going on your date?"
Delayed Follow-Up Questioning: Seeking additional information from the other person about previous information he or she shared.	"How's your mother doing after her operation yesterday?" "How was your date Saturday night?"
Adapting to Immediate Reaction/Feedback: Modifying your words or behaviour because of your partner's reaction.	If your friend starts to cry when you talk about her mother's death, you might quickly change the topic.

Source: © Mark V. Redmond, 1994. Used by permission.

Conversants also adapt non-verbal cues. Many times they raise or lower voice volume in response to the volume of a partner, or lean forward toward people in response to their leaning toward the speaker.

Adaptation across intercultural contexts is usually more difficult than within your own culture. Imagine shaking hands with a stranger, and having the stranger hold on to your hand as you continue to talk. In Canada, hand-holding between strangers is a violation of our non-verbal norms. But, in some cultures maintaining physical contact while talking is expected. Pulling your hand away from this person would be rude. As illustrated in *Understanding Diversity: Mind Your Manners—and Theirs*, on page 293–294, what may be mannerly in one culture is not always acceptable in another. Adapting to these cultural differences means developing that "third" culture that we talked about earlier in the chapter.

Taking an other-oriented approach to communication means considering the thoughts, feelings, background, perspectives, attitudes, and values of your interpersonal partners and adjusting your interaction with them accordingly. Other-orientation leads to more effective interpersonal communication, regardless of whether you are dealing with someone from your family or from another country.

By careful analysis of the factors that affect our communication partners, we can develop understanding and empathy. That understanding and empathy can then help us make the most effective strategic communication choices as we adapt our messages and responses.

In an effective interpersonal relationship, your partner is also orienting him- or herself to you. A competent communicator has knowledge of others, is motivated to enhance the quality of communication, and possesses the skill of being other-oriented.

If you learn the skills and principles we have presented here, will it really make a difference in your ability to relate to others? Recent evidence suggests the answer is "yes." A study by Lori Carrell found that students who had been exposed to lessons in empathy linked to a study of interpersonal and intercultural communication improved their ability to empathize with others.[30] There is evidence that, if you master these principles and skills, you will be rewarded with greater insight and ability to relate to others who are different from you.

Understanding Diversity

MIND YOUR MANNERS—AND THEIRS

If it be appropriate to kiss the Pope's slipper, by all means do so.
—Lord Chesterfield, founder of modern etiquette, in 1750

The saying "When in Rome do what the Romans do" suggests that international travellers should adopt an other-oriented approach to the host country's manners and customs. After interviewing hundreds of international businesspersons, Roger Axtell offers the following tips on etiquette when visiting with people from other countries or travelling to international destinations. Realize, of course, that these observations are not true of all individuals. As in Canada, in many of these countries there are dozens of different cultural groups with their own sets of values and customs.

Austrians
- Are punctual
- Use a firm handshake (both men and women)
- Consider it impolite to keep their hands in their lap when dining
- Are uncomfortable with first names until a friendship is established

English, Scots, Welsh
- Tend to use understatement in business matters
- Value punctuality
- Are accustomed to cooler room temperatures than Americans
- Call a Scot a Scotsman, not a Scotchman or Scottish

French
- Rarely use first names, even among colleagues
- Frequently shake hands but their grip is less firm than most
- Eat their main meal of the day usually at midday
- Make decisions after much deliberation

Irish
- Are not overly conscientious about time and punctuality
- Do not typically give business gifts
- Regard refusing a drink or failing to buy your round as bad manners

Italians
- Use strong and frequent hand and body gestures
- May grasp your elbow as they shake hands
- Do not consider punctuality a virtue, at least for social events
- Do not talk business at a social event

Russians
- Want to know what Americans really think
- When greeting, shake hands and announce their name
- Among friends, some give "bear hugs" and kiss cheeks

Egyptians
- Like all Muslims, rest on Friday
- Regard friendship and trust as a prerequisite for business
- Social engagements usually held late in the day

Zambians
- Often shake hands with the left supporting the right
- When dining, may ask for food; it is impolite not to
- Consider it improper to refuse food

Australians
- Speak frankly and directly; they dislike pretensions
- Will not shy away from disagreement
- Appreciate punctuality
- Have good sense of humour, even in tense situations

Indians
- When greeting a woman, they put palms together and bow slightly
- Do not eat beef and regard the cow as a sacred animal
- Show great respect to elders

Japanese
- Exchange business cards before bowing or shaking hands
- Consider it impolite to have long or frequent eye-to-eye contact
- Rarely use first names
- Avoid the word "no" to preserve harmony

Thais
- Regard displays of either temper or affection in public as unacceptable
- Have a taboo against using the foot to point, or showing the sole of the foot
- Don't like pats on the head

Brazilians
- Like long handshakes
- Like to touch arms, elbows, and backs
- When conversing, view interruption as enthusiasm
- Attach a sexual meaning to the OK hand signal

Mexicans
- Are not rigidly punctual
- Take their main meal at about 1:00 or 4:00 P.M.
- Refrain from using first names until they are invited to do so
- Consider hands in pockets to be impolite

Source: Adapted from Roger E. Axtell, *Do's and Taboos of Hosting International Visitors* (New York: John Wiley & Sons, 1989).

▶ Recap

DEVELOP SKILL TO ADAPT TO OTHERS

Develop Flexibility	Learn to "go with the flow."
Become Other-Oriented	Put yourself in the other person's mental and emotional mindset; adapt to others; listen and respond appropriately.
Adapt Your Communication to Others	Adjust your behaviour to others to accommodate differences and expectations.

Summary

A culture is a system of knowledge that is shared by a large group of people. It includes cultural elements, values, goals, and contexts. Cultural elements are categories of things and ideas that identify key aspects of cultural influence.

Cultural values reflect how individuals regard masculine and feminine behaviours and individual and collective achievements. They also reflect whether individuals can tolerate ambiguity or need a high degree of certainty, and whether they believe in concentrated or decentralized power structures. The goals of a culture depend upon the way it values individual versus group achievement. In high-context cultures, the meaning of messages depends heavily upon non-verbal information; low-context cultures rely more heavily upon words than upon context for deriving meaning.

Intercultural communication occurs when individuals or groups from different cultures communicate. There are several barriers that inhibit effective intercultural communication. Ethnocentrism is the belief that our own cultural traditions and assumptions are superior to those of others. Differences in language and the way we interpret non-verbal messages also interfere with effective intercultural communication. We stereotype by placing a group or a person into an inflexible, all-encompassing category. A related barrier is prejudice—we often prejudge someone before we know all of the facts. Stereotyping and prejudice can keep us from viewing people as unique individuals and, therefore, hamper effective, honest communication. Finally, assuming that we are similar to others can also be a barrier to intercultural communication. All humans have some similarities, but our cultures have taught us to process the world differently.

Although it is reasonably easy to identify cultural differences, it is more challenging to bridge those differences. To enhance understanding between cultures, we suggest the following: develop knowledge by seeking information about the culture, ask questions and listen effectively, and develop a "third culture." Increase your motivation to appreciate others who are different from you by tolerating ambiguity, developing mindfulness, and avoiding negative judgments about another culture. Finally, enhance your skill by becoming flexible. Be other-oriented by socially decentring, becoming more empathetic, and adapting your verbal and non-verbal behaviour to others.

For Discussion and Review

Focus on Comprehension

1. What is culture?
2. What are four contrasting cultural values?
3. What are the differences between high-context and low-context cultures?
4. What are the differences between individualistic and collectivistic cultures?
5. What is ethnocentrism?

Focus on Critical Thinking

6. Christine, a Canadian, has just been accepted as a foreign exchange student in Germany. What are potential cultural barriers that she might face? How should she manage these potential barriers?
7. What's the problem in assuming that other people are like us? How does this create a barrier to effective intercultural communication?

8. If you were to design a lesson plan for elementary school-age students about how to deal with racial and ethnic stereotypes, what would you include?
9. What are appropriate ways to deal with someone who consistently utters racial slurs and evidences prejudice toward racial or ethnic groups?

Focus on Ethics

10. Marla is the director of the campus multicultural studies program. She wants to require all students to take at least four courses in a four-year degree program that focuses on multicultural issues. Is it appropriate to force students to take such a concentration of courses?
11. Should an individual always speak out upon hearing a racist, sexist, or otherwise offensive remark? What if the listener is not a member of the target group? Are there contextual factors to consider before speaking out?
12. Is it ethical or appropriate for someone from one culture to attempt to change the cultural values of someone from a different culture? For example, culture A practises polygamy: one husband can be married to several wives. Culture B practises monogamy: one husband can be married to only one wife. Should a person from culture B attempt to make someone from culture A change his or her ways?

For Your Journal

1. Describe your perceptions of your cultural values, based upon the discussion of cultural values beginning on page 270 in this chapter. On a scale of 1 to 10, rate yourself on the value of masculine versus feminine perspective, individual versus group achievement, tolerance of uncertainty versus need for certainty, and centralized versus decentralized power. Provide an example of your reaction to an interpersonal communication encounter to illustrate each of these values.
2. Write a journal entry discussing how you have experienced one of the barriers to effective intercultural communication described in this chapter. Have you been ethnocentric in your thoughts or behaviour or a victim of ethnocentrism? Describe a situation in which communication was difficult because you and your communication partner spoke different languages. Have you been a victim of stereotyping or prejudice? Have you assumed someone was similar to yourself and, later, found that there were more differences than you suspected?
3. This chapter presented nine specific strategies or skills to help bridge differences in background and culture. Rank these skills and strategies in the order that you need to improve in your interactions with people from different backgrounds. Give a rank of 1 to the skill or strategy that you most need to develop, a rank of 2 to the next area you feel you need to work on, and so on. Rank yourself on all nine strategies.

Seek information about the culture   _____

Ask questions and listen   _____

Develop a "third culture"   _____

Tolerate ambiguity   _____

Be mindful   _____

Avoid negative judgments about another culture _____

Be flexible   _____

Become other-oriented   _____

Adapt your communication to others   _____

Based upon the areas in which you need greatest improvement, write a journal entry about how you will develop skill in these areas. How will you put what you have learned in this chapter into practice?

Learning with Others

1. Bring to class a fable, folktale, or children's story from a culture other than your own. As a group, analyze the cultural values implied by the story or characters in the story.

2. Working with a group of your classmates, develop an ideal culture based upon the combined values and elements of people in your group. Develop a name for your culture. Suggest foods, recreational activities, and other leisure pursuits. Compare the culture your group develops with those that other groups in your class develop. How would the communication skills and principles discussed in this chapter help you bridge differences among those cultures?[31]

3. As a group, go on an intercultural scavenger hunt. Your instructor will give you a time limit. Scavenge your campus or classroom area to identify influences of as many different cultures as you can find. For example, you could go to the cafeteria and make a note of ethnic foods that you find. Identify clothing, music, or architecture that is influenced by certain cultures.

4. In small groups, identify examples from your own experiences for each barrier to effective intercultural communication discussed in the text. Use one of the examples to develop a skit to perform for the rest of the class. See if the class can identify which intercultural barrier your group is depicting. Also, suggest how the skills and principles discussed in the chapter might have improved the communication in the situation you role-play.

Weblinks

www.abc.gc.ca This is the site for Aboriginal Business Canada. There are several links that can be accessed which focus on the development and promotion of Aboriginal business opportunities in Canada.

www.cacmall.com/homecra.html This is the Canadian Aboriginal Cyber-Mall. It is a site for learning about Aboriginal Canadians and for shopping. You can read legends, look at Aboriginal arts and crafts, and even make purchases.

www.infoability/resource/culture.html This is a large Canadian site with resources on society and culture. It offers information under categories such as race relations, gender relations, and language services.

www.seb.apc/~ara This is the site for Anti-Racist Action Toronto.

Suggested Readings

Lustig, M. W. and J. Koester. *Intercultural Competence: Interpersonal Communication across Cultures.* New York: Longman, 1999.
    A good text that delves into interpersonal communication among cultures and how to enhance intercultural competence.

Axtell, Roger E. *Do's and Taboos of Hosting International Visitors.* New York: John Wiley and Sons, 1989.
    This classic book is a "must-read" about international differences.

chapter 10
Understanding Interpersonal Relationships

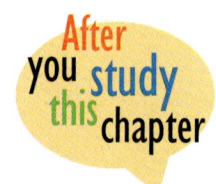

After you study this chapter you should be able to...

1. Explain how relationships are systems and a process.
2. Differentiate between relationships of circumstance and relationships of choice.
3. Describe three dimensions of interpersonal relationships.
4. Explain what interpersonal attraction is.
5. Describe the elements that contribute to interpersonal attraction.
6. Describe the principles of self-disclosure.
7. Construct two models for self-disclosure.
8. Describe two theories that explain how relationships develop.

- An Interpersonal Relationship as a System and a Process
- Relationships of Circumstance and Relationships of Choice
- Trust, Intimacy, and Power in Relationships
- Attraction in Relationships
- Self-Disclosure: A Foundation For Relational Escalation
- Two Models for Self-Disclosure
- Interpersonal Relationship Development Theories

> *You can hardly make a friend in a year, but you can lose one in an hour.*
>
> CHINESE PROVERB

Pat: Hi, aren't you in my communication course?

Jinping: Oh, yeah, I've seen you across the room.

Pat: What do you think about the course so far?

Jinping: It's okay, but I feel a little intimidated by some of the class activities.

Pat: I know what you mean. It gets kind of scary to talk about yourself in front of everyone else.

Jinping: Yeah. Plus some of the stuff you hear. I was paired up with this one student the other day who started talking about being arrested last year on a drug charge.

Pat: Really? I bet I know who that is. I don't think you have to worry about it.

Jinping: Don't mention that I said anything.

Pat: It's okay. I know that guy, and he just likes to act big.

This interaction between Pat and Jinping illustrates the reciprocal nature of interpersonal communication and interpersonal relationships. As you learned in Chapter 1, interpersonal relationships are connections that we develop with other people as a direct result of our interpersonal communication with them. The character and quality of interpersonal communication is affected, in turn, by the nature of the relationship.

The conversation between Pat and Jinping begins with a casual acknowledgment but quickly proceeds to a higher level of intimacy. Jinping confides in Pat. Pat, an other-oriented listener, offers confirmation and support; this response encourages Jinping to confide even more. In this brief encounter, Pat and Jinping have laid the groundwork for transforming their casual acquaintanceship into an intimate relationship.

In these last two chapters, we will explore the dynamic link between interpersonal communication and interpersonal relationships. Drawing from the understanding of communication you have acquired from the first nine chapters, you will learn about the nature of relationships, their development from initiation to termination, and the specific communication skills you can apply to maintaining them.

In this chapter we examine the nature of interpersonal relationships and the principles of how relationships work, building on the descriptions presented in Chapter 1.

An Interpersonal Relationship as a System and a Process

Interpersonal relationships are transactional just like interpersonal communication. This means that each person in a relationship affects the other person. Actually, relationships are affected by a wide range of factors that can best be understood by thinking of a relationship as a system. Systems theory was created originally to explain changes that occur in plant life,[1] but it also has proven valuable in explaining a variety of other phenomena including interpersonal relationships.

A **system** is a set of interconnected elements often described in terms of their relationships as *inputs, throughputs* (or *process*), and *outputs.* The most fundamental notion in systems theory is that a change in any system element affects all the other elements. Relationships can be thought of as a kind of system, which means that a change in one element of the relationship affects the other elements. For example, a change in your best friend's mood or behaviour affects your mood and behaviour as well. The more interdependent we are, the more impact each partner has on the other partner, and the more a change in one affects the other. Married couples can be classified according to how interdependent their relationship is and thus how much they are like a system.

One difficulty in analyzing a relationship as a system is deciding what elements are part of the system; that is, what are its boundaries. Is your job, your relationship with your father, your boss's mood, or your communication teacher an element of your relationship with your best friend? Certainly each of these can affect you, and thus can affect your relationship. If your communication instructor acts particularly nasty to you in class one day (this is just hypothetical, because we know how great communication instructors are), that might affect how you feel about yourself and influence your interaction with your best friend. For the purposes of this text, you don't need to worry about deciding what is in and what is out of the system; simply recognize that lots of factors affect your relationships, including ones of which you are unaware.

When one element of a system changes, the other elements also change, to adapt and to maintain balance. From a relational perspective, this might mean that you will counter your roommate's bad mood by attempting to provide comfort or diversion. Chapter 11 suggests a number of ways you can maintain relationships. Essentially, maintaining relationships requires you to develop strategies to counter efforts to escalate or de-escalate the relationships. Suppose you are dating someone but aren't interested in becoming very intimate; however, your partner wants to spend more time with you. What do you do? Your partner's actions represent a change in your relational system that affects you and your behaviour. You can either choose to spend more time with this person, or engage in behaviours to avoid that increase.

Systems represent a process in that they are constantly changing, evolving, and are dynamic. As a process, relationships are always moving to a new place, changing, and being redefined. The changes might not be enormous, but because it's a system, you change too. Part of the change is simply due to the fact that relationships are ongoing; they exist over a period of time. Existing over the passage of time means that relationships develop a history; they are accumulative. As you interact with a person, you gain a history together that becomes part of the

system. A set of interconnected elements in which change in one element affects all the other elements.

In an intimate, trusting relationship, we can feel safe in telling our deepest secrets to another person. (Peter Cade/Tony Stone Images)

relationship and affects each subsequent interaction. In the movie *When Harry Met Sally*, the two friends seem to initiate a relationship three different times. However, their first interaction has a direct impact on how they behave in their second interaction, and their second interaction affects the third. The accumulative nature of process means we can't undo something that has been done. Harry and Sally can't undo the impact they had on each other in their first interaction. However, this doesn't mean they can't overcome any negative impression they might have formed about each other.

Relationships of Circumstance and Relationships of Choice

In Chapter 1 an **interpersonal relationship** is defined as an ongoing connection that we make with another person and that we carry in our minds (and, metaphorically, in our hearts), whether the other person is present or not. These ongoing connections can be formed either because of unintentional circumstances or because of intentional choice. **Relationships of circumstance** form not because we choose them, but simply because our lives overlap with others' in some way. Relationships with family members, teachers, classmates, and co-workers fall into this category. In contrast, when we seek out and intentionally develop a relationship with someone, that is a **relationship of choice**. These relationships might include acquaintances, friends, lovers, spouses, or counsellors.

> It is chance that makes brothers but hearts that make friends.
>
> — *von Geibel*

We act and communicate differently in these two types of relationships because the stakes are different. The effect of the same interpersonal communication behaviour on different relationships can be dramatic. If we act in foolish or inappropriate

interpersonal relationships. Those connections we make with other people through interpersonal communication.

relationships of circumstance. Interpersonal relationships that exist because of the circumstances in which we are born, circumstances in which we work or study, and so on.

relationships of choice. Interpersonal relationships we choose to initiate, maintain, or terminate.

ways, our friends might end the relationships. If we act the same way within the confines of our family, our relatives may not like us much, but we will still remain family.

Of course, these categories are not mutually exclusive. Relationships of circumstance can also be relationships of choice: your brother or sister can also be your best friend. You can break off interacting with family members or quit your job to sever your relationships with fellow employees. In addition, the other individual can define and redefine the relationship. Your boss might fire you, a relative might cut you off, or a lover might desert you.

Trust, Intimacy, and Power in Relationships

We can further examine interpersonal relationships along three dimensions that are always present in varying degrees: trust, intimacy, and power. Although we have touched upon these elements in other discussions, we will now examine more closely the role that they play in forming and maintaining relationships. You should recognize the importance interpersonal communication has in the development of these dimensions.

Trust

Think about the kind of trust you have in people who are important to you. What does it mean when you trust your doctor? your lover or spouse? your accountant? More than likely, each of these relationships involves a different kind of trust, as shown in Table 10.1.

Table 10.1

Types of Trust

Types of Trust	Explanation	Example
Trust in someone's ability	You believe that the person has the skill, knowledge, will, and ethical standards to do a good job or fulfill some role expectation.	Your accountant
Trust in someone's regard for your welfare	You believe that this person will not cause you harm as you place your health, welfare, resources, and security in his or her hands.	Your doctor
Trust in someone's regard for privileged information	You believe that the person to whom you have disclosed personal information will not use this information against you.	Your counsellor or a friend
Trust in someone's relational commitment	You believe that when you disclose personal information, the other will acknowledge your feelings and vulnerability, will not exploit you, and will remain in the relationship.	Your lover or partner

In most interpersonal relationships, especially intimate ones, the last two categories of trust listed in Table 10.1 are the most important. Basically, **interpersonal trust** is the degree to which we feel safe in disclosing personal information to another person. We exhibit a variety of trusting behaviours: revealing intimate information about ourselves; displaying our vulnerability to another; displaying confidence in him or her.[2] As a relationship develops, we look for proof that our partner is **trustworthy**. We look for behaviours to assure us that he or she accepts our feelings and won't exploit them, and that he or she will protect our vulnerability and remain in the relationship. These behaviours include such things as not cheating, protecting information we have disclosed about ourselves, and continuing to show affection and closeness even when we reveal negative or threatening information. Our partner, in turn, expects the same from us. To sustain a close interpersonal relationship, both participants need to exhibit and expect trusting and trustworthy behaviour.[3]

There is a direct correlation between how much we trust someone and how much we can potentially gain from a relationship. The more we trust, the more information we are willing to share or disclose about ourselves (see the section on self-disclosure later in this chapter), and the closer the relationship becomes. Sometimes this sharing is selective. Students may tell their professors about very personal family problems, yet they would never tell them if they cheated on an exam. You may tell your parents about your finances and your academic progress, but you may be reluctant to tell them about the development of each of your new intimate relationships. Try the skill building activity below to discover more about whom you trust and who trusts you.

interpersonal trust. A quality of a relationship represented by the degree to which the partners believe it is safe to disclose personal information.

trustworthy. A quality we use to describe an individual who can be trusted to accept personal information without exploiting it, support vulnerabilities, and remain in the relationship.

Building Your Skills

Whom Do You Trust?

Create a list of names of those people with whom you have ongoing relationships: family members, co-workers, boss, friends, teachers, and so on. For each person on your list, write down the type of trust that characterizes your relationship: trust in ability, trust in regard for your welfare, trust in protecting privileged information, or trust in commitment to the relationship. You can put down more than one type for each person. Next, assign a number from 1 to 10 for the amount of trust you have in each person, with 1 being very little, and 10 being a lot.

Are your rankings consistently high or consistently low? What general observations can you make about how trusting you are of others?

Who Trusts You?

How trustworthy are you? Use the list of names of those whom you trust to protect privileged information and/or maintain a relational commitment. Using the same scale of 1 to 10, write down a number to indicate how much trust you believe the other person has in you.

How do your scores match up with those for "Whom Do You Trust?" What are some of the reasons for the similarities and differences? In what kinds of relationships do you share a high degree of mutual trust? In what kinds is there a large imbalance in the levels of trust?

Intimacy

In addition to the development of trust in interpersonal relationships, people also develop feelings of attraction and liking toward the other person. Attraction exists whenever you feel a positive regard for another person, or when you like someone;

interpersonal intimacy. A quality of a relationship represented by the degree to which a person's sense of self is accepted and confirmed by another person.

interpersonal power. A quality of a relationship represented by the degree to which one person can influence another in the direction he or she desires.

however, the intensity or strength of that attraction varies from relationship to relationship. Think about your feelings or liking for those people you regard as casual friends, and those you regard as best friends. You like your best friends more—you have greater attraction toward your best friends. There is a strong correlation between the level of intimacy in a relationship, and level of attraction. Feelings of attraction continually change as relationships change.

People are often led to initiate relationships because of some preliminary attraction toward another person; as the relationship becomes more intimate, so do the feelings of attraction. As you move closer to intimacy, that desire increases. In everyday usage, *intimacy* is often associated with sexual activity; however, interpersonal intimacy has a broader meaning that is generally independent of sexual intimacy. **Interpersonal intimacy** is a quality of a relationship represented by the degree to which each person's sense of self is confirmed and accepted by their partner; in essence, it means being able to be yourself and still be accepted by your partner. You can measure the intimacy of a relationship by the extent to which other people let you know that they see you the same way you see yourself while expressing positive feelings toward you. In essence, intimacy means that another person loves and accepts you in spite of your flaws and you don't have to hide those flaws from him or her.

One of the reasons this text includes a chapter on self is because the self is inextricably linked to intimate relationships. We depend on intimate relationships to provide us information about ourselves (as exemplified in the Johari Window discussed later in this chapter) and to bolster our self-confidence. The more intimate the relationship, the more we depend upon others for acceptance and confirmation of our self-image.[4] During periods when we might not have very intimate relationships, it is sometimes hard to maintain a strong positive self-image. Research confirms that having strong social support networks is related to subjective well-being.[5]

By now you have probably recognized the interactive nature of the qualities of interpersonal relationships about which you have been reading. A person becomes attracted to someone, and that can lead to interacting and developing trust, and that can lead to greater self-disclosing and attraction, and that can lead to intimacy. As relationships move toward greater intimacy, a number of changes occur in our communication and behaviours toward our partners (you'll read more about relationship stages later in this chapter). We directly and indirectly communicate our sense of intimacy through our words and actions. We might tell another person how we feel about him or her and how much we value the relationship. We might also use a variety of non-verbal cues, such as close physical proximity, eye contact, words of endearment, tone of voice, physical contact, and the amount of time we commit to the interacting.

Power

The third dimension in interpersonal relationships—power—might be the most significant of all. We might not realize it, but distributing power between partners requires a lot of subtle negotiation. Furthermore, our ability to do it successfully is a major factor in relational development. Power and control have been defined in a variety of ways,[6] but for our purposes **interpersonal power** means the ability to influence another in the direction you desire—to get another person to do what you want.

Chapter 10 Understanding Interpersonal Relationships

Power is present in each interpersonal interaction, and generally power is processed rather smoothly. For the power management to go smoothly, both parties must be willing to accept the way power is being played out. For example, you go into an office, approach the receptionist, and ask, "May I see Dr. Watson?" Initially, you are attempting to exert a small degree of power, because you initiated the interaction. By asking a question, you are also attempting to influence the receptionist. What if the receptionist looks up at you and doesn't reply? At that point, the receptionist might be resisting your attempt at influence. You've probably been in situations where someone has asked you a question and you have refused to answer. This usually results in an aggravated encounter that reflects some degree of power struggle.

🔸 Types of Power Relationships

In the discussion of attraction, you read about how one person who likes to make decisions would make a good partner with another person who likes other people to make decisions for him or her. This complementarity of needs is one form of attraction. This reflects one of the three patterns that characterize relationship power. In **complementary relationships**, one partner usually dominates and the other usually submits: One likes to talk, the other to listen; one likes to lead, the other to follow. You might find such a relationship undesirable to your own interests, but for many people such a relationship works to the satisfaction of both partners.

What happens when both partners want to call the shots, when both want to make the decision? Having both partners behaving in similar ways creates **symmetric relationships**.[7] Sometimes both partners want to dominate, and sometimes both want to be submissive. A **competitive symmetric relationship** exists when both partners are vying for control or dominance over the other person. For example, each might try to control which TV program they watch, or might insist on participating in every spending decision. Competition in such relationships often increases the amount of conflict and negotiation associated with decision making. At times neither partner wants to take control or make a decision, and this creates a **submissive symmetric relationship**. The following is an example of submissive symmetry (does it sound familiar to you?):

Barb: What movie do you want to rent?

Vic: Oh, I don't care. You decide.

Barb: No, you decide. I don't care either.

Most relationships, however, are neither purely complementary nor purely symmetrical; they are parallel. **Parallel relationships** involve a shifting back and forth of the power between the partners depending on the situation. For example, if Janene knows more about computers than her husband, Justin, then he might defer to her the decision about what new computer to purchase. However, Janene might defer to her husband to plan their upcoming vacation because of his travel-planning experience. Establishing who has power in various situations is a point of contention in developing relationships and takes time for the parties involved to resolve. Power in any relationship changes as individuals change. As Justin gains computer savvy, he might want more say in purchasing a new system. Having knowledge or expertise is one way we hold power over another person.

---

complementary relationship. Relationship in which the power is represented by one partner dominating and the other person submitting.

symmetric relationship. Relationship in which the power is represented by both partners attempting to have the same level of power.

competitive symmetric relationship. Relationship in which both partners vie for control or dominance of the other.

submissive symmetric relationship. Relationship in which neither partner wants to take control or make decisions.

parallel relationship. Relationship in which power shifts back and forth between the partners depending on the situation.

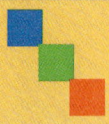

Building Your Skills

POWER IN YOUR RELATIONSHIPS

Think of one of your close relationships as you answer the following questions. Try this with several relationships such as your best friend, romantic partner, sibling, or parent.

Cp1.	I let my partner make most decisions.	Yes	No
Cp2.	I'm comfortable with the decisions my partner makes about our relationship.	Yes	No
Cp3.	I like how my partner plans our time together.	Yes	No
C1.	I make most of the decisions in the relationship.	Yes	No
C2.	My partner likes that I am the one who makes decisions in our relationship.	Yes	No
C3.	I'm usually the one who decides what we're going to do.	Yes	No
Sc1.	My partner and I both are pretty assertive about what we want.	Yes	No
Sc2.	There are times where both my partner and I want to make the decision.	Yes	No
Sc3.	We sometimes struggle because each of us wants to decide things.	Yes	No
Ss1.	Usually neither my partner nor I want to make the decision.	Yes	No
Ss2.	We get stuck sometimes because neither of us wants to decide.	Yes	No
Ss3.	Neither of us wants to be pushy, so we tend to be laid-back about decisions.	Yes	No
P1.	Sometimes I make decisions, and sometimes my partner makes them.	Yes	No
P2.	We each have areas where we defer to the other person's judgment.	Yes	No
P3.	If I can't decide something my partner will, and vice versa.	Yes	No

Look at your scoring for the five sets of items. Which ones have the most "Yes" responses? The "Cp" set reflects a complementary relationship in which your partner dominates as compared to the "C" set in which you are the dominant member. The "Sc" items reflect a symmetric relationship in which you and your partner compete for control. The "Ss" items cover a more submissive style of symmetric relationship. The "P" items are typical of the statements made in relationships that handle power within a parallel relationship.

Types of Power Distribution in Relationships

Why does one person in a relationship have power over the other? One pair of researchers developed a classic framework for defining bases of power that has been tested in several communication contexts, including classrooms and small group communication settings. The framework includes five power sources that we use to influence others.[8]

Legitimate power is power that comes because of respect for a position that another person holds. Teachers, parents, law officers, store managers, and company presidents all have power because of the position they hold relative to other people. When a police officer tells you to pull off to the side of the road you respond to this enactment of power by obeying the officer's command.

Referent power is power that comes from our attraction to another person, or the charisma a person possesses. We let people we like influence us. We change our behaviour to meet their demands or desires because we are attracted to them.

---

legitimate power. A type of power that comes from respect for a position that another person holds.

referent power. A type of power that comes from our attraction to another person, or the charisma a person possesses.

Expert power is based on the influence derived from a person's knowledge and experience. We convey power on those who know more than we do, or have some expertise we don't possess. This knowledge can even include knowledge about how to manage a relationship effectively. We grant power to partners who have more experience in relationships. There were frequent episodes of the *Seinfeld* TV series in which the characters defer to the expertise of their friends when it came to how to handle various relational crises.

Reward power is based on another person's ability to satisfy your needs. There are obvious rewards, such as money and gifts, but most rewards are more interpersonal in nature. In Chapter 2 we talked about the interpersonal needs of control, affection, and inclusion. The degree to which another person is able to satisfy these needs gives them a certain power. For example, those people who are able to help us meet your need to be included in social activities have power over you. You will do what they ask if you see that your need will continue to be met. Reward power is probably the most common form of power in interpersonal relationships. Withholding rewards is actually a form of punishment, or what is called coercive power.

Coercive power involves the use of sanctions or punishment to influence others. Sanctions include holding back or removing rewards. If you have a high need for physical affection, your partner might threaten to hold back that affection if you do not comply with a given request. You might threaten to end the relationship as a sanctioned form of power in order to accomplish a given goal. Punishment involves imposing something on another person that he or she does not want. Coercive power exists in relationships when one partner has the ability to impose the sanction or punishment on another. Your parents had the power to take away your allowance when you were younger, and therefore you did the chores they requested. However, once you have your own source of income, your parents no longer have this source of power over you.

expert power. A type of power based on a person's knowledge and experience.

reward power. A type of power based on a person's ability to satisfy our needs.

coercive power. A type of power based on the use of sanctions or punishments to influence others.

▶ **Recap**

TYPES OF POWER

Type	Definition	Examples
Legitimate Power	Comes because of respect for a position that another person holds	Teachers, parents, officials, law officers, clergy
Referent Power	Comes from our attraction to another person, or the charisma a person holds	Professional athletes, rock stars, evangelists, cult leaders
Expert Power	Derives from a person's knowledge or experience	Scientists, consultants, senior members of an organization
Reward Power	Comes from another person's ability to satisfy our needs	Bosses (giving money), friends (giving love or companionship)
Coercive Power	Stems from the use of sanctions or punishment to influence others	Boss (threatening to fire), parent (taking away privileges)

Attraction in Relationships

Knowing the types and dimensions of relationships helps our understanding of how relationships work, but it does not explain how and why they begin. What

interpersonal attraction. The degree to which you desire to form or maintain an interpersonal relationship.

short-term initial attraction. The degree to which we sense a potential for an interpersonal relationship.

long-term maintenance attraction. A liking or positive feeling that motivates us to sustain a relationship.

physical attraction. The degree to which we find another person's physical self appealing.

does it mean to say that you are attracted to another person? **Interpersonal attraction** is the degree to which you want to form or maintain an interpersonal relationship.

Short-Term Initial Attraction and Long-Term Maintenance Attraction

Interpersonal attraction occurs in the early stages of relational development as short-term initial attraction, and in the later stages of relational development as long-term maintenance attraction. You can understand the difference between the two by looking at your own relationships. Think of the dozens of people you initially found attractive but with whom you never developed an intimate relationship. **Short-term initial attraction** is the *degree* to which we sense a *potential* for developing an interpersonal relationship. For instance, you might find one of your classmates to be physically attractive, but never move to introduce yourself. The information you gather in your first interaction with someone can also generate a short-term initial attraction for a relationship, which you may or may not pursue, depending upon the circumstances. **Long-term maintenance attraction**, on the other hand, is the type that sustains relationships like your best friendships. It refers to a level of liking or positive feeling that motivates us to maintain or escalate a relationship. Short-term attraction gives way to long-term attraction as a relationship develops through the stages we will discuss in Chapter 11.

Think about your best friend. How did that relationship start? Perhaps it was because he or she was physically attractive, or, perhaps, you observed your friend laughing and joking with others and found that quality attractive. Why are you still friends with this person? Rarely (except in movies or TV shows) do we commit to, and maintain, a long-term intimate relationship, such as marriage, solely because we find another person physically attractive.[9] Perhaps you have discovered that you and your friend have a lot in common, or that you complement each other's personalities. For instance, your friend's calm, even disposition might balance your fiery temper.

Elements of Interpersonal Attraction

Why do we feel attracted to some people and not to others? The explanations are complex, but researchers have identified seven elements that influence our feelings of attraction. As you read about them, try to analyze your own feelings about people you find attractive.

Physical Attraction

The degree to which we find another person's physical self appealing represents our **physical attraction** to him or her. That appeal might be based on size, height, clothing, hairstyle, makeup, jewelry, vocal qualities, gestures, and so forth. The old adage, "Beauty is in the eye of the beholder," is particularly true in terms of explaining physical attraction. Each culture has its own definition of the physical ideal, which it teaches and perpetuates. In North America, for instance, advertisements and TV programs promote a slender ideal for both males and females. This certainly contributes to our society's fixation on losing weight and staying fit. In some cultures, and at various times throughout history, however, physical attractiveness was synonymous with bulkiness.

Physical attractiveness acts as a convenient filter to reduce relationship possibilities.[10] In general, we tend to seek out individuals who represent the same level of physical attractiveness as ourselves. Suppose you are really into physical conditioning and have a personal philosophy about good eating habits, exercise, avoiding drugs, and not smoking. You will probably seek out, and attract, a physically fit person to be your partner. To a certain degree, the physical image a person presents can reflect more substantive qualities. For example, there is a good possibility that a physically fit individual's philosophy about eating and exercise would be similar to yours. That similarity might serve as the basis for a long-term maintenance attraction. As you learned in Chapter 3, we use superficial information to make inferences about personality with varying degrees of accuracy, but whether we decide to escalate a relationship depends upon what happens in the initial and subsequent interactions.

🔸 Credibility, Competence, and Charisma

Most of us are attracted to individuals who seem competent and credible. We like those who are sure of themselves, but not full of themselves. We assume they are competent if they seem skilled, knowledgeable, and experienced. We find people credible if they display a blend of enthusiasm, trustworthiness, competence, and power. Competence, credibility, and, sometimes, physical attractiveness are all important elements in the composite quality we call *charisma*, which inspires strong attraction and allegiance. Political and other types of leaders often depend upon their charisma to attract supporters who are motivated to form relationships with them and willing to devote themselves to a chosen cause.

🔸 Proximity

We are more likely to be attracted to people who are physically close to us than to those who are farther away. In this class, you are more likely to form a relationship with classmates sitting on either side of you than with someone seated at the opposite end of the room. This is partly because physical **proximity** increases communication opportunities. We tend to talk with someone on a casual, offhand basis because he or she is right next to us. We are more likely to talk, and therefore to feel attracted, to neighbours who live right next door than those who live down the block. Any circumstance that increases the possibilities for interacting is also likely to increase attraction.

In impromptu surveys of students in our classes over the years, your authors have found that a high percentage form close friendships with residence roommates who were randomly assigned. There is a good chance that two individuals will become good friends simply because they share living accommodations. In one study on attraction, a researcher told pairs of people about one another, describing to each the other's dissimilar attitudes on a particular topic.[11] The participants were then asked to rate their attraction to the other person. All of the ratings were low. Then the partners were introduced to one another and allowed to interact. Even

proximity. That quality which promotes attraction because of being physically close to another and, therefore, in a position to communicate easily.

similarity. We are attracted to people whose personalities, values, upbringing, personal experiences, attitudes, and interests are similar to ours.

complementary needs. We are attracted to those whose needs complement our own; one person's weakness is the other person's strength.

when they discussed only the attitude on which they disagreed, they had significantly more attraction for one another. Clearly, the information exchange that communication affords increases our ability to make an informed decision about pursuing a relationship. In addition, in both of these examples, the interaction was between two college students—two individuals who already have a great deal in common. That commonality is the source of the next form of attraction.

Similarity

In general, we are attracted to people whose personalities, values, upbringing, personal experiences, attitudes, and interests are **similar** to ours. We seek them out through shared activities. You may, for example, join a folk dance group because you know the members share a dance interest with you. Within the group, you would be especially attracted to those who have a similar sense of humour, who share the same attitudes on certain issues, or who enjoy some of the same additional activities that you do. As we interact, we discover both similarities and differences between ourselves and others. We assess the relative weight of those similarities and differences and arrive at a level of attraction that may change over time as we continue to discover more information.

In the initial stages of a relationship, we try to emphasize positive information about ourselves to create a positive and attractive image. We reveal those aspects of ourselves that we believe we have in common with the other person, and the other person does the same.[12] Think about your initial interactions with strangers; typically, you spend the first few minutes trying to find topics of mutual interest. You discover that the person is from a place near your home town, has the same musical tastes, likes the same sports, frequents the same restaurants, has been to your favourite campground, has the same attitude about school, has had the same instructor for history class, and on and on. But the depth of this information is limited. We save our revelations about important attitudes and issues for a later stage in the relational development process.[13] Attitude similarity is more likely to be a source of long-term maintenance attraction than of short-term initial attraction.

Complementary Needs

You have heard the adage, "Opposites attract." Although we like people with whom we have much in common, most of us wouldn't find it very exciting to be stuck for the rest of our lives with someone who had identical attitudes, needs, values, and interests. Most of us look instead for someone with **complementary needs.** As we discussed in Chapter 2, Schutz identified three interpersonal needs that motivate us to form and maintain relationships with others: inclusion, control, and affection.[14] *Inclusion* represents the need to include others in your activities, or to be included in theirs. *Control* represents the need to make decisions and take responsibility, or the willingness to accept others' decision making. *Affection* represents the need to be loved and accepted by others, or the willingness to give love and acceptance to others.

If you have a high need to control and make decisions, and little respect for others' decision making, you will be more compatible with someone who does not have similar needs—someone who wants others to make decisions for him or her. In essence, we can view pairs of individuals as a team in which each side complements the other side's weaknesses. If you're not very good at keeping track of your bills and balancing your chequebook, you might pair up with someone who is good at maintaining a budget in order to create a strong personal finance team. In reality, there are no "perfect" matches, only degrees of compatibility relative to needs.

Building Your Skills

ARE YOUR NEEDS COMPLEMENTARY?

Evaluate your level of interpersonal needs for each of the following by putting your first initial along the rating scale.

1. How much do you like to include others in the activities you do?
   Very little 1―――2―――3―――4―――5―――6―――7―――8―――9―――10 A great deal

2. How much do you like to be included by others when they are involved in activities?
   Very little 1―――2―――3―――4―――5―――6―――7―――8―――9―――10 A great deal

3. How much do you like to take responsibility for decision making?
   Very little 1―――2―――3―――4―――5―――6―――7―――8―――9―――10 A great deal

4. How much do you like to let others make decisions for you?
   Very little 1―――2―――3―――4―――5―――6―――7―――8―――9―――10 A great deal

5. How much do you feel a need to be accepted and loved by others?
   Very little 1―――2―――3―――4―――5―――6―――7―――8―――9―――10 A great deal

6. How much do you feel a need to accept others and to give love to others?
   Very little 1―――2―――3―――4―――5―――6―――7―――8―――9―――10 A great deal

Now think of two close friends. Go back and place their first initials along each rating scale to indicate how much each item applies to them. Or ask your friends to initial the scale for themselves. Compare your ratings with those of your friends. Are there areas where you are similar? Complementary? Are there differences that cause difficulties in the relationship—for example, you both want to make decisions rather than accept others' decisions?

Relationship Potential

We need interpersonal relationships to confirm our self-image. The **predicted outcome value theory** claims that we assess the potential for any given relationship to meet this relational need and then weigh that assessment against the potential costs.[15] We are attracted to others with whom a relationship may yield a high outcome value (the rewards might exceed the costs). Over time, our assessments may change. In the movie *When Harry Met Sally*, for example, the main characters both thought initially that their relationship had little potential of meeting their needs. Over time, Harry and Sally developed a friendship that did meet certain needs. At that point they both thought the relationship had gone as far as it could. In the end, however, they discovered that they could have a more intimate relationship with a high outcome value.

Like Harry and Sally, most of us begin predicting outcome values in initial interactions and continually modify our predictions as we learn more and more about the other person. We pursue attractions beyond the initial interaction stage if we think they can yield positive outcomes, and generally avoid or terminate relationships for which we predict negative outcomes.[16]

relationship potential (predicted outcome value theory). We are most attracted to those relationships that potentially have greater rewards or benefits than costs.

Reciprocation of Liking

We like people who like us. One way to get other people to **reciprocate** is to show that we like them. In initial interactions, however, we are often reluctant to let other people know that we are attracted to them. We may hold back from showing our interest because we fear rejection or fear that we may give the other person a certain amount of power over us.

A study conducted by one of your authors and a colleague found that we often underestimate how much a new acquaintance is attracted to us.[17] Pairs of male and female college students interacted for the first time and then indicated their level of attraction for their partner, as well as their perception of how attracted their partner was to them. Most of the students significantly underestimated the amount of attraction the other person felt for them. It is unclear whether we underestimate because we don't have much confidence that others will like us as much as we like them, or because we, as North Americans, in general do not communicate effectively our level of attraction for others. Even in long-term relationships, people sometimes hold back in expressing their continued attraction for their friends or mates. As you interact with new acquaintances, keep in mind that they probably are more attracted to you than you realize, so you might want to adapt your decision making accordingly.

▶ Recap

ELEMENTS OF INTERPERSONAL ATTRACTION

Term	Explanation	Examples
Physical Attraction	The degree to which we find another's physical self appealing.	Body type and size, mannerisms, height, hairstyle, jewellery, facial features, clothes.
Credibility, Competence, and Charisma	We are attracted to individuals whom we perceive to be enthusiastic, knowledgeable, skilled, and trustworthy.	We find teachers, athletes, movie and TV stars attractive because we see them as skillful or credible.
Proximity	Physical proximity encourages attraction.	We are more attracted to immediate neighbours than to those who live down the block.
Similarity	We are attracted to those who share similarities with us.	We make friends with people who have personalities, interests, values, beliefs, and attitudes similar to ours.
Complementary Needs	We seek out people whose needs complement our own.	Those who want to control are compatible with those who want to surrender control.
Relationship Potential	We are attracted to those with whom we see the potential for a rewarding relationship.	As Humphrey Bogart said to Claude Rains in the movie *Casablanca*, "You know, Louie, this could be the beginning of a beautiful friendship."
Reciprocation of Liking	We are attracted to those who are attracted to us.	If someone indicates an interest in us, we tend to find him or her attractive.

reciprocation of liking. We like people who like us.

self-disclosure. Providing information about ourselves that another person would not learn if we did not tell him or her.

Self-Disclosure: A Foundation for Relational Escalation

Without a sharing of personal information or mutual self-disclosure, a relationship cannot proceed to a very intimate level. When we **self-disclose**, we provide information that others would not learn if we did not tell them. Others can learn our *approximate* age, height, and weight by just observing us. But they cannot learn our *exact* age, height, or weight unless we disclose it. Self-disclosure ranges from revealing innocuous information about who you are to admitting your deepest fears and most private fantasies. Disclosing personal information not only provides a basis for another person to understand you better, it conveys your level of trust and acceptance of the other person. To help explore relationships among self-concept, self-esteem, and self-disclosure, we will describe how self-disclosure occurs, note how people become aware of who they are through self-disclosure, and identify general characteristics of self-disclosure.

Interpersonal relationships cannot achieve intimacy without self-disclosure. Without true self-disclosure, you form only superficial relationships. You can confirm another person's self-concept, and have your self-concept confirmed, only if both you and your partner have revealed yourselves to each other. In the next chapter, you will see how self-disclosure changes as relationships begin, grow, and end.

As relationships move toward intimacy, they typically include periods of high self-disclosure early in the relationship. The *amount* of information that is disclosed, however, decreases as the relationship becomes more and more intimate. In other words, there is generally more self-disclosing activity earlier in a relationship than later. As a relationship proceeds, we begin sharing low-risk information fairly rapidly, move on to share higher-risk information, and then, finally, to share our most intimate disclosures. The more intimate the relationship becomes, the more intimate the information that is disclosed. The sculpture below represents the way we reveal ourselves when we are with close friends. Holding back from sharing intimate information signals a reluctance to escalate the relationship. The amount of information that we have to share about ourselves is finite, so we slow down as we have less left to disclose.

As we develop a relationship we reveal more of ourselves, removing the masks that we routinely use with strangers. (Sandra Rice)

Graph A in Figure 10.1 illustrates a typical disclosure pattern over the course of a long and intimate relationship. The peaks and valleys represent periods of variable disclosure. Note that most of the disclosure takes place in the beginning of the relationship. Not all relationships progress this way, however. The relationship in graph B represents two individuals who started to get to know each other but were

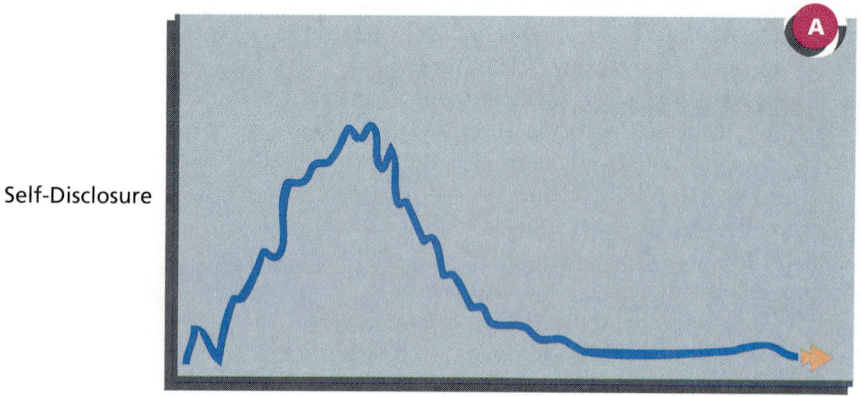

A A long and intimate relationship.

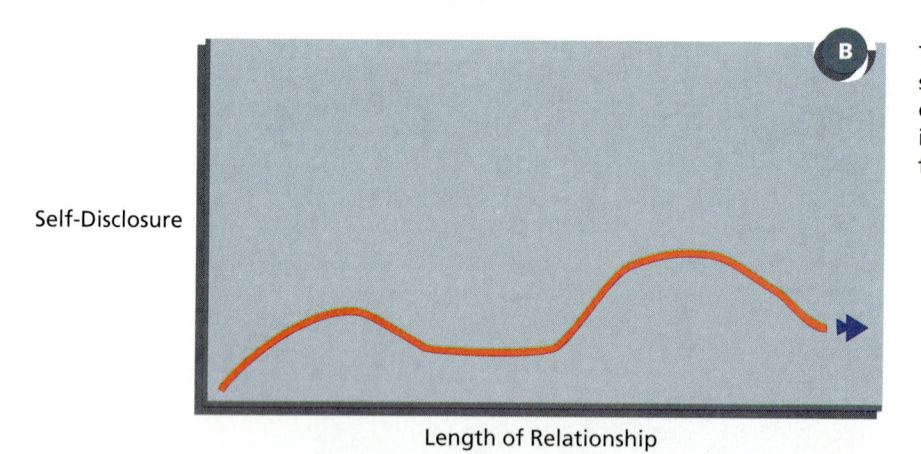

B Two individuals who started to get to know each other, but were interrupted before finally becoming friends.

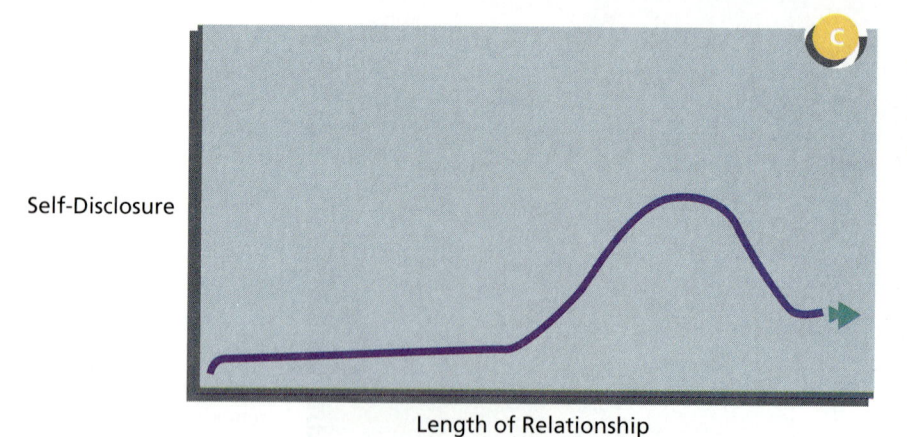

C Two individuals who knew each other as acquaintances before the relationship started to escalate.

Figure 10.1
Self-Disclosure and Relational Development

Building Your Skills

SELF-DISCLOSURE PATTERNS

Think about two of your current relationships and draw a graph like those in Figure 10.1 to show how the self-disclosure has progressed in each of them. How do the patterns compare? What do the differences or similarities reflect about the two relationships? What caused the peaks and valleys? Were there times when you or your partner tried to increase the rate of self-disclosure, and the other person rejected that attempt? What happened?

Self-Disclosure vs *Length of Relationship*

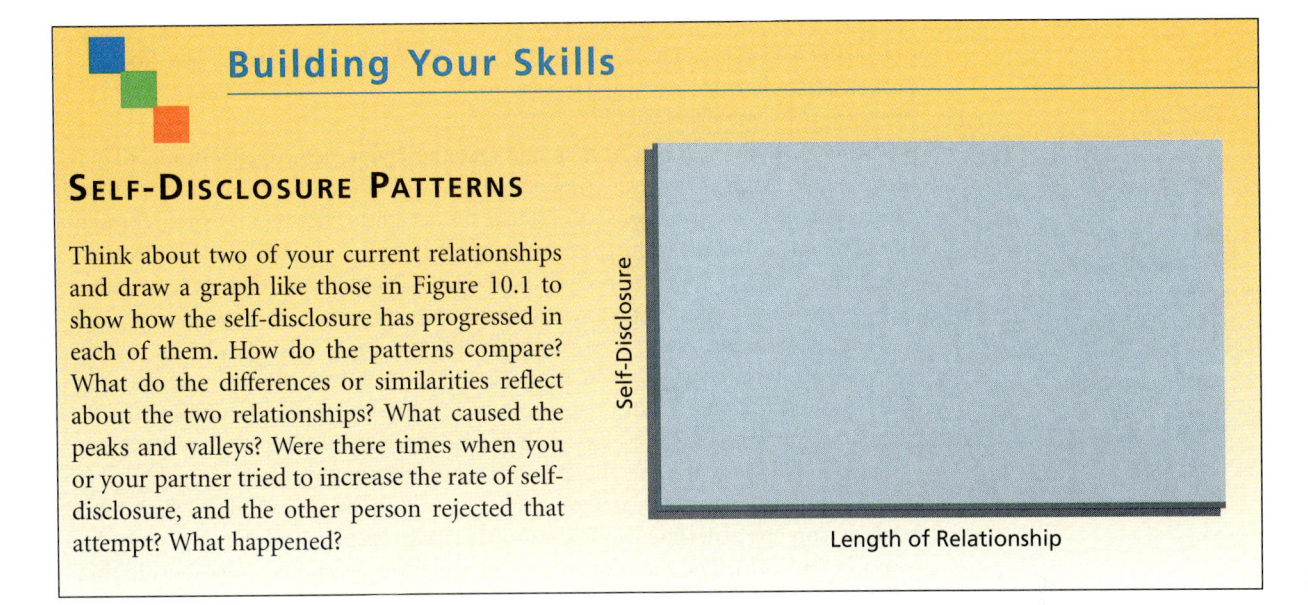

interrupted before they became close friends. They might have stopped because of some conflict, indecisiveness about pursuing the relationship, or external circumstances that limited opportunities for interacting. When the disclosure resumed, it became more intense. Graph C represents two individuals who probably knew each other as acquaintances for some time but never really had the opportunity or inclination to self-disclose. Once they did begin to escalate the relationship, however, there was a steep rise in self-disclosure. This graph might represent two co-workers who eventually start dating, or two students who have shared a class or two together before striking up a friendship.

Generally, a dramatic increase or decrease in self-disclosure reflects some significant change in the relationship. Even long-term relationships have significant increases and decreases in disclosure that signify changes. Before the birth of a first child, for example, both parents might disclose their fears and expectations about child rearing, and the information might have a profound effect on the relationship.

Interpersonal relationships cannot achieve intimacy without self-disclosure. Without true self-disclosure, we form only superficial relationships. You can confirm another person's self-concept, and have your self-concept confirmed, only if both you and your partner have revealed your selves to each other.

Two Models for Self-Disclosure

We have already seen that we self-disclose to move a relationship toward intimacy. Two models illustrate the process by which this happens. The first model, Social Penetration, shows how self-disclosure involves revealing a broad range of information about ourselves as well as delving deeper into more personal information. The Johari Window, the second model, uses imaginary window panes that correspond to the information we know and do not know about ourselves, as well as panes for personal information another person might, or might not, know about us.

Understanding the Depth and Breadth of Self-Disclosure: The Social Penetration Model of Self-Disclosure

A pair of researchers, Irwin Altman and Dalmas Taylor, developed a model of **social penetration** to illustrate how much and what kind of information we reveal in various stages of a relationship.[18] Their model starts with a circle that represents all the potential information about your self that you could disclose to someone (see Figure 10.2, circle A). This circle is divided like a pie into many pieces, with each piece of pie representing a particular aspect, construct, or dimension of your self. Some of the constructs in your personality pie might relate to athletic activities, religion, family, school, recreational activities, political interests, and fears. These pieces of pie represent the breadth of information available about you.

In addition, the concentric circles in the pie represent the depth of information. The smallest circle represents the most personal information. Each of your relationships represents a degree of social penetration, or the extent to which the other person has penetrated your concentric circles (depth) and shared pieces of your pie (breadth). The shading on circle B, for example, shows a relationship that involves a high degree of penetration, but on only one aspect of your self. Perhaps you have a good friend with whom you study and go to the library, but do not socialize with. You might have disclosed a depth of information to that friend about your academic skills and weaknesses, but nothing about your family, hobbies, politics, or other aspects of yourself.

social penetration. A model of self-disclosure and relational development that reflects sharing information that has both depth and breadth (how much and what kind of information we reveal).

Figure 10.2
Social Penetration Models

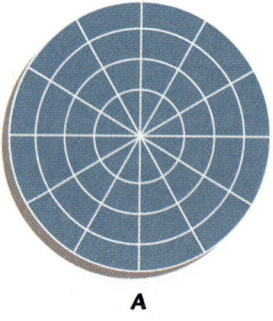

A
Your "self" with all its various dimensions. The pies represent the breadth of your "self," and the rings represent depth.

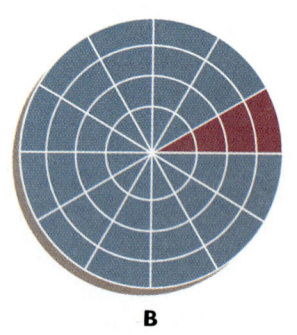

B
A limited relationship in which one dimension of your "self" has been disclosed to another person.

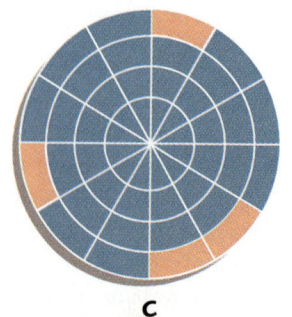

C
A relationship with greater breadth than B but with no intimacy.

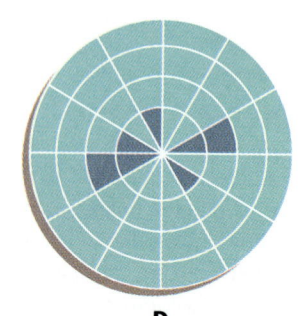

D
A highly intimate, close relationship in which there has been extensive breadth and depth of disclosure.

Your relationships with your instructors probably look a little like circle B, with its limited breadth. In circle C, more pieces of the pie are shaded, but the information is all fairly safe, surface information about yourself. This would probably be the kind of disclosure associated with a new or limited friendship. Circle D represents almost complete social penetration, the kind we achieve in an intimate, well-developed relationship, in which a large amount of self-disclosure has taken place.

Understanding How We Learn about Ourselves: The Johari Window Model of Self-Disclosure

To disclose information to others, you must first be aware of who you are. **Self-awareness** is your understanding of who you are. In addition to just thinking about who you are, asking others for information about yourself and then listening to what they tell you can enhance your self-awareness. By revealing yourself to others you learn about who you are as well as increasing intimacy with selected people in your lives. As well, others share information about you that they are aware of and that you may or may not be aware of yourself.

The **Johari Window model** nicely summarizes how your awareness of who you are is influenced by your own level of disclosure, as well as by how much others share information *about* yourself *with* you. (The name "Johari Window" sounds somewhat mystical and exotic, but it is labelled after the first names of the creators of the model, Joe and Harry—Joseph Luft and Harry Ingham.[19]) As Figure 10.3 shows, the model looks like a window. Like the circles in the social penetration model, the window represents your self. This self includes everything about you, including things even you don't yet see or realize. One axis is divided into what you have come to know about yourself and what you don't yet know about who you are. The other axis represents what a particular person knows about you and doesn't know about you. The intersection of these categories creates a four-panel window.

At first glance, all four quadrants in the window seem to be the same size. But that may not be the case (in fact, it probably isn't). Quadrant 1 is called the open area. It contains information that others know about you and that you are also aware of. The more information you reveal about yourself, the larger quadrant 1 will be. Put another way, the more you open up to others, the larger the open area will be. The open area might include such information as your age, your occupation, and other things you mention about yourself.

Quadrant 2 is called the blind area. This part of the window contains information that other people know about you, but that you do not know. Do you remember when, in elementary school, someone may have put a sign on your back that said, "Hit me"? Everyone was aware of it but you. The blind area of the Johari Window works in much the same way. For example, you may see yourself as generous, but others may see you as a tightwad. As you learn how others see you, the blind area of the Johari

self-awareness. Person's conscious understanding of who he or she is.

Johari Window. A model of self-disclosure that reflects the movement of information about ourselves from BLIND and UNKNOWN quadrants to HIDDEN and OPEN ones.

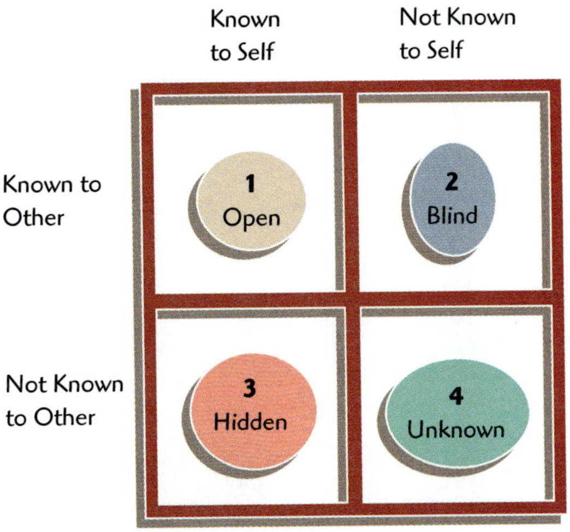

Figure 10.3
The Johari Window

	Known to Self	Not Known to Self
Known to Other	1 Open	2 Blind
Not Known to Other	3 Hidden	4 Unknown

Window gets smaller. Generally, the more you accurately know about yourself and about how others see you, the better your chances to establish open and honest relationships with others.

Quadrant 3 is the hidden area. This area contains information that you know about yourself, but that others do not know about you. You can probably think of many facts, thoughts, feelings, and fantasies that you would not want anyone else to know. They may be feelings you have about another person or something you've done privately in the past that you'd be embarrassed to share with others. The point here is not to suggest you should share all information in the hidden area with others. It is useful to know, however, that part of who you are is known by some people, but remains hidden from others.

Quadrant 4 in the Johari Window depicts the unknown area. This area contains information that is unknown to both you and others. These are things you do not know about yourself *yet*. Perhaps you do not know how you will react under certain stressful situations. Maybe you are not sure what stand you will take on a certain issue next year or even next week. Other people may also not be aware of how you would respond or behave under certain conditions. Your personal potential, your untapped physical and mental resources, are unknown. You can assume that this area exists, because eventually some, not necessarily all, of these things

Figure 10.4
Variations on the Johari Window

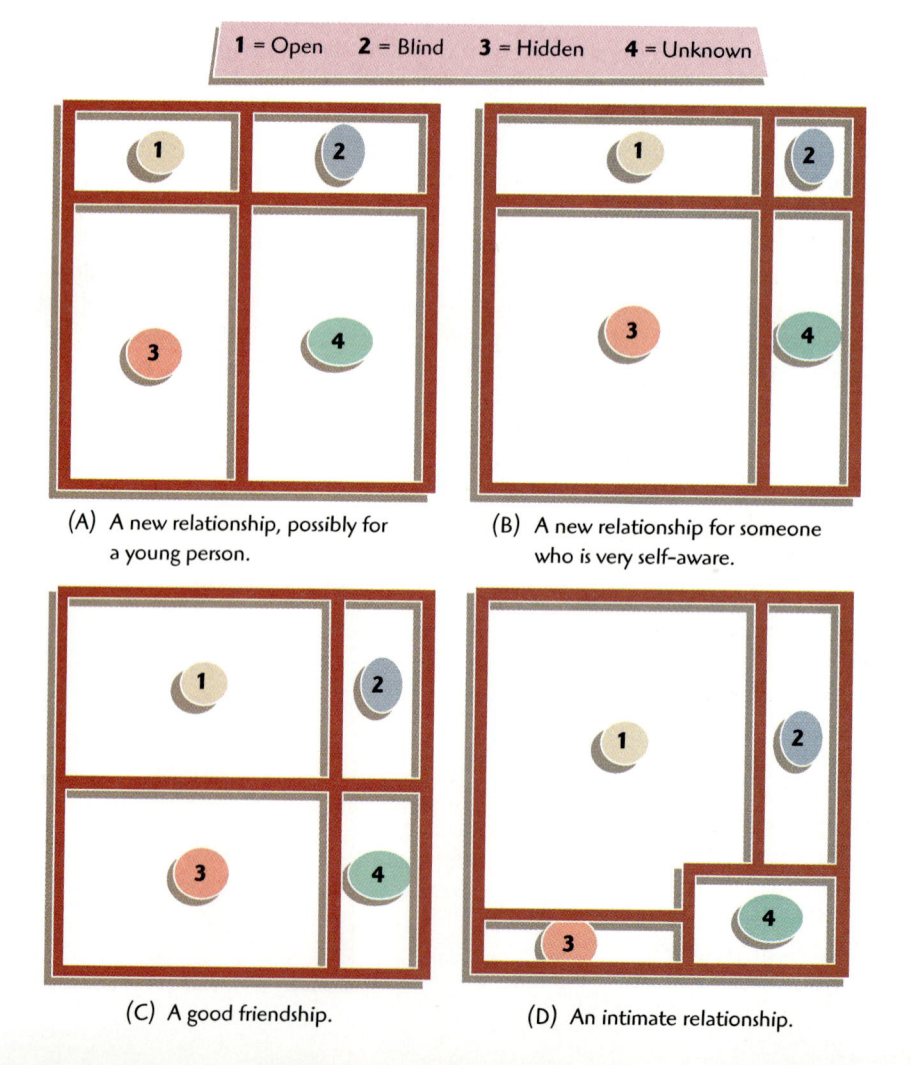

1 = Open   2 = Blind   3 = Hidden   4 = Unknown

(A) A new relationship, possibly for a young person.

(B) A new relationship for someone who is very self-aware.

(C) A good friendship.

(D) An intimate relationship.

become known to you, to others, or to both you and others. Because you can never know yourself completely, the unknown quadrant will always exist; you can only guess at its current size, because the information it contains is unavailable to you.

Sometimes our friends observe things about us that we don't realize about ourselves. This kind of unintentional self-disclosure is represented by the blind area. This quadrant is usually small when someone doesn't know us very well, and it grows larger as the person observes more and more information that is in our unknown quadrant. However, as the relationship becomes more intimate, the other person is more likely to reveal his or her perceptions of us, so the unknown and the blind quadrants shrink as information becomes known and accessible to us. As you can see, then, intimate relationships play an important role in the growth of what we know about who we are.

As we did with the social penetration model, we can draw Johari Windows to represent each of our relationships (see Figure 10.4). Window A depicts a new or very restricted relationship for someone who is probably young or at least not very self-aware. Very little information has been disclosed or observed by the other, so the open and blind quadrants are small. Window B shows a new or restricted relationship for someone who knows him- or herself very well. Again, the open and blind quadrants are small, but the unknown quadrant is also small. Window C represents a relationship that has evolved into a good friendship, and window D shows a very intimate relationship in which both individuals are open and disclosing.

We've discussed what self-disclosure is and described two models that explain how self-disclosure works and affects your understanding of who you think you are. Next we will describe characteristics of self-disclosure and discuss how disclosure, both appropriate and inappropriate, can affect our interpersonal relationships with others in both escalating and de-escalating relationships.

Characteristics of Appropriate Self-Disclosure

Mike was eating alone, sitting at the counter of his neighbourhood restaurant enjoying his favourite hamburger. Just as he was reaching for the ketchup bottle, a young woman on the stool next to him struck up a conversation with him. Within 10 minutes, Mike not only learned where this woman was from, but also whom she dated, how much money she made last year, and how embarrassed she was when her parents found her in a compromising position with her boyfriend on the front porch (which she described in vivid detail, complete with sound effects). Have you had the experience of meeting someone who told you more than you wanted to know about him- or herself? Although self-disclosure is a means to establishing relationships with others, as we presented in both the social penetration and Johari Window models, revealing too much too soon or making the disclosure only a one-way stream of revelatory information violates self-disclosure norms for most North Americans. The following discussion describes characteristics of appropriate self-disclosure.

Self-Disclosure Usually Moves in Small Increments

What made Mike so uncomfortable during his meeting with his dining neighbour was how much information he learned about his companion in such a short period of time. Most people usually reveal information about themselves a little bit at a time, rather than delivering a condensed version of their books-on-tape autobiography. Most North Americans would share Mike's discomfort at learning too much too soon. Monitor your own self-disclosure. Are you revealing information at a greater depth sooner than you should? If you do, others may find your disclosure disquieting. Appropriate self-disclosure should be well timed to suit the occasion and the expectations of the individuals involved.

Self-Disclosure Moves from Less Personal to More Personal Information

As the social penetration model illustrates, we can describe the depth of our self-disclosure by the intimacy level of the information we share. If we move too quickly to more intimate information before we've developed a history with someone, we violate social norms or expectations our partner may have. John Powell, author of the book *Why Am I Afraid To Tell You Who I Am?* notes that the information we reveal about ourselves often progresses through several predictable levels.[20]

Level 5: *Cliché communication.* We first establish verbal contact with others by saying something that lets the other person know we acknowledge his or her presence. Standard phrases such as "Hello" or "Hi; how are you?" or the more contemporary "What's up?" signal the desire to initiate a relationship, even if it is a brief, superficial one.

Level 4: *Facts and biographical information.* After using cliché phrases and responses to establish contact, we typically next reveal non-threatening information about ourselves, such as our names, hometowns, or majors.

Level 3: *Attitudes and personal ideas.* After noting our name and other basic information, it often follows that we begin talking about more personal information such as our attitudes about work or school, or other relatively safe topics. At this level, the information is not too threatening or revealing, but we do begin to talk about our likes and dislikes of what we might assume are non-controversial topics.

Level 2: *Personal feelings.* At this level, we discuss topics and issues that are exceedingly more personal. After we've developed rapport with someone, we then share more intimate fears, secrets, and attitudes about other people. Increasingly, we take risks when we share this information. It also involves trust to share these personal feelings.

Level 1: *Peak communication.* Powell calls this the ultimate level of self-disclosure that is seldom reached; his other name for level 1 is "gut level" communication. Only with our most intimate friends do we reveal such personal information. And it's possible, says Powell, that we may not reach this level of intimacy with our life partners, parents, or children. Peak communication is rare because of the risk and trust involved in being so open and revealing.

Self-Disclosure Is Reciprocal

In the mainstream North American culture, when people share information about themselves, they expect the other person to share similar information about her- or himself. If you introduce yourself by name to someone, you expect that person to respond by telling you his or her name. This cultural rule allows people to use disclosure as a strategy for gaining information and reducing uncertainty. The reciprocal nature of self-disclosure is called the **dyadic effect**. You disclose to me, and I'll disclose to you.

dyadic effect. Reciprocal nature of self-disclosure: "You disclose to me, and I'll disclose to you."

Self-Disclosure Involves Risk

Although self-disclosure is a building block for establishing intimacy with others, it can be risky. Once you disclose something to someone, that person can now share the information with others; that person has additional power if the information is something you'd rather not have others know.

There is also the risk of rejection when you tell someone something that is personal. As Powell comments, "If I tell you who I am, and you do not like who I am, that is all that I have."[21] Once you reveal what you believe is your true nature or personal feeling and you are rejected or rebuffed, you can't explain your rejection away by saying, "Oh, they don't know the real me." If you've revealed what you honestly believe is "the real you" and you experience disapproval from your partner, that can hurt worse than if your partner did not know "the real you."

Self-Disclosure Involves Trust

As we have already noted, to know something personal about someone is to have power over that person. If information has been shared with you, you have the power to reveal that information to others. To reveal personal information about someone that was shared with you in confidence is unethical. If you've made this promise, you should keep it. Using personal information against others to manipulate and control is a misuse of the trust that was placed in you.[22] According to British social psychologists Michael Argyle, Monica Henderson, and Adrian Furnham, keeping confidences of others is among the most valued expectation your friends have of you. Don't tell what you're not supposed to tell others. When you say, "Oh, I won't tell anyone. Your secret's safe with me," mean it.

> ### Recap
>
> #### CHARACTERISTICS OF APPROPRIATE SELF-DISCLOSURE
>
> | | |
> |---|---|
> | Self-disclosure usually moves in small increments. | Don't be in a hurry to tell someone too much too quickly about yourself. |
> | Self-disclosure moves from less personal to more personal information. | Revealing personal feelings and intimate information without establishing a foundation of sharing less personal information is likely to make your partner feel uncomfortable. |
> | Self-disclosure is reciprocal. | Appropriate self-disclosure involves dyadic interaction; it should not be a one-way monologue. |
> | Self-disclosure involves risk. | "But if I tell you who I am, you may not like who I am, and that is all that I have." You run the risk of being rejected by others when you disclose to them. |
> | Self-disclosure involves trust. | Disclosing to others means you trust them not to reveal your secrets to others or use the personal information against you. When others self-disclose, you have an ethical responsibility to keep confidential what you've learned. |

Interpersonal Relationship Development Theories

While we have discussed what interpersonal attraction is, the elements of attraction, and the importance of self-disclosure, we have not explored why relationships develop and change. In the next chapter, we will look at how relationships escalate and de-escalate. But what motivates us to move into a relationship or to develop a more or less intimate relationship? How did you move from acquaintanceships to being close friends? The earlier description of attraction theories provides a partial answer to this question by offering explanations of what evokes your interest in another person. However, they don't adequately explain why you might stay at one stage, back down from a stage, or move forward to the next. Noted relationship scholar Steve Duck suggests we go through a process of "filtering" in which we apply criteria at each stage of relational development that a potential close friend must pass.[23] In essence, a move from one stage to another toward intimacy means that a person has passed through another, finer screen filter. These screens represent decision points in which we make some assessment of the relationship and decide how we want to proceed. We can choose either to escalate, maintain, or de-escalate the relationship. Two theories reflect the kind of decision making that might be taking place: social exchange theory and dialectical theory (or dialectics).

Social Exchange Theory

Social exchange theory is an economic model of human behaviour that has been used to explain how people arrive at decisions in a variety of situations. **Social exchange theory** posits that people seek the greatest amount of reward with the least amount of cost. You've probably been in a difficult relationship where you have asked yourself, "Is this relationship really worth it?" What you are asking is whether the rewards you are gaining from the relationship are worth the trouble or expense necessary to sustain the relationship (the costs). Students frequently tell us about breaking up from long-distance relationships because the expense (driving time, telephone calls, missing activities where you live, and so on) ends up being greater than the rewards of the intermittent contact. Fortunately for some, the rewards associated with long-distance relationships remain greater than the costs, and those relationships continue to prosper.

Relationships can be evaluated in terms of immediate, forecasted, and cumulative costs and rewards.[24] **Immediate costs and rewards** occur in a relationship at the present moment in time. You can think about your current relationships and assess their present value. **Forecasted costs and rewards** are based on projection or prediction. We make guesses about the potential or future outlook of a relationship (communication scholar Michael Sunnafrank calls this predicted outcome value).[25] When you meet someone and begin to talk, you go through an initial assessment about whether a relationship with this person would be rewarding. You use forecasting to decide whether to remain in existing relationships during troubled times (costs escalate or rewards deteriorate). However, you don't immediately abandon long-term relationships at the first sign of trouble (low immediate rewards/high immediate costs) if you believe that things will improve (forecasted rewards).

---

social exchange theory. A theory that claims people make decisions on the basis of assessing and comparing the costs and rewards.

immediate costs and rewards. Those costs and rewards that are associated with a relationship at the present moment in time.

forecasted costs and rewards. The costs and rewards that an individual assumes will occur on the basis of projection and prediction.

Another reason people remain in ongoing relationships during periods of low immediate rewards has to do with cumulative rewards and costs. **Cumulative costs and rewards** represent the total rewards and costs accrued during the duration of the relationship. Just as with your finances, when you have greater income than expense, you put your extra money in savings. Analogously, you build up a relational savings account of the extra rewards. You can draw on that savings account during times when the relationship is not paying off well. You hold on to a relationship because you have invested a lot in it and have gotten a lot out of it. However, just as your savings account can run out of money, so can cumulative rewards, and at that point you might decide to terminate the relationship.

You can also consider rewards and costs in terms of their magnitude and the ratio. Suppose you have two friends, Kelsey and Moira. Kelsey makes you feel good about yourself, is helpful, and is lots of fun (rewards) but she is very needy and demanding (costs). Moira is lots of fun and helpful, but she is also needy. Which friendship would you pursue more? You might be inclined to pursue the relationship with Kelsey, because she is helpful, fun, and makes you feel good, whereas Moira is only fun and helpful. The magnitude of the rewards is greater with Kelsey than Moira. However, you might pursue a relationship with Moira because that relationship has a better ratio of rewards to costs (two rewards to one cost compared to Kelsey's three rewards to two costs). You might think that further developing a relationship with Moira might result in increased rewards with the same costs. However, relationships seem to have some point where there is maximum return for the investment; that is, a point where no matter how much you invest either the reward does not increase further or the costs increase significantly. Suppose you have a casual friend with whom your only shared interest is movies. Once a week you have a very rewarding visit with this friend about the latest releases. You decide to spend more time with this friend (cost) and find awkward dead spots in the conversation because there isn't really anything else of mutual interest to talk about (reward). In terms of your relationship with Moira, this means that having fun with her and getting her help is the only reward you will gain regardless of how much you invest in the relationship.

Finding that point where you maximize your rewards while minimizing costs is one challenge of relational development. You've probably been confronted with trying to decide whether to date someone whom you regarded as a friend. Your decision was probably a desire to see if you could increase the amount of reward. You or your partner might have been hesitant to change the relationship for fear that you might lose everything (similar to going bankrupt because of a bad investment). Decisions to spend more time with a given individual are usually attempts to garner more rewards; if we find the costs increase as well, we might reduce the time together.

The example of deciding between time with Kelsey or Moira reflects how people apply social exchange principles to relational decision-making by comparing relationships. We can compare a current relationship to previous relationships, ideal relationships, and potential relationships.[26] We hate to hear someone tell us, "You're just like my previous boyfriend" or "You're different from my last girlfriend; she was wild." Most of us are sensitive enough not to voice such comparisons, but nonetheless it seems to be a natural thing to do. One way to judge the value of a relationship is in terms of how it stacks up with other relationships you have experienced. You might savour a particular friendship because it is more rewarding than any other relationship you have had.

cumulative costs and rewards. The total costs and rewards accrued during the duration of a relationship.

expected costs and rewards. The templates we have for how much reward we should get from a given relationship in comparison to its costs.

dialectical theory. A theory that says relational development occurs in conjunction with various tensions that exist in all relationships, particularly connectedness versus autonomy, predictability versus novelty, and openness versus closedness.

People seem to construct templates in their minds for what relationships should be like. **Expected costs and rewards** represent expectations and ideals about how rewarding a relationship should be relative to its costs. We have a model of the ideal friend, the ideal lover, the ideal co-worker, and so on. We use the expected costs and rewards associated with these ideals to assess current relationships. We might abandon a relationship if we don't think it matches or has the potential to match our ideal. In essence, we set standards or criteria for our relationships by which we assess the desirability of a given relationship. Like Duck's filtering process, ideal images allow you to sort through relationships and focus on those that are closest to or exceed your ideal. The major difficulty associated with such comparisons rests in setting reasonable standards or ideals. For example, some parents adopt a philosophy of never arguing in front of their children. As the children become adults, they may have an expectation that happy marriages are ones that have no conflicts and thus evaluate their own marriages as a failure to reach their ideal. Continual disappointment in the ability to find relationships that measure up to your ideals suggests that you may need to reassess your standards.

Finally, we compare our current relationships to the rewards and costs we forecast for other potential relationships—this is where we leave someone for another person. We reduce our time spent with one friend when we believe we can have a more rewarding relationship with another person. Although we all dislike having someone "dump" us for another person, one way we assess the value of a given relationship is by how it compares to other prospects. You choose to spend time with some friends more than others because of how those relationships compare. You try to spend the most time with those relationships that have the best relative outcomes.

All these comparisons work in concert with one another. We compare our current relationships to previous ones, to the ideal, and to potential ones. For example, communication researchers Gerald Miller and Malcolm Parks have proposed that we will move quickly to terminate a relationship if it falls below our expectations and we think we have an opportunity to develop a new relationship that has the potential to exceed all of our expectations.[27]

Dialectical Theory

Dialectical theory looks at the human condition in terms of a set of opposing forces. When applied to interpersonal relationships, we can identify forces pulling us toward intimacy and opposing forces pulling us toward independence. Researcher Leslie Baxter has identified three dialectical tensions that have been widely used in interpersonal research.[28]

- *Connectedness versus autonomy.* We desire to connect with others and to become interdependent at the same time we have a desire to remain autonomous and independent. In one study of married couples, these desires to be connected and autonomous were found to be the most frequently occurring of the dialectical tensions.[29]
- *Predictability versus novelty (certainty versus uncertainty).* Knowing what to expect and being able to predict the world around us helps us reduce the tension that occurs from uncertainty. At the same time, we get bored by constant repetition and routine and therefore are attracted to novelty and the unexpected. This might explain why people relish horror movies where the unexpected jumps out at them. Fright becomes joyful because it meets a need for the unexpected.

- *Openness versus closedness.* We wish we could disclose information to others and to hear those we are attracted to disclose to us. One ideal we seem to have in relationships is the ability to be totally open with our partner. However, we also value our privacy and feel a desire to hold back information. Research conducted by one of your authors has found that the number one way that people adapt content in interactions is to hold back or modify information.[30] This tension was identified in the study of married couples mentioned earlier as the most important of the three tensions, although it did not occur as often as the other two tensions.[31]

According to the dialectical theory, each pair of tensions is present in every relationship but the impact of each polar force changes as a relationship progresses. Movement in relationships can be seen as a shift that occurs in the relative pull of one tension. For example, when you begin developing a new friendship, one issue you have to address is whether you want to give up some of your autonomy (freedom to do your own things) in order to spend time with this other person (connectedness). Notice how this is similar to social exchange theory in that you weigh costs (giving up autonomy) against rewards (becoming connected).

Both forces of autonomy and connectedness can be found even in close relationships.[32] Even though long-married couples have usually settled the issues of interdependence versus independence, dialectical theory asserts (and the research mentioned earlier supports) that tension is present from these forces. Generally, such tension diminishes as we become more intimate; however, many an engagement has been called off at the last minute because of the inability of the bride or groom to resolve this tension. This tension represents the challenge faced by individuals forming close relationships who are faced with maintaining their own identities, while at the same time melding their identity with another person.

Movement in relationships can be seen as moments during the developmental process in which some element of tension has been resolved or overcome.[33] For example, during the initial stages of a relationship you are restrained in your self-disclosures (closedness). As long as you remain closed, the relationship can only progress so far. You are confronted with the question of whether or not you should share information and increase the level of intimacy in the relationship. Thus a tension exists until you make your decision. Once you have decided, some of the tension is relieved. Thus if you decide on more openness, the reduction in tension is accompanied by a change in the relationship.

Both of these theories provide some framework to understand development and changes in relationships. However, these theories do not provide us with all the answers. People become involved, maintain, and end relationships for a wide variety of reasons. In the next chapter, we will examine relationships more closely, including how they develop, as well as offer skills for starting, maintaining, and ending relationships.

Dialectical theory posits that a tension exists between our desire for predictability and our attraction to the unexpected.
(Private Collection / Christian Pierre/Superstock)

Summary

As a system, an interpersonal relationship is a set of interconnected elements in which a change in one element affects all the others. The process nature of relationships means they are constantly changing. They can be considered relationships of circumstance when they occur, because surrounding conditions cause you to interact with someone. In contrast, you create relationships of choice when you intentionally seek to establish a relationship you could otherwise avoid.

We can also distinguish among relationships by looking at the degrees of trust, intimacy, and power in each one. Although there are many types of trust, interpersonal trust generally involves a belief that we can disclose information about ourselves to another person because he or she accepts who we are and is committed to the relationship. Intimacy is the degree to which our sense of self is accepted and confirmed by another person. Power is the degree to which we can influence another in the direction we desire.

Before you interact with a stranger or during your first interactions, you might experience short-term initial attraction, but as a relationship develops, you form more long-term maintenance attraction. Elements that influence our feelings of attraction include physical appeal; credibility, competence, and charisma; proximity; similarity; complementary needs; relationship potential; and reciprocation of liking. As interpersonal attraction increases, we self-disclose to the other person. Self-disclosure is a building block for intimacy. Increases or decreases in the amount of self-disclosure reflect changes in a relationship. Two models relate self-disclosure to the development of relationships. The social penetration model shows the depth and breadth of what we disclose to different people. The four quadrants in the Johari Window (OPEN, HIDDEN, UNKNOWN, and BLIND), reflect how much information we, and others, know about ourselves. As we develop relationships, the sizes of the quadrants in these windows change relative to one another.

Two theories that explain relationship development are social exchange theory and dialectical theory. Social exchange theory posits that we make decisions about becoming more or less intimate on the basis of the rewards and costs associated with the relationship. This decision is done in concert with forecasted and cumulative rewards and costs as well as in comparison with previous, potential, and ideal relationships. Dialectical theory sees our decisions being based on resolution of competing forces in our lives, particularly connectedness versus autonomy, predictability versus novelty, and openness versus closedness. As these forces are addressed, we move either toward or away from intimacy in our relationships.

For Discussion and Review

Focus on Comprehension

1. Distinguish relationships of circumstance from relationships of choice.
2. Define trust, intimacy, and power.
3. List and explain the seven elements of interpersonal attraction.

Chapter 10   Understanding Interpersonal Relationships

4. What are the elements of social exchange theory that people use in evaluating relationships?
5. What are the tensions that exist in relationships, according to dialectical theory?

Focus on Critical Thinking

6. Under what circumstances is it inappropriate for a person to use the power he or she has over another person to satisfy personal goals?
7. What is the relationship between interpersonal attraction and self-disclosure?
8. Under what circumstances in an intimate relationship might a person's OPEN quadrant in a relationship with another person actually become smaller?

Focus on Ethics

9. How can you judge whether information that has been disclosed to you is privileged and private information not to be shared with others? When is it okay to tell other people what you know about someone?
10. Under what conditions is it ethical or unethical to approach (a) a co-worker, (b) a subordinate, or (c) a superior to develop an interpersonal relationship because you feel attracted to him or her?

For Your Journal

1. Monitor a face-to-face, four-minute-long conversation between two or three of your friends. You should play the role of a quiet observer. Write down all of the ways in which your friends attempted to gain or concede power during the interaction. Include examples of the language they used and the non-verbal cues they exchanged.
2. At the end of a day, reflect upon your interactions with others. For each interaction you can recall, write down what you disclosed. What factors affected what you chose to disclose? How did the differences in your relationships with the various people involved affect your decisions about self-disclosure?

Learning with Others

1. Create two lists of names: people you regard as casual friends and people you regard as close friends. Identify what attracts you to the people on your list. Compare what attracts you to your casual and close friends with other students. How does your list fit with the categories for attraction identified in the text? What's different? What's the same?
2. *Johari Window Exercise*[34] The purpose of this exercise is to help you understand the Johari Window as presented in this chapter. In essence, we are asking you to construct a Johari Window for a group in which you participate. Of course, you should realize that the impression you have of the others and the

impression they have of you may be based on only a very brief opportunity to meet with one another. Your instructor will give you additional suggestions for completing this activity.

a. Form groups of three to five people.
b. Check five or six adjectives from the following list that best describe your personality as you see it.
c. Select three or four adjectives that describe the personality of each person in your group and write them on separate sheets of paper. Distribute these lists to the appropriate group members.
d. Fill in square number A ("known to self and known to others") with adjectives from the list that both you and at least one other member of your group have selected to describe your personality.
e. Fill in square number B ("not known to self but known to others") with those adjectives others in your group used to describe you, but you did not use to describe yourself.
f. Fill in square number C ("known to self but not to others") with adjectives you have used to describe yourself, but no one else used to describe you.

able	dependable	intelligent	patient	sensible
accepting	dignified	introverted	powerful	sentimental
adaptable	energetic	kind	proud	shy
bold	extroverted	knowledgeable	quiet	silly
brave	friendly	logical	reflective	spontaneous
calm	giving	loving	relaxed	sympathetic
caring	happy	mature	religious	tense
cheerful	helpful	modest	responsive	trustworthy
clever	idealistic	nervous	searching	warm
complex	independent	observant	self-assertive	wise
confident	ingenious	organized	self-conscious	witty

Weblinks

www-ai.ijs.si/eliza/eliza.html This site is called "Eliza." You can ask your new "friend" Eliza questions and Eliza will answer.

www.isspr.org/ This is the site for the International Society for the Study of Interpersonal Relationships. This association is dedicated to research on all areas of interpersonal relationships.

www.womentodaymagazine.com This is the site for *Women Today* magazine. It features many articles about relationships.

www.potsdam.edu/COUN/brochures/loneliness.html This is an online brochure about loneliness and some suggestions to reduce and cope with loneliness.

Suggested Readings

Brehm, S. *Intimate Relationships.* New York: Random House, 1995.
   This is a well-written overview of contemporary research about love and relationships.

Buss, D. M. et al. "International Preferences in Selecting Mates: A Study of 37 Cultures." *Journal of Cross-Cultural Psychology,* 21 (1990): 5–47.
   Is mutual attraction a necessary characteristic for a love relationship? Read about the most desired characteristics of a spouse across 37 cultures.

Dutton, Don and Arthur Aron. "Some Evidence for Heightened Sexual Attraction under Conditions of High Anxiety." *Journal of Personality and Social Psychology,* 24 (1974): 510–517.
   This is a classic study about interpersonal attraction done on the Capilano Bridge in British Columbia.

chapter 11

Developing and Maintaining Interpersonal Relationships

After you study this chapter you should be able to...

1. Explain the model of the stages of relational development.
2. Discuss the skills for starting relationships.
3. Identify and describe effective interpersonal communication skills and strategies for escalating, maintaining, and ending relationships.
4. Discuss the potential responses to relational problems.
5. Identify some of the causes for relational de-escalation and termination.
6. Compare face-to-face communication with computer-mediated communication.
7. Describe principles for using computer-mediated communication to initiate and maintain relationships.
8. Describe principles of upward, downward, horizontal, and outward communication.
9. Identify the characteristics of an effective leader and follower in an organization.

- Stages of Interpersonal Relationships
- Skills for Starting Relationships
- Interpersonal Communication Skills for Escalating and Maintaining Relationships
- De-Escalating and Ending Relationships
- Interpersonal Relationships on the Internet
- Interpersonal Relationships at Work

> *Love is not only something you feel. It is something you do.*
>
> DAVID WILKERSON

Jean: Hi. It's André, isn't it? We met at Mary Lynn's party, remember? It's good to see you again.

André: Sure, sure. I was hoping we'd run into each other again. How are you?

Jean: I'm fine. I've really been busy, though. I have a new job, and my parents have been in town visiting.

André: You do sound busy. What's the new job?

Jean: I'm working on some web page development projects for the university. What have you been up to?

André: Not much. How was the visit with your parents?

Jean: It was great. I had the chance to show them some of my favourite parts of town, like places I like to take walks and little coffee houses. They even came and watched me bowl with my league team. How's your job?

André: About the same as always. Well, I need to head out; I'll catch you again some time.

This interaction is the second encounter between André and Jean. In this interaction, who do you think is more interested in the other? How equal do you see the power between the two people? Who discloses the most?

In Chapter 10 we discussed why we are attracted to certain other people, how we communicate that attraction, and how we self-disclose to provide a foundation for greater intimacy. In this final chapter we explore **relational development**, the discernible stages relationships go through as they move toward or away from intimacy. We will also explore two special places where we develop relationships: the Internet and the workplace.

relational development. The process of moving from one stage to another as a relationship moves toward or away from greater intimacy.

Stages of Interpersonal Relationships

Although researchers use different terms and different numbers of stages, all agree that relational development does proceed in discernible stages. Understanding these stages is important to your studies because interpersonal communication is affected by the stage of the relationship. Individuals in an intimate stage discuss topics and display non-verbal behaviours that do not appear in the early stages of a relationship. We use interpersonal communication to move a relationship forward as we proceed from acquaintances, to friends, to lovers. Outsiders usually can tell what stage a relationship is in by observing the interpersonal communication.

We can think of the stages, from first meeting to intimacy, as the floors in a highrise. Relational development is an elevator that stops at every floor. As you get to each floor, you might get off and wander around for a while before taking the elevator to the next floor (see Figure 11.1). Each time you get on, you don't know how many floors up the elevator will take you, or how long you will stay at any given floor. In fact, sometimes you will never get back on the elevator, electing instead to stay at a particular stage of relational development. But, if you fall head over heels in love, you might want to move quickly from floor to floor toward intimacy. Part of the time you share this elevator with your partner, and the two of you make decisions about how high you will ride the elevator, how long to stay at each floor, and when and whether to ride the down elevator.

Just as there are lights on a panel to let us know the elevator has moved from one floor to another, we have markers that signal a move from one stage to another. These markers are called turning points. **Turning points** are specific

turning point. A specific event or interaction associated with positive or negative changes in a relationship.

**Figure 11.1
Elevator Model of
Relational Stages**

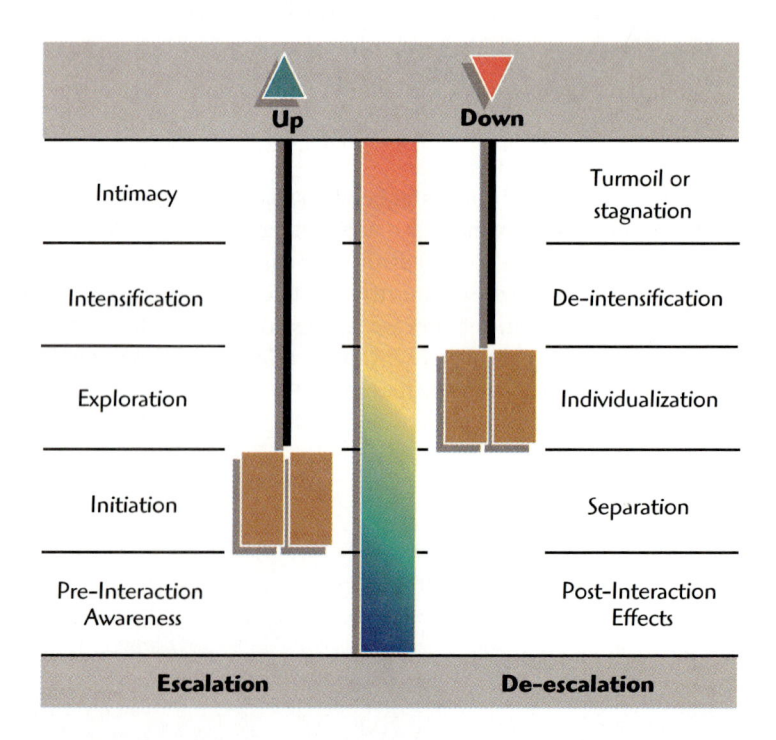

events or interactions that are associated with positive or negative changes in a relationship.[1] A first meeting, first date, first kiss, first sex, saying "I love you" for the first time, meeting a partner's family, going away together somewhere, making up after a conflict, moving in together, providing help in a crisis, or providing a favour or gift might all be turning points that indicate a relationship is moving forward. Two researchers found that, 55 percent of the time, these turning points inspired a discussion about the nature of the relationship.[2] Such discussion helps the partners reach mutual agreement about the definition of the relationship.

Relational Escalation

As you can see in the model in Figure 11.1, in a **relational escalation** the first floor is the *pre-interaction awareness stage*. Here, you might observe someone or even talk with others about him or her without having any direct interaction. Gaining information about others without directly interacting with them is a passive strategy for acquiring knowledge.[3] Through your passive observations, you form an initial impression. You might not move beyond the pre-interaction awareness stage if that impression is not favourable or the circumstances aren't right.

If you are attracted to the other person and the circumstances are right, you might proceed to the *initiation stage*, one of the first turning points in a relationship. In this stage, the interaction typically is routine; you might each respond to a large number of standard questions during the first four minutes of conversation,[4] sticking to safe and superficial topics, and presenting a "public self" to the other person. Your partner is now riding on the elevator with you, and any decision about whether the elevator should go up, down, or nowhere is a mutual one for the rest of the ride. You can never return to the initiation stage. Once you make an initial contact, you have created a relational history on which you will continue to build.

If you decide to go to the next floor, *exploration*, you will begin to share more in-depth information about yourselves. But you will have little physical contact, maintain your social distance, and limit the amount of time you spend together. This stage can occur in conjunction with the initiation stage.

If you proceed to the *intensification stage*, you will start to depend upon each other for self-confirmation and engage in more risky self-disclosure. You will spend more time together, increase the variety of activities you share, adopt a more personal physical distance, engage in more physical contact, and personalize your language. Also, in this stage you may often discuss and redefine the relationship, perhaps putting a turning-point label on yourselves such as "going steady," "good buddies," or "best friends." Other turning points associated with this stage include decisions to date each other exclusively, to become roommates, or to spend time with each other's family.

The top floor in the building is the *intimacy stage*. In this stage the two partners turn to each other for confirmation and acceptance of their self-concept. Their communication is highly personalized and synchronized. They talk about anything and everything. There is a free flow of information and self-disclosure. There is a commitment to maintaining the relationship that might even be formalized through marriage or some other agreement. The partners share an understanding of one another's language and non-verbal cues, and have a great deal of physical contact. They use fewer words to communicate effectively, and they have a clearer definition of their roles and of the relationship. Reaching this stage takes time—time to build trust, time to share personal information, time to observe each other in various situations, and time to build a commitment and an emotional bond.

relational escalation. The upward movement of a relationship toward intimacy through five stages: pre-interaction awareness, initiation, exploration, intensification, and intimacy.

As couples proceed from exploration to intensification, they have more physical contact and begin sharing more activities and confidences. Does it seem as if this couple is heading into the intensification stage? (Sandra Rice)

Building Your Skills

GRAPHING YOUR RELATIONSHIP CHANGES

Think of an interpersonal relationship that you have had for at least a year. On the graph at right, plot the development of that relationship from stage to stage reflecting the relative amount of time you spent in each stage. You can also indicate whether you backed up to a previous stage at any point.

If possible, have your relational partner fill out a similar graph and compare your perceptions of how the relationship has developed. What differences are there, and why? You also might want to share your graph and those of classmates to compare how different relationships develop. What can you tell from the graphs about the nature of their relationships?

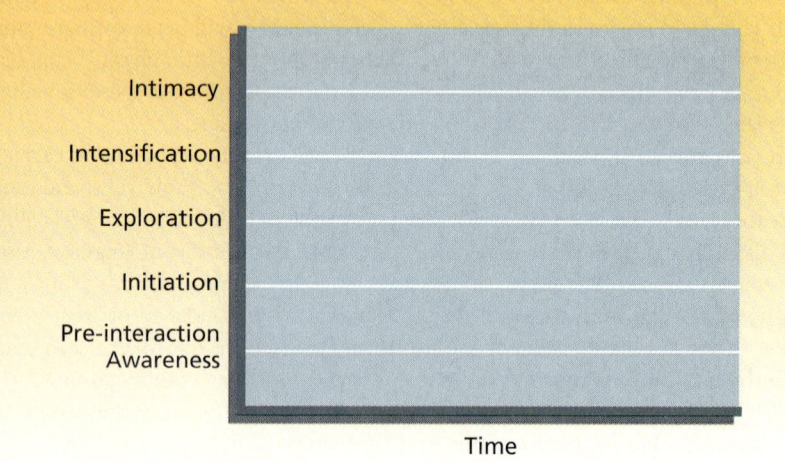

Relational De-Escalation

Sometimes, for a variety of reasons, you might decide that you want to leave an intimate relationship. But, as you may already know, the process of ending it is not as simple as going down the same elevator you came up on; it is not a reversal of the formation stage.[5]

In a **relational de-escalation**, when an intimate relationship is not going well, it usually enters the *turmoil* or *stagnation stage*. Turmoil involves an increase in conflict, as one or both partners tend to find more faults in the other. The definition of the relationship seems to lose its clarity, and mutual acceptance declines. The communication climate is tense and exchanges are difficult.

Stagnation occurs when the relationship loses its vitality and the partners become complacent. Communication and physical contact between the partners decrease; they spend less time together, but do not necessarily fight. Partners in a stagnating relationship tend to go through the motions of an intimate relationship without the commitment; they simply follow their established relational routines.

As with the up elevator, individuals can stop at this point on the down elevator and decide to quit descending. The relationship can remain in turmoil or stagnate for a long time, or the individuals can repair, redefine, or revitalize the relationship and return to intimacy.

If the turmoil or stagnation continues, however, the individuals might move down to the *de-intensification stage*, decreasing their interactions; increasing their physical, emotional, and psychological distance; and decreasing their dependence upon the other for self-confirmation. They might discuss the definition of their relationship, question its future, and assess each partner's level of satisfaction or dissatisfaction. The relationship can be repaired and the individuals can move back up to intensification and intimacy, but that is more difficult to accomplish now.

On the next floor down, the *individualization stage*, the partners tend to define their lives more as individuals and less as a couple. Neither views the other as a partner or significant other anymore. Interactions are limited. The perspective changes from "we" and "us" to "you" and "me," and property is defined in terms of "mine" or "yours" rather than "ours." Both partners turn to others for confirming their self-concepts.

In the *separation stage*, individuals make an intentional decision to eliminate further interpersonal interaction. If they share custody of children, attend mutual family gatherings, or work in the same office, the nature of their interactions will change. They will divide property, resources, and friends. Early interactions in this stage are often tense and difficult, especially if the relationship has been intimate. For relationships that never went beyond exploration or intensification, however, the negotiation is often relatively painless.

For former intimates, one of the awkward things about separating is their extensive personal knowledge about one another. Their talk is limited to superficial things, though they still know a lot about each other. This tends to make the interactions fairly uncomfortable. Over time, of course, each partner knows less about who the other person has become. For example, even after spending just a few years away from your high school friends, you might have difficulty interacting with them because the knowledge you both share is out of date.

relational de-escalation. The downward movement of a relationship away from intimacy through five stages: turmoil or stagnation, de-intensification, individualization, separation, and post-interaction.

Although interaction may cease altogether, the effect of the relationship is not over. Our relational stages highrise is like something out of the TV series, *Twilight Zone:* once you enter it, you can never leave it. The bottom floor on the down elevator, where you remain, is the *post-interaction effects stage.* This floor represents the lasting effects the relationship has on your self, and, therefore, on your other interactions and relationships. Steve Duck claims that in this final stage of terminating relationships we engage in "grave-dressing."[6] We create a public statement for people who ask why we broke up and also come to grips with losing the relationship. Sometimes our sense of self gets battered during the final stages of a relationship, and we have to work hard to regain a healthy sense of self.

Of course, we are all aware of people who hop on an express elevator to get out of a relationship, bypassing all the normal stages of decline. One study found that of all the various ways to terminate a relationship, abandoned partners most dislike the quick exit without discussion.[7] For the rest of this chapter, we will explore the skills for starting relationships and for escalating and maintaining relationships, and then examine the ending of relationships.

Skills for Starting Relationships

In Chapter 10 and in this chapter, we have seen how relationships progress toward intimacy and we have seen what helps make them grow. The movement from initial attraction to initiation of interaction is not always an easy one. There is a lot of uncertainty and apprehension involved in approaching a stranger and starting a conversation. The following section explains some of the principles to follow as you interact with others for the first time.

We can learn the skills that can help us reduce the interpersonal tensions that most of us feel at the start of a relationship. (B. Daemmrich/The Image Works)

Gather Information to Reduce Uncertainty

Meeting strangers and starting relationships is rarely easy. We all seem to share a fear of the unknown, which includes interacting with strangers whose behaviour we cannot predict. The research team of Charles Berger, Richard Calabrese, and James Bradac developed a theory to explain relational development.[8] Their **uncertainty reduction theory** is based on one basic cause–effect assumption: We like to have control and predictability in our lives; therefore, when we are faced with uncertainty, we are driven to gain information to reduce that uncertainty. Reducing uncertainty requires using a number of skills we have already covered, but primarily depends on effective perception and active listening. You need to gather as much information as you can about your partner to increase predictability and reduce anxiety.

We all are most comfortable in predictable situations, because we can call on familiar strategies to handle the situation. In initial interactions we often follow predictable, scripted behaviour that reduces uncertainty. What if you approached a stranger and said, "Hello," and the stranger responded by saying, "Bananas"? You would probably feel a little leery. You would feel even more uneasy if you then asked for the stranger's name, only to get the same reply, "Bananas." At this point you'd probably look for the nearest exit. If a person's response does not follow the normal initiation script, it might create so much anxiety that you will stop interacting.

Usually, however, we reduce uncertainty by gathering either cognitive or behavioural information about others.[9] Cognitive information relates to thoughts, attitudes, and opinions. Behavioural information relates to reactions and remarks in various situations. As you have seen, you gather some of this information during the pre-interaction stage of a relationship through observations and conversations with others who know the person. Later, you can directly observe the other's behaviours in interactions with him or her, and also ask direct questions. Usually people gather behavioural information through observation and cognitive information through interactions.

We are particularly motivated to gain information early in a relationship when uncertainty is greatest, and when we are trying to evaluate the predicted outcome

uncertainty reduction theory. A theory that claims people seek out information in order to reduce uncertainty, thus providing control and predictability.

Building Your Skills

ANXIETY LEVEL AND FAMILIARITY

Write down at least 10 different social situations you can recall having been in, such as attending weddings, funerals, or ball games; going to your grandmother's for dinner; visiting your best friend's parents for the first time; or meeting your new roommate. Next to each one, indicate how nervous you felt in that situation. Use a scale from 1 to 10, with 1 being calm and cool, and 10 being highly apprehensive. After you have rated each situation, go back and rate each one on how familiar or unfamiliar the situation was. Again use a scale of 1 to 10, with 1 being very familiar and 10 being very unfamiliar.

According to uncertainty reduction theory, there should be a strong correlation between your level of anxiety and the level of familiarity. Which situations caused the most anxiety? To what degree did your unfamiliarity with the situation affect your level of anxiety? What were you most uncertain about in each situation? In which situations were you most comfortable and why? Did you feel uncomfortable under some circumstances even though the situation was familiar? Why?

value.[10] We also are likely to seek out information if others behave in an unexpected way.[11] If your close friend who watches *South Park* every night suddenly begins reading during that time slot, you will probably ask why. Whether the friend shares with you what is going on will depend on how comfortable he or she is in revealing information about him- or herself.

Adopt an Other-Oriented Perspective

When, as a child, you were frightened by an encounter with a wild animal or a neighbour's pet, your parents probably told you, "It's just as afraid of you as you are of it." These words reflect an other-orientation and are useful to remember when we encounter new people as well. For all of us, meeting someone for the first time generally produces some degree of anxiety. When this happens to you, try to remember what other people did to make you comfortable in past encounters. They probably smiled a lot, actively listened, showed interest in you but didn't put you on the spot, disclosed information about themselves, and kept the conversation light. Try to use these techniques yourself to put your partner at ease.

Also, try to think about how you appear to the other person. If, for instance, you are speaking to someone you just hired, he or she may feel nervous and uncomfortable because of the power and status differences between you. Do your best to minimize the differences; for example, sit in chairs that face each other without a desk between you. In general, try to apply all the information that you have and that you observe about the other person to make decisions about your own behaviour. Don't just react; take the initiative to make the first interaction pleasant and satisfying to you both.

Observe and Act upon Approachability Cues

Subway riders learn to avoid eye contact because it is a signal for approachability. Other ways we can signal approachability include sustaining eye contact, turning toward another person, smiling, being animated (versus sitting very still), taking an open body posture, winking, and waving. In the absence of these cues, we generally conclude that a person wants to be left alone.

Sometimes circumstances prevent us from exchanging approachability cues. The seating arrangements in your class, for example, might discourage non-verbal exchanges. So, instead, you may try to develop some sensitivity to the way other people respond to your greetings. Saying "Hello" lets people know that you are approachable, and it tests approachability. If the other person responds with a warm smile and a few words, such as, "Have you finished today's assignment yet?" then the door might be open for further interaction. But if the person gives you a silent half smile and hurries on, you can take this as a signal that the door is closed.

Identify and Use Conversation Starters

We all give off a certain amount of "free" information that others can easily observe. You can use that information as a starting point for a conversation. Noting that someone is wearing a T-shirt from Jasper National Park, for example, you can ask when she or he went there and how she or he liked it. If someone is walking a dog of the same breed as your childhood pet, you can approach him or her to discuss the breed's peculiarities. If someone is carrying a book from a class you took last semester, ask him or her how the course is going.

Follow Initiation Norms

Many of the early interactions in a relationship are almost ritualistic, or at least scripted. In our culture, when two strangers meet for the first time they typically follow this pattern of conversation:[12]

Greetings:	Say "Hello," "Hi," or "How are you?"
Introductions:	Exchange names and pleasantries.
Topic 1:	Discuss the present situation or weather.
Topic 2:	Discuss current or past residences (where they live, home town, etc.).
Topic 3:	Determine whether they know people in common.
Topic 4:	Discuss their educational backgrounds or occupations.
Topic 5:	Discuss general topics such as TV, movies, music, family, sports, books, and/or travel.
Discuss Further Meeting (Optional):	Say something like, "Let's get together some time."
Exchange Pleasantries:	Say, "Nice to meet you," "Hope to see you again," and so on.
Close Conversation:	Indicate the intent to end the conversation with such statements as, "See you later," "Got to go to class now," or "Give me a call."
Good-byes:	Make final statements, "Bye," and move in different directions.

Following the script provides some comfort and security because both partners are able to reduce the level of uncertainty. If you deviate too much from this script, you might undermine your partner's sense of security and discourage him or her from pursuing a relationship.

As you follow the script, however, you should take advantage of opportunities to expand and develop the conversation in safe ways. Listen for details about the person's background and interests that you can inquire about, and share information about your own interests.

Provide Information about Yourself

Disclosing information about yourself allows the other person to make an informed decision about whether or not to continue the relationship. Remember, both of you need to be in a position to make such a decision. You might have found out what you want and decided that you have a lot in common with the other person, but he or she might not have reached that same point. However, you need to be careful not to violate the script or cultural expectations about what is appropriate to disclose in an initial conversation. You have probably had the experience of someone you have just met telling you his or her problems. As we mentioned earlier, such disclosures usually alienate the other, rather than advancing the relationship.

Present Yourself in a Positive Way

This may seem like a pretty obvious strategy. We tend to find people attractive who have positive self-images. And, as we have mentioned, it is also against our cultural norms to disclose negative information early on in a relationship. Do not try to provide false information about yourself, but simply be selective about the information you share. Also, keep in mind that we all have weaknesses and foibles, so the person interacting with you is probably also attempting to present a positive image. Practise the social decentring process you learned in Chapter 2 to think about the other person's thoughts and feelings as you listen to what he or she puts forward for your consideration. Being kind and responsive will win you more points than trying to act sarcastic and clever.

You can increase the likelihood of a positive response from other people toward you by engaging in appropriate non-verbal cues that communicate a friendly attitude. Such cues include the following:[13]

Proximity:	Move closer and lean forward if you are seated.
Orientation:	Sit directly in front of or closely beside the person.
Gaze:	Look the person in the eyes, especially when he or she looks at you.
Facial Expression:	Smile.
Gestures:	Nod your head; use lively movements.
Posture:	Keep an open posture, with your arms stretched toward the other person, rather than placing your arms on your hips or folding them.
Touch:	Touch the person in a friendly, non-sexual way.
Tone of Voice:	Raise your pitch; speak with a rising inflection and clear, pure tone.

Want to increase the likelihood of getting a positive response from others at a mixer? Look into the other person's eyes, smile, nod your head, and speak with a clear, pure tone. (Barbara Alper/Stock Boston)

Ask Questions

Asking questions will accomplish two goals: first, it will help you learn about the other person, and second, it will let the other person know that you are interested in her or him. Keep your questions open and non-invasive; don't interrogate the other person. Focus on things you know you have in common and that are safe. Use the situation as a resource for questions. For example, if you are standing in line to purchase tickets for an upcoming rock concert, you could ask the person next to you how he or she got interested in the group, which of their songs he or she likes best, how many live concerts he or she has seen, and so on.

Don't Expect Too Much from the Initial Interaction

Initial interactions do not necessarily determine the future of a relationship. In movies, such as *The Matrix,* initial interactions between the hero and the heroine are often brusque and unfriendly, but after sharing traumatic experiences, they eventually find love. Although real life does not usually work this way, keep in mind that the scripted nature of an initial interaction limits the opportunity for you and your partner to achieve an in-depth understanding of one another. Relax and arrange another meeting if you feel the spark of attraction. It will probably take a few interactions before you can make a sound cost-benefit analysis of the relationship.

Initiating conversation is only one step in the process of developing an interpersonal relationship. Later in this chapter, we will learn strategies for strengthening relationships with family members, friends, and colleagues.

▶ Recap

SKILLS FOR STARTING RELATIONSHIPS

Rule		Examples
1.	Gather information to reduce uncertainty.	Ask questions about interests and actively respond.
2.	Adopt an other-oriented perspective.	How does the other person perceive this situation? How would you like to be treated if someone approached you?
3.	Observe and act upon approachability cues.	Watch for smiles, eye contact, or someone turning toward you.
4.	Identify and use conversation starters.	"I see your T-shirt is from Paris. Have you been there?" "Isn't that the new Danielle Steel novel you've got there?"
5.	Follow initiation norms.	Use the script that begins with a greeting, proceeds through a series of socially acceptable topics, and ends in "Good-bye."
6.	Provide information about yourself.	Your name, interests, major, home town, family background.
7.	Present yourself in a positive way.	Be positive in tone. Smile. Tell about your successes and accomplishments without bragging.
8.	Ask questions.	"Where are you from?" "What's that place like?" "What do you do in your spare time?"
9.	Don't expect too much from the initial interaction.	"I've enjoyed talking with you. I'd love to hear more about your summer in Paris some time."

Interpersonal Communication Skills for Escalating and Maintaining Relationships

Initial interaction and attraction do not necessarily determine the success of a relationship. Our lives are filled with interpersonal relationships that are maintained at one of the lower levels of development. On the other hand, having reached even the most intimate stage of development does not mean that we can take a relationship for granted. A considerable amount of skill is needed to maintain intimate relationships.

Two of the most important categories of interpersonal relationships that we develop are friends and lovers. We use these two terms to distinguish relationships that differ in terms of their level of intimacy and sexuality. Both types of relationships are important. Our friendships are one of our most valuable sources of support. In a survey of more than 100 000 men and women, single women rated friends and social life as the most important source of happiness in their lives. Single men rated friends second only to their job duties.[14] Generally, lovers can be classified as relationships in which there is both a high degree of intimacy and attachment as well as sexual activity and/or attraction.[15] Historically, marriage was considered the most intimate relationship, rooted in the goal of procreation and forming a family.[16] Today, gay and lesbian relationships also reflect intimate romantic relationships with relational dynamics similar to heterosexual relationships, including marriage and child rearing.

We can use a variety of skills to escalate and maintain relationships such as tactful self-disclosure, active listening, and adapting. In this section we will cover some of the skills that are needed to move relationships toward intimacy and to maintain relationships at the stage we desire, including the most intimate.

Communicate Attraction

When we are attracted to people, we use both indirect and direct strategies to communicate our liking through non-verbal and verbal cues. Non-verbal immediacy represents those non-verbal cues we display when we are attracted to someone. For instance, we tend to reduce the physical distance between us; increase our eye contact and use of touch; lean forward; keep an open body orientation; and smile. We also use the courtship readiness behaviours, preening behaviours, positional cues, and appeals to invitation described in Chapter 7.

We also indirectly communicate our attraction verbally. We use informal and personal language, addressing the person by his or her first name and often referring to "you and I," and "we." We ask questions to show interest, probe for details when our partner shares information, listen responsively, and refer to information shared in past interactions. All these behaviours confirm that we value what the other person is saying.

We can also directly communicate our attraction verbally. Most of us don't do this very often. But think about how you feel when a friend tells you that he or she likes you. It raises your self-esteem; you feel valued. You can make others feel that way by communicating your liking for them, although in the early stages of relational development, there are social mores against doing so. We verbally communicate liking in other, more subtle ways as well. We might tell someone that we like a particular trait or ability, such as the way she tells jokes, or the way he handled an irritating customer. Or we might compliment someone's outfit, hairstyle, or jewellery. Each of these messages communicates attraction for the other person and is likely to elicit a positive response from him or her.

We also use **affinity-seeking strategies** to get people to like us. Table 11.1 summarizes strategies identified by the research team of Bell and Daly.[17] Deciding

affinity-seeking strategies.
Ways of getting other people to like you.

Table 11.1
Affinity-Seeking Strategies

	Strategies	Examples
1. Control	Present yourself as in control, independent, free-thinking; show that you have the ability to reward the other person.	• "I'm planning on going to grad school, and after that I'm going to Japan to teach English." • "You can borrow my notes for the class you missed if you'd like.
2. Visibility	Look and dress attractively; present yourself as an interesting, energetic, and enthusiastic person; increase your visibility to the other person.	• "Wow, that was a great show about Chinese acrobats. I do gymnastics too. Would you like to come watch me next week in our dual meet?"
3. Mutual Trust	Present yourself as honest and reliable; display trustworthy behaviours; show that you trust the other person by self-disclosing.	• "That guy you're having problems with called me and asked about you. I told him I didn't have anything to say." • "I've never told anyone this, but I've always hoped I could find my birth parents."
4. Politeness	Follow appropriate conversational rules; let the other person assume control of the interaction.	• "I'm sorry. I interrupted. I thought you were done. Please, go on." • "No, you're not boring me at all; it's very interesting. Please tell me more about it."
5. Concern and Caring	Show interest in and ask questions about the other person; listen; show support and be sensitive; help the other person accomplish something or feel good about him- or herself.	• "How is your mother doing after her operation?" • "I'd like to help out at the benefit you're chairing this weekend." • "That must have been really hard for you, growing up under those conditions."
6. Other-Involvement	Put a positive spin on activities you share; draw the other person into your activities; display non-verbal immediacy and involvement with the other person.	• "This is a great party, I'm glad you came along." • "A group of us are going to get a midnight snack; how about coming along?"
7. Self-Involvement	Try to arrange for encounters and interactions; engage in behaviours that encourage the other person to form a closer relationship.	• "Oh hi! I knew your class ended at two, so I thought I'd try to catch you." • "It would really be fun to go camping together this summer; I have this favourite place."
8. Commonalities	Point out similarities between yourself and the other person; try to establish equality (balanced power); present yourself as comfortable and at ease around the other person.	• I've got that computer game too. Don't you love the robots?" • "Let's both work on the project together. We're a great team." • "It's so easy to talk to you. I really feel comfortable around you."

Source: Adapted from R. A. Bell and J. A. Daly, "The Affinity Seeking Function of Communications," *Communication Monographs*, 51 (1984): 91–115.

to display non-verbal immediacy cues or to provide verbal self-confirmation are not only ways we communicate our attraction toward other people, they are also ways of getting other people to like us. Other affinity-seeking strategies include establishing mutual trust, being polite, showing concern and caring, and involving people in our activities. Apparently, these strategies do work. Bell and Daly found that individuals who seemed to use many affinity-seeking strategies were perceived as likeable, socially successful, and satisfied with their lives.[18]

Building Your Skills

AFFINITY SEEKING OBSERVATION

Put yourself in a place where you can observe strangers interacting, such as a party or a student centre. Without violating anybody's privacy, see if you can observe affinity-seeking behaviours or hear what is being said that communicates attraction between interactants. Which of the affinity-seeking strategies seem to be used the most? The least? How do people seem to respond to the affinity-seeking behaviours of their partners?

Monitor Your Perceptions, Listen Actively, and Respond Confirmingly

We have devoted two other chapters to perception and to listening and responding because of their importance to interpersonal communication. The skills we discussed in those chapters are also keys to success in ongoing relationships. If, for example, you can consciously attend to more of the cues you receive from others, you can learn more about how they react to different situations and then shape your relationship maintenance behaviours accordingly. By becoming more sensitive to your biases and working to counterbalance them, you can avoid overreacting to things your partner says and does. If you make a practice of checking the accuracy of your perceptions of others, you can avoid stewing and fretting over imagined slights and misunderstandings.

Listening skills are also crucial for developing and maintaining relationships. Listening clues you into others' needs, wants, and values and it enables you to respond to them in appropriate ways. In the initial stages of a relationship, partners share a great deal of information. The amount of information tapers off in the later stages and as a relationship continues over time. This tapering off creates the illusion that you don't have to listen as much, or as well, as you did early on. But listening is a way to demonstrate ongoing interest in another person. Even in long-term relationships, we do not know everything our partners have to say. It is still important to stop, look, and listen—to put down the newspaper or turn off the radio when our close friend begins talking to us.

You also need to listen actively and provide confirming responses. In Chapter 6 we discussed the notions of confirming and disconfirming responses. Using confirming responses increases your partner's sense of self-worth and communicates the value you place upon him or her. In addition, if you can develop an awareness of the biases that prevent you from responding with empathy, you can work deliberately to overcome them as you ask questions and paraphrase your partner's messages.

Be Open and Self-Disclose Appropriately

In Chapter 10 we wrote about self-disclosure being a critical element for movement toward intimacy. We cannot form truly intimate relationships without mutual self-disclosure. On the other hand, restricting the amount of self-disclosure is one way to control the development of a relationship. If a relationship is moving too fast, you might choose to reduce how much you are self-disclosing as a way to slow the progression of the relationship. In the interaction between Jean and André at the beginning of this chapter, André was apparently choosing to maintain the relationship as an acquaintanceship by restricting his self-disclosure. The level of self-disclosure needs to be appropriate to the level of development, and both partners must be sensitive to the timing of the disclosures. Failing to disclose or disclosing the wrong thing at the wrong time can damage a relationship.

You must also be willing to accept your partner's disclosures. You expect that you can disclose your most private secrets to your intimate partners. You also expect your intimate partners to listen and provide confirming responses to you when you make such disclosures. Imagine what effect it would have on an intimate relationship if your partner turned away from you every time you tried to self-disclose highly personal information. You would become frustrated and disenchanted. The relationship would lose value.

Express Emotions

Expressing emotions is a particular form of self-disclosure and is a skill that can be improved, as discussed in Chapters 5 and 7. Many of us are embarrassed about expressing our feelings, yet sharing feelings at the appropriate time during relational development is one way to continue its escalation. On the other hand, sharing the wrong feelings at the wrong time can have a detrimental effect.

There are two ways we share feelings with our partners. The first includes disclosing information about our past or current emotional states, such as sadness about the death of a family member, or fear about what we will do after we graduate. The second way we share emotions is the direct expression of emotions, such as expressing attraction, love, or disappointment toward our partner. As relationships become more intimate, we have a greater expectation that our partner will disclose emotions openly. The amount of risk associated with such emotional disclosures varies from person to person. Most of us are comfortable sharing positive emotions, such as happiness and joy, but are more reserved about sharing negative emotions, such as fear or disappointment. We might think expressing negative emotions makes us appear weak or vulnerable. In a study of 46 committed, romantic couples, researchers found that the number one problem was the inability to talk about negative feelings.[19] Partners often made the following types of observations: "When she gets upset, she stops talking"; "He never lets me know when he's upset with something he doesn't like"; and "He just silently pouts." We generally want to know how our partners in intimate relationships are feeling, even if those feelings are negative.

On the other hand, a constant barrage of negative expressions can also alienate our partner. Research has found that marital satisfaction rises with the number of positive feelings the partners disclose, not with the number of negative ones.[20] A balance has to be found that includes expressing both positive and negative emotions at the right time in a constructive and confirming manner.

Engage in Relationship Talk

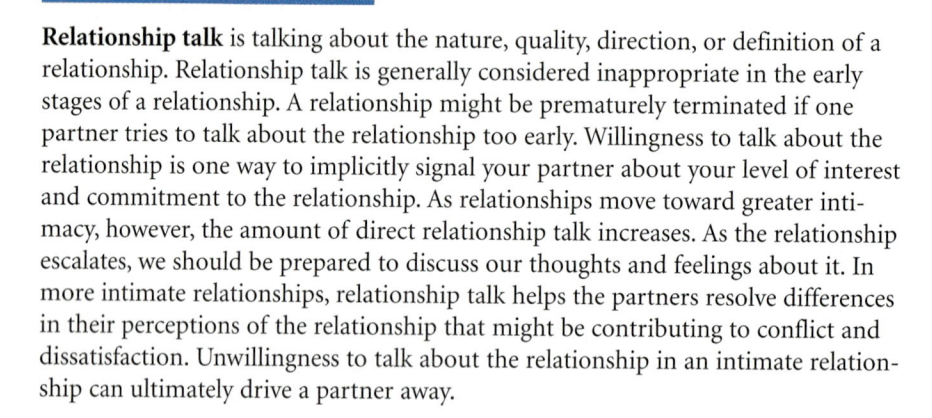

Relationship talk is talking about the nature, quality, direction, or definition of a relationship. Relationship talk is generally considered inappropriate in the early stages of a relationship. A relationship might be prematurely terminated if one partner tries to talk about the relationship too early. Willingness to talk about the relationship is one way to implicitly signal your partner about your level of interest and commitment to the relationship. As relationships move toward greater intimacy, however, the amount of direct relationship talk increases. As the relationship escalates, we should be prepared to discuss our thoughts and feelings about it. In more intimate relationships, relationship talk helps the partners resolve differences in their perceptions of the relationship that might be contributing to conflict and dissatisfaction. Unwillingness to talk about the relationship in an intimate relationship can ultimately drive a partner away.

Socially Decentre and Adapt

The skills covered in Chapter 4 for social decentring, empathizing, and adapting to others enhance both the escalation and maintenance of relationships. Social decentring helps you better understand your partner, which provides you with a basis for

relationship talk. Talking about the nature, quality, direction, or definition of a relationship.

choosing the most effective strategies for accomplishing your communication goals. We have been discussing the notion of "appropriateness" of your behaviours to the effective advancement and maintenance of your relationships. Determining appropriateness depends on your ability to read the situation and your partner, and then to adapt or choose the best behaviours. Essentially, you can either consider what your partner is thinking now, or will think in response to your actions—put yourself in your partner's shoes. For example, suppose you are on a first date and trying to decide whether to tell your partner about a very intimate relationship you had, which just ended. Put yourself in the other person's shoes. Would you want to hear on a first date about someone's recent breakup? What information do you have about your date that can help you determine your date's reaction? As relationships become more intimate, you receive more and more information that can improve decentring and adaptation.

Gaining information about your partners is one way you will be able to make decisions about how to help them in distressing situations. One pair of researchers, Ruth Ann Clark and Jesse Delia, studied how people wanted to be treated by their friends in response to six different distressing situations.[21] Clark and Delia found that there was not a strong desire to talk about the situation and a lot of variation in how people wanted their friends to approach it. When people were distressed, they wanted to be the ones to decide whether to bring up the issue or not. This means that rather than adopting a formulaic approach to distressed friends, you should use your ability to socially decentre and adapt to each one's particular needs. The abilities to provide comfort, social support, and ego support have been found to be associated with being a best friend.[22]

Well-adjusted couples display support and affection for each other through positive non-verbal cues. (Comstock Images)

Be Tolerant and Show Restraint

The most satisfying relationships are those in which both partners refrain from continually disagreeing, criticizing, and making negative comments to each other. Both individuals learn to accept the other and do not feel compelled to continually point out flaws or failures. One study found that well-adjusted couples focus their complaints on specific behaviours, whereas maladjusted couples complain about one another's personal characteristics. Well-adjusted couples are also kinder, more positive, and have more humour in their interactions. The partners tended to agree with one another's complaints, whereas the partners in maladjusted relationships launched counter-complaints.[23] In addition, happy couples, when compared to unhappy couples, display more affection through positive non-verbal cues, display more supportive behaviours, and make more attempts to avoid conflict.[24]

Maintaining a relationship requires tolerance. You must learn to accept your partner for who he or she is and put up with some things you dislike. When couples lose their tolerance, they begin focusing on, and criticizing, characteristics that they used to accept. Then the relationship begins to deteriorate.

Manage Conflict Cooperatively

The final skill for developing and maintaining relationships is to be able to manage conflict. Conflicts are inevitable in interpersonal relationships. As relationships develop, the individuals share more personal information and spend more time together, so the likelihood for conflict increases. The key to successful relational development and maintenance is *not* to avoid conflict altogether, but rather to manage it effectively. Because effective conflict management is a key to successful relationships, we have devoted an entire chapter to it. Because Chapter 8 discussed in detail the nature, causes, and methods of dealing with interpersonal conflict, we will simply mention at this time that using a cooperative management style can actually transform conflict into an experience that strengthens a relationship. It can clarify the definition of the relationship, increase the exchange of information, and create a cooperative atmosphere for problem solving.

Canadian Issues

WHO CHOOSES COMMON-LAW AS A FIRST CONJUGAL RELATIONSHIP?

When looking at the escalation of relationships, many young people choose to live with their lovers rather than to immediately marry them. These common-law relationships are on the increase. Set out below are some findings from a recent Canadian study of these relationships in Canada.

According to this study, which examined common-law relationships in Canada, "common-law unions are proliferating rapidly in Canada, and they are the major factor in the diversification of family behaviours." Common-law couples represented one couple in six in 1995. Quebec reported the most common-law unions with one out of every four couples living common-law. In fact, in Quebec, common law is the choice of the majority for their first conjugal union and is entered into earlier than in any other province. By the age of twenty, 12 percent of never-married Quebec women had already experienced a common-law union, compared to 8 percent of women in other provinces. This study found that Quebec women whose mother language was French were more likely to choose common-law unions. In fact, in other provinces, an analysis of women who spoke French as their mother tongue indicated that "common-law unions are more popular in the French group throughout the country."

Although becoming increasingly popular, common-law relationships are much less stable than traditional marriage relationships. According to this study, 70 percent of common-law unions end in separation within the first five years, with only a small minority of them ending in marriage (the estimate was three in every ten). This same study also estimated that 50 percent of Canadian women born between 1971 and 1980 will likely enter into a common-law relationship. The make-up of relationships is undergoing many transitions, common-law relationships being one of the many significant changes for Canadian families in the late 1990s and early 2000s.

Source: From Pierre Turcotte and Alain Belanger, "The Dynamics of Formation and Dissolution of First Common-Law Unions in Canada," Statistics Canada, 1998, 1–26. Adapted from "Moving in Together: The Formation of First Common-Law Unions," found in *Canadian Social Trends*, Cat. No. 11-008, winter 1997, No. 47.

> ## Recap
>
> ### INTERPERSONAL SKILLS FOR ESCALATING AND MAINTAINING RELATIONSHIPS
>
> | Skill | Example |
> |---|---|
> | Communicate attraction. | "We both like Céline Dion. I have her most recent CD. Perhaps we could listen to it together." |
> | Monitor your perceptions, listen actively, and respond. | "You look kind of sad. What's the matter?" "You've been to the CN Tower? Me too. What was your favourite part?" |
> | Be open and self-disclose appropriately. | "I'm glad you're my friend. I like how easy it is to talk to you." |
> | Express emotions. | "I'm happy you can come to the concert." |
> | Engage in relationship talk. | "I really like how close we are becoming." |
> | Socially decentre and adapt. | "I know it must have been hard for you to go to school when you felt so lousy." |
> | Be tolerant and show restraint. | "I never mentioned my dislike for that hat, because I knew you really liked it." |
> | Manage conflict cooperatively. | "We need to find a solution that both of us feel good about." |

De-Escalating and Ending Relationships

Given the process nature of relationships discussed in Chapter 10, you know that relationships are always changing. Sometimes the change is to a less intimate level, and sometimes it's the complete termination of the relationship. Part of effective relationship management involves being sensitive to cues that signal relational problems or change. As *Understanding Diversity: Gender and Ending Relationships* on page 352 indicates, women usually sense trouble in a relationship earlier than do men—but what exactly do they sense? Because each stage in a relationship has unique communication qualities, specific verbal and non-verbal cues can tip us off when a relationship begins to de-escalate.[25] There is a decrease in touching and physical contact (including less sexual activity), physical proximity, eye contact, smiling, vocal variety in the voice, and ease of interaction. In addition, there is a decrease in the amount of time spent together, an increase in time between interactions, and more separation of possessions. The interactions become less personal, and so does the language.

Understanding Diversity

GENDER AND ENDING RELATIONSHIPS

Men and women differ when it comes to dating and marital breakups. Women tend to be stronger monitors of the relationship, so they usually detect trouble before men do. Women's sensitivity to the health of the relationship may be one factor that makes them more likely to initiate the termination of a relationship as well.[26] However, when some men want out of a relationship, they engage in behaviours that women find totally unacceptable. This allows both partners to feel as if they were the ones who initiated the breakup and therefore lets them "save face."

Relationship-ending problems are sometimes associated with behaviours that appear early in a relationship. Marriages in which the men avoid interaction by stonewalling and responding defensively to complaints are more likely to end in divorce.[27]

In one study of divorce, men tended to see the later part of the process as more difficult, whereas the women said the period before the decision to divorce was more difficult. In addition, two-thirds of the women were likely to discuss marital problems with their children as compared to only one-fourth of the men; and men were twice as likely to say that no one helped them during the worst part of the process.[28]

Couples during de-escalation tend to use fewer intimate terms; they use less present tense and more past tense; they make fewer references to their future in the relationship; they use more qualified language ("maybe," "whatever," "we'll see"); make fewer evaluative statements; and spend less time discussing any given topic. They fight more, and they disclose less. If one person becomes less open about discussing attitudes, feelings, thoughts, and other personal issues, he or she is probably signalling a desire to terminate, or at least redefine, the relationship. Can you pick up the signals of the couple's difficulty reflected in the picture on page 356?

e-connection

BREAKING UP

The end of a romantic relationship has many effects, from emotional upheaval to lengthy introspection. A person's experiences in ending relationships obviously differ a great deal if he or she is the one choosing to end the relationship, rather than a partner choosing to end it. One way people work through their feelings is by writing about their experiences and even sharing them with others. The Internet is becoming a wonderful place where people can be expressive and share their experiences in a fairly safe environment. The following Web address accesses a site about teenagers:

http://teenwriting.about.com

After you log on to the site, type the words "breaking off relationships" into the search engine for a sampling of hundreds of poems written by teenagers about the ending of close relationships. You can also search this site for other writings on starting a new relationship, finding a new love, and a variety of other relational events. Even if you are beyond your teenage years, you may appreciate the feelings and thoughts expressed by people exploring the challenges of interpersonal relationship management.

Responses to Relational Problems

When you pick up signals of relational problems, you have three choices: wait and see what happens; make a decision to end the relationship; or try to repair the relationship. Repairing the relationship involves applying all the maintenance skills we talked about earlier. Some of the strategies for dealing with conflict, which you learned in Chapter 8, will also help you. Underlying the success of any repair effort, however, is the degree to which both partners want to keep the relationship going. The nature of the problem, the stage of the relationship, and the commitment and motivation of the partners all affect the success of repair efforts. There is no single quick solution to relational problems because so many factors influence each one. You need to focus on the specific concerns, needs, and issues that underlie the problem; then adapt specific strategies to resolve it. Professional counselling might be an important option.

What if it is your partner who wants to end the relationship? There is no pat answer for addressing this situation. If a friend stops calling or visiting, should you just assume the relationship is over and leave it alone, or should you call and ask what's up? People lose contact for a myriad of reasons. Sometimes it is beneficial to ask an individual directly if he or she is breaking off the relationship, although such direct requests place your self-concept on the line. How should you react if your friend confirms a desire to end the relationship? If possible, try to have a focused discussion on what has contributed to his or her decision. You might get information you need to repair the relationship. Or you might gain information that will help you in future relationships.

The Decision to End a Relationship

If you do choose to end the relationship, consider your goals. Do you want to continue the relationship at a less intimate level, or terminate it altogether? Do you care enough about the other person to want to preserve his or her self-esteem? Are you aware of the costs involved in ending the relationship? There is no one correct or best way to end a relationship. Ending relationships is not something you can practise to improve. But you can practise the effective relational management skills such as decentring and empathy, adaptation, and being tolerant. These skills will also help you in ending relationships.

We rely on our social networks for support and self-confirmation when an intimate relationship comes to an end. Advice about how to handle the loss of a close relationship is plentiful, but basically each person must find a way to compensate for the loss of intimacy and companionship. The loss of an important relationship hurts, but it need not put us out of commission if we make the most of our friends and family.

The de-escalation and termination of a relationship are not inherently bad. Not all relationships are meant to endure. Ending a relationship can be a healthy move if the relationship is harmful, or if it no longer provides confirmation of the self or satisfies interpersonal needs; it also can open the door to new relationships. Sometimes we choose not to end a relationship, but rather to de-escalate to a less intimate stage where there is a better balance between benefits and costs.

Breaking up an intimate relationship is hard because of the degree to which we become dependent upon the other person to confirm our sense of self. When a relationship ends, we may feel as if we need to redefine who we are. The most satisfying breakups are those that confirm both partners' worth rather than degrade it. "I just can't be what you want me to be"; "I'll always love you but . . ."; or "You're a very special person, but I need other things in life" are all examples of statements that do not destroy self-esteem.

The process of ending a relationship is considerably different when only one party wants out of the relationship (unilateral) than when both are agreeable to it (bilateral).[29] In **bilateral dissolutions**, both parties are predisposed to ending the relationship; they simply need to sort out details such as timing, dividing possessions, and defining conditions for the contact after the breakup. In a

bilateral dissolution. Ending a relationship when both parties are agreeable.

unilateral dissolution. Ending a relationship when only one party is agreeable.

fading away. Ending a relationship by slowly drifting apart.

sudden death. Ending a relationship abruptly and without preparation.

incrementalism. Ending a relationship when conflicts and problems finally reach a critical mass.

unilateral dissolution, the person who wants to end the relationship must choose a strategy (see pages 356–358) to get his or her partner to agree to the dissolution. Sometimes, however, people simply walk out of a relationship.

How Relationships End

A declining relationship usually follows one of several paths. Sometimes a relationship loses energy and runs down like a dying battery. Instead of a single event that causes the breakup, the relationship **fades away**—the two partners just drift further and further apart. They spend less time together, let more time go by between interactions, and stop disclosing much about themselves. You've probably had a number of friendships that ended this way—perhaps long-distance relationships. Because long-distance relationships require a great deal of effort to maintain, a move away can easily decrease the level of intimacy between two people.

Some relationships end in sudden death.[30] As the name suggests, **sudden death** moves straight to separation. One partner might move away or die, or, more frequently, a single precipitating event such as infidelity, breaking a confidence, a major conflict, or some other major role violation precipitates the breakup. Sudden death is like taking an express elevator from a top floor to the basement.

Between fading away and sudden death lies incrementalism. **Incrementalism** is the process by which conflicts and problems continue to accumulate in the relationship until they reach a critical mass that leads to the breakup; the relationship becomes intolerable or, from a social exchange perspective, too costly. "I just got to a point where it wasn't worth it anymore" and "It got to the point where all we did was fight all the time" are typical statements about incremental endings. For each of the three paths, individuals can choose from a variety of strategies to end the relationship.

Understanding Diversity

EMPATHY AND SEXUAL ORIENTATION

One of your authors once volunteered as a crisis phone counsellor in a large metropolitan area. Counsellors were trained to use effective counselling skills, such as empathy, in relating to the callers' crises. One night, a call came in from a very distressed and depressed man. He had broken up with his homosexual partner with whom he had had a long-term intimate relationship. At first I was uncomfortable dealing with the situation. Despite extensive training and role-playing, I wondered how I, as a heterosexual male, could empathize or relate to this caller. I continued to ask questions about how he felt, what he saw as his needs, and his perception of the problems. The more we talked, the more empathic I became, because I realized that his description was very familiar. I had been divorced some four years earlier, and this caller's descriptions of his feelings matched the feelings I had experienced during that time. I was able to talk about some of those feelings and this seemed to help him understand his own situation. I realized that though the sex of our partners was different, the overriding issue was the loss of an intimate relationship. I grew a little wiser that night.

Causes of De-Escalating and Ending Relationships with Friends and Lovers

The reasons for ending an interpersonal relationship are as varied as relationships themselves. In general, we end relationships when the costs are more than the rewards. This does not mean that as soon as a relationship becomes difficult we should dump it. Relationships are somewhat like savings accounts. If the relationship is profitable, you deposit your excess rewards into an emotional savings account. Then, at times when the costs exceed the rewards, you draw from your savings account to make up the deficit. In other words, if you have had a strong, satisfying relationship with someone for a long period of time, you will be more inclined to stay in the relationship during rough times. There might be a point, however, at which your savings account will run out, and you will decide to close your account—end the relationship. Of course, if you can foresee that you will reap more benefits in the future, you might decide to keep the account open, even when it is overdrawn. In addition, if you have had even less satisfying relationships in the past, or if your alternatives seem more dismal than your current relationships, you might decide to stick it out.[31] Of course, under those relational circumstances, when attractive alternatives do appear, relationships often suffer a sudden death.

One researcher found that most people attribute breakups to one of three main causes.[32] As Table 11.2 shows, "faults" are the number one cause. These are problems with personality traits or behaviours that one partner dislikes in the other. The number two cause, "unwillingness to compromise," represents a variety of failings on the part of one or both partners, including failure to put enough effort into the relationship, a decrease in effort, or failure to make concessions for the good of the relationship. The final cause, "feeling constrained," reflects one partner's desire to be free from the commitments and constraints of a relationship. But a variety of other elements can contribute to the breakup of both romantic and non-romantic relationships, including loss of interest in the other person, desire for independence, and conflicting attitudes about the definition of the relationship in areas such as sexual conduct, marriage, and infidelity.

Table 11.2
Reasons Given for Breakups

Faults
I realized that he/she had too many personality faults.
He/she behaved in ways that embarrassed me.
His/her behaviours were more to blame for the breakup than anything else.

Unwillingness to Compromise
I realized she/he was unwilling to make enough contributions to the relationship.
I felt that he/she no longer behaved toward me as romantically as he/she once did.
I felt that he/she took me for granted.
I felt that he/she wasn't willing to compromise for the good of the relationship.

Feeling Constrained
I felt that the relationship was beginning to constrain me, and I felt a lack of freedom.
Although I still cared for him/her, I wanted to start dating other people.
Although this relationship was a good one, I started to get bored with it.
He/she made too many contributions, and I started to feel suffocated.

Source: Adapted from M. J. Cody, "A Typology of Disengagement Strategies and an Examination of the Role Intimacy and Relational Problems Play in Strategy Selection," *Communication Monographs,* 49(3), (1982): 162.

Which of the three types of relationship termination do you think is evident here: fading away—where the partners drift slowly apart, sudden death—where separation is immediate, or incrementalism—where the conflicts gradually build until they reach the breaking point? (Donna Day/Tony Stone Images)

indirect relational termination strategies. Attempts to break up a relationship without explicitly stating the desire to do so.

direct relational termination strategies. Explicit statements of a desire to break up a relationship.

Strategies for Ending Relationships

When the vitality in long relationships fades away over a period of years, the individuals move slowly through the de-escalation stages before finally going their separate ways. Brand new relationships are far more likely to end abruptly. As you saw in Figure 11.1, the farther up the relational highrise you take the elevator, the longer the ride down.

But no matter what stage a relationship is in, partners use both direct and indirect strategies when they wish to end it. **Indirect strategies** represent attempts to break up a relationship without explicitly stating the desire to do so. **Direct strategies** involve explicit statements. The strategy that a person chooses will depend upon the level of intimacy in the relationship, the level of desire to help the partner save face, the degree of urgency for terminating the relationship, and the person's interpersonal skills. The Cathy cartoon on page 357 illustrates the difficulties we all face in coming up with a unique and non-threatening strategy for ending a relationship.

Indirect Strategies

One researcher identifies three strategies that people use to indirectly disengage: withdrawal, pseudo-de-escalation, and cost escalation. *Withdrawal* involves reducing the amount of contact and interaction without any explanation.[33] This strategy is the most dissatisfying for the other partner.[34] Withdrawal represents an attempt to avoid a confrontational scene and to save face.

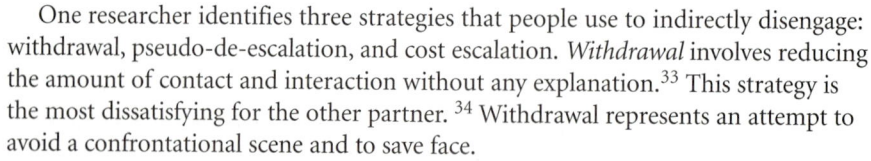

In *pseudo-de-escalation* one partner claims that he or she wants to redefine the relationship at a lower level of intimacy, but, in reality, he or she wants to end the relationship. Statements such as, "Let's just be friends" or "I think of you more as a sister" might be sincere, or they might reflect an unspoken desire to disengage completely. When both parties want to end the relationship, they sometimes use mutual pseudo-de-escalation and enter into a false agreement to reduce the level of intimacy as they move to disengagement.

Chapter 11 Developing and Maintaining Interpersonal Relationships

Cost escalation is an attempt to increase the costs associated with the relationship to encourage the other person to terminate it. A dissatisfied partner might ask for an inordinate amount of the other person's time, pick fights, criticize the other person, or violate relational rules.

Direct Strategies

The same researcher also identified four direct strategies that we use to terminate relationships: negative identity management, justification, de-escalation, and positive tone.[35] *Negative identity management* is a direct statement of the desire to terminate the relationship. It does not take into account the other's feelings, and it might even include criticisms. "I want out of our relationship"; "I just can't stand to be around you anymore"; and "I'm no longer happy in this relationship and I want to date other people" reflect negative identity management.

Justification is a clear statement of the desire to end the relationship accompanied by an honest explanation of the reasons. Justification statements may still hurt the other person's feelings: "I've found someone else who I want to spend more time with and who makes me happy" and "I feel as if I've grown a great deal and you haven't." A person who uses justification does not fault the other person, and he or she makes some attempt to protect both parties' sense of self. One researcher found that most people on the receiving end like this strategy best.[36]

De-escalation is an honest statement of a desire to redefine the relationship at a lower level of intimacy or to move toward ending the relationship. One partner might ask for a trial separation so that both people can explore other opportunities and gain a clearer understanding of their needs:[37] "Neither of us seems to be that happy with the relationship right now, so I think we should cool it for a while and see what happens."

Positive tone is the direct strategy that is most sensitive to the other person's sense of self. This strategy can seem almost contradictory because the initiator tries to affirm the other's personal qualities and worth at the same time that he or she calls a halt to the relationship. "I love you; I just can't live with you"; "I'm really sorry I've got to break off the relationship"; and "You really are a wonderful person; you're just not the one for me" are examples of positive tone statements.

> ### Recap
>
> #### STRATEGIES FOR DE-ESCALATING AND ENDING RELATIONSHIPS
>
> | | Term | Explanation |
> |---|---|---|
> | **Indirect Strategies** | Withdrawal | Reducing the amount of contact without any explanation. |
> | | Pseudo-de-escalation | Claiming a desire for less intimacy when you really want out. |
> | | Cost Escalation | Increasing relational costs to encourage the other to end the relationship. |
> | **Direct Strategies** | Negative Identity Management | Directly stating a desire to end the relationship without concern for the other person's feelings. |
> | | Justification | Directly stating a desire to end the relationship with an explanation of the reasons. |
> | | De-escalation | Directly stating a desire to lower the level of intimacy or move toward termination. |
> | | Positive Tone | Directly stating a desire to end the relationship while affirming the other person's value. |

Building Your Skills

HOW YOUR RELATIONSHIPS HAVE ENDED

Identify two relationships that you have ended and two relationships that the other person ended. For each relationship determine which of the indirect or direct strategies were used to end the relationship. What differences were there in how the relationships ended? What effects do you think the choice of strategy had upon you and your partner?

Conduct a survey of your friends by asking them these same questions. What conclusions can you draw about how people feel concerning different relationship-termination strategies?

Interpersonal Relationships on the Internet

Homes and workplaces have been dramatically altered by the introduction of the personal computer and computer-mediated communication. Relationships are no longer only developed face to face and you are probably forming many relationships over the Internet. **Computer-mediated communication (CMC)** was initially seen as a tool for accessing information, but it has quickly become an integral tool for human interaction. People have moved from using independent computers for word processing to using networked computers that allow them to send and receive messages and documents. This ability has proven invaluable at the workplace, where inter-office memos have been replaced by e-mail and attached documents. CMC has provided easy access to any member of an organization.

computer-mediated communication (CMC). Communication between and among people through the medium of computers (includes e-mail, chat rooms, bulletin boards, and newsgroups).

As the technology has been introduced to the home, more and more families use the Internet to keep in contact. E-mail and instant messaging provide another communication tool for maintaining interpersonal relationships with friends and lovers. With the introduction of chat rooms and discussion groups, you now have the ability to meet strangers and develop new interpersonal relationships. Thus, CMC allows you to meet two interpersonal goals: to make contact with strangers and thus initiate and develop new relationships; and to maintain existing relationships. These two goals differ greatly in directing your Internet interactions.

The use of CMC as a surrogate for face-to-face encounters creates some unique and intriguing challenges. One overriding rule that you should follow when communicating on the Internet is to follow all the rules you would normally follow in face-to-face interactions.[38] For example, in getting acquainted with someone, don't disclose too much too soon. Be a good "listener," and confirm the statements made by your Internet partners. Be other-oriented by considering how your Internet partners will react to what you have written.

The kind of information you provide and acquire through CMC has a direct impact on impression formation and relational attraction. Even though you are missing many of the usual non-verbal cues from which you draw impressions of other people (for example, their physical looks), you still form impressions about those with whom you interact. Prominent Internet researcher Joseph Walther has found that the impressions people develop about other people on the Internet become more similar to the impressions formed in face-to-face interactions the more users interact.[39] In Chapter 3 you read about the various biases that affect your perception of others. These biases must be guarded against in computer-mediated interactions as well. You need different skills for ascertaining the personal qualities of an Internet partner from those you need in face-to-face relationships.

You can manage the impressions others form of you on the Internet through the control of the information you provide about yourself. In face-to-face encounters, your behaviours impact other people's impressions of you, whereas in Internet encounters there are fewer behaviours to observe. What you type and how you type are the major factors by which impressions are drawn. Impressions are also affected by your language selection, expression of sensitivity, and responsiveness to other peoples' messages.

---

e-connection

CYBERSPACE AND RELATIONSHIPS

The development and maintenance of relationships in cyberspace are the subject of many articles and websites. The following website contains a number of interesting articles and links about various facets of computer-mediated communication, including cyberspace romance, identity management in cyberspace, and addiction to the Internet:

www.rider.edu/users/suler/psycyber/psycyber.html

Types of Computer-Mediated Communication (CMC)

Bulletin boards allow people to post messages without regard for who will read them, although threads often develop on bulletin boards where people respond to other postings. These can evolve into a kind of dialogue between or among posters,

Computer-mediated communication has made it easy for us to have access to family, friends, co-workers, and even complete strangers. The key to success is to apply the same skills that you would in a face-to-face relationship. (Hyacinth Manning/SuperStock)

reaching a point at which controversies can erupt in "flaming," with individuals calling each other names and insulting one another. Regular reading of the same bulletin board often lets you develop a sense of the more active posters.

CMC is used as a replacement for traditional "snail" mail. People can send and receive "letters" (e-mail) with relative ease. In this way e-mail is not really a form of interpersonal communication, although it can be used to develop and maintain relationships. The speed at which people can send and receive letters through e-mail makes it seem a lot more interactive than traditional postal service. One emerging Internet norm is that you are expected to respond as soon as possible to your e-mail; failure to do so sometimes evokes resentment from correspondents.

Chat rooms (also referred to as Internet relay chat or IRC), where people are actively involved in sending and receiving messages, are more similar to face-to-face (FtF) interactions than is e-mail. Discussion groups or public chat rooms often involve many people engaging in a kind of group discussion. However, one intriguing aspect of public chat rooms is that even though 10 or 12 people might be chatting at one time, the participants often pair up and simply respond to their partner's comments, ignoring the rest. Although at first confusing, chatters usually develop a knack for being able to discern relevant comments. Typed statements often start with the name to whom the message is intended. Such "interpersonal" dyadic exchanges often draw in the other chat room members, because everything that is written is open to public viewing. In this way it's like sitting in a small group in which you are talking with just one other member, but the other group members can still hear your conversation. Chatters often move to a "private room" where only those who are invited can participate. This allows chatters the privacy to carry on uninterrupted and confidential conversations. See if you can tell who is talking to whom in the following transcript of a fictional chat room:

SuperSteve:	Regis Philbin is cool.
Timeout:	I was bummed when they killed off the crew.
Beastie:	The first Star Wars is still the best—the story and effects were great.
SillySilk:	Can't believe the guy didn't know the Beatles made The White Album.
BrashnBold:	The effects stink. They're nothing compared to what they do now.

Super Steve:	Regis handled him well though—didn't make him feel too dumb.
BettyCracker:	But it was innovative for its time.
TinLizzie:	But if they were all saved, it wouldn't have been very realistic.
Beastie:	Yeah, and besides, Harrison Ford was great as Han.
Trouter:	I get enough realism from the news—I want to escape it at the movies.
BrashnBold:	I agree.
SillySilk:	I agree.
BettyCracker:	Right on.

In case you couldn't tell which comments went with which, we wrote this interaction so that all the names starting with the same letter are involved in a discussion with one another (regretfully, it doesn't happen this way on the Web). Often a chatter will use a unique colour or font so that you can easily pick out his or her comments, and this does help in following a given thread.

Instant messaging is similar to private chat rooms. Most Internet providers allow their members to create a friends and family list. When any of the "buddies" you've put on your list are logged on to the Internet, it lets you know. You can then send them a message and engage them in an "instant" exchange of messages. Instant messaging approximates a personal conversation or a small-group discussion if you are connected with several people at the same time. One disadvantage of instant messaging is that you might be involved in some other activity when someone contacts you. This creates a "listening" problem for you, because you might try to continue your other computer activity while still instant-messaging; this results in dividing your attention and often causes delays or disconfirming responses to your partners. Handling this situation is similar to handling the same dilemma in a face-to-face situation; you should either tell your partner you can't talk right now, or you should postpone your other activity.

Comparing Face-To-Face (Ftf) Communication to CMC

While we can use many of the strategies earlier in the chapter to initiate and maintain relationships using CMC, there are communication advantages and disadvantages to both FtF and computer-mediated interactions. In FtF, people obtain a lot of information by seeing how the other person behaves, how they react, and how they look. However, such visual information has a downside when we base biased attributions on what we see (reacting to a person's age, sex, race, or physical size) that may not be readily apparent in CMC. We might engage in fruitful and fulfilling chat with someone online that we might have avoided if we first had seen what he or she looked like. Besides differing in the use of non-verbals, CMC has interesting characteristics related to the importance of the written word, how much time delay there is between the interactants' messages, the occurrence of deception, and ease of simply disappearing.

Non-Verbal Communication

CMC is more limited in its use of non-verbal cues than FtF communication, lacking for instance the use of touch and smell and limited in the use of visual and aural cues. Thus words and graphics become more important in CMC than in FtF because you must rely solely on them to carry non-verbal messages. In FtF communication you can hear people's voices, see their facial expressions, and watch their body movements. These provide the context by which you attribute meaning to the words they speak. In CMC such cues are limited or non-existent, which means words are taken at their face value. There are some basic things users do to add emotion to their messages, including CAPITALIZING THE MESSAGE (which is considered "yelling"), making letters **bold,** or using emoticons—keyboard combinations used to represent some emotion—such as smiley faces : -). (See Chapter 1, page 19 for a list of common emoticons.) Despite these efforts, the ability to tease or make sarcastic remarks is limited because there is no tone of voice in the written message, which means the author must usually write out an accompanying interpretation. For example, "Boy, am I insulted by that or what?!!!! (just kidding)."

Technology already has been developed that lets users go beyond the limitations of using only written words. Several chat rooms now feature the use of audio links and take on the feeling of a large telephone party line. The introduction of spoken instead of written messages on the Internet adds non-verbal information for listeners. Just like the telephone, audio chat rooms provide information that gives you hints about the person's age, sex, and ethnicity (through accents). In addition, people can use the full range of vocal cues discussed in Chapter 7: pitch, tone, rate, volume, and silence. There are also visual chat rooms and teleconferencing that let you actually see the person with whom you are interacting.

Written Communication

Besides the restrictions on non-verbal communication, the use of the written word has other impacts on our Internet interactions. One online scholar suggests that a person's typing ability and writing skills affect the quality of any relationship that is developed.[40] The ability to encode thoughts quickly and accurately into written words is not a skill everyone has. Not only do writing skills affect your ability to express yourself and manage the relationship, but they also affect how you are perceived by others. Look at the following two e-mail messages and think about the impressions you form of the two authors.

> *GigoloMan:* "Hey, babe, whad's up? no what im thnking now we shuld do?"
>
> *GentleJim:* "Hi. Boy, have I been swamped with work lately. How's your day been?"

What's your impression of the two e-mailers? What affected your impression? The first example is filled with grammar and spelling errors that might create a negative impression because the author is not particularly skilled at writing. The second author uses correct grammar and spelling, which is more likely to produce a positive impression. The user name or nickname (also called a "nick" among CMC users) that is listed for each author also affects our impression.[41] "GigoloMan" sends a clear if politically incorrect message to those who see his moniker. The selection of words has a strong impact on the impression others draw about us from the Internet. All the material discussed in Chapter 6 on verbal communication and language is particularly relevant to the Internet, which is heavily word based.

Synchronous versus Asynchronous Interaction

In defining interpersonal communication in Chapter 1, we referred to the notion of being mutual. We described *mutual* as a transactional concept, meaning that the participants are influencing each other at the same time. In the cyber world, this notion is called *synchronicity*. A **synchronous interaction** involves both participants actively engaging in the interaction at the same time. Face-to-face interactions are, by their very nature, synchronous. Only some Internet interactions are synchronous, such as group or private chat sessions. Most Internet interactions are **asynchronous**, meaning that the participants are not necessarily logged on at the same time but rather send and receive posted messages. Bulletin boards, discussion forums, and e-mail represent asynchronous interactions. They are interactions to the degree that the participants post responses to what they have read. On bulletin boards a certain thread can continue for days or weeks about a particular subject. Your e-mails to friends often reflect responses to the e-mails they sent you, and they will then respond to your e-mails.

Even synchronous Internet interactions entail some response delay. It takes longer to formulate a typewritten response than a spoken or non-verbal one. The amount of delay (which is similar to silence in FtF interactions) can have an impact on the interpretation of the message's meaning. In chat sessions, participants expect to see a response very quickly to their posting. This is one reason chat sessions often involve very short and concise messages that can be rapidly written and sent. Most chat sessions involve a rapid succession of short messages that foster a sense of synchronicity and interaction. By the time a long message gets written and sent, it is often no longer germane to the discussion. The exception to this is when people are in private or small-group chat sessions, where they ask questions for which a longer, more developed response is expected.

E-mailing someone allows you time to compose your message and craft it more carefully than you might in a FtF interpersonal interaction. You can take time to consider your message and delete it before sending if you don't feel you have worded the message the way you want. Even in chat sessions, you might finish typing a line and then decide to delete it and write something else. In face-to-face interactions, people can think about what they want to say; but once having spoken, they cannot take it back. As a sender of Internet messages, you have more control over what you say and the impression you create; as the receiver of Internet messages, realize that the other person has had the chance to consider carefully his or her message for its greatest impact on you. Such deliberation is one reason you must be cautious about accepting the validity of Internet messages—deception is relatively easy.

Deception and Disappearance

The detection of deception in face-to-face encounters is aided by the presence of non-verbal cues. A 50-year-old white male (named Sam) could not claim to be a 20-year-old Chinese female (Samantha) without a major makeover. However, online such deception is almost as easy as simply typing the words. We say almost, because you can assess the content of the written message for clues to deceit. Sam writing as Samantha might talk about how much "she" enjoyed watching the Beatles live on the Ed Sullivan TV show (they appeared in 1964 and 1965) when she was growing up. This should alert you to the fact that Samantha would have to be older than 20, and probably not from China. College student respondents in one study reported the most common form of deception detection occurred when someone made an implausible statement or bragged.[42] The criteria for detecting deception apparently change as the Internet relationship becomes more intimate. As "friendships" develop over the Internet, to detect deception people come to depend on the personal knowledge and impressions of their partners acquired over the course of their correspondence.[43] Interestingly, this study also found that those who reported lying most were the ones most likely to suspect other users of lying.[44]

synchronous interaction. Occurs when participants are actively engaging in an interaction at the same time.

asynchronous interaction. Occurs when participants send and receive messages from each other with extended periods of delay between reception and response.

The ease with which someone can create a false persona means that you need to be cautious in forming relationships with Internet strangers. Besides developing relationships with people who falsely present themselves, another aspect about Internet relationships is that a person can simply disappear or assume another nickname without your ever knowing. Unless the person is using a site-specific user name, such as "iastate.edu" or "swt.edu," which represent university locations, you may have no direct knowledge about where they reside, much less their names. The use of a Sympatico, MSN, or Hotmail address means you are virtually in the blind about the people with whom you interact. People can simply change their e-mail addresses, and you are totally cut off. Disappearing is more difficult or at least impractical in face-to-face relationships; disappearing from a classmate with whom you've had a relationship would necessitate dropping the course and maybe even out of school. Knowing that you will be continuing to see a person puts different kinds of demands on relationship management and termination from the demands of the Internet.

> ### Recap

COMPARING FtF COMMUNICATION TO CMC

Non-Verbal Communication	The limitation of non-verbal cues in CMC means you depend on variations in the text to convey non-verbal meaning.
Written Communication	The selection and use of words convey important information about the sender.
Synchronous versus Asynchronous Communication	The different types of CMC vary in terms of the transactional activity from almost simultaneous to highly delayed.
Deception and Disappearance	The lack of FtF non-verbal cues reduces your ability to detect deception in CMC. Individuals can change their e-mail address and stop corresponding.

Using CMC to Initiate New Relationships

People are forming personal relationships over the Internet. In a study reported in 1996 about discussion groups, over 60 percent of the survey respondents reported forming personal relationships with someone they met on the Internet.[45] Further analyses of these relationships revealed an almost equal number of mixed-sex (55 percent) and same-sex relationships (45 percent), and only 8 percent were considered romantic. Over half of the respondents reported communication with their "friend" at least once a week. Interestingly, this study found women were more likely to form personal relationships in these newsgroups than men (72 percent of the female respondents, as compared to 55 percent of the males). There is an increasing likelihood that you will find yourself in a position of initiating and forming relationships with people you have met through the Internet. In general, the same principles and skills you read about in these last two chapters apply to the Internet. For example, similar strategies are used in the opening and closing of FtF and computer-mediated interactions.[46] However, there are some unique issues you should understand as you enter the world of CMC relationships.

Choose the Right Chat Room

One way we normally make friends is by engaging in activities where we meet people with similar interests. You probably have made friends with people who are members of your church, softball team, or math class. One form of attraction discussed in Chapter 10 dealt with being attracted to those who share similar interests. This same form of attraction exists on the Internet and can be used as the basis for starting relationships. Finding people with similar interests on the Internet is relatively easy, because chat rooms are often organized according to topics and interest groups. There are chat rooms or discussion groups for almost every sport, activity, and interest that you can imagine. And if there isn't one, you can actually create your own. There are also general social chat rooms that are very unstructured and have the same feeling as visiting a bar that has the reputation for being a "meat" market or a pickup place. At times the new information highway seems more like Bourbon Street than Sesame Street. Being a regular contributor to the more topically based chat rooms usually provides a safer environment for getting to know other chatters. As chatters share thoughts on the given topic, they often share more and more personal information as well, which allows for the development of online relationships.

Accept the Slower Pace of Relational Development

As mentioned earlier, the development of impressions is slower in CMC than FtF. This means that the process of forming interpersonal relationships is also likely to be slower. The major reason for this difference is that almost all information on the Internet must be put into text, whereas FtF interactions use a variety of non-verbal channels. Early researchers disputed the notion that true interpersonal relationships could be formed online, but subsequent research has found that the kind of effects that occur quickly in FtF interactions also occur on the Internet but just require more time.[47] CMC users can self-disclose honestly and openly with each other, to the point of forming truly intimate relationships. One advantage of the text-only medium is a reduction in our perceptual biases about a person's physical attractiveness.[48] At some point in Internet relationships, the users often provide a physical description of themselves (people seem to want to know the other person's sex, age, and location at the very beginning); eventually they exchange photographs and even arrange to meet in person. The process of building trust with another user to the point of feeling comfortable disclosing intimate information about yourself may take longer on the Internet than in person.

Apply Strong Verbal Skills

The point has been made repeatedly about the non-verbal communication limitations of CMC. Sending someone a hug and a kiss over the Internet does not provide the same kind of satisfaction as it does in person. Among the conversational skills used in FtF interactions are verbal and non-verbal expressiveness (including being articulate), listening and non-verbal sensitivity, humour, effective question asking, and responsiveness. These skills have their parallels in CMC, but for the most part are dependent on the ability to express yourself in writing. The reliance on verbal strategies is demonstrated by a study that found that e-mail pen pals apparently compensated for the lack of non-verbal feedback by increasing the use of personal questions.[49] Thus, having good question-asking skills would prove advantageous on the Internet.

The most skilled Internet communicators know CMC shorthand, incorporate emoticons and other devices to enhance their text, and adapt to their partners. As a listener/respondent, you can't use eye contact, head nodding, and "uh-huhs" to let the person know you are attentive and interested. You must write responses that show you are listening. This reflects another advantage of the Internet over FtF—you have a record of what was sent by your partner. So instead of not hearing what he or she said because your mind was wandering, you can simply review what was written if you spaced out during a chat session. It's a good idea to hang on to e-mail so you can look through previous correspondence if you are afraid you have forgotten some information your partner shared.

The limited non-verbal cues on the Internet mean that the principles of language discussed in Chapter 6 are probably more applicable to CMC than to FtF. The word is extremely important in our chat sessions and e-mails. Our words have power and can have a dramatic impact on the success of our Internet interactions. The impact of words is obvious during flame wars. Flaming hurts feelings and causes people to be turned off to a particular individual or website. The management of such conflicts requires application of the skills discussed in Chapter 8.

You may unintentionally hurt someone's feelings by what you write, and can apologize and repair the damage. However, e-mail has become an increasing medium for sexual harassment, aggressive behaviour, and harsh and unbridled criticism in the workplace.[50] One possible reason is that people feel less inhibited about what they write because of the physical separation they have from the person to whom they send the e-mail.[51]

Using CMC to Maintain Existing Relationships

A recent study found that the major use of home e-mail was for relationship maintenance.[52] This included using e-mail as a way to keep in touch with family and friends. E-mail is simple, quick, cheap, convenient, efficient, and provides a sense of interaction. For ongoing relationships, e-mail provides a kind of freedom from time zone and schedule conflicts, allowing users to send out messages at their convenience. Survey respondents reported that e-mail made it easier to share ideas, express opinions, and provide information with friends and family all over the world.[53] As of July 2000, the Internet provider America On Line (AOL) handled 110 million e-mails daily. Multiply this by the number of providers and add the growth that is occurring, and we get a glimpse of how important this medium is to interpersonal relationship maintenance. We use e-mail, instant chat, chat rooms, and discussion groups as a way of interacting with our friends and family. The expansion of CMC has begun to produce a virtual community, **computer-supported social networks (CSSNs)**.[54] The development of social networks is enhanced by the ability of users to create buddy lists. These lists result in personal networks of friends with whom you can exchange group-addressed e-mails or create group chat sessions.

For the most part, the rules and principles discussed in the last chapter on how to maintain relationships apply to the use of CMC. The Internet simply provides another tool by which you can implement the strategies that were discussed in that chapter. For example, you can send e-mails in which you engage in a discussion about the nature of your relationship, express your emotions, or engage in relationship talk. In some ways, such discussions might be easier online than face to face. You have time to consider your statements and not having to face someone in person as you talk about sensitive issues may help reduce feelings of threat. The following are some of the ways you can use the Internet to help you maintain and even escalate existing interpersonal relationships.

computer-supported social network (CSSN). A virtual community created by the social networking among individuals through CMC.

Communicate!

The very act of sending regular e-mails or engaging in chat sessions is probably the primary way the Internet helps maintain relationships. Maintaining an active line of communication with people is one of the best ways to preserve the relationship. Interest in the other person and commitment to the relationship is reflected in the very act of communicating. However, the amount of communication that is needed is defined by the people in the relationship. You might have one friend whom you e-mail daily and another whom you e-mail two or three times a year. Are these relationships different? Is one less intimate than the other? The answers are not really cut and dried. You might feel as close to both people, but the daily interactions create a sense of interdependence that is probably not found in the other relationship. Daily interactions mean you are both informed about each other's activities and probably providing daily support and confirming each other's value as a person.

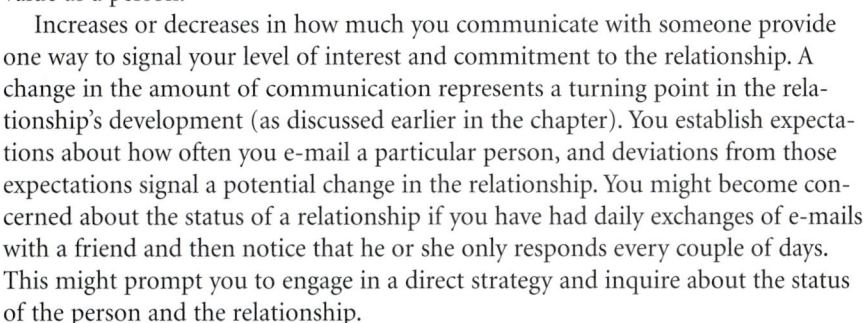

Increases or decreases in how much you communicate with someone provide one way to signal your level of interest and commitment to the relationship. A change in the amount of communication represents a turning point in the relationship's development (as discussed earlier in the chapter). You establish expectations about how often you e-mail a particular person, and deviations from those expectations signal a potential change in the relationship. You might become concerned about the status of a relationship if you have had daily exchanges of e-mails with a friend and then notice that he or she only responds every couple of days. This might prompt you to engage in a direct strategy and inquire about the status of the person and the relationship.

The Internet might actually result in increased communication among friends and lovers who are separated by distance. Information technologist Patricia Wallace speculates that the ease with which people can send each other things like e-mail greeting cards results in increased communication.[55] People are creative in the way they use the Internet to make contact and interact. One of your author's sons still manages to play games over the Internet with a school friend who has moved away. Wallace tells a story in her book, *The Psychology of the Internet,* about a couple who use the Internet to keep in contact when the husband is away on business trips and who link up to play bridge online with other people.[56]

Use Relational Maintenance Strategies

Keeping in contact with someone is one way to maintain the relationship and show your interest. You can also use a variety of the other strategies discussed earlier in this chapter. In your e-mails, you should appropriately disclose information about yourself. Remember that self-disclosure is related to relational development. Don't disclose too much if you are not interested in escalating the relationship; however, not disclosing anything might create stagnation and de-escalation. Some of these disclosures might include sharing your emotions. Having limited non-verbal cues means that your partner depends on you verbalizing your feelings. You can describe the feelings you have about events in your life and you can also express your feelings toward your partner. Talking about your feelings for your friend and engaging in other relational talk as well is another way to maintain your relationships over the Internet. Relationship talk and expressing feelings are fruitful when done within the norms appropriate to the relational stage. The Internet can seduce you into being too open about your feelings and thoughts about your relationships, as compared to face-to-face discussions. Just as you need to show restraint in face-to-face disclosures, you need to do the same in CMC.

Dependence on verbal messages means that you need to monitor your perceptions to ensure that you have accurately interpreted your partner's messages. Asking for clarification, expressing misunderstanding, or paraphrasing back what you think your partner means are good ways to enhance the accuracy of messages. Such strategies help maintain relationships because they reduce the impact of conflicts and stress associated with misunderstanding. Apply the principles of listening discussed in Chapter 5 to your behaviour during online relational interactions. Empathic listening on the Internet involves writing to let your partners know that you are sensitive to and understand their feelings. You can write back messages that show you are involved and engaged in the discussion of their situation. The use of confirming responses that show you understand their feelings will help maintain a positive relationship.

Be Other-Oriented and Adapt

The way you write back to your partner depends on your relationship and what you know about your partner. Throughout this text we have emphasized trying to look at interactions from your partner's perspective—to socially decentre and to

---

▶ **Recap**

USING CMC TO INITIATE AND MAINTAIN RELATIONSHIPS

Initiating

- Choose the right chat room. | Interact in places where you are likely to find other people who share your interests.
- Accept the slower pace of relational development. | The process of forming trust and getting to know another person online will probably be slower than FtF relationships.
- Apply strong verbal skills. | CMC favours those who have the ability to express themselves well in a written and graphic mode.

Maintenance

- Communicate. | The very act of regularly sending messages to another person is one way to help maintain the relationship.
- Use relational maintenance strategies. | Appropriate self-disclosing, sharing feelings, and relationship talk are among the strategies that can be used.
- Be other-oriented and adapt. | Use the knowledge you can acquire about other people through CMC to adapt your communication.

empathize. This principle is no less applicable to the maintenance of Internet relationships. As you acquire more and more knowledge about your partner through both your FtF and CMC interactions, apply that knowledge by adapting your communication. If anything, CMC provides you more time to take into consideration what you know about another person and create appropriate messages. As you compose your words on the computer, it is easy to forget that another human being will be reading and interpreting those messages—and not just any anonymous human, but one with whom you have formed a defined relationship, one with whom you share a bond and commitment. Accordingly, compose messages that reflect your understanding and appreciation of that other person.

Interpersonal Relationships at Work

While we have discussed informal relationships that we develop with varying degrees of intimacy, we have not examined the workplace. A large amount of your interaction time is spent at work, at school, and in other more formal organizations. Obviously, communication is important in any organization, but is *interpersonal* communication at work really important? As shown in the Canadian Issues box below and on the next page, many organizations seem to think so and put interpersonal communications skills high on the list of workplace skills. Note that skills such as teamwork, and planning and making decisions with others all require your ability to communicate effectively at the interpersonal level. More and more, organizations are looking for employees who can effectively relate to other people—bosses, subordinates, peers, and clients. These reflect the four directions of organizational communication: upward (to bosses), downward (to subordinates), horizontal (to peers), and outward (to clients). All the skills you have been studying throughout this text can improve your effectiveness in dealing with organizational relationships.

Your interactions in the workplace typically vary according to their degree of task versus social orientation. This variation is the source of both personal satisfaction and conflict. After you graduate, the workplace becomes a major source for developing interpersonal relationships. You make friends with the people with whom

---

Canadian Issues

WORKPLACE SKILLS IN A GLOBAL ECONOMY

What soft skills will Canadians need to work in a global economy? In other words, what skills, abilities, and knowledge will employers be seeking as they hire new workers in the next several years? A document developed by the Corporate Council of Education, a program of the National Business and Education Centre, the Conference Board of Canada, outlines the foundation skills for employability. The Corporate Council includes representation from numerous Canadian companies including Air Canada, Bell Canada, General Motors of Canada Limited, IBM Canada, Nortel, Shell Canada Limited, and Xerox Canada Limited, to name a few. Below is a summary of these skills. Note that many of the skills require interpersonal skills and the ability to communicate effectively.

Employability Skills 2000+

The skills you need to enter, stay in, and progress in the world of work—whether you work on your own or as a part of a team.

These skills can also be applied and used beyond the workplace in a range of daily activities.

Fundamental Skills The skills needed as a base for further development	**Personal Management Skills** The personal skills, attitudes, and behaviours that drive one's potential for growth	**Teamwork Skills** The skills and attributes needed to contribute productively
You will be better prepared to progress in the world of work when you can:	*You will be able to offer yourself greater possibilities for achievement when you can:*	*You will be better prepared to add value to the outcomes of a task, project or team when you can:*
Communicate • read and understand information presented in a variety of forms (e.g., words, graphs, charts, diagrams) • write and speak so others pay attention and understand • listen and ask questions to understand and appreciate the points of view of others • share information using a range of information and communications technologies (e.g., voice, e-mail, computers) • use relevant scientific, technological and mathematical knowledge and skills to explain or clarify ideas **Manage Information** • locate, gather and organize information using appropriate technology and information systems • access, analyze, and apply knowledge and skills from various disciplines (e.g., the arts, languages, science, technology, mathematics, social sciences, and the humanities) **Use Numbers** • decide what needs to be measured or calculated • observe and record data using appropriate methods, tools, and technology • make estimates and verify calculations **Think and Solve Problems** • assess situations and identify problems • seek different points of view and evaluate them based on facts • recognize the human, interpersonal, technical, scientific, and mathematical dimensions of a problem • identify the root cause of a problem; be creative and innovative in exploring possible solutions • readily use science, technology and mathematics as ways to think, gain and share knowledge, solve problems, and make decisions • evaluate solutions • make recommendations or decisions, implement solutions, check to see if a solution works, and act on opportunities for improvement	**Demonstrate Positive Attitudes and Behaviours** • feel good about yourself and be confident • deal with people, problems, and situations with honesty, integrity, and personal ethics • recognize your own and other people's good efforts • take care of your personal health • show interest, initiative, and effort **Be Responsible** • set goals and priorities balancing work and personal life • plan and manage time, money, and other resources to achieve goals • assess, weigh, and manage risk • be accountable for your actions and the actions of your group • be socially responsible and contribute to your community **Be Adaptable** • work independently or as a part of a team • carry out multiple tasks or projects • be innovative and resourceful: identify and suggest alternative ways to achieve goals and get the job done • be open and respond constructively to change • learn from your mistakes and accept feedback • cope with uncertainty **Learn Continuously** • be willing to continuously learn and grow • assess personal strengths and areas for development • set your own learning goals • identify and access learning sources and opportunities • plan for and achieve your learning goals **Work Safely** • be aware of personal and group health and safety practices and procedures, and act in accordance with these	**Work with Others** • understand and work within the dynamics of a group • ensure that a team's purpose and objectives are clear • be flexible: respect, be open to and supportive of the thoughts, opinions, and contributions of others in a group • recognize and respect people's diversity, individual differences, and perspectives • accept and provide feedback in a constructive and considerate manner • contribute to a team by sharing information and expertise • lead or support when appropriate, motivating a group for high performance • understand the role of conflict in a group to reach solutions • manage and resolve conflict when appropriate **Participate in Projects and Tasks** • plan, design or carry out a project or task from start to finish with well-defined objectives and outcomes • develop a plan, seek feedback, test, revise, and implement • work to agreed quality standards and specifications • select and use appropriate tools and technology for a task or project • adapt to changing requirements and information • continuously monitor the success of a project or task and identify ways to improve Source: *Employability Skills 2000+* brochure. Ottawa: The Conference Board of Canada, 2000. Visit the Conference Board of Canada's website at **www.conferenceboard.ca**

you work. You will socialize both on and off the job with various people from the organization. Conflicts arise when job-related decisions affect personal relationships, and vice versa. As a manager, you might become friends with some of your subordinates, but if the work performance of one of those subordinates falls below a satisfactory level, the friendship could interfere with your ability to address that problem. Many companies used to have policies prohibiting socializing among employees; however, this policy created strong dissatisfaction and discontent. Organizational policies that nurture relationships among employees build camaraderie and a supportive work atmosphere.[57]

Friendships at work are like any other relationships in terms of relational dimensions and development. One study, in which co-workers were extensively interviewed, identified three distinct transitions: acquaintance to friend, friend to close friend, and close friend to "almost best" friend.[58] Interestingly, the researchers found respondents hesitant to refer to a co-worker as "best" friend, opting instead for "best friend at work" or "very close." The initial development of workplace friendships occurred for a variety of reasons, such as proximity, sharing tasks, sharing a similar life event, or perceiving similar interests.[59] As the relationships developed, the changes identified in this study were similar to those typically found in any developing friendship—easier and more flexible communication, increased self-disclosing, more frequent interactions, more socializing, and increased discussion of both work problems and non-work topics.[60]

The challenge of workplace interpersonal relationships is to maximize the satisfaction that comes from healthy relationships, while minimizing the negative impact. Relationships often result in conflicts among the participants as they move through the relational development stages. They must resolve issues and establish rules regarding their workplace roles and interpersonal roles. The participants are expected to perform their required work in the face of these interpersonal struggles. Power is one of the most challenging factors that must be addressed in workplace interpersonal relationships. The position power of a manager over a subordinate can result in a harassment situation in which the subordinate feels forced into an undesirable interpersonal relationship. Power is defined by the organizational roles that each person plays and is thus a defining factor of workplace interpersonal relationships. These relationships can be identified by the direction the communication flows, as discussed in the following sections.

Interpersonal communication skills help us in our interactions with co-workers. Developing satisfying interpersonal relationships in an organization is often a rewarding part of a job. (D. Young-Wolff/PhotoEdit)

Upward Communication: Talking with Your Boss

"Please place your suggestions in the suggestion box," announces the boss. The suggestion box is the symbol for upward communication. **Upward communication** involves the flow of communication from subordinates up to superiors. The only person in an organization who does not communicate upward is the boss, president, or chief executive officer (CEO). Even those individuals usually answer to a governing board or to stockholders. Although today's organizational emphasis on quality encourages communication from lower levels to higher levels, effective

upward communication. Communication that flows from subordinates to superiors.

upward communication is still far from the norm. Many employees fear that their candid comments will not be well received. Others may wonder, "Why bother?" If managers offer no incentive for sharing information up the line, it is unlikely that their subordinates will make the effort. If a supervisor stays holed up in an office away from his or her employees, opportunities for sharing ideas will be limited. Remember the proximity hypothesis described in Chapter 10? People are more likely to talk with those people who are physically close to them.

If there is little upward communication, the organization may be in a precarious situation. Those lower down in the organization are often the ones who make contact with the customer, make the product, or work most closely with the development and delivery of the product or service; they hear feedback about the product's virtues and problems. If supervisors remain unaware of these problems, productivity or quality may suffer. In addition, if employees have no opportunities to share problems and complaints with their boss, their frustration level may be dangerously high. Upward communication helps managers to deal quickly with problems and to hear suggestions for improving processes and procedures.

The Broadway show *How to Succeed in Business without Really Trying* suggests that you can get ahead by manipulating your boss. Although we do not encourage you to try this approach, we do suggest that developing a positive relationship with your supervisor can help you succeed. One pair of researchers suggests that subordinates can "manage up" by being sensitive to the needs of supervisors.[61] If you know what your boss's most important goals are, along with his or her strengths, weaknesses, and preferred working style, you will be in a good position to establish a more meaningful relationship that will benefit both of you.

This process of managing might be mediated by how influential subordinates perceive their superiors. In 1952, an organizational researcher discovered that subordinates were more satisfied in their jobs when they felt their immediate supervisor had influence on decisions made at higher levels.[62] This is called the Pelz effect, after its discoverer, Donald Pelz. Subsequent research by organizational communication scholar Fred Japlin found that when subordinates perceived their supervisors as supportive, the Pelz effect was particularly strong in creating a sense of openness and satisfaction.[63]

If you are a manager yourself, encourage your subordinates to share both good news and bad. Be visible and cultivate their trust by developing a system that elicits feedback and comments. Use a suggestion box (paper or electronic), informal discussions, or more formal meetings and presentations. Making time for these exchanges will pay off in the long run.

Downward Communication: Talking with Your Subordinates

When the dean of your college tells your department chair that a course must be cancelled because of low enrolment, the department chair tells your instructor, and your instructor tells you, you have experienced downward communication. **Downward communication** is the flow of information from those higher up in an organization to those of lower rank. It can happen via memo, newsletter, poster, or e-mail or, of course, face to face. Most downward communication consists of instruction about how to do a job, rationales for doing things, statements about organizational policies and procedures, feedback about job performance, and information that helps develop the mission or vision of the organization.[64]

What is the best way to communicate with employees—in writing or face to face? It depends on the situation. Often the best method is oral, with a written follow-up or e-mail. In various situations, the best managers take care to develop

downward communication. Communication that flows from superiors to subordinates.

and send ethical, other-oriented messages. Then they follow up to ensure that the receiver understood the message, and that it achieved its intended effect. Managers need to be especially other-oriented when they are sharing sensitive information or broaching personal topics.

At the opposite end of the spectrum, the worst managers indulge in an egocentric abuse of the legitimate power that accompanies their rank within an organization. Sexual harassment, which may often take place through downward communication channels, appears to be a growing problem in the workplace. However, since it not only takes place via downward channels, a special section on sexual harassment is placed at the end of this section on workplace communication directions.

Horizontal Communication: Talking with Your Colleagues

You poke your head into your co-worker's office and say, "Did you hear about the possible merger between Byteware and Datamass?" Or, while you are tossing a crust at the Pizza Palace, one of your fellow workers asks how much pepperoni to put on a Super Duper Supreme. Both situations illustrate horizontal communication. **Horizontal communication** refers to communication among co-workers at the same level within an organization. In larger organizations you may talk with other workers in different departments or divisions who perform similar jobs at a similar level; that, too, is horizontal communication. Most often you communicate with your colleagues to coordinate job tasks, share plans and information, solve problems, make sure you understand job procedures, manage conflict, or get a bit of emotional support on the job.[65]

horizontal communication. Communication among colleagues or co-workers at the same level within an organization.

"I Heard It through the Grapevine," a popular song from the 1960s, describes the way gossip travels among friends. Messages travel through the workplace the same way. Grapevine messages tend to circulate within groups and departments rather than across departmental lines. Organizational communication researchers Davis and O'Connor found that information travels quickly through the organizational grapevine, and that it is also accurate from 75 to 90 percent of the time.[66] But errors do creep into these messages; details get lost and embellishments are added, much as when children play "Whisper Around the World" or "Telephone."

Although grapevine errors can cause problems for an organization, most continue to encourage co-worker communication because it enhances teamwork and allows the work group to develop a certain degree of independence. Some organizations even try to formalize it by forming *quality circles,* or groups of employees who meet together on a regular basis. These groups usually talk about such issues as how to improve the quality of services or products, reduce mistakes, lower costs, improve safety, or develop better ways of working together. This active participation in the work process encourages workers to do a better job. Moreover, the training they receive to participate in these groups—in group problem solving, decision-making skills, listening, relating, speaking, and managing conflict—applies to other areas of their work as well.

Outward Communication: Talking with Your Customers

"Attention, Zellers shoppers: Submarine sandwiches are now on sale for $1 each for the next 15 minutes." This is one kind of communication with customers. But in addition to just pitching to their customers, today's organizations are also asking

outward communication. Communication that flows to those outside an organization (such as customers).

sexual harassment. Unwanted sexually oriented behaviour in the workplace that results in discomfort and/or interference with the job.

customers what they think about the quality of the goods and services the organization produces. Increasingly, successful organizations are those that are other-oriented; they focus on the needs of those they serve through **outward communication**. They are spending time and money to find out what the *customer* perceives as quality, rather than relying solely on the judgments of their corporate executives. And they are training their staffs to develop more empathy, better listening skills, and more awareness of non-verbal messages from customers.

Sexual Harassment

The Canada Labour Code, the Canadian Human Rights Act, the Employment Equity Act, and provincial and territorial human rights codes prohibit all types of harassment including sexual harassment. The Human Rights Code covers the federal public service and federally regulated industries such as banks, communications, and inter-provincial transportation. A provincial code, such as that of Ontario, prohibits all types of harassment, and employers are responsible for preventing and discouraging harassment. If an employer fails to do so, the employee may file a complaint with the Ontario Human Rights Commission. Thus, business and industries not covered by the various provincial and federal codes still must provide harassment-free workplaces for all employees. According to Labour Canada, 41 percent of workers covered by major collective agreements have some form of negotiated protection against harassment including **sexual harassment**.[67] Division XV.1 of Part III of the Canada Labour Code establishes that all employees have the right to be free of sexual harassment in the workplace and requires employers to take positive action to prevent sexual harassment in the workplace. The Canada Labour Code defines sexual harassment as "any conduct, comment, gesture, or contact of a sexual nature that is likely to cause offence or humiliation to any employee or that might, on reasonable grounds, be perceived by that employee as placing a condition of a sexual nature on employment or on any opportunity for training or promotion."[68] The Supreme Court of Canada defines sexual harassment as unwelcome behaviour of a sexual nature in the workplace that negatively affects the work environment or leads to adverse job-related consequences for the employee.

Sexual harassment can include something as violent as rape or as subtle as making a sexually oriented comment about another person's body or appearance. Decorating the work area with pictures of nude people or displaying pornographic pictures on a computer are examples of more subtle sexual harassment. A Canadian Human Rights Tribunal identified three characteristics of sexual harassment. The first characteristic is that the encounters must be unsolicited and unwelcome to the complainant. An example of this type of behaviour is unwelcome sexual remarks. The second characteristic is that the conduct continues despite the complainant's protests, or if it does stop, there are negative employment consequences. For instance, the comments do not stop or the comments stop and the complainant is denied a promised promotion. Third, any perceived cooperation by the complainant must be due to employment-related threats or promises.[69] However, there is still much "grey area" when interpreting what is considered to be or not to be sexual harassment.

Despite codes, acts, and employer policies, sexual harassment continues to be a serious problem in the workplace. In the past decade, sexual harassment has received increasing attention due to the growing ranks of women in non-traditional work environments, recent high profile cases such as alleged cover-ups of harassment in the Canadian Armed Forces, a murder-suicide at a Sears Canada store in Windsor, Ontario, and increased numbers of men and women reporting sexual harassment. Recent surveys indicate that about half of working women experience some sort of sexual harassment in the workplace. The largest Canadian survey, *The Survey on Sexual Harassment in Public Places and at Work* (SSHPPW), reported that 56 percent of Canadian working women had experienced sexual harassment in the year prior to the survey.[70] The most common incidents were staring, jokes or comments about women, and jokes about the respondents themselves. While most research is devoted to men harassing women, this does not mean that women do not harass men, or that harassment does not take place between same-sex individuals. Of interest, a poll conducted in British Columbia indicated that 14 percent of 400 men polled said they had experienced sexual harassment at work.[71]

One researcher and her colleagues have worked on a typology of sexual harassment that includes gender harassment (behaviours that indicate demeaning attitudes about women), unwanted sexual attention (both verbal and non-verbal attention), and sexual coercion (the use of threats or rewards to solicit sexual favours).[72]

Building Your Skills

WHAT IS SEXUAL HARASSMENT?

Read each of the following situations, and write an A in the blank if you agree that the situation depicts some form of sexual harassment, or D if you disagree. Share your answers with your classmates and discuss those situations over which you disagree.

_____ 1. Marcia is wearing a low-cut blouse and a miniskirt; a male co-worker whistles at her as she is walking down the hall. In the past, Marcia has told her colleague that she does not appreciate his behaviour. The male co-worker is guilty of sexual harassment.

_____ 2. Susan is the branch manager of an insurance firm. She asks one of her employees, Steve, to stay after work and discuss some work-related ideas with her. When Steve arrives, the lights are dimmed, the door is locked, Susan offers Steve a glass of wine, and she asks Steve to sit next to her on the couch. Susan is guilty of sexual harassment.

_____ 3. Jesse, Lee, and Luc usually meet for lunch in the company cafeteria. They like to tell each other sexually explicit jokes that often portray women as sex objects. Juanita overhears the jokes and complains to her supervisor. Jesse, Lee, and Luc are guilty of sexual harassment.

_____ 4. Joao is a college professor who has a *Playboy* calendar displayed in his office. He requires all his students to visit him in his office for a private tutorial session in each of his classes. Joao is guilty of sexual harassment.

_____ 5. Liz, Joao's department chair, has received several complaints from female students about the calendar that Joao displays on his wall. She has not asked Joao to remove the calendar. Liz is guilty of sexual harassment.

_____ 6. At the weekly staff meeting several of the male workers secretly rate their female co-workers on a scale from 1 to 10 in terms of their physical attractiveness and then compare notes after the meeting. The supervisor knows this occurs but does not say anything about it. The supervisor is guilty of sexual harassment.

_____ 7. Barbara has left Ricardo several notes asking him for a date. Ricardo keeps refusing Barbara's requests. Now Barbara sends him e-mail messages about three times each week, asking Ricardo for a date. Ricardo asks Barbara to stop sending him messages, but she persists. Barbara is guilty of sexual harassment.

leadership. Behaviour that influences, guides, controls, or inspires others to take action.

Enhancing Leadership Skills

The preceding discussion of upward and downward communication is a reminder that workplaces are hierarchies of power and influence. Some workers—those with such titles as boss or manager—have assigned leadership roles, while others follow their directives. The most successful workplaces have both effective leaders and effective followers. In most organizations today all workers are expected to exhibit some degree of leadership skill. The essence of **leadership** is the ability to influence others.

Around 700 B.C., Homer warned his Athenian audience to be selective in their attempts to assume control: "You will certainly not be able to take the lead in all things yourself, for to one man a god has given deeds of war, and to another the dance, to another the lyre and song, and in another widesounding Zeus puts a good mind." The first qualification for leadership, as he was trying to tell them, is skill and knowledge about the task at hand. In addition, however, you need the skills necessary to motivate, inspire, and instruct others in their work. Because not all of us are born with these skills, Stephen Covey wrote a book called *The Seven Habits of Highly Effective People* to help those of us who want to sharpen our leadership skills. To be successful as a leader, Covey suggests the following:[73]

1. *Be proactive.* Don't wait until a situation becomes a problem to solve before starting to solve it. Don't simply react to problems, but anticipate them. Don't blame others. Accept responsibility for making decisions yourself.

2. *Begin with the end in mind.* Effective people have a vision of where they are going and what they want to accomplish.

3. *Put first things first.* In Covey's words, "Make sure the main thing is the main thing." Manage your time so that you can manage your life.

4. *Think win/win.* Don't assume someone must lose and someone must win. Approach situations attempting to maximize the benefits for all.

5. *Seek first to understand, then to be understood.* Listen effectively. Listening skills are essential in being other-oriented.

6. *Synergize.* Synergy means that working together results in more creativity than working alone.

7. *Sharpen the saw.* Take time out to enhance your skills rather than continuing to work with "unsharpened" tools.

The most effective leaders combine a task orientation with a relationship orientation to perform the following functions:[74]

Task Functions

1. *Initiate* new ideas or approaches to achieving the task.

2. *Provide information,* such as facts, examples, statistics.

3. *Seek information* by asking for facts and other data that can help get the work done.

4. *Seek opinions* and ask for clarification of opinions expressed by others.

5. *Offer opinions* about issues and ideas under consideration.

6. *Elaborate* and amplify the ideas of others.

7. *Evaluate* the advantages and disadvantages of issues, ideas, or proposed solutions.

8. *Energize* and motivate the group to take action and be productive.

Relationship Functions

9. *Encourage* others and offer praise and acceptance of others' ideas.

10. *Harmonize* and mediate disagreements and conflict.

11. *Compromise* and seek ways of finding common ground among group members.

12. *Be a gatekeeper* by encouraging less talkative members to participate and limiting lengthy orations from big talkers.

Enhancing Followership Skill

If you find yourself playing the role of follower in a group, remind yourself that you can still make an enormous contribution. Consider the following:

1. Seek opportunities to provide input and suggestions to leaders. Look for ways to communicate your interest in the goals of the group.

2. Listen well. This skill appears on any list for leaders or followers. Listening effectively and being able to comprehend and evaluate information is an essential followership skill.

3. Provide appropriate feedback. If you are not sure you understand directions from your superior, ask for further clarification.

4. Support your suggestions with evidence rather than with off-the-cuff opinions. Be able to document your suggestions with data, rather than relying only on emotion-based hunches. Although you should not ignore intuitive thoughts, most supervisors will respond more positively to those ideas you can support with evidence.

5. Don't abandon your ethical principles. If you are being asked to do something that violates your sense of right and wrong, you may need to suggest tactfully that the orders you have been given by your boss are not consistent with your ethical principles. "I was only following orders" or "I was just doing what I was told" usually don't hold up in court as an excuse for violating the law.

Summary

Relationships progress through stages, with the movement from one stage to another often signalled by turning points. As relationships escalate, they progress from pre-interaction awareness to initiation, to exploration, to intensification, and finally, to intimacy. Relationships de-escalate as we move to redefine or terminate them, moving from turmoil or stagnation, to de-intensification, to individualization, to separation, and finally, to post-interaction. Even after we end a relationship, its effects remain with us to shape our feelings and responses in other relationships. We use a variety of skills within each relational stage.

To move from initial attraction to initiation of interaction, we need to understand and utilize such skills as gathering information to reduce uncertainty, adopting an other-oriented perspective, observing and acting on approachability cues, identifying and using conversation starters, following initiation norms, providing information about ourselves, presenting ourselves in a positive way, asking questions, and not expecting too much from the initial interaction.

We disclose increasingly intimate and risky information as relationships escalate. Strategies for escalating and maintaining relationships include communicating attraction, monitoring perceptions, listening actively, and responding confirmingly; being open and self-disclosing appropriately; expressing emotions; socially decentring and adapting; being tolerant and showing restraint; and managing conflict cooperatively. People can react to relational problems by either ignoring them, trying to address and repair them, or by choosing to redefine or end the relationship. In a bilateral dissolution, both parties want to end the relationship, whereas in a unilateral dissolution one person wants to end the relationship and the other wants to maintain it. Relationships typically end in one of three ways: by fading away, through sudden death, or incrementally.

In general, relationships seem to end when the costs exceed the rewards over some period of time. The relationship no longer confirms an individual's sense of self enough to outweigh the demands the relationship places on the individual. The causes for ending a relationship fall into three categories: faults, unwillingness to compromise, and feeling constrained.

A new context for interpersonal relationships is cyberspace or the Internet. From an interpersonal perspective, you can initiate and develop new relationships totally through computer-mediated communication (CMC) or you can use the Internet as a tool for maintaining existing relationships. Compared to face-to-face (FtF) communication, CMC offers fewer non-verbal cues, more reliance on the written word, variation in terms of being synchronous (interacting at the same time) or asynchronous (interactive but not at the same time), and the ability of posters to be deceptive or even simply disappear.

In initiating new relationships over the Internet, you need to participate in the right kind of a chat room, generally one that reflects your interests. Follow the same rules in developing a new relationship over the Internet as you would in person, realizing that the process is generally slower through CMC. The very act of keeping up with communication through the Internet helps maintain existing relationships. The amount of CMC and changes in the amount provide some indication of a person's interest in and commitment to the relationship. CMC can be used as a tool for implementing the various relational maintenance strategies discussed earlier in this chapter.

Relationships at work can involve both a task and social dimension. Forming friendships at work is one way people meet social needs and often helps produce a positive work atmosphere. The challenge of workplace interpersonal relationships is maximizing the satisfaction derived from such relationships while minimizing any negative impact on work performance. In most organizations communication flows up, down, horizontally, and out to customers. Through upward communication you can share ideas and strategies for improving the work process; you can also enhance your relationship with your boss. Downward communication involves making contact with those who work for you. Horizontal communication concerns the communication you have with your colleagues on your level throughout the organization; most of the time, however, horizontal communication will occur with those who work in your immediate vicinity. Most organizations are encouraging better communication with customers and clients. Contacting those outside the organization who receive the organization's goods and services is an important way to ensure that what the organization offers is of high quality.

Leadership skills are important for success in most jobs. To enhance your leadership skills, cultivate people management skills such as listening, responding, organizing, and inspiring others. Leaders also need to know how to organize work, accomplish tasks, and relate well to others. An effective follower—a role most people play in organizations—makes relevant contributions, listens, follows directions, supports suggestions with evidence, and doesn't abandon ethical principles.

For Discussion and Review

Focus on Comprehension

1. What are the five stages of relational escalation and the five stages of relational de-escalation?
2. What skills are associated with starting a relationship?
3. What interpersonal skills are associated with maintaining and escalating relationships?
4. What are the direct and indirect strategies for ending a relationship?
5. How does computer-mediated communication (CMC) compare to face-to-face (FtF) communication?
6. What rules are suggested for initiating a relationship on the Internet? For maintaining an existing relationship on the Internet?
7. Jerri is president of Southwest Technical Computing. She has a sense that her managers are not tapping the wealth of ideas and suggestions that lower-level employees might have for improving productivity. What specific strategies could Jerri implement to improve upward communication?

Focus on Critical Thinking

8. Which two skills are probably the most important for starting a relationship and which two are least important? Why?
9. How do the strategies for escalating and maintaining a relationship relate to the indirect and direct strategies used for terminating a relationship?

10. Trace two close relationships that you have had—one with a friend of the same sex, and one with a friend of the opposite sex—through the applicable stages of relational escalation and de-escalation. What differences and similarities do you find at each stage? How can you explain them?

11. Despite the availability of relatively cheap interactive video setups for Internet use, people don't seem to be turning to them as much as they are to text-only interactions. Why might this be the case? Which would you use if you had a choice of the two? Why?

Focus on Ethics

12. You are in a romantic relationship that has become physically intimate. How ethical is it for you to say, "I love you" if you really aren't sure you do? If your partner says "I love you," should you say, "I love you too," even if you don't mean it?

13. In chat sessions on the Internet, is it really wrong to present false information about yourself just for fun when you know you will never meet the other people with whom you are interacting? Under what circumstances is describing yourself over the Internet as being of a different sex, age, race, or ethnicity ethical or unethical?

14. Lynn and Mario have had an intimate relationship and have been living together for over a year. The relationship has seemed to be comfortable for both of them. One day, Lynn comes home from work and finds that all of Mario's belongings are gone. A note from Mario says, "I couldn't bring myself to tell you I'm leaving. Sorry. Good-bye." Is Mario's behaviour ethical?

15. Kyle has e-mail at work, but not at home. His brother has e-mail at his home. Is it ethical for Kyle to use the computer at work on company time to send and receive e-mail messages from his brother three or four times a week?

For Your Journal

1. At the end of each day, for three or four days, stop and assess which of the interpersonal communication skills you used the most in your interactions that day. See if there is a consistent pattern in the skills you rely on. What skills do you seem to use the most? What skills do you use the least? How might using other skills affect your interactions and relationships?

2. Log on to a social chat room and then onto a topic-specific chat room. You don't have to post any messages; just be a "lurker" and watch what happens. What do people do to compensate for the lack of non-verbal cues? What do you notice about the messages themselves (for example, how long are they, what is the vocabulary like, how is the grammar, what jargon or slang is used?)? How do the two sites compare in terms of language? Focus on a couple of the posters on each site. What is your impression of these posters on the basis of what you observe?

3. Think about a close relationship you had and that you ended. What strategy did you first use? How well did this strategy work? What was your partner's reaction to this strategy? How did you feel using this strategy? What

other strategies were used, if any? What were the reactions to those strategies? If you had it to do over again, what other strategy might you have chosen to use? How do you think your partner would have reacted to that strategy? Why? If you can't think of any relationship that you have ended, use one in which your partner ended the relationship, and adapt the questions accordingly.

Learning with Others

1. In class, form at least five pairs of students. Each pair should choose a particular stage of relational development without telling the rest of the class. Then, each pair should spend two minutes discussing plans for the upcoming weekend in a way that communicates the stage they have chosen. The rest of the class should write down what stage they think each pair is portraying. After all the pairs have finished their dialogues, score each others' responses. Which stage was easiest to portray and identify? Which stage was most difficult? How easy is it to see differences in communication behaviour at various stages?

2. Internet Study Group

    Find three or four other students in your class with whom you feel comfortable and confident. Arrange some times where you can all be logged on to the Internet at the same time to do instant messaging, send e-mails copied to all the other group members, or create a chat room for your group. Share information with one another about the last assignments you had for this class such as examinations or papers. Discuss among yourselves through the Internet what is expected for the assignments, share any information each of you has that might help the others prepare better, and ask questions to help clarify information. If you are preparing for an exam, each of you might pose practice questions to the others, or each take a turn explaining some concept.

3. Working in groups of four or five students, use your own experiences to develop an answer to the following question: Do the reasons for breaking up a relationship change as the relationship becomes more intimate? To answer this question, start with casual relationships and identify reasons that people end those relationships. Next, talk about friendships and discuss reasons for ending them. And, finally, talk about intimate relationships and the reasons they break up. What are the similarities and differences among these relationships and why they break up?

Weblinks

http://dating.about.com/people/dating/gi/dynamic/offsite.htm?site=http%3A%2F%2Fwww.life-n-leisure.com%2Fdating%2Farticles%2Fquestions.htm   Here you'll find an article titled "Questions to Keep the Conversation Going During a Date" by Tim Arends.

www.campuslife.utoronto.ca/handbook/06-GettingFitAndHealthy.html This is a handbook that addresses various concerns of college and university students.

www.hcc.hawaii.edu/intranet/committees/FacDevCom/guidebk/teachtip/stress-1.htm
This site is about stress. There is a test you can take to assess your own level of stress.

www.queendom.com This site has all kinds of self-tests including leadership and other workplace-related tests.

Suggested Readings

Knox, David, Lakisha Sturdivant, and Marty E. Zusman. "College Students' Attitudes toward Sexual Intimacy." *College Student Journal*, 35(2), 241–244.
   An interesting study of attitudes about sexual intimacy including gender differences.

Conger, Rand D., Ming Cui, Chalandra M. Bryant, and Glen H. Elder. "Competence in Early Adult Romantic Relationships: A Developmental Perspective on Family Influences." *Prevention and Treatment*, 4, Article 11, posted May 14, 2001.
   Read the most current findings of this longitudinal study about the development of romantic relationships based on the type of family that began in 1989 when the subjects were in Grade 7.

Laiken, Marilyn E. *The Anatomy of High Performing Teams: A Leader's Handbook.* Toronto, ON: OISE Press, 1994.
   An excellent resource for the behaviours and skills required for people to become members in high-performing teams.

Notes

Chapter 1

1. E. T. Klemmer and F. W. Snyder, "Measurement of Time Spent Communicating," *Journal of Communication,* 20 (June 1972): 142.

2. F. E. X. Dance and C. Larson, *Speech Communication: Concepts and Behavior* (New York: Holt, Rinehart and Winston, 1972).

3. Dance and C. Larson, *Speech Communication.*

4. J. T. Masterson, S. A. Beebe, and N. H. Watson, *Invitation to Effective Speech Communication* (Glenview, IL: Scott, Foresman, 1989).

5. M. Buber, *I and Thou* (New York: Scribners, 1958); also see M. Buber, *Between Man and Man* (New York: Macmillan, 1965). For a detailed discussion of perspectives on interpersonal communication and relationship development, see G. H. Stamp, "A Qualitatively Constructed Interpersonal Communication Model: A Grounded Theory Analysis," *Human Communication Research,* 25(4), (June 1999): 531–47; J. P. Dillard, D. H. Solomon, and M. T. Palmer, "Structuring the Concept of Relational Communication," *Communication Monographs,* 66 (March 1999): 49–65.

6. Buber, *I and Thou.*

7. D. Yankelovich, *The Magic of Dialogue: Transforming Conflict into Cooperation* (New York: Simon & Schuster, 1999); for an excellent discussion of dialogue, also see S. W. Littlejohn and K. Domenici, *Engaging Communication in Conflict: Systemic Practice* (Thousand Oaks, CA: Sage, 2001), 25–51.

8. Buber, *I and Thou.*

9. V. Satir, *Peoplemaking* (Palo Alto, CA: Science and Behavior Books, 1972).

10. K. E. Davis and M. Todd, "Assessing Friendship: Prototypes, Paradigm Cases, and Relationship Description," in *Understanding Personal Relationships,* eds. S. W. Duck and D. Perlman (London: Sage, 1985).

11. B. Wellman, "From Social Support to Social Network," in *Social Support: Theory, Research and Applications,* eds. I. G. Sarason and B. R. Sarason (Dordrecht, Netherlands: Nijhoff, 1985).

12. R. Hopper, M. L. Knapp, and L. Scott, "Couples' Personal Idioms: Exploring Intimate Talk," *Journal of Communication,* 31 (1981): 23–33.

13. J. L. Freedman, *Happy People* (New York: Harcourt Brace Jovanovich, 1978).

14. M. Argyle and M. Hendershot, *The Anatomy of Relationships* (London: Penguin Books, 1985), 14.

15. W. M. Kephard, "Some Correlates of Romantic Love," *Journal of Marriage and the Family,* 29 (1967): 470–74.

16. M. Argyle, *The Psychology of Happiness* (London: Routledge, 1987).

17. J. J. Lynch, *The Broken Heart: The Medical Consequences of Loneliness* (New York: Basic Books, 1977).

18. D. P. Phillips, "Deathday and Birthday: An Unexpected Connection," in *Statistics: A Guide to the Unknown,* ed. J. M. Tanur (San Francisco: Holden Day, 1972).

19. F. Korbin and G. Hendershot, "Do Family Ties Reduce Mortality?: Evidence from the United States 1966–68," *Journal of Marriage and the Family,* 39 (1977): 737–45.

20. Korbin and G. Hendershot, "Do Family Ties Reduce Mortality?"

21. M. Argyle, *The Psychology of Interpersonal Behaviour* (London: Penguin, 1983).

22. Canadian Mental Health Association, Vancouver, "Understanding Depression" October, 1995.

23. Korbin and G. Hendershot, "Do Family Ties Reduce Mortality?"

24. H. Lasswell, "The Structure and Function of Communication in Society," in *The Communication of Ideas,* ed. L. Bryson (New York: Institute for Religious and Social Studies, 1948), 37.

25. See V. E. Cronen, W. B. Pearce, and L. M. Harris, "The Coordinated Management of Meaning: A Theory of Communication," in *Human Communication Theory: Comparative Essays*, ed. F. E. X. Dance (New York: Harper & Row, 1982), 61–89.

26. For an excellent discussion of the effects of computer-mediated communication and interpersonal communication, see J. B. Walther, "Interpersonal Effects in Computer-Mediated Interaction: A Relational Perspective," *Communication Research,* 19 (1992): 52–90; J. B. Walther, "Relational Aspects of Computer-Mediated Communication: Experimental and Longitudinal Observations," *Organization Science,* 6 (1995): 186–203; J. B. Walther, J. F. Anderson, and D. Park, "Interpersonal Effects in Computer-Mediated Interaction: A Meta-Analysis of Social and Anti-Social Communication," *Communication Research,* 21 (1994): 460–87; N. Negroponte, *Being Digital* (New York: Knopf, 1995); J. B. Walther and L. Tidwell, "When Is Mediated Communication Not Interpersonal?" in K. Galvin and P. Cooper, *Making Connections* (Los Angeles, CA: Roxbury Press, 1996); P. Wallace, *The Psychology of the Internet* (Cambridge, England: Cambridge University Press, 1999).

27. J. B. Walther and J. K. Burgoon, "Relational Communication in Computer-Mediated Interaction," *Human Communication Research,* 19 (1992): 50–88.

28. L. K. Trevino, R. L. Draft, and R. H. Lengel, "Understanding Managers' Media Choices: A Symbolic Interactionist Perspective," in *Organizations and Communication Technology,* J. Fulk and C. Steinfield (eds.) (Newbury Park, CA: Sage, 1990), 71–74.

29. Walther and Tidwell.

30. See D. Barnlund, *Interpersonal Communication: Survey and Studies* (Boston: Houghton Mifflin, 1968).

31. O. Wiio, *Wiio's Laws—and Some Others* (Espoo, Finland: WelinGoos, 1978).

32. S. B. Shimanoff, *Communication Rules: Theory and Research* (Beverly Hills: Sage, 1980).

33. M. Argyle, M. Hendershot, and A. Furnham, "The Rules of Social Relationships," *British Journal of Social Psychology,* 24 (1985): 125–39.

34. T. Watzlawick, J. Bavelas, and D. Jackson, *The Pragmatics of Human Communication* (New York: Norton, 1967).

35. See J. C. McCroskey and M. [J.] Beatty, "The Communibiological Perspective: Implications for Communication in Instruction," *Communication Education,* 49(1) (January 2000): 1–6; M. J. Beatty and J. C. McCroskey, "Theory, Scientific Evidence, and the Communibiological Paradigm: Reflections on Misguided Criticism," *Communication Education,* 49(1), (January 2000): 36–44. Also see J. C. McCroskey, J. A. Daly, M. M. Martin, and M. J. Beatty, (eds.), *Communication and Personality: Trait Perspectives* (Cresskil, NJ: Hampton Press, 1998).

36. See J. Ayres and T. S. Hopf, "The Long-Term Effect of Visualization in the Classroom: A Brief Research Report," *Communication Education,* 39 (1990): 75–78; and J. Ayres and T. S. Hopf, "Visualization: A Means of Reducing Speech Anxiety," *Communication Education,* 34 (1985): 318–23.

37. For a discussion of criticism of the communibiological approach, see C. M. Condit, "Culture and Biology in Human Communication: Toward a Multi-Causal Model," *Communication Education,* 49(1), (January 2000): 7–24.

38. M. Argyle, *The Psychology of Interpersonal Behaviour* (London: Penguin Books, 1983).

39. Argyle, *The Psychology of Interpersonal Behaviour.*

40. M. Argyle is widely acknowledged as the first scholar to suggest a systematic approach to apply learning theory to the development of social skills, including interpersonal communication skills. See: Argyle, *The Psychology of Interpersonal Behaviour.*

Chapter 2

1. K. Horney, *Neurosis and Human Growth* (New York: W. W. Norton & Co., 1950), 17.

2. J. M. Jones, S. Bennet, M. P. Olmstead, M. L. Lawson, G. Rodin, "Disordered Eating Attitudes and Behaviours in Teenaged Girls: A School-Based Study," *Canadian Medical Association Journal,* 165(5) (2001): 547–53.

3. S. L. Bem, "The Measurement of Psychological Androgyny," *Journal of Consulting and Clinical Psychology,* 42 (1974): 155–62.

4. For an excellent discussion of the role of gender and communication see J. C. Pearson, L. H. Turner, and W. Todd-Mancillas, *Gender and Communication,* 3d ed. (Dubuque, IA: Wm. C. Brown, Publishers, 1995). Also see D. K. Ivy and P. Backlund, *Exploring Gender Speak* (New York: McGraw-Hill, 1994).

5. Pearson, Turner, and Todd-Mancillas, *Gender and Communication*; Ivy and Backlund, *Exploring Gender Speak.*

6. D. G. Ancona, "Groups in Organizations: Extending Laboratory Models," in *Annual Review of Personality and Social Psychology: Group and Intergroup Processes,* ed. C. Hendrick (Beverly Hills: Sage, 1987): 207–31. Also see D. G. Ancona and D. F. Caldwell, "Beyond Task and Maintenance: Defining External Functions in Groups," *Group and Organizational Studies,* 13 (1988): 468–94.

7. This adaptation of S. L. Bem's work is from R. M. Berko, L. B. Rosenfeld, and L. A. Samovar, *Connecting: A Culture-Sensitive Approach to Interpersonal Communication Competency* (Fort Worth: Harcourt, Brace College Publishers, 1994).

8. L. A. Lefton, *Psychology* (Boston: Allyn & Bacon, 2000).

9. J. C. McCroskey and M. J. Beatty, "The Communibiological Perspective: Implications for Communication Instruction," *Communication Education,* 49 (January 2000): 1–28.

10. C. M. Condit, "Culture and Biology in Human Communication: Toward a Multi-Causal Model," *Communication Education,* 49 (January 2000): 7–24.

11. P. Zimbardo, *Shyness: What It Is, What to Do about It* (Reading, MA: Addison-Wesley, 1977).

12. S. Booth-Butterfield, "Instructional Interventions for Situational Anxiety and Avoidance," *Communication Education,* 37 (1988): 214–23.

13. J. C. McCroskey and V. P. Richmond, *Fundamentals of Human Communication: An Interpersonal Perspective* (Prospect Heights, IL: Waveland Press, 1996).

14. S. Booth-Butterfield, "Instructional Interventions."

15. Zimbardo, *Shyness.*

16. Our discussion of the Myers-Briggs Type Indicator is based on an excellent summary of research by L. A. Lefton, *Psychology* (Boston: Allyn and Bacon, 2000), 426–27.

17. E. Berne, *Games People Play* (New York: Grove Press, 1964).

18. F. E. X. Dance and C. Larson, *The Functions of Human Communication* (New York: Holt, Rinehart and Winston, 1976), 141.

19. M. V. Redmond, "The Functions of Empathy (Decentering) in Human Relations," *Human Relations,* 42 (1993): 593–606. Also see M. V. Redmond, "A Multidimensional Theory and Measure of Social Decentering," *Journal of Research in Personality* (1995).

20. B. Siegel, *Love, Medicine and Miracles* (New York: Harper & Row, 1986).

21. A. A. Milne, "Pooh Does a Good Deed," in *Pooh Sleepytime Stories* (New York: Golden Press, 1979), 44.

22. Summarized by D. E. Hamachek, *Encounters with the Self* (New York: Holt, Rinehart and Winston, 1982), 3–5, and R. B. Adler and N. Towne, (eds.), *Looking Out/Looking In* (Fort Worth: Harcourt, Brace Jovanovich College Publishers, 1993). Also see C. R. Berger, "Self-Conception and Social Information Processing," in *Personality and Interpersonal Communication,* eds. J. C. McCroskey and J. A. Daly (Newbury Park, CA: Sage, 1987), 275–303.

23. A. A. Milne, "Owl Finds a Home," in *Pooh Sleepytime Stories* (New York: Golden Press, 1979), 28.

24. Hamachek, *Encounters with the Self,* and Berger, "Self-Conception and Social Information Processing."

25. W. C. Schutz, *FIRO: A Three-Dimensional Theory of Interpersonal Behavior* (New York: Holt, Rinehart & Winston, 1958).

26. McCroskey and Beatty, "Communibiological Perspective."

27. See J. C. McCroskey and V. P. Richmond, *Fundamentals of Human Communication.*

Chapter 3

1. C. R. Berger, "Self-Conception and Social Information Processing," in

Notes

Personality and Interpersonal Communication, eds. J. C. McCroskey and J. A. Daly (Newbury Park, CA: Sage, 1987), 275–304.

2. P. R. Hinton, *The Psychology of Interpersonal Perception* (New York: Routledge, 1993).

3. D. W. Miller, "Looking Askance at Eyewitness Testimony," *Chronicle of Higher Education*, February 25, 2000: A19–20.

4. A. L. Sillars, "Attribution and Communication: Are People Naive Scientists or Just Naive?" in *Social Cognition and Communication*, eds. M. E. Roloff, and C. R. Berger (Beverly Hills: Sage, 1982), 73–106.

5. R. D. Laing, H. Phillipson, and A. R. Lee, *Interpersonal Perception* (New York: Springer, 1966).

6. C. R. Berger and J. J. Bradac, *Language and Social Knowledge* (Baltimore: Edward Arnold, 1982).

7. S. Asch, "Forming Impressions of Personality," *Journal of Abnormal and Social Psychology*, 41 (1946): 258–90.

8. D. M. Wegner and R. R. Vallacher, *Implicit Psychology: An Introduction to Social Cognition* (New York: Oxford University Press, 1977).

9. J. S. Bruner and R. Tagiuri, "The Perception of People," in *Handbook of Social Psychology*, ed. G. Lindzey (Cambridge, MA: Addison-Wesley, 1954).

10. F. Heider, *The Psychology of Interpersonal Relations* (New York: Wiley, 1958).

11. E. E. Jones and K. E. Davis, "From Acts to Dispositions: The Attribution Process in Person Perception," in *Advances in Experimental Social Psychology*, Vol. 2, ed. L. Berkowitz (New York: Academic Press, 1965).

12. G. A. Kelly, *The Psychology of Personal Constructs* (New York: Norton, 1955).

13. D. Hamecheck, *Encounters with the Self*, 3d ed. (Fort Worth: Harcourt Brace Jovanovich, 1992).

14. R. Nisbett and L. Ross, *Human Inference: Strategies and Shortcomings of Social Judgment* (Englewood Cliffs, NJ: Prentice-Hall, 1980).

15. Nisbett and Ross, *Human Inference*.

16. Nisbett and Ross, *Human Inference*.

17. E. E. Jones and R. Nisbett, "The Actor and the Observer: Divergent Perceptions of the Causes of Behavior," in E. E. Jones et al., *Attribution: Perceiving the Causes of Behavior* (Morristown, NJ: General Learning Press, 1972), 79–94; D. E. Kanouse and L. R. Hanson, Jr., "Negativity in Evaluations," in E. E. Jones et al., 47–62.

18. Hinton, *The Psychology of Interpersonal Perception*.

19. Asch, "Forming Impressions of Personality."

20. M. V. Redmond, "The Functions of Empathy (Decentering) in Human Relations," *Human Relations*, 42(4), (1993): 593–606.

21. Ronald B. Adler, Neil Towne, and Judith A. Rolls (2001). *Looking Out, Looking In*. Orlando, FLA: Harcourt Brace.

Chapter 4

1. L. Barker et al., "An Investigation of Proportional Time Spent in Various Communication Activities of College Students," *Journal of Applied Communication Research*, 8 (1981): 101–09.

2. K. W. Watson, L. L. Barker, and J. B. Weaver, *The Listener Style Inventory* (New Orleans: SPECTRA, 1995).

3. S. L. Sargent and J. B. Weaver, "Correlates between Communication Apprehension and Listening Style Preferences," *Communication Research Reports*, 14 (1997): 74–78.

4. M. D. Kirtley and J. M. Honeycutt, "Listening Styles and Their Correspondence with Second Guessing," *Communication Research Reports*, 13 (1996): 174–182.

5. Sargent and Weaver, "Correlates between Communication Apprehension."

6. W. Winter, A. J. Ferreira, and N. Bowers, "Decision-Making in Married and Unrelated Couples," *Family Process*, 12 (1973): 83–94.

7. O. E. Rankis, "The Effects of Message Structure, Sexual Gender, and Verbal Organizing Ability upon Learning Message Information," Ph.D. dissertation, Ohio University, 1981; C. H. Weaver, *Human Listening: Process and Behavior* (New York: The Bobbs-Merrill Company, 1972); R. D. Halley, "Distractibility of Males and Females in Competing Aural Message Situations: A Research Note," *Human Communication Research*, 2 (1975): 79–82. Our discussion of gender-based differences and listening is also based upon a discussion by: S. A. Beebe and J. T. Masterson, *Family Talk: Interpersonal Communication in the Family* (New York: Random House, 1986).

8. This discussion is based on A. Vangelisti, M. Knapp, and J. Daly, "Conversational Narcissism," *Communication Monographs*, 57 (1990): 251–74.

9. J. Thurber, "The Secret Life of Walter Mitty," in *Literature for Composition*, 3d ed., edited by S. Barnet et al. (Glenview, IL: Scott, Foresman, 1992), 43.

10. R. Montgomery, *Listening Made Easy* (New York: Amacon, 1981).

11. R. G. Owens, "Handling Strong Emotions," in O. Hargie, (ed.), *A Handbook of Communication Skills* (London: Croom Helm/New York University Press, 1986).

12. R. G. Nichols, "Factors in Listening Comprehension," *Speech Monographs*, 15 (1948): 154–63; G. M. Goldhaber and C. H. Weaver, "Listener Comprehension of Compressed Speech When the Difficulty, Rate of Presentation, and Sex of the Listener Are Varied," *Speech Monographs*, 35 (1968): 20–25.

13. J. Harrigan, "Listeners, Body Movements and Speaking Turns," *Communication Research*, 12 (1985): 233–50.

14. S. Strong et al., "Nonverbal Behavior and Perceived Counselor Characteristics," *Journal of Counseling Psychology*, 18 (1971): 554–61.

15. See: R. G. Nichols and L. A. Stevens, "Listening to People," *Harvard Business Review*, 35 (September–October 1957): 85–92.

16. C. W. Ellison and I. J. Fireston, "Development of Interpersonal Trust as a Function of Self-Esteem, Target Status and Target Style," *Journal of Personality and Social Psychology*, 29 (1974): 655–63.

17. "Canadian Issues: Languages in Canada," 1996, www.nais.ccm.emr.ca/school net/issues/html/langøø1.html

18. "Canadian Issues."

19. O. Hargie, C. Sanders, and D. Dickson, *Social Skills in Interpersonal Communication* (London: Routledge, 1991).

20. J. B. Weaver III and M. B. Kirtley, "Listening Styles and Empathy," *The*

Southern Communication Journal, 60 (1995): 131–40.

21. D. Goleman, *Emotional Intelligence* (New York: Bantam, 1995).

22. Goleman, *Emotional Intelligence.*

23. O. Hargie, C. Sanders, and D. Dickson, *Social Skills*; R. Boulton, *People Skills* (New York: 1981).

24. Boulton, *People Skills.* We also acknowledge others who have presented excellent applications of listening and responding skills in interpersonal and group contexts: Dennis A. Romig and Laurie J. Romig, *Structured Teamwork® Guide* (Austin, TX: Performance Resources, 1990); Sam Deep and Lyle Sussman, *Smart Moves* (Reading, MA: Addison-Wesley, 1990); Peter R. Scholtes, *The Team Handbook* (Madison, WI: Joiner Associates, 1988).

25. This discussion of logic fallacies is based on our discussion in S. A. Beebe and S. J. Beebe, *Public Speaking: An Audience-Centered Approach* (Boston: Allyn & Bacon, 2000), 89–392.

26. S. Gilbert, "Self-Disclosure, Intimacy, and Communication in Families," *Family Coordinator,* 25 (1976).

Chapter 5

1. R. A. Baron, B. Earhard, and M. Ozier, *Psychology* (Toronto: Pearson Education, 2001).

2. R. A. Baron et al., 2001.

3. D. Zillman, "Transfer of Excitation in Emotional Behavior" in *Social Psychophysiology,* eds. J. T. Cacioppo and R. E. Petty (New York: Academic Press, 1983); D. Zillman, "Cognition-Excitation Interdependencies in Aggressive Behavior," *Aggressive Behavior,* 14 (1988): 51–64.

4. D. Zillman, "Cognition-Excitation Interdependencies in Aggressive Behavior."

5. S. Schacter and J. E. Singer, "Cognitive, Social, and Physiological Determinants of Emotional States," *Psychological Review,* 69 (1962): 379–99.

6. P. Ekman, "Facial Expression of Emotion: New Findings, New Question," *Psychological Science,* 3 (1992): 34–38.

7. P. Ekman and K. G. Heider, "The Universality of a Contempt Expression: A Replication," *Motivation and Emotion,* 12 (1988): 303–308.

8. K. M. Prkachin, "The Consistency of Facial Expressions of Pain: A Comparison across Modalities," *Pain,* 51(3), (1992): 297–306.

9. Robert A. Baron, Bruce Earhard, and Marcia Ozier, *Psychology* (Scarborough, ON: Allyn and Bacon Canada, 1995).

10. M. Zuckerman, R. F. Simons, and P. Como, "Verbal and Nonverbal Communication of Deception," in L. Berkowitz, (ed.), *Advances in Experimental Psychology,* 14 (1981): 1–59.

11. J. B. Stiff, G. R. Miller, C. Sleight, and P. Mongeau, "Explanations for Visual Cue Primacy in Judgments of Honesty and Deceit," *Journal of Personality and Social Psychology,* 56 (1989): 554–564.

12. C. L. Kleinke, "Gaze and Eye Contact: A Research Review," *Psychological Bulletin,* 100 (1986): 78–100.

13. J. K. Burgoon, D. B. Buller and W. G. Woodall, *Nonverbal Communication: The Unspoken Dialogue* (New York: Harper and Row, 1989), 324.

14. Baron et al., *Psychology.*

15. Luigi Anolli and Rita Ciceri, "The Voice of Deception: Vocal Strategies of Naïve and Able Liars," *Journal of Nonverbal Behaviour,* 21(4), (1979): 259–284.

16. Baron et al., *Psychology.*

17. R. B. Zajonc and D. N. McIntosh, "Emotions Research: Some Promising Questions and Some Questionable Promises," *Psychological Science,* 3 (1992): 70–74.

18. Mary K. Devitt, Charles R. Honts and Lynelle Vondergreest, "Truth or Just Bias: The Treatment of the Psychophysiological Detection of Deception in Introductory Psychology Textbooks," *The Journal of Credibility Assessment and Witness Psychology,* 1(1), (1997): 9–32.

19. R. Plutchik, "A Language for the Emotions," *Psychology Today,* 14 (February 1980): 68–78.

20. J. W. Pennebaker, B. Rime, and V. E. Blankenship, "Stereotypes of Emotional Expressiveness of Northerners and Southerners: A Cross-Cultural Test of Montesquieu's Hypotheses," *Journal of Personality and Social Psychology,* 70 (1996): 372–380.

21. G. Hofstede, *Culture's Consequences: International Differences in Work-Related Attitudes* (Beverly Hills, CA: Sage, 1984).

22. J. A. Hall, "On Explaining Gender Differences: The Case of Nonverbal Communication," in P. Shaver and C. Hendricks, (eds.), *Sex and Gender* (Newbury Park, CA: Mayfield, 1987), 177–200.

23. L. Samovar and R. Porter (eds.), *Intercultural Communication: A Reader,* 7th ed. (Belmont, CA: Wadsworth, 1994).

24. L. R. Brody and J. A. Hall, "Gender and Emotion," in *Handbook of Emotions,* M. Lewis and J. M. Haviland, (eds.) (New York: Guilford, 1993): 451–452.

25. O. T. Goldshmidt, "'Talking Emotions': Gender Differences in a Variety of Conversational Contexts," *Symbolic Interaction,* 23(2), (2000): 117–135.

26. A. M. Kring and A. H. Gordon, "Sex Differences in Emotional Expression," *Harvard Mental Health Letter,* 16(3), (1999): 6–8.

27. A. M. Kring and A. H. Gordon.

28. Julia Wood, Ron Sept, and Jane Duncan, *Everyday Encounters: An Introduction to Interpersonal Communication* (Scarborough, ON: ITP Nelson, 1998).

29. E. Hatfield, J. T. Cacioppo, and R. L. Rapson, *Emotional Contagion* (New York: Cambridge University Press, 1994).

30. J. Dollard, L. W. Doob, N. E. Miller, O. H. Mowrer, and R. R. Sears, *Frustration and Aggression* (New Haven: Yale University Press, 1939).

31. L. Berkowitz, "Frustration-Aggression Hypothesis: Examination and Reformulation," *Psychological Bulletin,* 106 (1989): 93–106; L. Berkowitz, "On the Formation and Regulation of Anger and Aggression," *American Psychologist,* 45 (1990): 494–503.

32. Rene Martin and Choi K. Wan, "The Style of Anger Expression: Relation to Expressivity, Personality, and Health," *Personality and Social Psychology Bulletin,* 25(10), (1999): 1196–1208.

33. Andrew J. Dubrin and Terri Geerinck, *Human Relations for Personal and Career Success* (Toronto, ON: Pearson Education Canada, 2001).

34. Roland Ouellette, *Management of Aggressive Behaviour* (Powers Lake, WI: Performance Dimensions Publishing, 1993).

35. Roland Ouellette, "Management of Aggressive Behaviour," in Ed Nowicki, *Total Survival* (Powers Lake, WI: Performance Dimensions Publishing, 1996), 289–97.

36. See D. A. Infante and C. J. Wigley, "Verbal Aggressiveness: An Interpersonal Model and Measure," *Communication Monographs*, 53 (1986): 61–69; D. A. Infante and W. I. Gorden, "Superior and Subordinate Communication Profiles: Implications for Independent-Mindedness and Upward Effectiveness," *Central States Speech Journal*, 38 (1987): 73–80; D. A. Infante, B. L. Riddle, C. L. Horvath, and S. A. Tumlin, "Verbal Aggressiveness: Messages and Reasons," *Communication Quarterly*, 40 (1992): 116–126; D. E. Ifert and L. Bearden, "The Influence of Argumentativeness and Verbal Aggression on Responses to Refused Requests," *Communication Reports*, 11(2), (1998): 145–154; also see M. J. Beatty, K. M. Valencic, J. E. Rudd, and J. A. Dobos, "A 'Dark Side' of Communication Avoidance: Indirect Interpersonal Aggressiveness," *Communication Research Reports*, 16(2), (1999): 103–109.

37. See J. C. McCroskey and M. Beatty, "The Communibiological Perspective: Implications for Communication in Instruction," *Communication Education*, 49(1), (January 2000): 1–6; M. J. Beatty and J. C. McCroskey, "Theory, Scientific Evidence, and the Communibiological Paradigm: Reflections on Misguided Criticism," *Communication Education*, 49(1), (January 2000): 36–44. Also see J. C. McCroskey, J. A. Daly, M. M. Martin, and M. J. Beatty, (eds.), *Communication and Personality: Trait Perspectives* (Cresskil, NJ: Hampton Press, 1998).

38. Infante and Wigley, "Verbal Aggressiveness."

39. Infante et al., "Verbal Aggressiveness: Messages and Reasons."

40. American Psychiatric Association, *Diagnostic and Statistical Manual of Mental Disorders (IV)* (Washington, D. C.: American Psychiatric Press, 1994).

41. Zvia Breznitz, "Verbal Indicators of Depression," *Journal of General Psychology*, 119(4), (1992): 351–363.

42. Albert Ellis, *Humanistic Psychotherapy: The Rational-Emotive Approach* (New York: Lyle Stuart, 1973).

43. Albert Bandura, "Self-Efficacy: Toward a Unifying Theory of Behavior Change," *Psychological Review*, 84 (1977): 191–215.

44. T. J. Maurer and H. R. Pierce, "A Comparison of Likert Scale and Traditional Measures of Self-Efficacy," *Journal of Applied Psychology*, 83 (1998): 324–329.

45. Albert Bandura, "Exercise of Personal Agency through the Self-Efficacy Mechanism," in R. Schwarzer, (ed.), *Self-Efficacy: Thought Control of Action* (Washington, DC: Hemisphere, 1992), 3–38.

46. T. A Judge, J. J. Marocchio, and C. J. Thoresn, "Five-Factor Model of Personality and Employee Absence," *Journal of Applied Psychology*, 82 (1998): 745–755.

Chapter 6

1. C. K. Goden and I. A. Richards, *The Meaning of Meaning* (London: Kegan, Paul Trench, Trubner, 1923).

2. See G. H. Mead, *Mind, Self and Society* (Chicago: University of Chicago Press, 1934); H. Blumer, *Symbolic Interactionism: Perspective and Method* (Englewood Cliffs, NJ: Prentice Hall, 1969).

3. *The American Heritage Dictionary of the English Language* (Boston: Houghton Mifflin Company, 1969), 1162.

4. A. Korzybski, *Science and Sanity* (Lancaster, PA: Science Press, 1941).

5. G. Gusdorff, *Speaking* (Evanston, IL: Northwestern University Press, 1965), 9.

6. A. Ellis, *A New Guide to Rational Living* (North Hollywood, CA: Wilshire Books, 1977).

7. C. Peterson, M. E. P. Seligman, and G. E. Vaillant, "Pessimistic Explanatory Style Is a Risk Factor for Physical Illness: A 35-Year Longitudinal Study," *Journal of Personality and Social Psychology*, 55 (1988): 23–27.

8. D. W. Donakowski and V. M. Esses, "Native Canadians, First Nations, or Aboriginals: The Effect of Labels on Attitudes Toward Native Peoples," *Canadian Journal of Behavioural Science*, 28(3), (1996): 145–52.

9. Donakowski and Esses, "Native Canadians, First Nations, or Aboriginals."

10. J. E. Alcock, D. W. Carment, and S. W. Sadava, *A Textbook of Social Psychology*, (Scarborough, Ont: Prentice-Hall Canada, 1998).

11. F. K. Heussenstaunn, "Bumper Stickers and Cops," *Transaction*, 35 (1971): 32–33.

12. B. L. Whorf, "Science and Linguistics," in *Language, Thought and Reality*, ed. J. B. Carroll (Cambridge, MA: M.I.T. Press, 1956), 207.

13. W. Johnson, *People in Quandaries* (New York: Harper & Row).

14. A fascinating article, "The Melting of a Mighty Myth," in *Newsweek* (July 22, 1991) suggests that, contrary to popular opinion, Inuit do not have 23 words for snow, although they apparently do have more words to describe snow than most people who live in warm climates.

15. R. L. Howe, *The Miracle of Dialogue* (New York: The Seqbury Press, 1963), 23–24.

16. D. Yankelovich, *The Magic of Dialogue: Transforming Conflict into Cooperation* (New York: Simon & Schuster, 1999).

17. J. R. Gibb, "Defensive Communication," *Journal of Communication*, 11 (1961): 141–48. Also see R. Bolton, *People Skills* (New York: Simon and Schuster, 1979), 14–26.

18. H. S. O'Donnell, "Sexism in Language," *Elementary English*, 50 (1973): 1067–72, as cited by J. Pearson, L. Turner, and W. Todd-Mancillas, *Gender and Communication* (Dubuque, IA: William C. Brown, 1991), 96.

19. See D. K. Ivy and P. Backlund, *Exploring Gender Speak* (New York: McGraw Hill, 1994).

20. Associated Press. "'Canuck' No Slur, Editor Rehired," *Peterborough Examiner*, Sunday, February 28, 1999, B1.

21. We acknowledge and appreciate D. K. Ivy's contribution to this section on biased language. For an expanded discussion on this topic, see D. K. Ivy and P. Backlund, *Genderspeak* (New York: McGraw-Hill, 2000).

22. J. S. Seiter, J. Larsen, and J. Skinner, "'Handicapped' or 'Handicapable'?: The Effects of Language about Persons with Disabilities on Perceptions of Source Credibility and Persuasiveness," *Communication Reports*, 11(1), (1998): 21–31.

23. D. O. Braithwaite and C. A. Braithwaite, "Understanding Communication of Persons with Disabilities as Cultural Communication," in *Intercultural communication: A Reader*, 8th ed., edited by L. A. Samovar and R. E. Porter (Belmont, CA: Wadsworth, 1997): 154–64.

24. C. Rogers, *On Becoming a Person: A Therapist's View of Psychotherapy* (Boston: Houghton Mifflin, 1961); C.

Rogers, *A Way of Being* (Boston: Houghton Mifflin, 1980); C. Rogers, "Comments on the Issue of Equality in Psychotherapy," *Journal of Humanistic Psychology*, 27 (1987): 38–39.

25. E. Sieburg and C. Larson, "Dimensions of Interpersonal Response," paper delivered at the annual conference of the International Communication Association, Phoenix, April 1971.

Chapter 7

1. A. Mehrabian, *Nonverbal Communication* (Chicago: Aldine-Atherton, 1972), 108.

2. D. Lapakko, "Three Cheers for Language: A Closer Examination of a Widely Cited Study of Nonverbal Communication," *Communication Education*, 46 (1997): 63–67.

3. M. Zuckerman, D. DePaulo, and R. Rosenthal, "Verbal and Nonverbal Communication of Deception," *Advances in Experimental Social Psychology*, 14 (1981): 1–59.

4. P. Ekman and W. V. Friesen, "The Repertoire of Nonverbal Behavior: Categories, Origins, Usage and Coding," *Semiotica*, 1 (1969): 49–98.

5. E. Hess, *The Tell-Tale Eye* (New York: Van Nostrand Reinhold Company, 1975).

6. R. L. Birdwhistell, *Kinesics and Context* (Philadelphia: University of Pennsylvania Press, 1970).

7. N. Zunnin and M. Zunnin, *Contact: The First Four Minutes* (New York: Signet, 1976).

8. J. H. Bert and K. Piner, "Social Relationships and the Lack of Social Relations," in *Personal Relationships and Social Support*, eds. S. W. Duck with R. C. Silver (London: Sage, 1989).

9. P. Ekman, "Communication through Nonverbal Behavior: A Source of Information about an Interpersonal Relationship," in *Affect, Cognition and Personality*, eds. S. S. Tomkins and C. E. Izard (New York: Springer, 1965).

10. P. Ekman and W. V. Friesen, "Constants across Cultures in the Face and Emotion," *Journal of Personality and Social Psychology*, 17 (1971): 124–29; M. Argyle, *Bodily Communication* (New York: Methuen and Company, 1988), 157; I. Eibl-Eibesfeldt, "Similarities and Differences between Cultures in Expressive Movements," in *Nonverbal Communication*, ed. R. A. Hinde (Cambridge: Royal Society and Cambridge University Press, 1972); P. Collett, "History and Study of Expressive Action," in *Historical Social Psychology*, eds. K. Gergen and M. Gergen (Hillsdale, NJ: Erlbaum, 1984); E. T. Hall, *The Silent Language* (Garden City, NY: Doubleday, 1959); R. Shuter, "Gaze Behavior in Interracial and Intraracial Interaction," *International and Intercultural Communication Annual*, 5 (1979): 48–55; R. Shuter, "Proxemics and Tactility in Latin America," *Journal of Communication*, 26 (1976): 46–52; E. T. Hall, *The Hidden Dimension* (New York: Doubleday, 1966). For an excellent discussion of world view and the implications for intercultural communication see Carley H. Dodd, *Dynamics of Intercultural Communication* (Dubuque, IA: Brown and Benchmark, 1995).

11. Argyle, *Bodily Communication*.

12. W. G. Woodal and J. K. Burgoon, "The Effects of Nonverbal Synchrony on Message Comprehension and Persuasiveness," *Journal of Nonverbal Behavior*, 5 (1981): 207–23.

13. Argyle, *Bodily Communication*.

14. N. Blurton-Jones and G. M. Leach, "Behavior of Children and Their Mothers at Separation and Parting," in *Ethological Studies of Child Behavior*, ed. N. Blurton-Jones (Cambridge: Cambridge University Press 1972).

15. P. Ekman and W. V Friesen, "Constants across Cultures in the Face and Emotion," *Journal of Personality and Social Psychology*, 17 (1971): 124–29; Argyle, *Bodily Communication*, 157; I. Eibl-Eibesfeldt, "Similarities and Differences between Cultures in Expressive Movements," in *Nonverbal Communication*, ed. R. A. Hinde (Cambridge, England: Royal Society & Cambridge University Press, 1972); P. Collett, "History and Study of Expressive Action," in *Historical Social Psychology*, eds. K. Gergen and M. Gergen (Hillsdale, NJ: Erlbaum 1984); E. T. Hall, *The Silent Language* (Garden City, NY: Doubleday, 1959); R. Shuter, "Gaze Behavior in Interracial and Intraracial Interaction," *International and Intercultural Communication Annual*, 5 (1979): 48–55; R. Shuter, "Proxemics and Tactility in Latin America," *Journal of Communication*, 26 (1976): 46–52; E. T. Hall, *The Hidden Dimension* (New York: Doubleday, 1966). For an excellent discussion of world view and the implications for intercultural communication, see C. H. Dodd, *Dynamics of Intercultural Communication* (Dubuque, IA: Brown & Benchmark, 1995); G. W. Beattie, *Talk: An Analysis of Speech and Non-Verbal Behavior in Conversation* (Milton Keynes: Open University Press, 1983); O. Hargie, C. Sanders, and D. Dickson, *Social Skills in Interpersonal Communication* (London: Routledge, 1994); O. Hargie, (ed.), *The Handbook of Communication Skills* (London: Routledge, 1997).

16. This example originally appeared in Collett, "History and Study of Expressive Action."

17. Birdwhistell, *Kinesics and Context*.

18. A. E. Scheflen, "Quasi-Courtship Behavior in Psychotherapy," *Psychiatry*, 28 (1965): 245–57.

19. M. Moore, *Journal of Ethology and Sociology* (summer 1994); also see D. Knox and K. Wilson, "Dating Behaviors of University Students," *Family Relations*, 30 (1981): 255–58.

20. M. Reece and R. Whitman, "Expressive Movements, Warmth, and Verbal Reinforcement," *Journal of Abnormal and Social Psychology*, 64 (1962): 234–36.

21. A. Mehrabian, *Silent Messages* (Belmont, CA: Wadsworth Publishing Company, 1972), 108.

22. P. Ekman and W. V. Friesen, "The Repertoire of Nonverbal Behavior: Categories, Origins, Usage and Coding," *Semiotica*, 1 (1969): 49–98.

23. A. T. Dittman, "The Body Movement–Speech Rhythm Relationship as a Cue to Speech Encoding," in *Studies in Dyadic Communication*, eds. A. W. Siegman and B. Pope (New York: Pergamon, 1972).

24. A. A. Cohen and R. P. Harrison, "Intentionality in the Use of Hand Illustrators in Face-to-Face Communication Situations," *Journal of Personality and Social Psychology*, 28 (1973): 276–79.

25. A. Mehrabian and M. Williams, "Nonverbal Concomitants of Perceived and Intended Persuasiveness," *Journal of Personality and Social Psychology*, 13 (1969): 37–58.

26. M. Argyle, F. Alkema, and R. Gilmour, "The Communication of Friendly and Hostile Attitudes by Verbal and Nonverbal Signals," *European Journal of Social Psychology*, 1 (1972): 385–402.

27. A. Kendon, "Some Functions of Gaze-Direction in Social Interaction," *Acta Psychologica*, 26 (1967): 22–63.

Notes

28. S. W. Duck, *Understanding Relationships* (New York: The Guilford Press, 1991), 54.

29. M. Knapp and J. A. Hall, *Nonverbal Communication in Human Interaction* (New York: Holt, Rinehart and Winston, 1978), 313.

30. P. Ekman, W. V. Friesen, and S. S. Tomkins, "Facial Affect Scoring Technique: A First Validity Study," *Semiotica,* 3 (1971): 37–58; P. Ekman and W. V. Friesen, *Unmasking the Face* (Englewood Cliffs, NJ: Prentice-Hall, 1975).

31. A. Mehrabian, "Significance of Posture and Position in the Communication of Attitude and Status Relationships," *Psychological Bulletin,* 71 (1969): 363.

32. Ekman and Friesen, *Unmasking the Face;* Ekman, Friesen, and Tomkins, "Facial Affect Scoring Technique."

33. Ekman and Friesen, *Unmasking the Face;* Ekman, Friesen, and Tomkins, "Facial Affect Scoring Technique."

34. R. Buck, R. E. Miller, and C. F. William, "Sex, Personality, and Physiological Variables in the Communication of Affect Via Facial Expression," *Journal of Personality and Social Psychology,* 30 (1974): 587–96.

35. Ekman and Friesen, *Unmasking the Face.*

36. Ekman and Friesen, *Unmasking the Face.*

37. J. R. Davitz, *The Communication of Emotional Meaning* (New York: McGraw-Hill, 1964).

38. Davitz, *The Communication of Emotional Meaning.*

39. K. K. Sereno and G. J. Hawkins, "The Effect of Variations in Speakers' Nonfluency upon Audience Ratings of Attitude Toward the Speech Topic and Speakers' Credibility," *Speech Monographs* 34 (1967): 58–74; G. R. Miller and M. A. Hewgill, "The Effect of Variations in Nonfluency on Audience Ratings of Source Credibility," *Quarterly Journal of Speech,* 50 (1964): 36–44; Mehrabian and Williams, "Nonverbal Concomitants of Perceived and Intended Persuasiveness."

40. T. Bruneau, "Communicative Silences: Forms and Functions," *Journal of Communication,* 23 (1973): 17–46.

41. S. J. Baker, "The Theory of Silence," *Journal of General Psychology,* 53 (1955): 145–67.

42. E. T. Hall, *The Hidden Dimension* (Garden City, NY: Doubleday and Company, 1966).

43. R. Sommer, "Studies in Personal Space," *Sociometry,* 22 (1959): 247–60.

44. Sommer, "Studies in Personal Space."

45. See B. Stenzor, "The Spatial Factor in Face-to-Face Discussion Groups," *Journal of Abnormal and Social Psychology,* 45 (1950): 552–55.

46. A. Montague, *Touching: The Human Significance of the Skin* (New York: Harper and Row, 1978).

47. Montague, *Touching.*

48. N. M. Henley, *Body Politics: Power, Sex, and Nonverbal Communication* (Englewood Cliffs, NJ: Prentice-Hall, 1977).

49. J. Kelly, "Dress as Non-Verbal Communication," paper presented to the annual conference of the American Association for Public Opinion Research, May 1969.

50. J. Lefkowitz, R. Blake, and J. Mouton, "Status Factors in Pedestrian Violation of Traffic Signals," *Journal of Abnormal and Social Psychology,* 51 (1955): 704–06.

51. Mehrabian, *Nonverbal Communication.*

52. Argyle, *Bodily Communication.*

53. Mehrabian, *Nonverbal Communication.*

54. Argyle, *Bodily Communication.*

55. For an excellent review of gender and nonverbal cues see J. Pearson, L. Turner, and W. Todd-Mancillas, *Gender and Communication* (Dubuque, IA: William C. Brown, 1991); D. Ivy and P. Backlund, *Exploring Gender Speak: Personal Effectiveness in Gender Communication* (New York: McGraw-Hill, 1994).

56. Burgoon, Stern, and Dillman, *Interpersonal Adaptation.*

57. B. A. Le Poire and S. M. Yoshimura, "The Effects of Expectancies and Actual Communication on Nonverbal Adaptation and Communication Outcomes: A Test of Interaction Adaptation Theory," *Communication Monographs,* 66 (1999): 1–30.

58. See Birdwhistell, *Kinesics and Context.*

Chapter 8

1. J. W. Keltner, *Mediation: Toward a Civilized System of Dispute Resolution* (Annandale, VA: Speech Communication Association, 1987).

2. G. R. Miller and M. Steinberg, *Between People: A New Analysis of Interpersonal Communication* (Chicago: Science Research Associates, 1975), 264.

3. For a discussion of male and female gender roles see B. Bate, *Communication and the Sexes* (Englewood Cliffs, NJ: Prentice Hall, 1988); J. Pearson, L. Turner, and W. Todd-Mancillas, *Gender and Communication* (Dubuque, IA: Wm. C. Brown, 1991); D. Ivy and P. Backlund, *Gender Speak* (New York: McGraw-Hill, 1994).

4. C. M. Hoppe, "Interpersonal Aggression as a Function of Subject's Sex, Subject's Sex Role Identification, Opponent's Sex, and Degree of Provocation," *Journal of Personality,* 47 (1979): 317–29.

5. M. Olsen, *The Process of Social Organization* (New York: Holt, Rinehart, and Winston, 1978).

6. J. Hocker and W. Wilmont, *Interpersonal Conflict* (Dubuque, IA: Brown and Benchmark, 1994).

7. Olsen, *The Process of Social Organization.*

8. S. Ting-Toomey, "A Face Negotiation Theory," in *Theories in Intercultural Communication,* eds. Y. Kim and W. Gudykunst (Newbury Park, CA: Sage Publications, 1988).

9. G. R. Miller and M. Steinberg, *Between People: A New Analysis of Interpersonal Communication* (Chicago: Science Research Associates, 1975), 264.

10. R. J. Doolittle, *Orientations of Communication and Conflict* (Chicago: Science Research Associates, 1976), 7–9.

11. E. H. Mudd, H. E. Mitchell, and J. W. Bullard, "Areas of Marital Conflict in Successfully Functioning and Unsuccessfully Functioning Families," *Journal of Health and Human Behavior,* 3 (1962): 88–93; N. R. Vines, "Adult Unfolding and Marital Conflict," *Journal of Marital and Family Therapy,* 5 (1979): 5–14.

12. B. A. Fisher, "Decision Emergence: Phases in Group Decision-Making," *Speech Monographs,* 37 (1970): 60.

13. A. C. Filley, *Interpersonal Conflict Resolution* (Glenview, IL: Scott,

Foresman, 1975); R. H. Turner, "Conflict and Harmony," *Family Interaction* (New York: John Wiley and Sons, 1970); K. Galvin and B. J. Brommel, *Family Communication: Cohesion and Change* (New York: HarperCollins, 1991).

14. Hocker and Wilmot, *Interpersonal Conflict*, 10.

15. Adapted from D. W. Johnson. *Reaching Out: Interpersonal Effectiveness and Self-Actualization* (Boston: Allyn & Bacon, 2000), 314.

16. M. Deutsch, *The Resolution of Conflict* (New Haven, CT: Yale University Press, 1973).

17. R. Kilmann and K. Thomas, "Interpersonal Conflict-Handling Behavior as Reflections of Jungian Personality Dimensions," *Psychological Reports*, 37 (1975): 971–80.

18. L. L. Putnam and C. E. Wilson, "Communicative Strategies in Organizational Conflicts: Reliability and Validity of a Measurement Scale," in *Communication Yearbook*, 6, ed. M. Burgoon (Beverly Hills, CA: Sage Publications, International Communication Association, 1982).

19. V. Satir, *Peoplemaking* (Palo Alto: Science and Behavior Books, 1972).

20. J. T. Tedeschi, "Threats and Promises," in *The Structure of Conflict*, ed. P. Swingle (New York: Academic Press, 1970).

21. R. Fisher and W. Ury, *Getting to Yes: Negotiating Agreement without Giving In* (Boston: Houghton Mifflin, 1988).

22. Our discussion of conflict management skills is based upon several excellent discussions of conflict management prescriptions. We acknowledge Fisher and Ury, *Getting to Yes*; R. Boulton, *People Skills* (New York: Simon and Schuster, 1979); D. A. Romig and L. J. Romig, *Structured Teamwork® Guide* (Austin, TX: Performance Resources, 1990); O. Hargie, C. Saunders, and D. Dickson, *Social Skills in Interpersonal Communication* (London: Routledge, 1994); S. Deep and L. Sussman, *Smart Moves* (Reading, MA: Addison-Wesley, 1990); J. L. Hocker and W. W. Wilmot, *Interpersonal Conflict* (Madison, WI: Brown and Benchmark, 1994); M. D. Davis, E. L. Eshelman, and M. McKay, *The Relaxation and Stress Reduction Workbook* (Oakland, CA: New Harbinger Publications, 1982); W. A. Donohue and R. Kolt, *Managing Interpersonal Conflict* (Newbury Park: CA: Sage Publications, 1992).

23. Fisher and Ury, *Getting to Yes*; Boulton, *People Skills*; Romig and Romig, *Structured Teamwork® Guide*; T. Gordon, *Leader Effectiveness Training (L.E.T.): The No-Lose Way to Release the Productive Potential of People* (New York: Wyden Books, 1977).

24. A. Ellis, *A New Guide to Rational Living* (North Hollywood, CA: Wilshire Books, 1977).

25. S. R. Covey, *The Seven Habits of Highly Effective People* (New York: Simon and Schuster, 1989), 235.

26. Excerpts from *Transition*, Vanier Institute of the Family, Ottawa, March 1996, 4–10.

27. Fisher and Ury, *Getting to Yes*.

28. Canadian Human Rights Commission, "Human Rights in Employment," 1992.

29. Our prescriptions for assertiveness are based upon a discussion by R. Boulton, *People Skills*. Also see J. S. St. Lawrence, "Situational Context: Effects on Perceptions of Assertive and Unassertive Behavior," *Behavior Therapy*, 16 (1985): 51–62.

30. D. Cloven and M. E. Roloff, "The Chilling Effect of Aggressive Potential on the Expression of Complaints in Intimate Relationships," *Communication Monographs*, 60 (1993): 199–219.

31. J. W. Pfeiffer and J. E. Jones, (eds.) *A Handbook of Structured Experiences for Human Relations Training* (La Jolla, CA: University Associates, 1974), Vol. 2, 62–76.

Chapter 9

1. A. G. Smith, (ed.), *Communication and Culture* (New York: Holt, Rinehart and Winston, 1966).

2. P. Cateora and J. Hess, *International Marketing* (Homewood, IL: Irwin, 1979), 89; as discussed by L. A. Samovar and R. E. Porter, *Communication between Cultures* (Belmont, CA: Wadsworth, 1991), 52.

3. G. Hofstede, *Culture's Consequences: International Differences in Work-Related Values* (Beverly Hills, CA: Sage, 1980).

4. For an extensive summary and critique of Hofstede's research, see M. W. Lustig and J. Koester, *Intercultural Competence*, 111.

5. G. Hofstede, *Culture's Consequences*; also see G. Hofstede, "Cultural Dimensions in Management and Planning," *Asia Pacific Journal of Management* (January 1984): 81–98.

6. For an extensive review of communication gender differences see L. H. Turner, K. Dindia, and J. C. Pearson, "An Investigation of Female/Male Verbal Behaviors in Same-Sex and Mixed-Sex Conversations," *Communication Reports*, 8 (summer 1995): 86–96.

7. An excellent analysis and application of gender communication research has been compiled by A. Cornyn-Selby, "Are You from Another Planet or What?" presented at the Joint Service Family Readiness Matters Conference, July 14, 1999, Phoenix, Arizona.

8. See D. K. Ivy and P. Backlund, *Exploring GenderSpeak: Personal Effectiveness in Gender Communication* (New York: McGraw-Hill, 2000).

9. G. Hofstede, "Cultural Dimensions in Management and Planning," *Asia Pacific Journal of Management* (January 1984): 81–98.

10. Hofstede, *Culture's Consequences*.

11. W. B. Gudykunst, *Bridging Differences: Effective Intergroup Communication* (Newbury Park, CA: Sage, 1991), 45.

12. Gudykunst, *Bridging Differences*.

13. E. T. Hall, *Beyond Culture* (Garden City, NY: Doubleday, 1976).

14. Samovar and Porter, *Communication between Cultures*, 234.

15. M. V. Redmond and J. M. Bunyi, "The Relationship of Intercultural Communication Competence with Stress and the Handling of Stress as Reported by International Students," *International Journal of Intercultural Relations*, 17 (1993): 235–54; R. Brislen, *Cross-Cultural Encounters: Face-to-Face Interaction* (New York: Pergamon Press, 1981).

16. R. E. Axtell, *Do's and Taboos of Hosting International Visitors* (New York: John Wiley and Sons, 1989), 118.

17. J. S. Caputo, H. C. Hazel, and C. McMahon, *Interpersonal Communication* (Boston: Allyn and Bacon, 1994), 304.

18. S. Kamekar, M. B. Kolsawalla, and T. Mazareth, "Occupational Prestige as a Function of Occupant's Gender," *Journal of Applied Social Psychology*, 19 (1988): 681–88.

19. For an excellent discussion of world view and the implications for intercultural communication see: C. H. Dodd, *Dynamics of Intercultural Communication* (Dubuque,

IA: Brown and Benchmark, 1995).

20. Dodd, *Dynamics of Intercultural Communication,* 75.

21. Julia T. Wood, *Communication Mosaics: A New Introduction to the Field of Communication* (Belmont, CA: Wadsworth, 1997), 207; C. C. Innman, "Men's Friendships: Closeness in the Doing," in Julia T. Wood, (ed.), *Gendered Relationships* (Mountain View CA: Mayfield), 95–110.

22. C. R. Berger and R. J. Calabrese, "Some Explorations in Initial Interactions and Beyond," *Human Communication Research,* 1 (1975): 99–125.

23. Benjamin J. Broome, "Building Shared Meaning: Implications of a Relational Approach to Empathy for Teaching Intercultural Comunication," *Communication Education,* 40 (1991): 235–49.

24. F. L. Casmir and N. C. Asuucion-Lande. "Intercultural Communication Revisited: Conceptualization, Paradigm Building, and Methodological Approaches," in J. A. Anderson, (ed.), *Communication Yearbook,* 12 (Newbury Park, CA: Sage, 1989): 278–309.

25. Broome, "Building Shared Meaning."

26. W. B. Gudykunst and Y. Kim, *Communicating with Strangers* (New York: Random House, 1984); Gudykunst, *Bridging Differences.*

27. L. B. Szalay and G. H. Fisher, "Communication Overseas," in *Toward Internationalism: Readings in Cross-Cultural Communication,* eds. by E. C. Smith and L. F. Luce (Rowley, MA: Newbury House Publishers, 1979).

28. M. V Redmond, "The Functions of Empathy (Recentering) in Human Relations," *Human Relations,* 42 (1993): 593–606. Also see M. V. Redmond, "A Multidimensional Theory and Measure of Social Decentering," *Journal of Research in Personality* (1995); for an excellent discussion of the role of emotions in establishing empathy see Daniel Goleman, *Emotional Intelligence* (New York: Bantam, 1995).

29. See H. Giles, A. Mulack, J. J. Bradac, and P. Johnson, "Speech Accommodation Theory: The First Decade and Beyond," in *Communication Yearbook,* ed. M. L. McLaughlin, Vol. 10 (Newbury Park, CA: Sage, 1987), 13–48. For an excellent summary and application of accommodation theory, see R. West and L. H. Turner, *Introducing Communication Theory: Analysis and Application* (Mountain View, CA: Mayfield, 2000).

30. Lori J. Carrell, "Diversity in the Communication Curriculum: Impact on Student Empathy," *Communication Education,* 46 (1997): 234–44.

31. Adapted from Samovar and Porter, *Communication between Cultures.*

Chapter 10

1. L. von Bertalanffy, "Der Organismus als Physikalisches System Betrachtet," *Die Naturwissenschaften,* 28 (1940): 521–31.

2. F. E. Millar and L. E. Rogers, "A Relational Approach to Interpersonal Communication," in *Explorations in Interpersonal Communication,* ed. G. R. Miller (Newbury Park, CA: Sage, 1976), 87–103.

3. Millar and Rogers, "A Relational Approach to Interpersonal Communication."

4. Millar and Rogers, "A Relational Approach to Interpersonal Communication."

5. K. Chow, "Social Support and Subjective Well-Being among Hong Kong Chinese Young Adults," *Journal of Genetic Psychology,* 160 (September 1999): 319–316.

6. C. R. Berger, "Social Power and Interpersonal Communication," in *Handbook of Interpersonal Communication,* ed. M. L. Knapp and G. R. Miller (Newbury Park, CA: Sage, 1985), 439–99.

7. F. E. Millar and L. E. Rogers, "Relational Dimensions of Interpersonal Dynamics," in *Interpersonal Processes: New Directions in Communication Research,* eds. M. E. Roloff and G. R. Miller (Newbury Park, CA: Sage, 1987), 117–39.

8. J. R. P. French and B. H. Raven, "The Bases of Social Power," in *Group Dynamics,* eds. J. D. Cartwright and A. Zander (Evanston, IL: Row, Peterson, 1962), 607–22.

9. W. Stoebe, "Self Esteem and Interpersonal Attraction," in *Theory and Practice in Interpersonal Attraction,* ed. S. Duck (London: Academic Press, 1977).

10. S. W. Duck, *Personal Relationships and Personal Constructs: A Study of Friendship Formation* (New York: John Wiley and Sons, 1973).

11. M. Sunnafrank, "A Communication-Based Perspective on Attitude Similarity and Interpersonal Attraction in Early Acquaintance," *Communication Monographs,* 51 (1984): 372–80.

12. M. Sunnafrank, "Interpersonal Attraction and Attitude Similarity: A Communication-Based Assessment," in *Communication Yearbook* 14, ed. J. A. Anderson (Newbury Park, CA: Sage, 1991), 451–83.

13. Sunnafrank, "Interpersonal Attraction and Attitude Similarity."

14. W. Schutz, *Interpersonal Underworld* (Palo Alto, CA: Science and Behavior Books, 1966).

15. M. Sunnafrank, "Predicted Outcome Value During Initial Interactions: A Reformulation of Uncertainty Reduction Theory," *Human Communication Research,* 13 (1986): 3–33.

16. Sunnafrank, "Predicted Outcome Value During Initial Interactions."

17. M. V. Redmond and D. A. Vrchota, "The Effects of Varying Lengths of Initial Interaction on Attraction and Uncertainty Reduction," paper presented at the annual meeting of the Speech Communication Association.

18. I. Altman and D. A. Taylor, *Social Penetration: The Development of Interpersonal Relationships* (New York: Holt, Rinehart, and Winston, 1973).

19. J. Luft, *Group Processes: An Introduction to Group Dynamics* (Palo Alto, CA: Mayfield, 1970).

20. J. Powell, *Why Am I Afraid to Tell You Who I Am?* (Niles, IL: Argus Communications, 1969), 12.

21. Powell, *Why Am I Afraid?*

22. M. Argyle, M. Henderson, and A. Furnham, "The Rules of Social Relationships," *British Journal of Social Psychology,* 24 (1985): 125–39.

23. S. Duck, "Interpersonal Communication in Developing Relationships," in *Explorations in Interpersonal Communication,* ed. G. R. Miller (Newbury Park, CA: Sage, 1976), 127–47.

24. I. Altman and D. A. Taylor, *Social Penetration: The Development of Interpersonal Relationships* (New York: Holt, Rinehart and Winston, 1973).

25. Sunnafrank, "Predicted Outcome Value During Initial Interaction."

26. J. W. Thibaut and H. H. Kelley, *The Social Psychology of Groups* (New York: Wiley, 1959).

27. G. R. Miller and M. R. Parks, "Communicating in Dissolving Relationships," in *Personal Relationships 4: Dissolving Personal Relationships*, ed. S. W. Duck (London: Academic Press, 1982), 127–54.

28. L. A. Baxter, "Dialectical Contradictions in Relationship Development," in *Handbook of Personal Relationships*, ed. S. W. Duck (Chichester, England: Wiley, 1988), 257–73; L. A. Baxter and B. M. Montgomery, "Rethinking Communication in Personal Relationships from a Dialectical Perspective," in *Handbook of Personal Relationships*, 2d ed., edited by S. W. Duck (Chichester, England: Wiley, 1997), 325–49.

29. D. R. Pawlowski, "Dialectical Tensions in Marital Partners' Accounts of Their Relationships," *Communication Quarterly*, 46 (1998): 396–416.

30. M. V. Redmond, "Content Adaptation in Everyday Interactions," paper presented at the annual meeting of the National Communication Association, Chicago, 1997.

31. Pawlowski, "Dialectical Tensions."

32. L. A. Baxter, "Interpersonal Communication as Dialogue: A Response to the 'Social Approaches' Forum," *Communication Theory*, 2 (1992): 330–38.

33. Baxter, "Interpersonal Communication as Dialogue."

34. S. A. Beebe and J. T. Masterson, *Communicating in Small Groups: Principles and Practices* (New York: HarperCollins, 2000).

Chapter 11

1. L. A. Baxter and C. Bullis, "Turning Points in Developing Romantic Relationships," *Communication Research*, 12 (1986): 469–93.

2. Baxter and Bullis, "Turning Points."

3. C. R. Berger and J. J. Bradac, *Language and Social Knowledge: Uncertainty in Interpersonal Relations* (Baltimore: Edward Arnold, 1982).

4. W. Douglas, "Question Asking in Same and Opposite Sex Initial Interactions: The Effects of Anticipated Future Interaction," *Human Communication Research*, 14 (1987): 230–45.

5. S. W. Duck, "A Topography of Relationship Disengagement and Dissolution," in *Personal Relationships 4: Dissolving Relationships*, ed. S. W. Duck (New York: Academic Press, 1982).

6. Duck, "A Topography of Relationship Disengagement and Dissolution."

7. D. DeStephen, "Integrating Relational Termination into a General Model of Communication Competence," paper presented at the annual meeting of the Speech Communication Association, 1985.

8. C. R. Berger and R. J. Calabrese, "Some Explorations in Initial Interaction and Beyond: Toward a Developmental Theory of Interpersonal Communication," *Human Communication Research*, 1 (1975): 99–112; C. R. Berger and J. J. Bradac, *Language and Social Knowledge: Uncertainty in Interpersonal Relations* (Baltimore: Edward Arnold, 1982).

9. Berger and Bradac, *Language and Social Knowledge*.

10. S. Sunnafrank, "Predicted Outcome Value During Initial Interactions," *Human Communication Research*, 13 (1986): 3–33; and "Interpersonal Attraction and Attitude Similarity," in *Communication Yearbook*, Vol. 14, ed. J. A. Anderson (Newbury Park, CA: Sage, 1991), 451–83.

11. Berger and Bradac, *Language and Social Knowledge*.

12. Adapted from K. Kellerman et al., "The Conversation MOP: Scenes in the Stream of Discourse," *Discourse Processes*, 12 (1989): 27–61.

13. M. Argyle and M. Henderson, *The Anatomy of Relationships* (New York: Guilford Press, 1991).

14. For an excellent review of the nature of friendship, see M. Argyle, *The Psychology of Interpersonal Behavior* (London: Penguin, 1983).

15. A. M. Nicotera, "The Importance of Communication in Interpersonal Relationships," in *Interpersonal Communication in Friend and Mate Relationships*, ed. A. M. Nicotera and Associates (Albany: State University of New York Press, 1993), 3–12.

16. D. T. Kenrick and M. R. Trost, "Evolutionary Approaches to Relationships," in the *Handbook of Personal Relationships*, 2d ed., edited by S. Duck (Chichester, England: Wiley, 1997), 151–77.

17. R. A. Bell and J. A. Daly, "The Affinity Seeking Function of Communication," *Communication Monographs*, 51 (1984): 91–115.

18. Bell and Daly, "The Affinity Seeking Function of Communication."

19. A. L. Vangelisti, "Communication Problems in Committed Relationships: An Attributional Analysis," in *Attributions, Accounts, and Close Relationships*, eds. J. H. Harvey, T. L. Orbuch, and A. L. Weber (New York: Springer-Verlag, 1992), 144–64.

20. G. Levinger and D. J. Senn "Disclosure of Feelings in Marriage," *Merrill-Palmer Quarterly* 12 (1967): 237–49; A Bochner, "On the Efficency of Openess in Close Relationships," in *Communication Yearbook* 5, ed. M. Burgoon (New Brunswick, NJ: Transaction Books, 1982), 109–24.

21. R. A. Clark and J. G. Delia, "Individuals' Preferences for Friends' Approaches to Providing Support in Distressing Situations," *Communication Reports*, 10 (1997): 115–21.

22. S. A. Westmyer and S. A. Myers, "Communication Skills and Social Support Messages Across Friendship Levels," *Communication Research Reports*, 13 (1996): 191–97.

23. J. K. Alberts, "An Analysis of Couples' Conversational Complaints," *Communication Monographs*, 55 (1988): 184–97.

24. M. A. Fitzpatrick and D. M. Badzinski, "All in the Family: Interpersonal Communication in Kin Relationships," in *Handbook of Interpersonal Communication*, eds. M. L. Knapp and G. R. Miller (Beverly Hills: Sage Publications, 1985), 687–736.

25. G. R. Miller and F. Boster, "Persuasion in Personal Relationship," in *A Handbook of Personal Relationships*, ed. S. Duck (New York: Wiley, 1988): 275–88; M. G. Garko, "Perspectives and Conceptualizations of Compliance and Compliance Gaining," *Communication Quarterly*, 38(2) (1990): 138–157.

26. S. W. Duck, *Understanding Relationships* (New York: Guilford Press, 1991).

27. J. M. Gottman and S. Carrere, "Why Can't Men and Women Get Along? Developmental Roots and Marital Inequities," in *Communication and*

Relational Maintenance, eds. D. J. Canary and L. Stafford (San Diego: Academic Press, 1991): 203–229.

28. G. O. Hagestad and M. A. Smyer, "Dissolving Long-Term Relationships: Patterns of Divorcing in Middle Age," in Duck, *Personal Relationships*, Vol. 4: *Dissolving Personal Relationships*, ed. S. Duck (London: Academic Press, 1982), 155–88.

29. G. R. Miller and M. R. Parks, "Communication in Dissolving Relationships," in *Personal Relationships*, Vol. 4: *Dissolving Personal Relationships*, ed. S. W. Duck (London: Academic Press, 1982), 127–54.

30. Duck, "A Topography of Relationship Disengagement and Dissolution."

31. Miller and Parks, "Communication in Dissolving Relationships."

32. M. J. Cody, "A Typology of Disengagement Strategies and an Examination of the Role Intimacy, Reactions to Inequity and Relational Problems Play in Strategy Selection," *Communication Monographs*, 49(3), (1982): 148–70.

33. L. A. Baxter, "Accomplishing Relationship Disengagement," in *Understanding Personal Relationships: An Interdisciplinary Approach*, eds. S. Duck and D. Perlman (Beverly Hills: Sage, 1984): 243–65.

34. D. DeStephen, "Integrating Relational Termination into a General Model of Communication Competence," paper presented at the annual meeting of the Speech Communication Association.

35. Baxter, "Accomplishing Relationship Disengagement."

36. DeStephen, "Integrating Relational Termination into a General Model of Communication Competence."

37. Cody, "A Typology of Disengagement Strategies."

38. N. L. Buerkel-Rothfuss, "Rule-Breaking in Cyberspace Relationships: Netiquette vs. Interpersonal Competence," paper presented at the annual meeting of the National Communication Association, Chicago, November 1999.

39. J. B. Walther, "Impression Formation in Computer-Mediated Interaction," *Western Journal of Communication*, 57 (1993): 381–98.

40. J. Shuler, "E-Mail Communication and Relationships," in *The Psychology of Cyberspace*, www.rider.edu/users/suler/ psycyber/psycyber.html (August 1998).

41. P. Wallace, *The Psychology of the Internet* (New York: Cambridge University Press, 1999).

42. K. M. Cornetto, "Suspicion in Cyberspace: Deception and Detection in the Context of Internet Relay Chat Rooms," paper presented at the annual meeting of the National Communication Association, Chicago, November 1999.

43. Cornetto, "Suspicion in Cyberspace."

44. Cornetto, "Suspicion in Cyberspace."

45. M. R. Parks and K. Floyd, "Making Friends in Cyberspace," *Journal of Communication*, 46 (1996): 80–97.

46. E. S. Rintel and J. Pittam, "Strangers in a Strange Land: Interaction Management on Internet Relay Chat," *Human Communication Research*, 23 (1997): 477–506.

47. J. B. Walther, J. F. Anderson, and D. W. Park, "Interpersonal Effects in Computer-Mediated Interaction: A Meta-Analysis of Social and Antisocial Communication," *Communication Research*, 21 (1994): 460–87.

48. Walther et al. "Interpersonal Effects."

49. L. Pratt, R. L. Wiseman, M. J. Cody, and P. F. Wendt, "Interrogative Strategies and Information Exchange in Computer-Mediated Communication," *Communication Quarterly*, 47 (1999): 46–66.

50. J. C. Sipior and B. T. Ward, "The Dark Side of Employee Email," *Communications of the ACM*, 42(7), (July 1999); http://www.acm.org/pubs/citations/journals/cacm/1999-42-7/p88-sipior

51. Sipior and Ward, "The Dark Side of Employee Email."

52. L. Stafford, S. L. Kline, and J. Dimmick, "Home E-Mail: Relational Maintenance and Gratification Opportunities," *Journal of Broadcasting & Electronic Media*, 43 (1999): 659–69.

53. Stafford et al., "Home E-Mail."

54. B. Wellman, J. Salaff, D. Dimitrova, L. Garton, M. Gulia, and C. Haythornthwaite, "Computer Networks as Social Networks: Collaborative Work, Telework, and Virtual Community," *Annual Review of Sociology*, 22 (1996): 213–38.

55. Wallace, *The Psychology of the Internet*.

56. Wallace, *The Psychology of the Internet*.

57. See reviews in C. Conrad, *Strategic Organizational Communication: Toward the Twenty-First Century*, 3d ed. (Fort Worth, TX: Harcourt Brace, 1994); and T. D. Daniels, B. K. Spicer, and M. J. Papa, *Perspectives on Organizational Communication*, 4th ed. (Dubuque, IA: Brown and Benchmark, 1997).

58. P. M. Sias and D. J. Cahill, "From Coworkers to Friends: The Development of Peer Friendships in the Workplace," *Western Journal of Communication*, 62 (1998): 273–99.

59. Sias and Cahill, "From Coworkers to Friends."

60. Sias and Cahill, "From Coworkers to Friends."

61. J. Gabarro and J. Kotter, "Managing Your Boss," *Harvard Business Review*, 58 (1980): 92–100.

62. F. Japlin, "Superior's Upward Influence, Satisfaction, and Openness in Superior-Subordinate Communication: A Reexamination of the 'Pelz Effect,'" *Human Communication Research*, 6 (1980): 210–20.

63. Japlin, "Superior's Upward Influence."

64. D. Katz and R. Kahn, *The Social Psychology of Organizations* (New York: Wiley, 1966).

65. R. W. Pace and D. F. Faules, *Organizational Communication* (Englewood Cliffs, NJ: Prentice Hall, 1994).

66. W. L. Davis and J. R. O'Connor, "Serial Transmission of Information: A Study of the Grapevine," *Journal of Applied Communication Research*, 5 (1977): 61–72.

67. "Sexual Harassment Clauses," *Worklife Report*, 8(3), 4–7.

68. Human Resources Development Canada, *Information on Labour Standards*, 12, *Sexual Harassment*. Available: http://info.load-otea.hrdc-drhc.ca/publications/labour_standards/harassment.shtml.

69. H. F. Schwind, H. Das, W. Werther, and K. Davis, *Canadian Human*

Resource Management, 4th ed. (Toronto: McGraw-Hill Ryerson Canada, 1995).

70. Diane Crocker and Valery Kalemba, "The Incidence and Impact of Women's Experiences of Sexual Harassment in Canadian Workplaces," *Canadian Review of Sociology & Anthropology,* 36(49), (November 1999), 541–59.

71. M. Jimenez, "Sexual Harassment at Work Prevalent in B.C., Poll Shows," *Vancouver Sun,* May 4, 1998, A1, A2.

72. Crocker and Kalemba, "The Incidence and Impact of Women's Experiences of Sexual Harassment in Canadian Workplaces."

73. S. R. Covey, *The Seven Habits of Highly Effective People* (New York: Simon & Schuster, 1989).

74. K. D. Benne and P. Sheats, "Functional Roles of Group Members," *Journal of Social Issues,* 4 (spring 1948): 41–49.

Index

A

Aboriginal peoples, and wages, 279
abstract meanings, 166–167
acculturation, 270
action models of communication, 12–13
action-oriented listener, 198
active listening, 116–121
active perception, 76
adapt predictively, 291
adapt reactively, 291
adaptation, 291
adaptation skills
   adapt predictively, 291
   adapt reactively, 291
   communication accommodation theory, 291
   communication adaptation behaviours, 292
   computer-mediated communication (CMC), 368–369
   empathy, 289
   flexibility, 286
   intercultural context, 293
   other-orientation, 287–289
   skills, defined, 280
   social decentring, 287, 288, 348–349
adaptors, 203
affect displays, 203
affection, need for, 60
affinity-seeking strategies, 345–346
age, and cultural diversity, 268
aggression
   frustration-aggression hypothesis, 148
   verbal aggression, 150–151
aggressiveness, 253
agreement about judgments, 185
allness, 174–175
Altman, Irwin, 318
ambiguity
   of non-verbal communication, 197
   toleration of, 247
androgynous role, 46
anger
   and cardiovascular disease, 149
   dealing with your anger, 150
   defined, 149
   non-verbal signs of, 149
   understanding your anger, 154
   verbal aggression and, 151
appearance, 211–212
approachability cues, 340
argument style, 150
Argyle, Michael, 24, 214, 323
arousal, 213–214
Asch, Solomon, 77, 87
assertiveness
   vs. aggressiveness, 253
   defined, 60, 253
   describe, 255
   disclose, 255
   fair fighting, 257
   five steps in assertive behaviour, 254–256
   "I" language, 253
   identify effects, 255
   with non-other-oriented people, 253–257
   paraphrase, 255
   silence, 255
   visualization, 256
   when harassed, 254
asynchronous interaction, 363
attacking the person, 124
attending, 101
attitudes
   defined, 38
   and healing, 58
   self-disclosure, 322
attraction
   communication of, 344–346
   interpersonal. *See* interpersonal attraction
   physical, 310–311
attribution process, 82
attribution theory
   attribution process, 82
   attributional biases, 82–83
   causal attribution theory, 82
   correspondent inference theory, 82
   defined, 81
   self-handicapping strategy, 82
   self-serving bias, 82
attributions, 82
Aurelius, Marcus, 285
autonomic nervous system, 134, 137

B

back channel cues, 208
bafflegab, 172
bandwagon fallacy, 123
Barnes, Diane, 248
Baxter, Leslie, 326
behavioural effects of emotions, 136–137
beliefs, 39
Berne, Eric, 50
bias
   attributional, 82–83
   polygraph testing, 137
   self-serving, 82
biased language
   demeaning age, ability or social class, 181
   ethnic or racially biased language, 180
   sexist language, 179–180
   as word barrier, 176
big picture, 88
bilateral dissolutions, 354
Blake, Peter, 41
body movement, 200–201
brainstorming, 250–251
Braithwaite, Dawn, 181
breathing, and management of emotions, 154
Broome, Benjamin, 283
Buber, Martin, 7, 8
bulletin boards, 360
Burgoon, Judee, 196, 216
bypassing, 170–171

C

campus drinking, 50
Canadian issues
   Aboriginal peoples, and wages, 279
   Buzz Hargrove, 78–79
   campus drinking, 50
   common-law relationships, 350
   emotions in wake of traumatic event, 148
   immigration, 266
   labels, effect of, 168
   linguistic diversity, 118
   listening to Francophones and Allophones, 118
   non-verbal communication rules, 199–200
   perception of Americans, 70–71
   workplace skills in global economy, 369–370
   youth crime prevention, 247–248
categorizing, 73
causal attribution theory, 82
causal fallacy, 123
cell phones, 111
Centre for Addiction and Mental Health, 50
channel
   defined, 13
   richness of, criteria for, 20
charisma, and attraction, 311
chat rooms, 360–361, 364
clarifying response, 185
Client-Centered Therapy (Rogers), 29
closure, 73
co-culture, 267
coercive power, 309
cognitive complexity, 81
cognitive effects of emotions, 135–136
cognitive labels, 136
cognitive process, 287
colleagues, relationships with, 10, 373
collectivistic cultures, 140, 273
common-law relationships, 350
communibiological approach, 27, 47
communication
   computer-mediated. *See* computer-mediated communication (CMC)
   defined, 6
   downward, 372–373
   electronic. *See* mediated interpersonal communication
   horizontal, 373
   human, 6
   impersonal, 7
   intercultural. *See* intercultural communication
   interpersonal. *See* interpersonal communication
   intrapersonal, 9, 51
   mass, 9
   models of. *See* communication models
   non-verbal. *See* non-verbal communication
   outward, 373–374
   public, 9
   small-group, 9
   upward, 371–372
   verbal. *See* words
communication accommodation theory, 291
communication adaptation behaviours, 292
communication apprehension, 47
communication models
   action model, 12–13
   information source and transmitter, 13
   interaction model, 13–14
   message creation, 14–15
   message exchange, 13–14
   message transfer, 12–13
   transaction model, 14–15
communication style
   assertiveness, 60
   defined, 60
   development of, 60
   responsiveness, 60
   social learning approach, 60
   sociocommunicative orientation test, 61
comparisons
   avoidance of, 52
   social comparison, 43

competence, and attraction, 311
competitive symmetric relationship, 307
complementary needs, 312
complementary relationships, 307
compliments, 185
computer-mediated communication (CMC)
   adaptation skills, 368–369
   asynchronous interaction, 363
   bulletin boards, 360
   challenges, 359
   chat rooms, 360–361, 364
   communication, 367
   computer-supported social networks (CSSN), 366
   deception, 363–364
   defined, 358
   disappearance, 363–364
   e-mail, 360
   vs. face-to-face communication, 361–364
   instant messaging, 361
   non-verbal communication, 361–362
   other-orientation, 368–369
   relational maintenance strategies, 367–368
   relationship initiation, 364
   relationship maintenance, 366
   slower pace of relational development, 365
   strong verbal skills, 365–366
   synchronous interaction, 363
   types of, 359–361
   written communication, 362
computer-supported social networks (CSSN), 366
computing non-confrontational style, 238
concrete meanings, 166–167
confirming responses
   agreement about judgments, 185
   clarifying response, 185
   compliments, 185
   defined, 184
   direct acknowledgement, 185
   positive feeling, expressions of, 185
   and relationship escalation and maintenance, 347
   supportive response, 185
conflict
   constructive, 237
   defined, 226
   destructive, 237
   ego, 228, 231–232
   and emotions. *See* difficult emotional states
   and experiences, 227
   expressive, 229
   and goals, 226–227
   instrumental, 229
   myths, 232–234
   process of. *See* conflict process
   pseudo, 228, 229
   simple, 228, 230–231
   struggle spectrum, 226
   types of, 227–232
conflict management
   clear descriptions, 245
   confrontational style, 239–241
   cooperative style, 241, 350
   culture-based, 229
   and effective listening skills, 246
   emotion management, 242–245
   goal identification, 247
   goal management, 247–249
   goal overlap, 248–249
   "I" language, 245
   identifying your style, 239
   information management, 245–246
   mutually acceptable time and place for discussion, 244

   non-confrontational style, 238–239
   non-verbal messages, 244
   personal attacks, name-calling and emotional overstatement, 244
   plan your message, 244
   problem management, 249–253
   and relationship escalation and maintenance, 350
   self-talk and, 245
   skills, 242–253
   styles of, 237–242
   understanding of what others say and do, 246
conflict myths, 232–234
conflict process
   active conflict, 235
   follow-up, 236
   frustration awareness, 235
   resolution, 236
confrontational style of conflict management, 239–241
connotative meaning, 166
conscious competence, 112
conscious incompetence, 112
consistency, imposition of, 85
constructive conflict, 237
contempt, 138
content, 25
content-oriented listener, 104
context, 14
context-bound words, 162
continuous nature of non-verbal communication, 198
control, need for, 60
conversation starters, 340
conversational narcissism, 108
Cooley, Charles Horton, 42
cooperative style of conflict management, 241
correspondent inference theory, 82
cost escalation, 357
Covey, Stephen, 376
credibility, and attraction, 311
critical listening
   attacking the person, 124
   bandwagon fallacy, 123
   causal fallacy, 123
   defined, 122
   either/or fallacy, 123
   fact, 125
   faulty logic, 123–125
   hasty generalization, 123–124
   inference, 125
   and jumping to conclusions, 125
   non sequitur fallacy, 124–125
   red herring fallacy, 124
cultural context
   defined, 274
   high-context culture, 274
   low-context culture, 274
cultural diversity
   age, 268
   and conflict, 228–229
   dating customs, 271
   disability, 269
   and emotional expression, 139–140
   ethnicity, 269
   eye contract, 199
   facial expressions, 199
   gender, 269
   gestures, 199
   interracial relationships, 291
   language, 268–269
   manners and customs, 293–294
   non-verbal communication, interpretation of, 199
   race, 269

   range of differences, 268–269
   religion, 269
   sensitivity to, as perceptual skill, 91
   sexual preference, 269
   social class, 269
   space, 199
   and words, 163, 169–170
cultural elements, 267
cultural values
   defined, 270
   feminine, 270
   individualism, 270, 273–274
   masculine, 270
   masculinity, 270
   power distribution, 270, 273
   uncertainty avoidance, 270, 271–273
culture
   see also intercultural communication
   acculturation, 270
   co-culture, 267
   collectivistic, 140, 273
   defined, 139, 267
   enculturation, 267
   feminine, 270
   high-context, 140, 274
   individualistic, 140, 274
   low-context, 140, 274
   masculine, 270
   nature of, 267–275
   third, 282–283
culture shock, 276
cumulative rewards and costs, 325
customer relationships, 373–374

D

dating customs, 271
de-escalation, 357
de-intensification stage, 337
debilitating emotions, 153
deception, 137, 363–364
decoded, 13
Delaney, Bessie, 52
Delaney, Sadie, 52
denotative meaning, 166
depression, 11, 152
description of others, 79–81
destructive conflict, 237
dialectical theory
   certainty *vs.* uncertainty, 326
   connectedness *vs.* autonomy, 326
   defined, 326
   movement in relationships, 327
   openness *vs.* closedness, 327
   predictability *vs.* novelty, 326
difficult emotional states
   anger, 149
   and breathing, 154
   frustration, 147–148
   getting help, 155
   management of, 153–155
   positive self-talk, 155
   restructure your thoughts and feelings, 154–155
   sadness, 152–153
   understanding your anger, 154
   verbal aggression, 150–151
direct acknowledgement, 185
direct perception checking, 90
direct relational termination strategies, 356, 357–358
disability, and cultural diversity, 269
disappearance, and computer-mediated communication, 363–364

Index

disconfirming responses
  defined, 184
  impersonal response, 187
  impervious response, 186
  incoherent response, 187
  incongruous response, 187
  interrupting response, 186
  irrelevant response, 186
  tangential response, 186
discrimination, 181, 279
distracters, 238
distractions, 110–111
diversity
  conflict, and gender, 228
  cultural differences, and misinterpretation, 31
  cultural manners and customs, 293–294
  empathy and sexual orientation, 354
  ethnocentric thinking, 281
  gender differences and non-verbal communication, 215
  gender styles at work, 164–165
  immigration in Canada, 266
  interracial relationships, 291
  linguistic, in Canada, 118
  non-verbal communication, interpretation of, 199
  other-oriented communication, 44
  range of differences, 268–269
  relationship de-escalation and ending, 352
dominance, 214
downward communication, 372–373
Duck, Steve, 338
Duncan, H.D., 22
dyadic effect, 323

E

e-connections
  argument style, 150
  bafflegab, 172
  breaking off relationships, 352
  cultural traditions, 275
  cyber shorthand, 164
  cyberspace and relationships, 359
  electronic perceptions, accuracy of, 80
  electronic relationships, 18–19
  emoticons, 19
  emotional intelligence quotient, 118
  impersonal America, 17–18
  Japan and emoticons, 141
  Myers-Briggs Personality Test, 49
  netiquette, 146
  non-verbal messages, interpretation of, 213
  sexist language, avoidance of, 180
e-mail
  see also e-connections; mediated interpersonal communication
  emoticons, 19
  emotions, communication of, 19
  relationship development and maintenance, 360
  social information-processing theory, 20
effective communication
  ethics, 29
  flexibility, 28
  improvement of effectiveness, 27–31
  knowledgeable, becoming, 28
  motivation, 28
  other-oriented, 29–31
  skilled, 28
ego conflict, 228, 231–232
either/or fallacy, 123
elaborated code, 184
electronic communications. *See* mediated interpersonal communication

electronic perceptions, accuracy of, 80
Ellis, Albert, 155
emblems, 202
emoticons, 19, 141
emotional contagion theory, 143
emotional expression
  and culture, 139–140
  and etiquette, 142
  and gender, 141–142
  and non-verbal cues, 196
  and roles, 142
emotional health, 11–12
emotional "hot buttons," 109
Emotional Intelligence (Goleman), 117
emotional intelligence quotient, 117, 118
emotional noise, 108–109
emotions
  behavioural effects of, 136–137
  characteristics of, 134–137
  cognitive effects of, 135–136
  and conflict. *See* difficult emotional states
  dealing with your own emotions, 144–147
  debilitating, 153
  defined, 134
  depth and breadth of, 138–139
  difficult emotional states. *See* difficult emotional states
  e-mail communication of, 19
  emotional contagion theory, 143
  excitation transfer theory, 135
  expression of, 347–348
  factors influencing emotional expression, 139–142
  fight or flight response, 134
  heightened arousal, 134–135
  and humour, 144
  intensity of, 139
  know when to feel, talk or act, 146–147
  management of, and conflict, 242–245
  mixed, 138
  non-verbal expression of, 143
  number of, 138
  perception checking, 143–144
  physiological effects of, 134–135
  primary, 138
  recognize your feelings, 144
  schemas, 136
  skills for dealing with others' emotions, 143
  take ownership of your feelings, 145
  think before speaking, 146
  universality of emotional expression, 137
  in wake of traumatic event, 148
empathic listening and responding
  active listening, 116
  emotional intelligence, 117
  empathic responding, 117–119
  empathizing, 116
  empathy ability, 117
  understanding others' feelings, 119
empathizing, 116
empathy
  ability, 117
  defined, 289
  vs. detachment, 183
  and other-orientation, 289
  relational, 283
  and sexual orientation, 354
  vs. sympathy, 291
employment skills, 11
encoding, 13
enculturation, 267
episodes, 15
ethics
  defined, 29
  in workplace, 178
ethnic or racially biased language, 180

ethnicity, and cultural diversity, 269
ethnocentrism, 276–277, 286
etiquette
  and emotional expression, 142
  on the Internet, 146
excitation transfer theory, 135
expectancy violation theory, 216
expectations, and healing, 58
experiences, and conflict, 227
expert power, 309
exploration stage, 335
expressed struggle, 235
expressive conflict, 229
external noise, 110–111
eye contact, 113, 204–205, 215, 340

F

facial expressions, 206–207, 215
fact, 125
fading away, 354
fallacies
  attacking the person, 124
  bandwagon fallacy, 123
  causal fallacy, 123
  defined, 123
  either/or fallacy, 123
  hasty generalization, 123–124
  non sequitur fallacy, 124–125
  red herring fallacy, 124
family relationships, 9
faulty logic. *See* fallacies
feedback, 14, 126
feminine cultures, 270
fight or flight response, 134
first impression, 77
Fisher, Roger, 249
flexibility
  development of, 286
  vs. rigidity, 183
followership skill, 377
forecasted rewards and costs, 324
friends, 10, 344
frustration, 147–148
frustration-aggression hypothesis, 148
Fuller, Rodney, 80
Furnham, Adrian, 323

G

gender and gender differences
  and conflict, 228, 229
  and cultural diversity, 269
  and emotional expression, 141–142
  eye contact, 215
  facial expressions, 215
  gestures, 215
  listening skills and, 107
  and non-verbal communication, 215
  partnership perspective, 228
  posture, 215
  relationship de-escalation and ending, 352
  space, 215
  stereotypical labels for males and females, 45
  styles at work, 164–165
  touch, 215
  vocal cues, 215
generalization, 174–175
generalized-other perspective, 55
genuine *vs.* manipulative, 182–183
gestures, 200–201, 215
Gibb, Jack, 177
giving in, 239
Gliksman, Louis, 50

goals
   and conflict, 226–227
   and conflict management, 247–249
   and problem management, 250
Goffman, Erving, 40
Goleman, Daniel, 117, 118
grapevine messages, 373
The Greek Interpreter (Doyle), 74
groups, association with, 43–44
Gudykunst, William, 285

H

Hall, Edward T., 209
halo effect, 80, 84
harassment, 254
Hargrove, Buzz, 78–79
hasty generalization, 123–124
Having Our Say (Delaney and Delaney), 52
hearing, 100
Heider, Fritz, 82
heightened arousal, 134–135
Henderson, Monica, 323
high-context culture, 140, 274
Hill, Barb, 247, 248
Hofstede, Geert, 270
horizontal communication, 373
horn effect, 80, 84
Horney, Karen, 38
Howe, Ruel, 170
human communication, 6
humour, and emotions, 144

I

"I" language, 181–183, 245, 253
illustrators, 203
immediate rewards and costs, 324
immigration in Canada, 266
impersonal communication, 7
impersonal response, 187
impervious response, 186
implicit personality theory, 79–80
imprecision, 172–174
impression formation theory, 77
impression management, 79
impressions, 77
inattentive listening, 106
inclusion, need for, 60
incoherent response, 187
incongruous response, 187
indexing, 175
indirect perception checking, 90
indirect relational termination strategies, 356, 357
individualism, 270
individualistic cultures, 140, 274
individualization stage, 337
inference, 125
information
   ignoring, and inaccurate perception, 84
   management of, and conflict, 245–246
   organization of. *See* organization of information
   overload, 110
   self-disclosure, 322
   source, 13
information triage, 122
initiation norms, 341
initiation stage, 335
instant messaging, 361
instrumental conflict, 229
intensification stage, 335

interaction adaptation theory, 195–196
interaction models of communication, 13–14
intercultural communication
   communication codes, differences in, 278, 283
   culture shock, 276
   defined, 275
   discrimination, 279
   ethnocentrism, 276–277
   mistranslated advertisements, 278
   prejudice, 279
   similarity, assumptions of, 280
   stereotypes and, 278–279
intercultural competence
   adapt predictively, 291
   adapt reactively, 291
   ambiguity, toleration of, 284–285
   ask questions, 282
   communication accommodation theory, 291
   communication adaptation behaviours, 292
   empathy, 289
   flexibility, 286
   knowledge of others, enhancement of, 280, 283
   listen effectively, 282
   mindfulness, 285
   motivation, 280, 284–286
   negative judgments, avoidance of, 286
   other-orientation, 287–289
   seek information from culture, 281–282
   skills in adaptation, 280, 286–293
   social decentring, 287, 288
   third culture, development of, 282–283
Internet communication
   see also e-connections; mediated interpersonal communication
   asynchronous interaction, 363
   bulletin boards, 360
   chat rooms, 360–361
   computer-mediated communication (CMC), 358–369
   e-mail. *See* e-mail
   instant messaging, 361
   interpersonal relationships, 358–369
   netiquette, 146
interpersonal attraction
   charisma, 311
   competence, 311
   complementary needs, 312
   credibility, 311
   defined, 310
   elements of, 310–314
   long-term maintenance attraction, 310
   physical attraction, 310–311
   predicted outcome value theory, 313
   proximity, 311–312
   reciprocation of liking, 314
   relationship potential, 313
   short-term initial attraction, 310
   similarity, 312
interpersonal communication
   and categories of non-verbal behaviour, 203–204
   defined, 6
   distinctive form of communication, 6–7
   effectiveness of, 27–31
   evolving model, 12–15
   vs. impersonal communication, 7, 8
   importance of, 9–12
   and interpersonal perception, 75–76
   mediated, 16–21
   mutual influence between individuals, 7–8
   myths, 25–27
   occurrence of, 7
   relationship management, 8–9
   self-concept, effect of, 54–61

   self-esteem, effect of, 54–61
interpersonal communication principles
   complexity, 23
   connection to others, 21–22
   content dimension, 25
   irreversibility, 22–23
   relationship dimension, 25
   rules, 23–24
interpersonal conflict, 226
   see also conflict
interpersonal intimacy, 306
interpersonal needs, and self, 59–60
interpersonal perception
   see also perception
   defined, 67, 69
   and interpersonal communication, 75–76
   interpretation stage, 74
   organization stage, 71–73
   of others. *See* perception of others
   process, 68–74
   selection stage, 69–70
interpersonal power, 306
   see also power
interpersonal relationship development theories
   dialectical theory, 326–327
   social exchange theory, 324–326
interpersonal relationships
   see also relationships
   attraction, 309–314
   of choice, 303–304
   of circumstance, 303–304
   computer-mediated communication, 364
   defined, 8, 303
   friends, 344
   on Internet, 358–369
   intimacy, 306
   lovers, 344
   power, 306–309
   as process, 303
   relational development. *See* relational development
   self-disclosure, 314–323
   stages of, 334–338
   as system, 302
   trust, 304–305
   at work. *See* workplace relationships
interpersonal trust, 305
interpretation
   cultural differences, misinterpretation of, 31
   and interpersonal perception, 74
   of message, and self, 58–59
   of others' behaviour, 81–83
interracial relationships, 291
interrupting response, 186
intimacy, and interpersonal relationships, 306
intimacy stage, 335
intimate space, 209
intrapersonal communication
   defined, 9
   and self-esteem, 51
irrelevant response, 186

J

James, William, 40, 41, 42
Japan, and emoticons, 141
jargon, 174
Johari Window model, 319–321
Johnson, David W., 237
Johnson, Wendell, 167
jumping to conclusions, 125
justification, 357

Index

K

kinesics, 201
knowledge
  ask questions, 282
  defined, 280
  development of, 280–283
  listen effectively, 282
  seek information from culture, 281–282
  third culture, development of, 282–283
Korzybski, Alfred, 167

L

labels
  effect of, 168
  for sexual orientation, 180
language, and cultural diversity, 268–269
Lasswell, Harold, 12
leadership, 376–377
Lefton, Lester, 47
legitimate power, 308
L'Heureux-Dubé, Claire, 169
life position, 50
linguistic determinism, 170
listening
  active listening, 116–121
  attending, 101
  barriers to. *See* listening barriers
  critical. *See* critical listening
  defined, 100
  empathy and. *See* empathic listening and responding
  goals, 113–114
  inattentive, 106
  remembering, 102
  respond, 103
  selecting, 100
  skills. *See* listening skills
  styles, 103–105
  understanding, 101–102
listening barriers
  cell phones as distraction, 111
  conversational narcissism, 108
  criticism of the speaker, 109–110
  distractions, 110–111
  emotional "hot buttons," 109
  emotional noise, 108–109
  external noise, 110–111
  information overload, 110
  internal thoughts, 106
  in intimate relationships, 106
  into listening goals, 114
  self-absorption, 107–108
  speed rate *vs.* thought rate, 110
listening skills
  ask questions, 114–115
  assessment of, 105
  and conflict management, 246
  critical listening. *See* critical listening
  empathic. *See* empathic listening and responding
  eye contract, 113
  and gender, 107
  improvement of, 112–115
  listen, 113–114
  look, 113
  paraphrasing, 112, 115
  practise, 114
  relationship escalation and maintenance, 347
  stop, 112
listening styles
  action-oriented listener, 198
  content-oriented listener, 104
  defined, 103
  people-oriented listeners, 103
  second-guessing, 104
  time-oriented listener, 104
logic, 123
long-term maintenance attraction, 310
looking glass self, 42
love, 138
Love, Medicine, and Miracles (Siegel), 58
lovers, 10, 344
low-context culture, 140, 274
lying, 137

M

malapropism, 173
male-dominated culture, 46
management, relationships with, 371–372
marriage, 344
masculine cultures, 270
masculinity, 270
Maslow, Abraham, 112
mass communication, 9
material self, 41
McCroskey, James, 47, 61, 277
Mead, George Herbert, 42
mediated interpersonal communication
  see also computer-mediated communication (CMC); e-connections
  defined, 17
  emoticons, 19
  meaningful relationships through, 18
  non-verbal cues, reduced level of, 20
  social information-processing theory, 20
Mehrabian, Albert, 194, 201, 212
men. *See* gender and gender differences
message
  content, 25
  creation, 14–15
  defined, 13
  exchange, 13–14
  grapevine, 373
  interpretation, and self, 58–59
  relationship dimension, 25
  transfer, 12–13
mindfulness, 285
mixed emotions, 138
motivation
  ambiguity, toleration of, 284–285
  defined, 280
  development of, 284–286
  mindfulness, 285
multi-channelled nature of non-verbal communication, 198
mutual influence between individuals, 7–8
mutual transaction model of communication, 14–15
Myers-Briggs Personality Test, 49
myths of interpersonal communication, 25–27

N

need for affection, 60
need for control, 60
need for inclusion, 60
negative identity management, 357
netiquette, 146
Neuliep, James, 277
noise
  defined, 13
  emotional noise, 108–109
  external noise, 110–111
non-confrontational style of conflict management, 238–239
non sequitur fallacy, 124–125
non-sexist language, 180
non-verbal communication
  ambiguity of, 197
  believability, 194–195
  in Canada, 199–200
  codes. *See* non-verbal communication codes
  computer-mediated communication (CMC), 361–362
  conflict management and, 244
  continuous nature of, 198
  culture based interpretation, 198
  defined, 193
  and emotional messages, 196
  feelings and attitudes, communication of, 194
  interaction adaptation theory, 195–196
  interpersonal relationships, role in, 195
  interpretation of. *See* non-verbal communication, interpretation of
  multi-channelled nature of, 198
  skill assessment, 217
  understanding, purpose of, 193–196
  verbal cues, working with, 195–196
non-verbal communication, interpretation of
  arousal, 213–214
  challenges, 197–199
  clusters of non-verbal cues, 216
  in context, 216
  dominance, 214
  expectancy violation theory, 216
  immediacy, 213
  and past experiences, 217
  perception checking, 218
non-verbal communication codes
  adaptors, 203
  affect displays, 203
  appearance, 211–212
  body movement, 200–201
  categories of, 201–204
  emblems, 202
  eye contact, 204–205
  facial expressions, 206–207
  gestures, 200–201
  illustrators, 203
  intimate space, 209
  perceptions of liking, 201
  personal space, 209
  posture, 200–201
  public space, 209
  quasi-courtship behaviour, 201
  regulators, 203
  social space, 209
  territoriality, 210–211
  touch, 211
  vocal cues, 207–208

O

openness, 347
organization of information
  categorizing, 73
  patterning, 72
  punctuating, 72
  superimpose, 73
other-orientation
  as adaptation skill, 287–289
  assertiveness, 253–257
  communication, 293
  computer-mediated communication (CMC), 368–369
  and culture-based conflict management, 229
  and effective communication, 29–31

empathy, 289
empathy ability, 117
ethics in the workplace, 178
generalized-other perspective, 55
intergenerational conflict, and empathy, 243
lying, 137
in other cultures, 44
and perceptual skill, 89, 90
as relationship-starting skill, 340
self and, 54–55
social decentring, 287, 288
specific-other perspective, 55
talkaholic scale, 171
words, use of, 188
words to value others, 184–185
outward communication, 373–374
overgeneralization, 84

P

parallel relationships, 307
paraphrasing, 112, 115, 120–121, 255
partnership perspective, 228
passive perception, 76
patterning, 72
Pennel, Joan, 247
people-oriented listeners, 103
perception
 see also interpersonal perception
 active perception, 76
 awareness and, 88
 barriers to accurate perceptions, 83–87
 big picture, 88
 cultural differences, sensitivity to, 91
 defined, 69
 electronic perceptions, accuracy of, 80
 elements to which you attribute meaning, 88–89
 improvement of perceptual skills, 87–89
 monitoring, and relationship escalation and maintenance, 346
 and organization, 71–73
 and other-orientation, 89
 of others. See perception of others
 others' perceptions of you, 88
 passive perception, 76
 selective perception, 69–70
perception checking, 90, 91, 143–144, 218
perception of others
 description of others, 79–81
 implicit personality theory, 79–80
 impression formation, 77
 interpretation of behaviour, 81–83
 personal constructs, 81
perceptual barriers
 consistency, imposition of, 85
 ignoring circumstances, 86
 ignoring information, 84
 negative, focus on, 86
 overgeneralization, 84
 oversimplification, 85
 preconceptions, 84
 stereotypes, 85–86
perceptual differences, 68
personal constructs, 81
personal space, 209
personality
 communication apprehension, 47
 defined, 47
 implicit personality theory, 79–80
 interaction style, 47
 Myers-Briggs Personality Test, 49
 shyness, 47
 willingness to communicate, 47, 48

physical attraction, 310–311
physical health, 11
physiological effects of emotions, 134–135
Pitts, Leonard, 17, 18
placating response, 238
polarization, 176
polygraph testing, 137
positive feeling, expressions of, 185
positive self-presentation, 342
positive self-talk, 155, 245
positive tone, 358
post-interaction effects stage, 338
posture, 200–201, 215
power
 coercive, 309
 distribution in relationships, 308–309
 distribution of, and cultural diversity, 270, 273
 expert, 309
 interpersonal, 306
 in interpersonal relationships, 306–309
 legitimate, 308
 referent, 308
 reward, 309
 types of power relationships, 307
power relationships
 competitive symmetric relationship, 307
 complementary relationships, 307
 parallel relationships, 307
 submissive symmetric relationship, 307
 symmetric relationships, 307
preconceptions, 84
predicted outcome value theory, 313
prejudice, 279
primacy effect, 77
primary emotions, 138
problem management
 analyze the problem, 250
 define the problem, 249–250
 evaluation of solution, 251–253
 goals, determination of, 250
 multiple solutions, generation of, 250–251
 select the best solution, 251–252
problem solving vs. control, 182
prototypes, 73
proxemics, 209
proximity, and attraction, 311–312
pseudo conflict, 228, 229
pseudo de-escalation, 356
psychology, 47
The Psychology of the Internet (Wallace), 80, 367
public communication, 9
public space, 209
punctuating, 72

Q

quality circles, 373
quasi-courtship behaviour, 201

R

race, and cultural diversity, 269
racially biased language, 180
rational de-escalation, 337–338
rational emotive therapy, 155
rational escalation, 335–336
received signal, 13
receiver, 13
recency effect, 77
reciprocation of liking, 314
red herring fallacy, 124
reference groups, 43
referent power, 308

referents, 162
reflected appraisal, 42
reflecting content through paraphrasing, 120–121
reframing, 52–53
regulators, 203
relational development
 and computer-mediated communication (CMC), 365
 de-escalation and ending, 351–358
 de-intensification stage, 337
 defined, 333
 escalation and maintenance of relationships, 344–350
 exploration stage, 335
 individualization stage, 337
 initiation stage, 335
 intensification stage, 335
 intimacy stage, 335
 post-interaction effects stage, 338
 rational de-escalation, 337–338
 rational escalation, 335–336
 relationship-starting skills, 338–343
 separation stage, 337
 stages of interpersonal relationships, 334–338
 stagnation, 337
 turning points, 335
relational empathy, 283
relational problems, responses to, 352–353
relationship de-escalation and ending
 bilateral dissolutions, 354
 causes of, 354–355
 decision to end relationship, 353–354
 direct strategies, 356, 357–358
 fading away, 354
 how relationships end, 354
 incrementalism, 354
 indirect strategies, 356, 357
 relational problems, responses to, 352–353
 strategies for ending relationships, 356–358
 sudden death, 354
 unilateral dissolution, 354
relationship dimension, 25
relationship escalation and maintenance
 affinity-seeking strategies, 345–346
 appropriate self-disclosure, 347
 attraction, communication of, 344–346
 computer-mediated communication (CMC), 366, 367–368
 confirming responses, 347
 cooperative conflict management, 350
 expression of emotions, 347–348
 listening skills, 347
 openness, 347
 perceptions, monitoring, 346
 relationship talk, 348
 restraint, 349
 socially decentre and adapt, 348–349
 tolerance, 349
relationship functions, 377
relationship potential, 313
relationship-starting skills
 approachability cues, 340
 ask questions, 343
 computer-mediated communication (CMC), 365
 conversation starters, 340
 expectations fro initial interactions, 343
 information gathering, 339–340
 initiation norms, 341
 other-orientation, 340
 positive self-presentation, 342
 self-disclosure, 341–342
 uncertainty reduction, 339–340
relationship talk, 348

Index

relationships
see also interpersonal relationships
of choice, 303–304
of circumstance, 303–304
colleagues, 10
defined, 8
electronic, 18–19
with family, 9
friends, 10
honesty in, and self-esteem, 53
initiation and formation of, 8
interracial relationships, 291
lovers, 10
and non-verbal communication, 195
power. See power relationships
power distribution in, 308–309
relational development. See relational development
and rules, 24
self-concept, effect of, 54–61
self-esteem, effect of, 54–61
stage of, 9
supportive, and words, 177–184
at work. See workplace relationships
religion, and cultural diversity, 269
remembering, 102
residual arousal, 135
respond, 103
responding skills
confirming responses. See confirming responses
critical responding, 126–127
descriptive vs. evaluative, 127
empathic, 117–119
reflecting content through paraphrasing, 120–121
unnecessary details, avoidance of, 127
useable information, 126–127
well-timed responses, 126
responses
clarifying, 185
confirming. See confirming responses
disconfirming responses. See disconfirming responses
fight or flight, 134
impersonal, 187
impervious, 186
incoherent, 187
incongruous, 187
interrupting, 186
irrelevant, 186
placating, 238
supportive response, 185
tangential, 186
responsiveness, 60
restraint, and relationship escalation and maintenance, 349
restricted code, 174
reward power, 309
Richmond, Virginia, 47, 61
rigidity, 175
risk, and self-disclosure, 323
Rogers, Carl, 29, 118, 183
roles
androgynous role, 46
assumption of, 44–46
and emotional expression, 142
rules, 23–24

S

sadness, 152–153
schemas, 136
Science and Sanity (Korzybski), 167
second-guessing, 104

Seiter, John, 181
selecting, 100
selective exposure, 59
selective perception, 69–70
self
and communication style, 60–61
defined, 38
and interpersonal needs, 59–60
and interpretation of messages, 58–59
looking glass self, 42
material self, 41
and other-orientation, 54–55
social self, 41
spiritual self, 41
self-absorption, 107–108, 285
self-awareness, 319
self-concept
attitude, 38
beliefs, 39
defined, 38
development of, 42–46
dimensions of self, 40–41
groups, association with, 43–44
interaction with individuals, 42–43
interpersonal communication, effect on, 54–61
perception of, 40
and personality, 46–47
relationships, effect on, 54–61
roles, assumption of, 44–46
self-labels, 46
social comparison, 43
values, 39
self-disclosure
characteristics of appropriate self-disclosure, 321–323
defined, 315
dyadic effect, 323
intimacy and, 315
Johari Window model, 319–321
from less personal to more personal information, 322
reciprocal, 322
and relational development, 316–317
and relationship escalation and maintenance, 347
as relationship-starting skill, 341–342
risk, 323
small increments, 321–322
social penetration model, 318–319
trust, 323
typical disclosure pattern, 317
self-efficacy, 155
self-esteem
and campus drinking, 50
comparisons, avoidance of, 52
defined, 49
honest relationships and, 53
improvement of, 51–54
interpersonal communication, effect on, 54–61
letting go of the past, 53
life position, 50
reframing, 52–53
relationships, effect on, 54–61
self-talk and, 51
support, 53–54
and visualization, 52
self-fulfilling prophecy, 55–58
self-handicapping strategy, 82
self-image, 342
self-labels, 46
self-reflexiveness, 46
self-serving bias, 82
self-talk, 155, 245
self-worth, 49
see also self-esteem

semantics, 165
Seneca, Shauna, 248
separation stage, 337
Seven Habits of Highly Effective People (Covey), 376
sexist language, 179–180
sexual harassment, 374–375
sexual orientation, 180
and cultural diversity, 269
empathy and, 354
intimate romantic relationships, 344
Sherman, Anne, 248
Shimanoff, Susan, 24
short-term initial attraction, 310
shyness, 47
Siegel, Bernard, 58
signal, 13
similarity, and attraction, 312
simple conflict, 228, 230–231
skills, 280
see also adaptation skills
small-group communication, 9
social class, and cultural diversity, 269
social comparison, 43
social decentring, 287, 288, 348–349
social exchange theory
comparisons of forecasted rewards and costs, 326
cumulative rewards and costs, 325
defined, 324
expected costs and rewards, 326
forecasted rewards and costs, 324
immediate rewards and costs, 324
magnitude of rewards and costs, 325
ratio of rewards and costs, 325
social information-processing theory, 20
social learning approach, 60
social penetration model, 318–319
social self, 41
social space, 209
social style. See communication style
sociocommunicative orientation test, 61
soft skills, 11
source, 13
space, 208–209, 215
spatial zones, classification of, 208–209
specific-other perspective, 55
speed rate vs. thought rate, 110
spiritual self, 41
stagnation, 337
static evaluation, 175
stereotypes
defined, 73, 85, 278
and intercultural communication, 278–279
labels for males and females, 45
as perceptual barrier, 85–86
submissive symmetric relationship, 307
subordinates, relationships with, 372–373
sudden death, 354
Sullivan, Harry Stack, 42
superimpose, 73
support
for dealing with difficult emotions, 155
and self-esteem, 53–54
supportive relationships
empathy vs. detachment, 183
equal rather than superior, 183–184
ethnic or racially biased language, 180
flexibility vs. rigidity, 183
genuine vs. manipulative, 182–183
"I" language, 181–183
language that demeans age, ability or social class, 181
problem solving vs. control, 182
sexist language, 179–180

supportive response, 185
Survey on Sexual Harassment in Public Places and at Work, 375
symbolic interaction, 165
symbols
   defined, 23, 162
   words as, 162
symmetric relationships, 307
sympathizing, 120
sympathy, 291
synchronous interaction, 363
system, 302

T

talkaholic scale, 171
tangential response, 186
Tannen, Deborah, 107
task functions, 376–377
Taylor, Dalmas, 318
termination of relationships. *See* relationship de-escalation and ending
territoriality, 210–211
think before speaking, 146
third culture, 282–283
thought, 162
thought rate *vs.* speed rate, 110
time-oriented listener, 104
tolerance, and relationship escalation and maintenance, 349
touch, 211, 215
transaction model of communication, 14–15
trust
   interpersonal, 305
   and potential relationship gains, 305
   in relationships, 304–305
   and self-disclosure, 323
   types of, 304
trustworthy, 305
turning points, 335

U

uncertain meaning, 172–174
uncertainty avoidance, 270, 271–273
uncertainty reduction theory, 339–340
unconscious competence, 112
unconscious incompetence, 112
understanding, 101–102
unilateral dissolution, 354
universality of emotional expression, 137
upward communication, 371–372
Ury, William, 249

V

values, 39
verbal aggressiveness, 151
verbal communication. *See* words
visualization, 52
vocal cues, 207–208, 215

W

Wallace, Patricia, 80, 367
Walther, Joseph, 20
Wiio, Osmo, 23
willingness to communicate, 47, 48
withdrawal
   from conflict, 238
   and ending relationships, 356
women. *See* gender and gender differences
word barriers
   allness, 174–175
   bafflegab, 172
   biased language, 176
   bypassing, 170–171
   generalization, 174–175
   jargon, 174
   language of extremes, 176
   malapropism, 173
   polarization, 176
   restricted code, 174
   rigidity, 175
   static evaluation, 175
   uncertain meaning, 172–174
words
   abstract meanings, 166–167
   arbitrary nature of, 162
   behaviour, effect on, 169
   concrete meanings, 166–167
   confirming responses, 184, 185
   connotative meaning, 166
   context-bound, 162
   creation, power of, 167–168
   culturally bound, 163
   culture, effect and reflection on, 169–170
   denotative meaning, 166
   disconfirming responses, 184, 186–187
   as labels, 168
   and meaning, 161–167
   policies and procedures, effect on, 169
   power of, 161, 167–170
   semantics, 165
   and supportive relationships, 177–184
   as symbols, 162
   thoughts and actions, effect on, 168
   to value others, 184–185
   and world view, 170
workplace relationships
   challenges of, 371
   with colleagues, 373
   with customers, 373–374
   downward communication, 372–373
   followership skill, 377
   horizontal communication, 373
   interactions in workplace, 371
   leadership skills, 376–377
   with management, 371–372
   outward communication, 373–374
   sexual harassment, 374–375
   with subordinates, 372–373
   upward communication, 371–372
workplace skills in global economy, 369–370
world view, 170, 281
written communication, 362

Y

Yankelovich, Daniel, 8, 177
youth crime prevention, 247–248